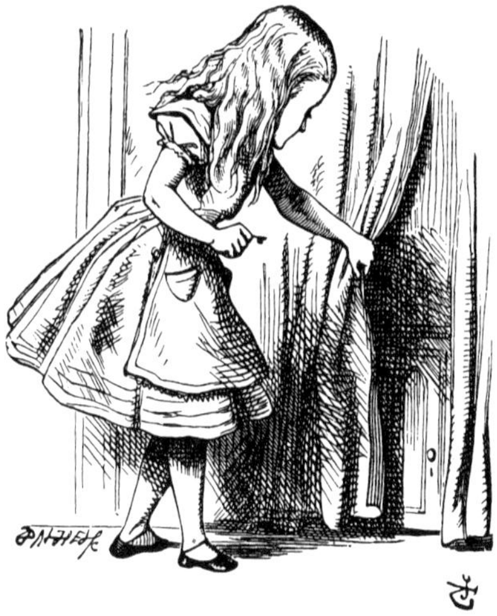

LEWIS

CARROLL

Anne Higonnet

'And what is the use of a book,'

thought Alice,

'without pictures or conversations?'

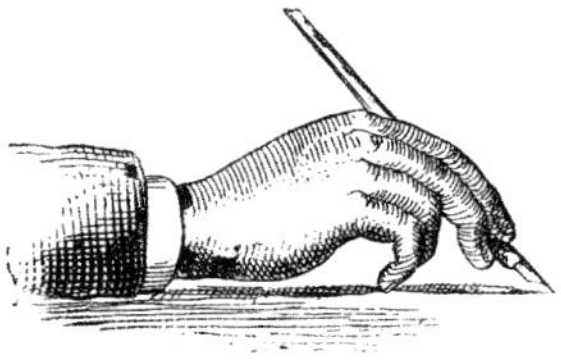

Alice's Adventures in Wonderland, Chapter 1

Lewis Carroll is the pen name with which Charles Lutwidge Dodgson signed two of the best-known books in the English language, *Alice's Adventures in Wonderland* and *Through the Looking Glass and What Alice Found There*. Professionally, Dodgson was a mathematician. On the side, as an amateur, he made photographs. Over time, these photographs have come to be seen as almost as great among photographs as his writings are among books. Many of his best photographs, not coincidentally, are about the same people his books were written for — children. Technically, the photographs are by Dodgson, but the relationship between the photographs and the books is so important, and the name Lewis Carroll simply so famous, that we can say the photographs are by Carroll.

Carroll was born Charles Lutwidge Dodgson in 1832, one of the eleven children of a formidable minister, also named Charles Dodgson (PLATE 3). He attended excellent schools (not always happily) and conducted his career at the last of them, Christ Church College in Oxford University. Carroll spent his entire adult life there, unmarried, holding various positions and leaving only for holidays or to participate in the London intellectual scene. He specialized professionally in mathematical logic, a field in which he regularly published and also taught. Carroll was a skilled mathematician, a distinguished professor whose *Symbolic Logic* (1896) and *The Game of Logic* (1887) are still in print. He was keenly aware of new trends in the fine arts, literature, theatre and photography, and he cultivated friendships with prominent figures in those fields, often facilitated by the popularity of the *Alice* books. Carroll also enjoyed the company of people he called his 'child-friends', most of them girls, and many of whom he photographed. Excruciatingly shy in some ways and often afflicted with a stutter, Carroll nonetheless loved to tell stories and jokes, as well as to perform tableaux vivants and theatricals, especially for children. Up to the end of his life, he continued to behave playfully with children, and to write to them. He died in 1898.

Carroll took up photography when the medium was new and difficult. There is some debate about exactly when he first experimented with photography, but the safest guess is around 1855, when Carroll was twenty-three. He probably began at the instigation of a fellow member of Christ Church, the medical student Reginald Southey (PLATE 5) but may also have been inspired by an adventurous uncle who we know was practising photography at the time. One technique for permanently fixing images chemically had been publicly announced in Paris in 1839, and had triggered an explosion of technical and aesthetic invention. Yet by the mid-1850s, photography still required a great deal of time, space, money, precision, determination and imagination. The chemicals and procedures Carroll had to master were as numerous and complicated as his visual antecedents were few and primitive. Carroll could only invent, and he invented with genius.

'It is my one recreation, and I think should be done well,' Carroll wrote of photography. For close to twenty-five years, Carroll devoted his energy to photography in a manner that was far from what we would call recreational. His class position, as well as the cultural climate of Victorian Britain, allowed him to pursue sustained and serious occupations outside the teaching that earned him a living — 'amateur' was not then a pejorative term. Carroll worked in a painstaking photographic process called 'wet collodion'. Wet collodion photography involved glass plates, slow exposures, several noxious chemical solutions and many procedures, each of them required to be delicate and swift. Glass-plate negatives had to be developed immediately and positive contact prints were made in sunlight. The creation of contact prints meant that final images were exactly the same size as the glass-plate negatives, enhancing the precision of the medium's minute detail. While he sometimes employed professional printers, Carroll usually did his own printing and successes came at the price of many failures. Estimates suggest that Carroll produced about 3,000 photographs of which at least 2,500 negatives survive. His output began at a high level, peaked in 1863 — a year in which he made more than 250 images — and tapered off to almost nothing by the late 1870s. Alongside the making and printing of photographs, Carroll spent many hours organizing and assembling them into albums. He also kept almost obsessive records of his activity: he made lists, numbered many of his negatives and prints, and included records of his photography in his thirteen notebooks and diaries. With the exception of four volumes of his diary and a missing ten pages in another volume, all of these records survive.

Of course Carroll is more famous for his books than for his photographs, especially *Alice's Adventures in Wonderland*, published in 1865, and its 1871 sequel, *Through the Looking Glass*. Carroll's delightful sense of humour connected his various accomplishments. Mathematical logic may not appear to be a very funny subject, but Carroll managed to introduce jokes in his mathematical publications. A few of these even refer to pictures. For example, in his *Symbolic Logic*, one exercise entitled 'Pairs of Concrete Propositions, proposed as Premisses [*sic*]: Conclusions to be found' reads: 'No portrait of a lady, that makes her simper or scowl, is satisfactory; No photograph of a lady ever fails to make her simper or scowl.'

Carroll's writings always involved images, whether evoked or actually accompanying his texts. Carroll himself illustrated the first written version of the *Alice* story, with drawings whose skill he deemed insufficient for publication, but which today seem utterly charming. Ever since Carroll decided to publish his book with illustrations by John Tenniel, the works of eminent illustrators, artists, filmmakers and photographers over the years have expanded the story's impact. Notable among them are the plates made by Arthur Rackham in 1907 and the animated film by Disney (1951).

The *Alice* story is known around the world, not so much because everyone has read Carroll's books, but because his words have merged with the generations of illustrated versions of the book to become iconic. 'Wonderland', 'going down the rabbit hole' and 'off with her head!' are among the many expressions used ubiquitously to refer to any unexpected transformation of the ordinary into the magical or ludicrous. 'Curiouser and curiouser' (to use another famous Carroll phrase) are the decidedly adult versions of the *Alice* stories that have proliferated over time: photographs, films, novels and computer games that overtly explore repressed sexuality and violence. Several of them, such as Salvador Dalí's illustrations (1969), Jan Švankmajer's semi-animated film (1988) and Anna Gaskell's photographs (1996–98) are significant works of art in their own right. The visual qualities of Carroll's written work help explain how he could be almost as great a photographer as he was an author. His photography was no secret in his lifetime and he often made photographs for display in his albums, and also occasionally for exhibition. However, his photographs were not published in his lifetime, nor in the years immediately following his death — except as rare illustrations to early biographies about him. Carroll's photographs remained the least well-known aspect of his work until the pioneering photo-historian Helmut Gernsheim began to draw attention to them in 1949. Gradually, scholarship on the photographs accumulated and now it lags only slightly behind the dauntingly impressive mass of work on Carroll's books. As the academic study of childhood becomes increasingly layered and challenging, and in particular as we gain critical distance from Victorian ideas about childhood, our understanding of Carroll's photographs of children becomes correspondingly more nuanced.

Carroll was a great photographer of childhood. He also made very beautiful portraits of adults, as well as some excellent landscapes and still lifes, but it is his photographs of children that are truly exceptional. His photographs of children represent individuals, and they also brilliantly illuminate the whole Victorian ideal of childhood, showing us how and why that concept was so vital to its time and place.

Victorians rigidly divided childhood innocence from adult experience. To be more precise, they attributed an innocence to the young of the privileged English upper and middle classes. This idea of humanity was invested with religious force, so childhood was seen as almost divinely ideal, while adult experience was equated with sin. Carroll wrote: 'Anyone that has ever loved one true child will have known the awe that falls on one in the presence of a spirit fresh from God's hands, on whom no shadow of sin [...] has yet fallen.' The child was every Victorian adult's perfect but lost self and the concept by which adulthood was negatively defined. Any such concept based on extreme opposition always threatens to collapse — witness Carroll's language, which cannot evoke the child's 'spirit fresh from God's hands' without fearing the 'shadow of sin'.

In his writings about photography, Carroll often mocked the deluded pretensions of adult subjects. Parodying Henry Wadsworth Longfellow's sonorous poem *The Song of Hiawatha* (1855) in his *Hiawatha's Photographing* (1857) Carroll relates a family's ludicrous reaction to their portrait:

> *Then they joined and all abused it.*
> *Unrestrainedly abused it.*
> *As 'the worst and ugliest picture*
> *They could possibly have dreamed of.*
> *Giving one such strange expressions —*
> *Sullen, stupid, pert expressions.*
> *Really any one would take us*
> *(Any one that did not know us)*
> *For the most unpleasant people!'*

The photographer flees, cursing his subjects. In another satirical piece, *A Photographer's Day Out*, published in 1860, Carroll skewers the parents' pompous plans for their family portrait:

> *This was to have been the great artistic triumph of the day; a family group, designed by the two parents, and combining the domestic with the allegorical ... Such, I say, was the intention; the result, to any unprejudiced observer, was capable of but one interpretation — that the baby was in a fit — that the mother (doubtless under the erroneous notions of the principles of Human Anatomy), was endeavouring to recover it by bringing the crown of its head in contact with its chest — that the two boys, seeing no prospect for the infant but immediate destruction, were tearing out some locks of its hair as mementoes of the fatal event — that two of the girls were waiting for a chance at the baby's hair, and employing the time in strangling the third — and that the father, in despair at the extraordinary conduct of his family, had stabbed*

himself, and was feeling for his pencil-case,
to make a memorandum of having done so.

Meanwhile, Carroll's writings about images of children tend to opposite extremes. In his poetry and prose he often veered towards the sentimental, as in a poem which appeared at the end of *Through the Looking Glass*, dedicated to the real life 'Alice', Alice Liddell:

Still she haunts me, phantomwise,
Alice moving under skies
Never seen by waking eyes.

Alternatively, his humorous writing cloaked his feelings in absurdity. Yet in his photographs, Carroll observed the conditions of Victorian childhood more clearly and discerningly than anyone else in his time.

Carroll's albums provide the immediate context and purpose for his photographs. Thirty-four of these albums were listed among Carroll's effects at his death, and twelve are now known. Carroll used the albums, which sometimes also contained photographs by other people, to display his photographs to family and friends, and also to initiate new relationships. He would send albums to people he hoped to meet, including eminent figures such as the poet laureate Alfred Lord Tennyson (PLATE 13) or the artist John Everett Millais (PLATES 44, 46), hoping they would request similar photographs of themselves or their children. It is possible that Carroll did so to advance himself another rung on the exquisitely cruel and calibrated English social ladder. While, by our standards, all the subjects of Carroll's photography appear to have belonged to the same comfortable middle class, by the standards of Victorian England many belonged to one remarkably consistent segment of the upper-middle class who aspired to the lowest rungs of the aristocracy and were therefore eager to distance themselves from people like Carroll who were barely one rank lower. Alice Liddell, for instance, the child of whom Carroll made his most memorable early photographs (PLATES 7, 15, 16, 17, 22), and who was the muse of his books and namesake of *Alice's Adventures in Wonderland*, was a gorgeous girl who also happened to be the daughter of Carroll's direct professional superior, the Dean of Christ Church College.

This adds a new twist to the traditional interpretation of Carroll's motives for photographing children. It has always been assumed that Carroll was fascinated with children because of a genuine delight in their natural charm. The charm, however, may have been a complicated mixture of the natural and the social. Carroll could have been attracted to the signs his child subjects displayed of a social status he aspired to but might not ever reach. Or perhaps only the manners inculcated by upper- or middle-class family life seemed naturally charming to him.

The issue of Carroll's motives inevitably confronts us with the scandal surrounding his photographs. The discovery of four photographs of nude girls made by Carroll in the Rosenbach Library collection in Philadelphia has increased suspicion of his motives. Many people suggest there is evidence of paedophilia in Carroll's photographs. Some argue his sexual desire for little girls was conscious; others concede it might have been unconscious. Either way, the photographs, particularly those of Alice Liddell, have been used to explain the erotic energy that some scholars believe is evident in the *Alice* books. Carroll's relationships with children, especially Alice Liddell, have been submitted to renewed scrutiny. Much is made of a break in social relations with the Liddell family and the destruction of Carroll's diary entries for that period. In her 2001 novel, *Still She Haunts Me*, for instance, Katie Roiphe speculates (albeit in a fictional context) that the Liddells were reacting to photographs Carroll took of a naked Alice. It is a biographical fact that towards the end of his photographic career, Carroll often sought parents' permission to take photographs of their daughters undressed. Almost fifty percent of Carroll's photographs portray children and of those the most erotic pictures are all of girls — no one can reasonably deny the sensual appeal of such images. At the very least, Carroll felt an unerring attraction to photogenic children whose beauty was enhanced by his abilities as a photographer.

Some caution, however, is in order. Consider first that Carroll solicited parents' permission to photograph their children by showing them albums of his work, and that most Victorians accepted a high degree of sensuality in images of children — paradoxically because they believed so adamantly in children's purity. Tennyson, for instance, whose sons Carroll did photograph (PLATES 11, 12, 13), called a picture of Alice Liddell with rags falling off her shoulders the most beautiful photograph he had ever seen (PLATE 17). Consider also Carroll's subjects' social position — if abusive gratification was his aim, he could not have chosen better defended prey. Lastly, consider the overall subject matter of Carroll's work and its defining traits. If half of Carroll's photographs were devoted to children, half were not. Among his other subjects were landscapes, still lifes and many portraits of adults who were recognized in Victorian society for their books, paintings, poetry, marriages or academic careers — in other words, for their moral and intellectual qualities.

What truly sets Carroll's treatment of his subjects apart from other painted, sculpted or photographic portraits of the time is not the sensuality in his portraits of children, but something quite different. Carroll consistently represented children and women deep in thought, in an era that commonly associated intellect with masculinity and disassociated thoughtful activity from femininity and childhood. Time and again, Carroll chose to represent children and women — including older women — reading books (PLATES 9, 31, 39, 48, 50), pondering a chess move (PLATE 21), or even peering through a microscope (PLATE 20). The clarity of the gazes directed straight at the photographer in Carroll's portraiture is itself a kind of tribute to intelligence. In Victorian culture, as in ours, direct eye contact was considered a sign of integrity, as well as of seduction, and Carroll's photographs very often make such a connection.

Like all great photographs, Carroll's are the product of his artistic choices, never the result of random mechanical chance. Those characteristic gazes, which are apparently so intent on the communication of an inner self, are illusions staged and seized by Carroll's art. His sitters all described how Carroll distracted them from his photographic activity with stories and jokes, as he waited for the perfect moment to click the shutter. However difficult it may be to see the formal characteristics of Carroll's photographs without recalling his writing or the photographer's own biography, it is worth the effort. His photographs express their meanings visually, through formal choices about light, space, depth, format and composition. If they were merely illustrations of his life, or even instruments of his sexual desires, Carroll's photographs would not be worth looking at.

Carroll framed his subjects so that their physical presence would dominate his photographs. Several famous scenes in *Alice's Adventures in Wonderland* alert us to the importance of how Carroll situated bodies in space. As Alice drinks magic potions, she suddenly shrinks or expands, rapidly becoming either much too small or much too big for the rooms in which she finds herself. In his illustrations to his manuscript, Carroll further dramatized this idea of not fitting properly into space by drawing Alice folded into tiny boxes, squeezed not only by the borders, but also by the text, or popping out of his drawings altogether with her head cut off ('off with her head!'). By contrast, in his photographs, Carroll's subjects are neither too small nor too large in relation to the spaces they occupy (exactly what Alice longs for). Also by contrast, some of the best-known photographers working around the same time as Carroll made consistently different choices when they positioned their subjects. Julia Margaret Cameron specialized in intimate and softly-focused close-ups of faces, which emphasized the spiritual intensity of her subjects, while O.J. Rejlander, at the other end of the spectrum, preferred complex groups of figures and moral narratives. In Carroll's portraits, typically, the photographer's point of view places the subject in a space that belongs to them – a pictorial space able to contain an entire body, yet immediately contiguous to the viewer's. One step closer and we would be with the people in the photographs, but the figures remain just beyond reach.

The expressive use of space in Carroll's photographs is heightened by the relationship between the format of the images and their degree of detail. The photographs' actual dimensions are very small. The wet collodion technique with which they were made allowed an almost uncannily minute degree of detail, as well as a perfectly even gradation from light to dark, and Carroll consciously pushed that possibility to the limits of technical perfection. The viewer is therefore pulled towards the photographs, lured by the density of optical information to stay close. The intimacy of the album format in which they were originally seen would only have added to this effect.

Yet Carroll's subjects do not blend into a photographic fiction, into another imaginary world. In this respect, Carroll's photographs are fundamentally different from the fantasy of his writings. The settings of his photographs are adamantly realistic and contemporary. Though never to be confused with a professional studio, the spaces of Carroll's photographs are clearly planned and intentionally plain, and often marred near the edge by something not quite right, something wrinkled or askew, which insists on the reality of the photographic accident. Carroll presses his figures compositionally against a few props, constraining them with devices such as the corner of a room, chair and sofa edges, or foliage. The visible pressure of body against prop, seen in the folds of clothing and angles of limbs, locates Carroll's bodies in real space while preventing the figures from merging into their settings. And those settings include their clothes. By far the largest surface area of Carroll's photographs is occupied by the busy, geometric, patterned Victorian clothing. Tailored, boned, scalloped, ruffled, printed, ribboned and pleated, the fashions worn by Carroll's subjects are translated by the camera into optically dense zones that catch and retain the viewer's eye.

In spite of all the fashionable clutter, these are not fashion plates. Just as the wet collodion technique captures the details of Victorian clothing, so it also heightens the realism of flesh, hair and eyes, and the individuality of facial features, registering above all the radiant luminosity of the children's skin and gaze. The drama of Carroll's vision depends on optical contrasts, on the difference between the glow of skin and the starch of a cuff, the wisp of a curl and the knot of a bow, between the flash of an eye and the glitter of a jewel. Carroll believed that the essence of humanity was only to be found in childhood. His photographs show how his Victorian belief in the ideal of childhood innocence allowed him to see, at another level of understanding, something essential in all the people he photographed.

Carroll's life and work were characterized by oppositions: between whimsy and formality, humour and reason, nonsense and logic, spontaneity and ritual and, in our post-Freudian age, we could add another — between unconscious and conscious. In his daily and professional life Carroll abided by rules and regularity. In his imaginative creations he invoked rules in order to play with them and to subvert them. The camera must have appealed to Carroll because it turned the world upside down on its lens just as, in his books, Carroll's humour turned everything upside down, inside out, and backwards. As Carroll wrote in *Through the Looking Glass:*

> *'Living backwards!' Alice repeated in great astonishment, 'I never heard of such a thing!' '— but there's one great advantage in it, that one's memory works both ways.'*

The looking glass that is the camera turns the world backwards in another way, too, by rendering the world as negatives, then using a chemical magic to turn the world back into positive images.

Carroll consciously thought of childhood, too, in terms of positive and negative reversals. He associated children with the light of innocence, a light which could all too easily be reversed by the shadow of experience, sin or death. Yet in his photographs, Carroll could not help showing both the light and the shadow. His photographs reveal all the tensions and contradictions that he and his society believed could be resolved by their notion of childhood. Innocent and erotic, powerfully present and tamed by society, alluring and unattainable, eternally beautiful and tragically ephemeral, the Victorian child was an impossible ideal. When Alice ends her adventures in Wonderland by calling them a 'dream within a dream' we know we have been awakened to what lies below Alice's ordinary life and ours. By using a camera to record surfaces, Carroll also revealed something deeper.

PLATE 1

Alice Murdoch
Park Lodge, Putney, London

19 JUNE 1856

This portrait of Alice Murdoch was one of the first photographs that Carroll made. As if by instinct, he has chosen the basic composition and point of view that would characterize his photographs of children: the image centres on the face and hands, and includes all or most of the figure. Yet this early experiment reveals some problems with his choices. The child's body appears collapsed in the middle as well as legless, and the visual relationship between her skirt and the seat of the chair is confusing. Alice married Andrew Charles Armstrong, a captain in the Prince of Wales's Leinster Regiment, in 1874. Carroll placed this portrait in the first of his albums with a poem he wrote and dedicated to his subject: 'O Child! O new born Denison / Of life's great city! On thy head / The glory of the morn is shed / Like a celestial benison!'

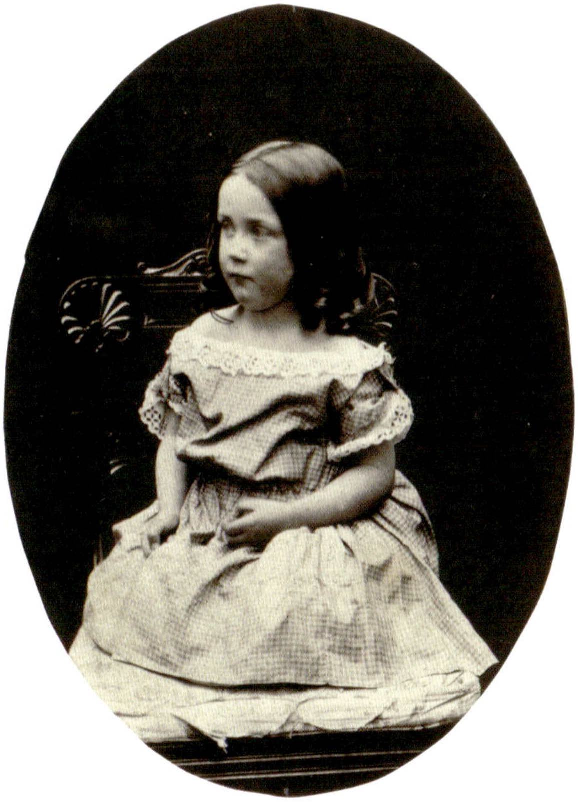

Alice Murdoch.

PLATE 2

Skeffington Hume Dodgson
Croft Rectory, Yorkshire

JULY 1856

In this portrait Carroll contrasts the calm, pale face of his brother Skeffington Dodgson, set against the solid dark upper half of the photograph's background, with an array of dense textures: the knot of his bow tie, check of his jacket, rubber of his gaiters, thick knit of his socks, leather of his shoes, mesh of his net, weave of his basket and turned legs of his chair, as well as the more muted patterns of the curtain behind and the rug beneath him. The Dodgson family was very large and very lively. Of eleven children, four were boys — Carroll the eldest and Skeffington the second — and seven girls. The brothers and sisters all played elaborate games together, some involving witty family newsletters filled with delightfully improbable stories and pictures. Carroll stayed close to his family his whole life.

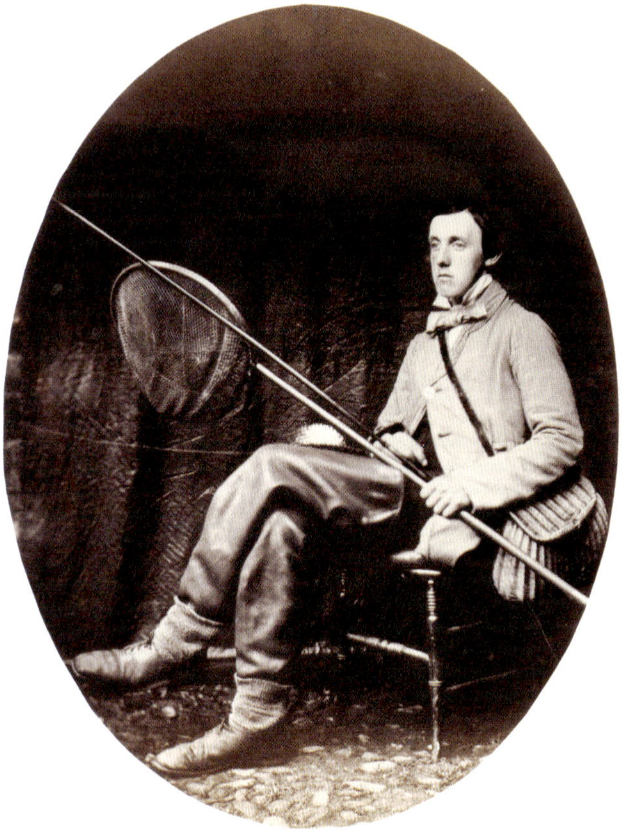

Skeffington Dodgson

PLATE 3

Charles Dodgson
Croft Rectory, Yorkshire

JULY 1856

At ease in his armchair and yet upright, Carroll's father dominates his portrait. The blending of dark costume and dark background makes the figure seem to belong in its space and highlights, by contrast, the face and hands, which are visually connected to the gleams reflected off the chair's handles. Both face and hands are subtly turned towards the photographer, so the viewer feels the subject's attention. Charles Dodgson had been a brilliant student and become an eminent professional cleric. He earned the high honour of a Double First in Classics and Mathematics at Christ Church, Oxford. As an adult, he was awarded the positions of first perpetual curate at Daresbury in Cheshire, then of rector at Croft in Yorkshire, archdeacon of Richmond in London and canon of Ripon, again in Yorkshire.

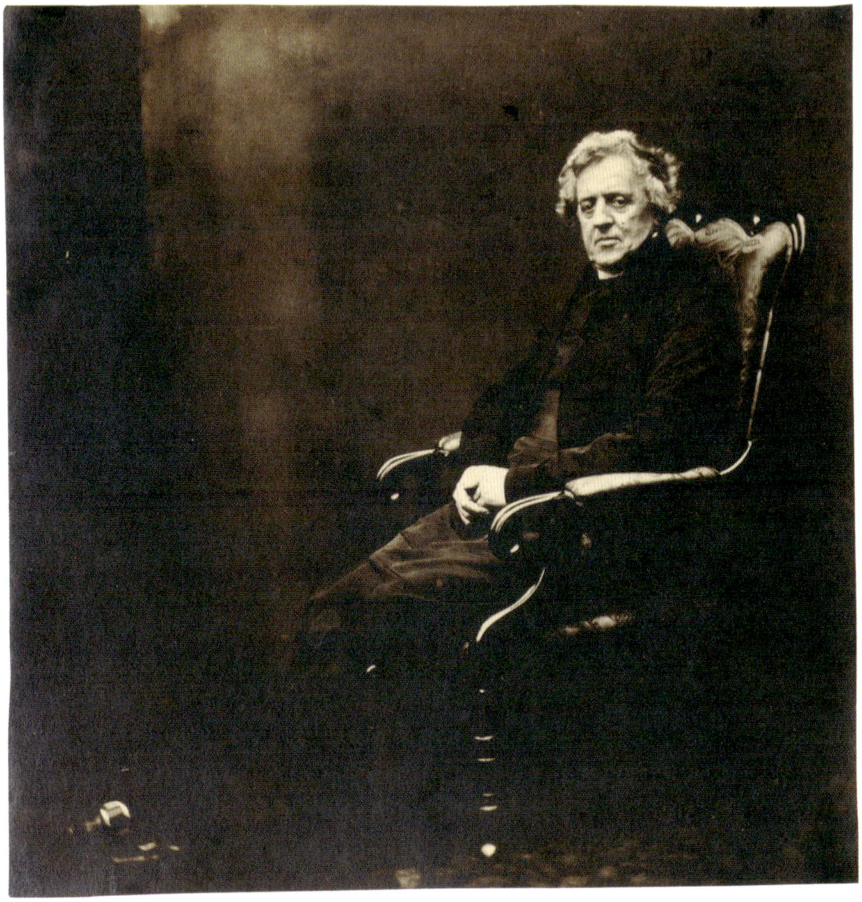

C Dodgson.

PLATE 4

Broad Walk with Figures
Christ Church, Oxford

JUNE 1857

Seen from high above, the Broad Walk of Christ Church appears even more solemn than it would have from below. With the delicate tracery of tree branches covering the top half of the picture as well as both left and right sides, the manicured walk seems in harmony with nature. The four young undergraduates are photographed standing on the Broad Walk, three of them in their characteristic students' mortarboards. Carroll's entire adult life revolved around Christ Church and its rituals, as it was both his official workplace and his home. This photograph was taken from a window in the rooms of his friend and colleague, Reginald Southey (PLATE 5).

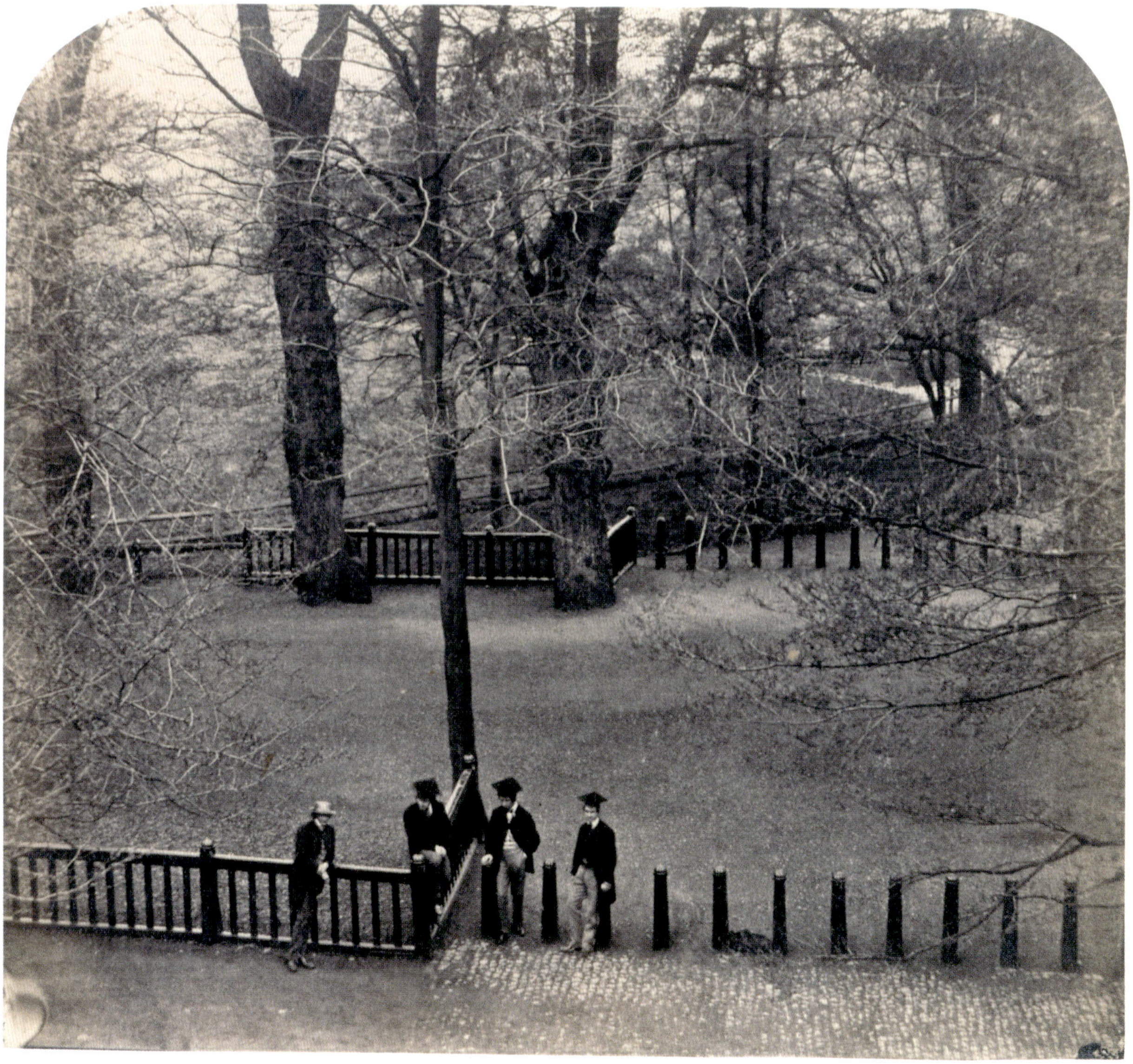

PLATE 5

Reginald Southey and Skeletons
Anatomical Museum, Christ Church, Oxford

JUNE 1857

A human skeleton stands in the centre, with Reginald Southey, Carroll's friend and fellow photographer standing on the left and a monkey skeleton on the right. Below, a gorilla's and a human's skull face right. Clearly, Carroll intended his photograph to elicit a comparison between Southey's living face and the specimen skulls. Carroll scholar Roger Taylor has suggested that the comparison had a distinctly scientific connotation. He speculates that Southey and the human skeleton face the rising sun, and therefore the future, while the monkey, by contrast, faces the past. The comparison between the two skulls, meanwhile, taps into heated contemporary debates on the theory of evolution. This was the moment, Taylor continues, at which Oxford was turning its priorities from theology, to modern and more scientific studies.

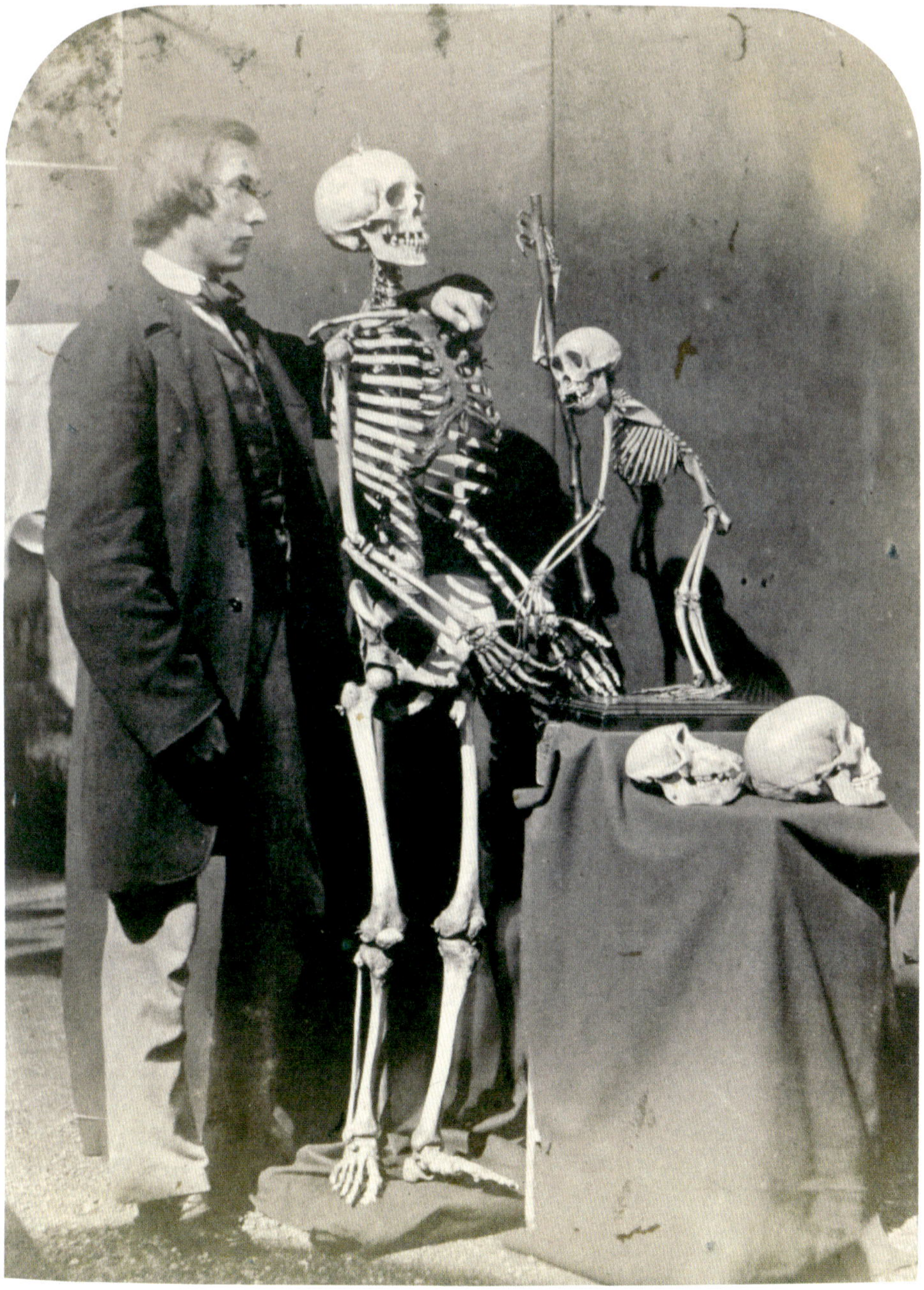

PLATE 6

Skeleton of Sunfish
Anatomical Museum, Christ Church, Oxford

JUNE 1857

Light against dark, the skeleton appears to be a lesson in both natural history and graphic design. The pattern of the skeleton is echoed yet altered by its deep shadow. This is perhaps the most formally dynamic in a series of photographs of anatomical specimens Carroll made in June 1857 for Dr Henry Acland, Regius Professor of Medicine at Christ Church. The specimens belonged to Christ Church and Acland wished to preserve some record of them while they were on loan to the new University Museum. On the page facing the picture, Carroll wrote the following excerpt from *The Song of Hiawatha* by Henry Wadsworth Longfellow: 'Slowly upward, wavering, gleaming / Rose the Ugudwash, the sun-fish'

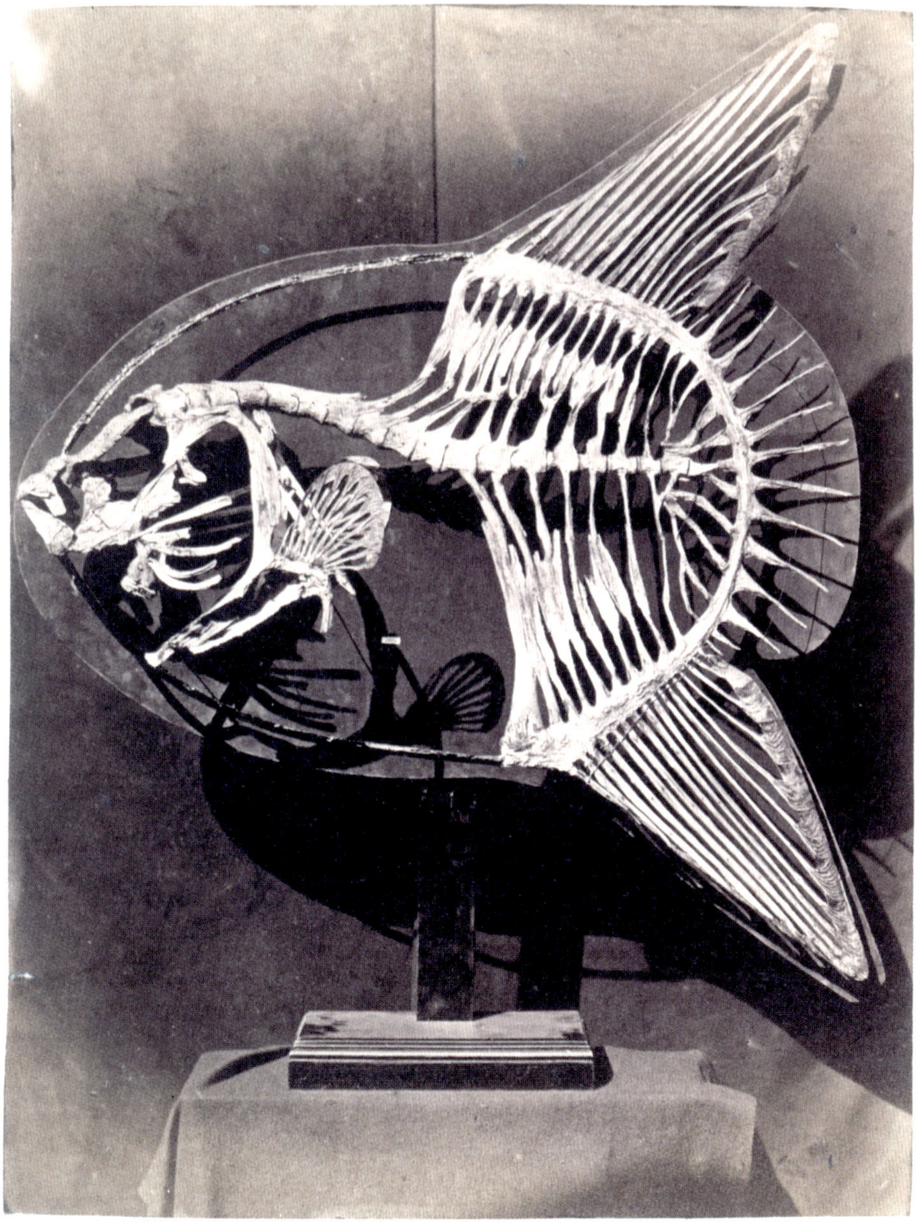

PLATE 7

Lorina and Alice Liddell
Deanery Garden, Christ Church, Oxford

2 JUNE 1857

On 25 April 1856, Carroll met the three daughters of the Dean of Christ Church, Henry George Liddell: Lorina (left), Alice (right) and Edith. Their father had recently moved into the college with his famously beautiful and socially ambitious wife, Lorina. Later Alice would inspire the children's literature classics, *Alice's Adventures in Wonderland* (1865) and *Through the Looking Glass* (1871). In these two photographs Carroll has arrived at a solution to the formal problems of his earlier portraits of children (PLATE 1). The photographs crop the figure at the lap to reduce spatial complexity and the folded hands clarify the body's position in space. The two pictures were taken on the same day and pasted together in one of Carroll's albums. Indeed the two photographs were taken so as to resemble each other closely, to the point of seating both sisters in the same chair, as well as ensuring that lighting, point of view and pose were similar.

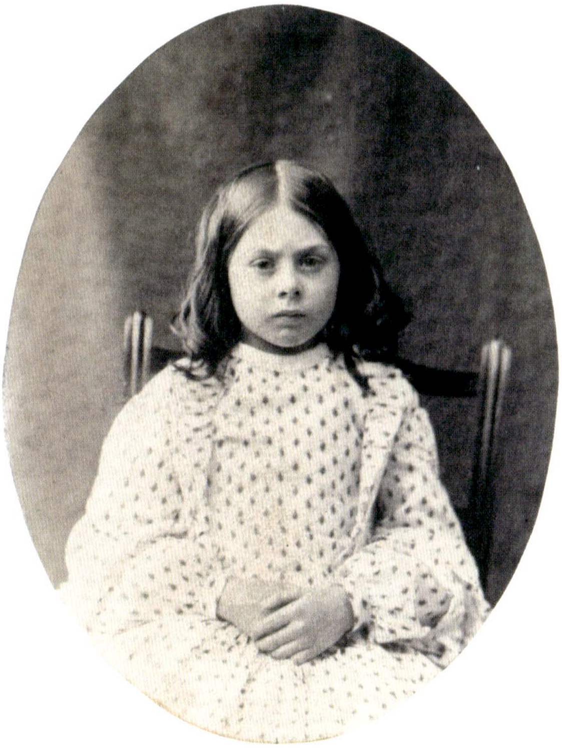

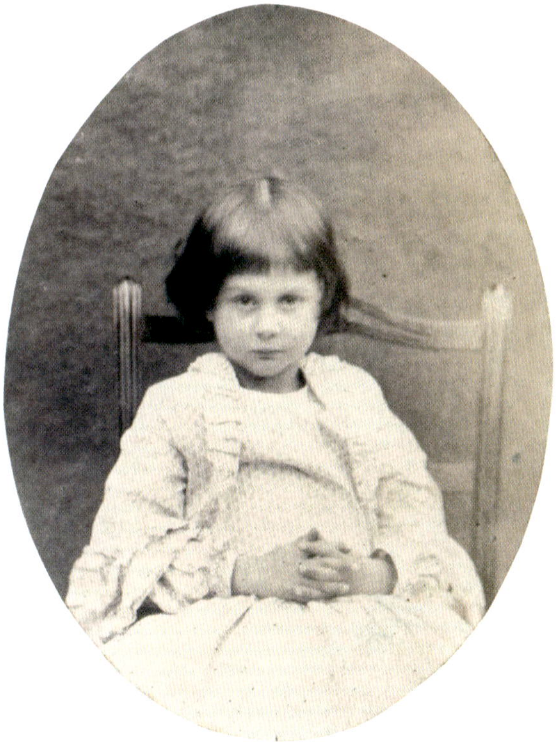

PLATE 8

Edwin Dodgson as 'The Young Mathematician'
Croft Rectory, Yorkshire

JULY – AUGUST 1857

The young mathematician has seemingly fallen asleep on the job, while his dog remains alert and guards the scene. The dog occupies the centre of the image, while on one side the boy's hand limply holds his writing tool over his tipping slate, and on the other the boy's leaning head echoes the slant of the slate. Edwin Dodgson was the youngest Dodgson child. He did in fact study mathematics at Twyford School, Hampshire, and then went on to study at Rugby. Later, he took holy orders and became a missionary, first serving in Zanzibar, then on the island of Tristan da Cunha, a very remote and isolated community in the south Atlantic Ocean, and also nearby in Cape Verde and Saint Helena. He returned to England in 1899 and passed away at the family home in 1918.

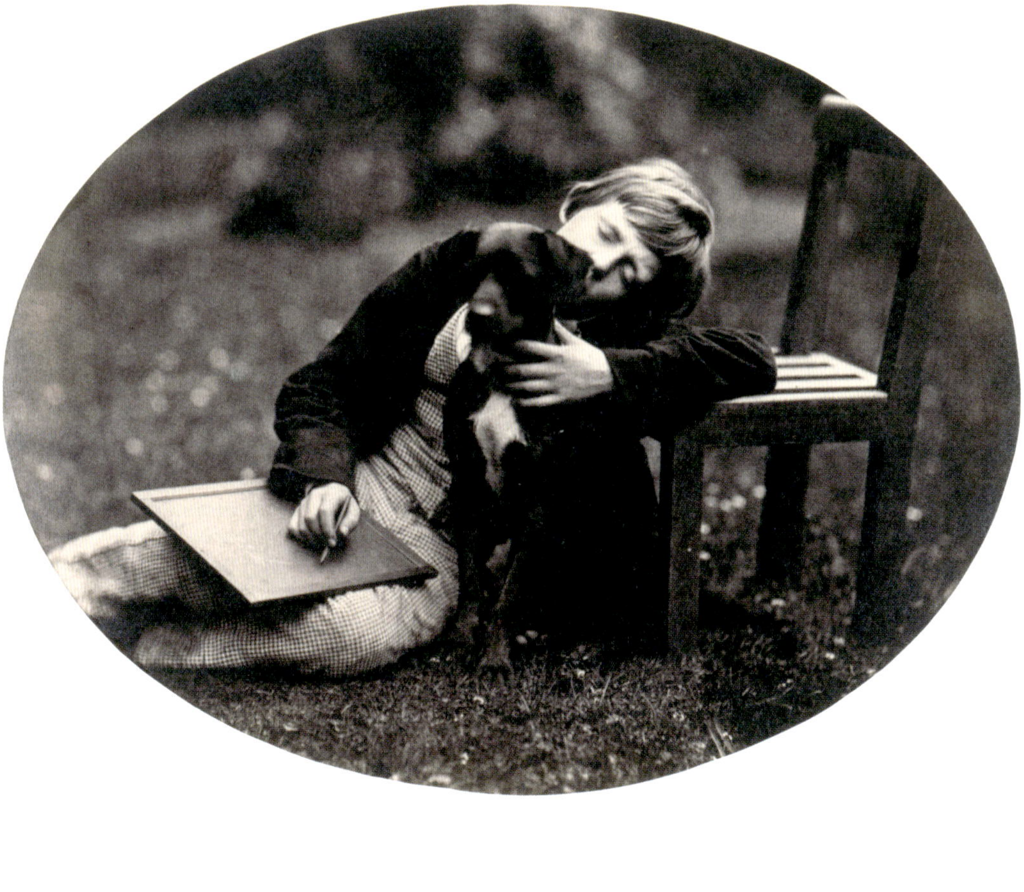

PLATE 9

Edwin Dodgson and 'The New Book'
Croft Rectory, Yorkshire

JULY — AUGUST 1857

Carroll represents six of his sisters and his youngest brother Edwin Dodgson, in a group portrait. Seated in the drawing room of their home, The Old Rectory in Croft, the siblings cluster around a new book, in a picture which commemorates their love of learning. Their heads form a frieze running across the centre of the image, which rhymes with the vases and the candelabra on the mantelpiece behind them. The sister on the right is turned slightly towards the light, echoing the luminous curtain next to her. The children in the Dodgson household held their parents in an unusual awe. Their father provided moral guidance and intellectual discipline, while their mother's love seemed to them (largely in their memories, because she died when her oldest child was nineteen), nearly divine in its patience and purity. Interestingly, Carroll and four of his siblings stuttered, and six of his seven sisters remained unmarried.

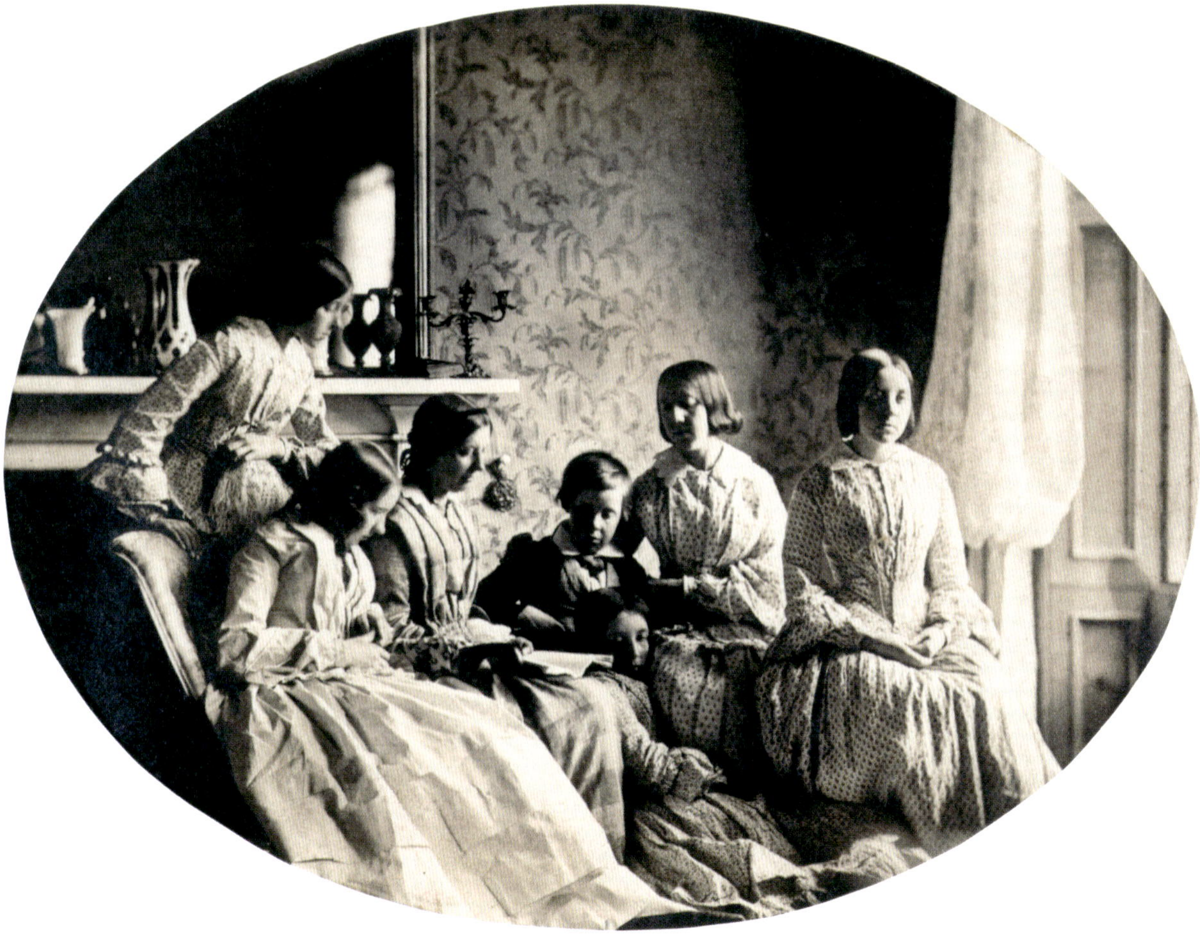

PLATE 10

Agnes Weld as 'Little Red Riding-Hood'
Croft Rectory, Yorkshire

18 AUGUST 1857

Carroll photographed Agnes Weld in the hope of gaining access to her uncle, the famous and revered poet laureate, Alfred Lord Tennyson (PLATE 13). Carroll wrote of Agnes: 'She hardly merits one [photograph] by actual beauty, though her face is very striking and attractive, and will certainly make a beautiful photograph. I think of sending a print of her, through Mrs Weld, for Tennyson's acceptance.' In the album where this picture appears, Carroll had written a poem inspired by the picture: 'Into the wood – the dark, dark wood – / Forth went the happy Child / And in it's [*sic*] stillest solitude / Talked to herself and smiled; / And closer drew the scarlet Hood / About her ringlets wild [...]'

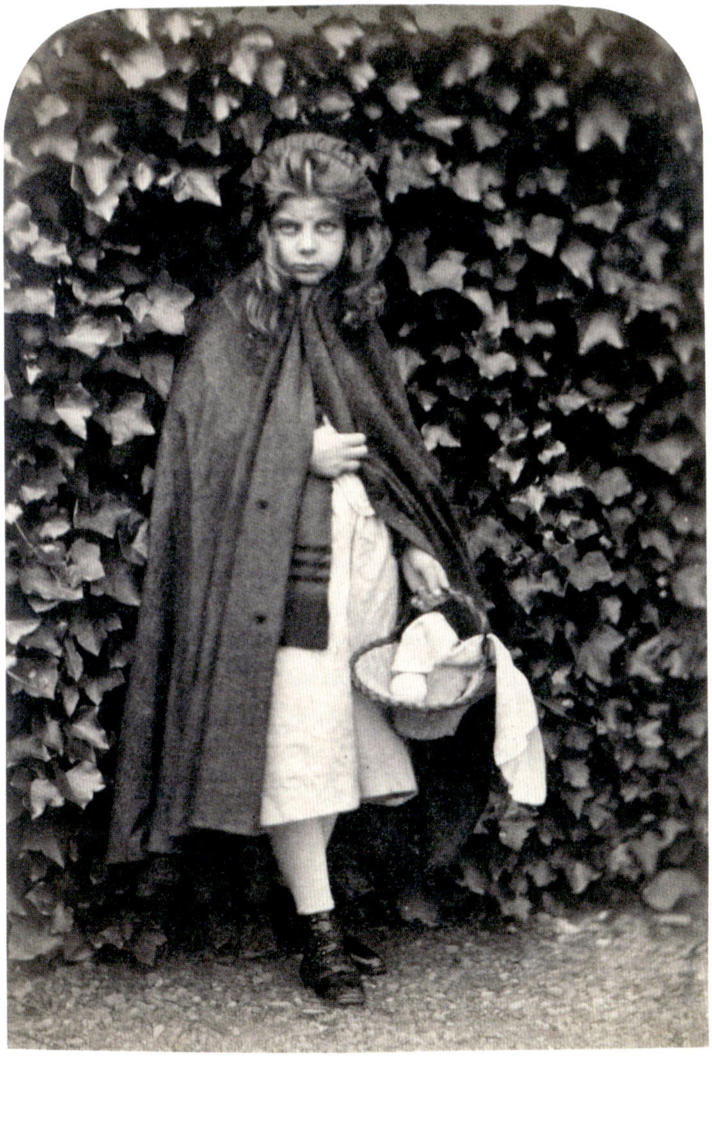

PLATE 11

Hallam and Lionel Tennyson with Julia Marshall
Monk Coniston Park, Ambleside, Lake District

28 SEPTEMBER 1857

This photograph was made at a holiday home in the Lake District owned by the Tennyson family's friend, James Garth Marshall, a wealthy industrialist from Leeds. The closeness between the two sons of Alfred Lord Tennyson, Lionel (left) and Hallam (right), and the daughter of their host, Julia Marshall, is visually expressed by Carroll's use of the corner in which they are posed, which draws together the small group. Just as he had with the Liddells, Carroll took advantage of people's desire to have good photographs of their children. Tennyson himself did not much like to be photographed, but he made an exception for Carroll (PLATE 13). Carroll was genuinely delighted by Tennyson's children and wrote that they were 'the most beautiful boys of their age I ever saw.' Hallam's signature was added into Carroll's album several years after the photograph was made.

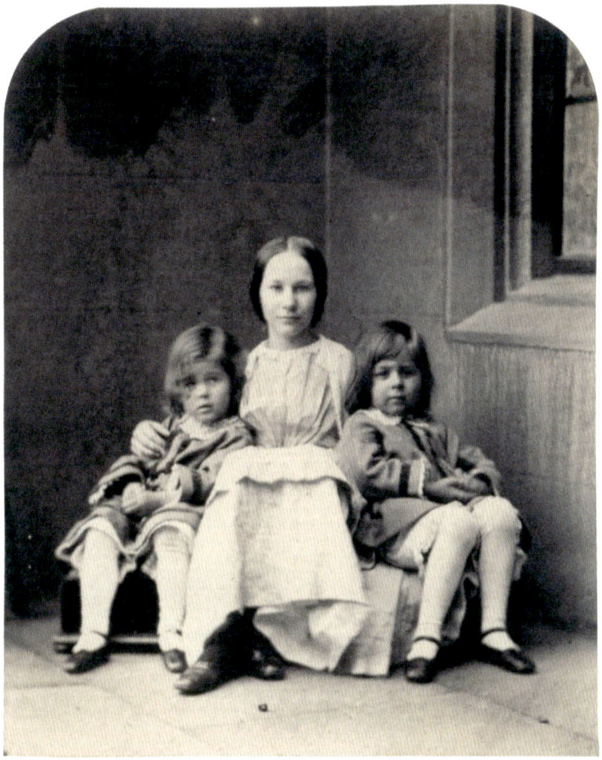

Lionel Tennyson

Hallam Tennyson
April 19th 1862

PLATE 12

Hallam Tennyson
Monk Coniston Park, Ambleside, Lake District

28 SEPTEMBER 1857

Grand and yet miniaturized, Hallam Tennyson lords over the scene. He stands high above the camera, so that we see his whole body, and raps his stick with assurance, ankles crossed in a casually haughty stance, just like an adult in a stately portrait. Yet he perches precariously on the stuffed seat of a chair, which reminds us playfully of how young he is. Hallam's smooth round face looks even more beguilingly natural by contrast with the sharp reflections of light off the complex chair carving. Hallam devoted his adult life to his father's work, leaving Cambridge University without a degree to become Tennyson's companion and secretary. He also wrote the official biography of his father, which was published in 1897.

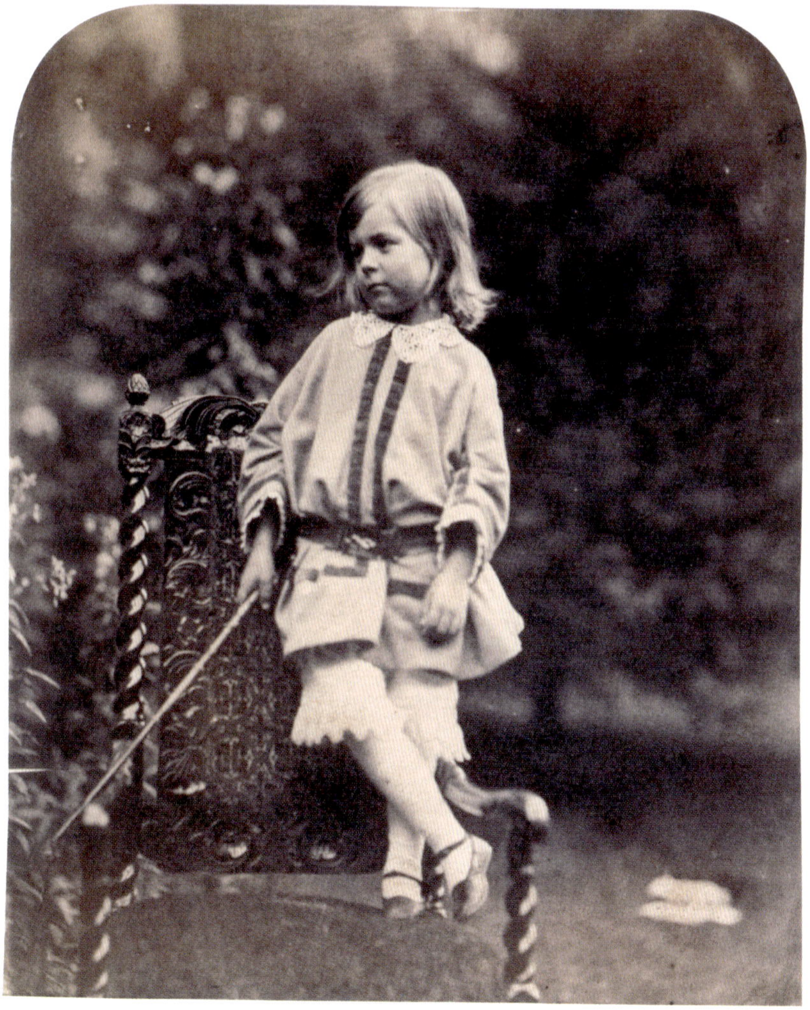

Hallam Tennyson

PLATE 13

Tennysons and Marshalls
Monk Coniston Park, Ambleside, Lake District

29 SEPTEMBER 1857

On the right are Tennyson's hosts, the Marshalls: young Julia Marshall is seated on the floor between her parents. On the left is Tennyson with his son Hallam on his lap. Each group is given its own space — the Tennysons' space is defined by the window, while the Marshalls' is set apart by the areas of wood panelling and curtains. The photograph is unusual for Carroll in its distance from his subjects. The representation of Tennyson and his son is less conventional than the pose of the Marshalls, which appears somewhat impersonal despite the affection evident in Julia's physical closeness to her parents. Carroll continued to make similarly striking images of fathers with their children, in which the closeness of the relationship coexists with the concentration of the father on something else (PLATES 25, 34, 36, 46). Here Tennyson is the only figure staring straight at the camera.

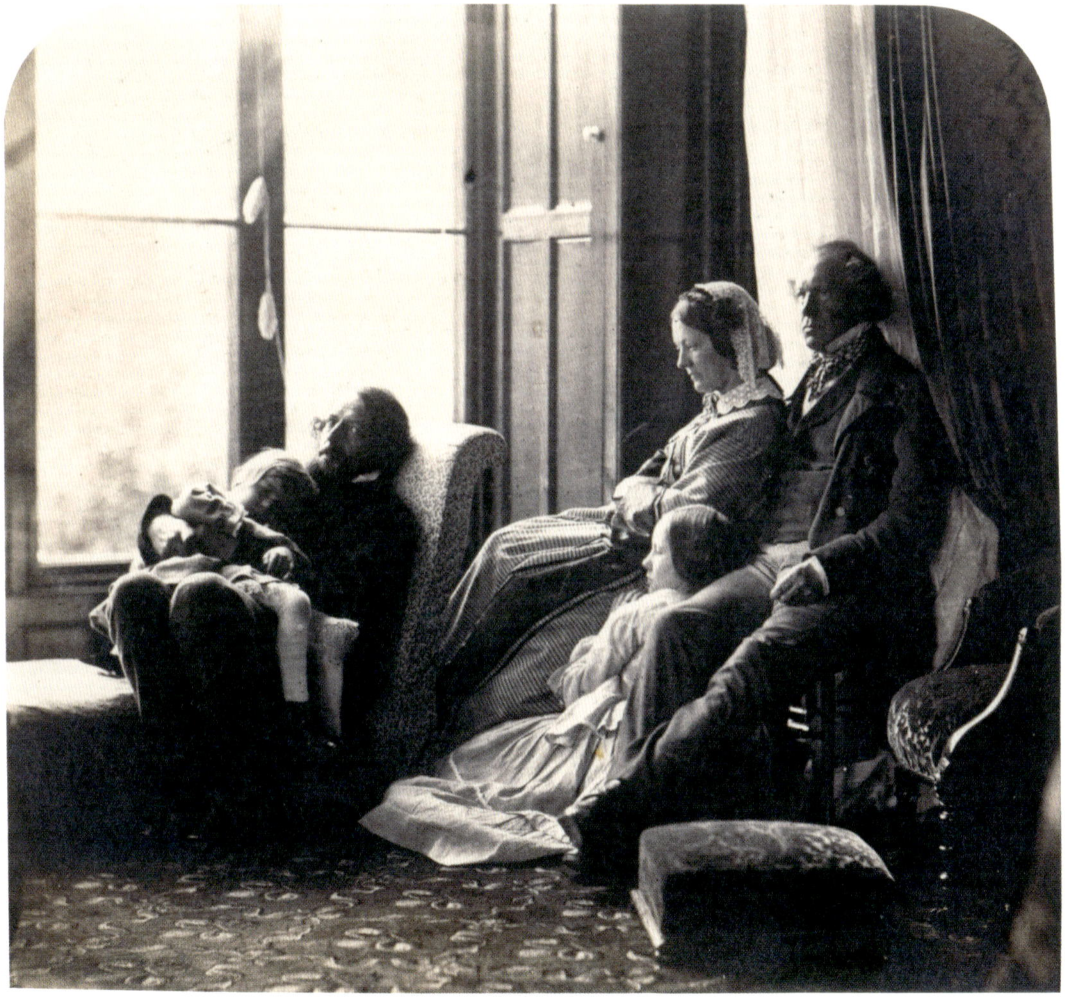

PLATE 14

Kathleen Tidy
Ripon, Yorkshire

1 APRIL 1858

A screen of branches is daringly placed between us and the subject. The variations in the arrangement and size of the branches is markedly natural in comparison with the strict geometric plaid of the child's hat-ribbon and skirt, but stiffer and barer than the child's young face. Kathleen Tidy is the first child-friend about whom a letter from Carroll survives. It was written in 1861. Kathleen was the daughter of Thomas Holmes Tidy, a friend of Carroll's in Yorkshire, and a lieutenant colonel with the 14th Buckinghamshire Foot Regiment. The photograph was made on the occasion of her seventh birthday and required several attempts.

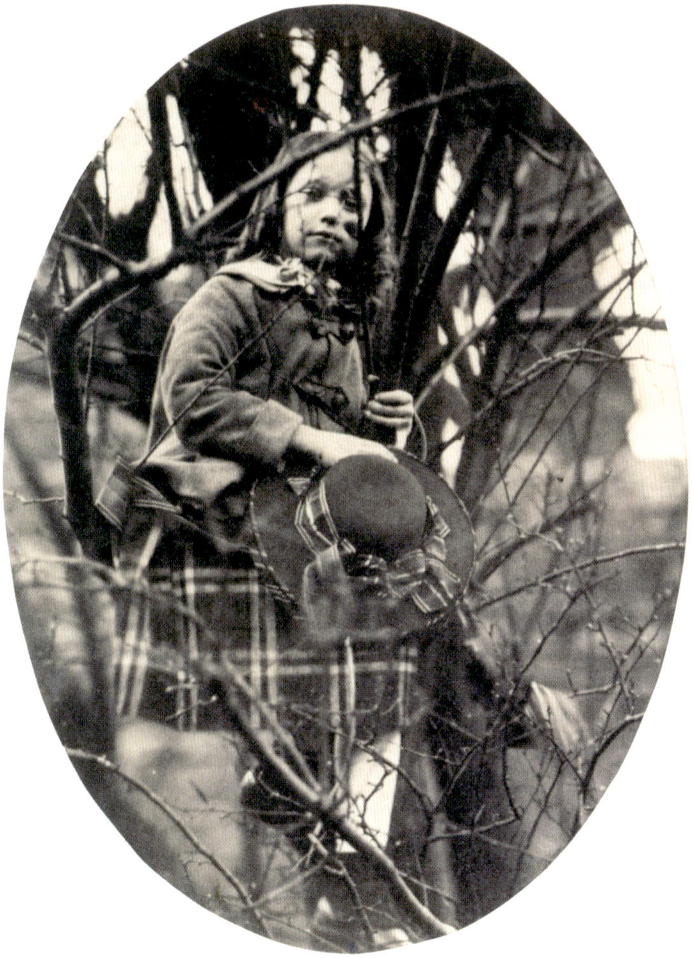

Kathleen H Tidy

PLATE 15

Edith, Lorina and Alice Liddell
Deanery Garden, Christ Church, Oxford

SUMMER 1858

On 4 July 1862, Carroll and a friend took Edith, Lorina and Alice Liddell on a boat trip, during which Carroll told the girls the first version of the *Alice* story. At the sisters' insistence, especially Alice's, Carroll expanded the story and wrote it down. While Alice became the heroine, Lorina and Edith were also cast as characters. The children at first seem slumped in a heap, while the sofa's tilt implies spontaneity. In fact, the children had to pose for about forty-five seconds, and closer examination reveals the image's careful composition. Lorina's head crowns the triangular group against a light background, while Edith's and Alice's heads are framed by the dark sofa behind them. Sleeve ruffles, hands and skirt hems form a layer of intricate detail, and the curved edge of the sofa's patterned upholstery provides a dense base.

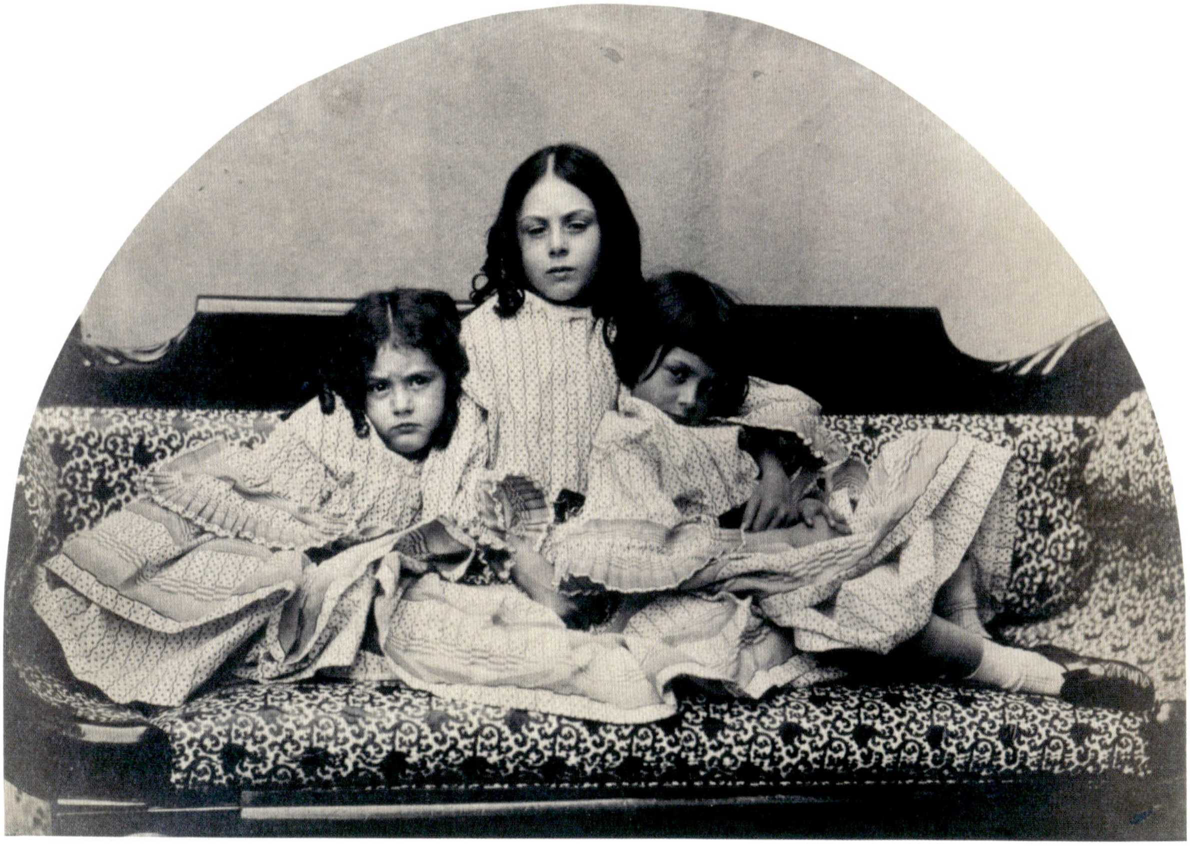

Lorina Charlotte Liddell

Edith Mary Liddell *Alice Pleasance Liddell.*

PLATE 16

Alice Liddell
Deanery Garden, Christ Church, Oxford

SUMMER 1858

Of the Liddell sisters, indeed of all children, Alice was clearly the most fascinating to Carroll. In 1885, Carroll wrote to a grown-up Alice that she had been 'my ideal child-friend.' He said: 'I have had scores of child-friends since your time: but they have been quite a different thing.' It was to Alice that Carroll gave the first manuscript version of *Alice's Adventures Under Ground* in 1864, with an inscription that read: 'A Christmas Gift to a Dear Child, in Memory of a Summer Day.' Unlike most of his portraits, this one of Alice is completely in profile. The sideways direction of her gaze is emphasized by the slat of the chair, which leads our eye from her face to her fingers. This pose removes her from emotional contact with us and thus hints at her own inner thoughts.

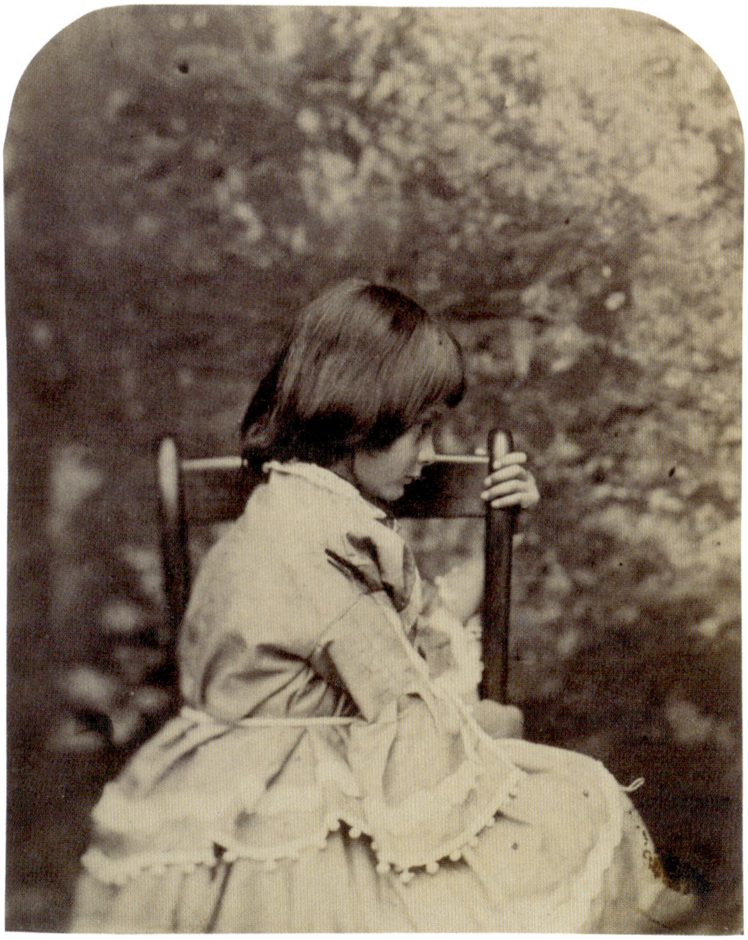

Alice Pleasance Liddell.

PLATE 17

Alice Liddell as 'The Beggar-Maid'
Deanery Garden, Christ Church, Oxford

SUMMER 1858

This picture is one of the most famous photographs in the history of the medium. It portrays a child who is manifestly affluent and alluringly charming in the guise of a wretched beggar. The photograph's lighting and point of view emphasize how completely clean the child's face, hands and feet are, how neatly trimmed and brushed her hair is. Carroll has caught the sparkle of her eyes, and the utter confidence of her gaze. At the very centre of the image, her cupped hand is conspicuously turned sideways, not held outwards in supplication – she asks for nothing. No one in Carroll's audience would have been fooled for an instant into thinking this was a real beggar even though she is barefoot with her clothing in rags. Carroll did make a few photographs of working-class children and, when compared to these, the superficiality of this representation of 'poverty' is made evident.

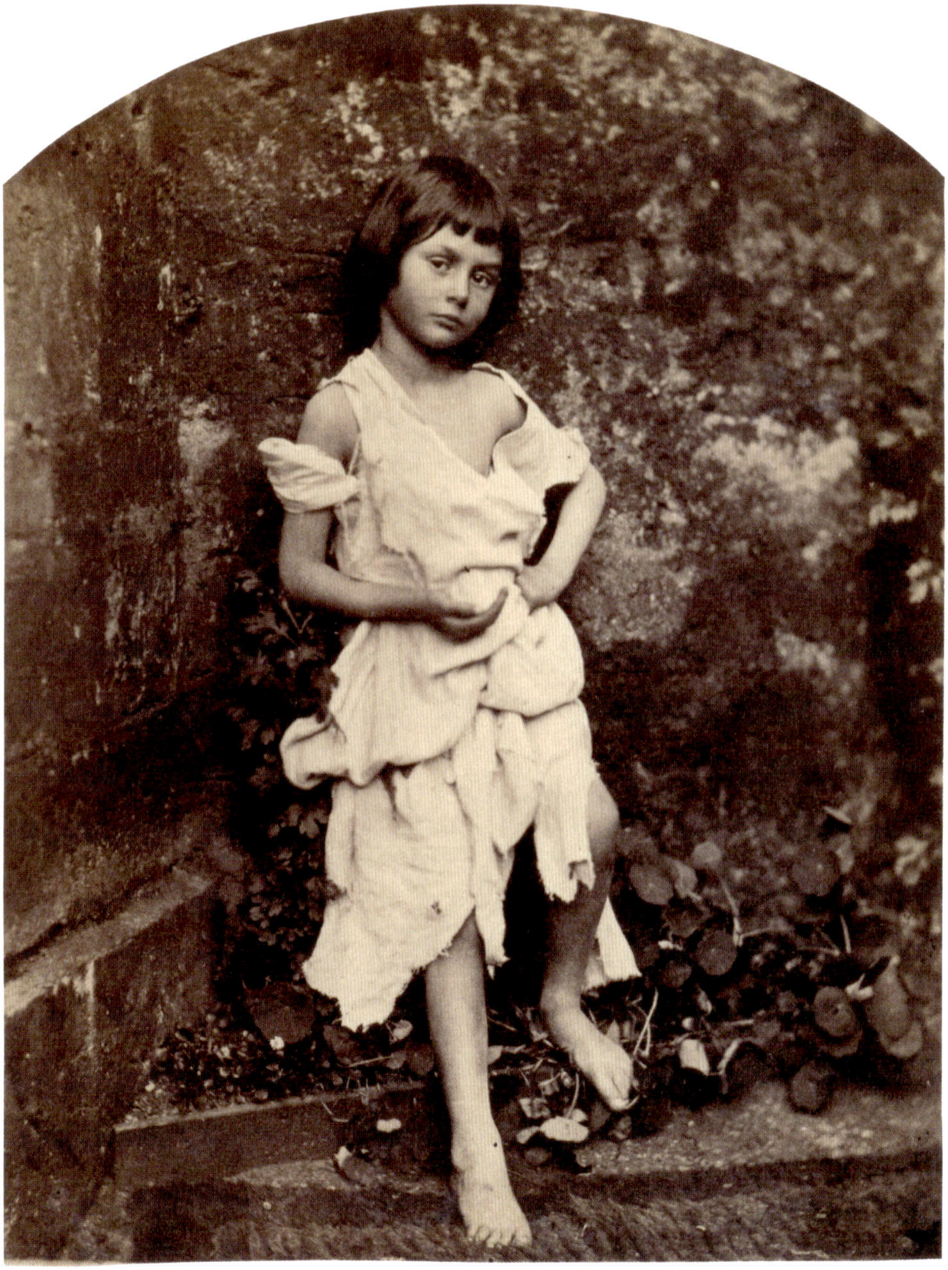

The Beggar. A.L. Oxford.

PLATE 18

Five Twyford Schoolboys
Twyford School, Hampshire

SUMMER 1859

Contrary to current myths about Carroll's work, he took many photographs of boys. Here, five boys on the verge of adolescence strike would-be manly poses. Carroll has posed the boys standing close together as a group, side by side, and the darkness of their jackets blends one boy into the next. At the same time, Carroll has also marked the boys out from the group as individuals: their legs are each positioned in slightly different ways and they appear in front of various backgrounds — a white wall, an open door and foliage on a gate trellis. Twyford was the school attended by Carroll's younger brother, Edwin (PLATE 8). From left to right, the boys have been identified as Clement Drake Elton Malet, Frederick George Richardson, John Henry Clutton, Ralph William Clutton and John St John Frederick.

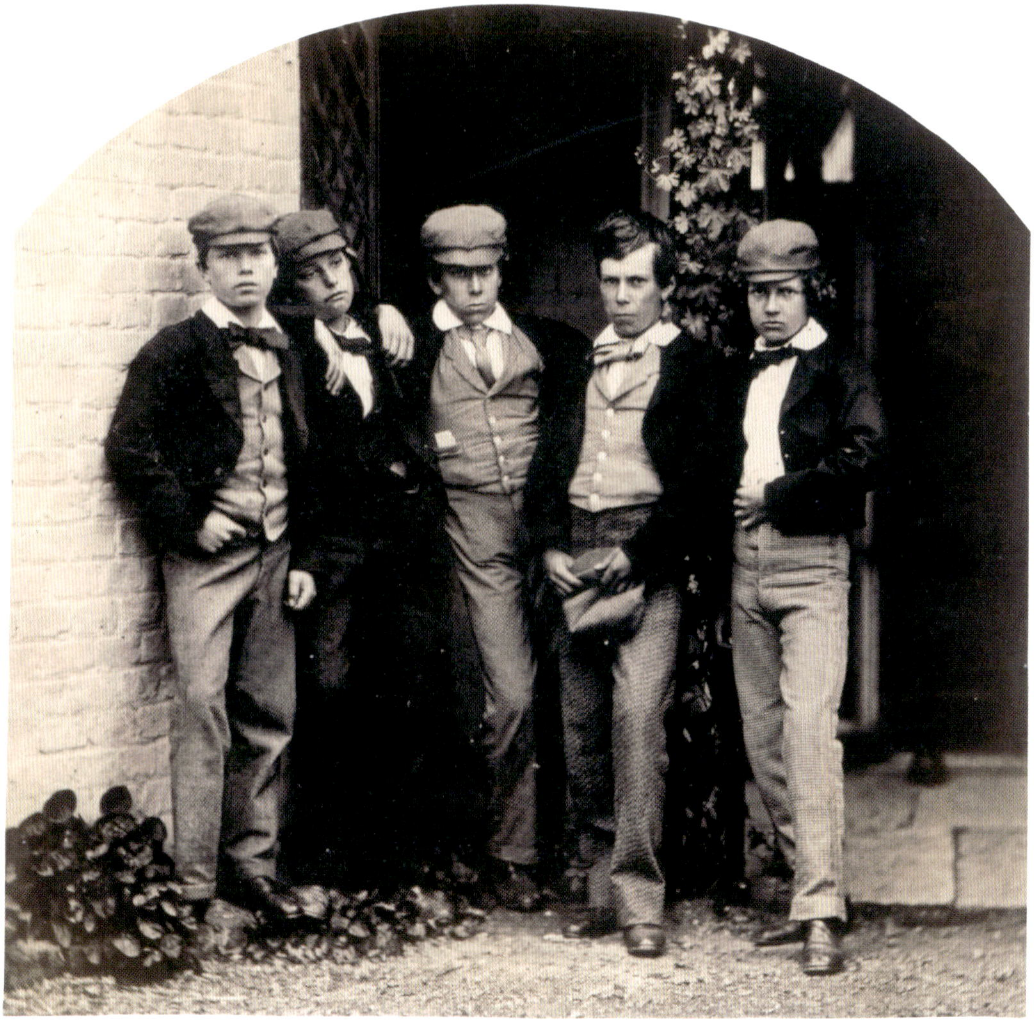

Clement D'E Malet
John Henry Clutton
Ralph Clutton
F. G. Richardson
John St J Frederick

PLATE 19

Joanna and Fanny Grey Smith
Dinsdale Rectory, Yorkshire

SUMMER 1859

Joanna and Fanny Grey Smith were two of the four daughters of Carroll's friends in Yorkshire, the Reverend John and Maria Smith. Staying with them in August 1857, Carroll wrote in his diary that all the Smith children 'were much what one might expect from their free country life, strong, active, handsome, and with a strong aversion to books'. Indeed, when Carroll made a group portrait of all four girls, he showed them with a pet, a doll and a game of chess, but never with a book. These two single portraits also illustrate, formally, how Carroll paid attention to the differences between children, even siblings. The portrait of Joanna (left) is dutiful, the portrait of Fanny (right) is inspired. With Fanny's direct gaze, her flower 'offering', and the crisp and variegated play of light and shadow across her face and hands, her portrait makes a connection with the viewer that her sister's does not.

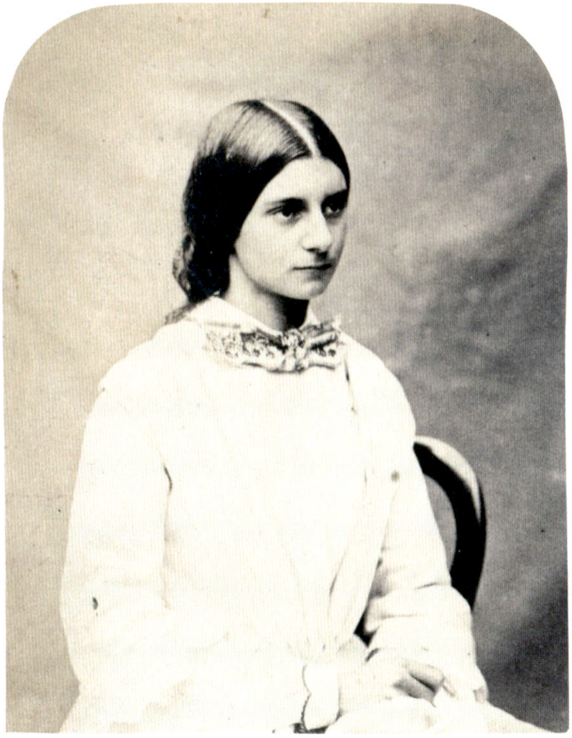

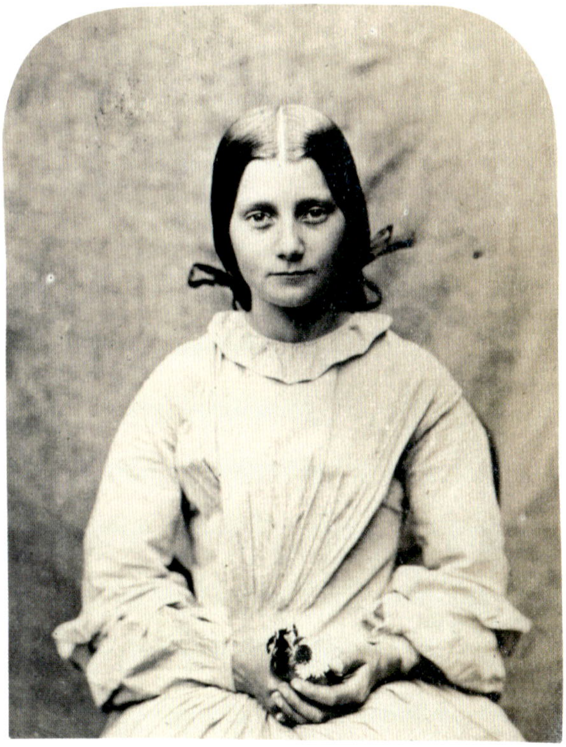

PLATE 20

Lucy Lutwidge
Croft Rectory, Yorkshire

SUMMER 1859

In this rare Victorian image of female scientific curiosity, a middle-aged woman gazes avidly and happily into a microscope. On the table next to the microscope are other scientific paraphernalia, which by pulling our attention downwards and to the left, increase the energy of the direction in which the woman looks. Lucy Lutwidge took over the care and management of the Dodgson household after her sister Frances, Carroll's mother, died in 1851, soon after he left for university. She was thus like a second mother to the Dodgson children. She remained with the family for the rest of her life — first at the Croft Rectory in Yorkshire, where Carroll grew up, and later at The Chestnuts in Guildford, Surrey.

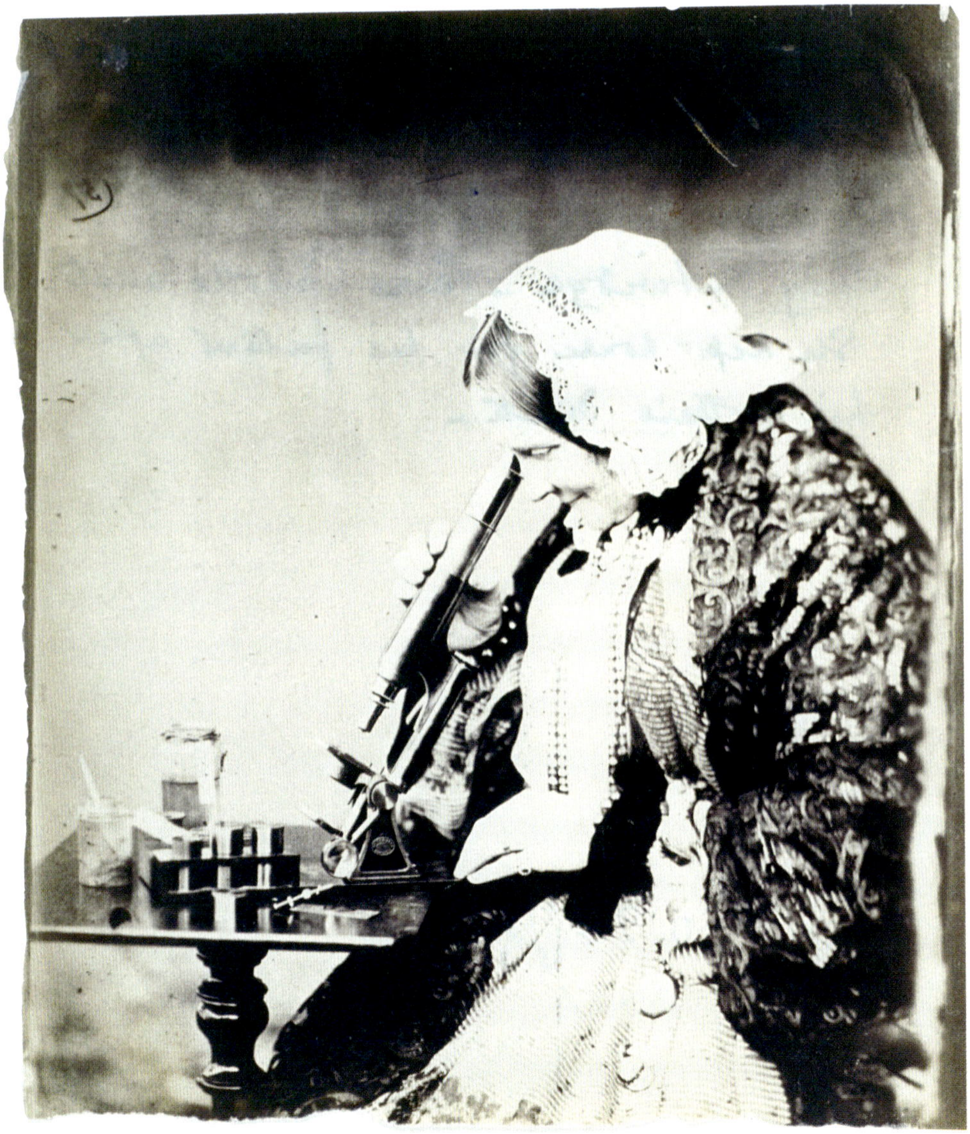

PLATE 21

Henrietta Mary and Margaret Anne Lutwidge
Croft Rectory, Yorkshire

SUMMER 1859

As in his portrait of Lucy Lutwidge (PLATE 20), this portrait of her two sisters Henrietta Mary and Margaret Anne represents the intelligence of his aunts – here by showing them engaged in a game of chess. The two women are both likened and differentiated from each other, just like the opposing chess pieces with which they play. Margaret, who plays the white side, is set against a light background, while Henrietta, who plays the black side, is set against a dark background. While most of the details of the sisters' clothing and hair arrangements are individual, the basic style of their costume is the same, and they both wear distinctive beaded bracelets. Chess figures prominently in *Through the Looking Glass*: 'It's a huge game of chess that's being played – all over the world – if this is the world at all, you know. Oh what fun it is! How I *wish* I was one of them! I wouldn't mind being a Pawn, if only I might join – though of course I should *like* to be a Queen, best.'

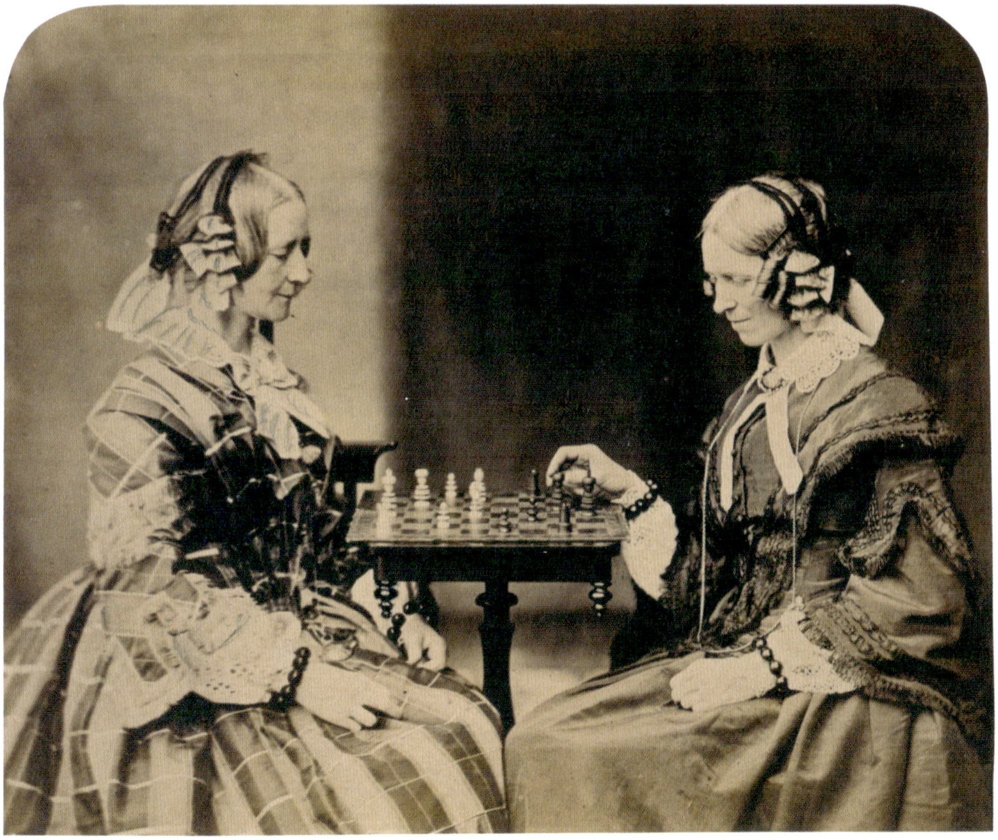

PLATE 22

Alice Liddell as 'Queen of the May'
Deanery Garden, Christ Church, Oxford

MAY – JUNE 1860

In this portrait, Alice Liddell is crowned with flowers as the traditional Queen of the May – the young girl chosen each year to represent purity and the potential of a renewed earth in the traditional British May Day celebrations. A few years after this picture was made, by the end of 1863, Carroll had become estranged from the Liddell family. No one knows why, but the best guesses revolve around the social ambitions of Lorina Liddell, Alice's mother, for whom Carroll would not have seemed advantageous company. For his part, Carroll made disparaging remarks in his diary about Alice's passage into adolescence, and later made a photograph of her as a young woman in which she looks both miserable and trapped. Alice went on to make a good marriage to a country gentleman, Reginald Hargreaves, on 15 September 1880.

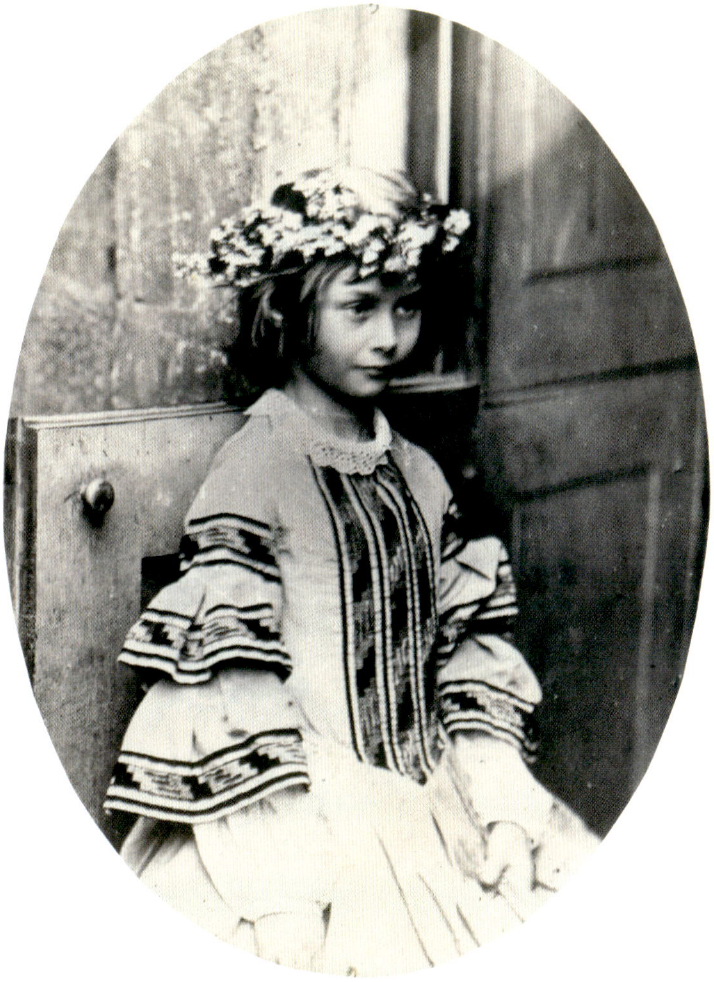

Alice Liddell.
daughter of the Dean of Ch. Ch.

PLATE 23

Mr and Mrs Henry Hobson and Family
Croft Rectory, Yorkshire

SUMMER 1860

This is one of Carroll's most straightforward family groups. Despite the intended starched formality of the sitters' costumes and posture, Carroll manages to capture glimmers of the parents' protective affection and of the children's boredom with posing. In his writings on photography, Carroll took particularly devastating comic aim at photographic family portraits, which may explain why he made few of them himself and also why this example is so carefully symmetrical and planar in its composition. Henry Hobson and his wife, Sarah, both taught at the Croft National School which was established by Carroll's father. They are here photographed with their daughters and son who were named (from left to right), Lydia, Henry and Eliza.

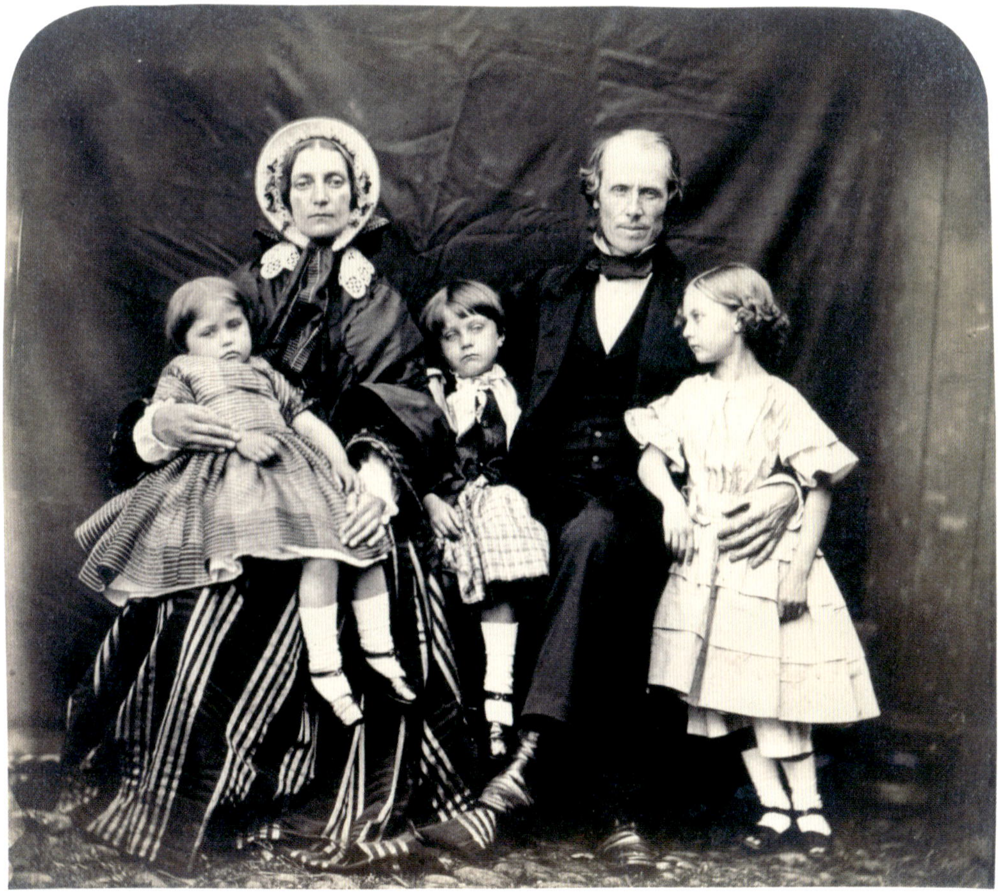

PLATE 24

Magdalen Tower
Oxford

SUMMER 1861

The tower of Magdalen College, Oxford, has always been much admired. Carroll was particularly appreciative of the city's architecture and, at several points in his academic career, he argued for the preservation of old buildings. Like the many landscape paintings of the era, for which English art is famous, this photograph obeys the conventional rules of representation. The foreground of grasses offers a space to enter into the picture imaginatively, a horizontal middle-ground presents a variety of incidents, and the far background disappears into a haze. Carroll also includes some figures in his composition – four girls in their short skirts and a nursemaid, identifiable by her bare head, near the water.

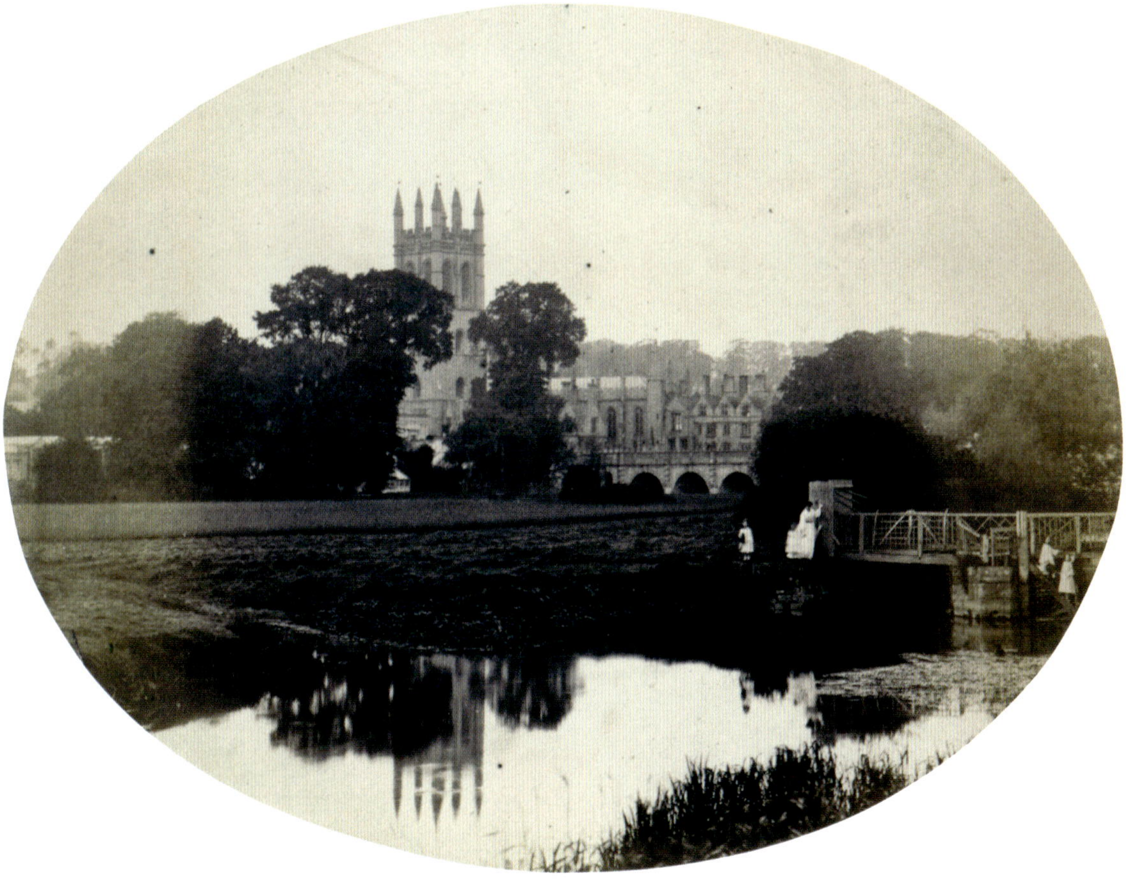

PLATE 25

Professor Robert Gandell and his daughter Florence
Iffley Rectory, Oxford

10 JULY 1862

Florence Gandell's body provides the photograph's central axis, extended by one of her father's legs, while her leg and the chaise establish a stable base for the image. Her delicate embrace of her father is made to seem closer because he is placed right next to the upholstered curve of the chaise's backrest, and is further emphasized by their joint focus on the same bright white letter. Professor Robert Gandell was a colleague of Carroll's at Oxford and was a tutor of Magdalen Hall at the time this picture was made. In an era in which 'Madonna' pictures of mothers and children were ubiquitous, Carroll showed an unusual sensitivity to the relationships between men he knew and their children (PLATES 13, 34, 36, 46).

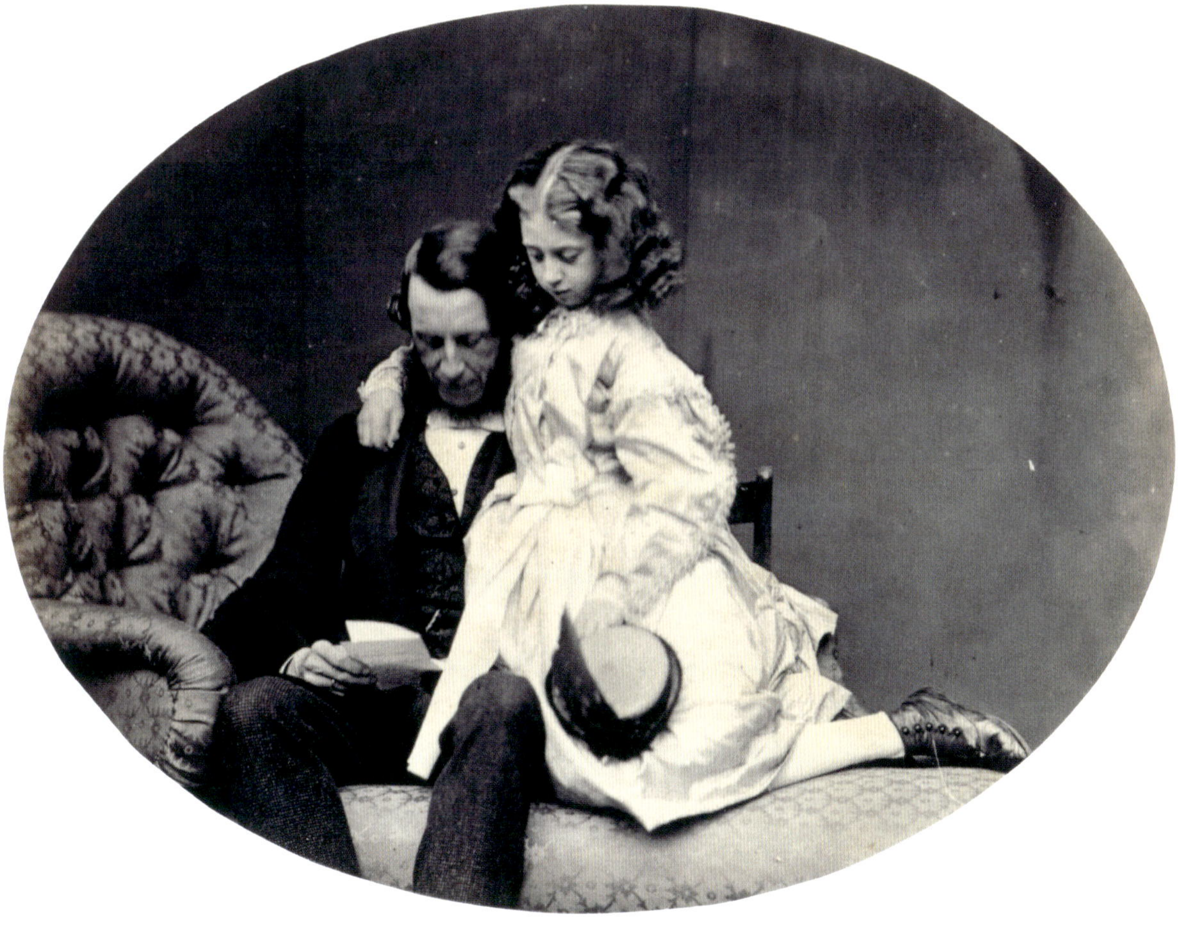

R Gandell
Florence Gandell
July 10. 1862.

PLATE 26

Alice Jane Donkin in 'The Elopement'
Barmby Moor, Yorkshire

9 OCTOBER 1862

Although the girl in this photograph wears the short skirts that identify her as a young girl, Carroll entitled this image *The Elopement*. In 1862, Alice Jane Donkin was only eleven but already romantically attached to Carroll's brother, Wilfred Dodgson (PLATE 52), and the couple were married nine years later. Very unusually for Carroll's photographs, this portrait is elaborately staged out-of-doors and illustrates an episode in a narrative story — the moment when the woman escapes out of a window to join her intended companion. Carroll admired Victorian painting, which was similarly narrative and often contained a moral message. In his photography, however, he preferred to capture a still and realistic moment, one without any obvious moral or dramatic content.

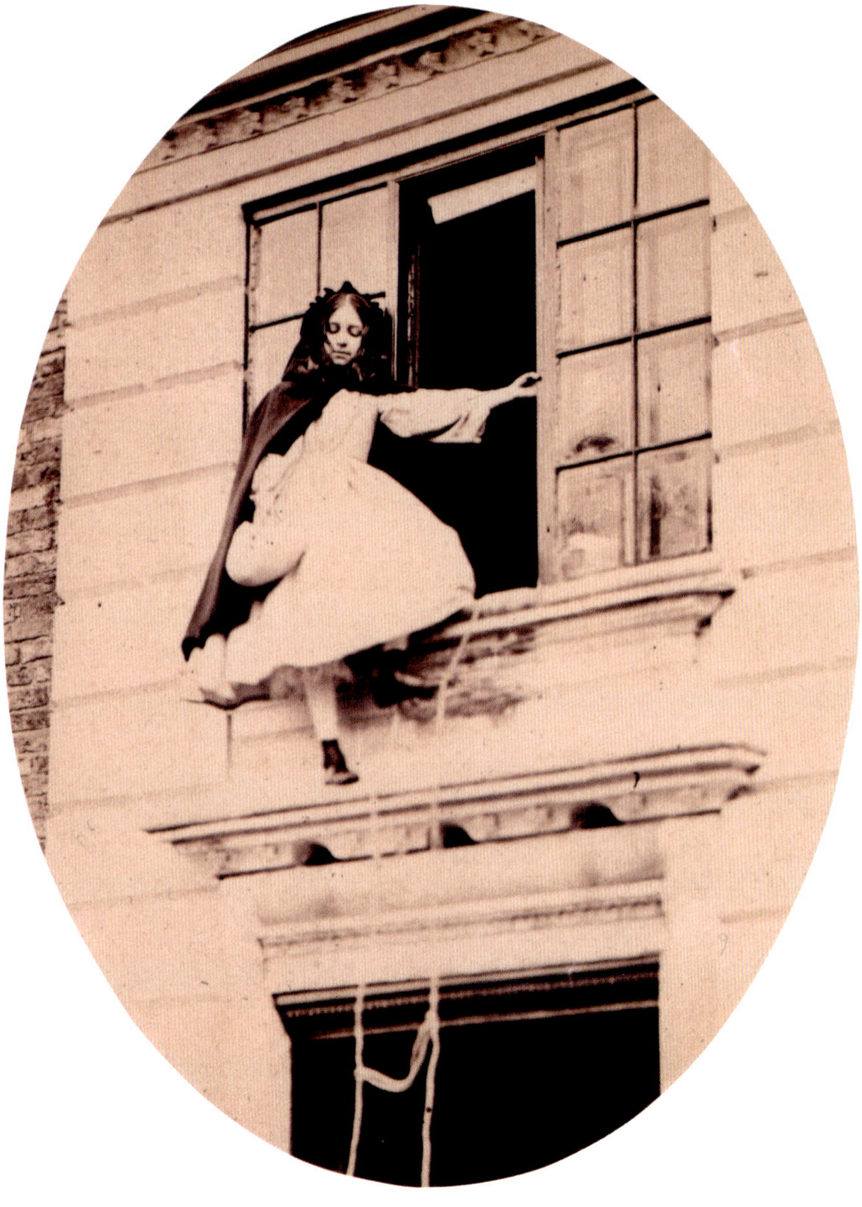

Alice Jane Donkin

PLATE 27

Irene MacDonald in 'It Won't Come Smooth'
Elm Lodge, Hampstead, London

25 — 31 JULY 1863

The girl's slightly large head, her blousy, buttoned white nightgown and the inward curl of her toes on one foot all register as signs of childhood innocence, and are reinforced by the title, which echoes the complaint of generations of little girls obliged to wear their hair long: 'it won't come smooth.' The feminine ideal of the time demanded hair that was long, yet perfectly groomed. (However the young Alice Liddell wore her dark hair short and straight, unlike the depiction of Alice in John Tenniel's illustrations where she appears with long blonde hair). The empty chair next to Irene MacDonald emphasizes her diminutive size, yet her brush and mirror hint at the world of the adult woman. 'It won't come smooth' could also serve as the motto of *Alice's Adventures in Wonderland* during which Alice cannot satisfy anyone's expectations of her.

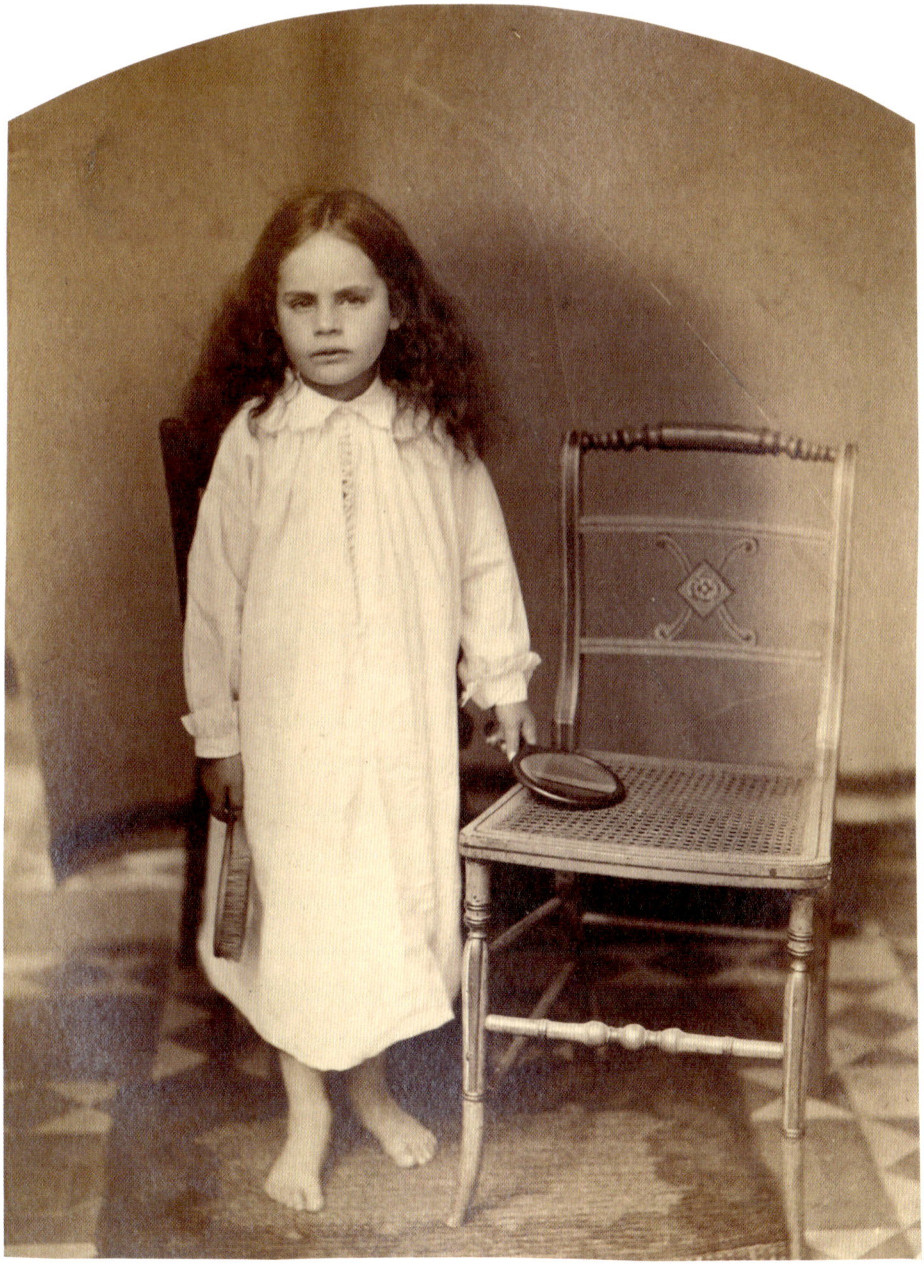

PLATE 28

Irene MacDonald
Elm Lodge, Hampstead, London

25—31 JULY 1863

Arms and shins bare, heavy-lidded gaze meeting the viewer's eyes, wrapped in luxurious fabrics and reclining on animal skins, this child could almost be seen to be posing as a harem girl. Western Europeans then associated North Africa, the Middle East, India and East Asia with indolent sensuality, in an attitude we now call Orientalism. Irene MacDonald was the daughter of George MacDonald, a close friend of Carroll's who also wrote children's books. The family had recently been to Algiers, which may have inspired this picture. Whatever evocation of the Orient Carroll or the family intended, they are contradicted by the neat and shiny strapped black shoes and immaculate white ankle socks typical of the clothing of affluent European girls.

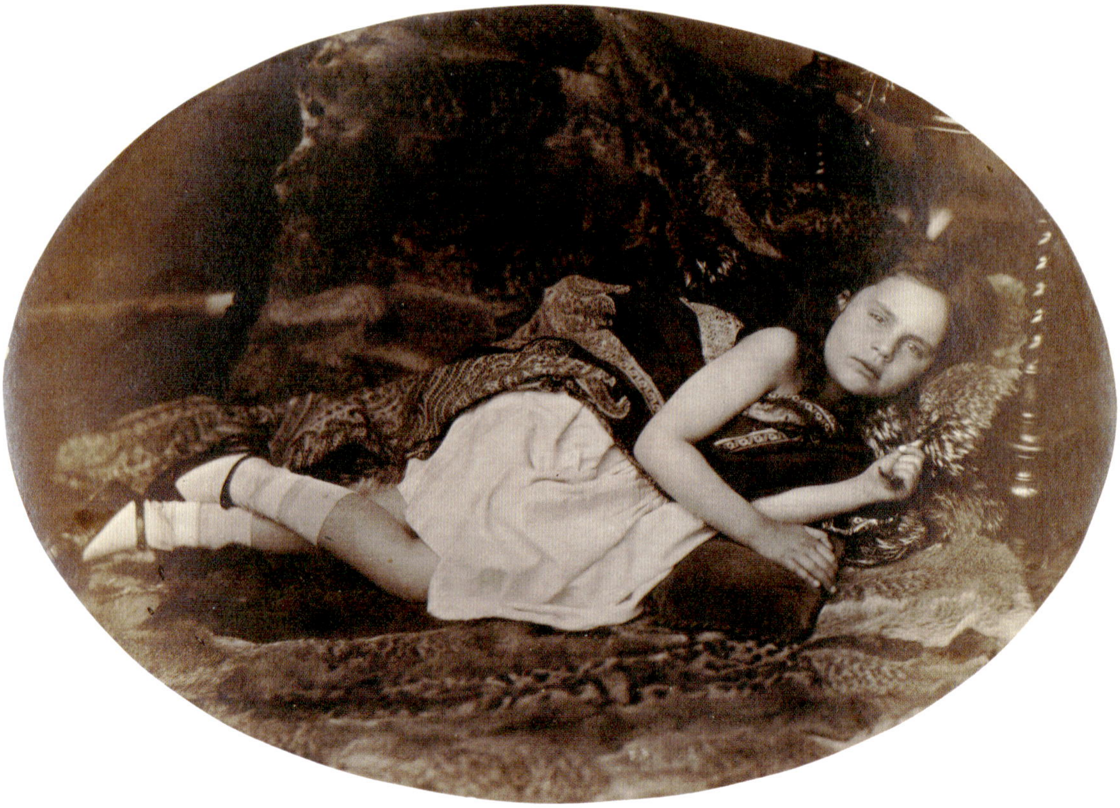

IRENE MAC DONALD

PLATE 29

Marcus Keane
Whitby, Yorkshire

26—29 AUGUST 1863

Just as it is a myth that Carroll only photographed girls, so it is untrue that all his most sensual photographs were of girls. Perhaps this picture has added to the confusion, because very young Victorian boys wore skirts. Yet Carroll has included a hint of his sitter's gender: a toy horse, rather than a doll. Horses were associated with masculinity and boys were often posed with toy horses in Carroll's portraits (PLATES 47, 55). This horse is quite small, reminding us that this is a very young boy. From deep within his pillow, tightly clutching his toy horse, Marcus Keane looks out intensely — whether he is sulky, scared or sultry is hard to tell.

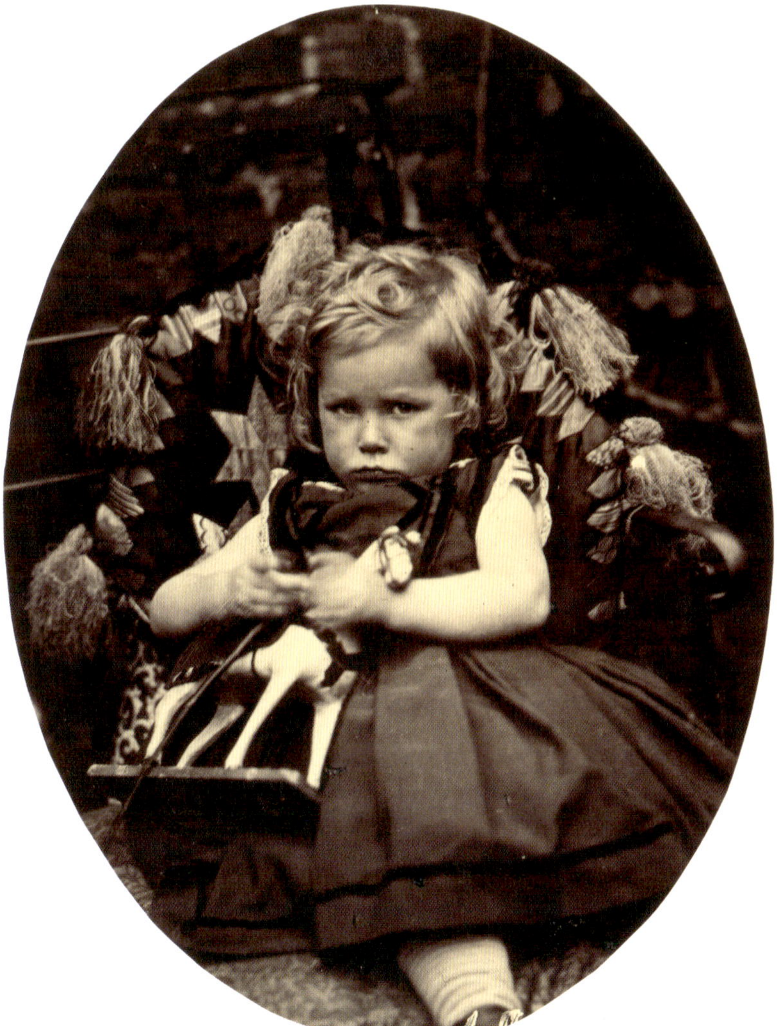

by L.C.

PLATE 30

Tom Taylor
Wandsworth, London

3 OCTOBER 1863

This portrait captures Tom Taylor's intelligent gaze and relaxed posture, and also shows Carroll's careful use of setting. The striped blanket behind Taylor directs attention towards the most expressive part of the portrait — his face and hands. This picture was taken at Taylor's home in south London, where Carroll stayed for three days from 3 to 6 October 1863. In his diary, Carroll notes that he 'had the cellar as a dark room, and the conservatory as a studio, and succeeded in getting some very good portraits'. Like Carroll, Taylor was an extraordinary polymath who was, among other things, Professor of English Literature at University College London, a journalist, an art critic for *The Times*, editor of *Punch* magazine, and one of the most popular playwrights of his generation. It was Taylor who introduced Carroll to John Tenniel, who illustrated the first editions of the *Alice* books.

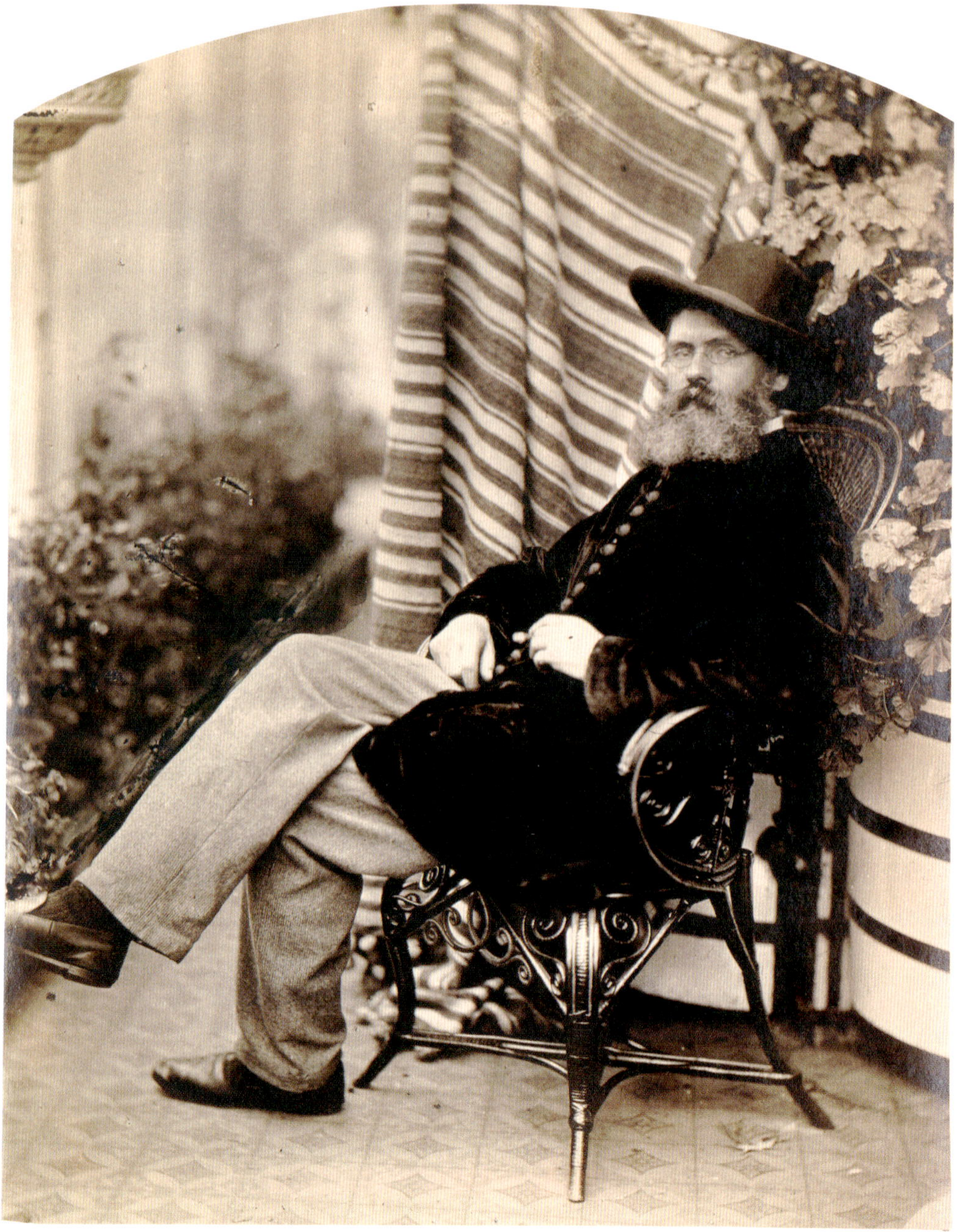

Tom Taylor
Oct: 3: 1863.

PLATE 31

Christina Georgina Rossetti
and her mother Frances Rossetti
16 Cheyne Walk, Chelsea, London

7 OCTOBER 1863

Christina Georgina and Frances Rossetti were the sister and mother of the famous Pre-Raphaelite painter and poet Dante Gabriel Rossetti. Carroll seems to have been intrigued by the women's close relationship to each other, here shown by the merging of the daughter and mother into one single mass. Both women look at the same book, which is tantalizingly out of focus. Frances Rossetti (née Polidori) was also the sister of John William Polidori, the personal physician and companion of the poet Lord Byron. Her daughter lived with her until she died. Christina Georgina Rossetti is now widely considered to be among the most important Victorian poets. Reclusive in her own lifetime, and in the shadow of her better-known siblings, she wrote works such as *Goblin Market* (1862), whose powerful imagery and sensuality has been increasingly appreciated, particularly by feminist scholars, since the 1970s.

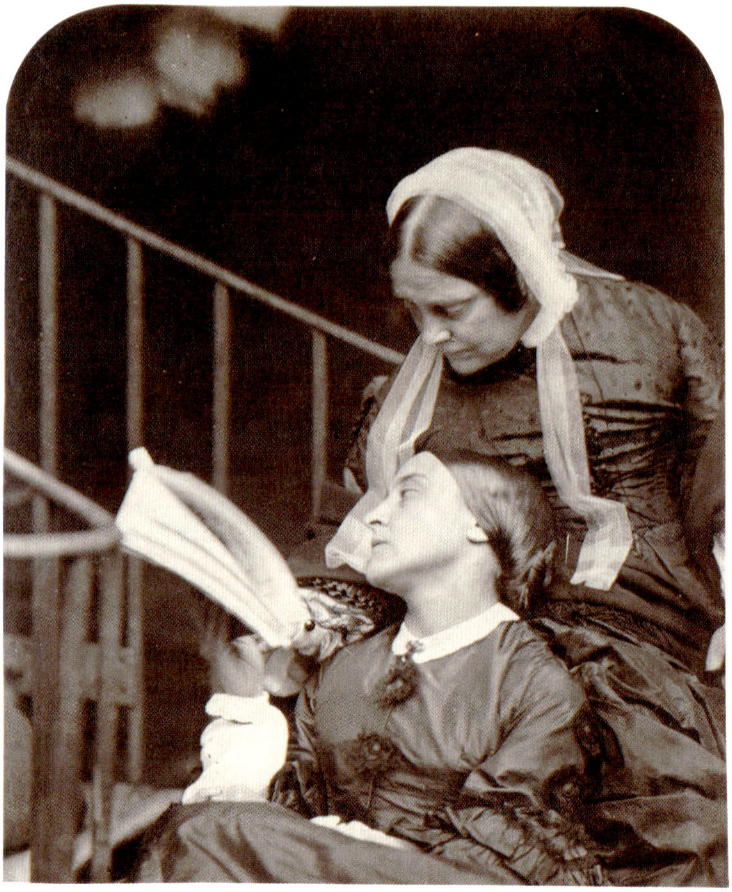

Frances Rossetti
Christina G. Rossetti

PLATE 32

Alexander and Mary Munro
16 Cheyne Walk, Chelsea, London

7 OCTOBER 1863

The mutual trust and affection manifest on the faces of the couple here is visually reinforced by the alignment of their gazes towards each other along the angle of the stair railing behind them. Even the placing of Alexander's hand on his wife's shoulder, directly above her own clasped hands, creates a visual link between them that again emphasizes their intimate relationship. Alexander Munro was a close friend of Carroll's. He was a sculptor who frequently exhibited at the Royal Academy and was well known for his charming images of children. One of Munro's most popular sculptures, *Boy with Dolphin*, is now the statue on the fountain in Hyde Park, London. Carroll included several photographs of Munro's sculptures in his albums, which shows his high esteem for his work, but also the affinity he felt between their representations of children.

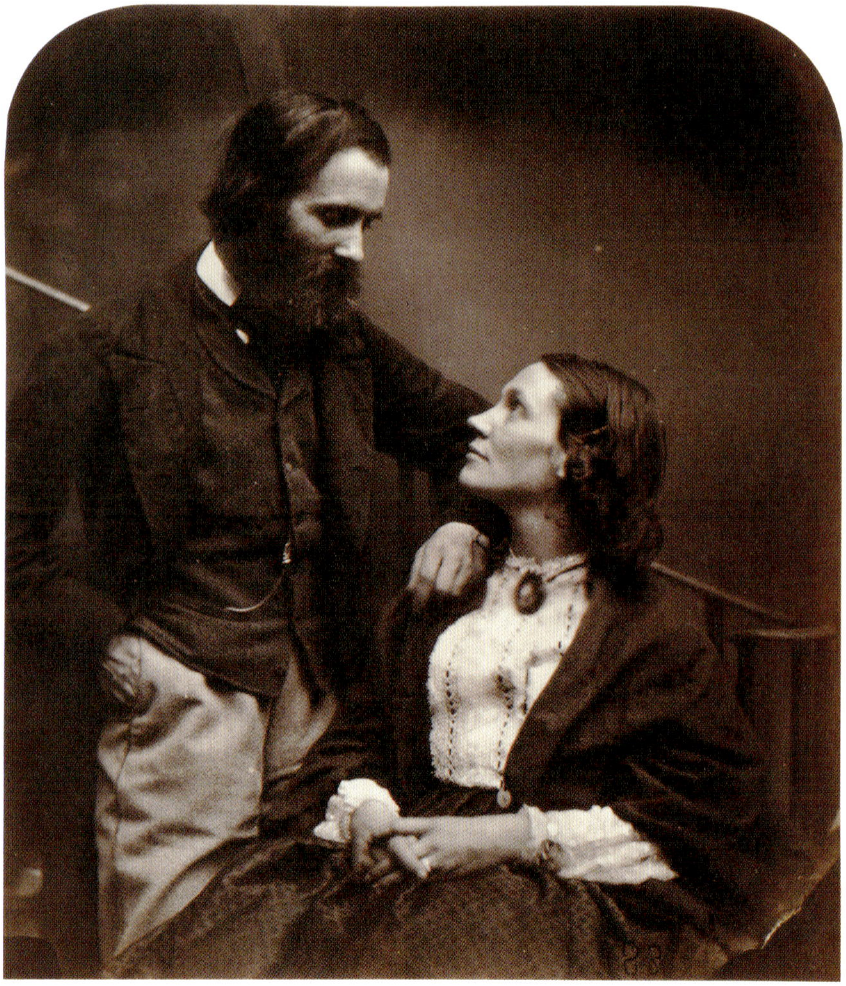

PLATE 33

Helene Beyer
16 Cheyne Walk, Chelsea, London

9 OCTOBER 1863

Helene Beyer — referred to in Carroll's diary as 'Madame Beyer' — was a model for several Pre-Raphaelite artists who were friends of Carroll, including the sculptor Alexander Munro (PLATE 32) and the painter Dante Gabriel Rossetti. This photograph was taken on the staircase of Rossetti's London home, 16 Cheyne Walk, where Carroll stayed in early October 1863, before returning to stay with the MacDonalds (PLATES 27, 28) in north London. Carroll's formal invention is evident when comparing his three different uses of a similar setting on the staircase of the Rossetti's home (PLATES 31, 32, 33).
In light of Carroll's fondness for photographing children, it is interesting to note the handsome strength of many of the adult women that he photographed, as is particularly evident here.

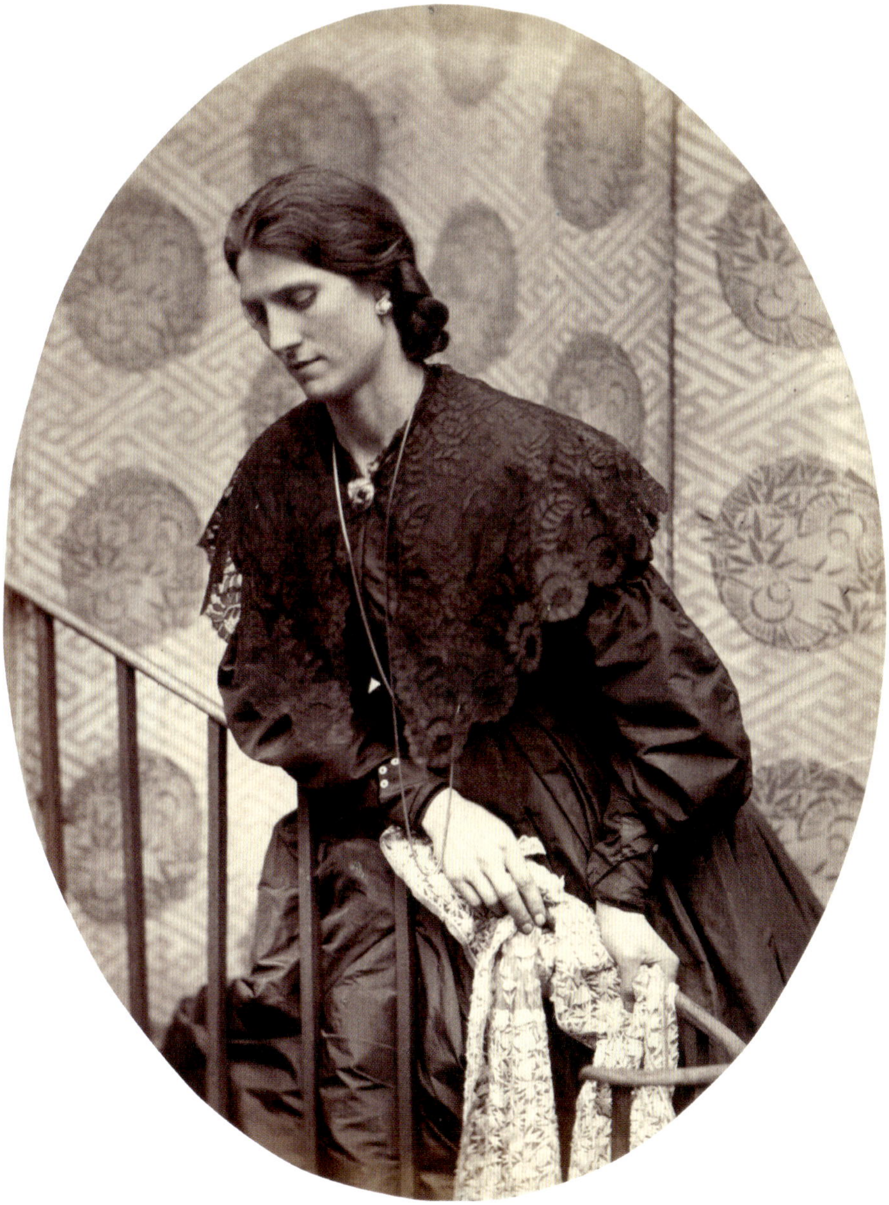

Johanna Unger

PLATE 34

Arthur Hughes and his daughter Agnes
12 Earl's Terrace, Kensington, London

12 OCTOBER 1863

At the heart of the image is a circle of intimacy, created by the heads of the father and daughter, his hand on her arm, their joined hands, the curve of his sleeve and her tiny fingers on the back of his collar. Arthur Hughes was a Pre-Raphaelite painter and illustrator whose work Carroll greatly admired. Carroll had a strong appreciation of the fine arts and bought a number of works to hang in his rooms at Christ Church, including Hughes's *The Lady with the Lilacs* (1863). He took a number of photographs of the Hughes children and particuarly admired Agnes. In recalling making this portrait he wrote in his diary: 'Got a splendid picture of him [Arthur Hughes] with Agnes.'

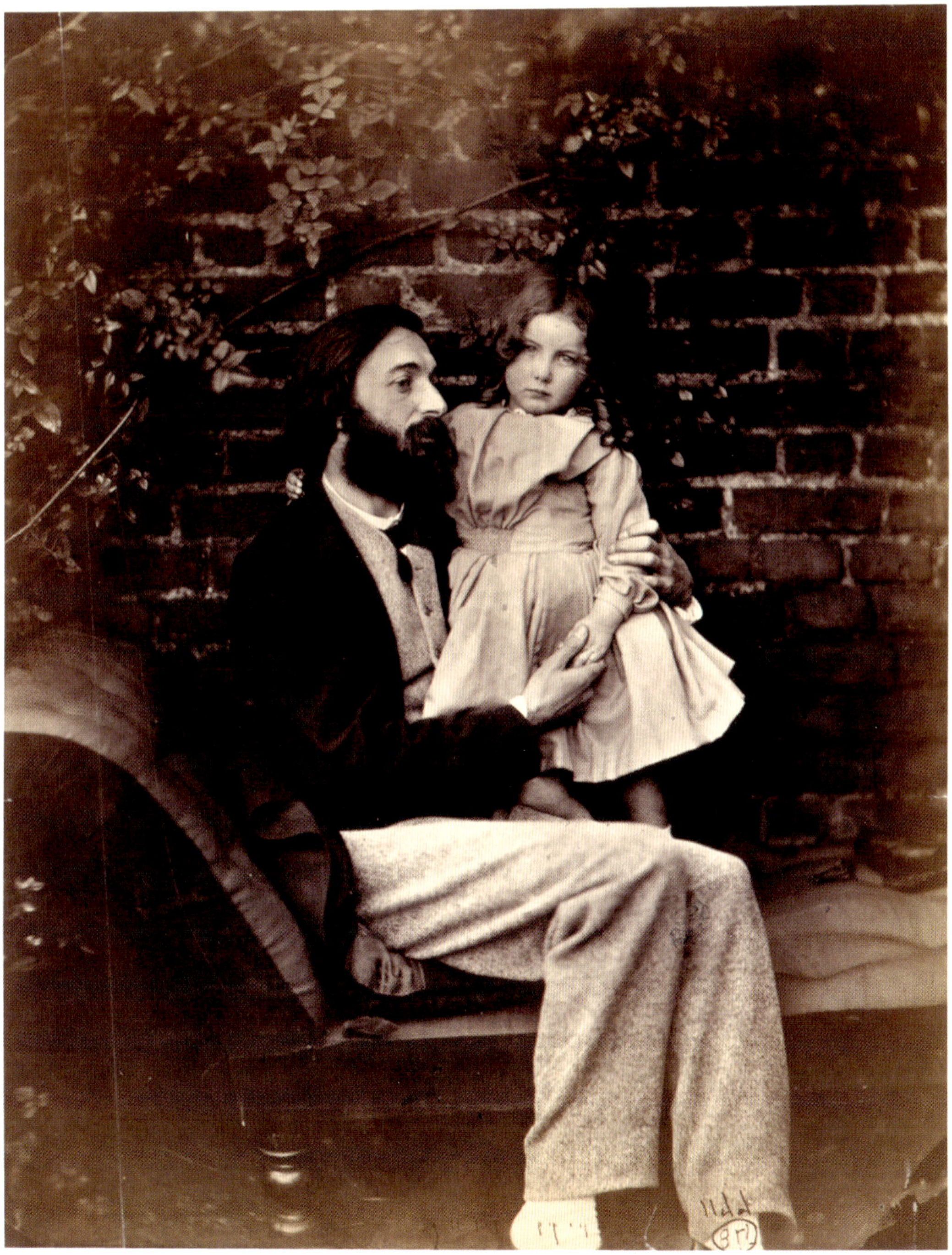

PLATE 35

Arthur Foord Hughes
12 Earl's Terrace, Kensington, London

12 OCTOBER 1863

The rhyming ovals of the caned chair back and straw hat, the turn of the boy's face towards the left, and the ribbon flying over his shoulder all give this photograph a sense of movement. The impression of natural spontaneity in Carroll's child-portraits, notably this one, is all the more remarkable when one remembers how painstakingly long Carroll's wet collodion photographic technique forced his exposures to be. Arthur Foord Hughes was the son of the artist, Arthur Hughes, and brother of Agnes (PLATE 34). The Hughes family was another of the families, like the MacDonalds and the Munros, whose company Carroll enjoyed and whose relationships he celebrated in his group portraits.

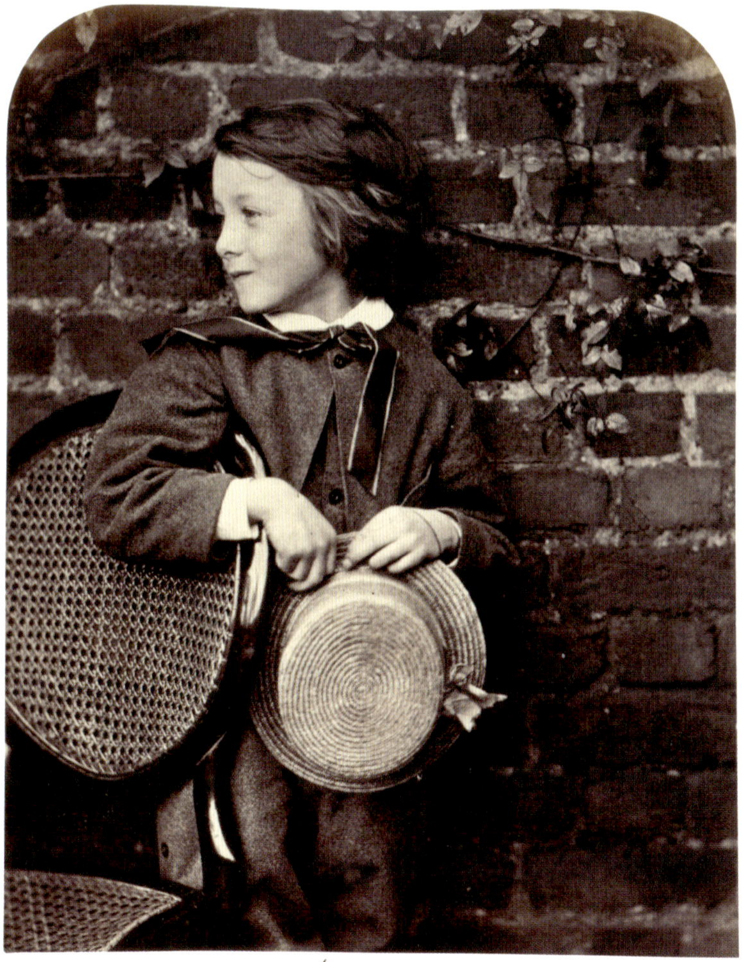

Arthur Hughes.

PLATE 36

Reverend Thomas Childe Barker and his daughter May
Badcock's Yard, Oxford

6 JUNE 1864

May Barker dominates the image, winding confidently through its centre, while her father, Reverend Thomas Childe Barker leans his head evocatively at the exact corner of a window frame, so that his gaze barely escapes outdoors. Again, in his diary Carroll records his pride in his photography. Writing about this picture he states: 'Barker arrived with his eldest child, May, whom I begged he would bring over to be photographed. Took three pictures of her. One, with him, looks first rate.'

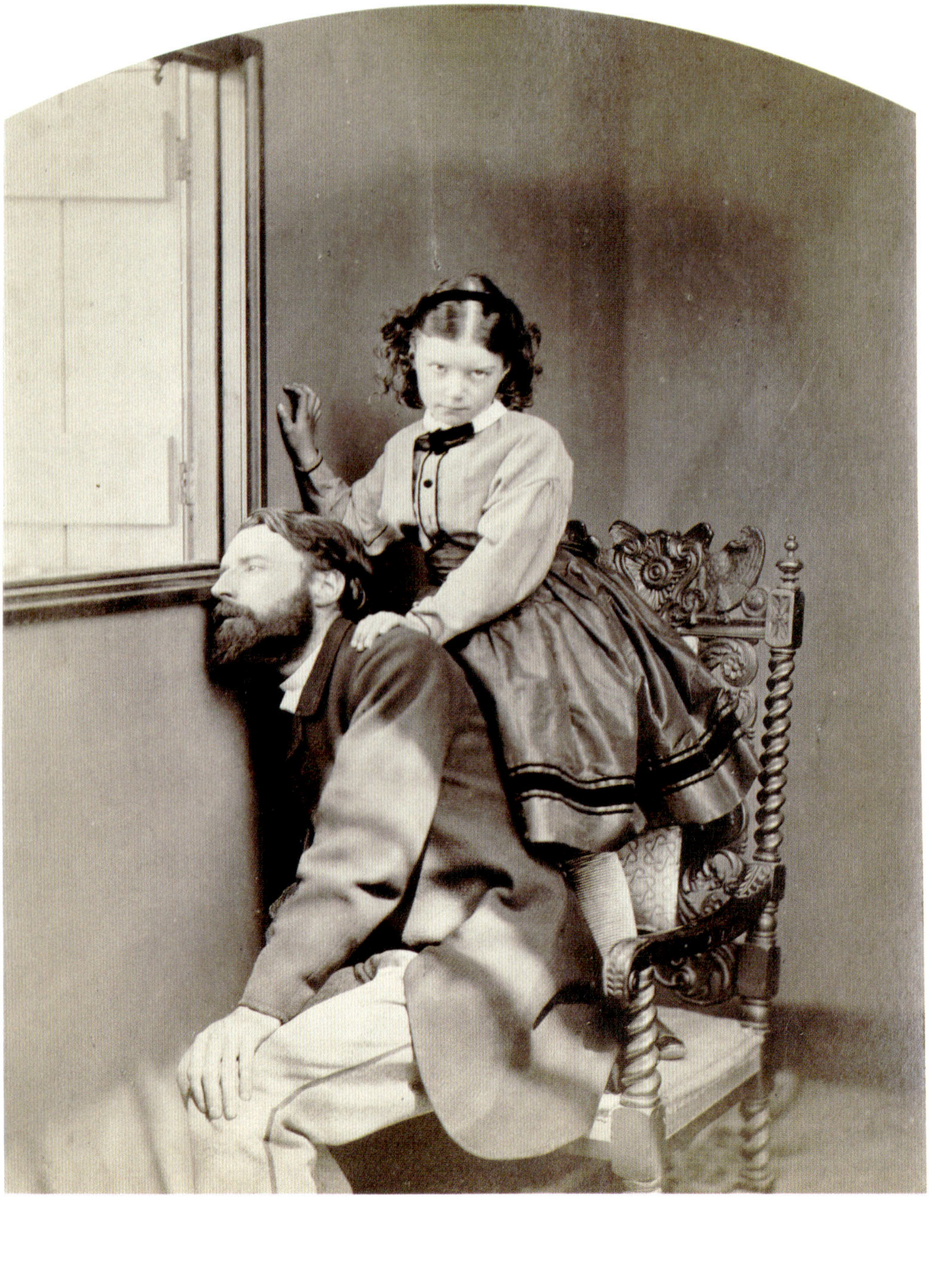

PLATE 37

Grace Denman
Lambeth Palace, London

8 JULY 1864

The handle of the croquet mallet and the rising steps emphasize the linearity of the image, while the chequered dress fabric adds another element of geometry. Against these patterns the face, hands and calves of the little girl stand out. Five-year-old Grace was the daughter of George Denman, an MP and Judge of the High Court. This picture calls to mind a famous croquet scene in *Alice's Adventures in Wonderland*: 'Alice thought she had never seen such a curious croquet-ground in all her life; it was all ridges and furrows; the balls were live hedgehogs, the mallets live flamingoes, and the soldiers had to double themselves up and to stand upon their hands and feet, to make the arches [...] it was a very difficult game indeed.'

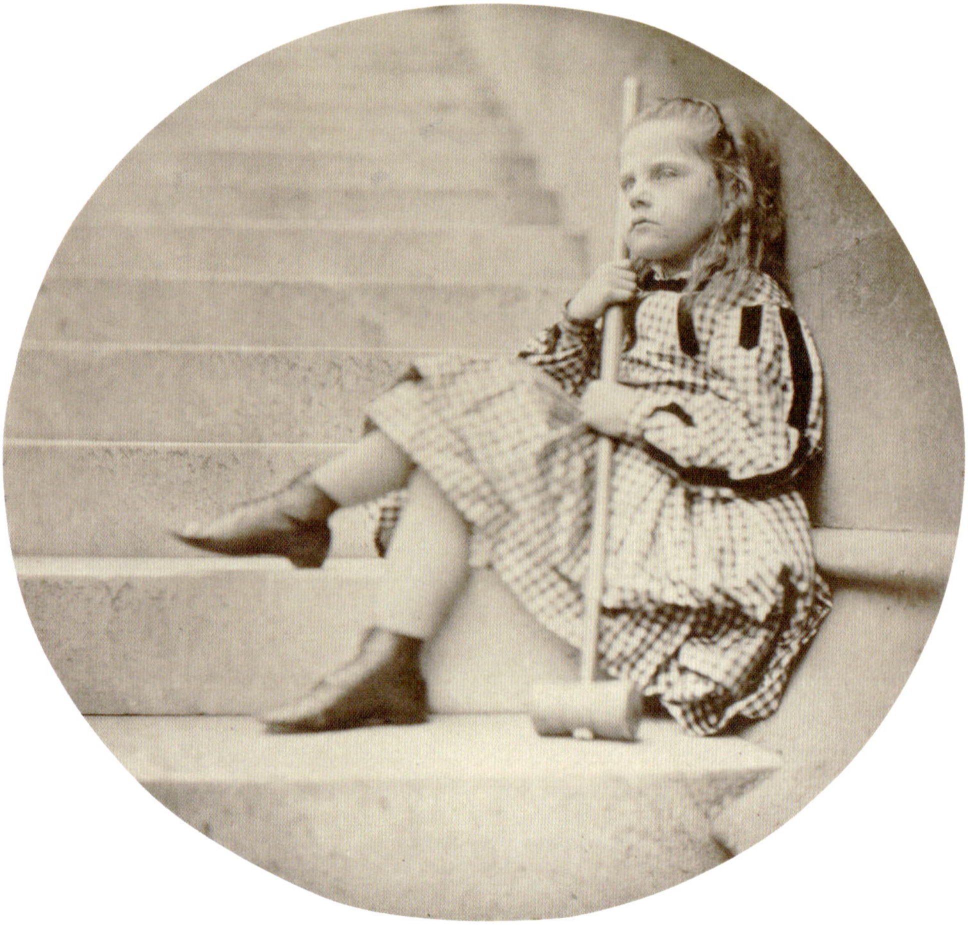

PLATE 38

Alice Constance Westmacott
Lambeth Palace, London

9 JULY 1864

In comparison with his portrait of Grace Denman, made in the same location (PLATE 37), Carroll makes a different use of the stairs in this composition – here the stripes of a blanket repeat the pattern of the steps boldly in the foreground. Carroll presented his photographs in albums and often asked his subjects to sign their name below their portrait — Alice Constance Westmacott's childish cursive, reproduced here, is particularly charming. By displaying the signatures, Carroll confirmed the subject's approval of their portrait and also added a personal touch that appealed to the friends and acquaintances to whom he showed his albums. Alice was the daughter of Richard Westmacott, another member of Carroll's artistic circle who was a sculptor and Professor of Sculpture at the Royal Academy, and is best known for his design of the pediment of the Royal Exchange in London.

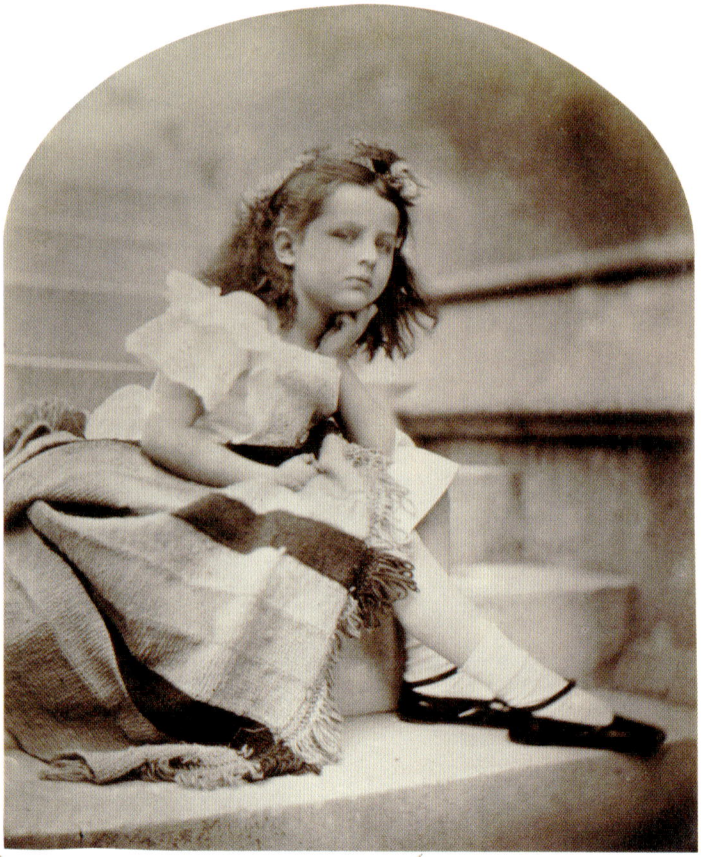

Alice Constance

PLATE 39

Tryphena Hughes
and her children Arthur Foord, Amy and Agnes
Lambeth Palace, London

19 JULY 1864

While Carroll made several photographs of close relationships between fathers and single children, his pictures of mothers tend to include several children (PLATE 23). The exception is his portrait of the Rossettis, which portrays a mother with her adult child (PLATE 31). Carroll's family group portraits are none the less loving – witness here the three different forms of tender attention the children pay their mother: the boy leans on her shoulder with clasped hands, the older daughter gazes at her, and the younger daughter leans on her lap. Tryphena Hughes (née Foord) was the wife of the painter Arthur Hughes (PLATE 34) and the mother of their three children: Arthur Foord (PLATE 35), Amy and Agnes (PLATE 34). It is likely that the book at the Hughes' feet is one of Carroll's own photograph albums.

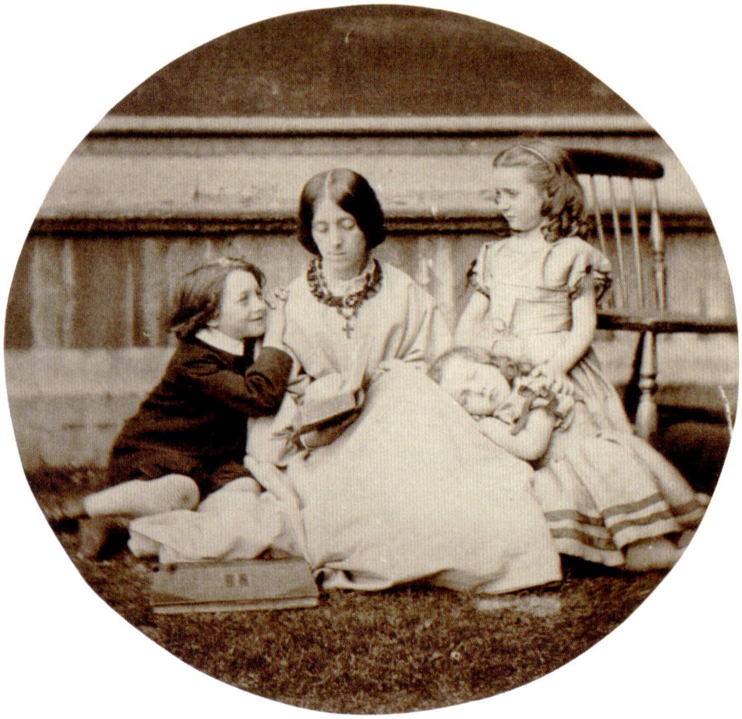

[illegible] Hughes

PLATE 40

Beatrice Mary Henley
Lambeth Palace, London

20 JULY 1864

This portrait shows Carroll's skill in capturing the expressions of his young subjects. Here the viewer is drawn to the winsome upwards look and the gentle smile of Beatrice Mary Henley. Carroll appears to have spontaneously caught a natural moment — Beatrice leans casually against the corner of the building and looks away from the camera lens. However, the picture is actually carefully constructed: Carroll focuses our attention on her face and hands by leaving the rest of the image softly blurred, and the angles of the architecture behind the girl reinforce the composition. Beatrice was the daughter of Robert Henley, Vicar at Putney. This picture was among several that Carroll made at Lambeth Palace (PLATES 37, 38, 39) — the official London residence of the Archbishop of Canterbury — in summer 1864.

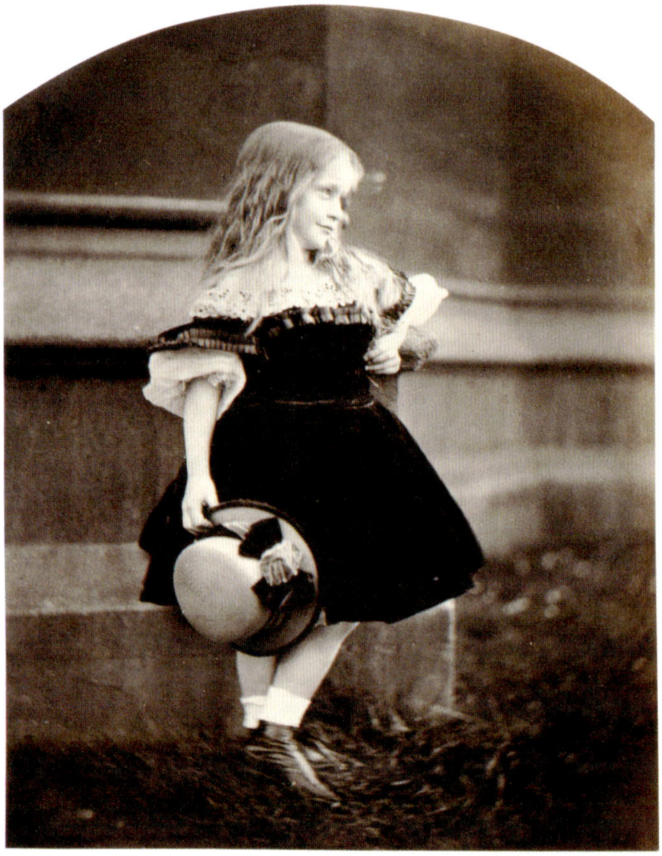

Beatrice Henley.

PLATE 41

Last Page of the
Alice's Adventures Under Ground
Manuscript

SEPTEMBER 1864

Carroll illustrated the original manuscript of *Alice's Adventures in Wonderland* himself and gave it to Alice Liddell in 1864. Then entitled *Alice's Adventures Under Ground*, the manuscript ended with a pen-and-ink portrait drawing of Alice. At some point, Carroll (or could it have been Alice herself?) covered the hand-drawn portrait with this photograph of Alice aged seven. Curiously, when Carroll asked Alice for the loan of the manuscript in order to publish a facsimile version, she must have raised the issue of the photograph. Her response to Carroll's initial request is lost, but he replied to her on 7 March 1885: 'My own wishes would be distinctly *against* reproducing the photograph' [his emphasis]. It was not until the late 1970s or early 1980s that the Carroll scholar Morton N. Cohen rediscovered the drawing beneath the photograph. The manuscript has been kept at the British Library in London since 1948.

of her own little sister. So the boat wound slowly along, beneath the bright summer-day, with its merry crew and its music of voices and laughter, till it passed round one of the many turnings of the stream, and she saw it no more.

Then she thought, (in a dream within the dream, as it were,) how this same little Alice would, in the after-time, be herself a grown woman: and how she would keep, through her riper years, the simple and loving heart of her childhood: and how she would gather around her other little children, and make <u>their</u> eyes bright and eager with many a wonderful tale, perhaps even with these very adventures of the little Alice of long-ago: and how she would feel with all their simple sorrows, and find a pleasure in all their simple joys, remembering her own child-life, and the happy summer- days.

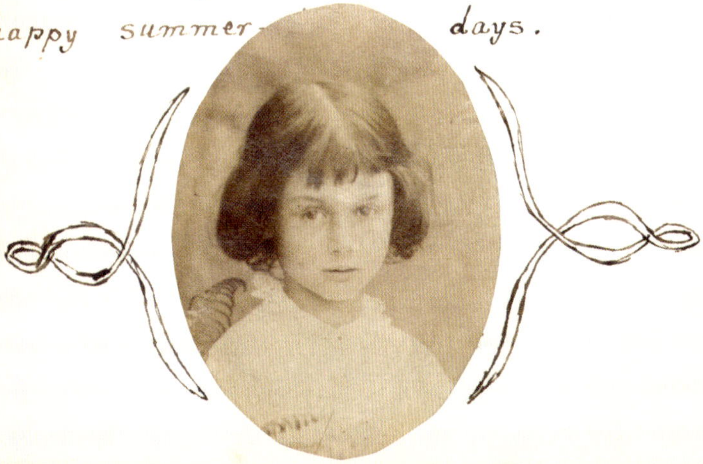

PLATE 42

Dame Ellen Alice Terry
92 Stanhope Street, London

13 JULY 1865

Dame Ellen Alice Terry was the leading Shakespearean actress in Britain, and one of the most famous actresses of her day. Carroll felt a strong affection for her, as well as professional admiration, although his moral principles caused him to break their friendship while she lived out of wedlock with the architect/designer, Edward William Godwin, between 1868 and 1874. They could not marry while she awaited the finalization of her divorce from her first husband, the artist George Frederick Watts — a very scandalous situation for the time. The portrait was taken at Terry's London home. Terry's addition to her signature, 'Believe me / Truly yours' is evidence of their close relationship.

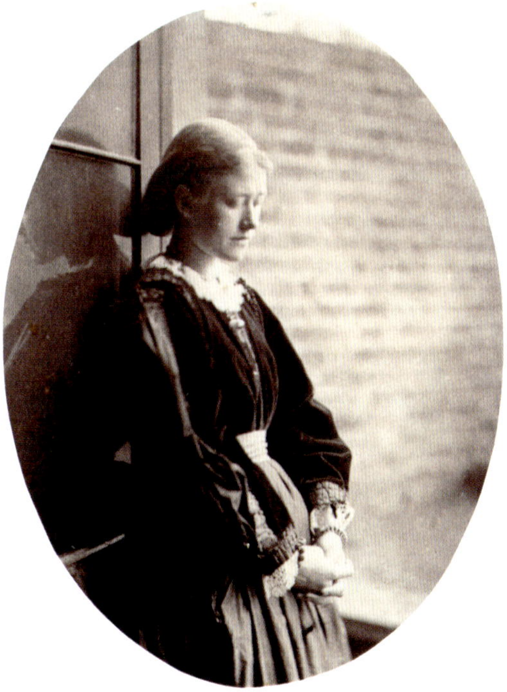

Believe me /

Truly yours

Ellen Alice Watts:

PLATE 43

Florence 'Flo' Maude and Marion 'Polly' Terry
92 Stanhope Street, London

14 JULY 1865

This is one of many images in which Carroll captures the bond between siblings or cousins (PLATES 9, 15, 21, 48). A strong connection is formed by the pressing of one sister's cheek against the other's forehead and the blending of their slightly differently shaded dresses. Florence 'Flo' Maude and Marion 'Polly' Terry were the younger sisters of the actress, Dame Ellen Alice Terry (PLATE 42). Of the eleven children in the Terry family, several also joined Ellen in becoming noted actors, including both the sisters photographed here. The theatrical line continued to future generations and one of the Terry sisters was the grandmother of the legendary Shakespearean actor Sir John Gielgud. Florence was one of the privileged people to whom Carroll sent a special morocco-bound edition of *Alice Through the Looking Glass* when it was published in 1871.

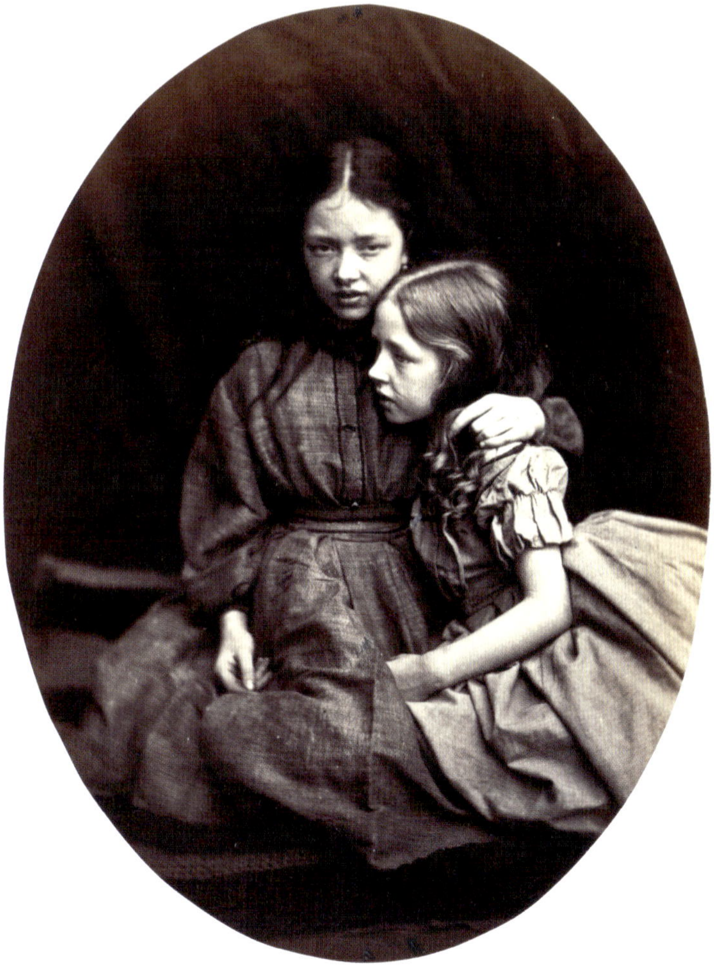

Polly Terry

PLATE 44

John Everett Millais
7 Cromwell Place, London

21 JULY 1865

John Everett Millais's handsome profile, crisply placed against a luminous background, his solid torso and his strong yet sensitive hands clasping a book, together create an image of perfect Victorian intellectual masculinity. Millais was one of the great painters of late nineteenth-century Britain. He began his career as a controversial founder of the Pre-Raphaelite brotherhood, together with William Holman Hunt and Dante Gabriel Rossetti, and went on to paint some of the most popular pictures of his age, including his famous painting of Shakespeare's *Ophelia* from 1852. He also made several paintings that are iconic images of Victorian childhood — like Carroll's photographs — such as his *Bubbles* (1886), a portrait of Millais's four-year-old grandson, Willie James.

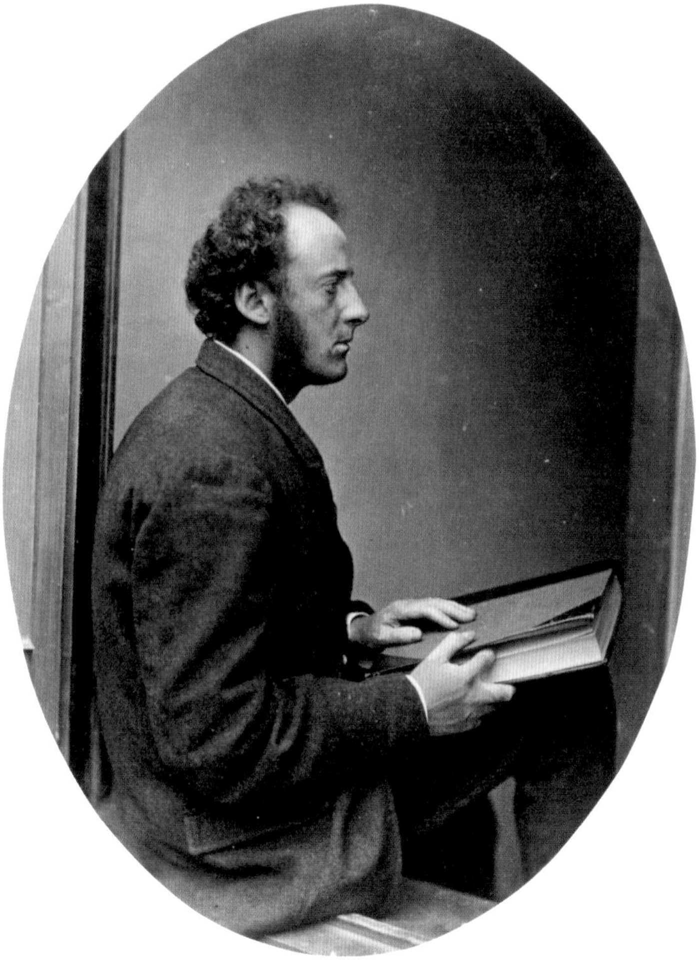

J. E. Millais. (Artist).

PLATE 45

Mary Hunt Millais
7 Cromwell Place, London

21 JULY 1865

Seated in a corner with her legs tucked sideways, the simplicity of the child's simple, loose, white nightgown focuses the viewer's attention on her face and hands. Unlike most of Carroll's photographs, which rely on Victorian clothing fashions to provide optical variety and geometric density at the centre of his pictures, this one works with tonal gradations. Mary Hunt Millais' seated pose allows her nightgown to form a graceful play of fluid folds, which the camera translates into shades of grey. Mary was one of the daughters of John Everett Millais (PLATE 44). The photograph was made at the Millais family home and Carroll was pleased with his work from his visit, writing: 'Finished photographing at the Millais', by taking beautiful negatives of Mr M. and Mary.'

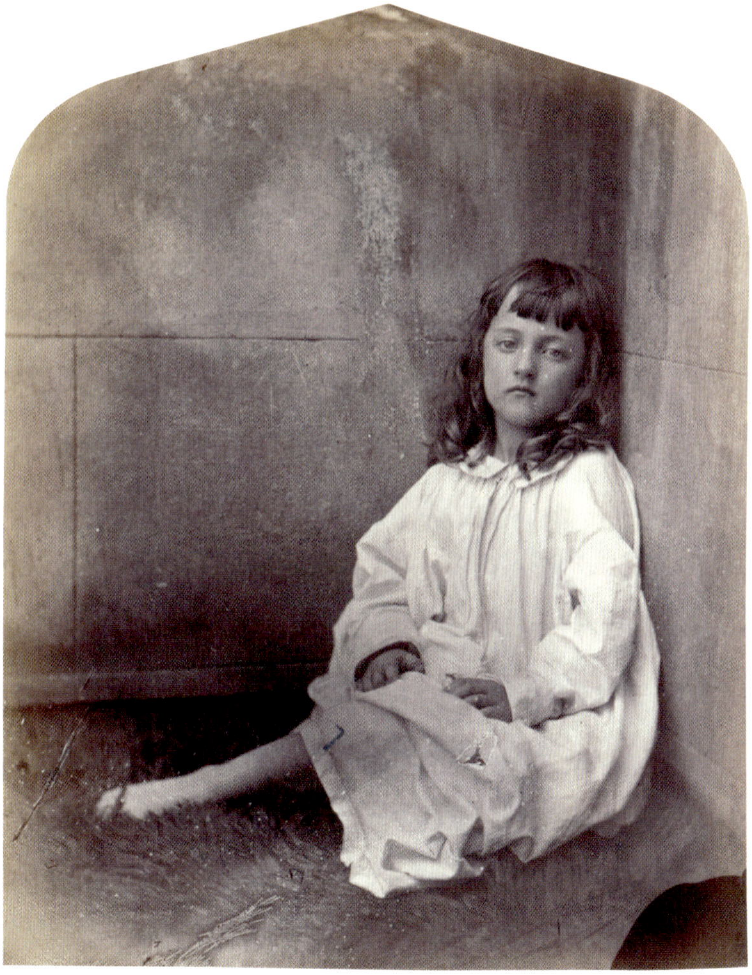

Mary Millais.

PLATE 46

John Everett Millais, his wife Euphemia 'Effie' and their daughters Effie Gray and Mary Hunt
7 Cromwell Place, London

21 JULY 1865

Unlike the conventional family portraits he derided in his writings, and even unlike some of his own, more straightforward portraits of families (PLATE 23), this portrait visualizes the ideal intimacy of a family. The two parents are alike in their postures, almost mirror-images of each other, yet are differentiated by their clothing — her garments are silky and ornamented, his are plain and tailored. The children are held both within their parents' arms and the secure frame of the window, while the parents perch on the edge between the domestic interior and the outside world. The marriage of John Everett Millais (PLATE 44) to Euphemia 'Effie' Chalmers Gray was notorious in their time, because her first marriage to the art critic, John Ruskin, was annulled for non-consummation after she ran away with Millais.

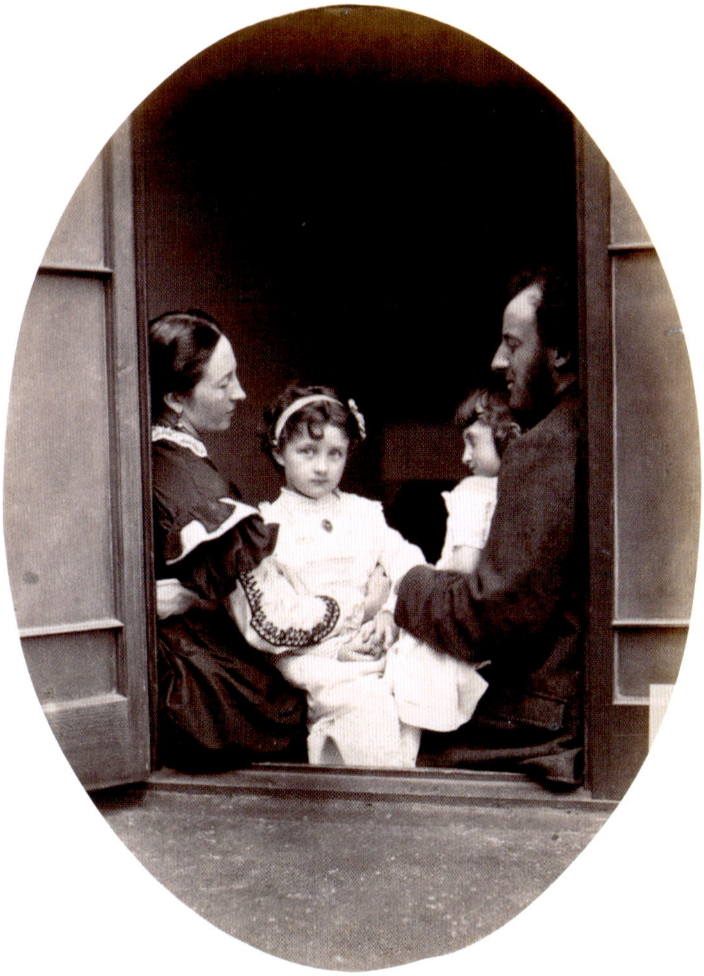

Effie C. Millais

PLATE 47

Montague Cyril Bickersteth
Bishop's Palace, Ripon, Yorkshire

7 SEPTEMBER 1865

Men, especially aristocrats and military figures, have been represented with their horses in countless portraits throughout the history of art. Carroll plays with this tradition, and its conventional masculinity, in this portrait of Montague Cyril Bickersteth. Not only is the horse in this case a toy, mounted on wheels, but it is too small even for the boy who is riding it. The small horse, moreover, contrasts with the stern solidity of the stone pillars against which the boy leans. With tiny steed on one side and massive architecture on the other, Bickersteth stands in-between — just as a boy is neither a baby nor a man. Montague was the son of Robert Bickersteth, the Bishop of Ripon, and this was among a number of pictures of the family that Carroll made at the Bishop's Palace during his stay in Yorkshire.

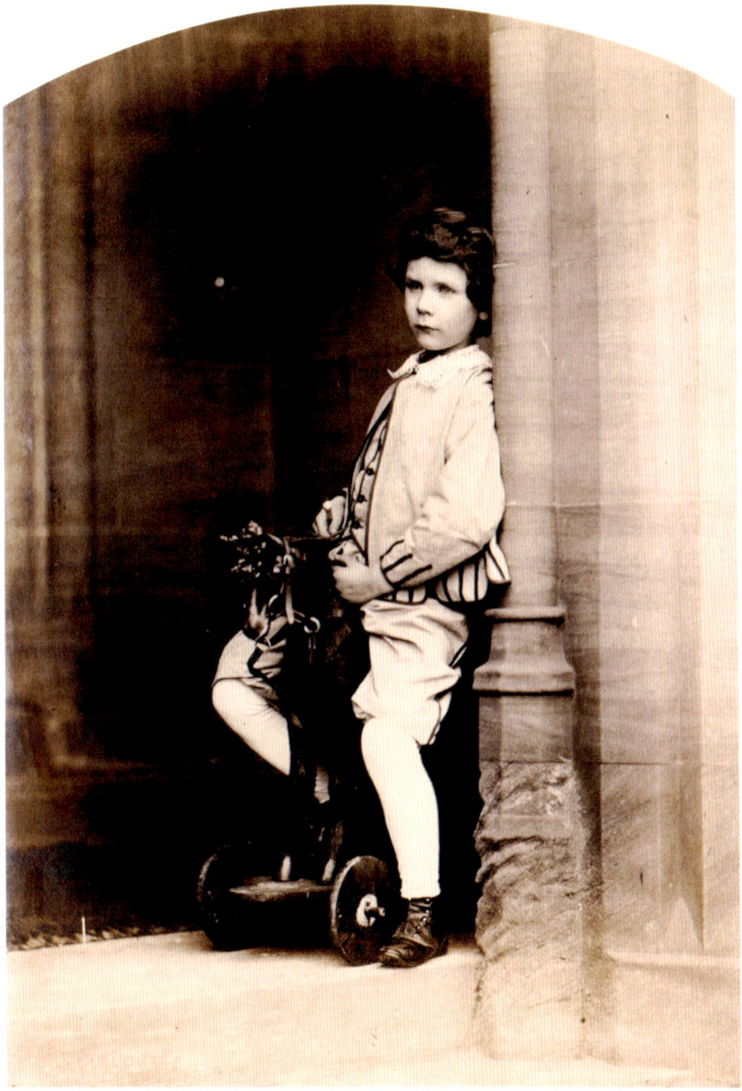

Cyril Bickersteth

PLATE 48

'Two Alices':
Alice Emily and Alice Jane Donkin
Badcock's Yard, Oxford

14 MAY 1866

One of these Alices is the same Alice Jane Donkin pictured in *The Elopement* (PLATE 26), who later became Carroll's sister-in-law. The other is Alice Emily, daughter of William Fishburn Donkin, a Professor of Astronomy at Oxford. The two girls were cousins. Alice Emily later became an artist and made an oil painting inspired by one of Carroll's photographs of Xie Kitchin (PLATES 53, 55, 56), which he hung in his rooms at Christ Church. Not only did Carroll's photographs often show women absorbed in intellectual pursuits, but he also often portrayed them sharing these activities. This may reflect the atmosphere in his childhood home (PLATE 9), as well as the relationship he saw between his aunts (PLATE 21).

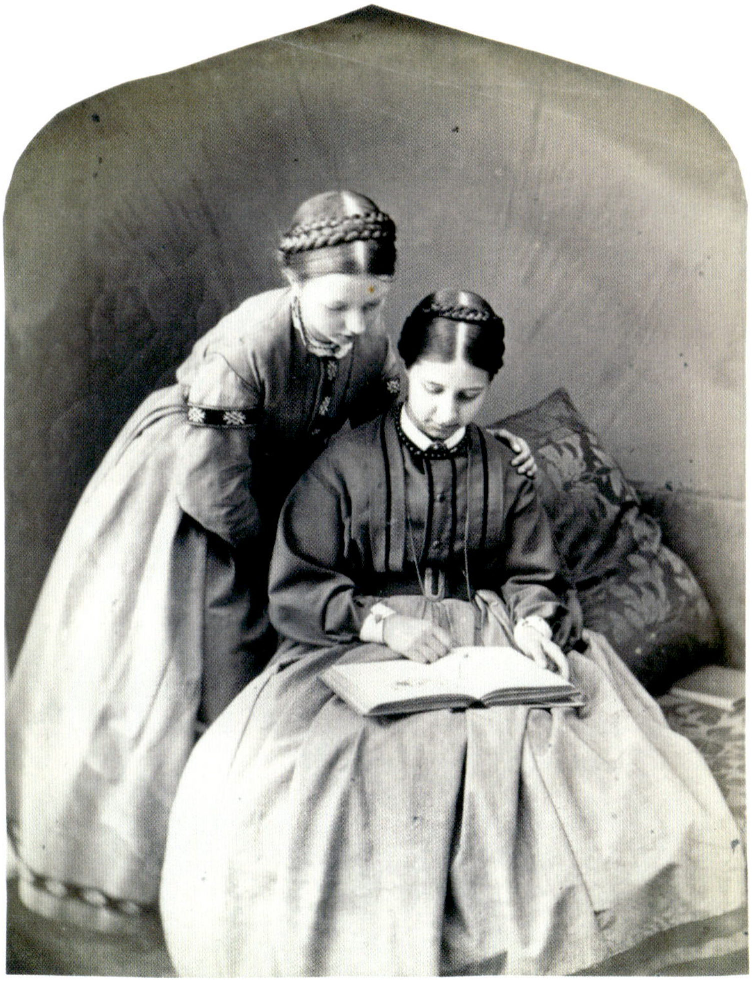

Two Alices. (Donkin)

PLATE 49

Ella Chlora Faithfull Monier-Williams
Badcock's Yard, Oxford

24—28 MAY 1866

Ella Chlora Faithfull Monier-Williams, the daughter of Sir Monier Monier-Williams, a scholar of Asian languages at Oxford, was one of the privileged child-friends who received a special, inscribed copy of *Alice's Adventures in Wonderland*. She vividly remembered being photographed by Carroll: 'As a child he gave one the sense of such perfect understanding, and this knowledge of child nature was the same whether the child was only seven years of age, or in her teens. A "grown-up" child was his horror. A visit to Mr Dodgson's rooms to be photographed was always full of surprises. Although he had quaint fancies in the way he dressed his little sitters, he could never bear a dressed-up child. A "natural child" with ruffled untidy hair suited him far better, and he would place her in some ordinary position of daily life, such as sleeping, or reading and so produce charming pictures.'

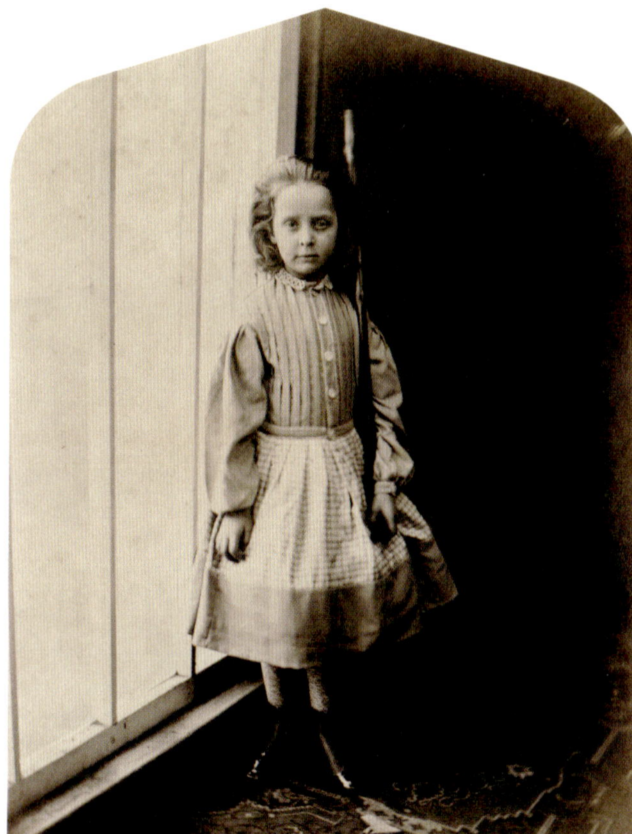

Ella Chlora Williams

PLATE 50

Catherine 'Katie' Gram Brine
Badcock's Yard, Oxford

16 JUNE 1866

This portrait of Katie Brine epitomizes Carroll's image of his ideal reader. Katie is pictured with a book, but appears to have been inspired by the story into an imaginative world of her own. She holds the book open and looks thoughtfully into the distance. In his writings, Carroll often expressed his pleasure at his young readers' enthusiasm for what he called his books 'of nonsense'. Alongside his personal correspondence to his child-friends, he also wrote letters to his readers that appeared in his books as prefaces, signed 'Your affectionate Friend'. In 1876, Carroll wrote in *An Easter Greeting to Every Child Who Loves 'Alice'*: 'I think — nay, I am sure — that some children will read this gently and lovingly, and in the spirit in which I have written it.'

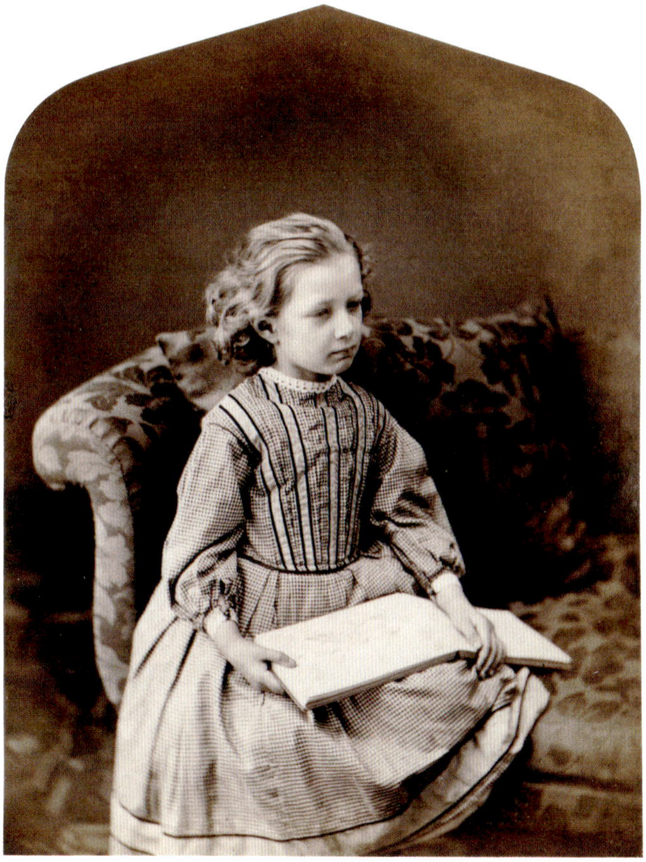

Katie Brine.

PLATE 51

John Phillips
Badcock's Yard, Oxford

11 JULY 1866

Light picking out the white tendrils of his hair, securely lodged in the curving corner of a sofa, John Phillips holds emblems of his geological profession: a mineral sample and hammer. Phillips was a prominent figure at Oxford. He was Keeper of the Ashmolean Museum from 1854 until 1870, when he was elected Keeper of the new University Museum, a post he held until the year he died. He was also Professor of Geology. The separation of scientific material from the collection of the Ashmolean and the creation of the new University Museum as a centre for the study of science marked a new commitment to empirical academic disciplines at the university – a move which Phillips helped lead. This change is also evident in Carroll's series of pictures of anatomical specimens, made for Dr Henry Acland (PLATES 5, 6).

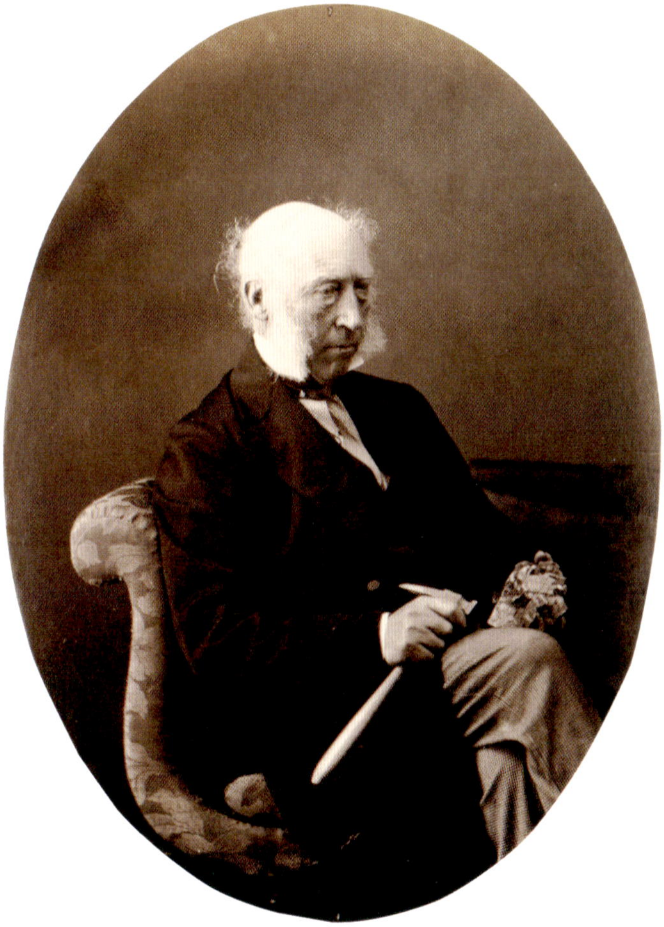

John Phillips
July 11 1866

PLATE 52

Wilfred Longley Dodgson
The Chestnuts, Guildford, Surrey

4 – 17 SEPTEMBER 1869

Wilfred Dodgson, one of Carroll's three brothers, married Alice Jane Donkin and they had nine children. Alice had known Wilfred since childhood and appeared in portraits by Carroll as a girl and a young woman (PLATES 26, 48). Like his brother Edwin, Wilfred attended Twyford School and like Carroll, he completed a degree at Christ Church. Unlike his brother and father, however, he did not excel academically and went on to become a land agent in Shropshire. Carroll made two portraits of Wilfred, both with an unusual point of view. This portrait is taken from quite a distance to fit in the whole of the impressive Victorian bicycle Wilfred is seated on, while another is a rare close-up of his brother's face.

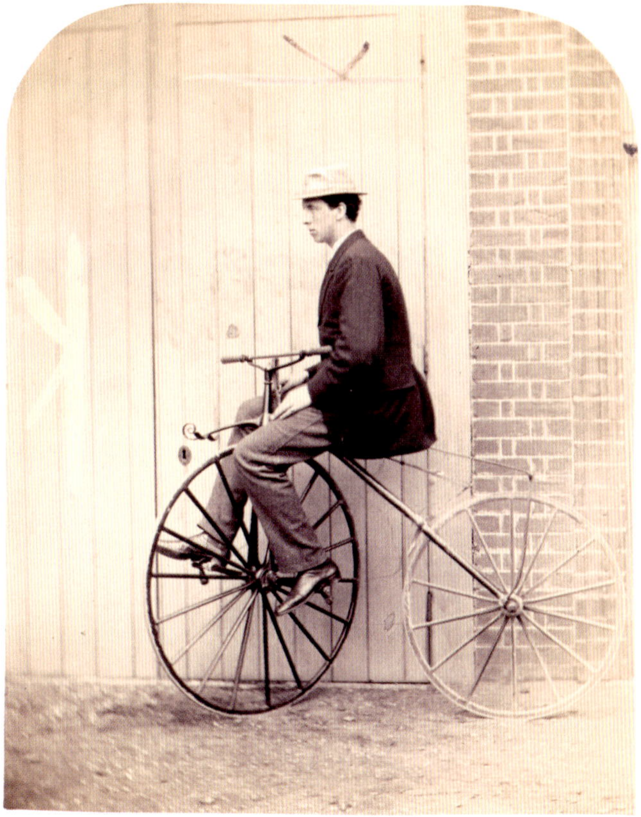

W. E. Dodgson.

PLATE 53

Alexandra 'Xie' Rhoda Kitchin as a Chinese Merchant
Christ Church Studio, Oxford

14 JULY 1873

Like many of his contemporaries, Carroll believed that black-and-white photographs were improved by hand-colouring. Carroll gave two hand-coloured photographs of the Liddell children to their mother in 1856, and for the rest of his photographic career continued to employ artists to colour some of the photographs he wished to give as special gifts. In this portrait of Xie Kitchin, the colourist has not only added colour to what was already in the black-and-white version of this photograph, but also created a foreground of large cobblestones and a background of Chinese ships at port. These additions, presumably suggested by Carroll, reveal the Orientalist associations Carroll invoked every time he dressed his subjects in Chinese dress.

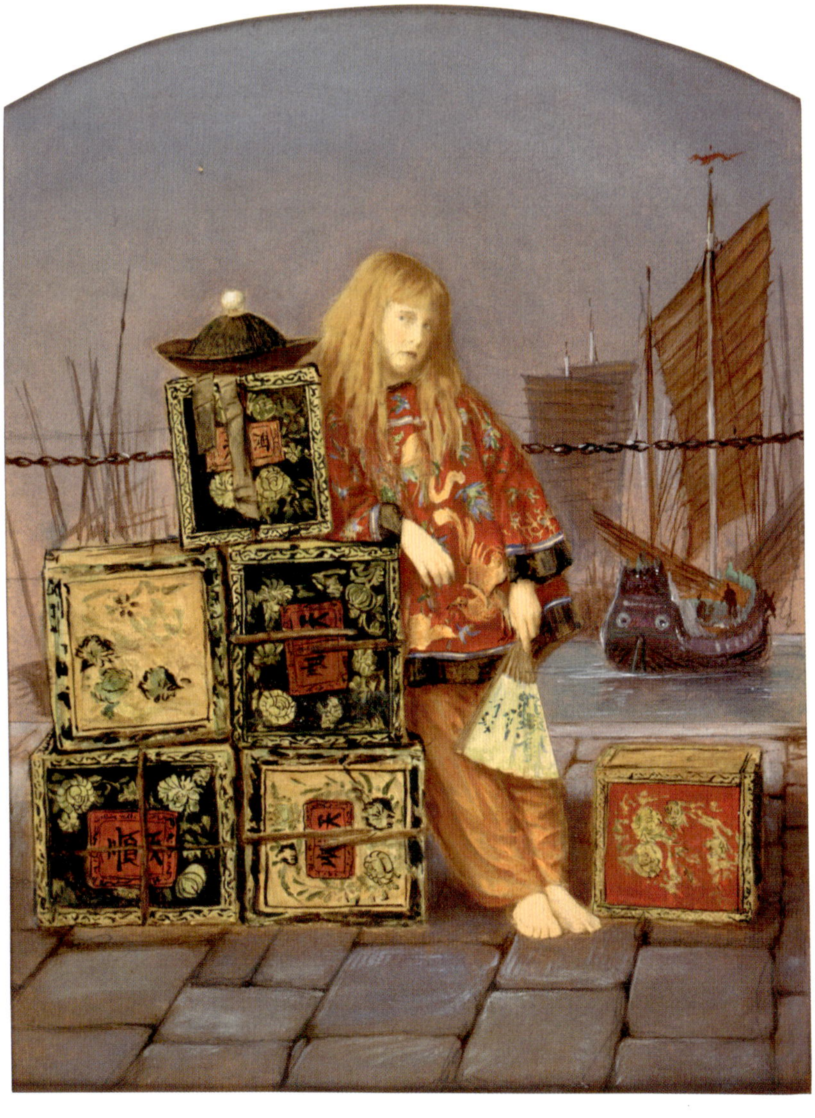

PLATE 54

Beatrice Sheward Hatch
Christ Church Studio, Oxford

24 MARCH 1874

In 1898, Beatrice Hatch remembered when, as a child, she had watched the magical transformation of the photographic negative for a self-portrait with Carroll: '[I stood] in the tiny dark room and watch[ed] him while he poured the contents of several little, strong-smelling bottles onto the glass picture of [you] that looked so funny with its black face.' Beatrice was the daughter of another of Carroll's Oxford colleagues – Reverend Edwin Hatch, the Vice-Principal of St Mary Hall, Oxford. Like Beatrice, several of Carroll's child-friends published memoirs or articles about their friendship after interest in him grew as a result of the success of the *Alice* books.

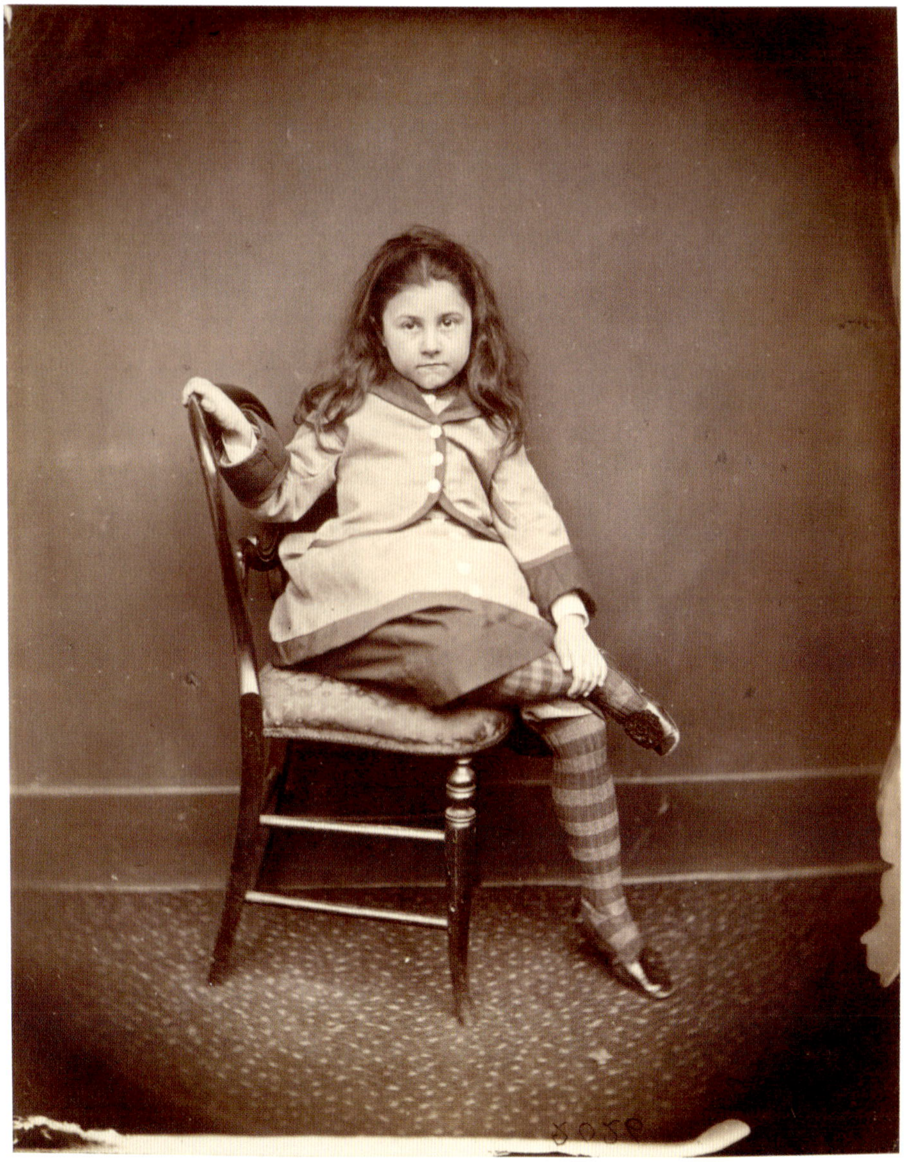

PLATE 55

Brook, Herbert, Hugh and Alexandra 'Xie' Rhoda Kitchin in 'St George and the Dragon' Christ Church Studio, Oxford

26 JUNE 1875

Brook plays St George on a rocking horse, Herbert has collapsed, Hugh substitutes a leopard skin for dragon hide and Xie wears a flimsy crown. This is perhaps the most insistently staged of Carroll's photographs. The theme is ancient, the costumes makeshift and the scenery contrived. The photograph is a revelation of the impromptu devices involved in children's pretence, disrupting the illusion of the performance. Even during his marvellous stories of the imaginary *Alice* worlds, Carroll the narrator occasionally interrupts with a humorous reminder of Alice's ordinary life, or makes fun of his own story-telling: 'Alice laughed. "There's no use trying," she said: "one *can't* believe impossible things." "I daresay you haven't had much practice," said the Queen. "When I was your age I always did it for half-an-hour a day. Why sometimes I've believed as many as six impossible things before breakfast!"'

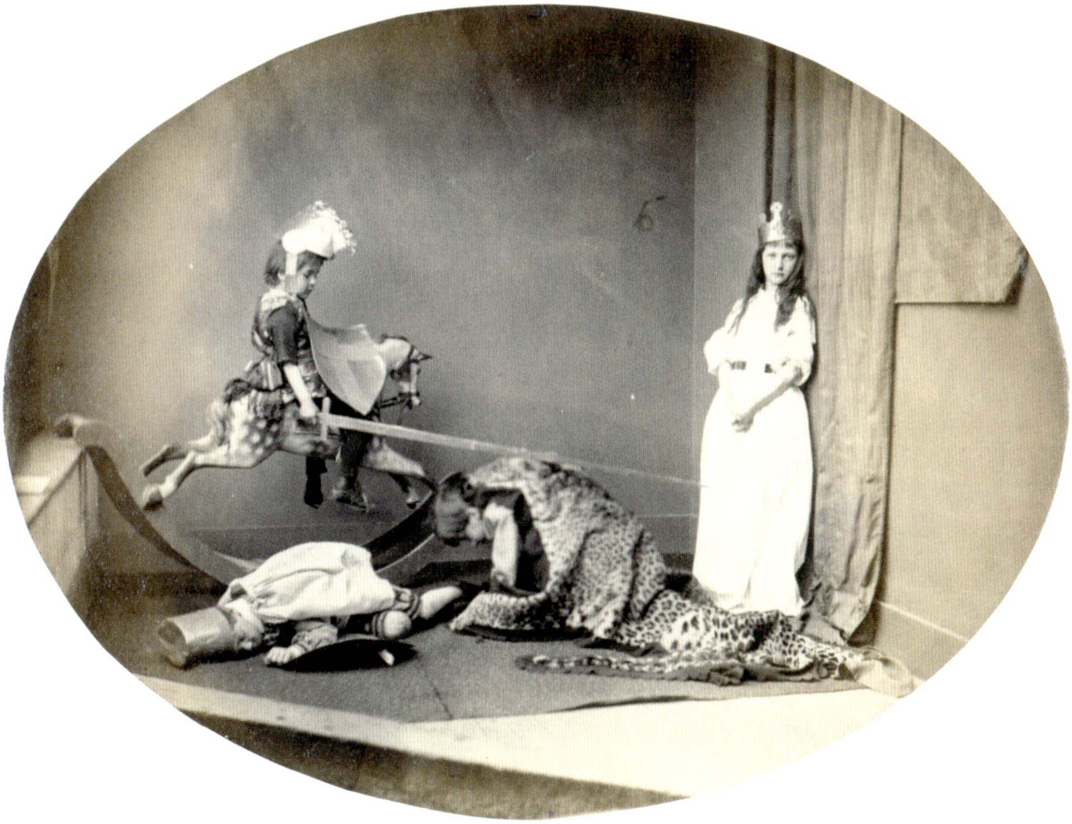

S. George and the Dragon.
(children of Rev. G. W. Kitchin).

PLATE 56

Alexandra 'Xie' Rhoda Kitchin
Christ Church Studio, Oxford

1 JULY 1876

The geometry of her parasol spokes and the wicker chaise caning, together with the bold stripes on her stockings, create a dynamic frame for Xie Kitchin's beauty, self-possession and direct gaze. Carroll took more photographs of Xie Kitchin than of any other child, close to fifty, over the course of many years from 1869 to 1880. She was named after Alexandra Princess of Wales, a friend of her mother's, which gives a sense of her family's social standing. Her father was George William Kitchin, who was a Junior Censor at Christ Church, but went on to become dean of Durham and chancellor of Durham University. He also authored the words to the popular hymn, *Lift High the Cross*. The words include the stanza: 'Each newborn servant of the Crucified / Bears on their brow the seal of Him who died', which vividly conveys the importance of children to ideas of Christan redemption at the time.

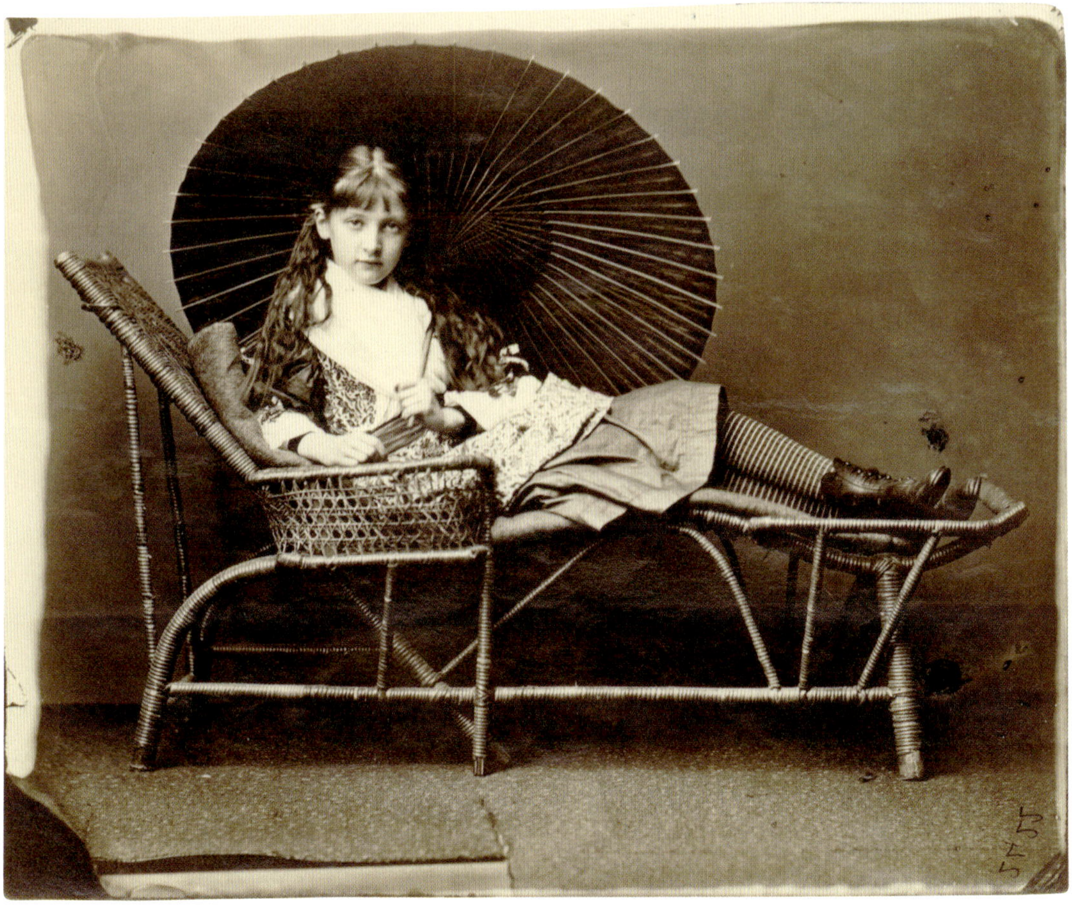

'Who are **YOU**?' said the Caterpillar.

This was not an encouraging opening for a conversation.

Alice replied, rather shyly, 'I – I hardly know, Sir, just at present –

at least I know who I **WAS**

when I got up this morning,

but I think I must have been changed several times since then.'

Alice's Adventures in Wonderland, Chapter 5

1832	27 January, Lewis Carroll (Charles Lutwidge Dodgson) is born in Daresbury, Cheshire
1839–51	Photography in England is characterized by competing daguerreotype and calotype processes
1843	Dodgson family moves to Croft Rectory in north Yorkshire. He begins formal education at a local school in Richmond
1846–49	Attends Rugby School
1850	Matriculates at Christ Church at Oxford University
1851	Takes up residence as a Christ Church scholar Great Exhibition in Hyde Park London, where Frederick Scott Archer introduces the collodion process that he was to use throughout his career
1852	His name is put forward for a studentship at Christ Church Formation of the Photographic Society in London; opening of the first exhibition dedicated solely to photography by the Society of the Arts and the Photographic Society in London
1854	Spends time with his uncle, Robert Skeffington Lutwidge, photographing the countryside around Croft
1855	Discovers a shared interest in photography with his fellow Christ Church student, Reginald Southey Publishes 'Photography Extraordinary', an article about photography's application to literature, in the *Comic Times* Appointed a full-time mathematics lecturer at Christ Church

1856	First publication under the pen name Lewis Carroll
	Writes to his uncle asking for 'some photographic apparatus, as [he wanted] some occupation here [other] than mere reading and writing'
	Purchases his first camera from Ottewill & Co., one of London's pre-eminent camera makers
	Goes to stay with his uncle Hassard Hume Dodgson in Putney, which becomes his first photographic excursion
	Sets up his first darkroom in Christ Church
	Following the example of Southey and John Dillwyn Llewellyn, begins making his own photographic albums
1857	Dr Henry Acland, Regius Professor of Medicine at Christ Church, commissions him to photograph anatomical specimens at the university museum
	Spoof on portrait photography *Hiawatha's Photographing* is published
1858	Submits four portraits, including *Alice Weld as 'Little Red Riding Hood'* (PLATE 10), to the Fifth Annual Exhibition of the Photographic Society
1860	*A Photographer's Day Out* is published
	Publishes *A Syllabus of Plane Algebraical Geometry*
1861	Ordained as a deacon
1862	4 July, takes a boat trip with Lorina, Alice and Edith Liddell during which he tells the first version of *Alice's Adventures in Wonderland*
1863	Takes first photograph at his new studio, Badcock's Yard, in Oxford
1864	Presents Alice Liddell with a manuscript version of what is then titled *Alice's Adventures Under Ground*, with his own illustrations

1865	Publishes *Alice's Adventures in Wonderland*, with illustrations by John Tenniel, but is unsatisfied with the quality of the printing. A new edition is printed, which is released in November, but is dated 1866
1867	Publishes *An Elementary Treatise on Determinants*
1871	Begins taking carte-de-visite portraits, the preferred photographic format after 1860 Publishes *Through the Looking Glass and What Alice Found There*
1872	Moves his premises to a purpose-built studio above his college rooms at Christ Church
1875	Begins organizing and numbering his photographic inventory
1879	Publishes *Euclid and his Modern Rivals*
1880	After July, gives up photography
1881	Resigns Mathematical Lectureship
1887	Publishes *The Game of Logic*
1888	Publishes *Curiosa Mathematica Part I: A New Theory of Numbers*
1892	Resigns Common Room Curatorship, the last of his major responsibilities at the university
1896	Publishes *Symbolic Logic, Part I Elementary*
1898	14 January, dies of bronchitis and is buried in Guildford, Surrey

Acknowledgements

My first debt is to scholars of Carroll's photography, on whose work I have depended, notably: Helmut Gernsheim, Morton N. Cohen, Roger Taylor, Edward Wakeling and Douglas R. Nickel. Diane Waggoner and Victoria Sears began to work on Carroll as my students, but I quickly realized it was they who were teaching me. My thanks go to the whole Phaidon team who made this project possible: Denise Wolff, Paul McGuinness, Rebecca Cooper, Sonya Dyakova and especially Samantha Woods. Most of all, I want to thank my beloved children Constantin and Philip, who do not always find it easy to live with my work, and yet who inspire it every day.

Picture credits

Harry Ransom Humanities Research Center, The University of Texas at Austin: 13, 15, 17, 53, 65, 67, 69, 71, 73, 75, 77, 79, 81, 83, 85, 87, 89, 91, 95, 97, 103, 105, 109, 111, 113, 117, 123, Morris L. Parrish Collection, Department of Rare Books and Special Collections, Princeton University Library: 19, 21, 23, 25, 27, 29, 31, 33, 35, 37, 39, 41, 43, 45, 47, 49, 55, 57, 59, 61, 63, 99, 101, 107, 115, 119, 121, National Museum /SSPL Bradford, UK: 51, British Library Board. All Rights Reserved, Add. 46700, f.46v: 93

Phaidon Press Limited
Regent's Wharf
All Saints Street
London, N1 9PA

Phaidon Press Inc.
180 Varick Street
New York, NY 10014

www.phaidon.com

isbn: 978 0 7148 4282 0

A CIP record of this book is available from the British Library.

Designed by Sonya Dyakova
Printed in China

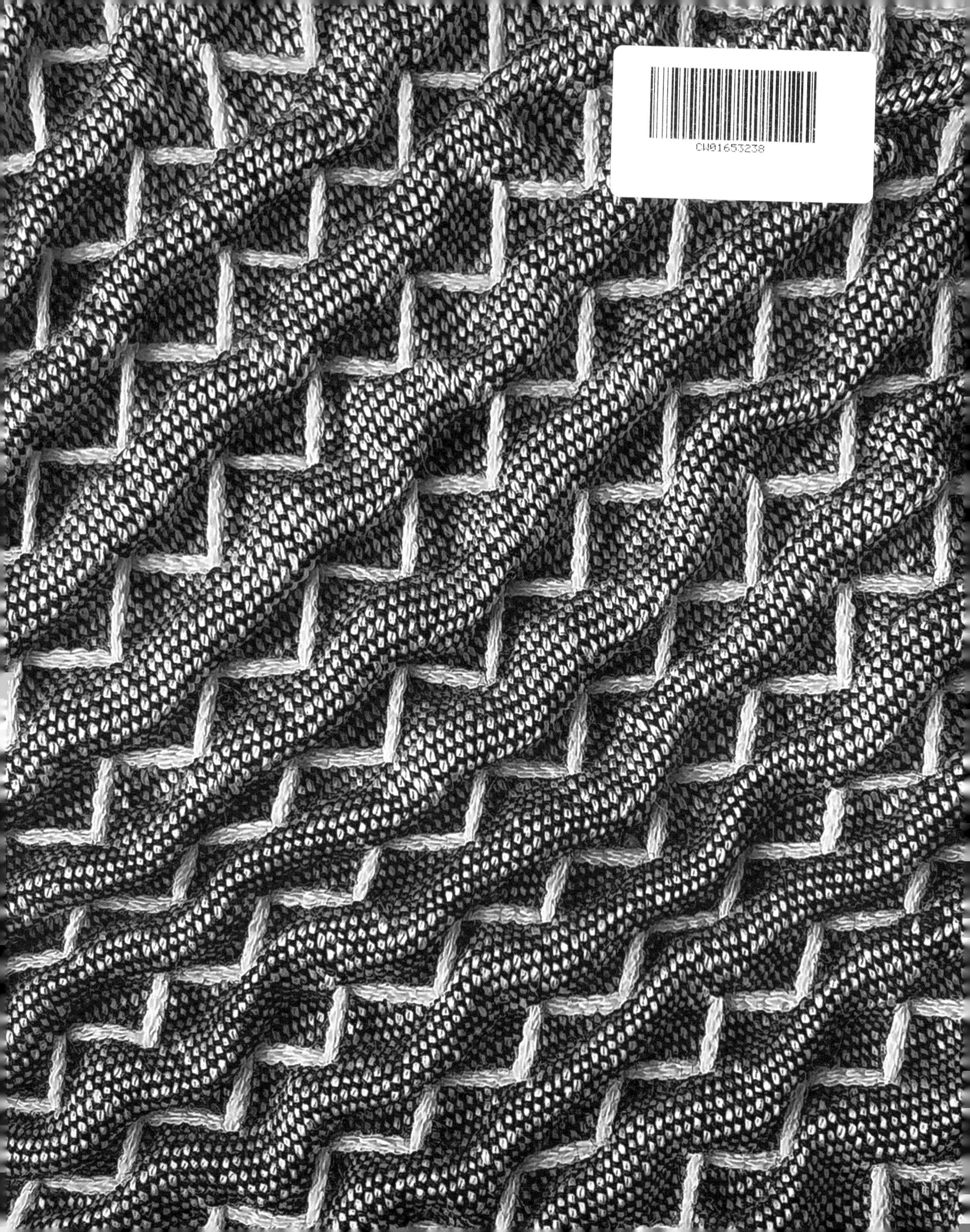

CREATIVE DIMENSIONS in WEAVING

A HANDWEAVER'S GUIDE
TO 3D TEXTURE

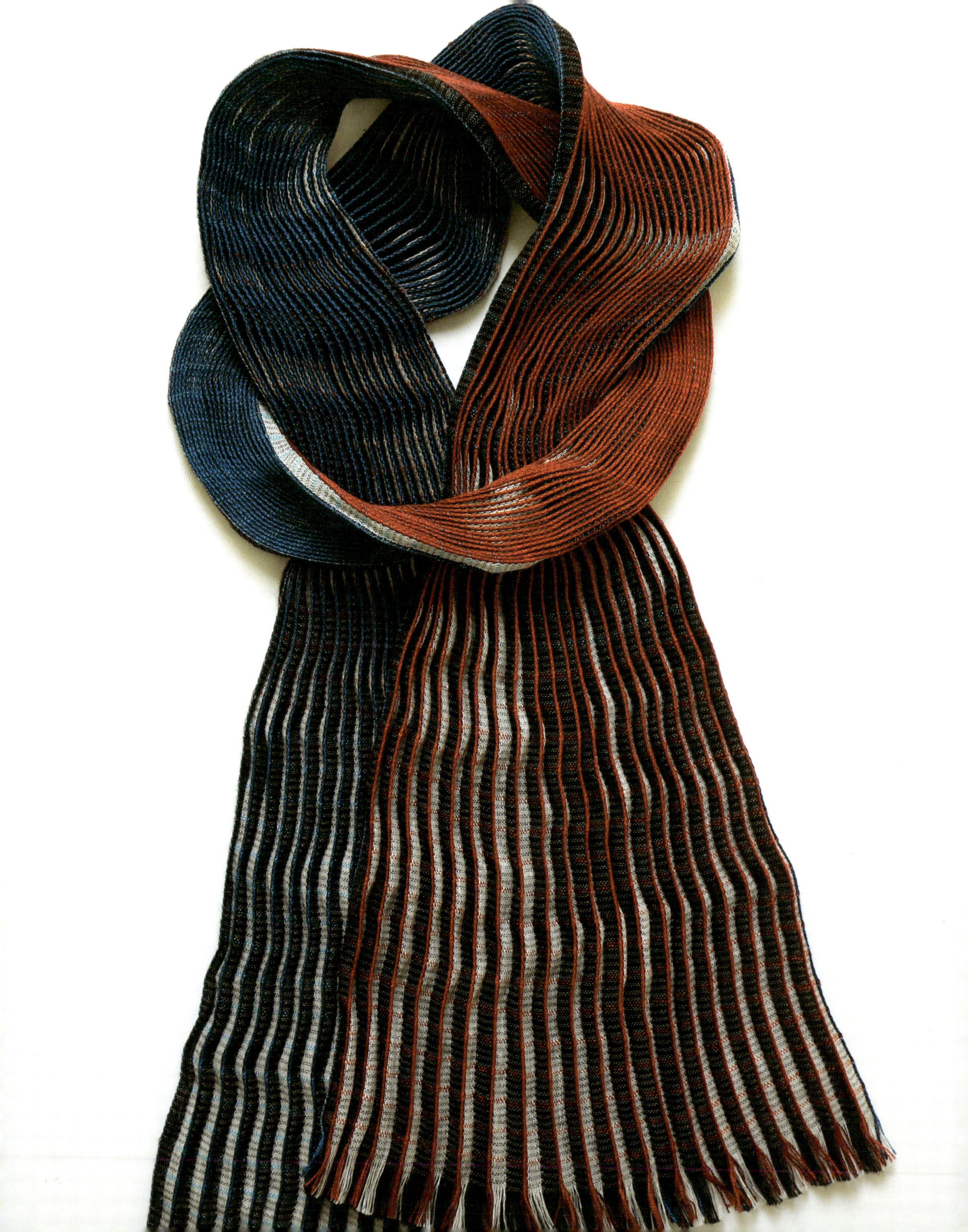

Stacey Harvey-Brown

CREATIVE DIMENSIONS in WEAVING

A HANDWEAVER'S GUIDE TO 3D TEXTURE

THE CROWOOD PRESS

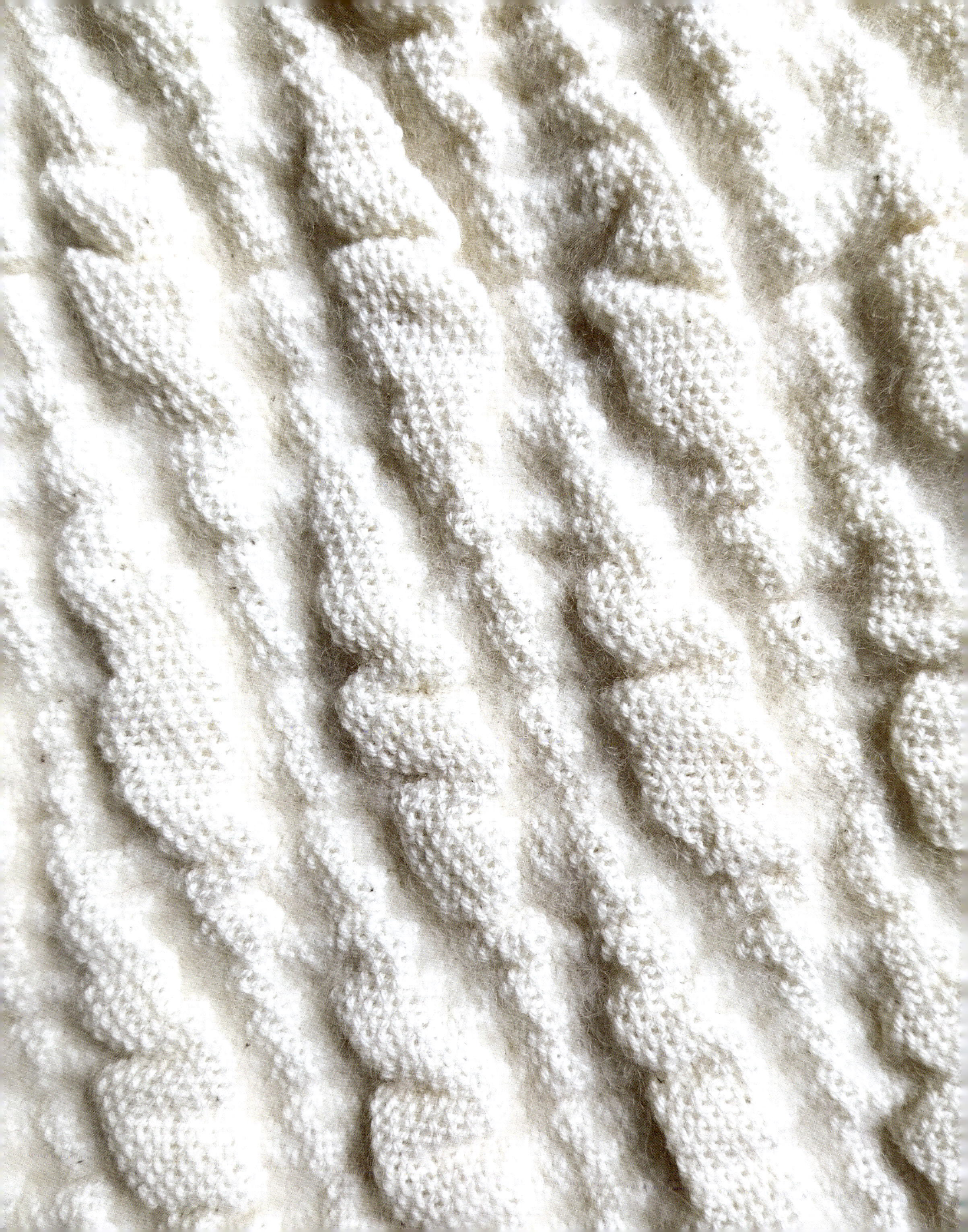

CONTENTS

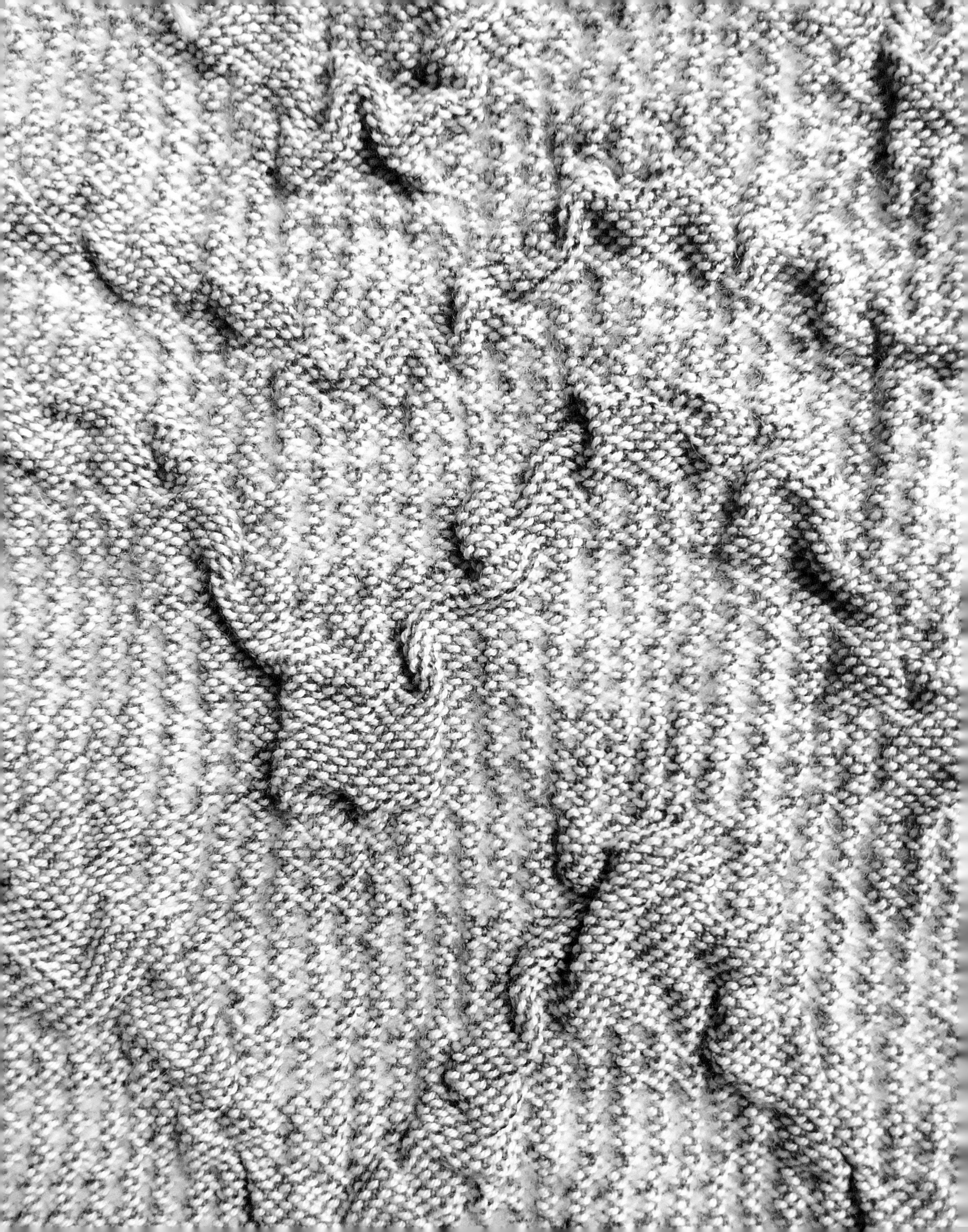

INTRODUCTION

> *The basis of texture in cloth lies, first in the fiber and the construction and size of yarns; second, in the weave which includes the manipulation of sett, the grouping of yarns, and combining of weaves; and third, in the finishing process.*
>
> —Azalea Stuart Thorpe and Jack Lenor Larsen, *Elements of Weaving*, 1967

Exploring three dimensions in weaving is both fascinating and magical. At first glance, the woven grid appears to be constraining – verticals and horizontals on a flat plane. However, that grid can be distorted in many ways, including rising above and below the flat plane to give physical depth to cloth.

Dimensional woven fabric is cloth that, when appropriately finished, changes from a flat (or flat-ish) piece into a three-dimensional form. This deep texture is not merely created on the surface but is fundamental in the construction of the fabric, through material selection, weave structure and finishing. Texture in weaving terms usually refers to yarns and fabrics that are not completely smooth or which have a slight surface texture. Dimensional texture takes surface texture and adds three-dimensional depth.

Dimensional surfaces, or dimensional textures, are created through various means, often including a mixture of yarns that do and do not shrink. These yarns behave in different ways on wet-finishing and can create folds, furrows, puckered or blistered surfaces, mounds, valleys, ridges, puffs, pleats and even spirals. The effects can be all over or confined to specific areas, although invariably there are boundary areas that have a smaller element of texture before subsiding into 'flat' fabric. Everything depends on the combination of the weave structure, materials, sett, and finishing treatments applied to the fabric. And that's where the fun starts – there are infinite combinations of even those four elements that give rise to variations on the theme.

Weaving does not necessarily have a front and a back; it can be reversible. There are examples of work hanging freely in space, as well as others that are supported by a wall but are not necessarily flat against it. Weaving is allied with design, technology and architecture as well as craft and art applications. It can be utilitarian and art, functional and decorative. It can be a sculpture exploring volume and space, a room divider, an absorber of sound, the lightest of airy scarves or a window covering. For those weavers who wish to explore dimensional texture in any of these contexts, it is a medium that welcomes exploration, pushing and crossing boundaries, manipulating the woven grid.

The textile artists of the 1970s broke many accepted rules of the time and pushed the understanding of textiles as art. Kay Sekimachi and Ruth Asawa brought woven and knitted sculpture to the public eye. Paul O'Connor also created many interesting double cloth dimensional pieces, which both he and his friend and weaver Margaret Coe have brought to public attention.

Dimensional Surfaces as Tactility

People who love textiles love touching things. After all, anyone who is in contact with cloth (which is everyone) connects with it on a very personal level. Even the most untactile of people hold their clothes before putting them

Combining single and double layers gives many different dimensional effects.

on. We often select garments simply because of the feel of them, sometimes because of the yarn content and sometimes because the provenance of them matters a lot. If the fabric doesn't feel good, it's often not selected. Our sense of touch is imperative, even now in our electronic world. In fact, it could be argued that close contact with different textures is more important now than ever as we are more absorbed into the world of keyboards and touchscreens.

We also live in a highly visual world and texture is often pushed into a very minor position, but tactility helps us make sense of the world. Especially if we are not allowed to touch something, our fingers itch to get the information that can only come through the fingertips or in direct connection to the skin. Because of our personal tactile history, we know what something is supposed to feel like when we see it, even if we're not allowed to touch it physically at that moment. But can you imagine what it would be like *not* to have that innate tactile knowledge?

Inspiration

Inspiration is everywhere – a new yarn; a different way of looking at a familiar weaving structure; natural forms; books on origami, pleats and sashiko stitching; and other crafts like ceramics, glass and wood. All of these can inspire the wish to create something that will capture the textural essence of the image or object. But how to translate that wish, that desire, into woven form?

That's one of the big parts of this book. It does not contain specific projects in order to recreate a particular effect found in nature. Instead, it is a guide to dimensional texture through exploring different structures and specific techniques – the tools to enable you to create your own tactile and dimensional experience through weave.

Even if you are a new weaver, so long as you know how to calculate a warp, wind it and put it on your loom ready to weave, and can read a weaving draft, you'll get value from this book. Weaving texture is very approachable and forgiving. Basically, you can't get it wrong! If you use different yarns, a different sett, or finish the fabric differently, you'll get different results. They may not be the results you were expecting, but that's part of the learning and of the fun. Sometimes even the dyes on yarns, especially overtwisted yarns, can change how the same yarn will react during wet-finishing (*see* Lotte Dalgaard and Paulette Adam's book, *Thread Magic*).

Book Structure

This book has been compiled with all experience levels in mind. It gives an overview and a detailed dive into two areas.

Part 1 begins with looking at materials and their properties as well as the basics of finishing processes. This is followed by individual chapters covering ten different techniques. Within each of these chapters, the bulk of the information will be for those who have not tried these techniques before – technical information and drafts – to facilitate the weaving of dimensional surfaces easily and quickly. However, there will also be suggestions of materials, ratios and finishing considerations for intermediate weavers or those who have already learned the basics and want to extend themselves. Specific yarn sizes are not often mentioned – this is deliberate so that the weaver can use yarns already in a stash and try other proportions and yarn mixes. Other ideas will be put forward, with some drafts and images, to develop knowledge, skill and experience. This is intended to be inspirational, to push you out of your comfort zone, giving suggestions of a different way of approaching things or maybe a little challenge....

Part 2 looks at three methods of sculptural weaving: multi-layering in various ways, tubular weaving and shaping weaving on and off the loom. There are different approaches for all experience levels here too.

There is an extensive bibliography, artist links and appendices. Please note: current information on suppliers is not included as this changes continuously and all around the world. Some of the yarns (such as polyester) can easily be found through other textile suppliers such as sewing or knitting shops. Metals can be sourced from various suppliers, including hardware or electrical stores. Weavers tend to be 'out-of-the-box' thinkers, and chatting to other craft practitioners can often turn up an unusual source for materials.

The book has largely been written with the eight-shaft weaver in mind as eight shafts are what the majority of weavers have. For those with fewer shafts, there are indeed some textural forms that will provide many variations for four or six shafts. For those with more, there are occasional drafts for multi-shaft looms, and the majority of the techniques that are featured here can be expanded from eight shafts upwards, allowing the weaver to develop more complex designs using the principles given.

Threading

Different threading conventions are used throughout the book – some might be familiar, others might be new. There are also many different methods of approaching tie-ups and the associated ways that treadlings will be organised under each tie-up.

People's minds work in different ways and one method might not be logical to you, whereas another will make perfect sense. Explore until you find the system that suits you. Organise threading, tie-ups and treadling plans to make sense to your mental processes to give you the results you want.

Tie-ups

Tie-ups are largely used in this book as they give a clearer visual appearance on the page. However, if table or dobby looms are used, then a conversion from the tie-up and treadling to a liftplan might be required. This information is given in Appendix 1.

Hints and Tips

We are all different in our approach and our practice. Any hints and tips that are given in the book have been gleaned from many people and through personal weaving experience over the years. Some may work brilliantly for you, others might not, so please feel free to discard the suggestions that either do not work for you or do not compute with your way of thinking. The way that works for you is the right way for you.

Drafting

Drafts have been largely created using Fiberworks PCW and WeavePoint but most weaving software will give the same results, albeit in slightly different ways. In this book, WeavePoint has been used to give the clearest graphic result.

The tie-up is in the top right-hand corner, threading is from right to left and treadling is from top to bottom. It is generally not a problem if something is woven from the reverse direction, especially when it is a textural effect rather than a graphic one. If you find something a little confusing, try reversing the order of the treadling or liftplan and it might make more sense to you, depending on how you normally read a draft.

Wet-finishing

There is much to learn from very subtle variations in wet-finishing. Texture weaving seems to bring these varied results to the fore more than regular weaving. Experimentation is encouraged, and no result is 'wrong' – just different to what was intended. Unless a woollen fabric has been wet-finished to felting point so that it is rigid (which might be the intention), a textural effect will be achieved. In addition, a result that might be too gentle or subtle at first can be re-finished to give a more dramatic effect, if that is desired.

Analysis of Results

The different techniques that the book covers allow for pleating, soft puffs, distortions, depth, gentle emphasis and shifting of the woven grid. The more these techniques are explored, changing the parameters, trying different yarn combinations and wet-finishing techniques, the more a textural weaving vocabulary will develop and give further tools to express what it is that you wish to bring out in your weaving, whether that is for garments or interiors, accessories, artwork, or having fun for sampling's sake.

Keep an open mind when analysing the results of your explorations. What might not suit something that you are looking for at the moment could well be just what is needed for a future project. Careful notes will assist in finding that particular technique when required.

I hope that this book will provide many of the tools that you are looking for to express different modes of texture. It is not a project book, although that would be fun. But that would be to deprive you, the creative weaver, of your personal expression of texture. Once you have the tools and techniques, you can do whatever you like!

PART ONE: DIMENSIONAL SURFACES

No fabric is totally flat – by incorporating twist, yarns are generally round and therefore interlacements of those round yarns are going to give a slightly dimensional result. However, in this book, we are going another step further, taking the fabric out of the flat plane and into the realm of three dimensions. This is created through various means, often mixing active and passive yarns such as wool (which is active and shrinks), and cotton (which is passive and does not generally shrink). The tension differences between them create puckering in various ways on the surface of the cloth. This is the emphasis of Part One.

We shall be exploring ten different methods of creating dimensional texture, featuring wool, elastane and gathering threads as our active yarns. These give different results, sometimes before wet-finishing, but mostly during and after wet-finishing.

The techniques and structures shared in Part One have varying levels of difficulty. The book is not compiled in order of complexity so you can explore any chapter in the order that suits you.

As a guide for newer weavers, seersucker can easily be explored with four shafts. With eight shafts, waffle would then be a good one to try. Overshot and shibori are weft-based techniques and so are perhaps the next ones to discover, followed by sashiko (and warp shibori from the shibori chapter) which bring in supplementary warps and/or wefts. Pleats are a whole world in themselves, with lots of different approaches and varying levels of difficulty. Deflected double weave is a fun and helpful topic bridging the gap between supplementary warps and wefts and double cloth techniques. Double cloth blocks incorporating dimensional shrinkage, stitched double cloth, and four-colour double weave (4cDW) are the final elements in Part One and perhaps the most challenging for newer weavers.

For more experienced weavers, jump in wherever your curiosity takes you. Distorting the flat plane can give unexpected results as well as planned ones and the skills you develop from Part One will enable you to incorporate many different effects in your own creative designing for original and personal fabric.

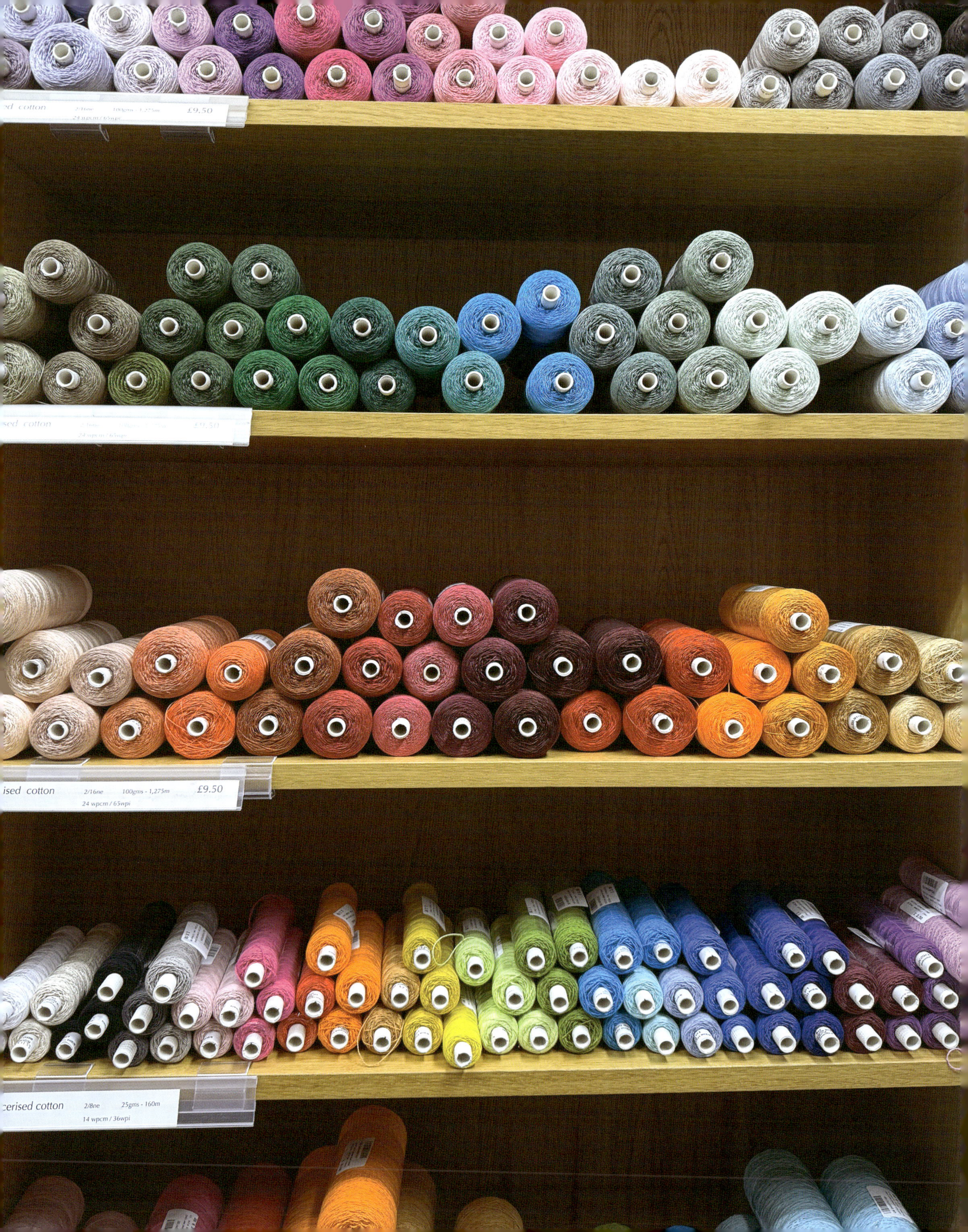
£9.50
ised cotton 2/16ne 100gms - 1,275m £9.50
24 wpcm / 65wpi
cerised cotton 2/8ne 25gms - 160m
14 wpcm / 36wpi

CHAPTER 1

MATERIALS AND FINISHING

Texture has always been part of weaving and cloth. Together with mixes and contrasts of fibre and finishes, the woven grid can be manipulated by design or accident into many different forms. Some gently ripple across the surface, some are temporary and disappear either through pressing or washing, some can be fused into place, while others are more structural. Many material properties are harnessed to create certain effects, such as seersucker, which became wider known when industrial developments in looms and finishing processes arose to make their production in bulk much easier and faster. Chemical developments led to processes to create blistering and puckering in cloth, which were utilised in industrial settings but much more rarely in studio settings due to their toxicity and the necessity for protective clothing and equipment.

A big sea-change occurred in Japan during the 1980s, where Junichi Arai in particular stimulated the development of dimensional textile surfaces by using a yarn collection of 150 different synthetic and natural yarns, mostly in black and white, incorporating many variations in shrinkage, twist, sheen and stability. He integrated those with his design sensibilities of construction, using the properties and contradictions of materials in often complex layers and structures. The Miyake Design Studio had also brought traditional Japanese fabrics such as shibori and sashiko into the mainstream, and created fabrics by extreme methods such as burning, melting and laminating – all highly experimental using new methods and materials. This took the Western world by surprise and inspired textile designers to take risks and try new drastic adaptations in their turn. Once that genie was out of the bottle, it wasn't going to be constrained again!

An exhibition called *Textural Space,* curated by Lesley Millar in 2001, showcased Japanese textile artists who demonstrated that 'through their textural understanding and sense of space, [they] are challenging our expectations of the material nature of textiles'. The rigorous technical skills employed combined with detailed knowledge of the materials each artist had used brought exquisite sensitivity, structure, order and presence to the art through deliberate and rhythmical making processes.

Now textural fabrics are part of the mainstream but for many handweavers they are still shrouded in mystery. This book aims to bring a collection of techniques and information together so that you can try out different methods, materials and finishes to include dimensional surface relief into your fabric and also to go even further, diving into sculptural methods. It is mostly concerned with yarns and fibres that are easily accessible to a modern handweaver, and also processes that can be undertaken in the home or studio settings.

MATERIALS, YARN PROPERTIES AND SAMPLING

Material properties of fibres and yarns are a starting point for dimensional weaving. The following section gives brief information on some of the fibres and yarns used for dimensional effects. Further details and descriptions can be found in the Glossary.

Throughout the various techniques used in the book, you will find frequent reference to 'active' and 'passive' yarns.

A colourful selection of yarns at the Handweavers Studio & Gallery. (Photo: Alan Willey)

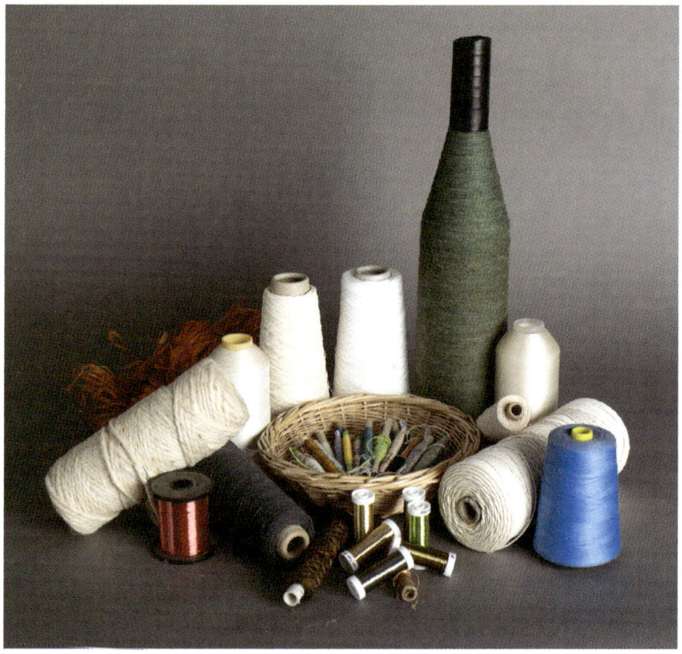

This collection of yarns includes: enamelled copper yarn, rug wool, raffia, highly twisted buttonhole cotton, paper tape, mercerised cotton, Harris tweed singles, monofilament, cottolin, paper cord, polyester, various metals, viscose, stainless steel and wool. The central basket contains many small spools of various yarns including linen, silk, cotton and blends for wefts. (Photo: Colin Usher)

Passive Yarns

'Passive' yarns are yarns that do not have any – or have very limited – capacity in them to alter their state and do not require extra care in the finishing. These are used for non-shrinking areas or layers, and include yarn such as cotton, linen, silk, bamboo viscose, cottolin, superwash wool, polyester, Tencel™ and viscose rayon, among others. They can also be filament yarns – those that are not spun but are extruded in long strands of various thickness, more often to be found in man-made yarns and silk. All of these yarns are often woven in plain weave and provide the surface that is forced into dimensionality by the 'active' yarns.

Cottolin

Cottolin is a durable blend of cotton and linen that is not mercerised and shares the properties of both fibres.

Bamboo Viscose

Bamboo viscose is a regenerated fibre – a man-made fibre artificially created using bamboo leaves and shoots. A heavy yarn, similar to cotton in appearance, it is generally cooler,

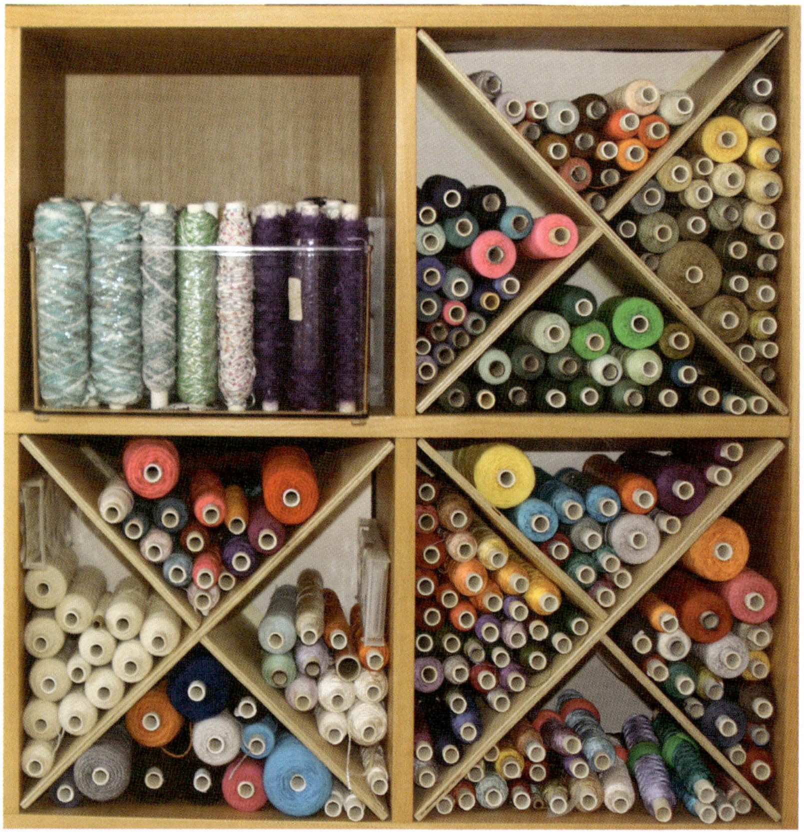

An excellent way to store pirns or bobbins of yarn is with this X arrangement within a box shelf. (Photo: Wendy Morris)

feels softer and has better moisture-absorption properties. It is hypoallergenic and antibacterial. However, production methods can be toxic (*see* Appendix II).

Superwash Wool
Superwash wool is wool that has been chemically treated to remove the ability to full, so it can be washed in a washing machine without shrinking or felting.

Synthetics
Polyester – A man-made yarn, invented in the 1940s. It is derived from oil and is thermoplastic, capable of being heat set with steam to take on a new form, It is useful for holding pleating and other shaping after heat-finishing.

Viscose rayon – A regenerated yarn from a natural source, such as wood pulp, which is chemically treated to create a half-natural, half-synthetic fibre. The yarn is absorbent, hard-wearing and can be blended with natural and synthetic fibres. However, production methods can be toxic (*see* Appendix II).

Lyocell (also trademarked as Tencel™, Newcell™ and Seacell™) – A semi-synthetic fibre made using non-toxic solvents (no hazardous waste – see Appendix II). It is resistant to wear, tearing and pilling and shares many properties with bast fibres such as cotton, linen, ramie and hemp but also silk and viscose rayon. It has minimal shrinkage, blends well with natural and synthetic fibres and is fully biodegradable.

Balanced Yarns

Balanced yarns have two or more strands/plies. Each separate ply is spun in one direction (either S or Z). They are then combined and twisted in the opposite direction to ensure they wrap around each other. The number of twists in the reverse direction is around half the number of twists in the individual singles yarn. This is the usual method for a regular two-ply yarn.

Experienced hand-spinners can create yarns with three or more plies, which are either balanced or unbalanced. A balanced yarn will not distinctly torque in one or other direction when held in a gentle arc.

Active Yarns

Active yarns, in the sense used in this book, are yarns that are used to create dimensional effects. That can be through differential shrinkage, overspinning to create tensions within the yarn, or even a regular thread used to gather up the fabric in a technique such as shibori, for instance. If no specific use is suggested, it will refer to yarns that will shrink before or during wet-finishing to give the desired effect.

There are many different yarns that can be used for active yarns.

Elastane or Elastomeric Yarns
Elastane or elastomeric yarns are made from polyurethane and have stretch incorporated within them with qualities similar to rubber. Sometimes referred to as Lycra™ or Spandex™, elastane yarns do perish over time. They can be used at 100 per cent elastane, but are often found in blends, using 3–12 per cent elastane with wool, linen, silk or cotton, which are easier to use for both warp and weft.

When used in the warp, the warp ends are under tension. As soon as the tension is released, the elastomeric element will return to its pre-stretched state, causing instant puckering of the cloth with which it is interacting. Used in the weft, there is more control over how much tension is applied per pick, which can be interesting to explore in any technique.

It is advisable to use a temple or a system that will ensure that the width of the warp remains consistent during weaving, and that it will not be pulled up tightly while on the loom (*see* Appendix I). Not using a warp-width device could result in many broken ends on the selvedges as they are subject to much higher abrasion levels. Elastane or elastomeric yarns will always strive to return to a relaxed state.

Colcolastic™ by Venne is an elastane yarn that is plied together with a cotton yarn. This is a useful yarn in a structure that does not contain floats as when the tension is removed from the fabric and the elastic element contracts, the two yarns can separate, leaving loops of cotton standing proud of the surface if the yarn is not contained within a weave structure.

Overspun or High-twist Spun Yarns

Overspun or high-twist spun yarns (also known as crepe yarns) are classed as unbalanced. They incorporate a lot of captured kinetic energy during the spinning process and require a certain amount of care when used (*see* Appendix II).

Singles Yarns

A singles yarn is a yarn with only one strand/ply and is twisted only in one direction. It will want to unwind from the cut end when left dangling. Singles yarns can be found most often in linen, wool and paper, among others. Wool and other absorbent fibres also have the potential to 'bloom' a little on wet-finishing, as there is no other ply to contain each strand.

Other 'Active' Yarns

Other 'active' yarns can include some novelty or fancy yarns such as bouclé. Any plied yarn that has one ply as a stable element, and another ply at a different twist ratio is called 'unbalanced' and will have an effect when used as a floating element in the weaving. How much of an effect it has will depend on the fibre content, the amount of variation in the spinning, the weave structures used with it, and the finishing methods applied.

Wool

Wool can be used for both active and passive yarns. Depending on how the fibre is prepared and the mode of spinning, plus the variability in plying or not plying, many kinds of effects are possible. Even 'balanced' wool, if prepared and spun in a certain way, will full (and eventually felt) if agitated during wet-finishing, and so it can be used to take an active role in creating the dimensional textures.

Different methods of spinning are woollen-spun, worsted-spun and semi-worsted (*see* Appendix II).

TOP TIP

If you have not worked with overspun or elastane yarns before, it is a good idea to do some sampling, both of the yarn itself and of the weave you intend to use so that the amount of energy and contraction they hold can be determined. Overspun samples need to be placed into hot water for around ten minutes, although the reaction can be almost immediate, and observed to see what happens.

Blended or Mixed Yarns

Blended or mixed yarns such as wool/silk, wool/Tencel™ or wool/stainless steel will have differing wet-finishing properties than either yarn on their own. Wool/silk, depending on the proportion of wool to silk, might not shrink on wet-finishing as much as expected. As usual, sample to ascertain the amount of shrinkage prior to weaving a specific project.

Metal Wires

Metal wires include copper, brass and stainless steel (*see* Appendix II). They can be used in dimensional weaving, especially in sculptural settings. To use metal wires in the warp, please refer to Arline M Fisch or Christine K Miller's books (*see* Bibliography). For warp uses, these books are invaluable.

For our dimensional texture purposes, we are using metal solely in the weft. A malleable wire is required to ensure that the selvedge can be woven well. If it is necessary to unweave at any point, a suitable wire that will not break at the selvedge is favourable. The more malleable a metal is, the finer it can be drawn or rolled, giving high-gauge numbers, so the lower the gauge number, the thicker the metal is. The thicker the wire, the more challenging!

Sampling is required to determine the material's suitability, but another consideration when weaving sculpture includes weight and the effects of gravity on the finished piece.

Paper Yarns

Paper yarns for weaving are often made from flax, hemp or cotton (*see* Appendix II) and spun as a singles.

SAMPLING

Throughout the book, you will find many examples to try. Before starting on a full-scale project, it is highly recommended that some time is spent sampling, trying out combinations of yarns, setts, structures and wet-finishing. While this might not be initially appealing, the information you learn will repay your effort many times over. You will get an instinctive feel for the 'hand' and look of the fabric – the drapability/stiffness, amount of texture you want to achieve, practicality of the fabric for the end use you envisage, and so on.

It is perfectly possible to make a warp from two different materials and use the same warp beam. A little more care is required so that the non-shrinking yarns are kept under the same tension as the shrinking yarn, especially when transferring the warp from mill or warping frame to the loom, and in beaming.

If you are proposing to make something much larger than your samples, you will need to sample again at the beginning of the project warp to ensure that the wet-finishing and shrinkage will give the results you want. When scaling up, the increase in width and number of ends involved in the warp increases the amount of resistance you encounter when weaving and beating up. Therefore, there might not be the same number of picks per inch/cm on a wider cloth as on a narrower one. There is also a natural tendency to beat harder on a narrower warp.

If you don't get the results you want with this sampling, there is then the opportunity to adapt the sett by re-sleying in order to open out the fabric a little bit so that the picks per inch/cm match your initial samples. It is also advisable at this stage to wet-finish the new sample to ensure that the new sett will give the result you want after washing. Weave structures with many interlacements within a repeat will require a more open sett to create any texture. The longer the active yarn floats, the greater the contraction of the yarn, and used in combination with plain weave in the passive yarns will give effective dimensional texture. This might seem like a lot of effort, but it will avoid potential disappointment after your project is woven.

Your collection of samples will form a directory of various techniques, yarns, setts and finishing methods to which you can refer for future projects.

RECORD KEEPING

Careful record keeping is an important element of these experiments in order to replicate your results at any future time. Useful elements to record are:

- Wraps per inch/cm (wpi/cm)
- Ends per inch/cm (epi/cm)
- Picks per inch/cm (ppi/cm)
- Yarn samples
- Yarn count
- Yarn supplier (if known)
- Warping order
- Threading order
- Reed size
- Sleying order
- Treadling order
- Size of sample on the loom
- Size of sample once it is taken off the loom
- Wet-finishing treatment (including timings)
- Finished size of the sample
- Shrinkage percentage (dividing finished sizes by pre-finished sizes)

WET-FINISHING

Wet-finishing is one of the most important aspects of this book and is used in many of these techniques. Throughout the book, specific finishing details will be mentioned, but an overview is given here.

Where fulling is required to achieve the textural effect, wet-finishing with hot sudsy water and agitation, or hot air and agitation, is necessary. There is a tendency for the shorter dimension of a piece of weaving to pull in more than the longer direction, which is something to be aware of if specific dimensions are important. If so, it is a good idea to stay-stitch selvedges (for width) or the beginning and end (for length) together prior to wet-finishing. If floats are on the underside of the fabric, consider turning the fabric inside out (so that the floats are now on the outside) prior to wet-finishing, so that they cannot full the fabric to itself.

Activating Active Yarns

In most cases, wet-finishing is necessary. For samples, it's a good idea to see how easily the yarns that have been used will shrink by hand-washing. Normally, when washing wool fabric, other than to close up the weave, you would hardly touch the fabric, but for dimensional texture, active yarns need to be activated. This can be done in several ways.

Overtwist

When overtwist or high-twist yarns are used, all that is needed is hot water – around 60°C – and a little agitation.

As soon as the fabric is placed into the hot water and the water is absorbed, the pent-up twist in the overtwist float areas releases and the floats try to coil up on themselves. If you need to encourage a specific direction of activity, then gently pull opposite corners of the sample to effect the correct orientation. Ann Richards describes the effect clearly in her book, *Weaving Textiles That Shape Themselves* (*see* Bibliography). Pleats will be assisted by pulling the fabric along the pleat length, and left to drain and air dry naturally. If detergent has been used, rinse in a similar temperature before squeezing out the excess water and laying on towels to dry on a flat surface.

High-twist wool can be steamed for at least an hour before cooling and drying slowly to hold its new shape permanently.

Fulling by Hand

When using woollen-spun or less tightly spun worsted yarns, you will probably need to add soap. This can be olive-oil soap, hand-washing solutions or powder that is thoroughly dissolved, or dish-cleaning liquids.

The idea is to eliminate any lanolin, grease or oils that might have been added to the yarns during the industrial or hand-spinning process, and allow the rough edges of the wool fibres to act on themselves. Rubbing the wool against itself or against a slightly rough surface will start the fulling process. If you have a washboard, rub the sample against the washboard until it begins to shrink. It might take some time to get started, but once it starts, it will full quickly.

Once the fabric has started to shrink and pucker, great attention must be given to the process. Stop as soon as you like the effects. Once it has gone 'too far', it cannot be undone. Further samples would need to be woven to do more wet-finishing, stopping a little earlier. In fact, that is an interesting set of samples all on its own!

FULLING

Fulling is the process of using hot water, soap and agitation to make fabric shrink by friction and pressure. It is traditionally used in woollen clothmaking to tighten up the weave in the cloth to insulate and repel water.

Felting

Felting more generally refers to the meshing or interlocking of loose wool fibre, rather than woven fabric form, although if fulling is carried through to excess, felting is the result.

Fulling by Machine

Top-loading washing machines can also be used on a regular wash cycle, taking the samples out to inspect the progress. However, these are not readily available in

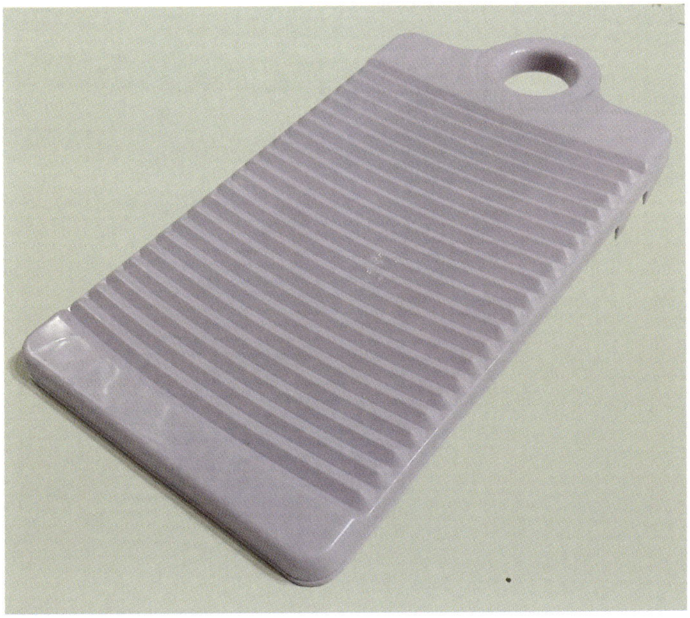

Washboards can be inexpensively obtained from many sources. These are useful for assisting with wet-finishing, especially with wool as the active shrinking yarn.

Europe, where you can either wash by hand, take your chances in a front-loading machine, or use the tumble-drying method, which isn't so ecological in electricity consumption. If there is not much in the tumble dryer, add one or more wet towels to speed up the process. Another suggested method is to add one or more tennis balls. Other methods of wet-finishing are required for specific techniques, such as shibori and these will be covered in their respective chapters.

Personal experience has shown that with front-loading washing machines, the action on the wool-wash programme is usually non-effective and the action on other programmes is quite often too effective. The best control is not with the washing, but with the drying, so if you have access to a tumble dryer, use a wool-wash programme on the washing machine, or hand wash, and then place the dripping wet fabric into the tumble dryer on normal heat and check it every five to ten minutes or so.

Do not forget that samples can always be put in for a little more time, but if overdone, it is unlikely that the process will be reversible. Usually around 30 to 40 minutes in the tumble dryer gives effective results, but that is dependent on how much texture is desired, the materials used and the wet-finishing methods before tumble-drying. It is down to the individual weaver as to how much shrinkage is required.

COMPARING DIFFERENT AMOUNTS OF WET-FINISHING

To compare different amounts of wet-finishing, one suggestion is to weave a set of identical samples (or cut up one larger one and stitch the edges to prevent unravelling) and put them all through the same initial wet-finishing process.

Remove one sample, continue the wet-finishing on the others. After a certain amount – of time or shrinkage – remove another sample. Continue the wet-finishing, repeating this format until there are no more samples left. The full group of samples will provide a lot of useful information.

Once the fabric has been fulled to your satisfaction, it can be air-dried by suspending from a line, or dried flat on a towel. Because the texture is the feature, it is not advisable to use a dry towel to roll the fabric in. Be patient. The results will be worth it.

Pressing/Ironing

Generally speaking, pressing or ironing is not required for dimensional texture. However, if you are wanting directional *pleating* effects, then an iron can be a useful addition, with gentle pressing on the closed pleat in the direction you wish the pleat to lie, using a soft cloth between the iron and the pleats being ironed. Care needs to be taken when pressing to avoid flattening the dimensional area.

Also, if you have texture and flat areas juxtaposed, ironing might be desirable for the flat areas to ensure the contrast is clear.

Reviving a Flattened Texture

If a dimensional texture fabric is squashed and needs to be rejuvenated, usually a little steam and a shake will revive it, leaving it to air dry or place onto a dry towel on a flat surface. However, if the fabric contains thermoplastic yarns and has been ironed, then reinstating the texture is not generally possible, as the heat causes thermoplastic yarns to change their form permanently once the specific melting point for that yarn has been reached and exceeded.

Pleats have specific requirements:

- **Round pleats** will be assisted by steam, dampening them slightly and pulling them along their length.
- **Vertical pleats** are encouraged by twisting them into a skein.
- **Knife pleats** need a little pressing after steaming or dampening.
- **Finger-pleating** is always an option for fine detail assisted by pressing, if required.

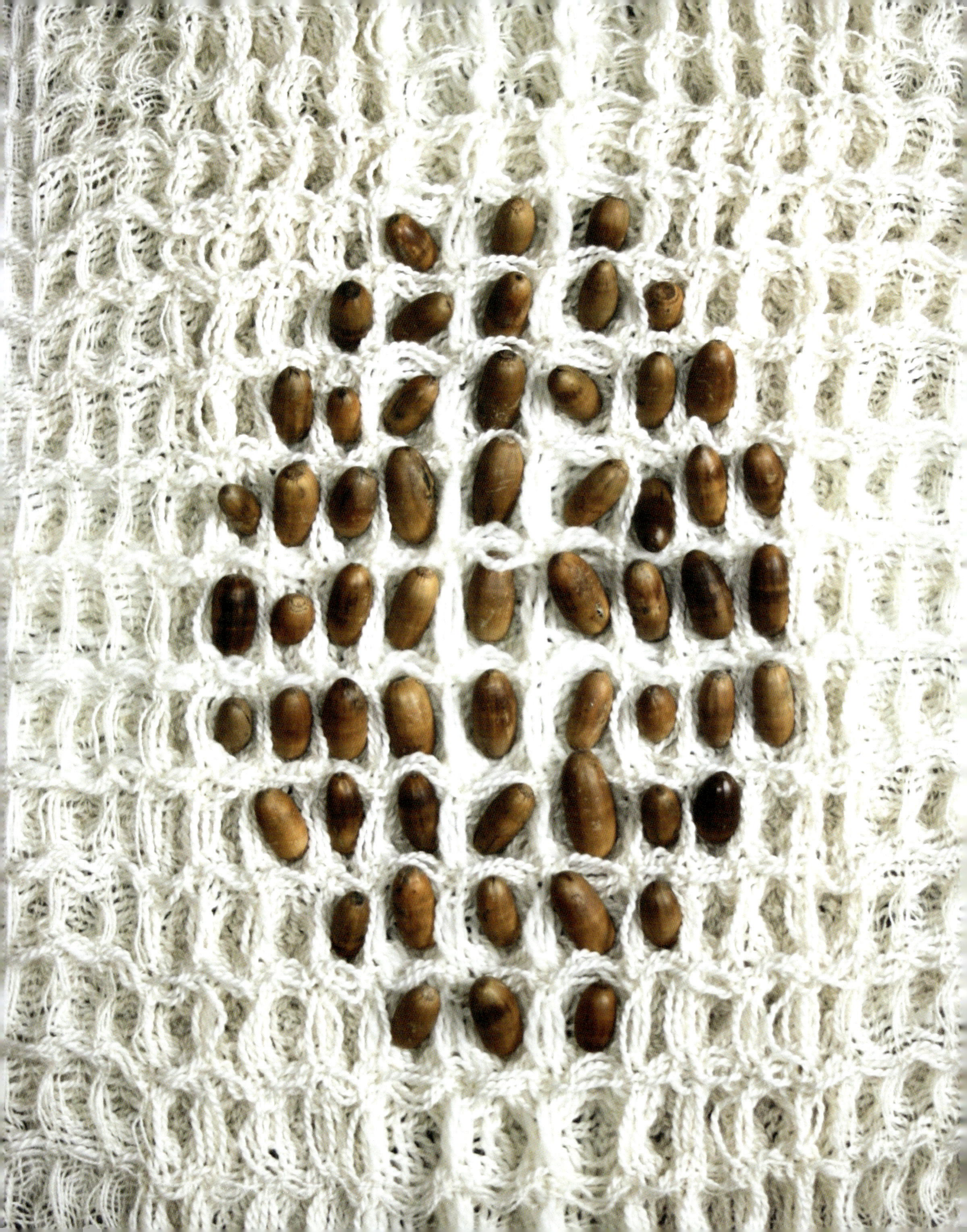

CHAPTER 2

WAFFLE

Waffle (sometimes known as honeycomb in the UK) is one of the most approachable of the dimensional effects. Most weavers have come across the magic of waffle weaves for collapsing into depth. In this book, waffle refers to the weave structure that looks like the American breakfast waffle. It is the most dramatic of all weave structures, even before wet-finishing occurs, as it automatically creates surface dimension as soon as it is released from the loom. The three-dimensional hollow that results is called a 'cell'.

Waffle is known for its thermal properties, often being used for lightweight blankets, which trap air in the cell pockets providing an insulating layer. Less well known are its acoustic properties. With its large surface area and depth, waffle can effectively mute echoes and dampen sound. The egg-box shape of many acoustic coverings for recording studios are based on the visual surface of waffle weave, even though many of them are non-woven products.

STRUCTURE

The structure of waffle itself is quite straightforward. It consists largely of floats in both vertical and horizontal directions and is designed with a point threading. What contains the floats is a diagonal formation of plain weave outlining them. Ridges form along the longest of the vertical and horizontal floats on both sides of the fabric, which are offset to each other. What is the longest set of floats based around the top point of the threading on one side is also the centre point of a square on the opposite side. The reverse is true around the bottom point of the threading. The floats introduce a shrinking element, and once tension is relaxed, the floats contract, pulling the two sides into relief against each other.

Waffle Variations

The main variations that can be derived are the size of the waffles and the materials used.

Four-shaft Waffle

The smallest size of waffle is possible on just four shafts.

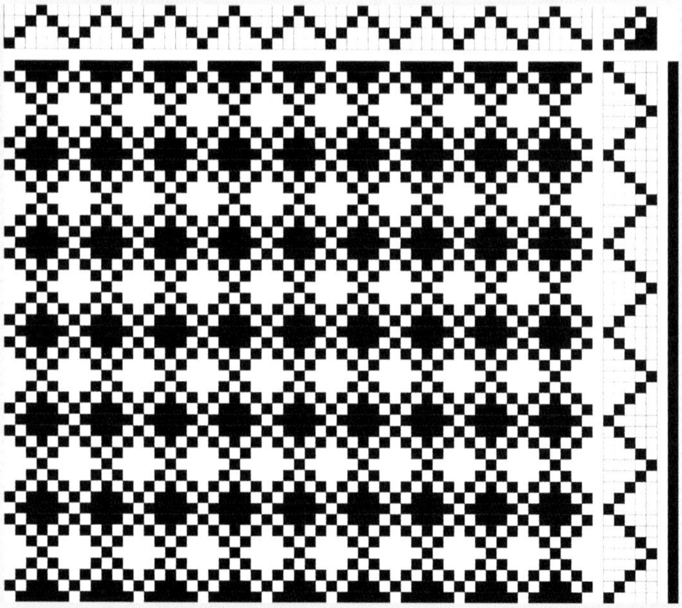

Four-shaft waffle on a point threading and treadling. Because of the nature of a point threading and treadling, only one-half of the full waffle is needed in the tie-up.

Incubator Waffles of different sizes in various wools have been used for this artpiece.

Six-shaft Waffle

Six shafts will give a more distinct result.

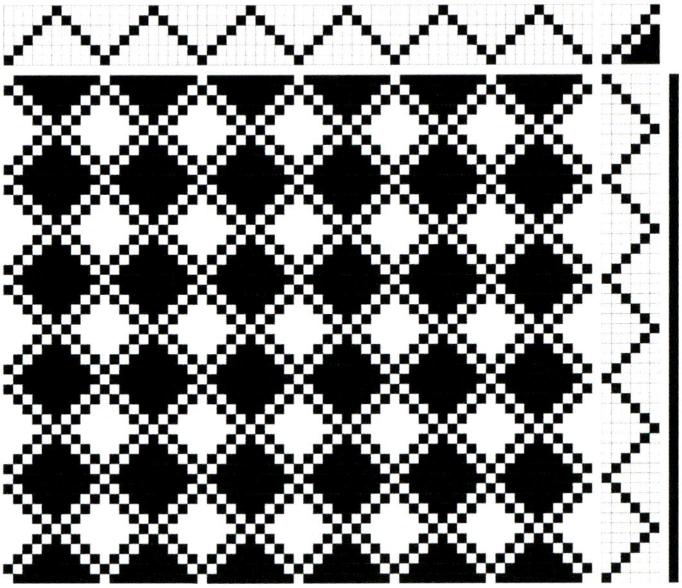

Six shafts give a more distinctive waffle.

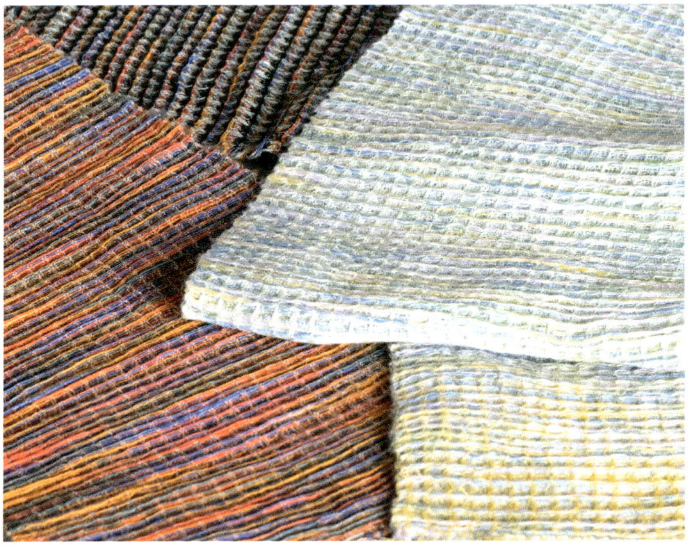

These eight-shaft waffles explore the impact of a variegated cotton singles weft on a spaced-dyed 60/2 silk warp. (Photo: Colin Usher)

Eight-shaft Waffle

The more shafts that can be used, the larger the floats and the deeper the resulting cells. Thicker yarns in warp and weft will enhance this. The effect will happen regardless of the material property of the yarn but using yarns that will full does encourage more shrinkage of the floats and a deeper cell. Different materials used within the same warp and/or weft give graded variations.

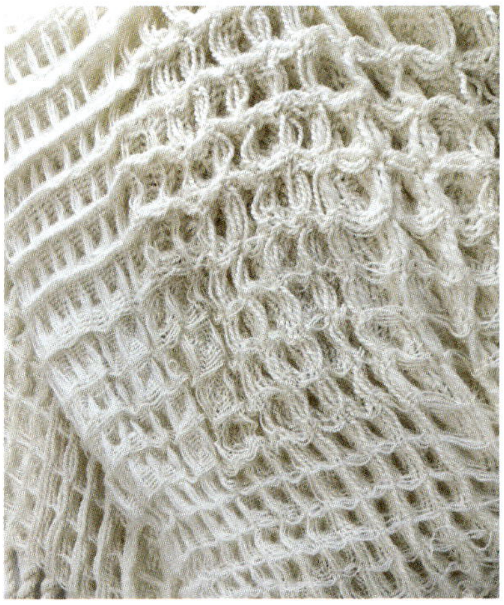

Incubator (detail): This piece demonstrates using different materials with the same threading to vary the sizes of the waffle.

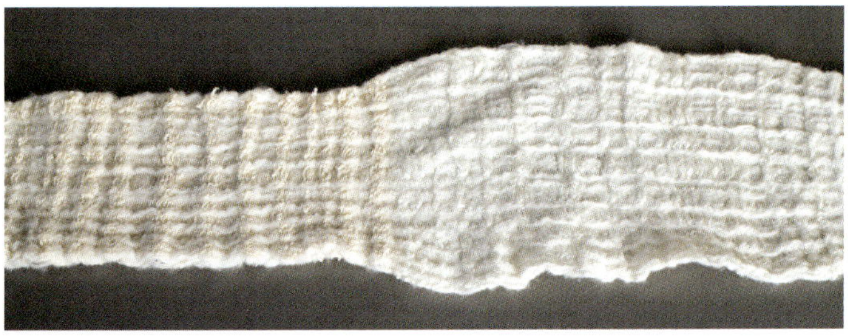

Different weft materials impact the waffle. The cream singles silk noil weft forces the plied white wool warp to contract widthwise in the left of this sample. To the right, a 60/2 silk interspersed with the same wool as in the warp forces the sample out again. (Photo: Colin Usher)

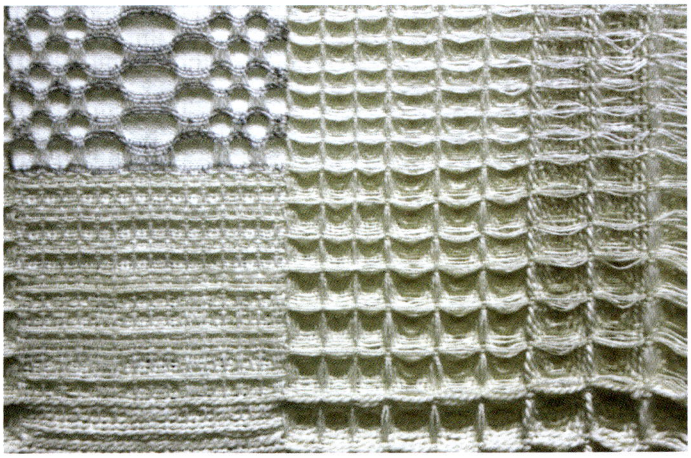

The Collective (detail): This piece amalgamates different sizes of waffle and honeycomb, using point threadings. (Photo: Colin Usher)

12-shaft Waffle

With more shafts comes the ability to grade the size of the waffle cells and create interesting surfaces; 12 shafts will allow for two main sizes of compatible waffles.

Another option is to split the threading into two blocks of six shafts.

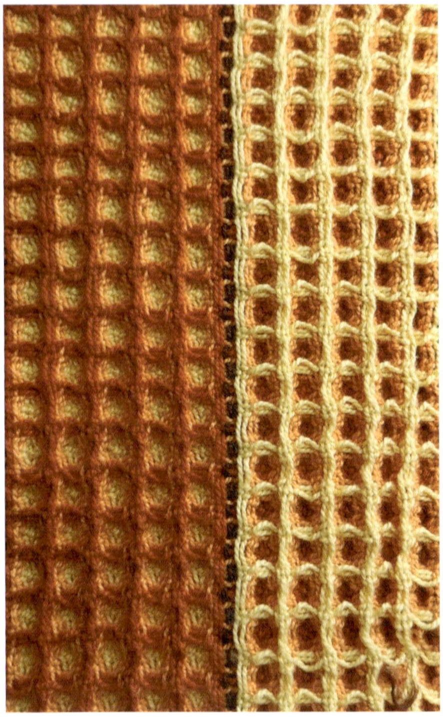

Two sets of six-shaft point threading were used for this waffle by Jennifer Verrall, using colour to highlight the cell ridges and valleys.

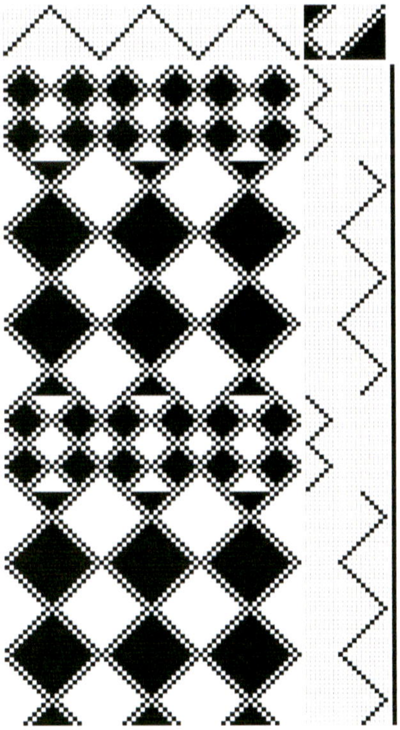

This 12-shaft draft gives two waffle sizes in the tie-up, but variations of shape can be created through the treadling and the extended tie-up.

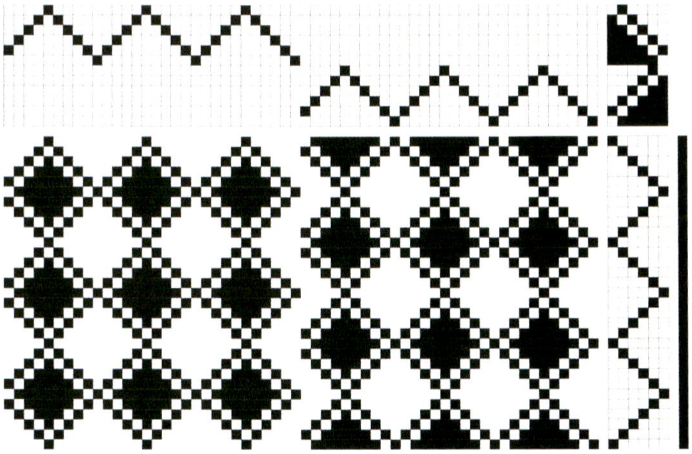

Twelve shafts can also be divided up into two six-shaft point threadings. Note that each block has to end before the return point is complete in order to maintain an odd–even threading order.

16-shaft Waffle

With 16 shafts, there are further options.

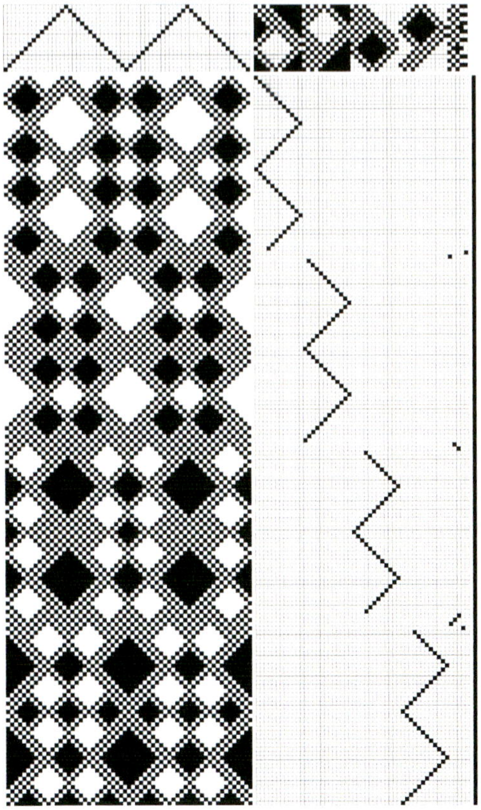

Sixteen shafts allow for more variations in waffle sizes, and in the amount of plain weave that can be incorporated.

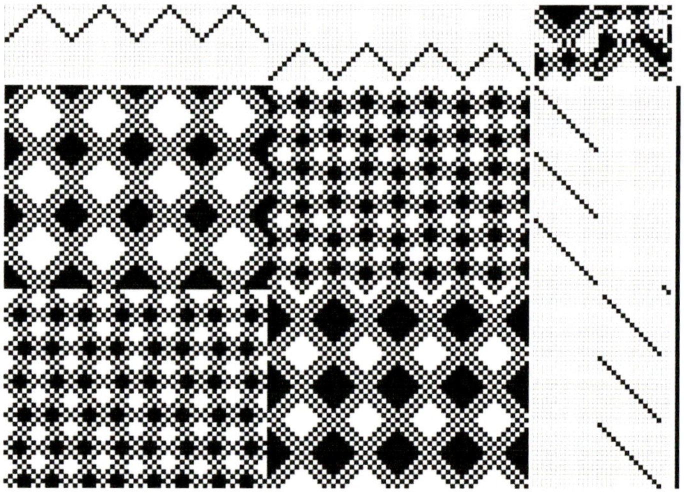

Sixteen shafts also allow for two sets of eight-shaft waffles and their variations to be used.

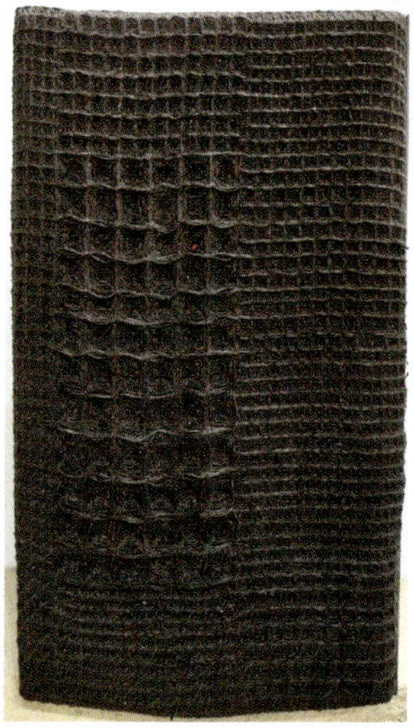

Different-sized waffles, in black linen interspersed with red lurex, give a distinctive look to this speaker cover by Wendy Morris.

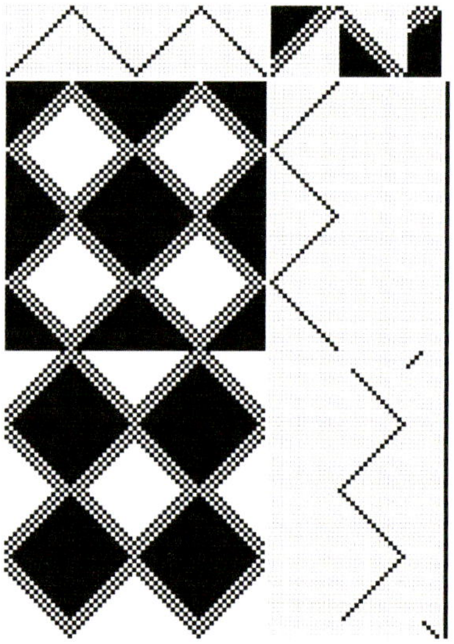

Very large waffles can be created with 16 shafts, but it can be advisable to stabilise the fabric with wider outlines of plain weave.

24-, 32- and 40-shaft Waffles

With 24 shafts, you can combine a 16-shaft with an eight-shaft waffle or have two groups of eight shafts and two groups of four shafts, and various other combinations. With 32 or 40 shafts, even more variations can be achieved.

Using Different Structures with a Waffle

So far, only waffle and plain weave have been used. However, with multiple shafts, and point threading in blocks, different structures can be woven in addition.

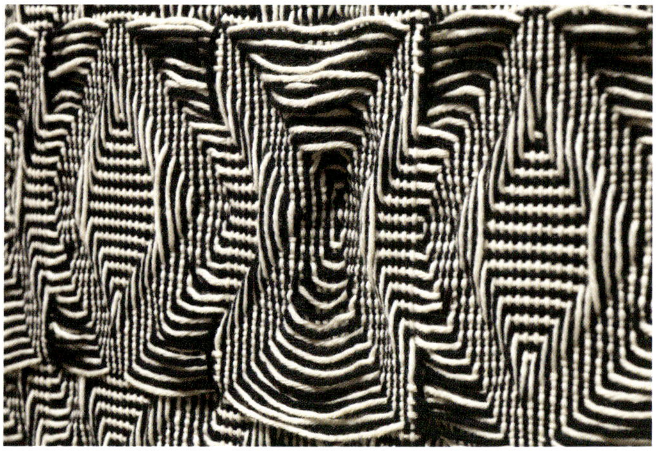

A detail of Heather Macali's *Black + White XO* shows shadow weave and waffle combined. The black wool was dyed with acid dyes. (Photo: Dan Jarvis)

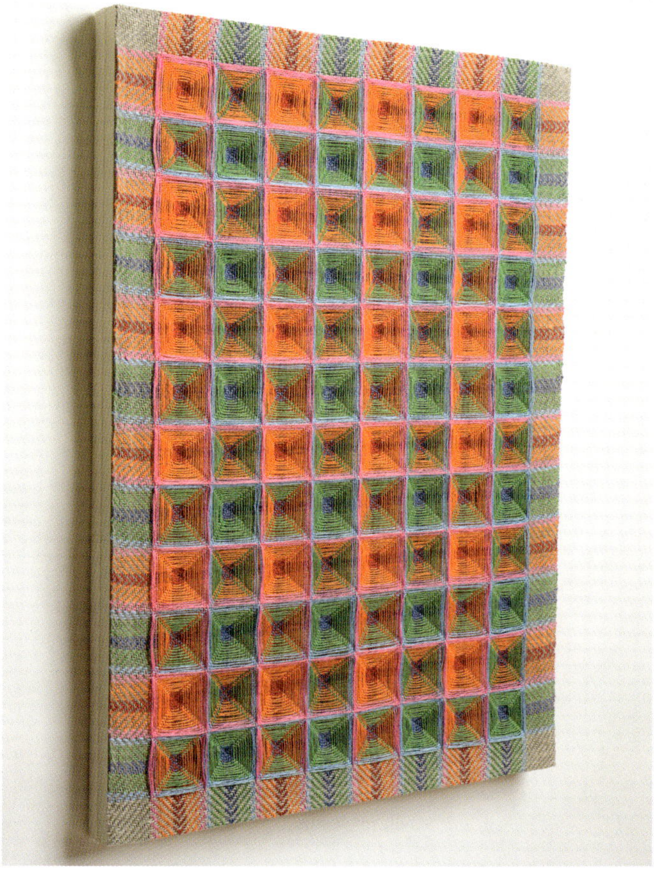

Susie Taylor's *Sanctum 2* shows colourplay as well as waffles being combined with twills for the border areas. (Photo: James Dewrance)

SHAPING

Waffle can be useful for shaping garments. Putting a waffle band down one side of a length of cloth while weaving the remainder in a regular balanced cloth, such as plain weave derivatives, twills, crepe weaves or satins, will create shrinkage in the waffle area only. This will lead to curvature of that side of the cloth and crinkles or pleating at the border between the two weave structures as the shrinkage works on the warp and weft.

A single waffle band can also be to create seersucker effects (*see* Chapter 4).

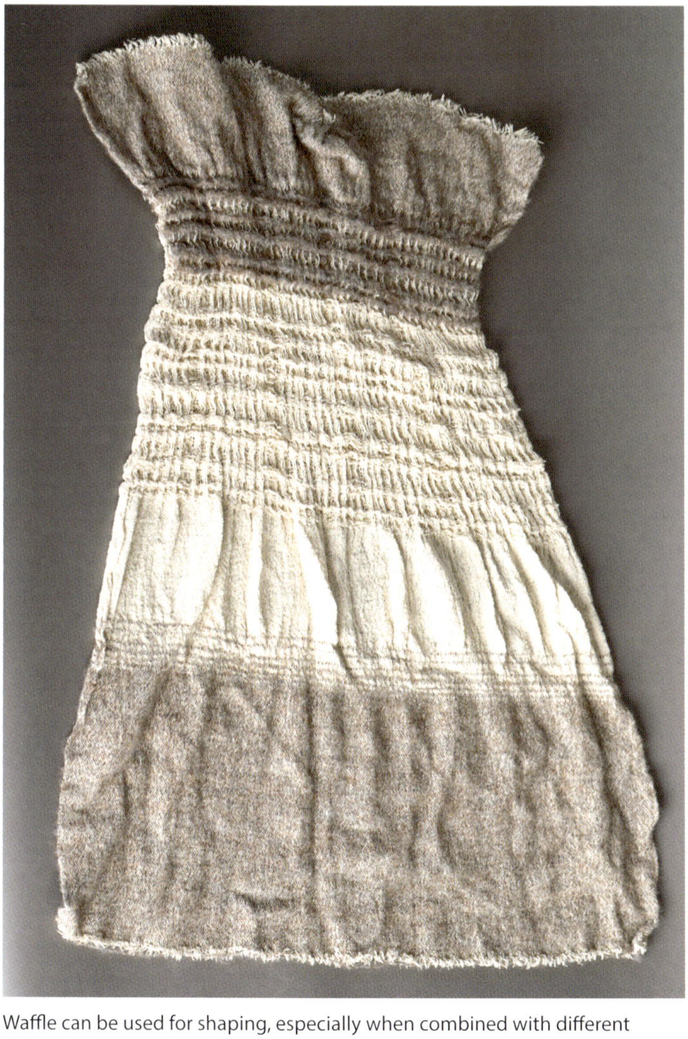

Waffle can be used for shaping, especially when combined with different material properties. The silk noil warp was woven in plain weave and waffle using both a Harris tweed weft (in the heathery colour) and silk noil weft.

Waffle in Double Cloth

With two blocks of point threading, two separate layers can be created to allow for waffle on one side versus plain weave on the other, which can be swapped over. The shrinkage created by the waffle will cause puckering in the plain weave layer, which can give deep dimensional effects (*see* Chapter 10).

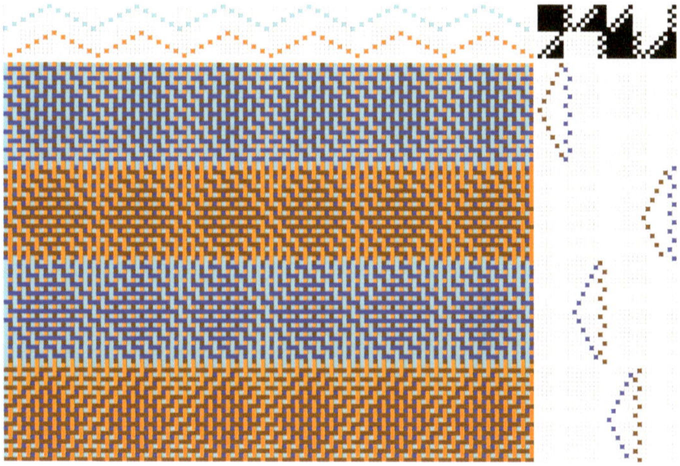

A double-layer waffle – two waffles created on two layers – can be explored. The tie-up and treadling give a plain weave on one layer with the waffle on the other. This draft shows horizontal bands. The plain layer will pucker on wet-finishing.

Alternatively, there could be two layers of waffles, which can switch layers in various ways, as the weaver wishes.

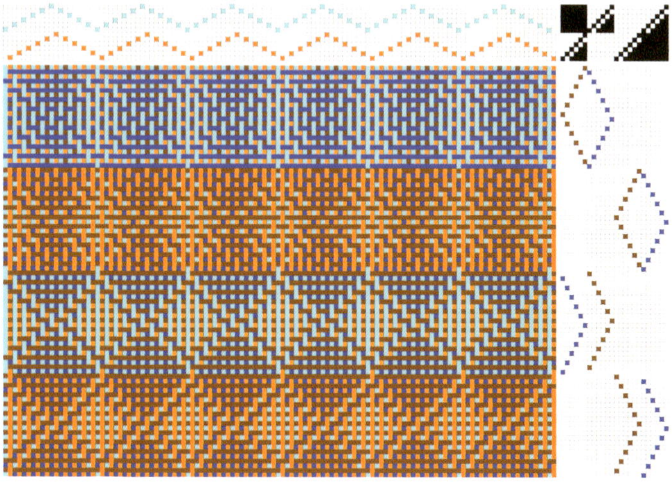

A double waffle created with waffle on both sides of the fabric at the same time can be woven. This draft has stitching points to keep the two sides attached to each other.

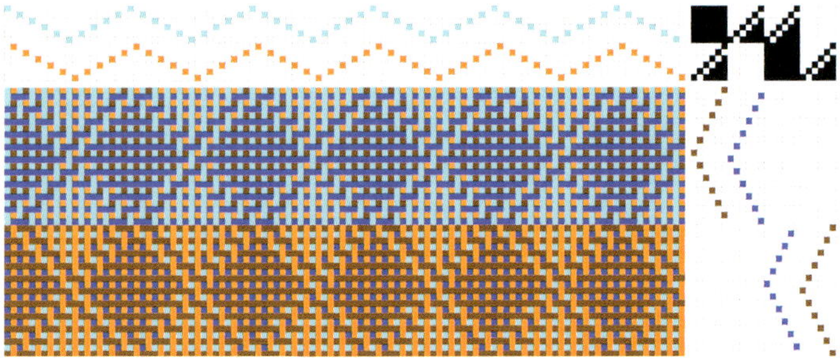

This draft shows the two waffle layers exchanging position as a way of securing them together.

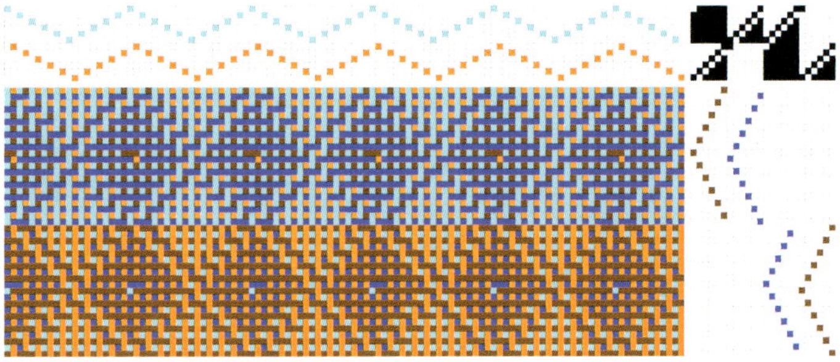

This draft adds additional stitching points in the centre of the waffle.

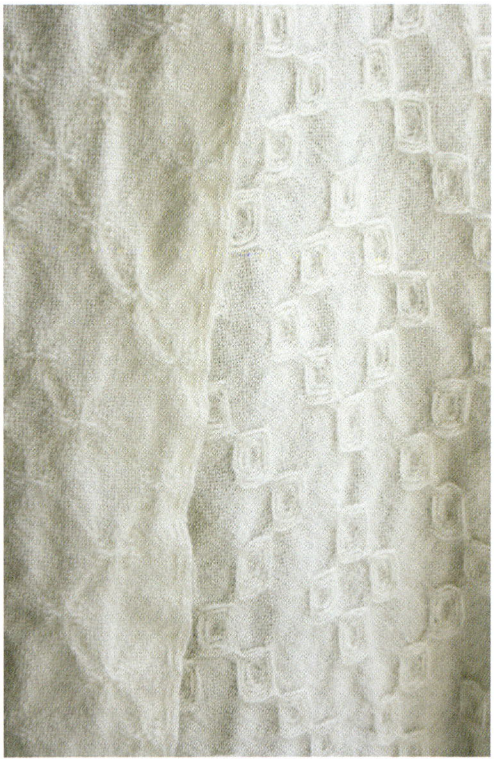

Waffle can also be used as a design feature. Three blocks of eight-shaft waffles were threaded randomly, used independently and combined to make a design that is different on either side of the lambswool scarf.

Playing with Waffle Layers

Switching over different waffle layers and playing with colour in the threading and weaving will give many colour combinations, which can be fun to explore, as well as the dimensional effects.

Interchanging waffles in warp bands continuing with these six-shaft point threadings would require 24 shafts – 12 shafts for each warp block.

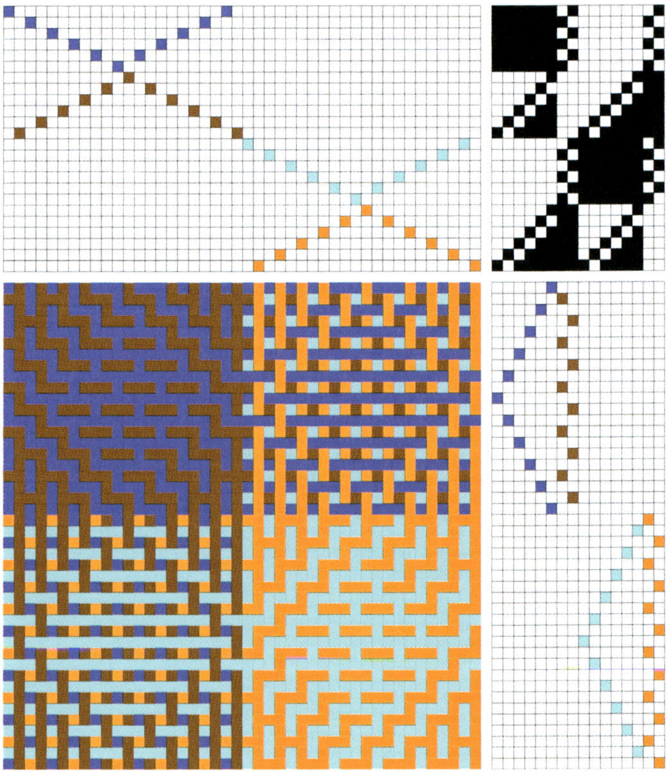

One side of each block is weaving plain weave and the other is weaving the waffle, switching roles in adjacent blocks in warp and weft.

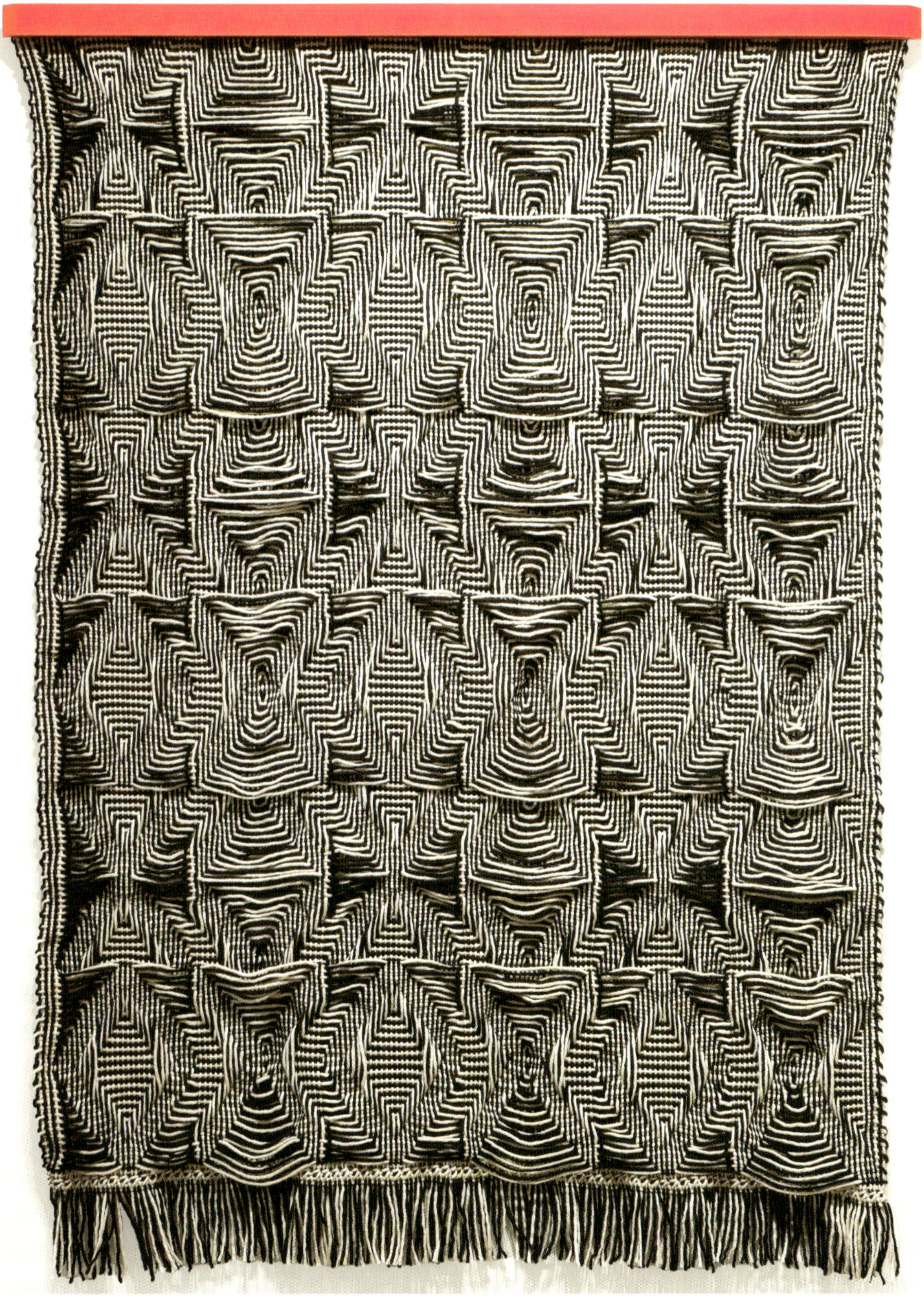

Heather Macali combines waffle with shadow weave in *Black + White XO*. The black wool was dyed with acid dyes. (Photo: Dan Jarvis)

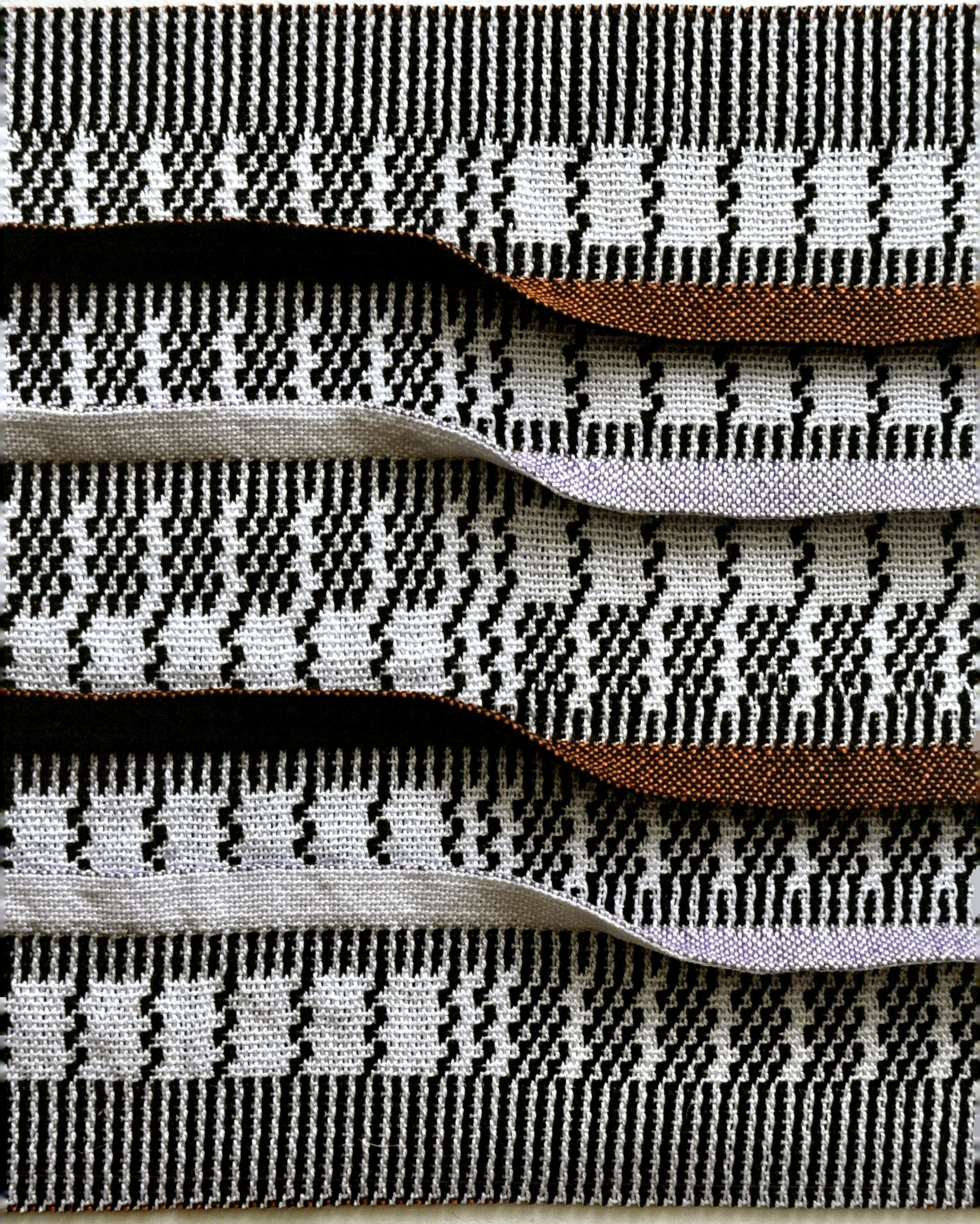

CHAPTER 3

PLEATS

The first thing many people think of when considering dimensional cloth is a pleat. Pleats can be created in several different ways, including shibori, which has its own chapter (*see* Chapter 6). This chapter looks more closely at different methods of creating pleats through structure. There are various ways and experimentation is always recommended to find the right sett and materials for the result you wish to achieve.

There are some very good books on specific elements of pleating, for example using overspun yarns. These include Ann Richard's *Weaving Textiles That Shape Themselves,* and Lotte Dalgaard and Paulette Adam's *Thread Magic* (*see* Bibliography). I recommended that you consult these if this is an area that you want to investigate further.

WHAT IS A PLEAT?

According to Paul Jackson, from his book *Complete Pleats*:

> *A pleat is a sheet of material folded back and forth; the pairing – to use terminology borrowed from origami – of a 'valley' fold with a 'mountain' fold. A pleat can be straight or curved, sharp or soft, geometric or organic. It can create a two-dimensional surface or a three-dimensional form.*

This book and *Folding Techniques for Designers*, by the same author, are indispensable if the interested reader wishes to explore pleats deeply.

PLEATS USING VALLEY AND MOUNTAIN FOLDS

Using these two fold directions, different pleats can be created:

- **Accordion pleat** – Equal spacing of a valley/mountain fold pairing.
- **Knife pleat** – Unequal spacing between folds (think of mill skylights).
- **Box pleat** – Pairing two mountain folds and then two valley folds.
- **Upright pleat** – Valley, mountain, valley; a version of this can be made to twist from side to side.
- **Non-parallel pleat** – Vertical mountain folds and long diagonal valley pleats.
- **V-pleat** – Accordion pleat that changes its emphasis from mountain to valley or valley to mountain on the same fold.
- **Twisted pleat** – Pleats designed to collapse into a spiral directly related to the angle of pleat.

Accordion and knife pleats can both be formed easily in weaving in several ways, some giving sharper edges than others. Accordion pleats are created by using equal amounts of both weave structures. Knife pleats are the result when using one weave with a longer run compared to the other, but consistency and a clean break between the two weave structures are key. Upright pleats can be pressed into the required direction after wet-finishing. Ann Richards uses cord weaves to create V-pleats for her beautifully crisp and elegant pleated necklaces.

The three pleat structures featured here are:

Lynn Smetko's colourful upright horizontal pleats are interspersed with an interchanging double cloth design, using white and black cotton warps in a 1:1 ratio. (Photo: Lynn Smetko)

1. Twill- and satin-based pleats
2. Plain weave cord pleats
3. Double-weave pleats.

TWILL- AND SATIN-BASED PLEATS

Opposing warp and weft dominance in twill or satin weaves creates a soft ridge effect where the two effects border each other, forcing one to curve slightly over the other. That change is the basis behind pleating using twills or satin weaves. These are sometimes referred to as 'furrow' pleats, which describes the rounded look of them.

Horizontal pleats can be formed with a minimum of three shafts, although vertical pleats require a minimum of four (to give a cord effect), six or eight shafts (using twills). Pleats that move across the surface, either diagonally or organically, will require at least eight shafts – often many more.

One main feature of pleats is that they create a large reduction in the length or width of the fabric once finished. In this book, that reduction is called the 'fold factor'. When planning projects, do bear in mind and sample to take account of the fold factor to avoid inadvertently running out of warp before your project is complete or not planning a wide enough piece for the effect you want. One recommendation is three to five times the width (for vertical pleats) or the length (for horizontal pleats), depending on the method of construction of the pleat, number of pleats, their height etc. Sampling is essential to ascertain the desired amount of pleat.

Horizontal Pleats

These need a minimum of three shafts in order to create a 2/1 and 1/2 twill. Four shafts allow for a longer float with a 3/1 and 1/3 twill, which helps to give structure to the pleat. The changeover of warp to weft dominance and back again causes torsion between the two areas, leading to the pleat crest being midway in the more dominant band, an effect that is highlighted if different thicknesses are used in warp versus weft.

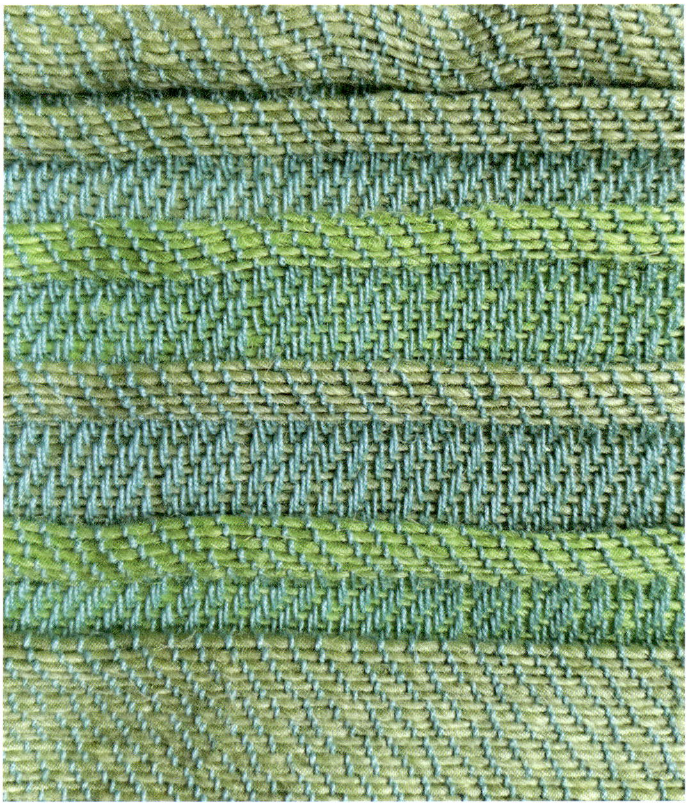

A cotton warp and a heavier linen weft help with the fold potential of this four-shaft horizontal pleat. The overview shows the lighter weft-faced twill standing proud above the larger darker warp-faced twill stripes.

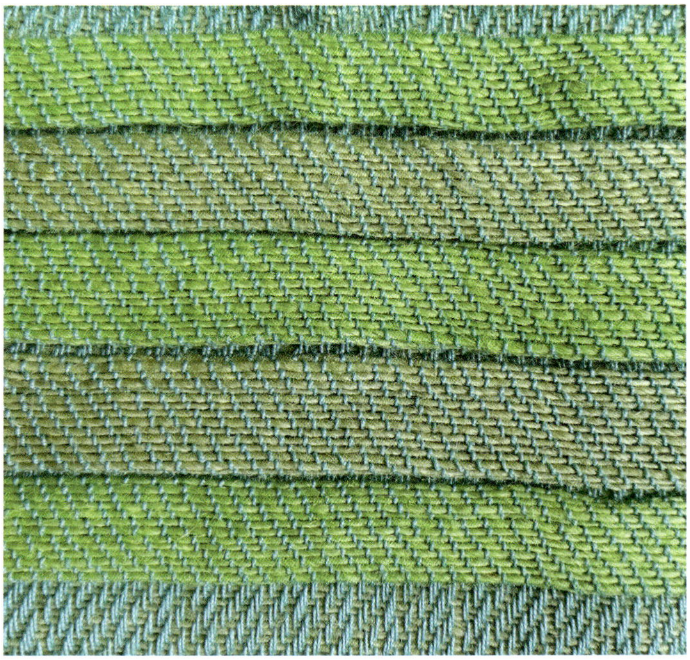

The reverse side shows the role reversal. What appeared as a weft-faced twill in the first image now appears as a warp-faced twill on the reverse. The larger stripes dominate, showing their weft-faced surface.

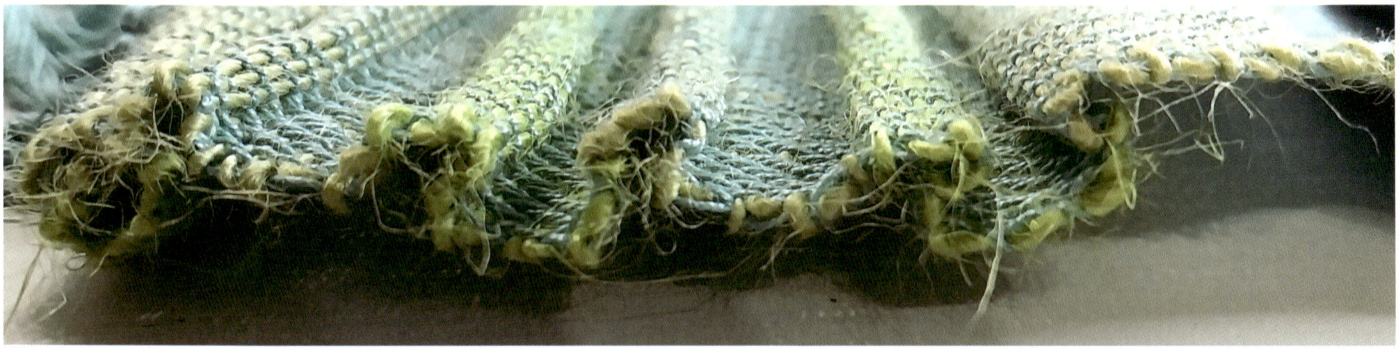

The side view highlights the tendency of the warp-faced side to be overshadowed by the weft-faced side when the weft is much heavier than the warp.

Four-shaft Twill

With a four-shaft loom, a weft stripe of 1/3 twill can be employed, creating a weft-faced twill. When this is followed by a weft stripe of the same or different width in 3/1 twill (a warp-faced twill), the two opposing twills create a visual and textural disturbance to the surface of the fabric. If a thicker weft than warp yarn is used that will help with the shift in surface tensions, creating a more dominant surface in the 1/3, which causes the finer warp 3/1 twill area to curve away from the strength of the 1/3 twill. Different setts and strength of beat will affect the result. Reversing the twill line with the cleanest break will help form pleat formation. In this scenario, the mountain pleat will be where the 1/3 is dominant, and the valley where the 3/1 is dominant.

The best effects arise when the pleats are neither too narrow nor too wide, so sampling is imperative. A general rule of thumb is around $^{1}/_{8}$–½in (0.5–1.25cm) before changing to the other twill, depending on the thickness of yarns used and whether you are using regular- or irregular-sized pleats.

Consider using a finer warp with the potential to shrink a little, so exploring material changes. For instance, a fine crepe wool warp could give an enhanced effect, or a fine singles linen warp might give the cloth a firmer hand, especially when combined with thicker wefts, particularly of linen or other stiffer, less pliable yarns.

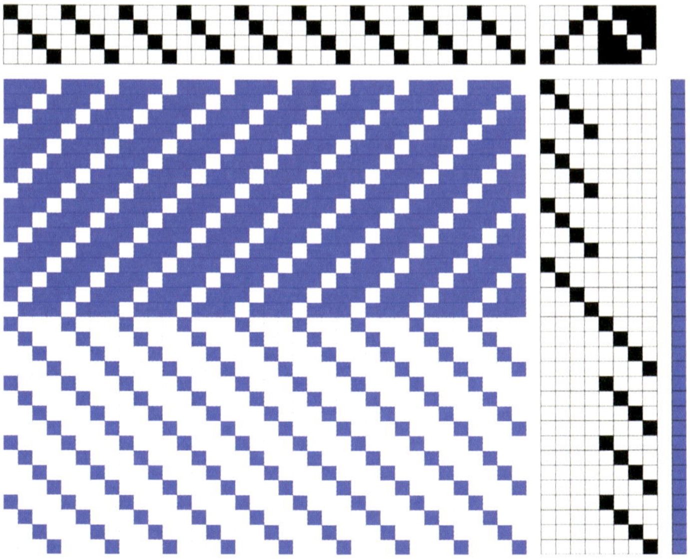

Four-shaft draft showing 1/3 3/1 horizontal pleats created through changing the twill from 1/3 in the weft to 3/1 in the weft. Different yarns, colours and proportions can be used for variations.

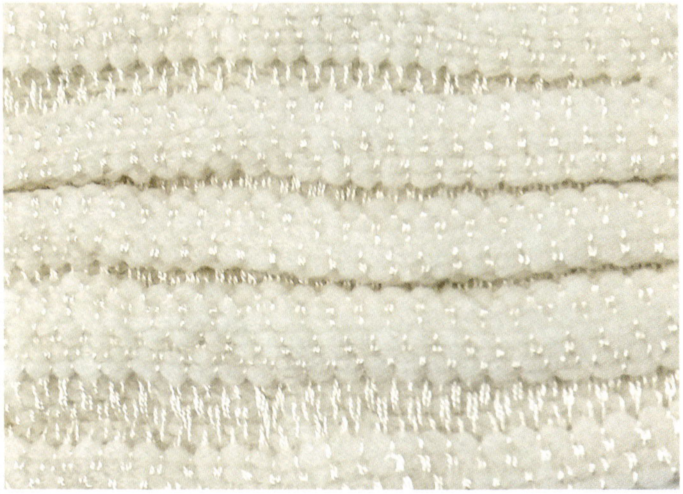

Jane Deane's four-shaft sample uses a 30/2 silk for the warp and a pencil roving in wool for the weft. The combination of thick versus thin leads to a pronounced pleat with a very soft hand.

Five-end Satin or Twill

The same information holds for satin weaves. A five-end satin is the smallest satin weave that is possible.

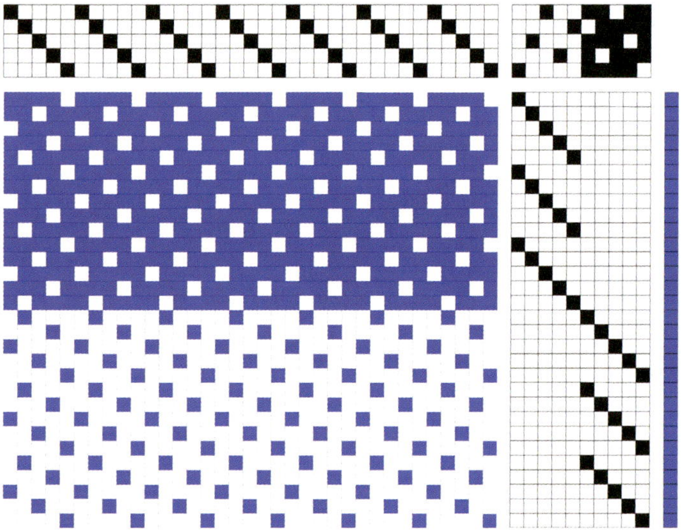

A five-end satin structure can also be used in its two extremes: warp-faced – satin and weft-faced (sateen).

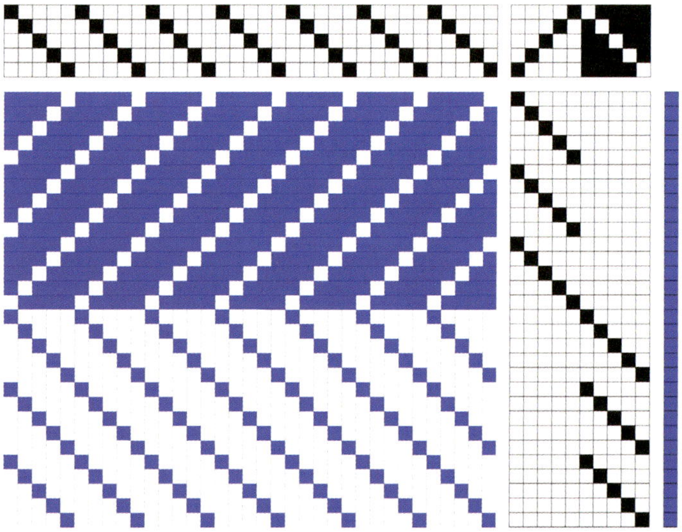

A five-end twill can be substituted. It will have a more distinctive diagonal line moving through both faces. Compare the two five-end drafts.

Eight-end Satin

Eight-end satin is the other more frequently used satin. This can be created in two different versions: step 3 or step 5. Again, the contrast between the warp-faced satin and the weft-faced sateen will give the most effective pleat construction. Material choices make a big difference in whether the pleats will be crisp or soft. Pressing after wet-finishing will help to set the direction of the pleats.

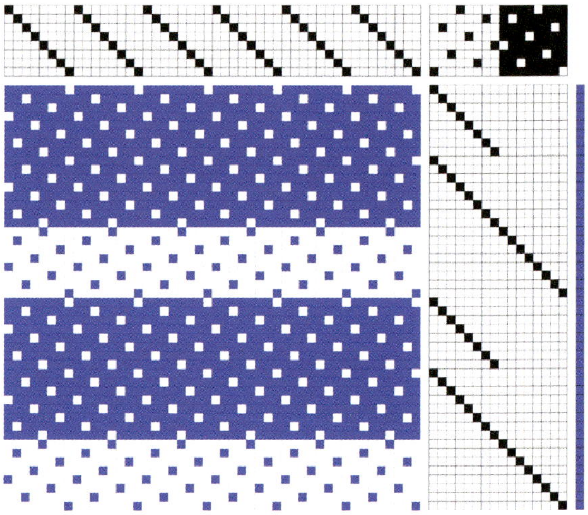

An eight-end satin is more usual. This draft shows the step 5 version. This means that there are five shafts between the first end and the second end in the tie-up, and this wraps around (going up) for every end in the tie-up. The inverse can be seen in the second half of the tie-up, where one shaft is removed from the warp-faced tie-up five shafts lower. A clean break is required between the two horizontal surfaces.

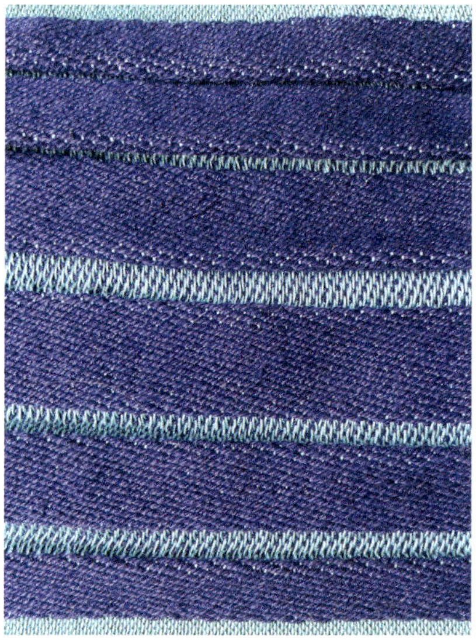

Blue unmercerised cotton was used as the weft for the eight-shaft satin knife and box pleats in this sample. The knife element is created through weaving the leading edge of the pleat for at least twice as long as the pleating element. In this case, the weft-faced sateen was woven in increasing amounts compared with the warp-faced satin, which remained at two repeats of the satin. The box pleat is then developed by weaving larger amounts of the sateen either side of a larger satin before reducing gradually in a mirror image of the first part of the sample.

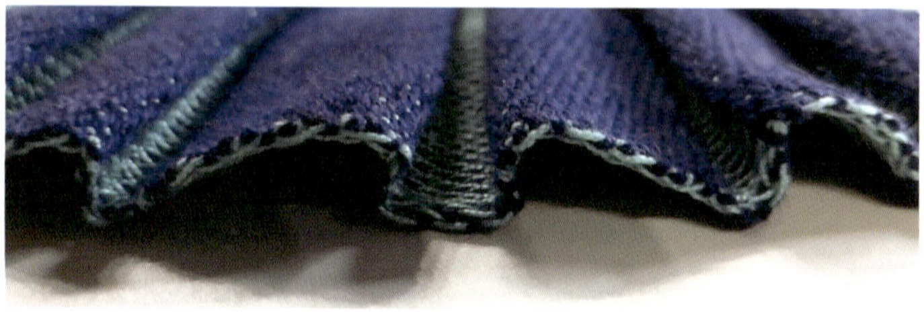

The side view showing the box pleat element bordered by knife pleats. The pleats were pressed with an iron after wet-finishing, while still slightly damp.

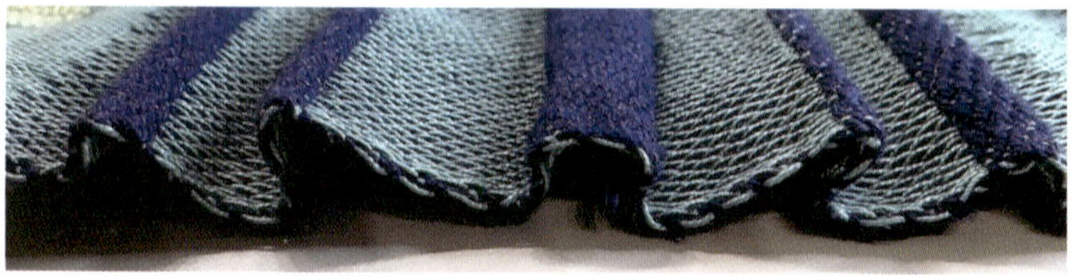

Reversing the fabric shows the box pleat element and the knife pleats going in opposite directions.

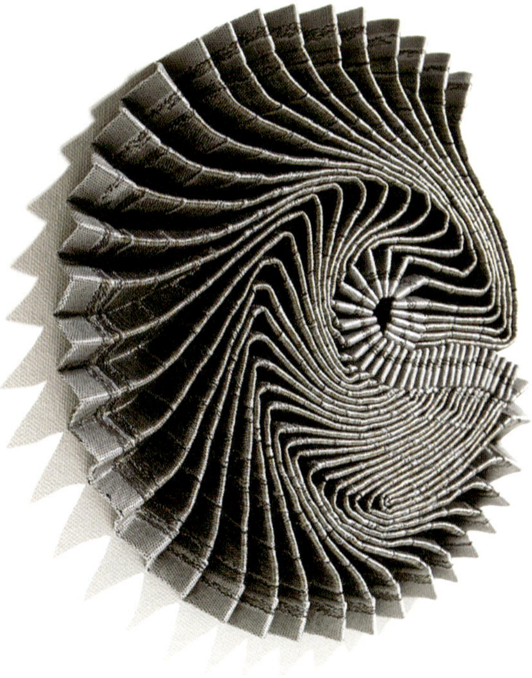

This artwork, *Ammonite Shadow: Ardescia Swirl* by Dr Hannah White, captures the essence of its natural inspiration through the creative use of pleats, hand-manipulation and stitching. Materials: Trivera thread, jacquard woven double cloth fabric. Processes: Hand-pleated, heat set, sculpted and stitched. (Photo: Dr Hannah White)

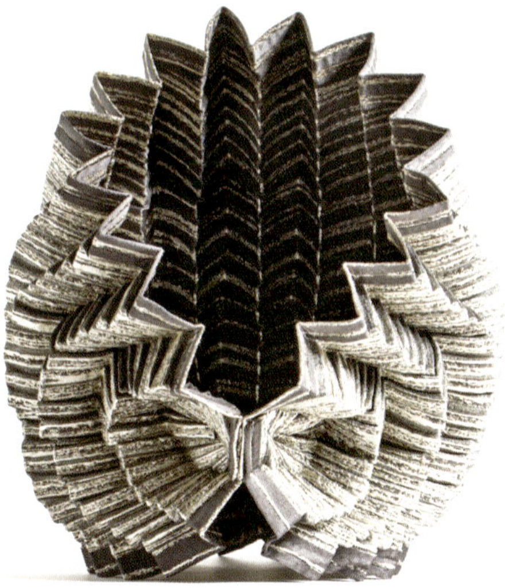

Dr Hannah White's *Fluidity and Rigidity: Sculpture Number 4* combines her experience as a weaver with electroforming to create a hybrid material called 'Metal Integral Skeleton Textiles'. Metal only grows onto conductive threads specifically designed within the weave, creating hard and soft areas. The sculptural forms emerge through interaction with the contrasts between textile's fluidity and metal's rigidity. Hannah describes this process as 'engineering with thread'. Materials: Trivera thread, conductive thread, jacquard woven double cloth fabric. Processes: Hand-pleated, heat-set fabric, selectively electroformed, sculpted and stitched. (Photo: Beytan Erkmen)

Vertical Pleats

Vertical pleats usually need a minimum of six shafts (using two three-end threading blocks), although eight shafts is usually preferred with two four-end threading blocks.

One of the principal methods to create vertical pleats is to sett the warp much closer than you might expect. Density is directly related to the yarn twist and fibre content that is being used, as well as the end use required, so experimentation is always recommended. To facilitate the lengthwise collapse into pleats, try beginning with a sett around 70–75 per cent of maximum warp density if using softer yarns. The stiffer the warp yarn, the more open the sett, moving towards a regular balanced sett.

Eight-shaft Twills

Looking at four-shaft twill weaves, a threading block of 1/3 twill versus another of 3/1 twill or broken twills require a total of eight shafts. The threading blocks need to be wide enough to create a distinct area of each particular weave structure. If there are not enough ends per threading block, there will be insufficient action of the two stripes against each other. If there are too many ends, the pleats may flatten out. The finer or softer the warp threads, the more ends will be required per threading block. Sampling is recommended exploring different setts and widths of threading blocks for the specific yarns being used to get the desired result. Pleating will occur only when each block is of a significant length.

Consistency and a clean break between the two weave structures are key to getting effective pleats. As with the horizontal pleat, the structure itself forces the creation of the pleat as the two twill blocks change position. Spacing the pleats is also possible by adding plain weave bands at either side of the twill areas.

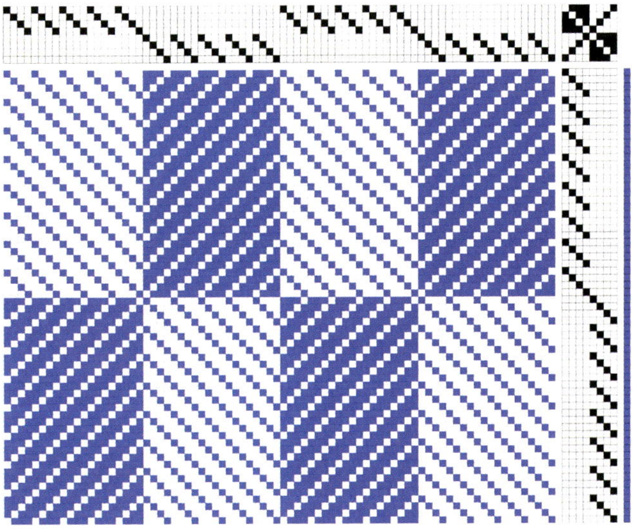

Vertical pleats can be formed on eight shafts. This draft has been divided into two threading blocks: Shafts 1–4 for one block and shafts 5–8 for the second block. Each block can then weave a 1/3 or 3/1 twill independently of the other to allow for the contrasting surfaces vertically. Please note that the draft is contracted for illustration purposes and shows only small amounts of treadling for each block. In order to create the pleat effect, significantly longer treadling blocks are required before switching treadling blocks, or the pleating effect will be greatly reduced.

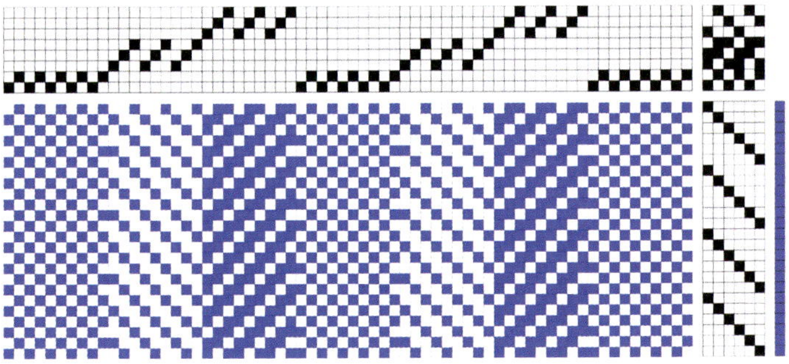

A variation with plain weave and 1/2 and 2/1 twills can be used to space the pleats.

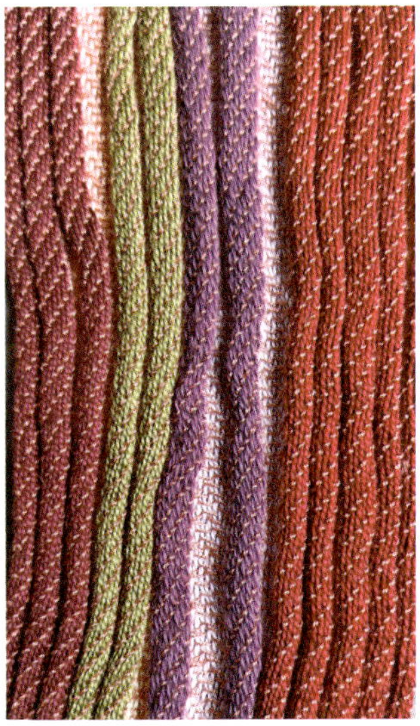

One side of this sample by Jennifer Verrall shows various colours used in the warp stripes. These can give dramatic peep-through effects. One set of stripes uses lighter colours, the other darker tones.

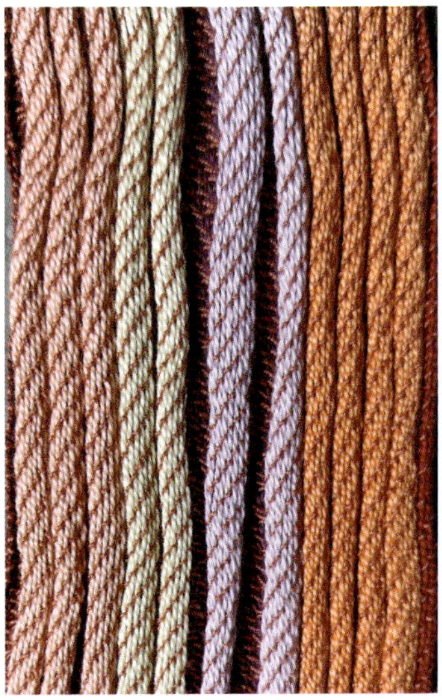

The other side of the sample gives the opposite effect. A fine weft complements the warp colours used.

TOP TIP

Using a finer weft yarn with shrinkage potential, for instance a wool (not superwash), crepe, elastane or singles yarn (with twist only in one direction), normally assists with the pleating effect.

Plain Weave

Plain weave can be used to emphasise and visually deepen the changeover between pleats by creating an interruption between the warp and weft float blocks. If four-end twills are used for the blocks, then two more shafts are required for the plain weave, but using a three-end construction, such as three-end warp- and weft-faced twills, would permit two shafts for plain weave.

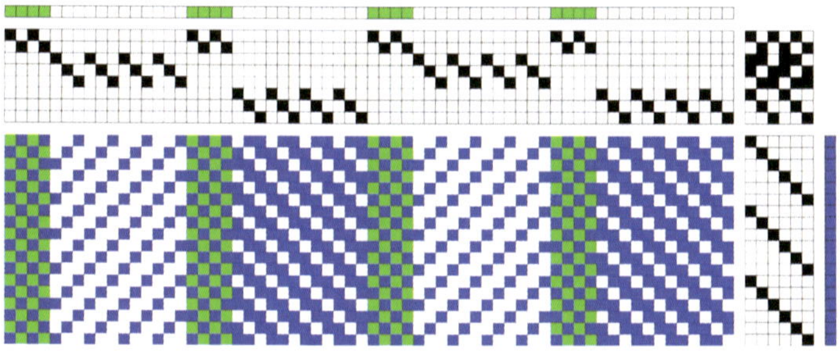

Plain weave can create the boundary between two areas of the twills, as shown in the green warp bands in this draft. This threading has the plain weave on shafts 7 & 8, but it could just as easily be placed on shafts 1 & 2, shifting the twills up to 3–5 and 6–8.

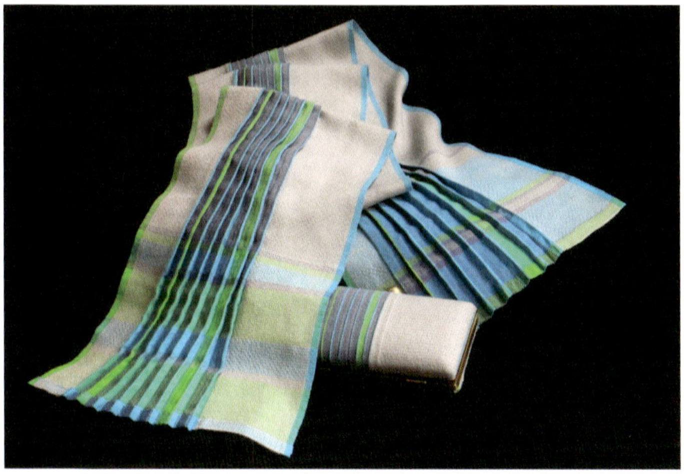

The two mini point twills act as hinges between the areas of plain weave. The 1/2 twill creates a valley, the 2/1 creates a mountain. Wendy Morris's scarf and clutch purse show this lighter weight alternative to full pleats with less fold factor. (Photo: Wendy Morris)

Small Point Threading

Additionally, a small point threading between areas of plain weave can give a pleat – the plain weave on two shafts providing the walls of the pleat, and the remaining six shafts providing two three-shaft points.

Small point threadings can be used to shape the fabric in various ways, including spiralling forms and for shaping. This area gives such varied results and rewards further exploration.

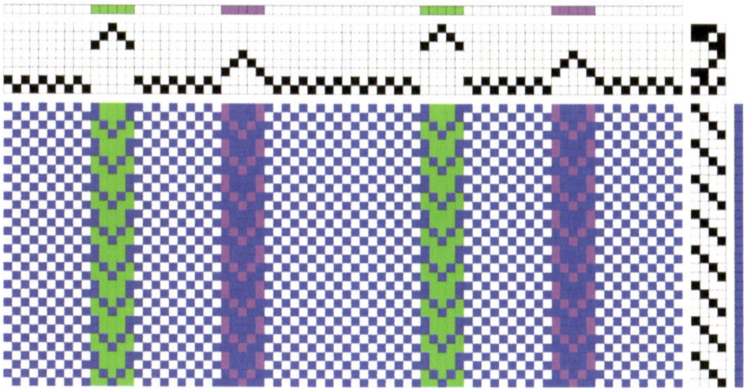

This version of a knife pleat can be formed by using separate point effects that can be threaded on dedicated shafts, while weaving the pleat walls in plain weave. Wendy Morris developed this draft to create a pleated scarf without the full bulk of an accordion pleat. The point causes a float on the inside of the pleat, effectively creating a hinge. The hinge can be highlighted further by using a contrasting accent colour along the length of the pleat crest. This is yet another variation incorporating ideas across these different but closely related methods.

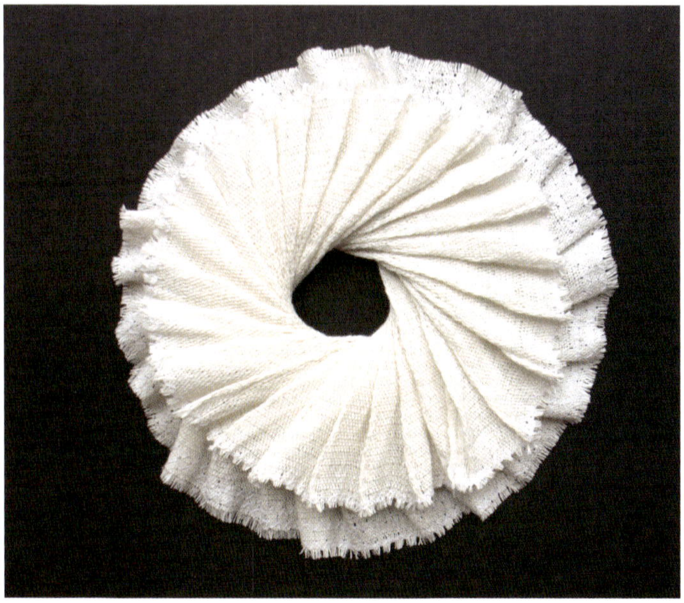

The same principle of small points in the threading combined with plain weave gave Suzanne Townshend the idea to weave a fabric that spirals. A fine linen and a manila hemp used together in the warp gives a crisp hand to this sample, accompanied by wefts of fine and high-twist wool to create the pleating. (Photo: Suzanne Townshend)

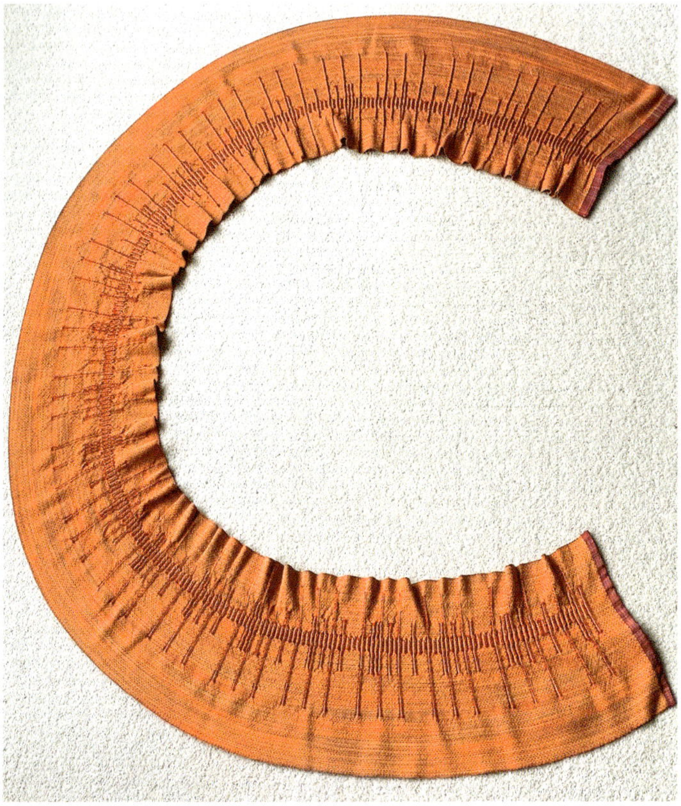

The pleated underside of mushroom caps is the inspiration behind this development for a shaped scarf by Wendy Morris. The warp is silk, the weft a mercerised cotton. Small point designs in the treadling with bands of warp- or weft-dominance gives the fabric an amazing amount of elasticity. Highlighted with an accent yarn at the crests of the pleats. (Photo: Wendy Morris)

Design

Different widths of blocks can be explored. Effective results can arise from irregularity in the widths of the pleats. With more shafts available (eight or more), organic development of these kinds of pleats can be explored.

Greater visual effects can be achieved through combining the threading blocks with different colours for the two different areas. A repeating lighter block for the warp-emphasis stripe (3/1) alternating with a darker block in the weft-emphasis weave (1/3) gives a sense of highlights and shadows and therefore more dimensionality visually. The warp-emphasis stripe will sit proud, and the weft-emphasis stripe will move underneath, creating shadow effects. It is possible to press the pleat edges to firm up the edge from a soft pleat to a crisp one. This is an area ripe for exploration.

If plain weave is used to interrupt and deepen the effect of the pleats, then a highlight colour can be placed there. Two different colours at the peak and trough gives a dramatic appearance.

Twills

Explore different thicknesses of warp versus weft to see which combinations of materials, tightness of yarn twist and sett work best for the desired result. Using broken twills in a warp versus weft variation will give additional textural effects. Other four-end warp versus weft weave structures can also be used to contrast with each other, such as four-end Han damask.

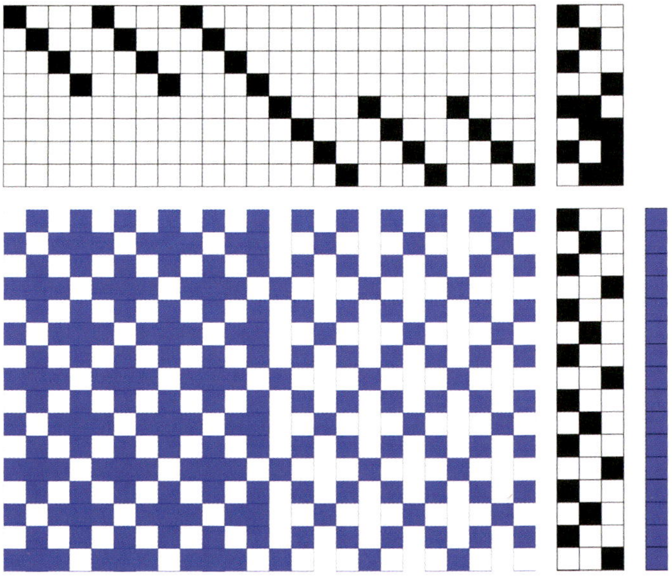

Han damask gives small textural effects to the surface of the cloth, as does a broken twill. A vertical pleat can be created with this structure in the same way as for twills.

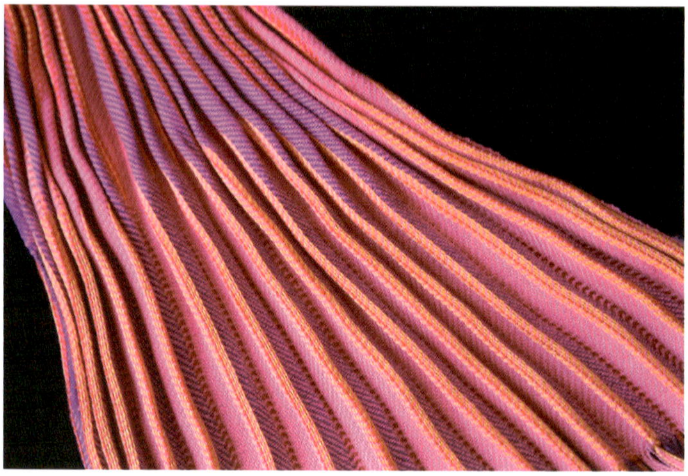

Eye-catching and dramatic colour highlights the pleats in this straight and point twill scarf. (Photo: Wendy Morris)

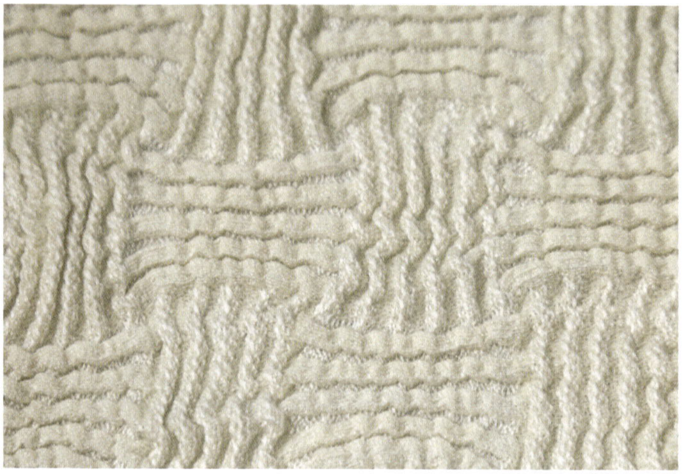

With equal prominence in warp and weft effects, Wendy Morris' dramatically furrowed cloth uses twill blocks in its construction. (Photo: Wendy Morris)

For those weavers who do not like to sett their warps closely, a fairly thick warp yarn threaded in the same way but sett a little more loosely than a normal twill for the yarn selected can create effective pleats when woven with an overtwisted weft. The slightly more open sett will allow for the overtwisted weft, which is usually quite fine, to be able to wrestle the warp into submission. As usual, sampling is required to determine the most effective sett for the amount of overtwist in the weft yarn.

Satin-based Weaves

Satin-based weaves follow the same principle as for twills, requiring more shafts – a minimum of ten when juxtaposing two five-end satins, or 16 shafts for two eight-end satins. The break-off point between the warp and weft effects needs to be considered carefully to create the cleanest break. Often a satin-based pleat will be softer as the fabric contains more natural drape because of the longer floats. The use of a tighter twist, linen yarns or other yarns with stiffness helps to give more body to the fabric.

Finishing

Normally, these kinds of pleats need a little encouragement by pulling firmly along the direction of the pleat and air-drying. In other words, pull across the width of the fabric for horizontal pleats and down the length of the fabric for vertical pleats.

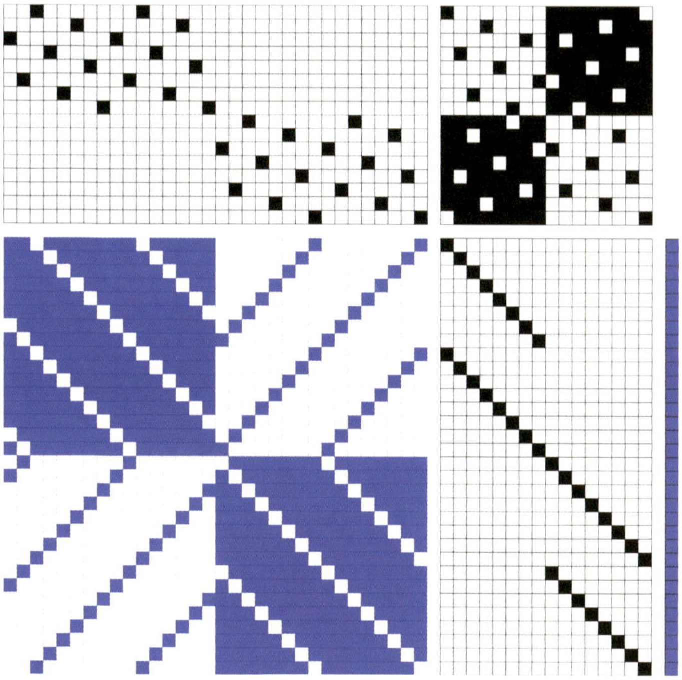

If using eight-shaft satins for a vertical pleat, 16 shafts are required. The warp and weft emphasis can be changed from one group of shafts to the other to give differing effects, depending on the frequency of the change.

Warp and Weft Effects

Both warp and weft effects can be used in the same cloth for great results, depending on materials used, sett and finishing treatments.

CORD PLEATS

These fabrics use plain weave combined with floats. As usual for pleats and cords, too few ends or picks (depending on whether the cords are vertical or horizontal) per block will not give a satisfactory result. Conversely, too many ends or picks in a cord have a tendency to flatten out and lose their impact.

Materials used for the active element will also have a big impact on the resultant cord – woollen wefts tend to give a softer effect after wet-finishing while overtwisted yarns give a crisper result, more like the sharp folds in origami.

Horizontal

Four Shafts

Plain weave requires only two shafts per cord so alternating cords on four shafts can be used. This uses two

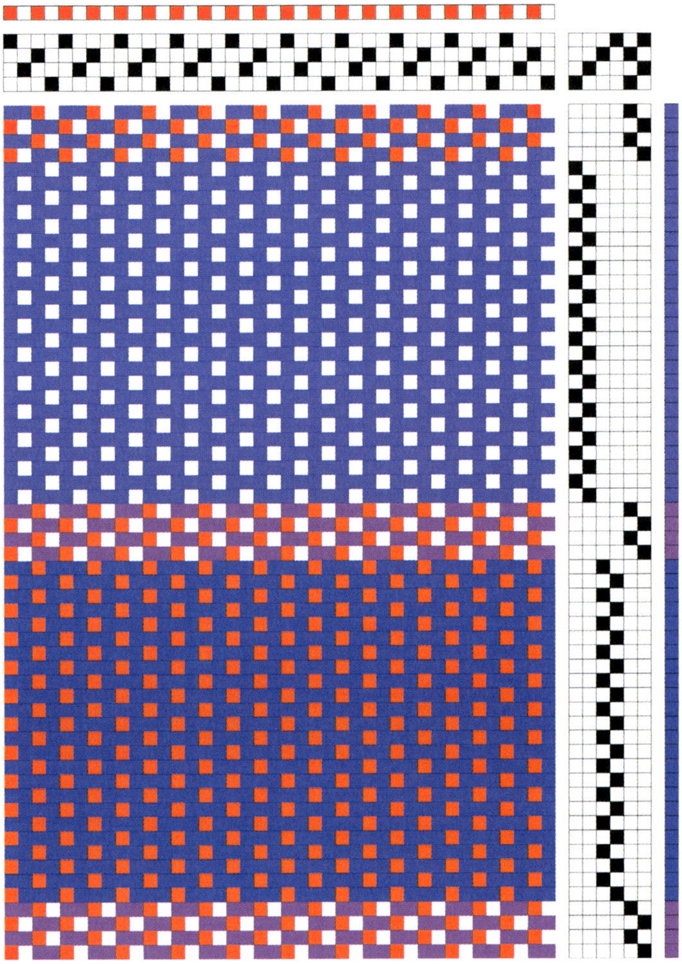

The draft illustrates four-shaft horizontal cord weaving on the top with the second warp floating underneath the woven cord. The two layers alternate.

warps. Separate warp beams are advised for this due to uneven take-up during weaving as one cord weaves and the other does not. Some regard this as a double cloth

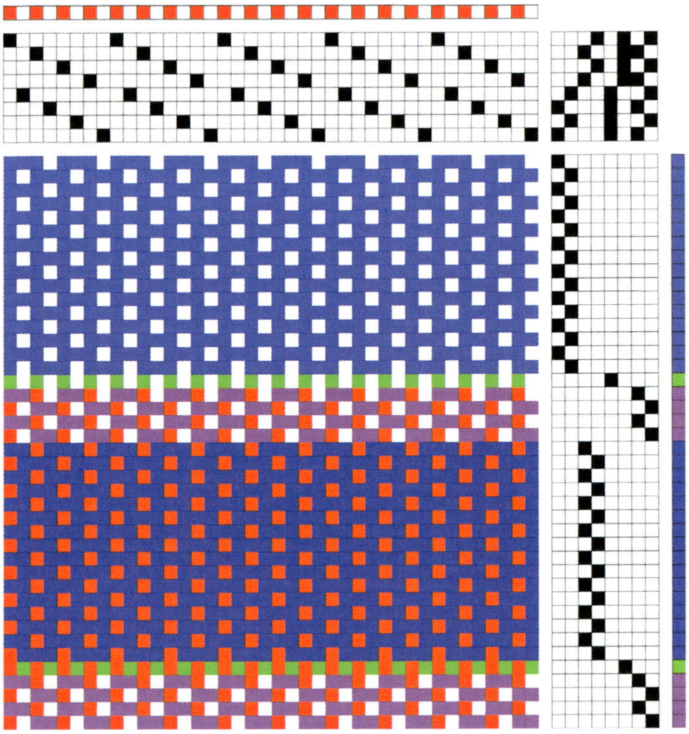

Wadding can be inserted to plump up the cord effect on this eight-shaft draft. The draft shows the positioning of the wadding with a green weft showing the face cloth only. The thickness of the wadding and the impact it has on the cord produced cannot be shown on a graphic draft. The wadding is placed in the weft just before the two layers are combined (with the purple weft) so that it remains fixed between the front and back layers of the section just woven.

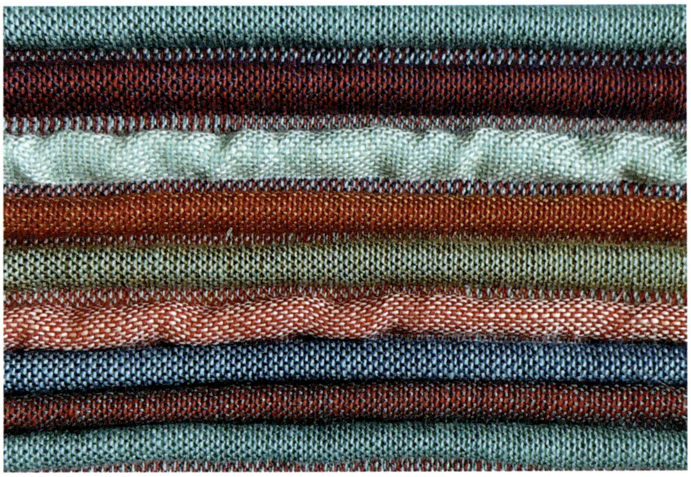

Cotton warps in green and red are used for these horizontal cord pleats on four shafts, leaving the other layer unwoven. Wadding is inserted into each cord with two picks of thick rug wool in the same shed before changing the shed to weave a few picks of plain weave.

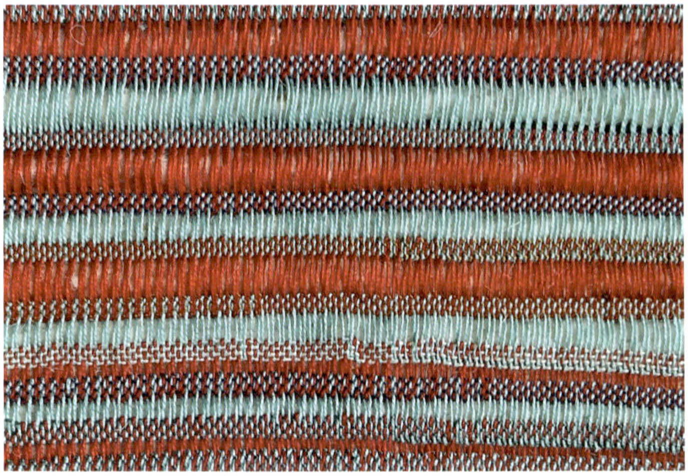

The underside shows the unwoven warp floats where the cord is being woven on the surface with the wadding weft between the floats and the woven top layer. This is also known as a loose-backed piqué cord.

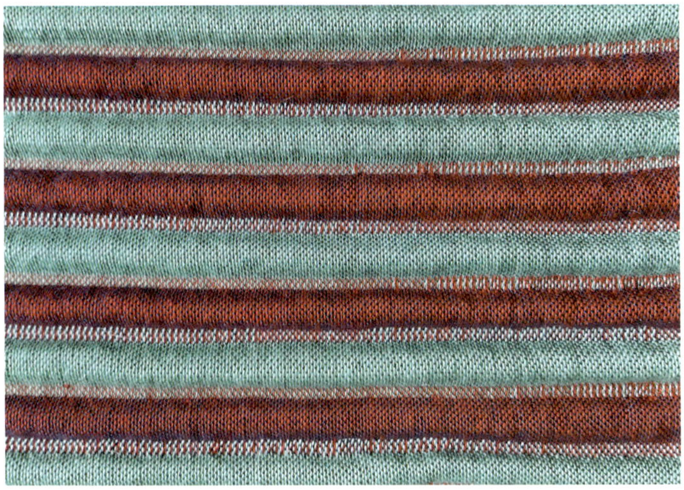

This sample shows the same thing, but this time with a woven underlayer – also called a fast-backed piqué cord.

derivative, with the threading block that is not being used for the cord weaving as a second layer, or it can be left simply floating in which case it can be thought of as a supplementary warp.

The four shafts are used as two individual cords with two colours for optional colourways on a double cloth threading. Each cord is woven on its own two shafts for twice as long as the proposed height of the cord, plus a few more picks to allow for curvature. Weaving a minimum of two picks of plain weave across all shafts at the changeover between the two cords ensures clean transitions between the cords.

Using wool for both warps will give maximum dimension on wet-finishing, although passive warps can also be used. If an active yarn such as wool is used only for the supplementary warp, shrinkage during wet-finishing will aid in the contraction of the yarn, adding to the dimensional effect of the top cloth.

A wadding weft can be inserted between the woven layer and the floating warps to emphasise the contours, either for each cord or randomly for variations in the fabric. The thickness of the wadding weft, combined with the height of the woven cord, will affect the prominence of the cord, so exploring variations of these will give differing effects and could lead to some interesting designs.

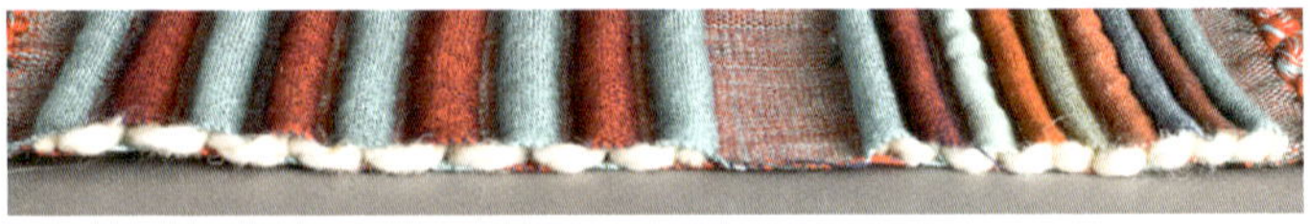

The edge of the fabric shows the two white rug wool wadding wefts as they move from cord to cord. (Photo: Colin Usher)

Vertical

Four Shafts

Traditional warp Bedford cord creates vertical plain weave cords on a four-shaft single cloth by using two wefts: one that will weave across the whole warp and a fine shrinking yarn that will weave only in the areas not required for pleating and will float underneath the area that is to form the pleat. This can give one vertical cord block at a time or switch cords on demand. A shrinking yarn can also be used for both wefts, which will give pleats in both threading areas. The sett is a very firm plain weave.

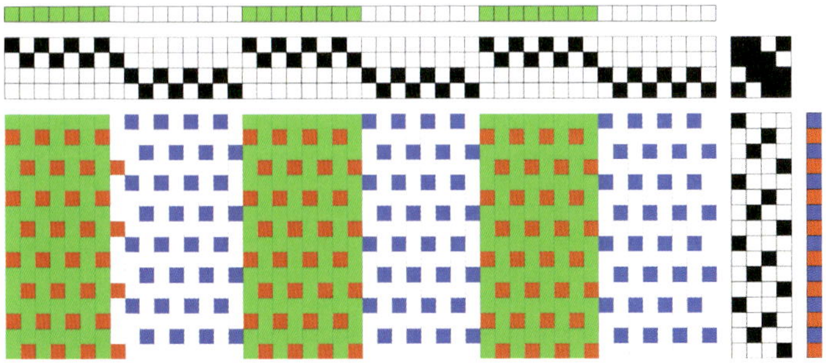

Traditional Bedford cord is a vertical cord using two wefts alternating over two threading blocks, requiring two shafts each to allow for two different cords. The red active weft weaves with the green warp and the blue weft, which could be either passive or active, weaves with the white warp, leaving floats across the block that is not woven for each of the wefts.

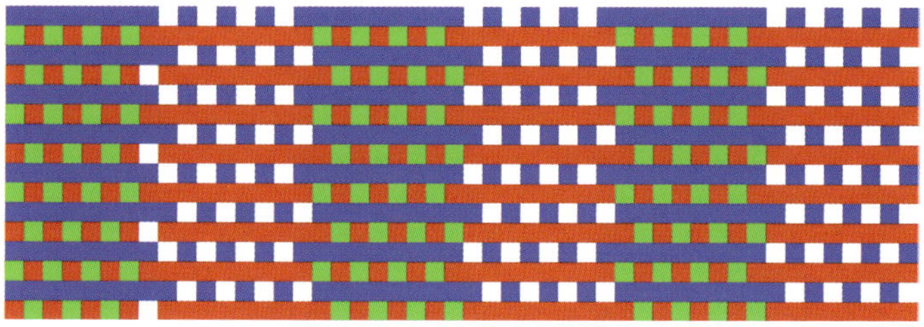

The reverse side, showing the floats used to create the undulation in the cords.

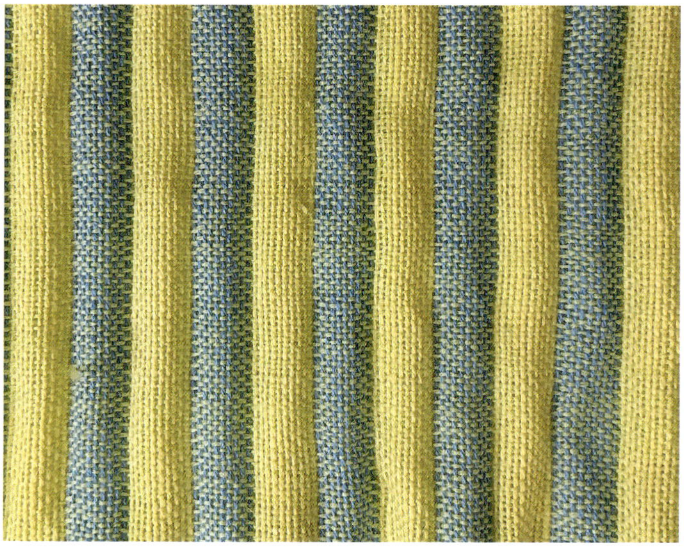

Traditional Bedford cord on four shafts with two warp colours, shown just as it came off the loom. The cotton warp was woven with a wool weft.

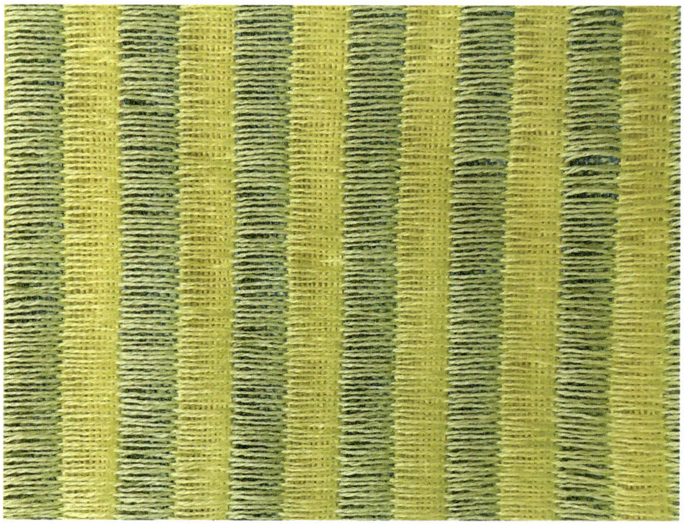

The underside shows the single weft used to weave both the cords alternately floating across the cord not being woven on that pick. This was also just as the sample came off the loom.

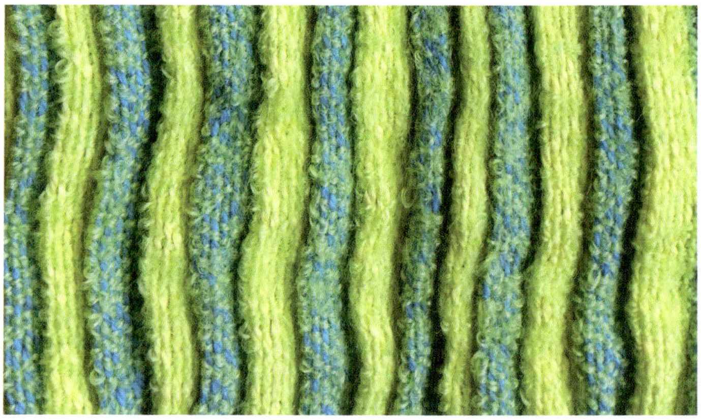

The sample wet-finished.

With four shafts, there are options – weaving a cord on one two-shaft block can be combined with weaving half hopsack for the other block to give gentle undulations. Either a shrinking wool or an overspun yarn can be used for the second weft.

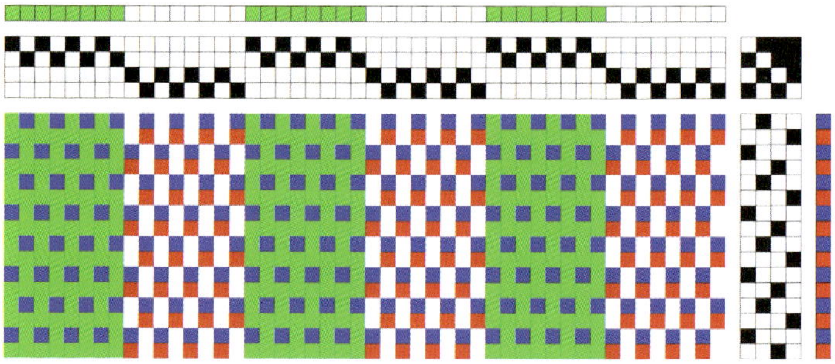

A variation using half-hopsack for one of the blocks gives gentle undulations. Both red and blue wefts use the same lifts as each other before changing to the opposite shafts. If one of the wefts is an active weft, the undulations can be formed.

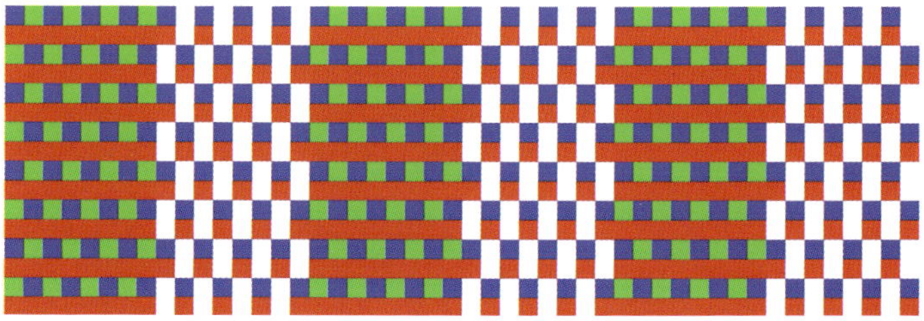

The reverse side.

If a more defined separation between cords is required, stitching ends can be created by switching over the last and first ends of adjacent threading blocks on four shafts when using shrinking weft yarns. The two ends at the beginning and end of each block are switched over so that the

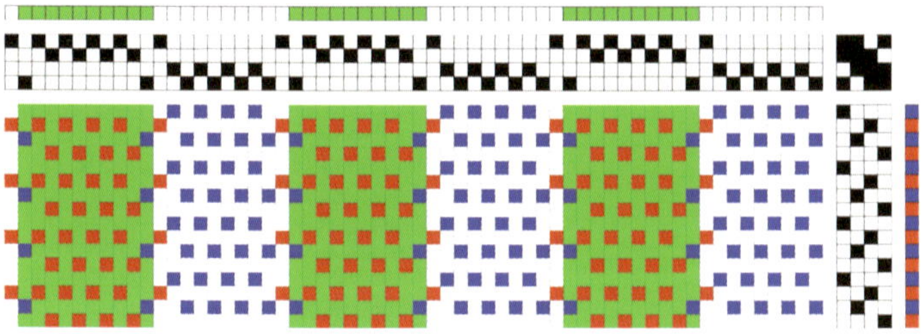

Stitching ends are introduced at each end of each threading block. Note that the last end of the first white block is threaded on shaft 4, and the first end of the first green block is threaded on shaft 1. This gives distinct separation between the cords.

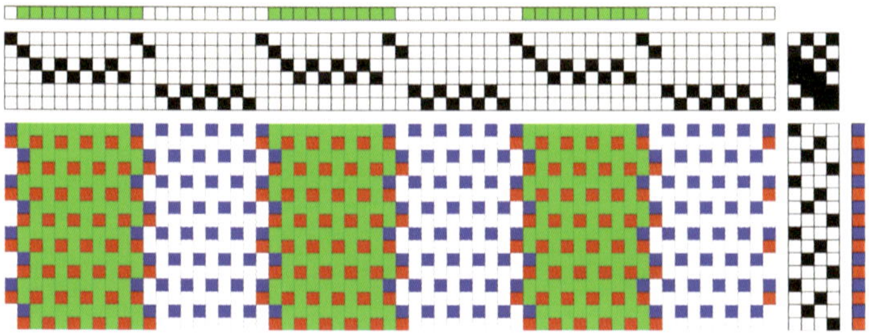

The same effect can be produced on six shafts, using two dedicated shafts for the stitching ends. Here, shafts 5 & 6 create the stitching element, while the cord blocks are on shafts 1 & 2 and 3 & 4.

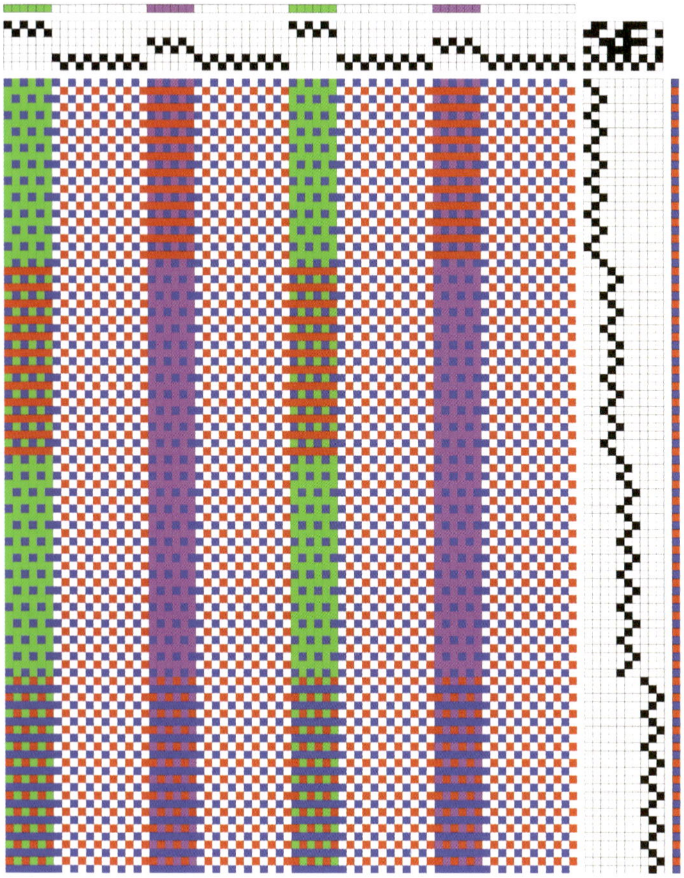

Mountain and valley folds alternate with plain weave between each cord band on a six-shaft draft. The tie-up allows for both sets of cords to operate together in the same direction, in the opposite direction, and to be independent from each other in both directions.

respective wefts are trapped, ensuring that each cord will form, but without any gaps in the fabric.

However, it is more usual to dedicate this job to two extra shafts to create the stitching ends separating the two cords, especially if you are using slippery yarns for your cords as it gives a distinctive separation between them.

Six and More Shafts

So far, all the cords have been one-sided. Ann Richards, in her book *Weaving Textiles That Shape Themselves*, talks about adapting Bedford cord floats to incorporate plain weave areas in between alternating ridges, where the cord floats are on one face with the next cord highlighting the floats on the other face. She also discusses how using overlapping reversals either of the mountain or the valley cords can give a wide variation of pleated shapes, especially when exploring variations in the amount of overlap.

These are possible on six shafts. If the cords are kept relatively narrow, this encourages sharp pleats to form on both sides of the fabric, which gives the origami effect. Ann recommends a fairly stiff yarn for the plain weave weft, and a high twist for the floating picks, although a fine fulling wool weft or other shrinking yarns would also do the job well.

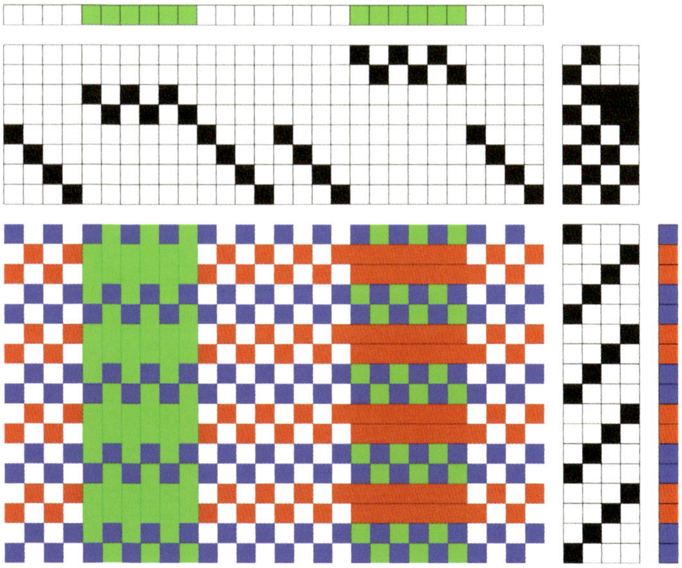

With eight shafts, the plain weave can be spread over four shafts and the two cords giving mountain and valley folds can be on their own two shafts each. This is the method that Ann Richards uses.

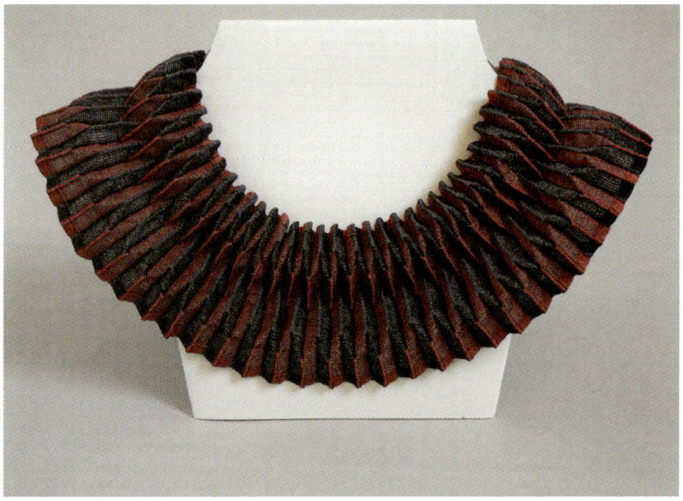

To achieve the extra stiffness that is required for this neckpiece, half-hopsack is woven for the pleat sides. Combined with the material properties of spun silk and silk/steel in the warp, together with paper and crepe silk yarns in the weft, the floats behind the cords create the intricacies of this work. (Photo: Ann Richards)

During wet-finishing, the overtwisted weft(s) will force the cord pleats into position. Further explanations for her self-folding woven origami pieces are given in her book *Weaving Textiles that Shape Themselves* (*see* Bibliography).

Design

It is most usual to see regular widths of cord, but variation in width can be very effective. Again, colour can be introduced to create dramatic emphasis, whether in horizontal or vertical cords.

With more shafts, occasional cords could give way to an area of tighter pleats, or an organic design could be outlined by more structured texture. So much can be played with here and different combinations adopted. Slight variations in materials or structures can give very different results.

Finishing

Wet-finishing can be used to highlight contrasts in yarn shrinkage. Depending on the yarns used, finishing will vary slightly, although the technique is basically the same. Immersing the fabric into hot water, with a little dishwashing detergent to remove any grease or dirt, is sufficient on its own for overtwist cords. Woollen-spun weft floats will require agitation in hot sudsy water to aid in shrinking the floats (*see* Chapter 1).

DOUBLE CLOTH PLEATS

Even though there is a dedicated double cloth chapter (*see* Chapter 9), double cloth pleats belong here.

While this chapter is concerned more with structural pleats, if one of the layers is not to be pleated, and the non-pleating layer consists of an active yarn, pleats on the passive layer will be held and enhanced after wet-finishing as the active yarn shrinks and pulls the pleat tighter.

Horizontal Pleats

These require two warp beams for best effects, although a separate warp can be suspended from the back of the loom with weights. Alternatively use the warp beam of a separate loom as the second warp beam (*see* Appendix I). It is not necessary to use active yarns in these pleats. Two warps of non-shrinking yarns are very effective, although if pleating is kept to one warp only, an active non-pleating warp can help with keeping the pleats in place.

Plain weave double cloth pleats can be made on four- or eight-shaft looms, while twill pleats require six shafts as a minimum, and other weaves such as crepes might require more than eight shafts.

Upright Pleats

Upright pleats are created through weaving two or more picks of combined single cloth before weaving one layer for a certain length, then releasing the tension on that beam, using the beater to bring the fell of that fabric up to the fell of the base layer, weaving the two layers together in a combined single cloth plain weave to hold the pleat in place, then re-tensioning the pleated layer. This is the same as unstuffed horizontal Bedford cords but with two warps as opposed to one.

Highlights in colour can be woven midway through the chosen pleat to create a visual highlight when the pleat is pulled up. Extra stiffness and foldability at the crest of the

TOP TIP

Care and attention when joining the two layers together again is vital if the fabric is to look seamless. If it is proving difficult to get the pleat layer tight against the base layer, tighten the base warp so that it provides a smoother path for the pleat warp.

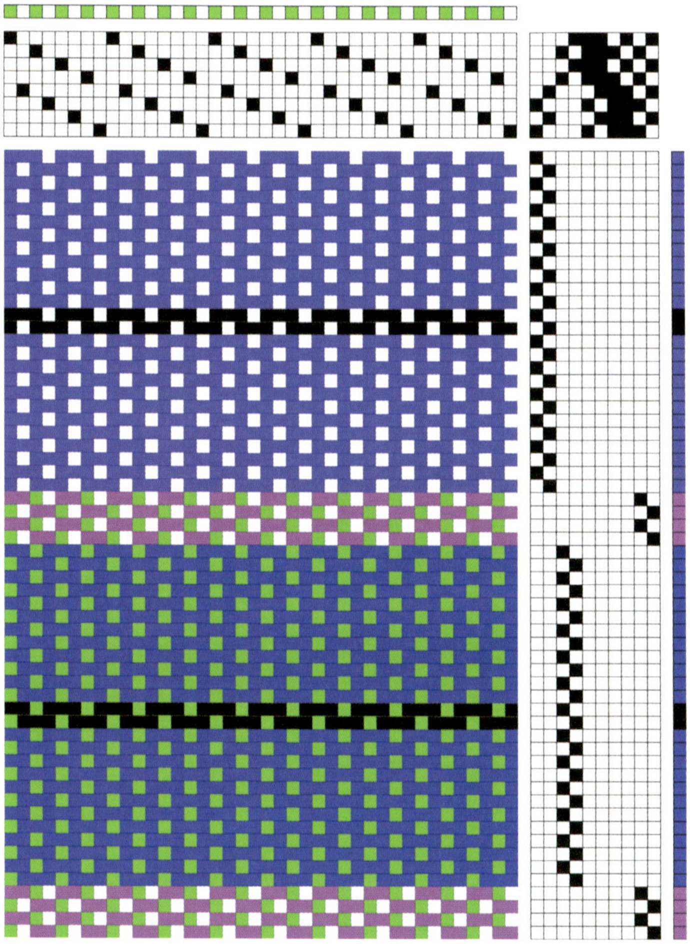

A divided parallel threading on eight shafts is useful for double cloth upright pleats. There is no active warp here and the threading is in white and green for the two layers. The tie-up here allows for either layer to weave plain weave, and for a combined plain weave giving a single layer to act as a stitching boundary. The treadling in this draft begins with one layer weaving plain on the top layer, leaving the other layer to be warp floats underneath. The black weft showing for two picks is the middle point of each pleat. The purple weft is where the two layers are joined together in a single cloth before the other layer comes to the surface and weaves its pleat, while the previous pleat warp floats underneath.

pleat can be created by weaving a few picks on either side of the crest in a stiffer yarn, such as linen or metal blend; for instance, stainless steel blended with other fibres.

An upright pleat that is not tightly against the base cloth turns into more of a cord, with a softer crest.

If softer, less upright, cord-type forms are desired, one or more wadding wefts (depending on the roundness and height of the cord) can be added.

Pleats are usually made to show on one side only, using solely one layer or switching layers.

If using one layer only for pleating, that warp needs to be at least three or more times as long as the non-pleating layer.

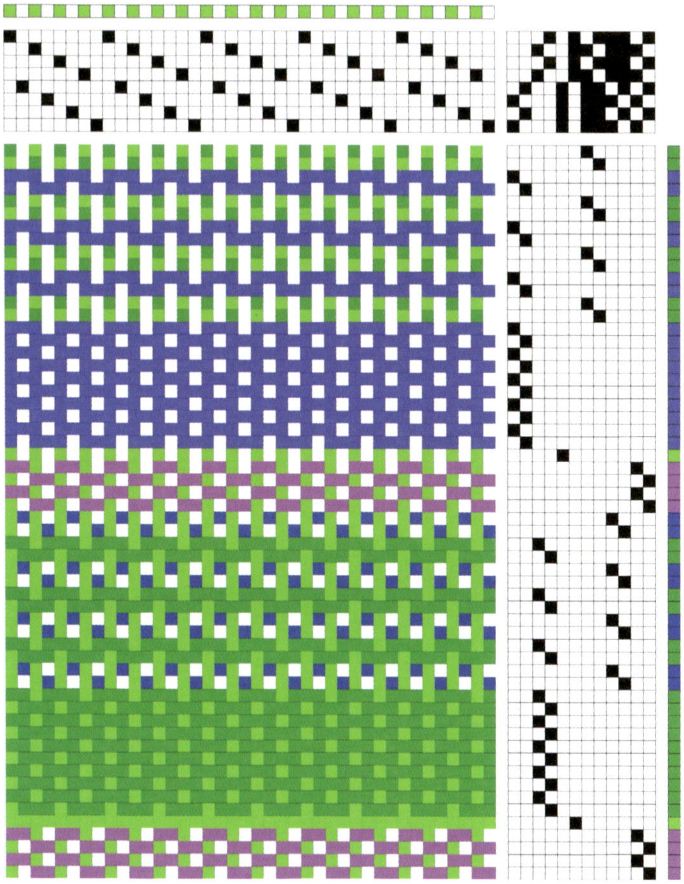

This draft shows one way to create fast-backed (woven underlayer) cords. The areas where there are two picks of blue alternating with two picks of darker green show the weaving on both layers. The areas where just the plain weave shows on one layer (the white warp with mid-blue weft and the light green warp with dark green weft) have floats on the underneath layer. The bright green pick is the wadding weft, which can be a much thicker yarn or multiple yarns in the same shed to allow for the stuffing. The purple weft is the plain weave combining both layers together.

WEAVING THE PLEATS IN PLACE

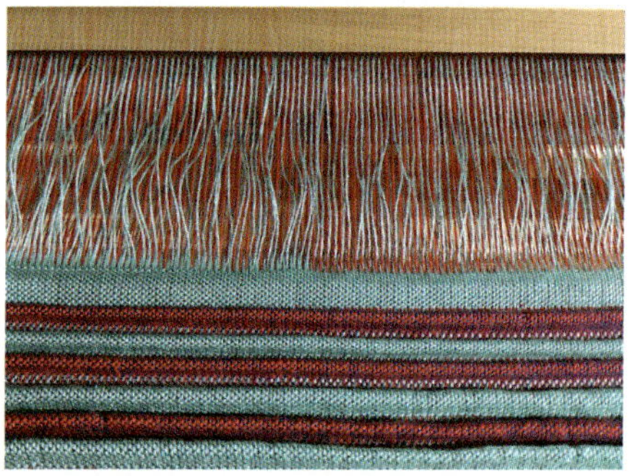

After weaving the fabric intended for the pleat, release the tension off the pleat warp beam enough to allow it free movement forwards but not so much that the warp cannot form a weavable shed. Tighten the warp that is not moving to enable a smoother surface for the pleat to fold against.

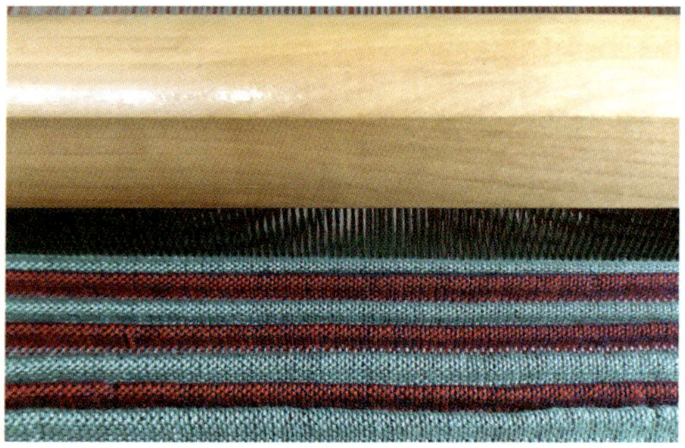

Squeeze the pleat into place and, keeping the beater against the fell of the cloth, open the next shed, weave the pick, close the shed then beat firmly on the closed shed. Hold the beater against the fell of the cloth when changing shed for the next few picks. Beat hard. Also tighten the tension gradually on the pleat layer to ensure evenness in the fabric.

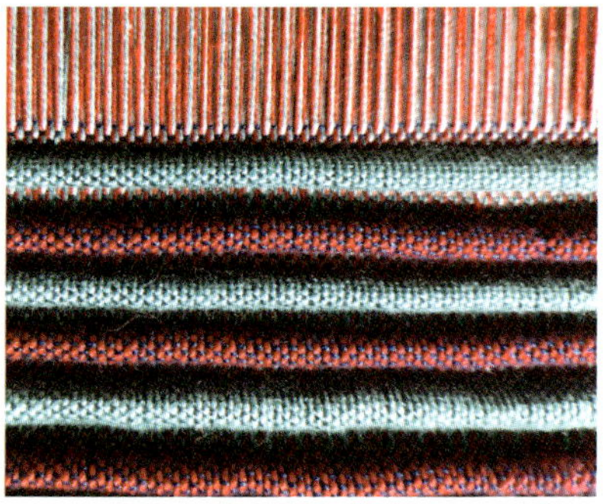

Ensure that several picks are woven to hold the pleat in place. By now your warps should both be at the same tension and ready for you to continue onto the next pleat. Ensure that the new pleat begins with a clean shed.

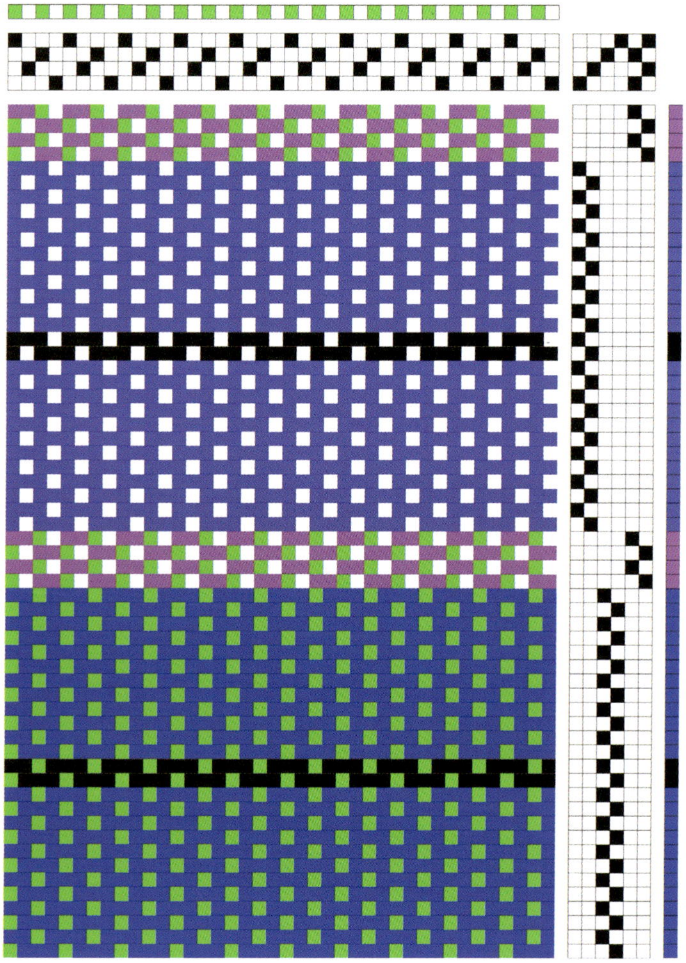

The two warps are pleating on just the face of the cloth, switching positions after the combined plain weave. The underneath warp is floating.

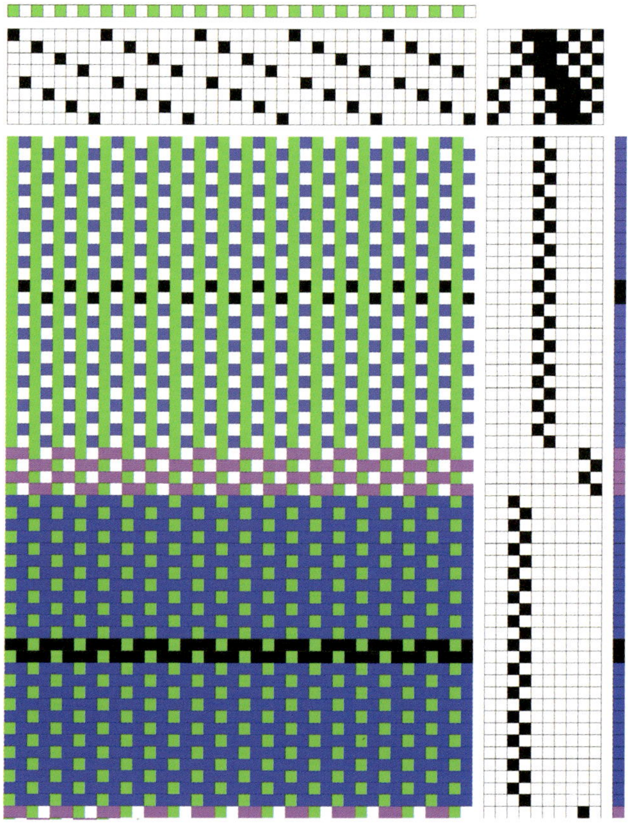

The two warps here are pleating on opposite sides of the cloth. The tie-up shows how either layer can weave alternately and on either side. The green warp is floating above the white warp, which is weaving plain weave on the underside of the fabric. The white layer will be pulled up to create an underneath pleat before the combined plain weave (purple weft) is woven. Then the dark blue weft will weave the next pleat on the top of the fabric before it too is pulled up into the pleat before weaving the next combined plain weave.

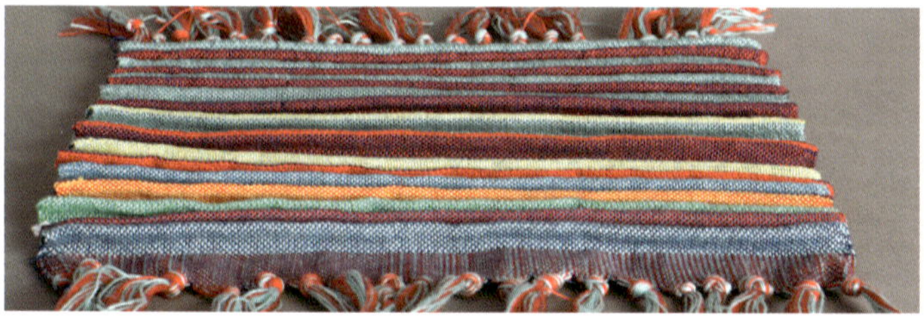

Upright pleats seen from one direction. The multiple colours are visible.

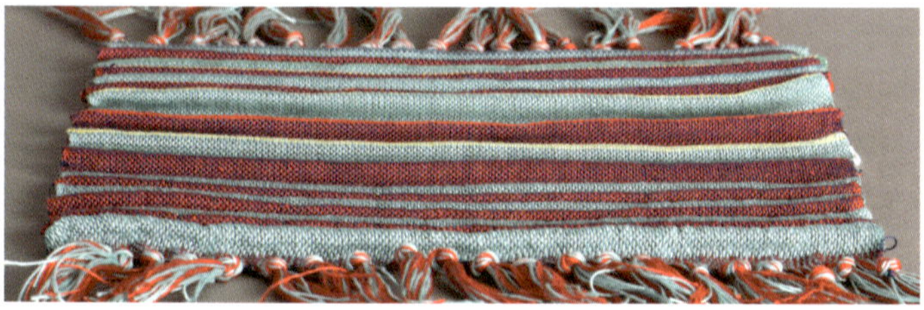

The same pleats seen from the opposite direction. The colours have changed.

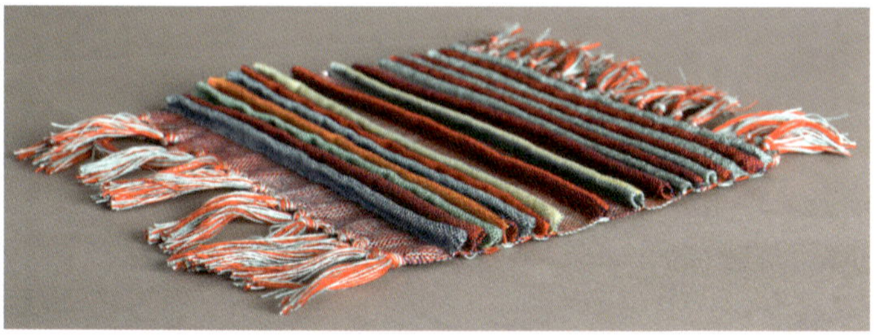

The angled view shows how upright the pleats are and how closely they are pulled and held in place by the combined plain weave. (Photos: Colin Usher)

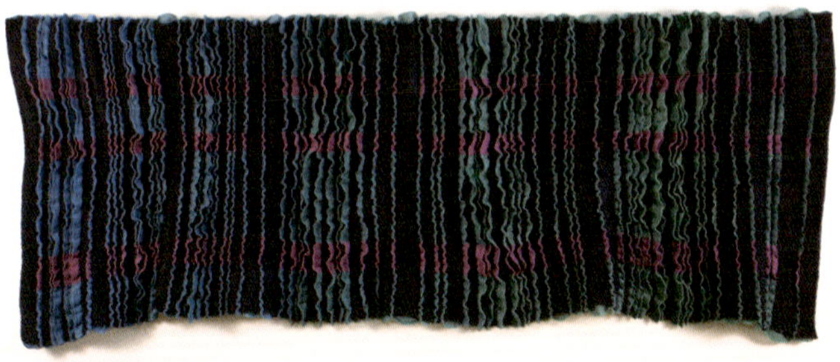

Sara Nordling's wall piece *Transposition* was woven in wool and cotton using crepe weaves for structure. All her yarns were hand-dyed. The piece is 27 × 67 × 1½in (69 × 170 × 4cm). (Photo: Sara Nordling)

A more sculptural piece could utilise double cloth's ability to create the pleating on both sides of the fabric.

Occasional upright pleats are also possible by weaving the two layers as a single cloth for longer between pleats. This can be effective if the two layers are interchanged for the pleats, and different visual rhythms can be created through the selection of which layer is to make the pleat. With different coloured warps for the two layers and/or wefts for each pleat or for each side of a pleat, many visual patterns are possible, and directional pressing can also add highlights and interest to the resultant cloth.

TOP TIP

A tip from experienced pleat weaver Sara Nordling is to tack down the outside edges of the pleat to the base warp with T-pins once woven. This helps to keep the tension on the warps more even. The T-pins can be removed after several inches of additional weaving.

Accordion Pleats

Accordion pleats are approached differently and require equal distances on both sides of the pleat – an equilateral pleat, but with a woven base underneath to provide the third side.

It is important to begin with two or more plain weave picks in a combined single cloth so that there is a firm start to the accordion pleat. Then weave the two layers as a regular double cloth (separate layers) until the desired distance for the first half of the accordion pleat is reached.

For a right-angled accordion pleat, i.e. a mountain Λ, repeat the number of picks on the pleating layer without weaving any more on the base layer.

Release the tension on the pleating layer and move the woven fabric up to the fell of the base layer. Secure with a minimum of two picks of plain weave to create a single combined cloth.

The next accordion pleat can be created in the same way immediately or with more single combined cloth woven between pleats, if desired. As before, the pleat crest can be highlighted with a contrast colour or stiffer yarns.

For a steeper-angled accordion pleat, weave the two layers as for regular accordion pleats until the desired distance for the *base* of the pleat is reached. Then continue weaving the pleat layer only, making a note of the number

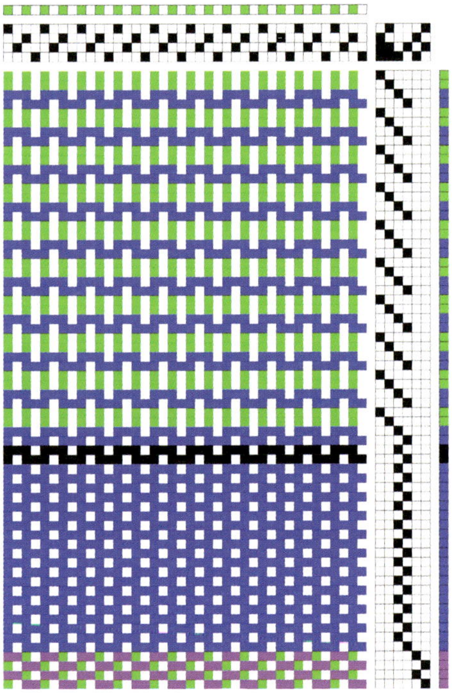

A four-shaft double cloth accordion pleat is created by weaving half the pleat length as two layers of plain weave. At the half-way point, the black weft indicates the fold and then the top layer continues to weave the remainder of the pleat (blue weft). At the end point of the pleat, the top layer is pulled up to meet the lower layer and secured in place by the combined plain weave in purple.

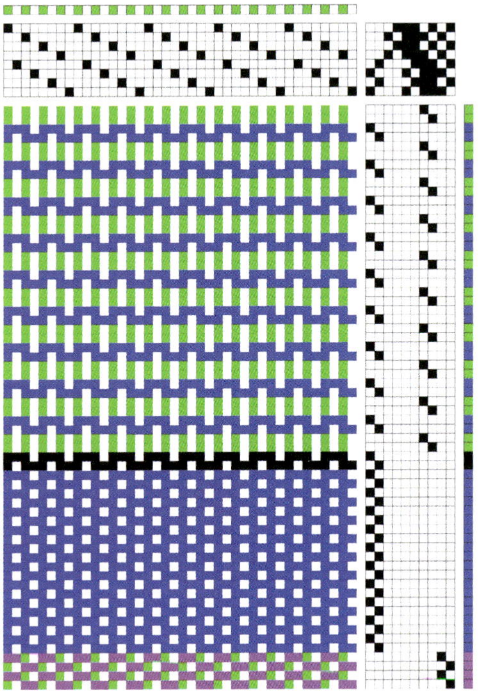

An eight-shaft draft shows the same thing from the top side…

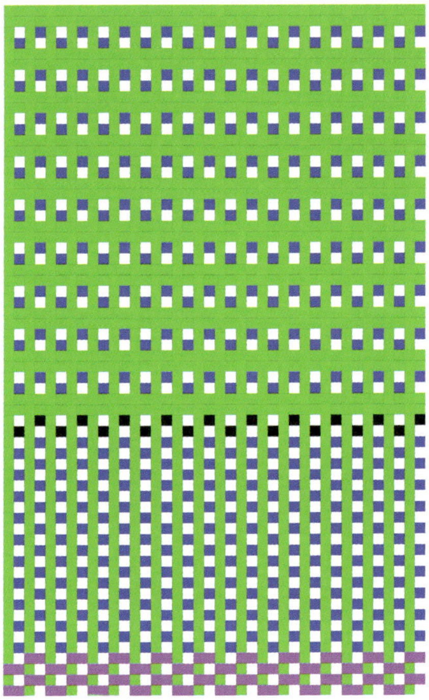

…and looking at the reverse side.

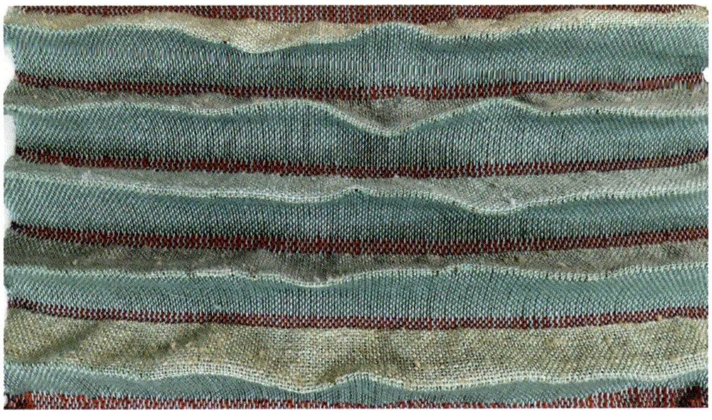

Accordion pleats with their equal sides are separated by a few picks of plain weave to hold the pleats in place. In this sample, two picks of a fine metal weft have been inserted at the fold point. The intractability of metal compared to cotton has given the top of the pleats some extra dimensional angles. Each pleat is woven with two colours: one side in green, the other side in yellow.

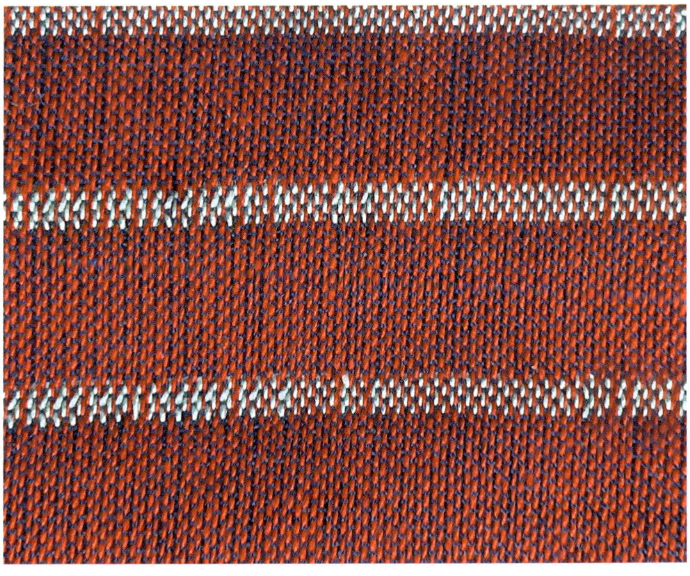

The underneath of the pleat shows the ground cloth. This was woven in conjunction with the first half of the top pleat.

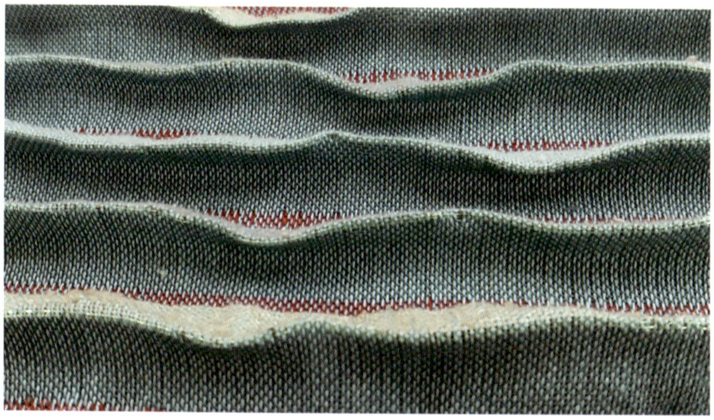

A view of the green side with a hint of the yellow. The undulations created by the metal crests can be clearly seen here.

of picks in the first half of the pleat when complete. When the planned crest is reached, weave the same total number of picks for the other side of the pleat. Then follow the previous instructions to move the pleat layer up to the fell of the base layer, and secure as before. An important design consideration is the material strength of the proposed pleat. The pleat needs to be stiff enough to stand up under its own weight. If the fabric is not robust enough, a tall pleat will collapse over itself. This might be the desired result, or not.

Accordion pleats can be supported by the addition of inclusions, which are discussed in Chapter 14.

Knife Pleats

Knife pleats are similar, but the two layers are woven separately for just one-third of the length of the pleat. The pleat layer then continues for another third. At that point, the highlight colour or stiffening wefts for the crest of the fold are woven, followed by the pleating layer, again only for the remainder of the pleat length (the remaining one-third), perhaps using a darker weft for shading effects.

When the end of the pleat weaving is reached, ensure that the two layers are combined to lock the pleats into the fabric, releasing the tension of the pleat layer, and bringing the woven fabric up to the fell of the base layer, securing with at least four picks of plain weave single combined cloth, incrementally tightening the tension on the pleat warp as for the accordion and upright pleats.

You can hand press or pin the pleats into place while on the loom. As knife pleats are considerably longer on the top layer than the bottom, it can be useful to pin the pleat just woven to the previous fabric as a temporary measure to aid with the weaving of the next pleat, but it will be necessary

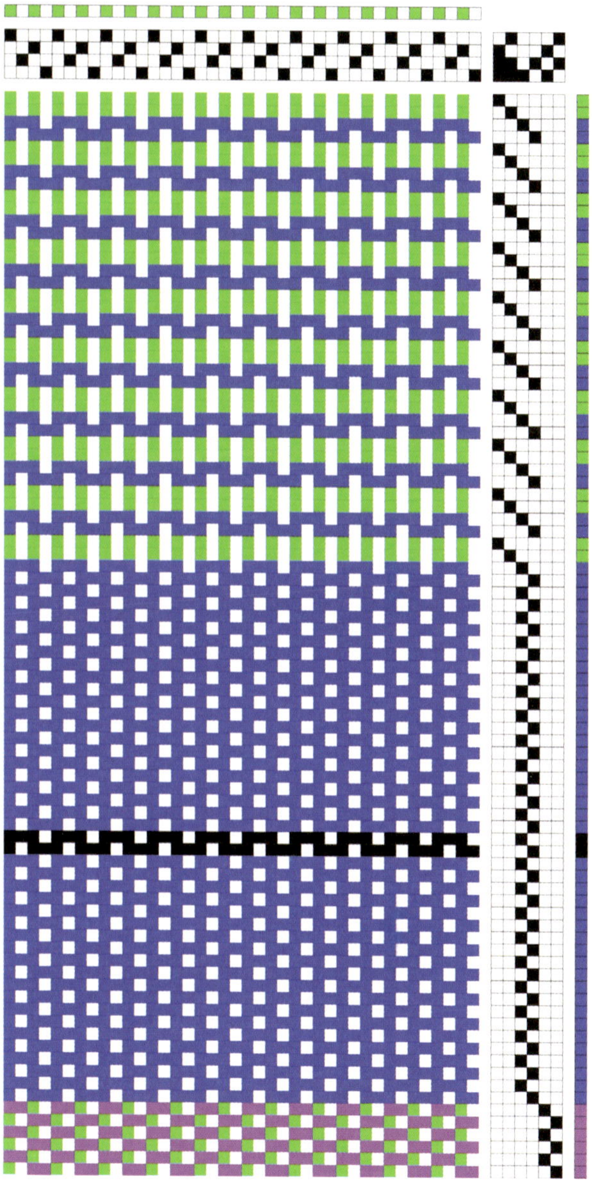

A four-shaft double cloth knife pleat uses the same method as the accordion weave for the first third of the length of the pleat. The second third of the pleat is the top layer alone. The highlight picks in black denote the fold, then the underside of the knife pleat can be woven with a different colour weft, weaving only the top cloth for the remaining third of the total length.

to pin or fold the pleat forward into its correct position prior to the woven fabric going around the front beam and onto the cloth beam.

The fabric can be wet-finished gently and the pleats folded or pressed into place by hand or with an iron.

All the illustrations show both cloths being the same width. However, you may decide to have a narrower width for your pleating layer, if using only one layer for pleating.

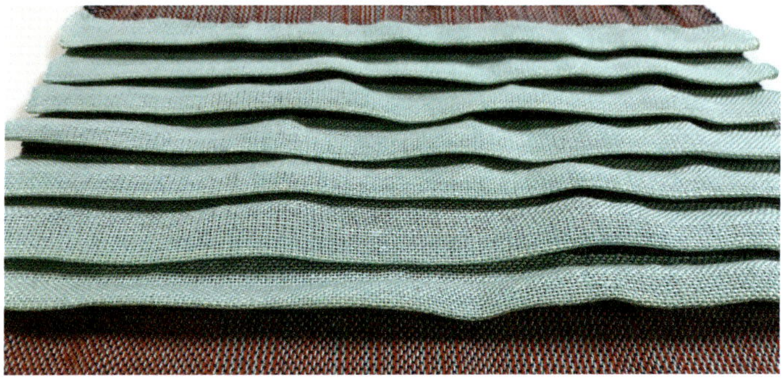

Knife pleats in double cloth can be pressed down so that only one surface is visible.

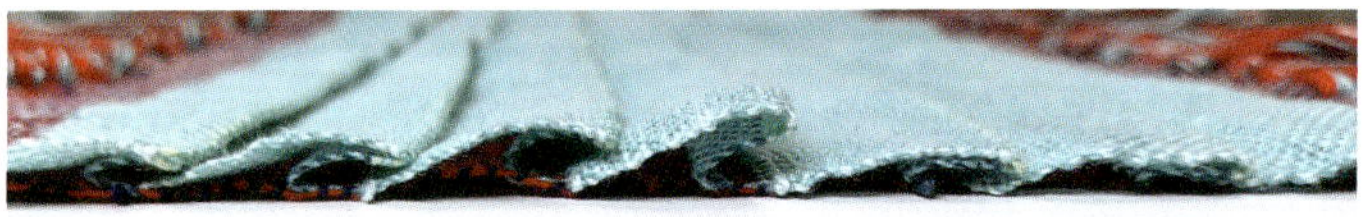

The side view shows the structure of the knife pleat with a minimum of two-thirds of the pleat woven in parallel to the bottom layer before the final third of the pleat layer being woven.

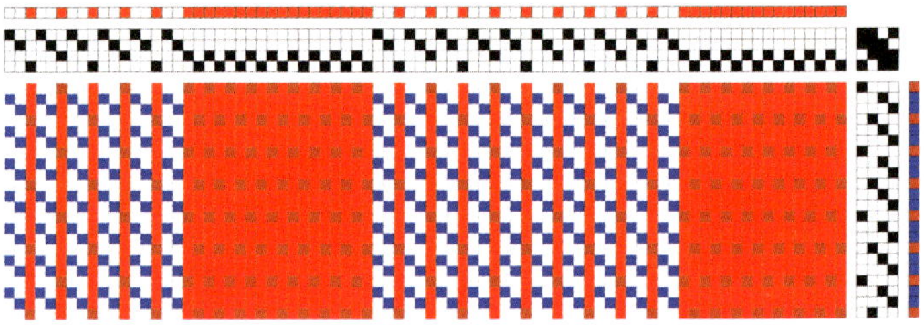

Four shafts can be used to create individual vertical pleats using active and passive yarns. The draft shows single cloth areas in red and double cloth areas in light and dark red, white and mid-blue.

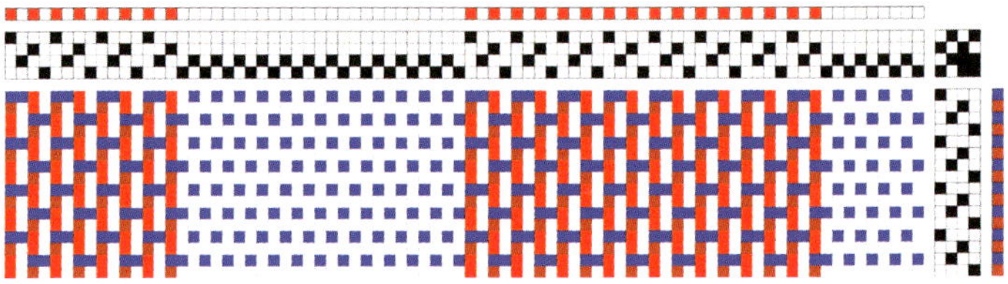

Combined double and single cloth threadings in a 1:1 ratio of active to passive yarns for the double cloth area gives the opportunity to create a vertical pleat when weaving the passive weft in both the single and double cloth areas.

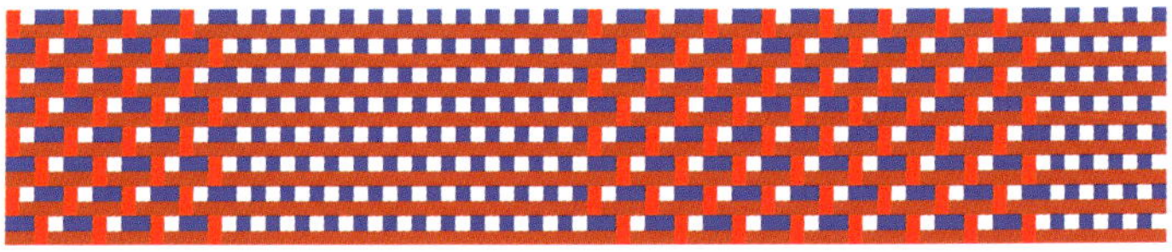

The active weft only interacts with double cloth, weaving an integrated half-hopsack, leaving floats across the underside of the single cloth area.

TOP TIP

Ensure that the pleats remain in situ when wet-finishing by stay-stitching them lightly in place prior to the finishing process.

Vertical Pleats on Eight Shafts

Often, as it is relatively easy to create horizontal pleats, work is created horizontally and then turned so that the pleats appear to be running vertically. However, it is possible to create vertical pleats in double cloth stripes on four shafts using active yarns alongside the passive yarns, with a ratio of 1:2 active to passive combined with narrower single cloth areas, although the result will not necessarily be crisp pleats.

There are two options:

1. Use an active warp for the whole width of the warp with passive yarns forming the top layer of the double cloth bands in a 2:1 (or more) passive to active ratio.
2. Use a passive warp for the whole width of the warp with the active yarns forming the bottom layer in the double cloth areas, this time in a 1:2 (or 1:3) ratio.

Two wefts are required: one active, one passive.

For option 1, the active weft will weave across the full warp in plain weave. The passive weft will interact only with its passive warp, floating underneath the active single cloth layer. These passive floats can be cut away, if desired, after finishing.

For option 2, the passive weft will weave across the full warp in plain weave. For most effective results, the active weft interacts only with its active warp, weaving the bottom layer in the double cloth with weft floats underneath the single cloth area. If less texture is required, it can also weave in a half hopsack along with the passive weft in the passive warp areas.

Another option uses a 1:1 ratio in the two warp stripes.

A translation to eight shafts in the larger ratio allows four shafts to act as one layer, and two of the remaining four shafts becoming one of the warps for the double, with the remaining two for the other.

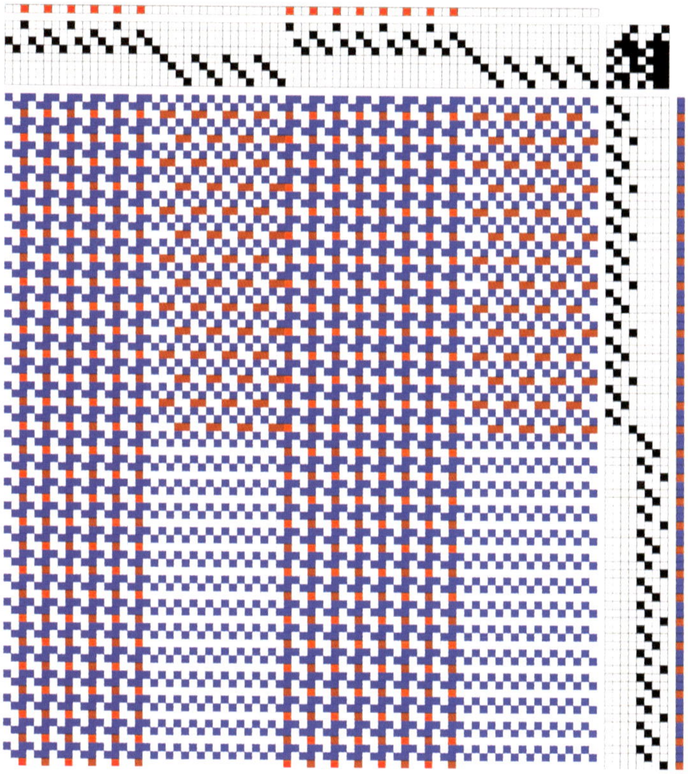

A mix of half-hopsack and plain weave are demonstrated in the face and back views of this eight-shaft draft. The long floats can be cut shorter after wet-finishing if the length of them are a problem.

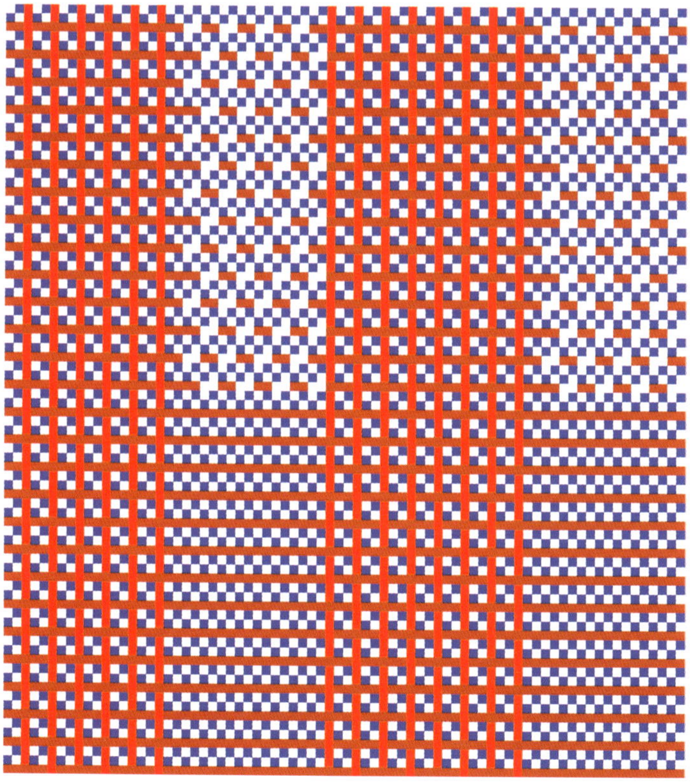

The view of the underside.

Using Vertical and Horizontal Pleats Together

Vertical and horizontal pleats can be formed in the same cloth. This is done by weaving the above method for the vertical pleats and 'framing' the combined double cloth areas by weaving the cotton weft across the entire cotton warp for a number of picks above and below the combined single layer in the double cloth warp areas. The active warp floats that are not required shrink on wet-finishing to form the horizontal pleat.

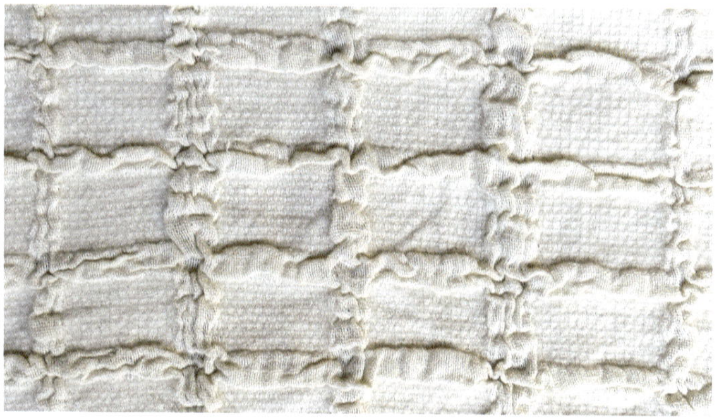

The same double cloth, single cloth combination in the warp can also allow for grids. The cotton and wool warp is woven with linen and wool in the weft.

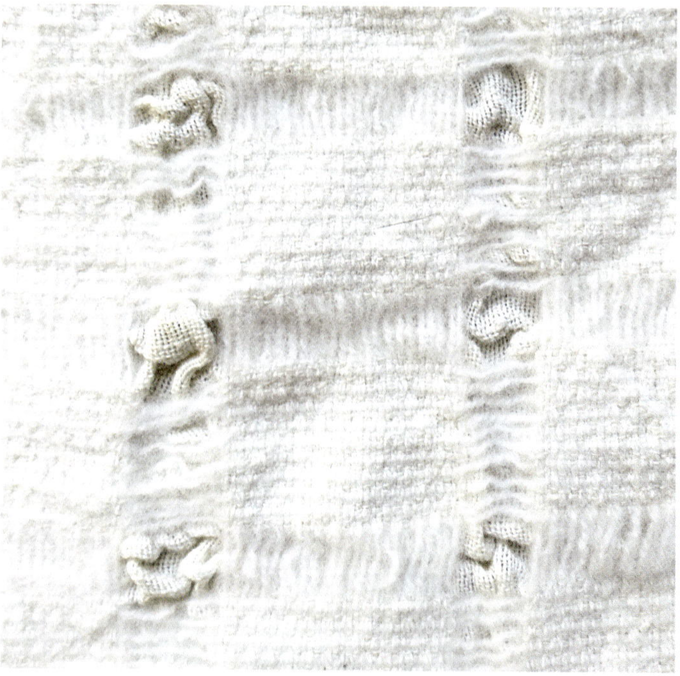

The reverse view shows where the same treadling principles are followed as for the warp. Wool and linen are woven together in the combined areas, and only the linen is woven in the areas where horizontal puckering is desired, allowing the wool warp to float in these areas. On wet-finishing, the retraction of the wool allows for the puckering of the passive areas.

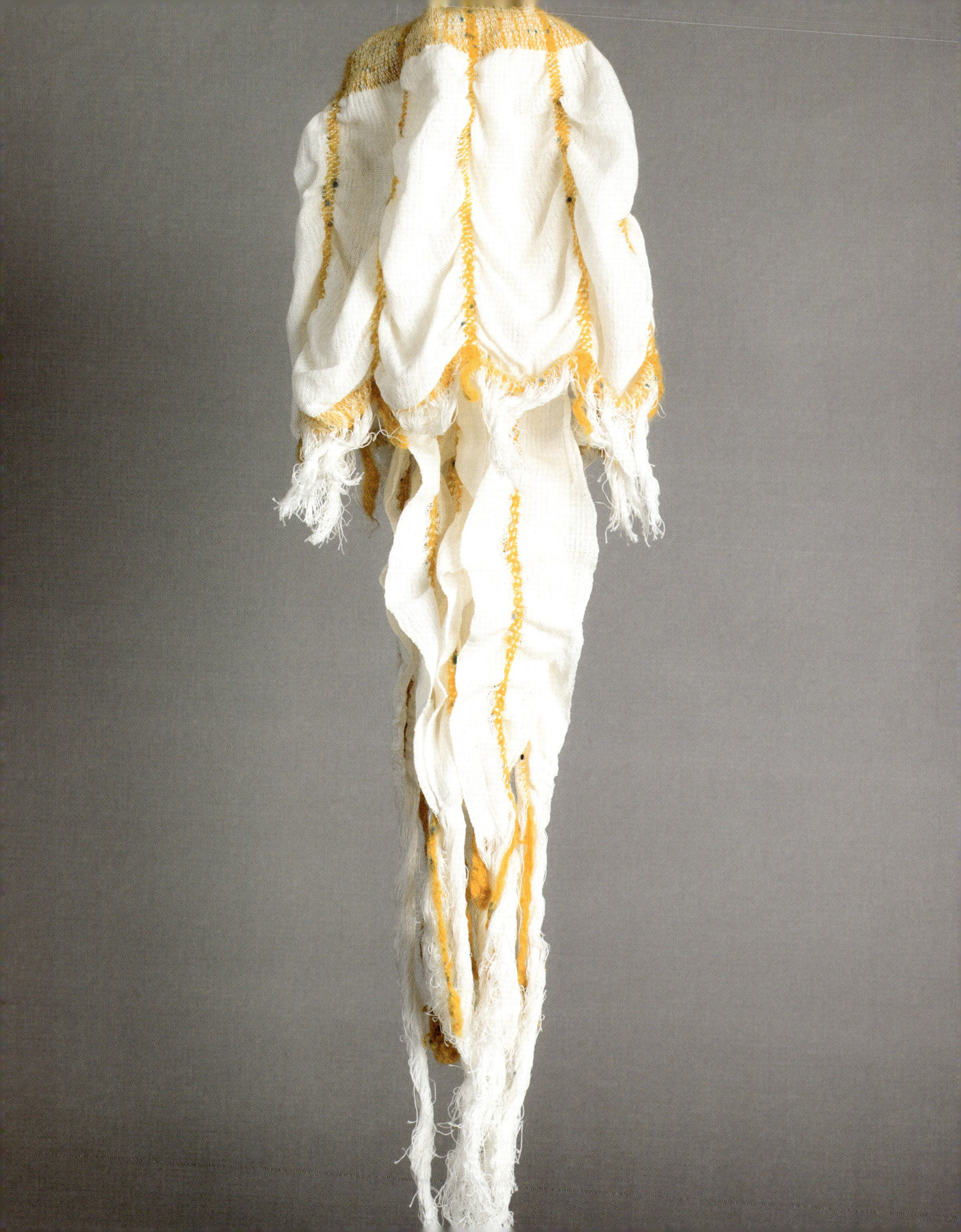

CHAPTER 4

SEERSUCKER

Seersucker is a fabric that usually intersperses warp bands of a puckered appearance with warp bands of ribbed appearance. It is a very approachable technique for creating dimensional texture and is generally regarded as a warp technique, which means that the fabric will shrink in length.

It is associated industrially with light, summer cotton clothing, tea towels or picnic tablecloths and serviettes. The stripes have widely differing tensions; those with normal tension end up puckering when the tighter warp bands are relaxed.

There are two ways to create seersucker. One involves the use of two warp beams, tensioning each one differently. The other uses just one warp beam but utilises wool or another active yarn to create shrinkage in warp stripes, causing the puckering of non-shrinking areas when it is wet-finished.

ONE-BEAM SEERSUCKER

This is a very simple technique. The warp uses alternating bands of a shrinking yarn and non-shrinking yarn, so wool stripes alternating with cellulosic yarns such as cotton, cottolin, linen, Tencel™, silk, bamboo viscose or polyester stripes would work well.

The warp can be wound as one, knotting the active and passive warps together when changing yarns during winding, especially if the warp is not a long one. For longer warps, it can be helpful even when using one warp beam to add a second warp stick to the warp beam. This allows the two warp yarns to be wound separately and put onto their own back stick, which are both attached to the warp beam. This is a useful technique for sampling, especially on table looms. It is particularly useful when using an elastic or overtwisted yarn, as the two warp yarns can be kept apart and tensioned separately in between samples as required even, when they are wound together onto the same warp beam.

The weave is usually plain weave or simple small-scale designs such as hopsack, twill variants or small crepe weaves in the non-shrinking areas. The warp yarns that are going to shrink are usually woven in plain weave or rib weaves. If plain weave is used across both stripes or if a simple rib is used in the shrinking warp stripe with plain weave across the other, this can easily be woven on four shafts as only two blocks of two shafts are required: one set per stripe.

The wool and cotton warp stripes alternate. The stripes can be any size, although larger is not always better, and this is where personal choices come to play. It is useful to keep the sett of the active yarn more open than a regular plain weave to allow the wool room to shrink and full. The non-shrinking stripes can be sett with a regular plain weave sett or with a twill sett if a twill or twill derivative is being used. Crepe weaves need careful perusal to see how many interlacings there are in the repeat to decide on the most

TOP TIP

When tying on the seersucker warp using knots rather than lashing, tie the passive warp first then tie the active yarn, adding the desired tension.

Medusa. A thin seersucker stripe using Shetland singles yarn is the driving force behind the gentle rippling of the jellyfish. (Photo: Colin Usher)

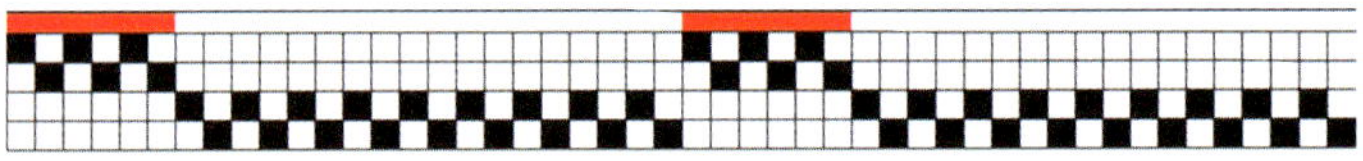

Seersucker on four shafts has two threading blocks – one smaller than the other – with two shafts per block. It is useful to use an active warp yarn for the smaller threading block.

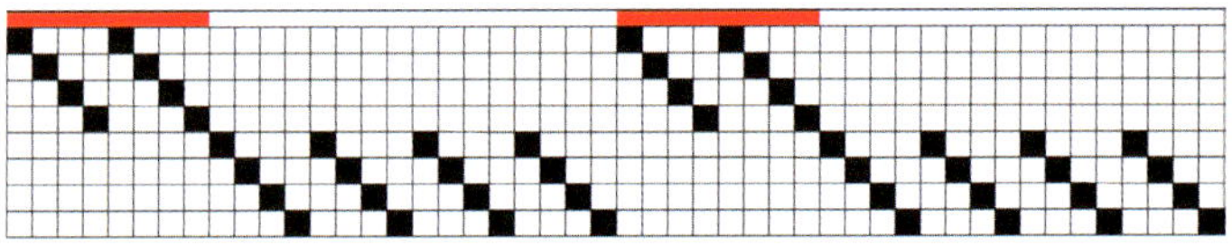

Seersucker on eight shafts.

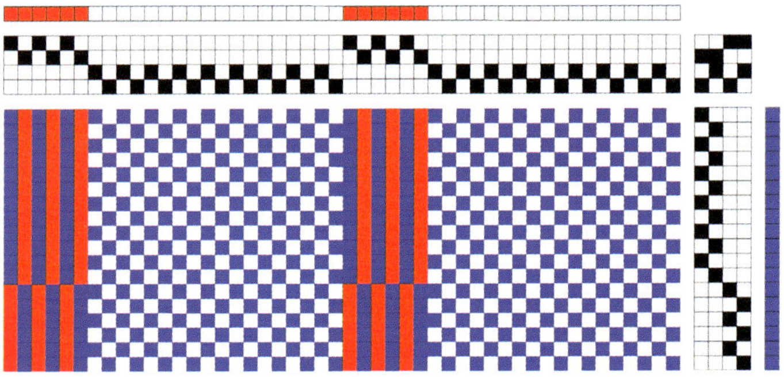

Weaving the four-shaft seersucker uses one weft, two warp yarns and plain weave plus a rib in the active warp.

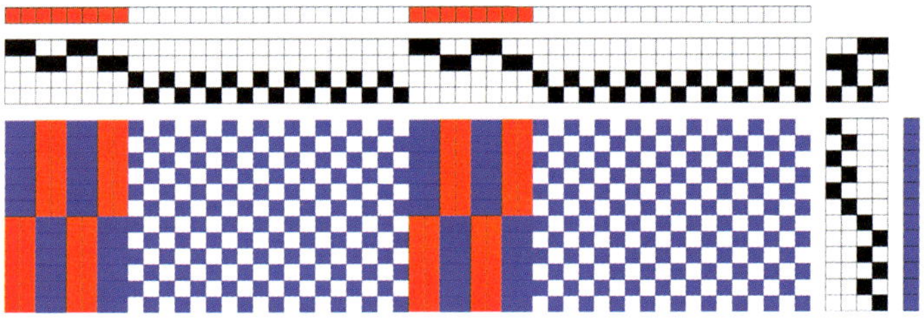

Changing the wool threading to a hopsack helps to increase the shrinkage during wet-finishing.

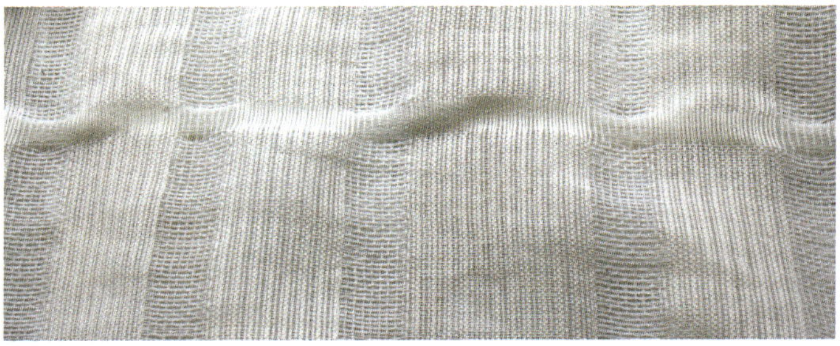

Weaving seersucker gives an easy result if delayed gratification is not an issue. However, it does not show its effects prior to wet-finishing, unless using elastane for the active warp yarn. This sample is prior to wet-finishing.

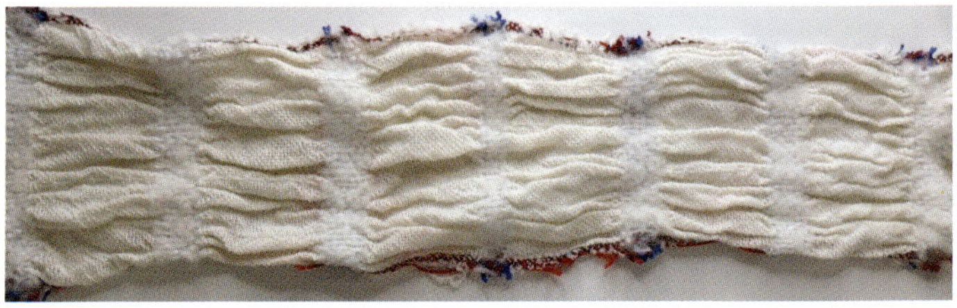

This four-shaft sample uses hopsack for the rib and weaves four picks before changing rib. This was wet-finished for around 15 minutes.

appropriate sett, depending on whether it is predominantly twill-based or plain weave-based.

For eight shafts, the threading can be spread over four shafts per block.

Weaving Seersucker: Four Shafts

Weaving seersucker using wool stripes is incredibly simple. If you can weave plain weave, you're good to go! For a greater textural impact, a rib can be used in the wool areas.

Ribs allow for longer warp floats. The passive weft will use repeated lifts in the same rib shed while changing the ground weave shed every pick. This allows for the weft to be condensed within the rib while being expanded in the passive areas. The active warp will have more room to full during wet-finishing as it has longer floats. This will force the non-shrinking areas into deeper puckers.

Weft yarns can be changed whenever desired. Texture variation comes from different weft yarns, so many variations and 'looks' are possible with the same weaving draft. Try slub yarns, noils, various textures, different non-shrinking yarns such as man-made, wool, metals, monofilament (fishing line), polyester, and paper.

Weft stripes of shrinking yarns can also be introduced, including elastane-based yarns, and other yarns that will full on wet-finishing.

Weaving Seersucker: Eight Shafts

Eight-shaft looms provide the same options.

Additionally, there is the option of adopting different four-shaft weaves for the ground weave – and the active wool stripes too, if desired.

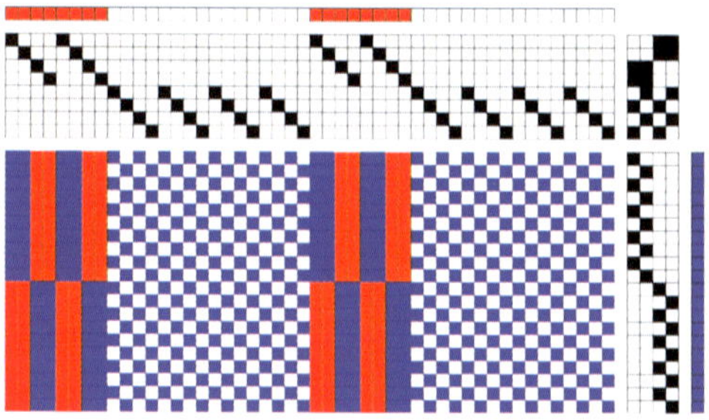

Eight shafts can also be used to weave a rib in the active warp area alongside plain weave in the passive warp block.

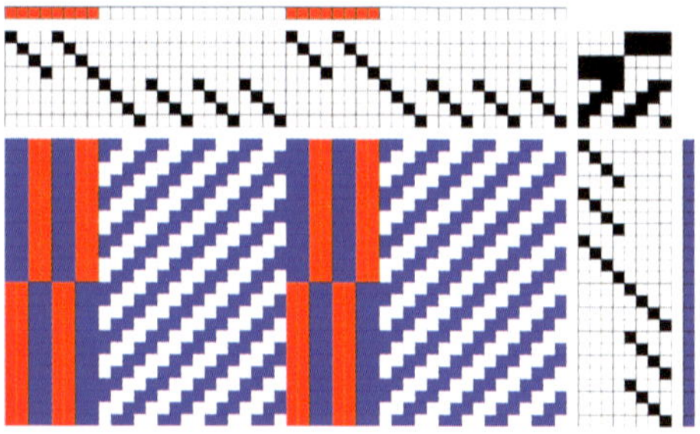

With eight shafts, there are other options such as a 2/2 twill with the rib.

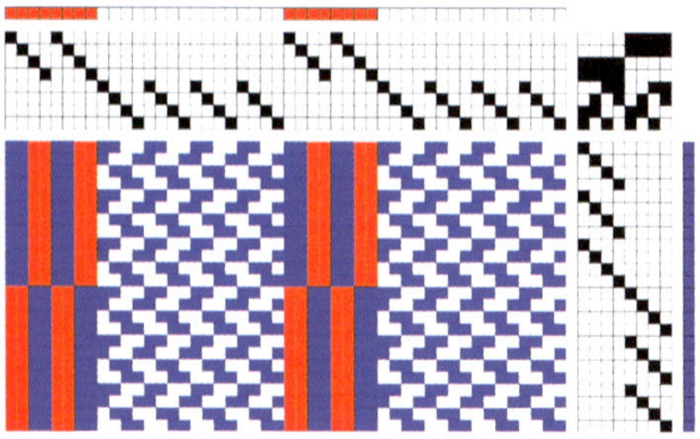

Broken twill gives a textural surface to the cloth while still maintaining the rib for the shrinkage.

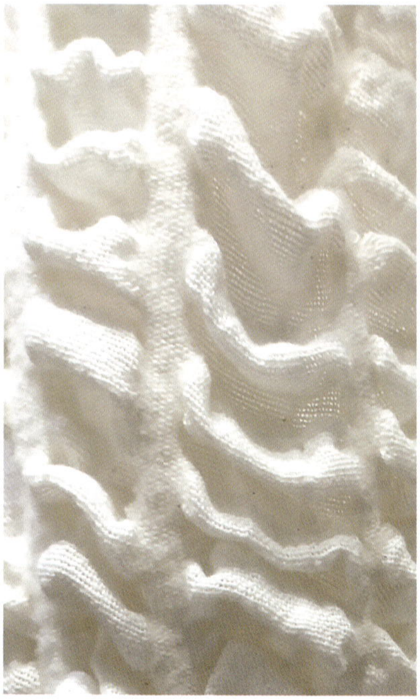

Different wefts give different results. Here, the same cotton has been used for warp and weft for a large effect seersucker.

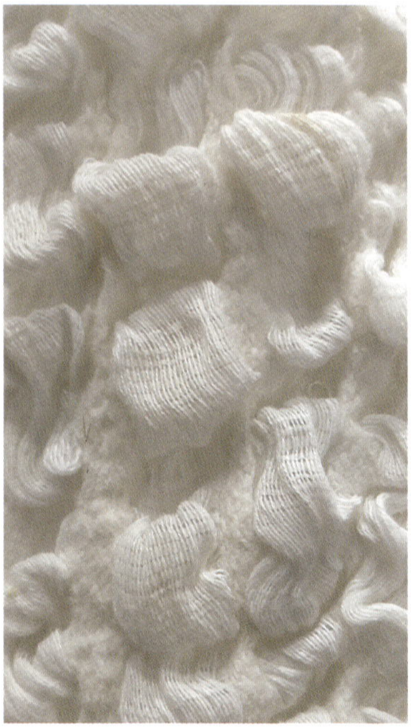

A fine paper weft is used on the same warp, resulting in a very different effect. The twist of the singles paper yarn contained while weaving is released on hitting the water during wet-finishing. The relaxing of the twist in the yarn forces a torque reaction into the woven cloth, giving characteristic coiling surfaces that vary according to the thickness and angle of twist of each type of paper yarn.

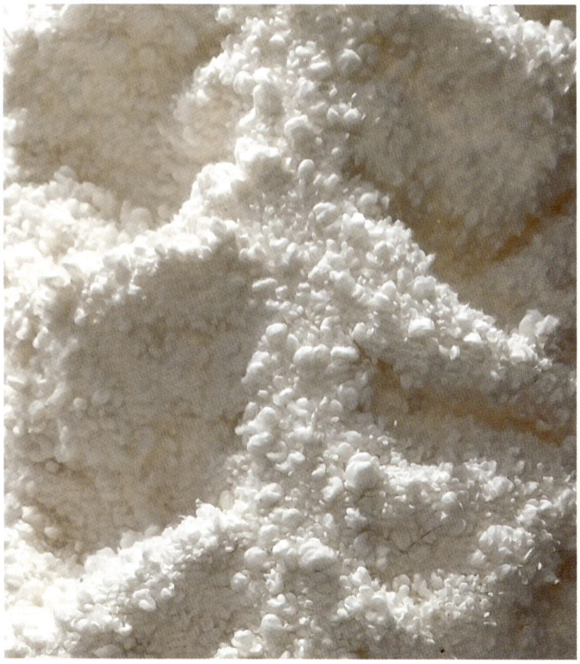

A novelty 'popcorn' cotton weft is used here. Because of the size of the popcorn texture, large areas of one rib are woven before switching over to the other rib. This creates long wool floats in the warp, which allows the fabric to be pulled up into this ruched result during vigorous wet-finishing. The centre of the image is the wool warp; the festoon areas to the sides are the cotton warp.

Other Variations: Six Shafts

Shrinking warp stripes can be teamed up with double cloth to give an interesting double-sided effect. Use hopsack or rib weave on two shafts for the active yarn (if wool, it is useful to dedicate the front two shafts for this to ensure that the potentially 'sticky' yarns are visible at the front of the castle) and the remaining four shafts as two layers of regular double cloth in passive yarns. Opening the sett of the shrinking warp stripes a little can assist with the shrinkage during wet-finishing, especially for some singles yarns.

Hopsack gives a balance to the two weft picks required for the double cloth areas so there is no excess weft build-up in the active warp area, which can occur if plain weave is used here. Separate wefts can be used for the front and back layers of the double cloth, which leaves room for varying the weft yarns.

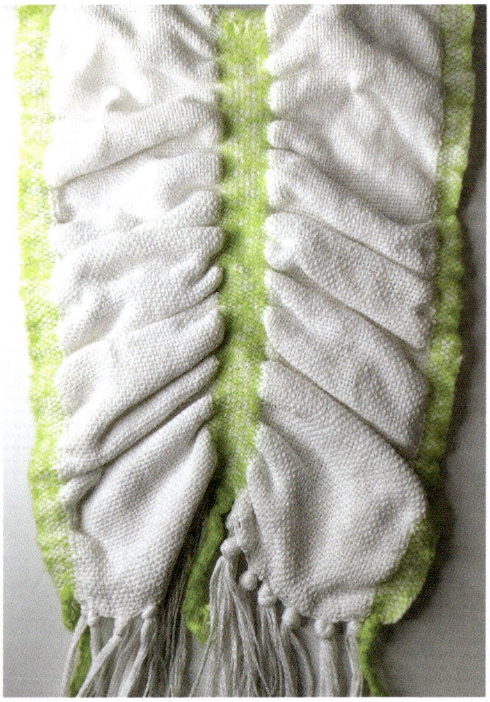

Double cloth can be combined with seersucker to give quite a dramatic result. The weft is the same cotton as the warp and the wool warp stripe is a lambswool.

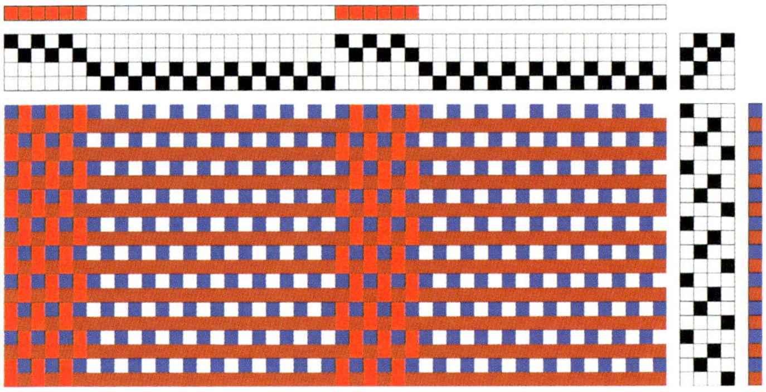

Using a secondary active weft on a single cloth seersucker, floats can be created across the passive warp areas to increase the amount of contraction on wet-finishing. This is easiest done weaving face down, so the floats will be on the surface as you weave.

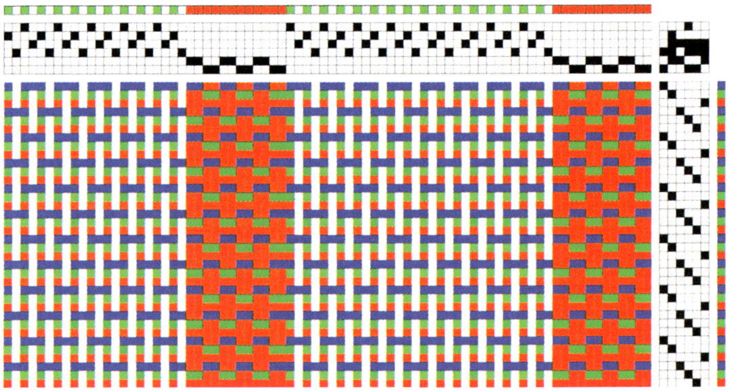

With the double cloth scenario, the active weft floats (red in the draft) can be hidden between the two passive layers and only interact with the active warp.

As with any double cloth, when winding this fabric onto the cloth beam, do it little and often, weaving only in the 'sweet spot' of the loom to ensure that the beater is at as small an angle from the perpendicular as possible.

Weft Floats in Active Yarns

To achieve a more dramatic dimension in a single cloth fabric, the addition of a secondary weft of active yarn with picks that interact only with the active warp in regular seersucker leaves long floats over the non-shrinking areas. When wet-finished, these floats will also retract, creating deeper lengthwise puckering of the passive stripes, as well as the horizontal puckering that will occur through the active warps. This is woven face down if weaving a single cloth so that the floats appear on the top of the fabric as it is woven. They will be the underneath surface when it is finished.

If used in conjunction with the six-shaft double cloth version, the active weft floats could be hidden between the two passive double cloth layers.

TOP TIP

Hold the beater against the fell while re-applying the warp tension to keep the two layers closely allied after advancing your cloth.

As seersucker does not show its effect until wet-finishing, have faith during the weaving process that it will become something completely different at the end of the process.

Wet-finishing

Because a mixture of active and passive yarns – usually of wool and cotton – are used together in the warp, the wool will shrink during wet-finishing and the non-shrinking areas will therefore pucker up. If different weft materials are introduced, the results will vary.

In all cases, except for elastane-based active warp stripes, wet-finishing is necessary to create the desired result using soap, hot water and agitation.

Once it has been fulled to the desired state, it can be air-dried by suspending from a line or laid flat on an absorbent surface. Because texture is what is desired in this instance, it is not advisable to iron the fabric, and wringing the fabric in a dry towel can impart permanent creasing, depending on the yarns used. Be patient and allow the cloth to dry naturally.

TWO-BEAM SEERSUCKER

Two warp beams can be used to weave the same drafts, if preferred. Warp tensioning then becomes a matter of choice rather than serendipity through wet-finishing.

With two beams, there is the option to dispense with shrinking versus non-shrinking yarns for the warp and instead use just one material. Non-mercerised cotton is often used, mostly for its traditional role of being absorbent and soft for garments or kitchenware.

The secret behind seersucker using two warp beams is the difference in tension applied to each warp beam. The warp is generally designed as a single cloth, but alternating bouts are wound onto each beam. The weave is usually plain weave across the two, but one of the beams is woven with a balanced end/pick ratio, while the other beam is tightened considerably. The weaving progresses with the balanced weave. As the woven cloth is wound on, the more tightly tensioned stripes can be seen to have more widely spaced picks, and when the tension is relaxed to normal, they force small puckers into the balanced weave stripes. The amount of texture is much less than with the shrinking/non-shrinking stripe combination but can give a really wonderful subtle surface effect.

Waffle Seersucker

One variation that is a little surprising can be the introduction of a point threading band and the weaving of waffle instead of the rib. Because the long floats in warp and weft of the waffle area lead to more shrinkage, small waffle warp stripes can lead to a seersucker effect in the alternating plain weave stripes. A soft wool used in either warp, weft or both will allow for more effect. It will be held securely in the plain weave stripes but shrink a little in the waffle stripes. This can also be exaggerated through wet-finishing techniques.

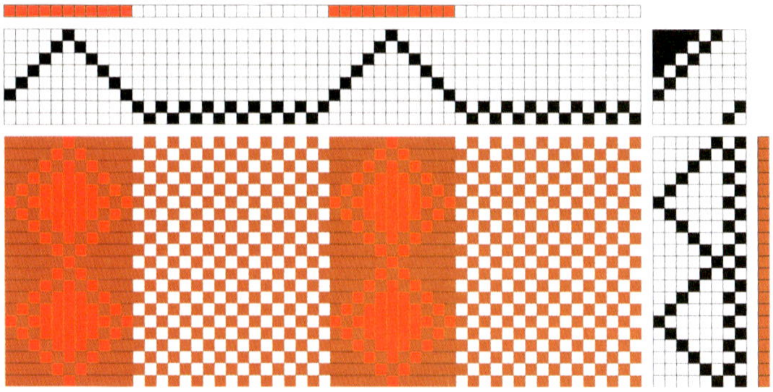

Another weave structure with great contraction is the waffle. Used as an active warp band and contrasted with a plain weave passive warp along with an active or a passive weft, the shrinkage can be very effective for a seersucker effect. This draft uses a skeleton tie-up for a floor loom. Two treadles are required for each pick.

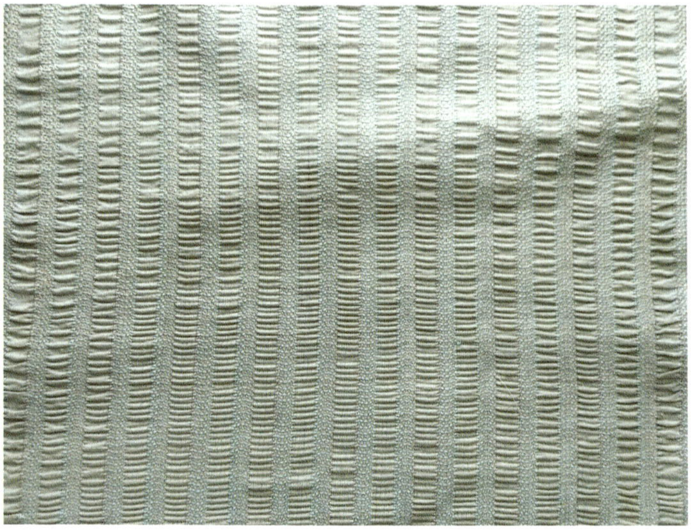

Two back beams can be tensioned separately to give a very effective seersucker. This fine all-over silk seersucker is typical of beam-tensioned effects as opposed to differential shrinkage created by using warp stripes of wool and relying on wet-finishing to create the effect.

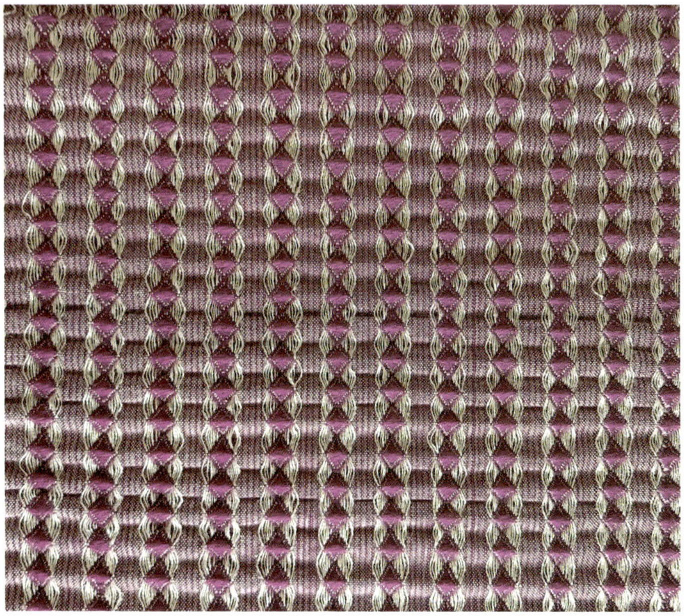

This fine fuchsia cashmere weft in conjunction with a silk warp allows the structure itself to create the effect, rather than wet-finishing processes.

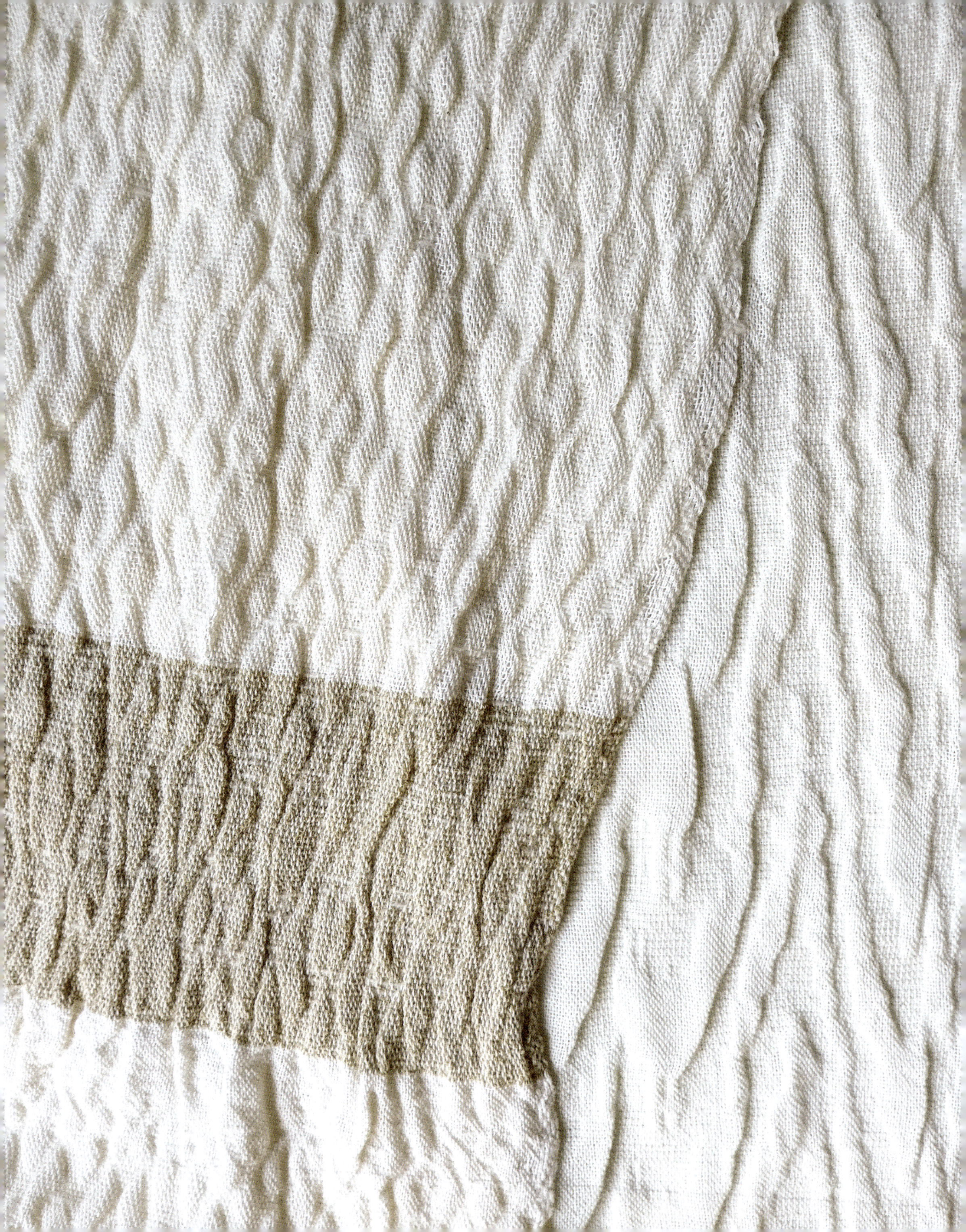

CHAPTER 5

OVERSHOT

We are so used to overshot being synonymous with colonial coverlet designs with heavy weft floats creating patterns on both sides of a fabric that it is difficult to think of it in any other way. But overshot is more than that. It is a threading style that alternates odd and even shafts in a two-shaft pattern block that can either overlap with or be distinct from its neighbour. It has a basic ground weave of plain weave and the patterning is caused by using a secondary or supplementary weft yarn. In traditional overshot, this is usually of a thicker yarn contrasting in colour from the ground weft. In overshot for texture, subtle interplay of light and shade can be highlighted in self-coloured ground cloths of light natural colours.

Using overshot for texture is a relatively easy and interesting way to create ripples and other three-dimensional effects in the surface of the cloth. This is not usually a method for creating deep texture, so for weavers who prefer subtler methods, this will be one to explore. The trick is to ensure that the secondary weft has some shrinkage potential, whether that is through being overspun, unbalanced, or with fulling or elastic properties. To create the best three-dimensional effects, all the floats need to be used on just one side, and not on both face and reverse as is usual in traditional overshot designs. The rest of the time, the secondary weft is woven in with the ground cloth.

If texture is required on both sides of the cloth, traditional overshot designs can be used with elongated float lengths so that the fabric is pulled up by the active weft contracting during wet-finishing. However, with texture on both sides of the cloth, the shrinking floats will remain visible on both surfaces in a similar way to sashiko-style weft shibori (*see* Chapter 6).

YARN CHOICES FOR OVERSHOT

The end use of the fabric will determine what the ground warp and weft will be. More usual yarns are: cotton, silk, bamboo viscose, rayon, linen and various blends. It is usually advised not to use a shrinking yarn for the ground weave, but this could give an interesting surface if tried. Textured yarns such as noils and slubs can be effective in the ground weave, but care has to be taken to ensure that the yarn selected is not too stiff because it needs to respond to the floats' shrinkage. Generally, the warp and ground weft are in the same yarn, but this depends on the end use. A scarf might need a finer weft to give more drape, but a jacket might require something a little firmer.

The warp does not have to be sett with a traditional plain weave sett. To create lighter weight but warm winter scarves when using a lambswool or a merino for an overshot weft, a more open ground weave sett can be used. Sampling is needed to ascertain the correct weight that suits the materials being used.

Wefts for the ground weave can be explored, but it is often most effective to keep the ground weft the same as the warp yarn. The weft used for the overshot is really where the experimentation comes in. High-twist or overspun yarns are fun to use as they spring into action once the fabric touches hot water during finishing. However, these are often spun in fine counts and may not be of sufficient strength to force the rippling of the fabric unless the ground yarns are also carefully considered and are fine enough to allow the overspun to release its energy effectively during wet-finishing. Also, if the fabric is destined for clothing accessories, as the floats are on the 'skinside' of the fabric,

Different scales of design can be exploited using overshot techniques for subtle texture.

any coiling of overspun floats could be scratchy next to the skin.

Elastic yarns get going straight away and may have to be stretched during weaving through using a temple or by suspending weights from the selvedges over the side of the loom (*see* Appendix I for further details.)

Woollen-spun and other fulling yarns are very good to use as the overshot yarn. Their effects do not appear until well on through the wet-finishing process. Care has to be taken not to overdo the shrinkage once it has begun because if the fabric becomes over-fulled, the result cannot be undone.

DESIGNING

The patterns are created through using the overshot yarns to float in certain areas and interweave with the ground fabric in other areas. When the fabric is removed from the loom and wet-finished, the shrinkage potential of the yarn is released, causing the ground fabric to be raised above the floats, thus creating the dimensional effect.

The long floats of the overshot weft yarn are what give the pattern. The longer the float, the more potential it has to contract in finishing. The more the interlacements, the less the yarn can move and the less the shrinking effect.

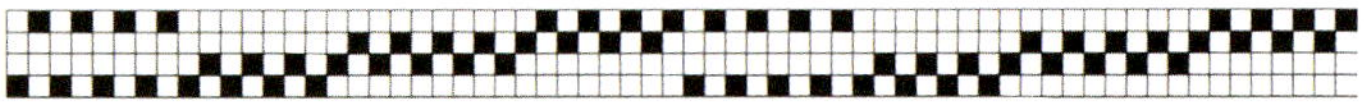

In this detail, the first design section of the Snail Trail draft (not including the selvedge) has been elongated. This could continue in the same vein for the remainder of the original draft or alterations can be made to change the design.

However, both the surface dimensionality and the float lengths have to be compatible with the end use of the fabric, unless it is to be lined.

Four Shafts

One of the wonderful things about overshot for texture is that just four shafts can be used to create quite complex designs. Any of the overshot designs found in weaving books can be used for texture. *A Handweaver's Pattern Book* and *A Handweaver's Source Book*, both by Marguerite Porter Davison, are two such excellent resources for interesting patterns (*see* Bibliography).

Four-shaft overshot designs most often have four blocks overlapping each other: Block A on shafts 1 & 2, Block B on shafts 2 & 3, Block C on shafts 3 & 4 and Block D on shafts 1 & 4. An odd shaft is followed by an even shaft, and an even shaft is followed by an odd shaft to allow for plain weave.

If the results are not distinct enough, blocks can be extended to give a longer float area.

DRAFTING YOUR OWN DESIGNS

When drafting your own designs, and the fabric is designed to be balanced, one square on the profile draft usually represents four ends and four picks – odd ground/pattern shaft/even ground/ same pattern shaft.

Double check to ensure that the fabric is weaving up square. For instance, if the pattern requires two repeats of each design line, but the scale of the design is elongating too much, the number of pattern picks can be reduced to one for each individual element of the design. If the design is too squashed, more pattern picks will be required for each individual element.

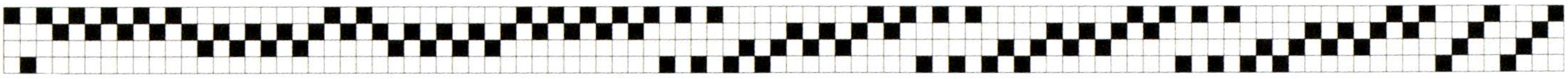

This is the four-shaft threading for Wandering Vine, also known as Cat Track and Snail Trail, used as a colonial overshot design.

WEAVING

Two weft shuttles are used, as in traditional overshot: one containing the ground weft and the other the overshot weft. The patterning is all done with the overshot weft.

The difference between regular overshot and a one-sided overshot for texture is found in the tie-up.

Beginning with a four-shaft draft, the plain weave tabby progresses as usual for regular overshot. However, instead of a 2/2 twill tie-up for the pattern picks, a 1/3 tie-up is substituted. That increases the floats on one side only, giving small areas of interaction on the other side.

As seen on the 'face' side of the draft, with only one shaft raised, there are very long weft floats sitting on the surface of the fabric. This is intentional. The 'right' side – the texture side – is revealed once the fabric has been taken off the loom but is actually on the underside during weaving. This is called weaving 'face down' and is the recommended

The tie-up shows a 1/3 twill along with plain weave. The treadling shows that two wefts are used alternately: one passive (blue) and one active (dark red). The blue weaves plain weave, the red weaves the 1/3 twill, according to the treadling draft.

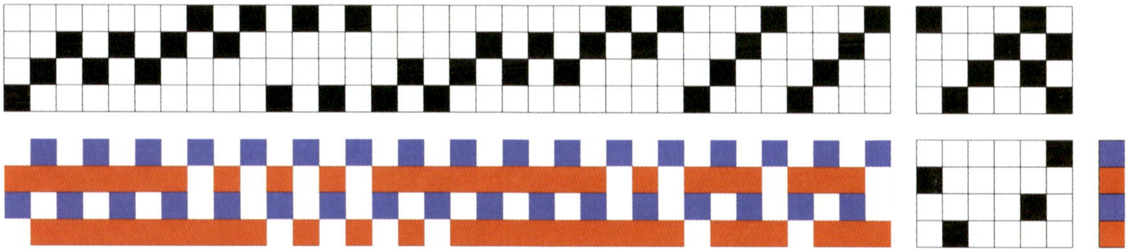

This draft shows the pattern (red) weft design. The plain weave (tabby) is not included in order to see the design more clearly.

The tabby ground has been added here. It is harder to see the design and the draft appears elongated. In practice, the red weft will cover most of the white tabby where the floats occur.

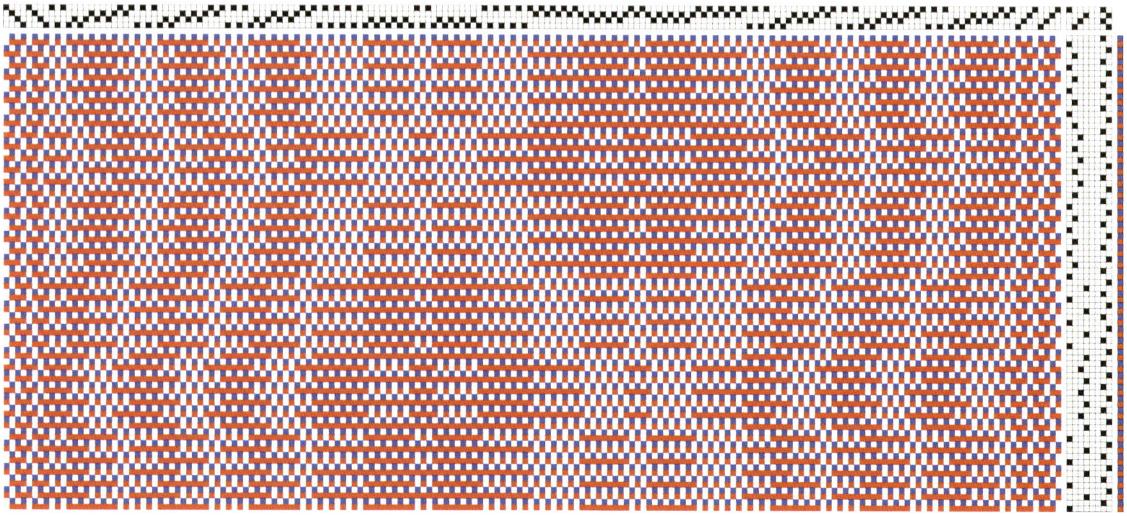

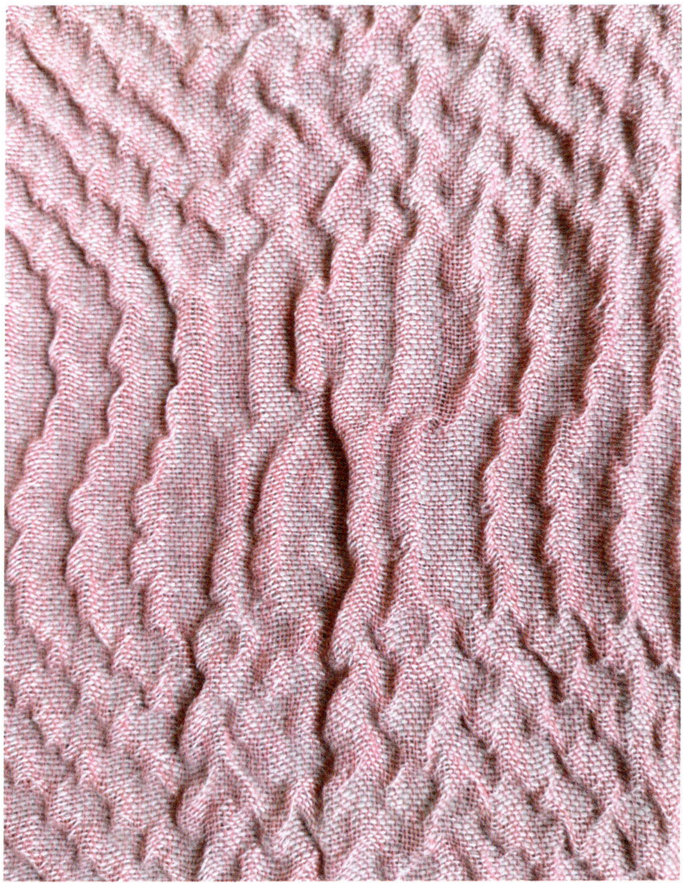

This elongated version of Snail Trail uses a 2/12 ne cotton warp and polyester (passive) and merino (active) wefts. The green-grey merino gives a mellow background where it is woven into the ground weave, leaving the brighter influence of the pink warp to come to the fore in the soft ridges created through the shrinkage of the merino on wet-finishing.

way to weave any draft that has many shafts to lift for each or alternate picks. To weave the draft to see the 'right' side during weaving, the opposite shafts would need to be lifted, so instead of lifting shaft 1 on its own, shafts 2, 3 and 4 would have to be raised.

Weaving overshot for texture as a technique does not have to be based around overshot designs. A four-shaft two-block design can give graphic but subtle results.

Four blocks on four shafts can be created without an overshot design to give a raised pattern.

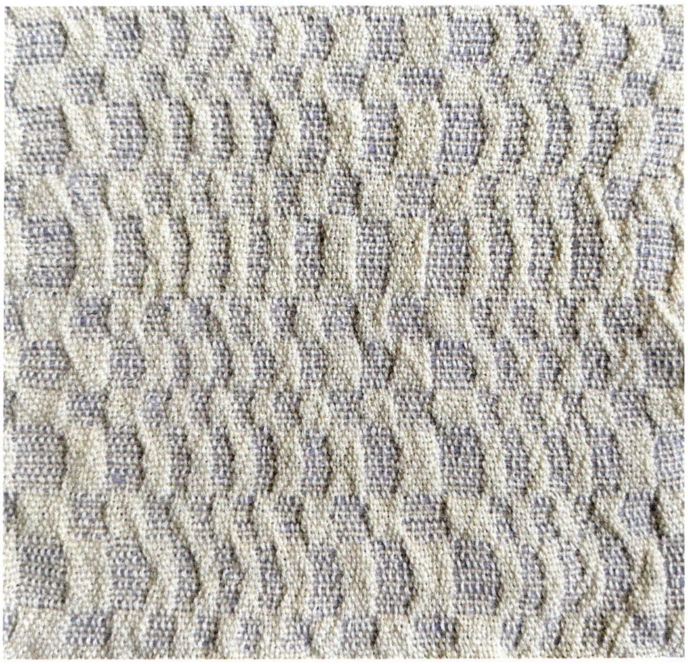

Varying the sizes of the two threading blocks plus gradual changes in the length of the blocks give a sophisticated look to a simple overshot. The use of 2/18 ne mercerised cotton contrasts with the softness of the 28/2 Nm lavender lambswool.

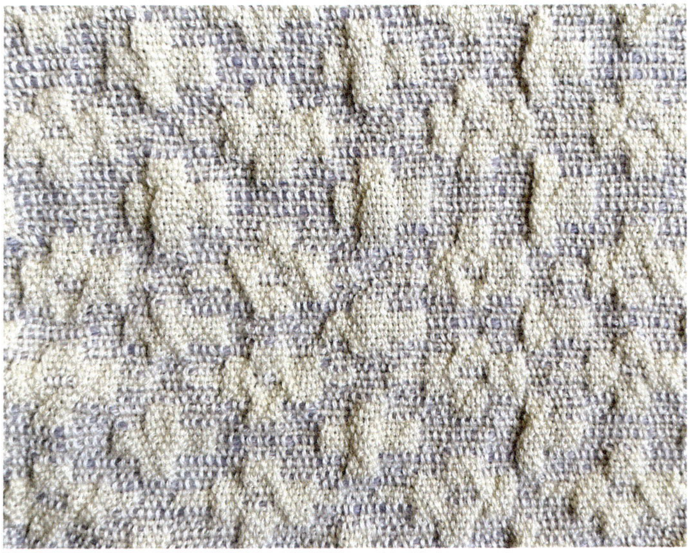

The same cotton ground warp is threaded here in four blocks on four shafts, as is traditional in overshot designs, but a typical overshot pattern has not been used. The same ground weft cotton and overshot wool were used.

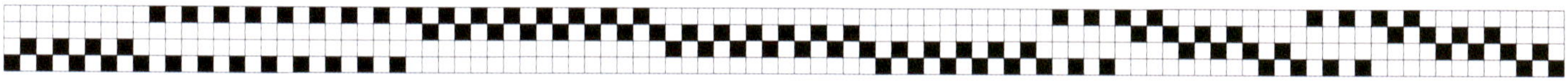

Jitterbug overshot threading on four shafts. Note the four threading blocks are on shafts 1 & 2 (A), 2 & 3 (B), 3 & 4 (C) and 1 & 4 (D).

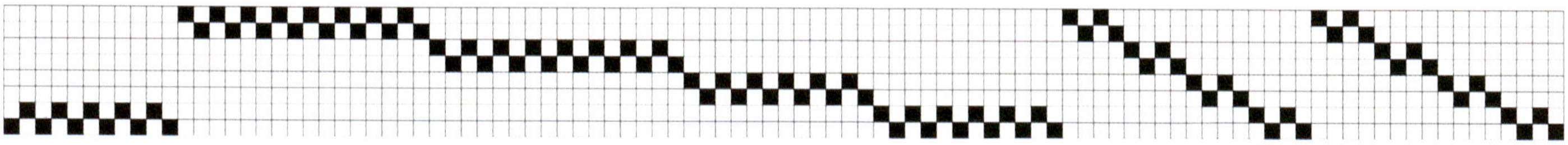

When converted for eight shafts, the four blocks now have two discrete shafts each. Block A is on shafts 1 & 2, B is on shafts 3 & 4, C is on 5 & 6 and D is on 7 & 8.

Eight Shafts

With eight shafts, there are more variations available. The most immediate results can be created by using four discrete blocks, converting the four-shaft overshot designs with their half-tone overlaps into very distinct and clear blocks, with Block A on shafts 1 & 2, Block B on shafts 3 & 4, Block C on shafts 5 & 6 and Block D on shafts 7 & 8.

Jitterbug, attributed to Bertha Gray Hayes and found in Marguerite Porter Davison's *A Handweavers' Source Book*, gives asymmetric shapes and good texture.

In order to convert the treadling into a sequence that will give texture, the first step is to use a technique called 'woven as drawn in'. The treadling uses the same order that was used for the threading. In weaving software, it is very swift. The pattern design will be the overshot weft in an active yarn that will alternate with the passive ground tabby weave.

Add the alternating tabby wefts of 1, 3, 5, 7 (Tabby A) versus 2, 4, 6, 8 (Tabby B), in the same way that is used in the four-shaft overshot.

When discrete blocks are used, they can be moved around far more easily. 'A' does not have to be before 'B' or after 'D', so profile drafts can be explored to create more variation in the block designs, including breaks in the design. There are many books to help with block drafting and profile drafting (*see* Bibliography).

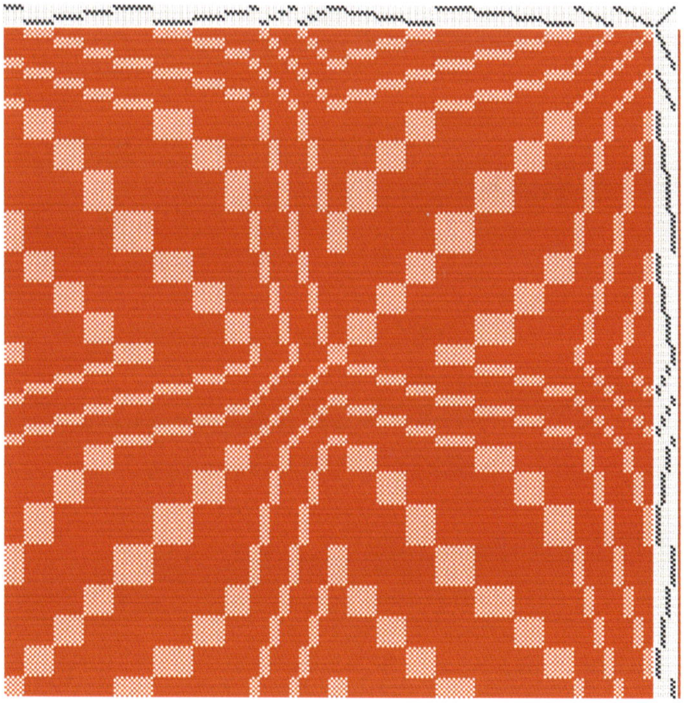

The draft now has the addition of the woven-as-drawn-in treadling, showing the floats side without any tabby.

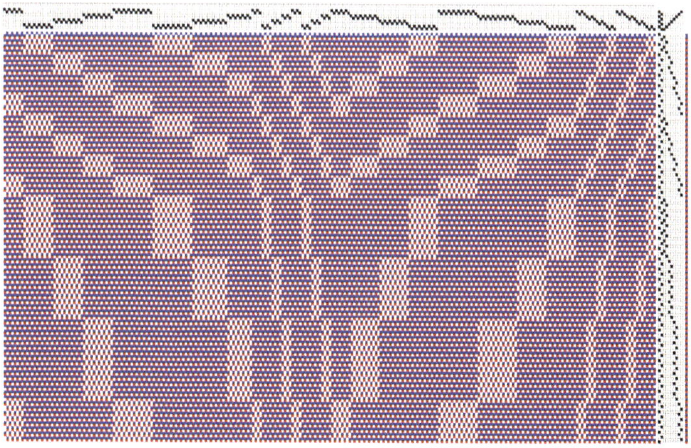

This shows a detail with the tabby ground added.

TOP TIP

Remember that a consistent plain weave ground is required. The easiest way to do this is to thread the loom with odd and even shafts alternating.

Another development is to overlap blocks to get the half-tone effect of traditional overshot, so that Block A is on shafts 1 & 2, Block B is on shafts 2 & 3, Block C is on shafts 3 & 4, etc. This gives areas where the overshot is integrated into the non-shrinking ground, producing the half-tone effect. This will give eight blocks with which to experiment.

A useful eight-shaft draft to show variations on the theme is a star pattern, adapted from Carol Strickler's *A Weaver's Book of 8-Shaft Patterns* (*see* Bibliography). It is designed to demonstrate a range of angles in the design lines and how the angles impact the resulting texture.

Different tie-ups have varying impacts on the resulting fabric, and therefore on the potential for more or less dimensional effect.

Other tie-ups are possible – try different variations to explore their effects.

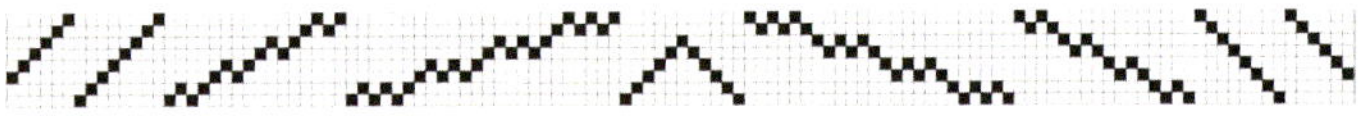

Adapted overshot star threading for eight shafts. This shows half the threading.

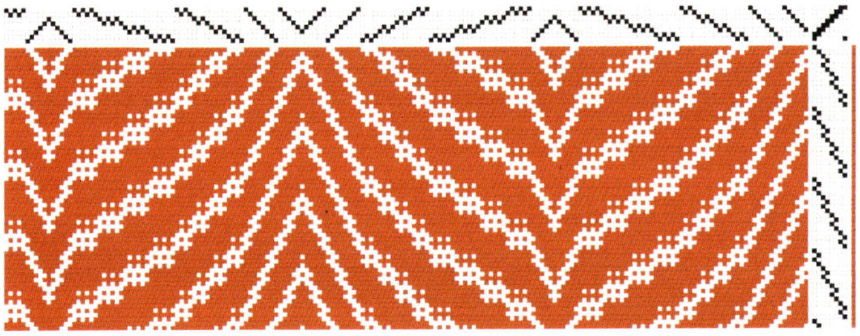

In the profile tie-up, two shafts are raised twill fashion, which means that alternate pattern picks lift a complete threading block. The pattern weft will pass under a complete block and then surface cleanly to pass over three other blocks. However, every other pattern pick engages with one shaft each from two successive blocks, so that it will be integrated into those and only pass completely over two blocks. This allows for longer floats with stability provided by the integration every second pattern pick.

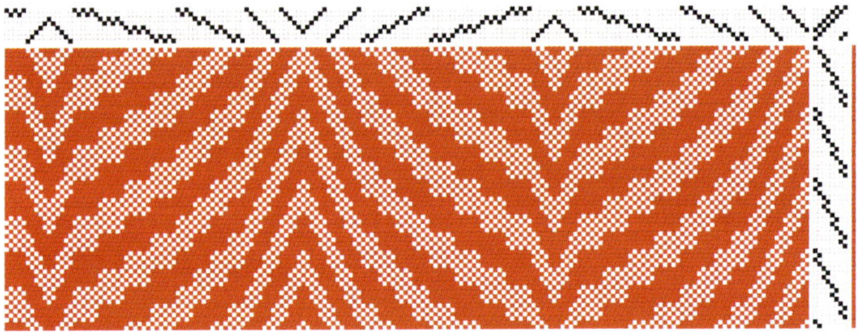

This draft still has two shafts being raised at a time for the pattern, but this time using one end each from two successive threading blocks. This ensures that the pattern weft is integrated into the fabric for every pick but the float length is necessarily reduced as two blocks are involved in the integration each time.

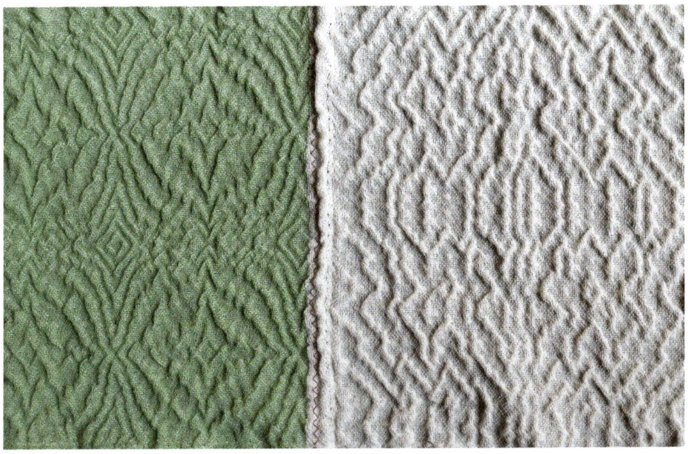

Two different eight-shaft overshot drafts have been threaded in two groups on 16 shafts to allow different permutations with the two drafts. The green is a variation of Blooming Leaf and is woven as drawn in. The white sample is an original draft based on a thistle and is weaving a different treadling plan.

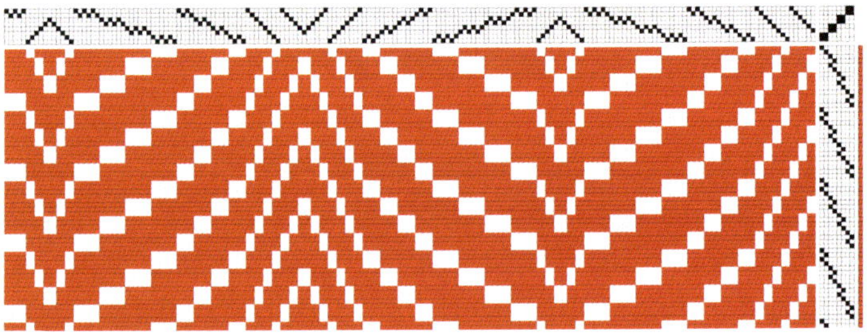

In this draft, the overshot weft uses a block tie-up of 2/6 twill.

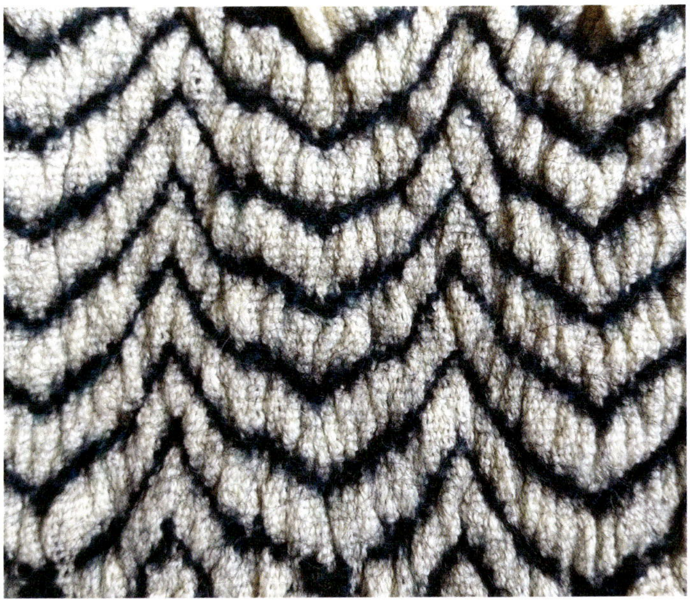

A design woven with the tie-up as blocks of 2/6 rather than the twill line and a shorter repeat length of treadling per block gives a compact and graphic pattern.

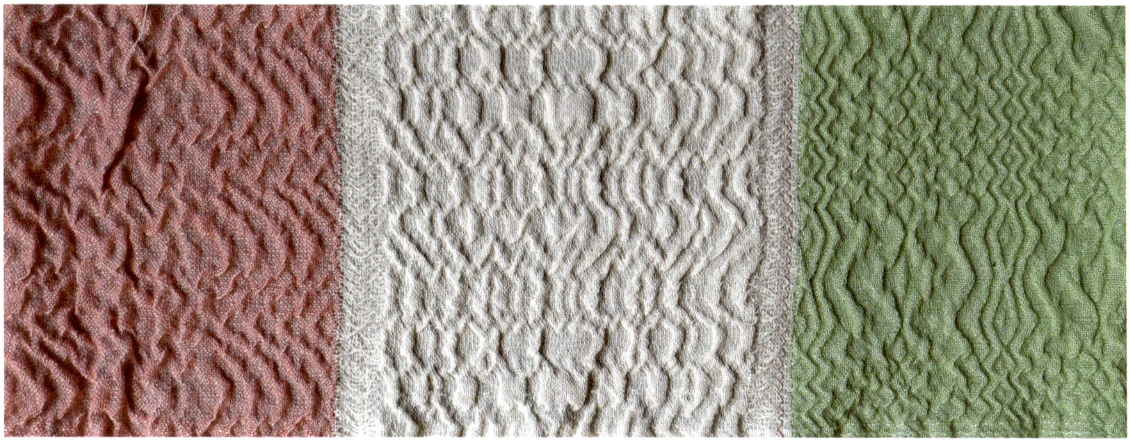

Variations on the four-shaft Wandering Vine (Cat Track and Snail Trail) in pink, a thistle design in white and the Blooming Leaf in green play with scale and movement within each sample.

Treadling

Treadling patterns can be simple or complex. Starting suggestions for profile treadlings are for:

1. Straight
2. Point
3. Advancing
4. Woven as drawn in

Just remember to add the plain weave ground. There are many varieties of treadling, such as M&Ws, and other overshot pattern treadlings can be adapted and original treadling patterns designed.

A cross between shibori and overshot can be small wool floats on one side of the fabric and large floats on the other, which are not removed.

With more shafts, many more options for designing are available, including differing sizes of design.

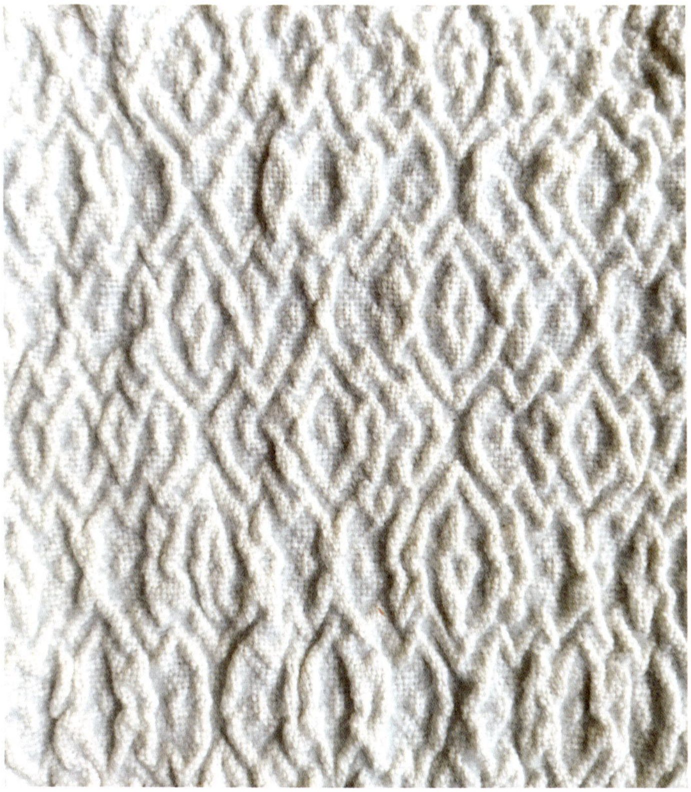

A smaller scale design has been woven as drawn in with a finer overshot weft in pale blue.

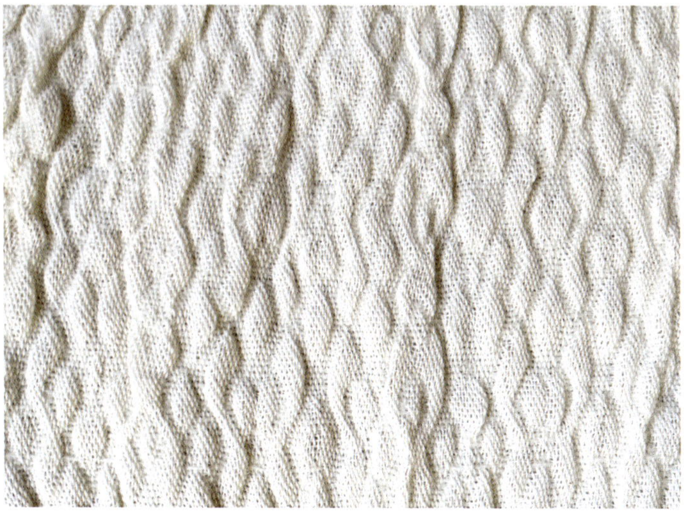

Gentle ripples are a feature of this scarf exploring material, multiple design lengths and organic movement. The cotton warp was sett more openly than a regular plain weave so that the wool overshot would not have to contract too much to create the effect in order to keep the scarf light.

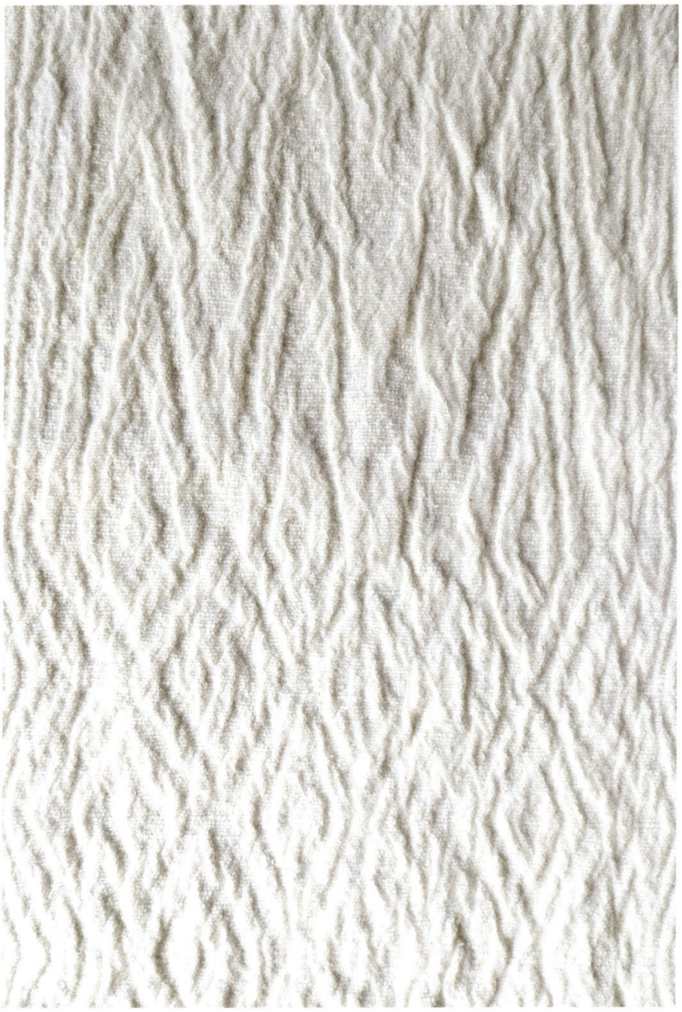

This scarf is completely in wool. The wet-finishing has left a subtle design visible.

Finishing

Once the fabric is woven, it will need wet-finishing, especially if wools or high-twist yarns are used for the overshot weft. With the elastomeric yarns, the fabric can be stretched out, so it is useful for close-fitting garments. With wool, the long floats act as an insulating layer, so this can be quite useful for a lined garment or scarves.

Variations

Many motifs can be created with the use of a point overshot threading, i.e. trees and stars.

Vary the threadings and treadlings using a mixture of ends and/or picks per block to create undulating and more organic results.

Advancing threading patterns will also give different options.

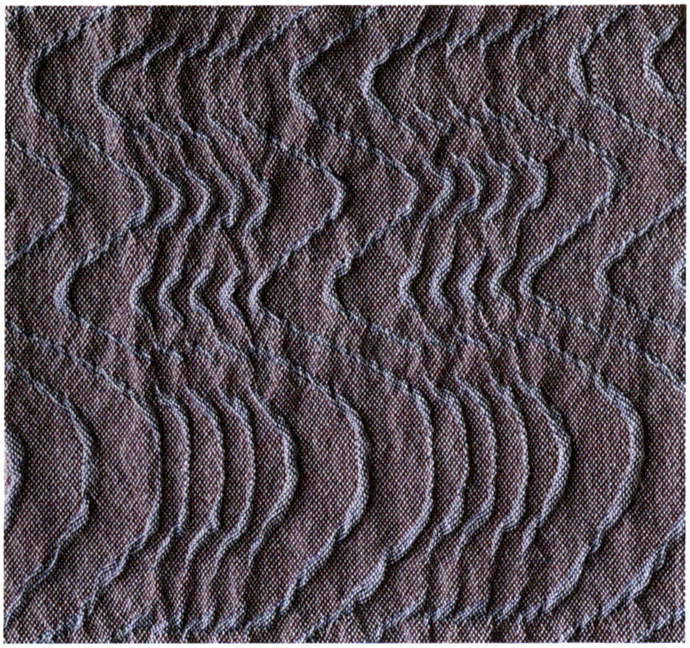

This overshot by Lynn Smetko uses 20/2 mercerised cotton in the warp, a 20/2 different cotton in the weft and an elastane viscose yarn for the overshot weft.

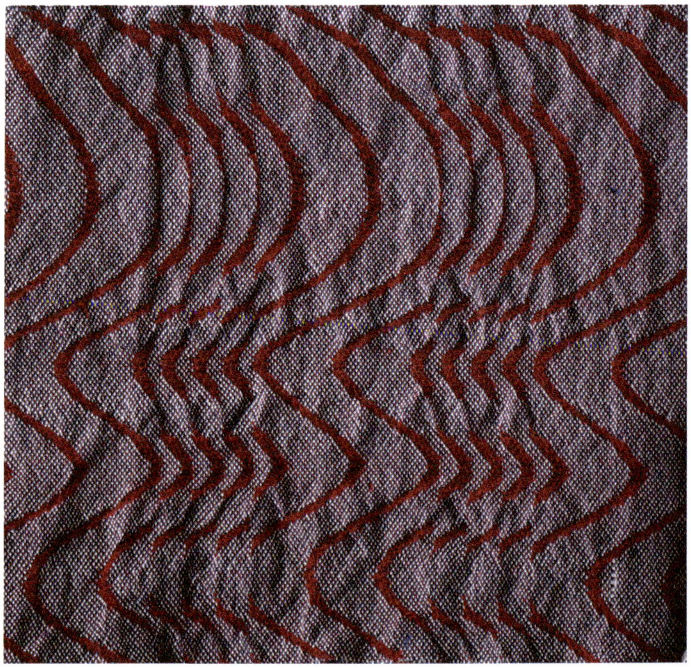

The reverse of this multi-shaft design wanders organically. The red floats of the elastane viscose yarn show clearly. (Photos: Lynn Smetko)

Different weft ground yarns – including fancy yarns such as glitter yarn or interesting textures such as noils or slub yarns – will add character and variety but may detract from the textural effect.

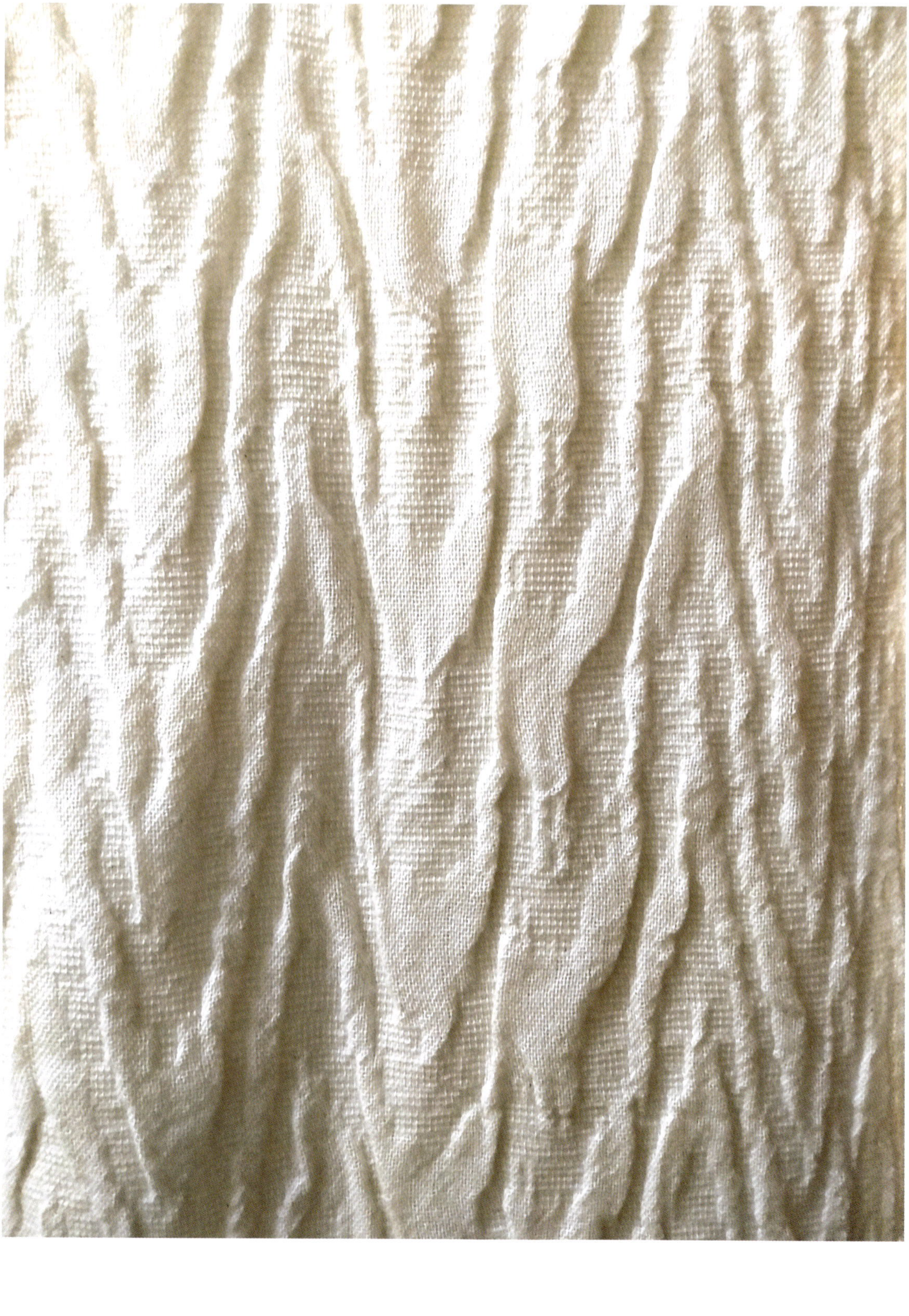

This cotton scarf using overshot for texture has wool as its shrinking weft. In plain white, it is simple but effective.

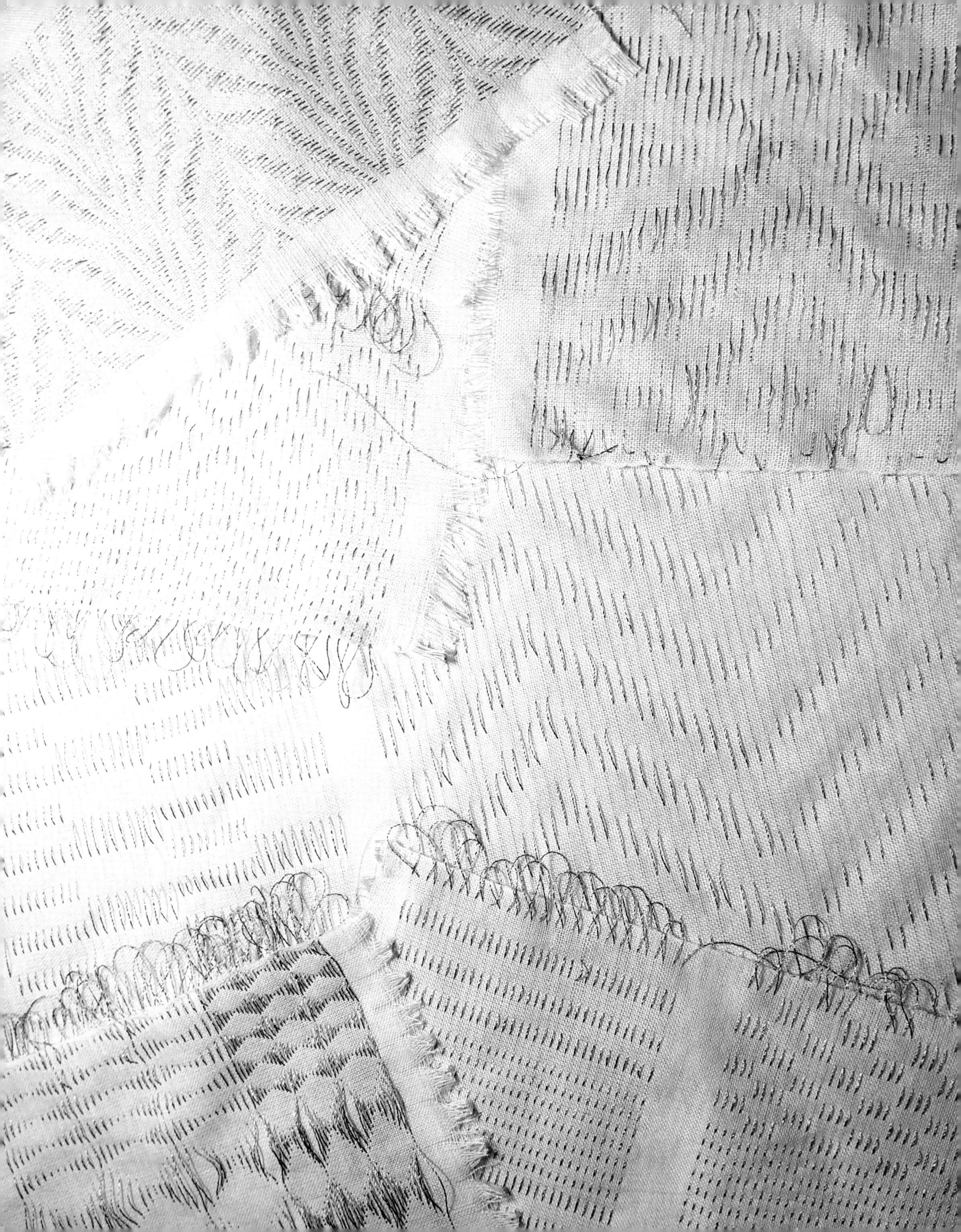

CHAPTER 6

SHIBORI

Using shibori methods for permanently pleating or shrinking cloth creates miraculous surfaces.

—Jack Lenor Larsen (Introduction to *Memory on Cloth*, 2002)

Traditionally, shibori is associated with gathering material tightly in different pattern modalities using various equipment to provide a resist when dyeing. Woven shibori is an effective way for weavers to create intricate patterning for interesting dyeing effects – you can dye the projecting surfaces different colours – but it also can create dimensional texture in cloth as another end result.

The first International Shibori Symposium, held in Nagoya in 1992, redefined shibori as 'a process of manipulating two-dimensional fabric into three-dimensional shapes'. This led to an expansion of how artists use and identify with shibori, resulting in much experimentation within the handweaving community.

The meaning of shibori (root verb *shiboru*) is 'to wring, squeeze, press' and it is this squeezing and pressing in predetermined patterns through the pulling up of supplementary warps and/or wefts that gives the three-dimensional possibilities. It can be used for dramatic and effective surfaces that act against each other and create shadows, especially with effective lighting. To that end, white or ecru yarns work best, with the added bonus that they can also dye easily. If you wish, you can use coloured yarns to create your textured cloth, which can be overdyed as required for different effects.

The textural version requires you to select certain warp and/or weft yarns, which are formed into shape prior to wet-finishing. How you wet-finish depends on the yarns you have selected to use.

The terms 'shibori warp/weft' and 'pattern warp/weft' are interchangeable in this book.

Textured shibori is created by weaving gathering threads into fabric, then pulling the gathering threads tightly up before wet-finishing the cloth. Pleats, puckers and folds are etched into the cloth by using thermoplastic yarns such as polyester that 'remember' the gathered shape through permanent alteration of the yarn's properties. Less permanent alterations are effected through the finishing of silk or cotton, but this is prone to disappearing during future washing.

If weaving for garments, shibori can be used to shape the edges of a length of cloth – for cuffs, or perhaps a waistline.

Shibori can be useful in clothing, as the amount of 'ease' in the fabric created through the expanding of the gathered area can flatter the underlying body shape.

One adaptation of shibori is known as 'crimp cloth' and was devised by Dianne Totten specifically for clothing.

Shibori samples prior to being pulled up.

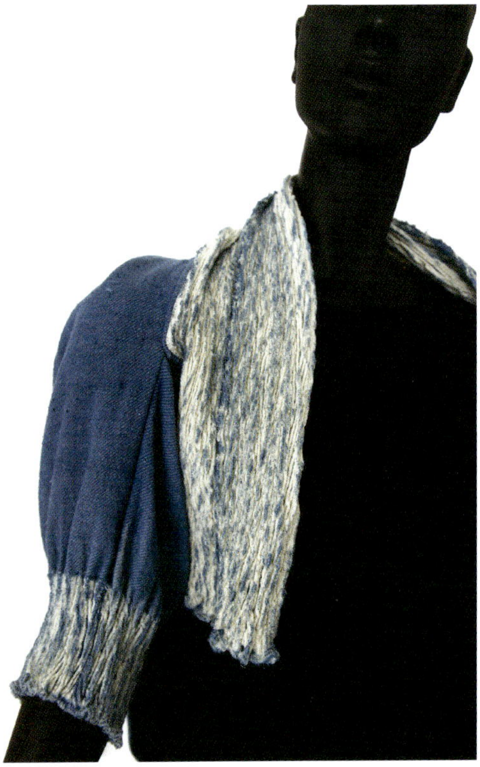

Eileen Hallman's indigo jacket illustrates shibori used for effective cuffs and collars. (Photo: Rebecca D'Angelo)

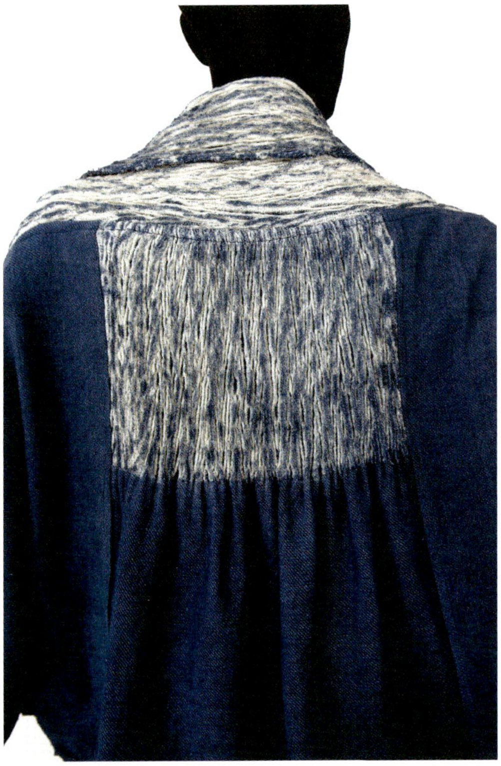

The shibori here is used to gather the fabric at the shoulder and upper back, allowing for a fuller fabric at the bust and waist. (Photo: Rebecca D'Angelo)

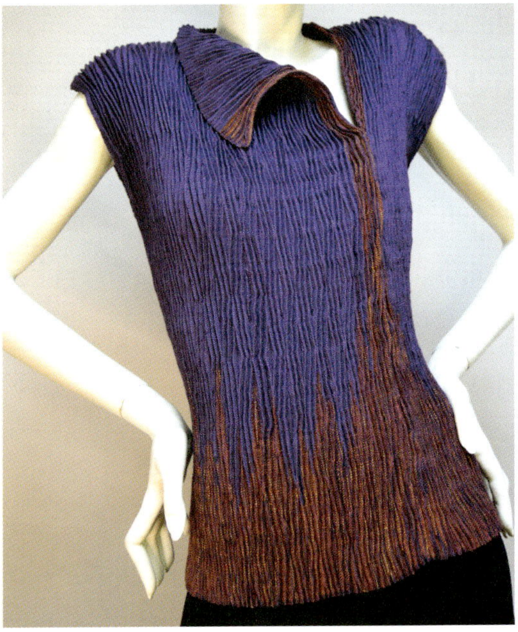

Dianne Totten's crimp fabric with its extended point-effect design makes a lovely top using clasped weft to achieve the clear colour distinction at the base of the fabric and down one seam. (Photos: Dianne Totten)

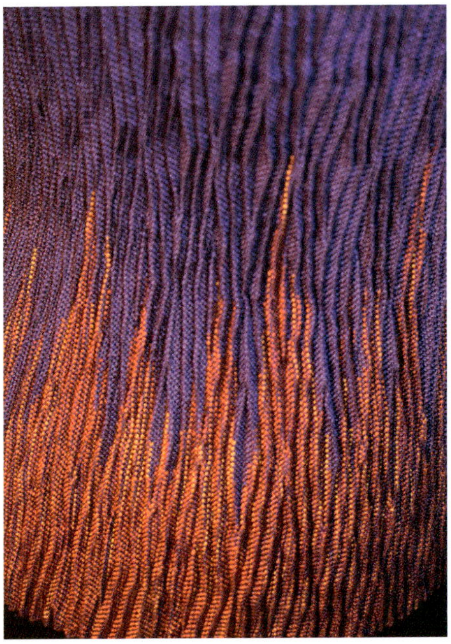

This shows how the clasped weft (the fabric is woven sideways) has been used effectively for a contrast in colour.

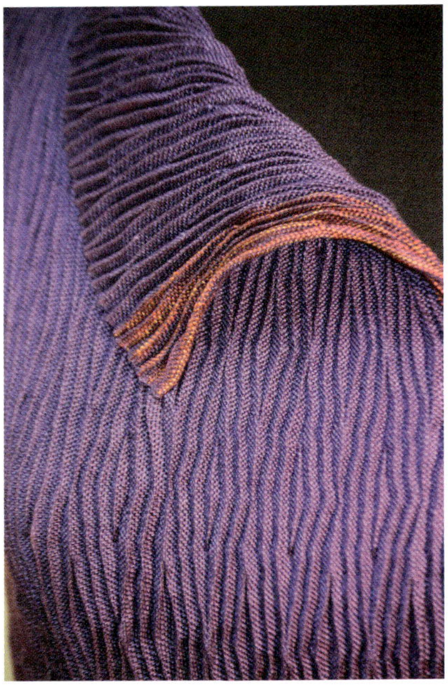

Colour used in this way helps to highlight the neckline.

TECHNICAL INFORMATION

The basic ground cloth for shibori is most often plain weave, interspersed in the weaving with a supplementary pattern weft, which is placed where you wish the texture to be anchored. The most readily recognisable form of supplementary threads are the pattern wefts in the overshot designs, especially recognisable in colonial coverlets.

Woven shibori allows us to place the pattern wefts in specific places as the fabric is being woven. With two shafts, such as a rigid heddle or a two-shaft loom, the shibori weft can be placed exactly where you wish by hand manipulation, selecting which individual threads to pass the shibori weft over, where to separate the warp threads to allow the shibori weft to pass underneath the warp, and where to bring it back up again, plus how many times you wish to do this in the passage of one pattern pick.

The resulting floats of the shibori weft between anchor points dictate which way the fabric will be distorted once it is gathered. Wherever a float is above or beneath the fabric, the cloth will fold or pucker away from the float. The shibori weft does not have to weave in like a normal thread. It is in one of two positions in the pattern picks:

1. On the surface of the fabric
2. On the underside, or reverse, of the fabric

The design freedom on these simpler looms is the reward; however, the hand manipulation takes time.

Using two more shafts (i.e. a four-shaft loom) to create the shibori, there is less creative freedom in exactly where and how you create your floats, but it is an easier and faster weaving experience. Decisions can be made in advance as to how to thread the two shafts not required for the ground weave fabric in order to create warp shibori patterns, or alternatively to thread two different plain weave blocks for weft shibori effects.

The book *Woven Shibori* by Catharine Ellis is an invaluable tool to understanding and creating shaft-woven shibori designs.

More shafts give more design possibilities.

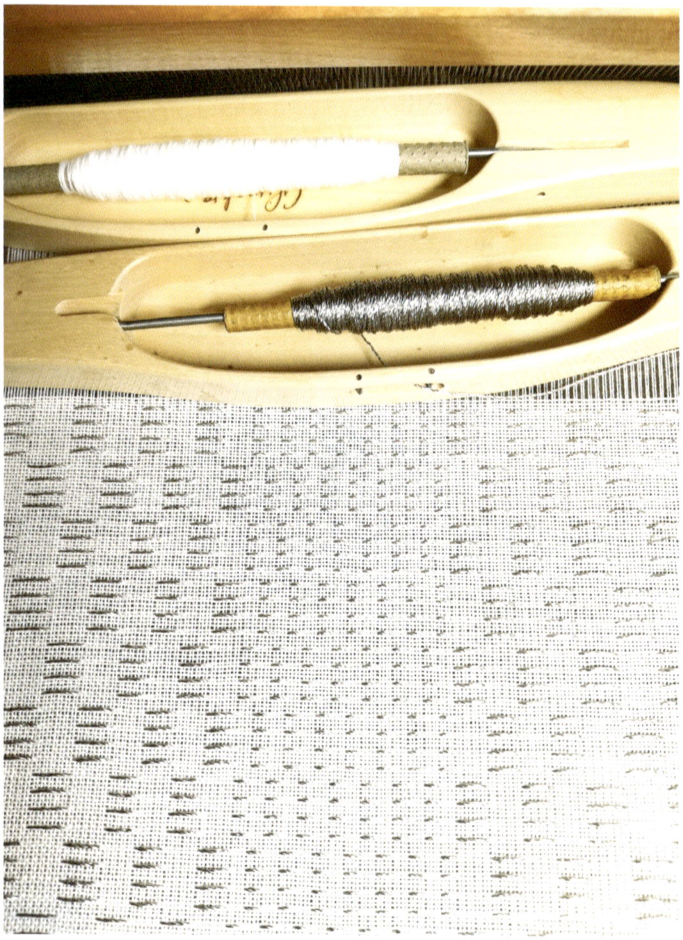

Four-shaft weft shibori on the loom showing both the ground weft (white) and the shibori weft (silver).

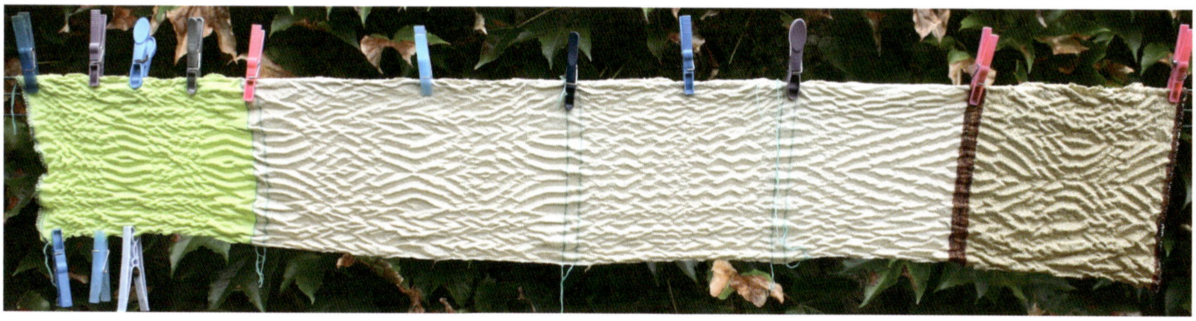

Eight-shaft samples hung on a washing line after steaming. Here, clothes pegs have been attached to add a little weight to the edge of one sample.

GROUND WEAVE

The ground weave is usually plain weave for several reasons:

- It only requires two shafts per block, leaving the remainder of the shafts on the loom for more blocks to create more intricate designs; for including warp shibori ends; or for a combination of both block areas and warp shibori ends.
- The weave structure is so simple that it does not visually detract from the action going on with the dimensional texture created by the shibori gathering. The eyes and brain tend to see visual cues before textural ones.
- It is easy to focus on weaving the shibori pattern if the ground weave is a simple plain weave.

Other weaves are possible, including twills and twill derivatives, and crepe weaves, which give the fabric a textured surface. An all-over design such as a crepe is less likely to detract from the dimensional texture and can give extra subtle depth cues, but these are usually only available to weavers with more than eight-shaft looms.

Yarn Choices: Ground Weave

It is the ground weave that will hold the shaping so specific types of yarns are generally used in order for the shibori patterning to remain after wet-finishing. Anything thermoplastic will hold the shape if it is fixed through steaming.

Polyester

Polyester is probably one of the easiest of these to get hold of – it can usually be found in sewing or weaving shops. Use either in the warp or weft, or both together to create many different texture surfaces. If the pleating is to be horizontal (created through the use of shibori pattern threads in the warp), then use the polyester in the warp. If vertical folds are desired (weft shibori), use polyester in the weft. For both directions, it can be used in both warp and weft.

If shaping is desired in one direction only, the cloth can combine a polyester or similar yarn with a more organic one, such as cotton. This combines the softness and comfort of cotton with the thermoplastic qualities in the polyester. Cotton allows for a certain softness in visual appearance, especially if you choose not to tighten the pleats to their maximum when pulling up the shibori threads.

Different effects will also occur between the cotton and the polyester when using some dyes, which could be really effective, especially when using a natural cotton and a very white ('optic' or 'polar' white) in the polyester. Of course, many pre-dyed colours of both yarns are available, which can be used for tonal or contrasting effects. Experimentation is the name of the game.

Wool

Another yarn choice could be wool. This can either be steamed or washed with agitation to full, or washed and tumbled dried to give differing results. Harder twists will give a different texture and look than merino or softer-spun worsteds. As ever, sample before committing to a specific project warp.

Linen, Paper or Elastane Yarns

Other yarn choices can be linen, paper or yarns spun or plied with elastane. To avoid nasty surprises, it is advisable to sample fabric with any yarns that do not contain wool, thermoplastic or elastane. You could wet-finish them twice: once to set the texture and then again to check whether or not they will hold the shibori effects when laundered further.

The choice of weight of yarn is also important as finer ground weaves will pucker, fold and pleat more readily than thicker yarns. Bear in mind the quality of yarns too – fine linen will allow for crisper folds compared to fine wool. The sett needs to be one that will allow for pliability, so regular plain weave with a plain weave sett is recommended. It can be sett a little closer for crisper pleats. As woven shibori

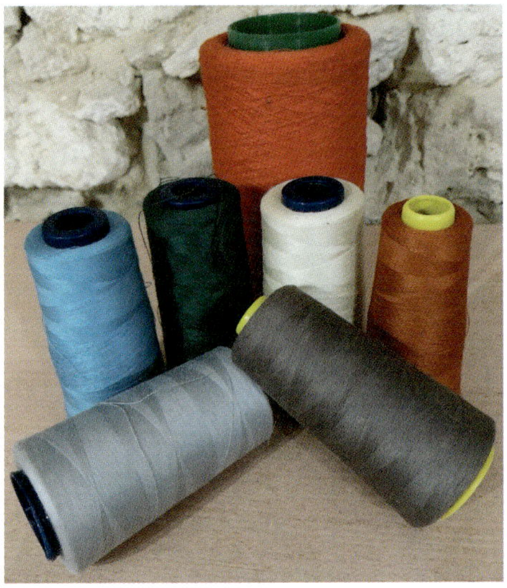

Polyester cones like this can be bought cheaply in notions areas of home-products outlets. Although intended for sewing, if the thickness is one that suits the fabric, it is perfect for use in the ground.

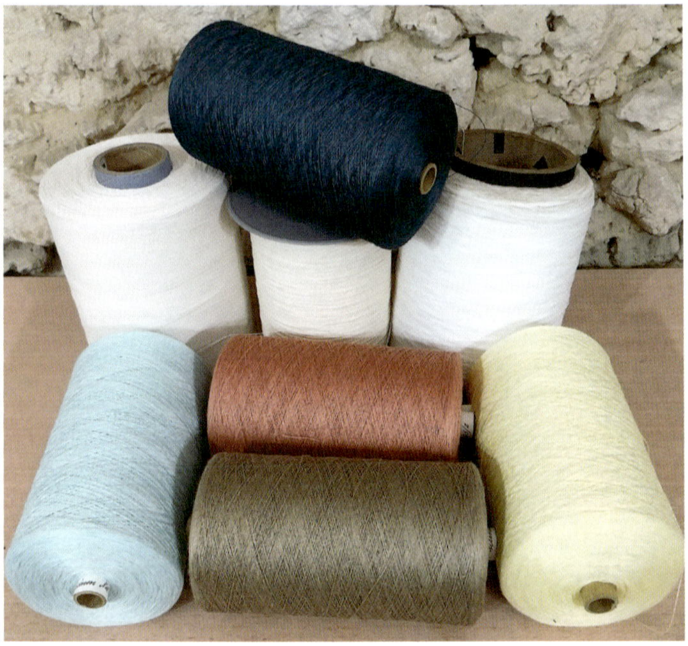

Linen yarns can give a firm hand to a ground cloth. Ironing the folds after the fabric is dry but before removing the shibori wefts can assist with crisp effects. However, test before committing to a large project that they will hold the texture if re-washed after the shibori has been removed. It is often best to use these in conjunction with a polyester in the other direction. Paper yarns (back left and centre) can be effective as they have enhanced twist, although they are largely contained within the ground weave. Elastane (back right) can be used in conjunction with other fibres.

relies on the physical pulling up of gathering threads, it is possible to get away with pushing the envelope, but as always, you need to sample to check that the end result is the one you want!

Yarn Choices: Shibori

The shibori warp or weft is known as a 'supplementary' warp or weft. A supplementary thread is one that is not integral to the cloth; a ground cloth provides the functionality of the cloth, and supplementary threads give an extra pattern to it. In shibori, these supplementary threads can be used as warp ends, weft picks, or both warp and weft. They are generally spaced out and are the gathering threads. It is useful to use a thicker, slippery yarn for these. Highly mercerised cotton will be slick enough to remove easily after finishing and drying. Mercerisation strips the tiny fibres that stick out from the spun cotton and fluffs out the fibres, creating a very smooth surface.

TOP TIP

Check for colour fastness before steaming.

Other shibori threads can be viscose rayon, but be warned that some dyed viscose rayon can lose its colour during the steaming process, bleeding into the fabric.

Alternatively, monofilament (fishing line) can be used. Monofilament can be difficult to knot unless it is quite fine, with the knots slipping undone quite easily, so special care must be taken to ensure that they do not undo during finishing. Above all, ensure that the yarn is slippery or smooth. In America, perle cotton is one that is frequently used.

The thickness of the shibori thread can also be varied. The thicker the shibori yarn, the larger the holes that the removal of the shibori thread leaves in its wake. This can be used as a feature, especially if you intend to use the final fabric as a window dressing, lamp covering or artwork. Because shibori threads are mostly purely floats and do not often interact with the fabric other than passing from one side of the surface to the other – and mostly from one edge to the other – the fabric can be concertinaed along the shibori thread as tightly or loosely as you wish to create different effects from the same patterning.

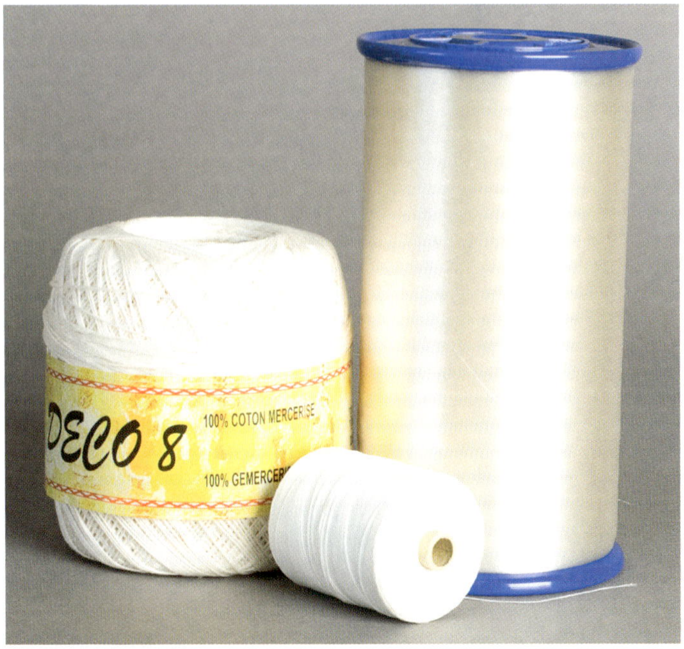

Three shibori wefts: perle (or crochet) cotton (left), hard overtwisted cotton (front) and monofilament (right). Monofilament can be bought in smaller quantities from fishing supply stores as well as haberdashery suppliers. Overtwisted cotton can be found in sailing shops and upholsterers.

WEAVING: SHIBORI WEFT

Shibori is not a difficult technique to learn. It is very similar to traditional overshot in that two shuttles are used: one containing the ground yarn and the other the shibori pattern weft yarn (marked in turquoise on the drafts).

Two or more plain weave picks are woven with the ground weft, followed by a shibori pattern pick. It is useful to have a floating selvedge sleyed at a distance from the body of the warp on one side, or both, so that it can be used to create loops for the shibori weft if weaving the shibori across the full width of the warp. It is not needed for the ground weave if weaving plain weave. A floating selvedge is not a definitive requirement because the shibori wefts can easily be looped without it, but it does help as a reminder for new shibori weavers.

Drafts

Simple shibori designs are very effective. Strong pleats can be formed with just two blocks, tightly pulled. A minimum of two picks of plain weave are required between each shibori pick.

More designs can be explored with eight shafts and four blocks.

If designing with a diagonal line, the more ground weave woven between shibori picks, the more vertical the shibori design. Conversely, the fewer picks between shibori wefts, the shallower the diagonal line.

Merging pleats can be created.

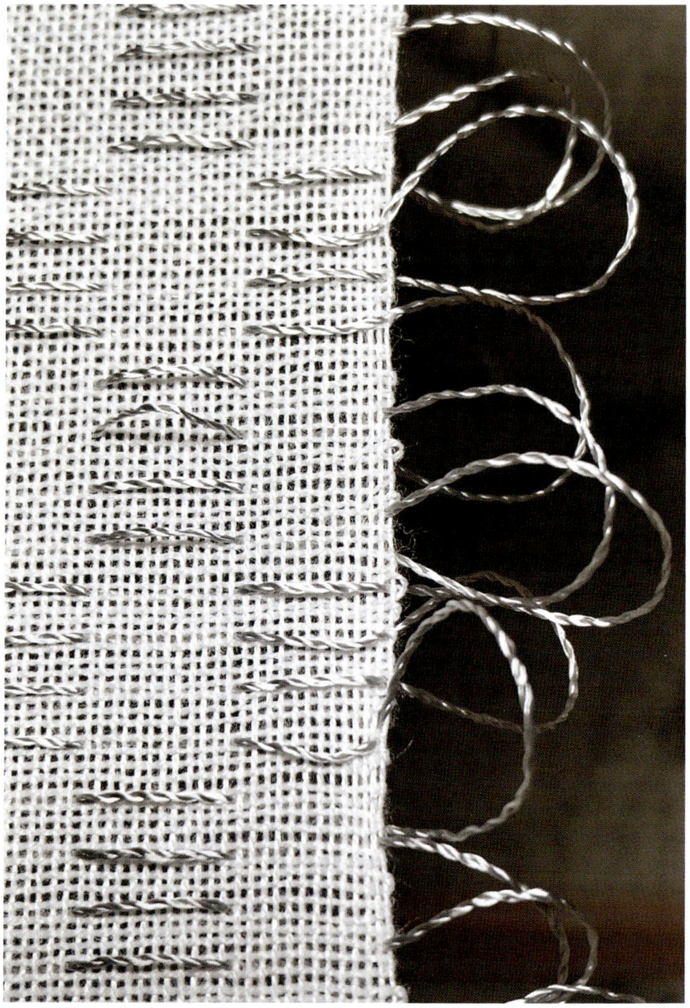

The shibori selvedge loops are shown here. Either a floating selvedge can be placed several dents away from the real fabric selvedge or the shibori weft can be looped, so long as there is sufficient weft available at the ends of the fabric to be able to pull up the shibori weft.

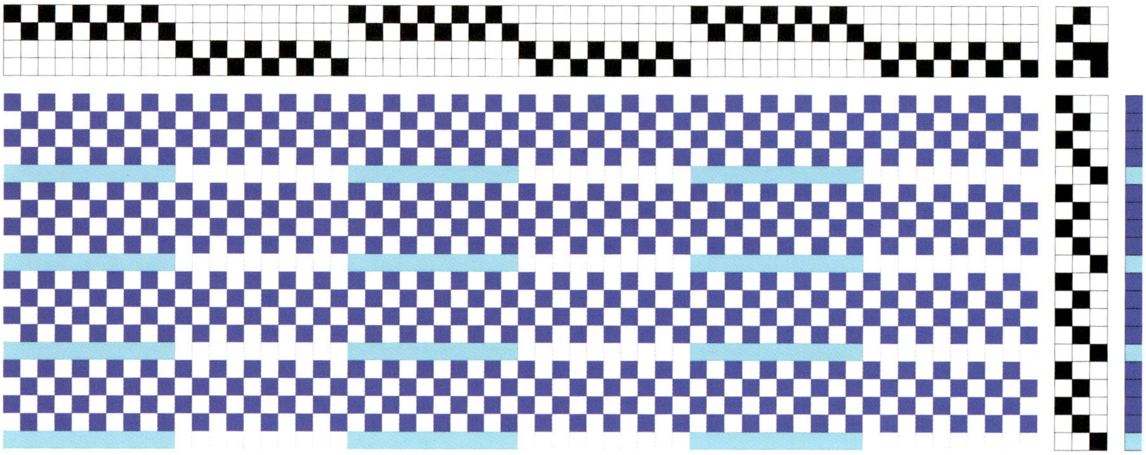

A four-shaft loom allows for two threading blocks for shibori design, using plain weave for the ground. Shibori blocks repeated continually in the same block give straight vertical fold lines in the finished fabric. Weft shibori creates vertical folds in the fabric.

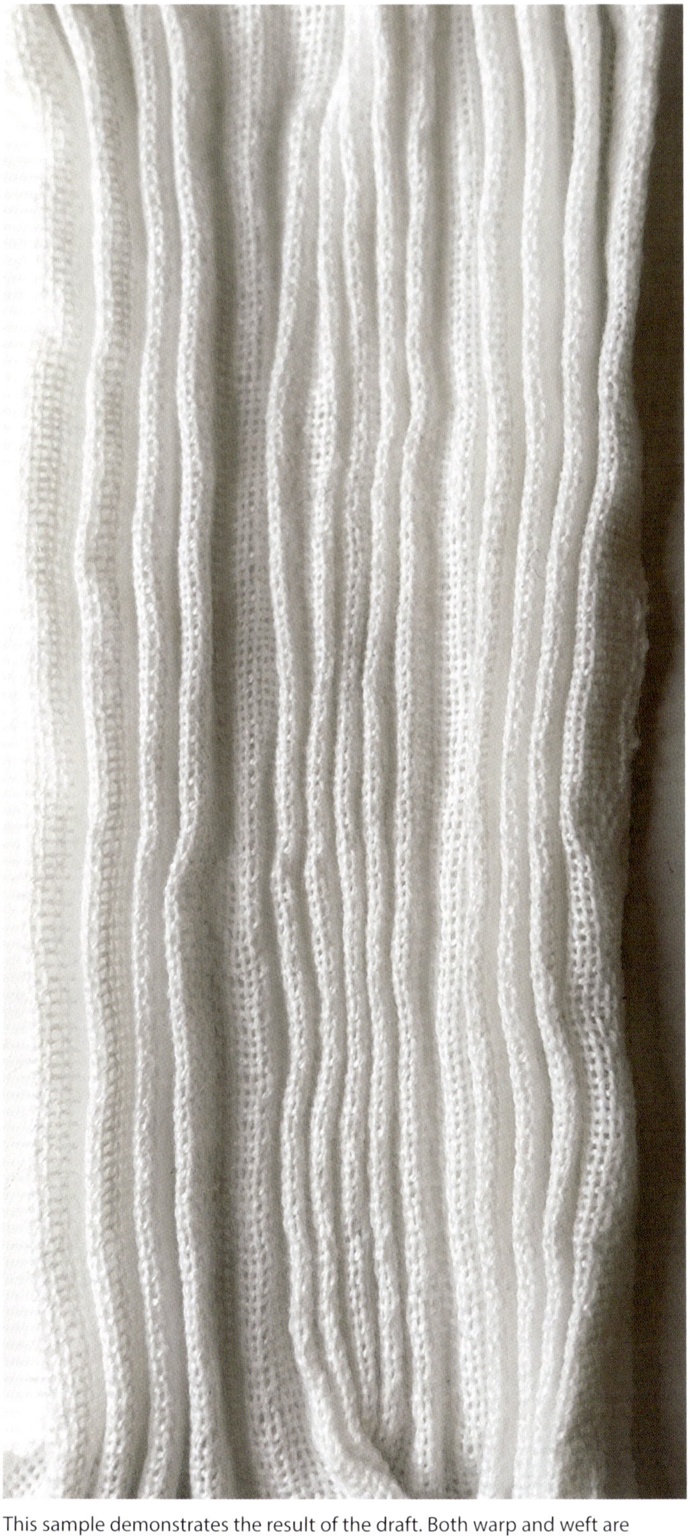

This sample demonstrates the result of the draft. Both warp and weft are polyester, but the warp could be another fibre such as cotton. The result is created through the polyester ground and weft shibori.

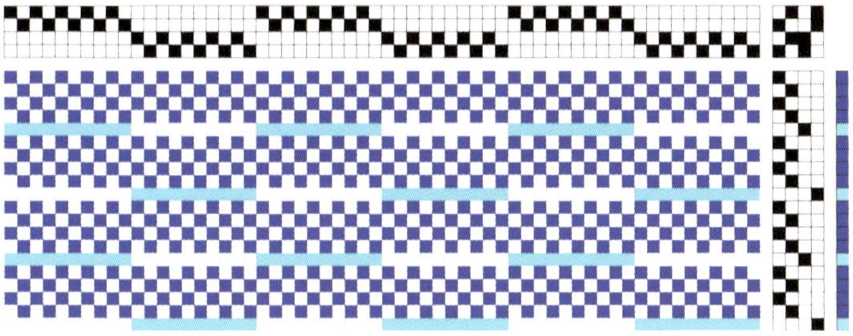

Alternating shibori blocks create a more complex series of folds and textures.

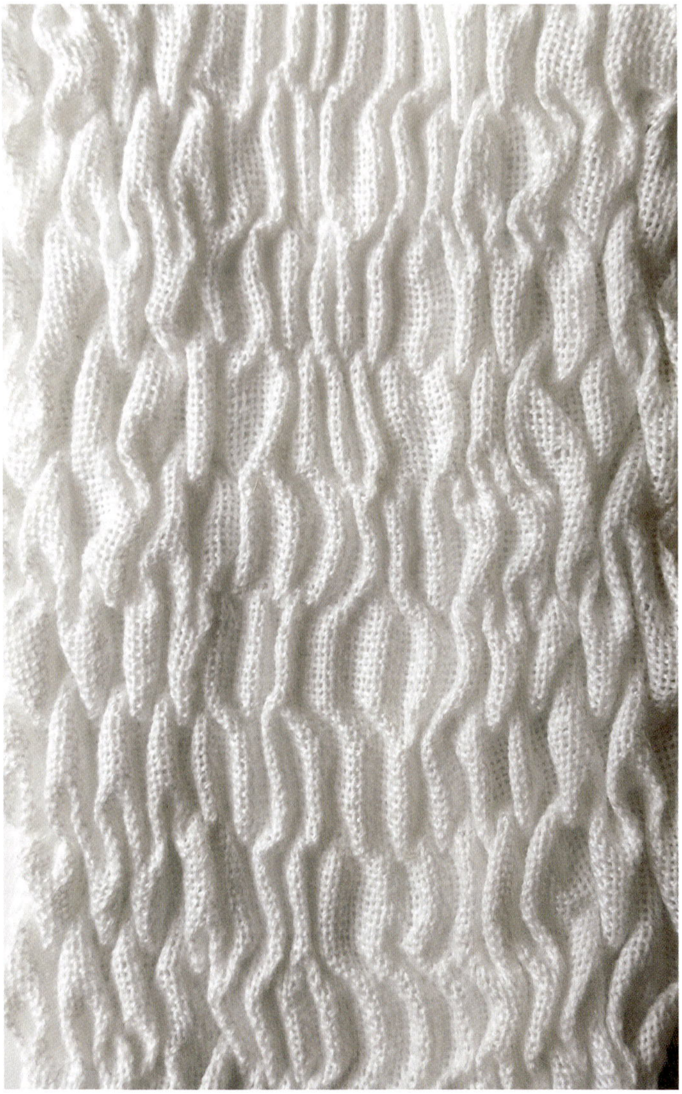

Alternating blocks give a more interesting end result. The shibori was not pulled up tightly across the whole sample and shows a more open area where the fabric was not so compacted during steaming. Additionally, different patterns can be created simply by changing the number of repeats of the shibori weft before switching to the opposite block.

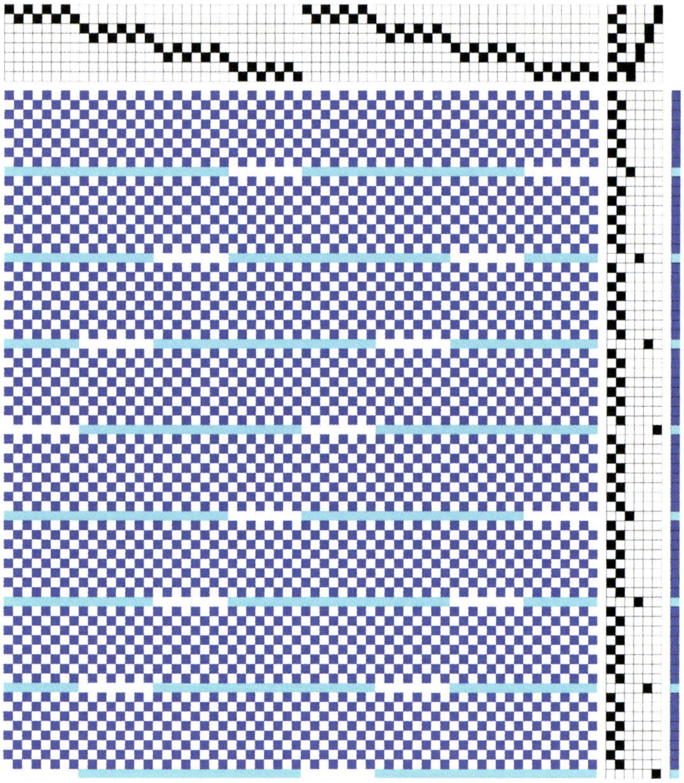

Eight shafts allow for four threading blocks. Increased numbers of plain weave ground picks between shibori picks increases the angle of the shibori design.

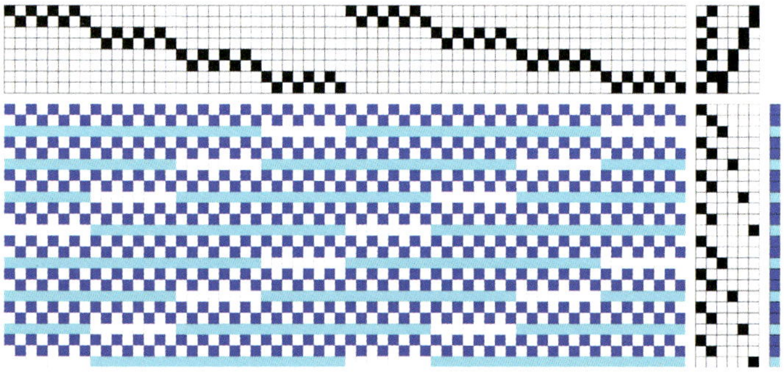

Reduced plain weave ground picks between shibori picks makes the design line shallower.

PROFILE DRAFTS

Shibori drafts are often profile drafts – a shorthand way of giving all the design information required without including absolutely everything. No ground weave is included, just the patterning.

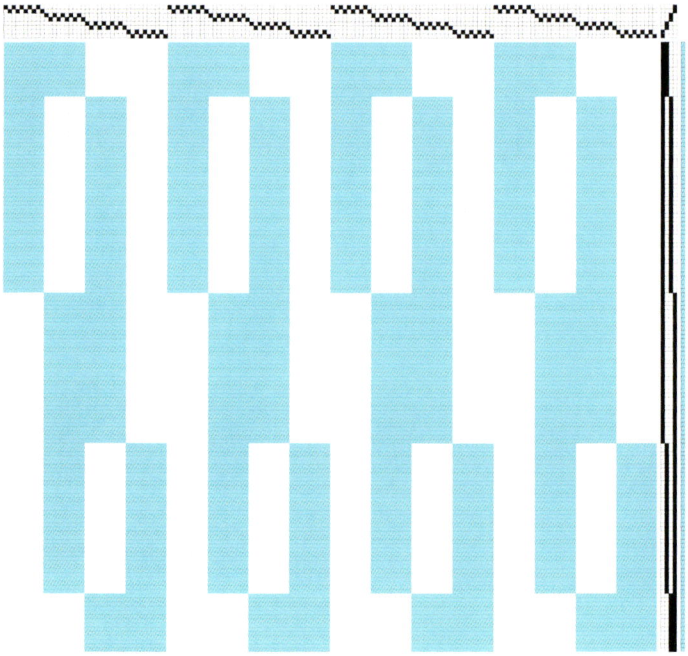

This profile draft shows four ways of combining two threading blocks for shibori to give various folding results.

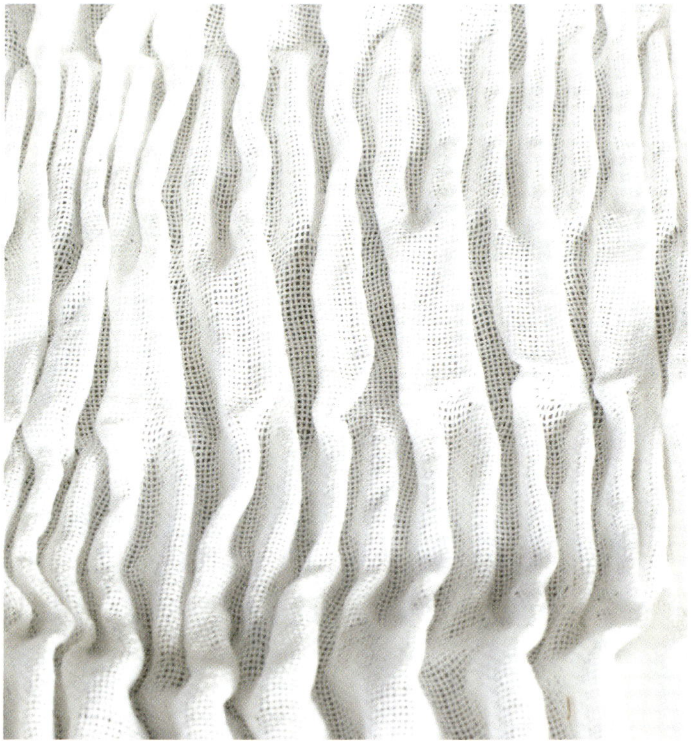

Four threading blocks on eight shafts can be combined to create a series of merging pleats in any combination desired. Polyester is used in warp and weft. (Photo: Colin Usher)

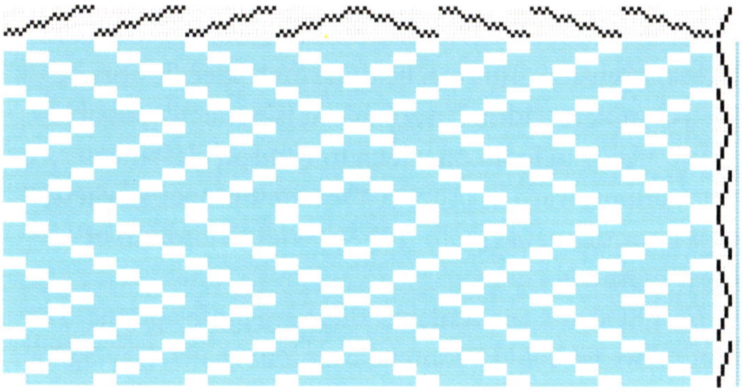

The profile draft shows the result of using only one block with both an extended point block threading and a different point block treadling. The long shibori float will pull the opposite side into a deep peak moving away from the float. The white areas will be the small peak coming up from the fabric.

Diamond pleats can be formed using the same shibori weft block principles. Using two adjacent blocks and advancing twill fashion, the texture will be the same amount on both sides. However, using a single block twill fashion, the two sides of the fabric have differing amounts of pleating. With only one block being raised, the top of the fabric will have small shibori peaks, while the reverse will have deeper ones.

Rather than blocks, a regular twill tie-up can also be used to give a more interrupted edge to the pleat formation, as we saw in Chapter 5.

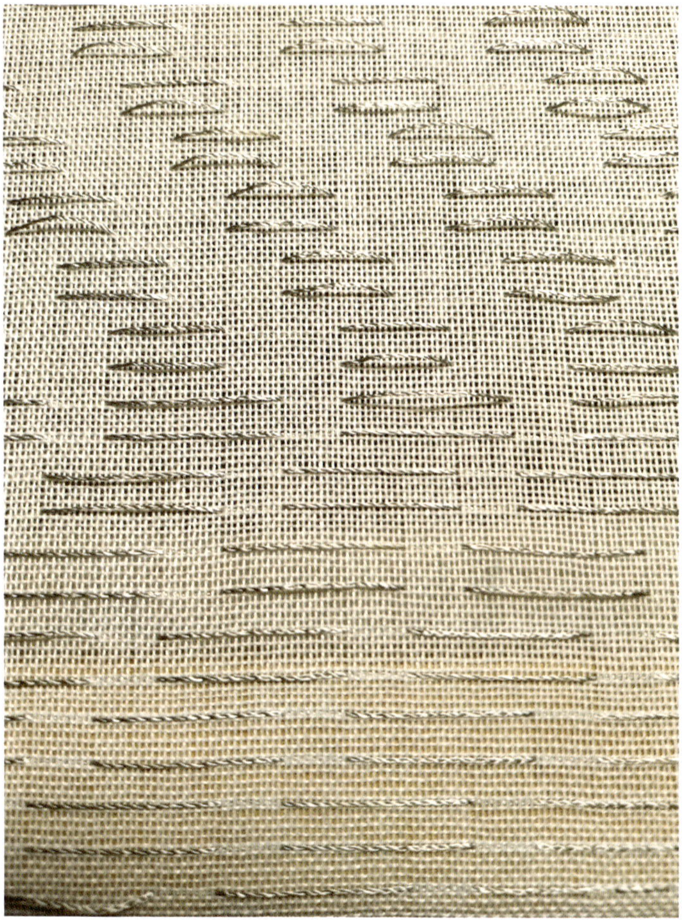

Weft shibori in a block point design on the loom.

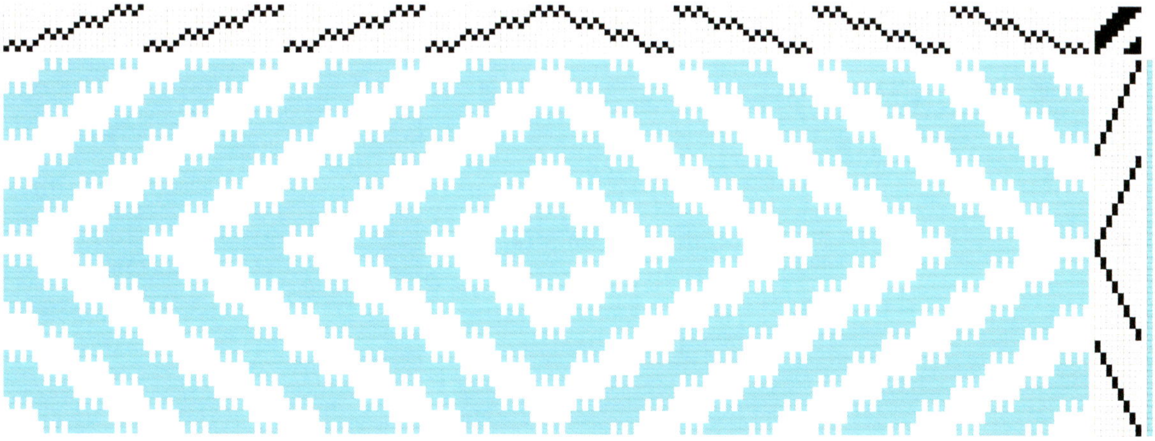

Using two blocks and moving through the blocks in a twill fashion in the tie-up will give areas of semi-texture as well as the pleats. The treadling is now a longer mirrored design.

Weft Only or Warp Only

To create differing texture areas, the shibori weft does not have to be pulled up with the same intensity across the whole design.

TOP TIP

When pulling up tightly, use a chopstick or other tool to make it easier on both your hands and your patience!

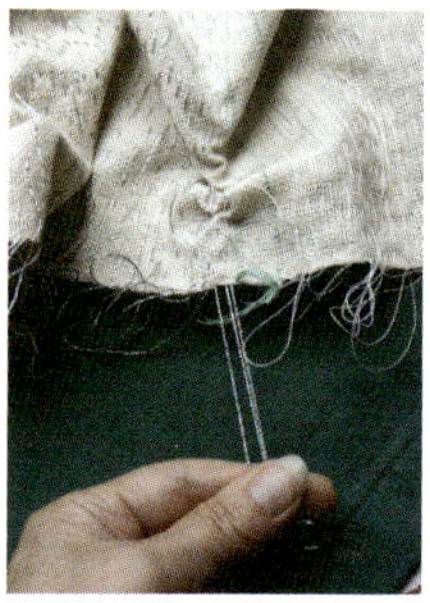
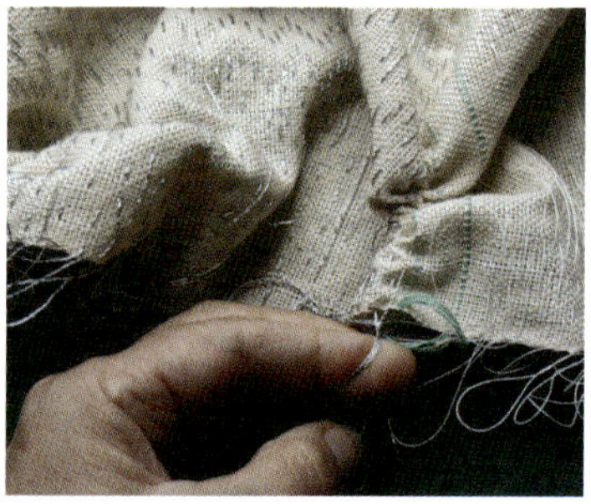
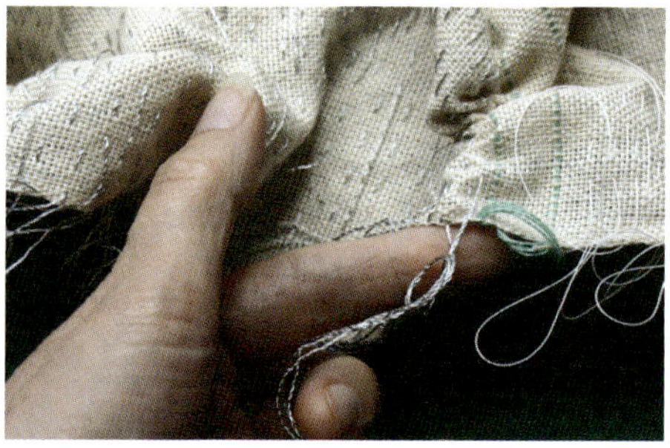
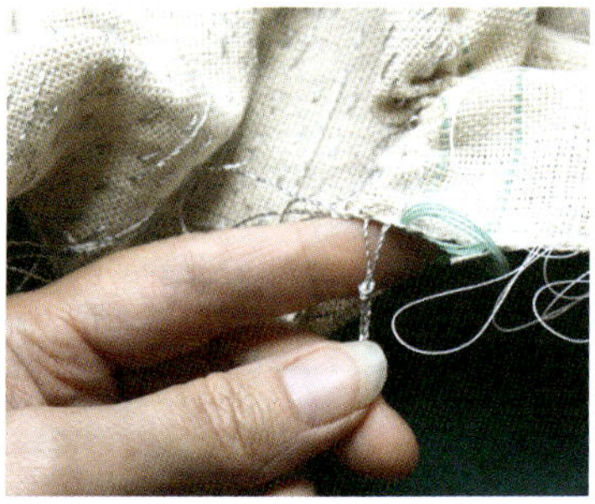

Once the fabric is woven in the desired weave structure, the shibori threads are then pulled up. If it is in the weft and there are shibori loops on both sides of the fabric, work your way along one side, tying small groups of shibori wefts into overhand knots. If there are irregular or odd numbers of shibori wefts, it can be preferable to group them in twos or threes and pull them up together. If it is in the warp, group the threads into roughly ½in (1.3cm) bundles.

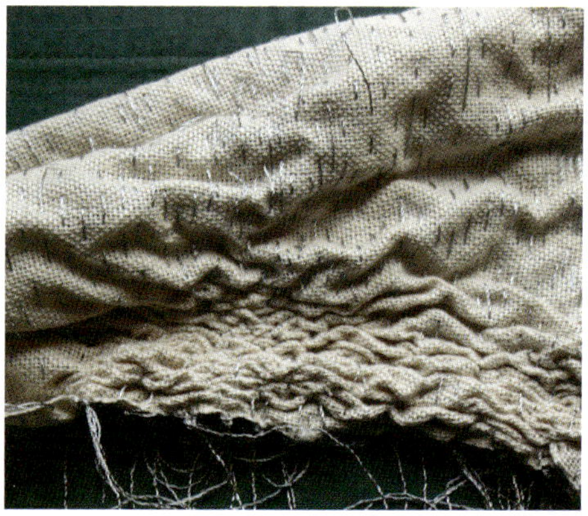
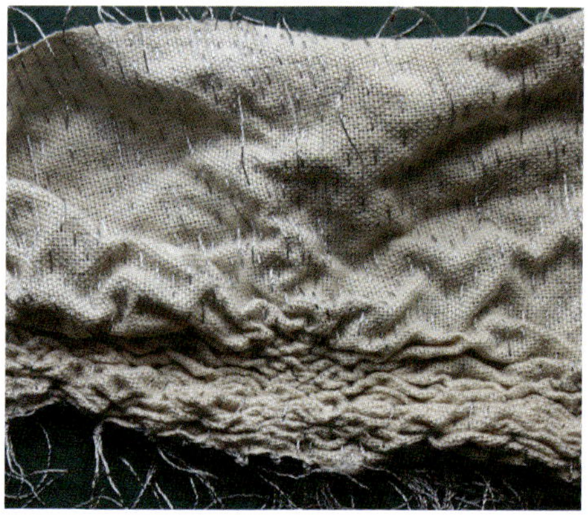

When doing the initial pulling up, it is useful to knot groups if around one-third of the width is initially pulled up. Move on to the next group. Pulling one side at a time makes the job easier. Once one side is completed, start on the other side. If loops are only on one side, then pull up on one side only. It is a useful rule of thumb to use loops on one side only when it is a narrow cloth, but to use loops on both sides and pull from each side towards the centre of the cloth if the fabric is wider than around 6in (15cm).

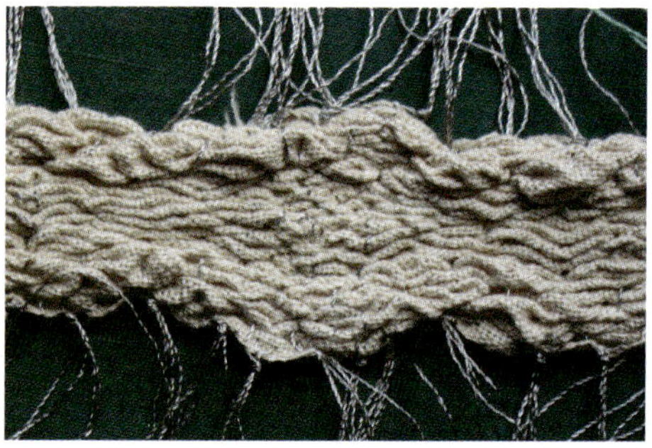
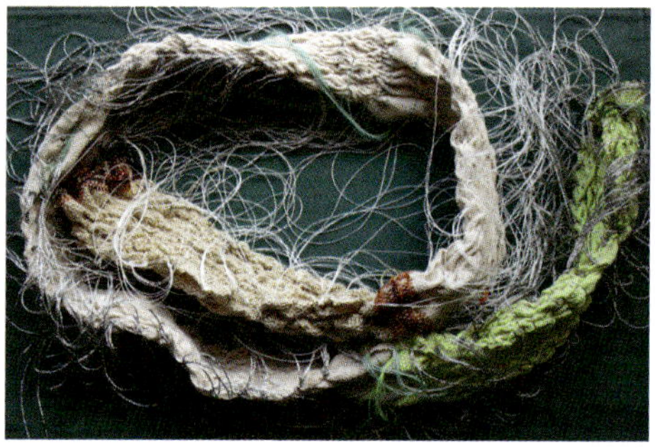

All the shibori threads can be pulled up tightly or the amount of gathering can be varied along the length. It is awkward to pull up a wide piece tightly in one go as the extreme angles created through pulling up individual groups of shibori wefts makes it difficult to see which group to pull up next. In this situation, pull up to a convenient and easy stage for the second side, then go back to the beginning of that side and pull up some more.
Once the whole length is pulled up, the fabric can be coiled ready to be put in a steaming receptacle.

Pulling Up

SHIBORI FOR DYEING

The gathering threads need to be pulled tightly if the dyes are not to penetrate into the centre of the fold.

Shibori for texture only
Tight gathering is not required. In fact, the tighter the pulling, the less apparent the design can be.

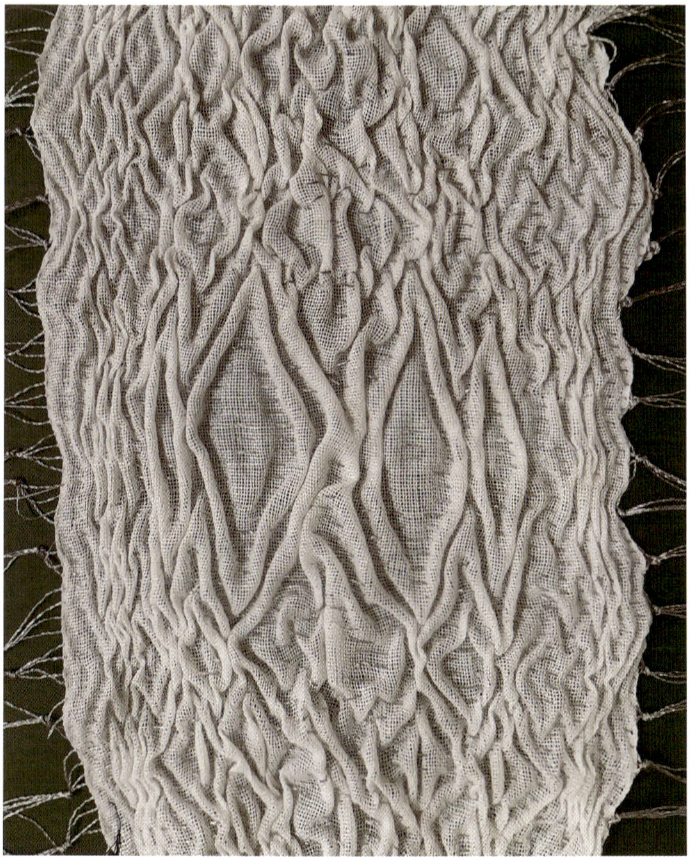

This diamond design shows the shibori pulled up loosely in the middle before steaming.

Textured Features

It is perfectly possible to isolate an area for pulling up to make a textured feature or for that textured feature to move across the surface of the cloth.

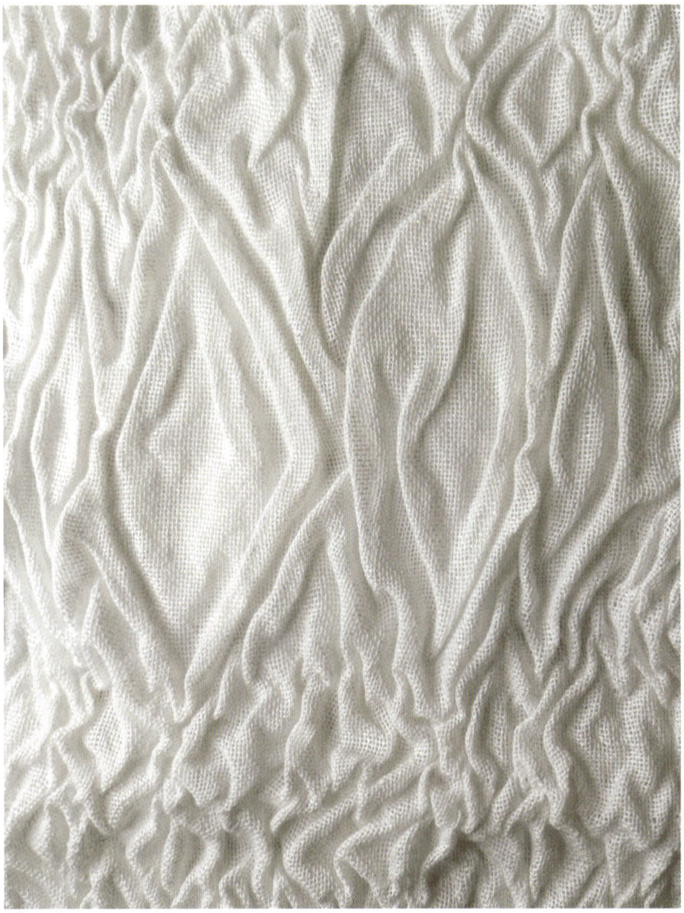

The same fabric after steaming. It is clear to see that the central diamonds have not been pulled as tightly as surrounding areas.

Wet-finishing

Wet-finishing is vital in order to 'fix' the shaping created through the gathering of the fabric. At this point, decisions can be made whether to dye the fabric, or whether to go ahead with just the texture. If dyeing, follow the dyeing instructions for both the yarns and the dye products being used.

As mentioned before, steaming of polyester or man-made petrochemical yarns is ideal. If you need to immerse the fabric into very hot water (wearing protective gloves if required), it may not need to be steamed afterwards if the heat-setting temperature has been reached during the

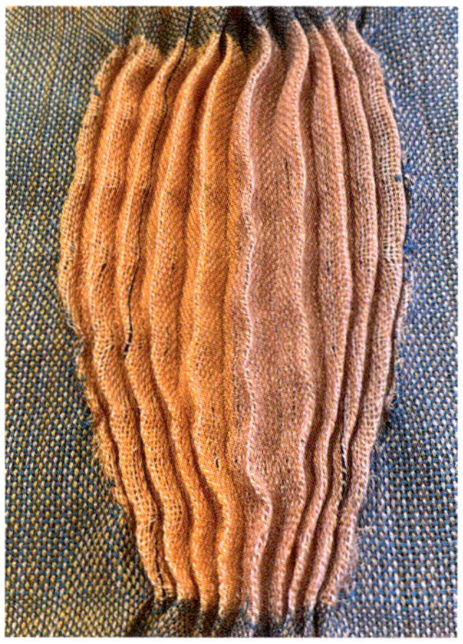

Amy Parker has experimented with what is possible when using shibori for specific areas. Here, an isolated area has been placed in the middle of a flat fabric, inspired by the underside of mushrooms.

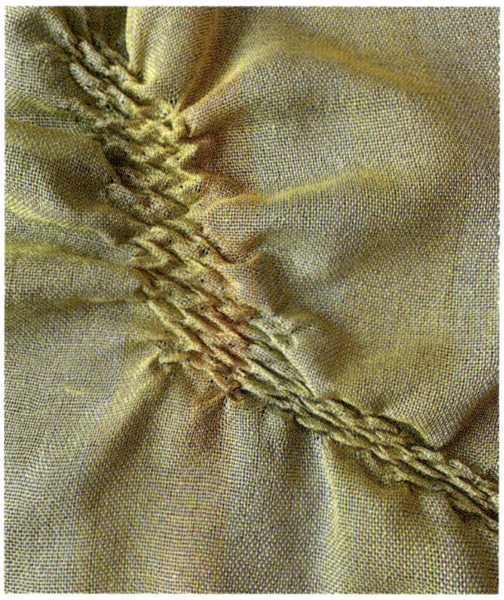

The shibori is going for a walk across the fabric.

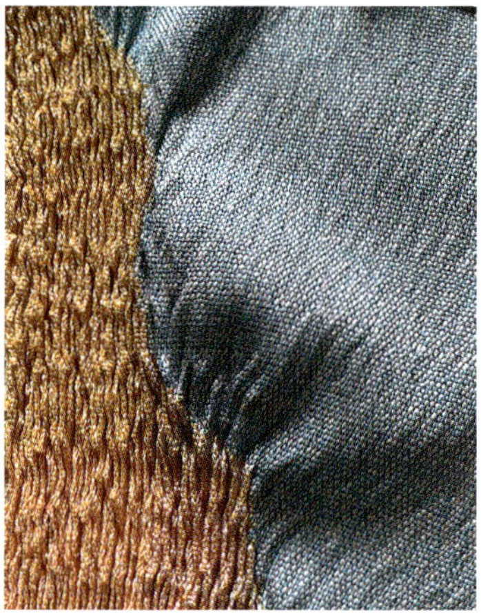

Here she uses clasped weft, but only using the shibori in one of the weft areas. The shibori area ground yarn is polyester used double and the blue ground has a 60/2 silk weft.

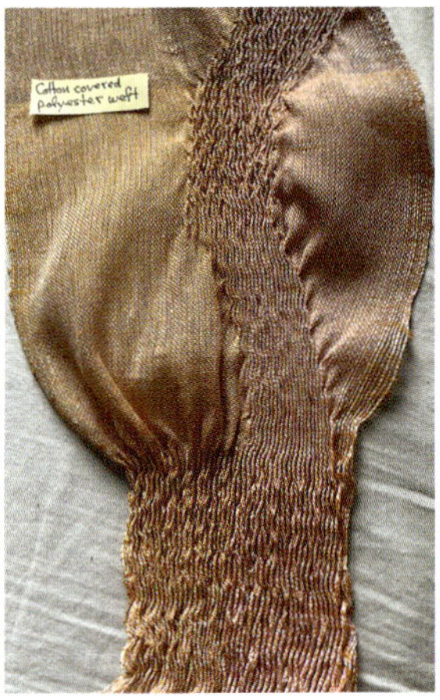

This sample includes both shaping and meandering areas. (Photos: Amy Parker)

dyeing process. It is advisable to check the temperature required by the heat-setting yarn to enable this.

If using a cold-dyeing process, or one that doesn't reach the temperature that the heat-setting yarn requires to change its form, then steam prior to dyeing.

A regular food steamer can be used for steaming. Other devices such as a microwave or pressure cooker can also be used, as can specialised fabric-steaming equipment. For health and safety reasons, please devote any kitchen equipment involving dyeing to textile use only – do not use for food purposes.

Wet out the fabric thoroughly before putting it into the steam receptacle. Steaming for an hour is often recommended, but successful samples have resulted with as little as 20 minutes, depending on the yarn. Leave to cool before removing from the steamer and place to air dry.

If a ground weft such as wool has been used, hand wash the fabric before removing the shibori threads, using hot sudsy water, agitating if desired to help the folds full a little, assisting the fabric with its shibori 'memory'. A little fulling will only impact the exposed folds of the pleating. More fulling will affect more of the fabric and make the pleats tighter and harder to open. It is another design choice.

Rinse fully to remove the soap and leave to air dry.

With tightly gathered fabric, ensure it is fully dry before removing the shibori wefts as wet fabric will 'grab' the weft, making it difficult to remove easily. When dry, select one side and pull the first group of knotted shibori wefts away from the fabric so that the individual shibori wefts can be seen. Cut just below the knot, ensuring that the woven cloth is not accidently snipped! Either pull the other end of that same group and release the fabric immediately or work down one side cutting all the knots away and then pull out the freed shibori wefts to reveal the textural fabric in all its glory.

TOP TIP

Line the steaming baskets with a wet tea-towel as this prevents scorching of the fabric.

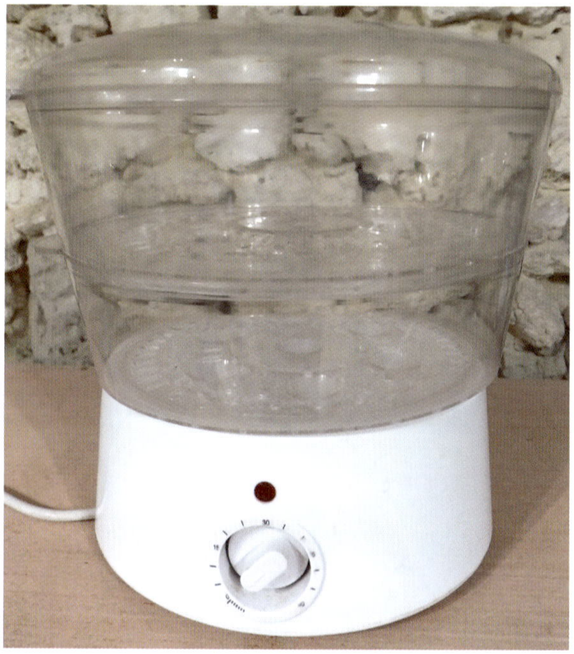

A plastic food steamer is a very good method for setting thermoplastic or wool yarns for shibori.

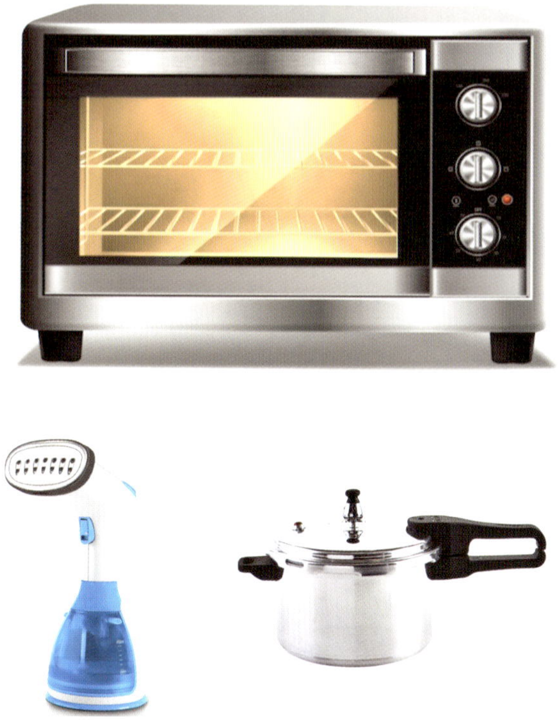

Other steaming appliances include microwave, pressure cooker and garment steamers.

WEAVING: WARP AND WEFT SHIBORI COMBINED

Designing for warp and weft shibori combined is a little trickier. Sampling is required to ensure that the required effects are achieved in both directions. The draft included here is just a starting point. Geometric designs can be a lot of fun as well as more organic lines.

Which direction is pulled up first can be important. As usual, it is a personal choice and might require some sampling if a specific effect is desired. For an overall effect, the trick is to do little and often, pulling up a small amount first in one direction then in the other direction. Return to the first direction and pull up a bit more, then pull in the other direction. Repeat until the chosen amount of gathering is made in both directions. Again, a chopstick or knitting/crochet needle can be helpful to protect hands, especially when pulling up tightly.

If the threads are pulled up tightly in one direction first, and then gathered up in the other direction, this has a direct impact on the results as the already-pulled fabric will inhibit the pulling in the other direction. As usual, sample to get the desired effect.

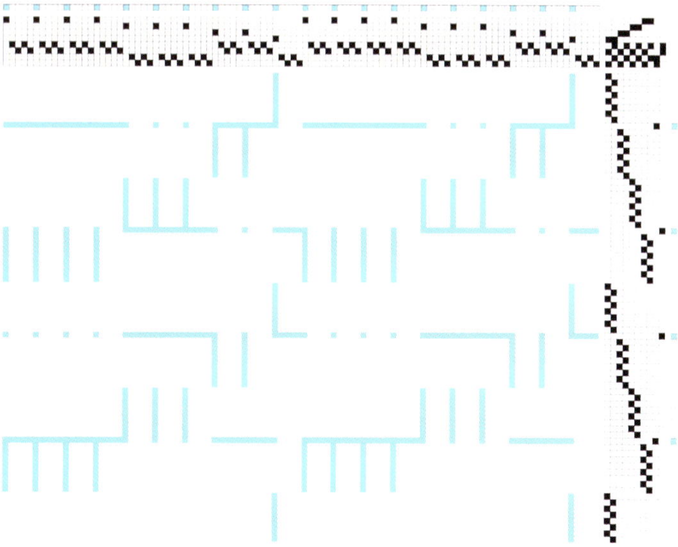

Warp and weft shibori can be combined in the same cloth, as seen in this draft detail.

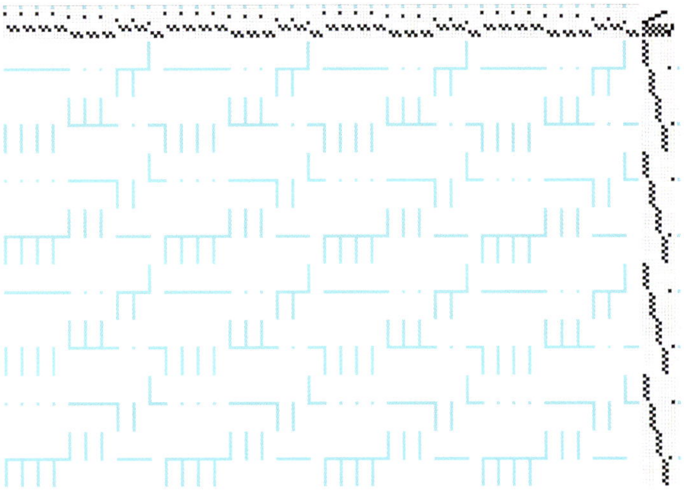

The design might not look particularly inspiring in draft form but it can create a wave effect in the cloth. This has been adapted from an original 24-shaft version.

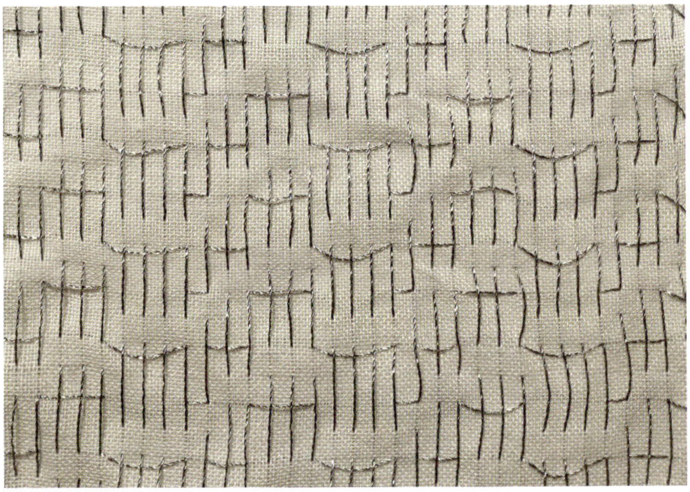

This sample is shown prior to wet-finishing...

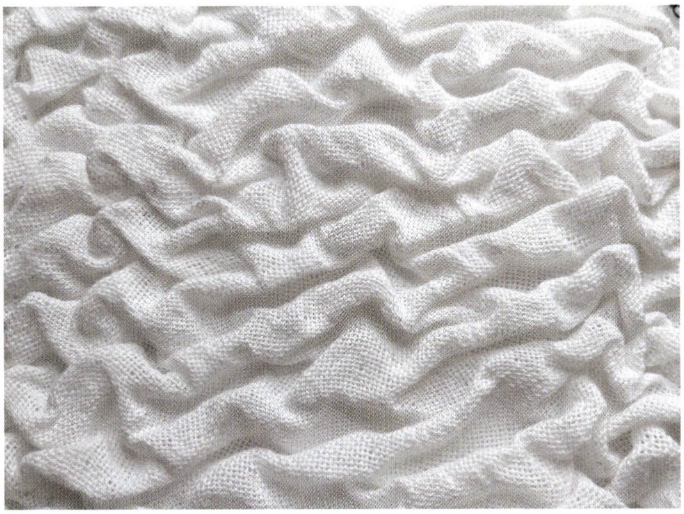

...And after steaming for one hour.

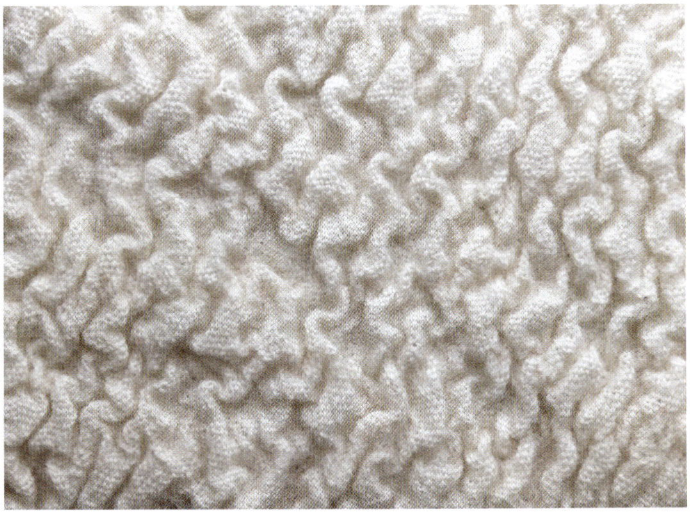

Merino wool was used in this warp and weft shibori sample, which was finished in the steamer. The warp shibori was half-pulled and then the weft shibori was half-pulled before repeating the process until the desired gathering was achieved.

OVERSHOT DESIGNS

Overshot designs can be used as inspiration for shibori. In a typical overshot design, there are areas of weft floats on top, weft floats underneath and places where the pattern weft is also woven into the ground cloth. This is different to normal shibori where there are no sections where the ground cloth is woven with the shibori weft.

Four Shafts

For four-shaft looms there is a variation where all three of the overshot elements are used, including integrating the shibori weft with the ground weave in places to give the effect of the half-tone areas of overshot. There will still be folds created by the areas of pure weft floats on top and underneath the fabric. In shibori, this leads to areas of tighter, more prominent folds either above or below the fabric and areas of flatter fabric in between. This is especially interesting if flat areas or very small puckers are combined with larger folds.

It is fun to explore favourite overshot threadings and to experience which ones give clearer fold lines. More repeats in the ground weft and enlarging threading blocks will give variations.

Eight Shafts

With eight-shaft looms, both traditional shibori and traditional overshot methods can be used.

With traditional shibori, there are four threading blocks (for an eight-shaft loom) and the tie-up can be designed to vary the number of blocks used.

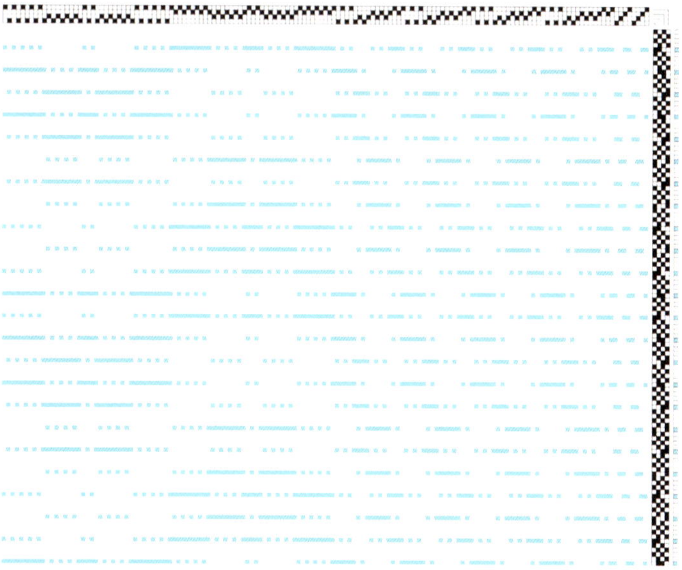

This draft shows the insertion of the plain weave ground at a ratio of four ground picks to one shibori pick.

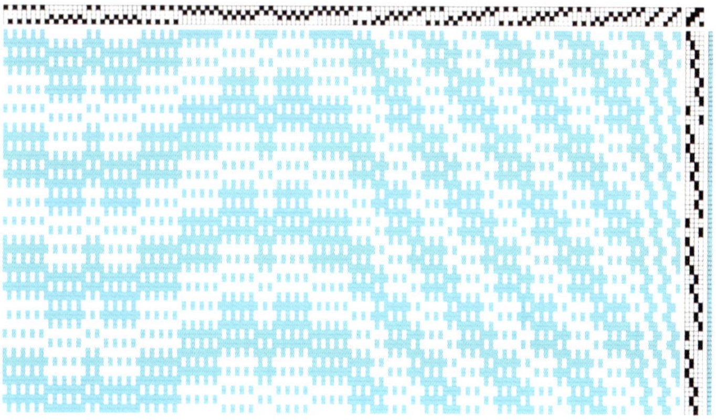

A profile treadling can be very useful to give an idea of the effects of a treadling design on the threading to ascertain whether the result might be something to weave physically. The 2/2 twill-progression tie-up combined with the advancing treadling profile is going to give areas of integration in an overshot fashion.

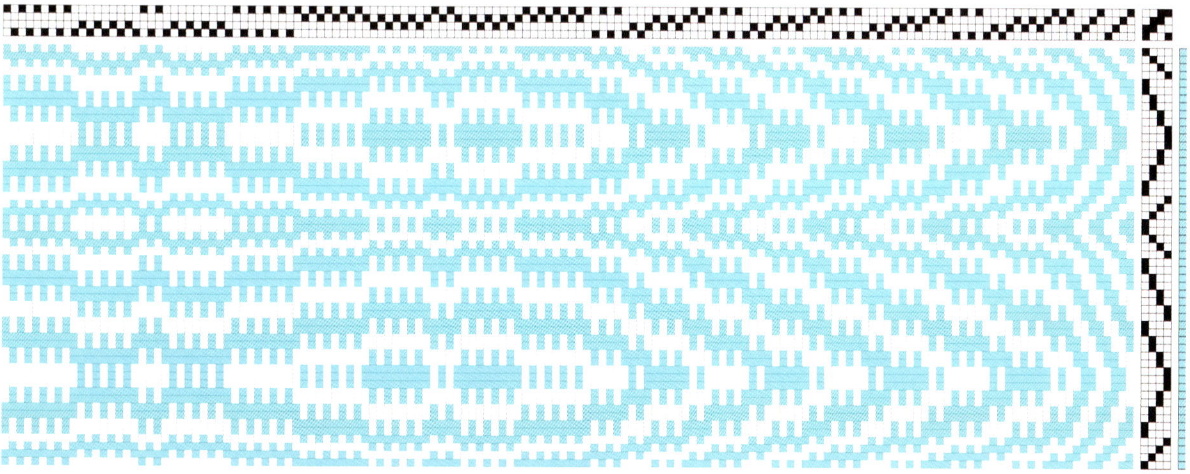

The variation here gives larger areas of solid colour, leading to a higher chance of pleating that will create a desired effect. If this is woven, the plain weave ground needs to be put into the treadling plan, spacing out the shibori wefts. The same principle applies to all the following profile treadling drafts.

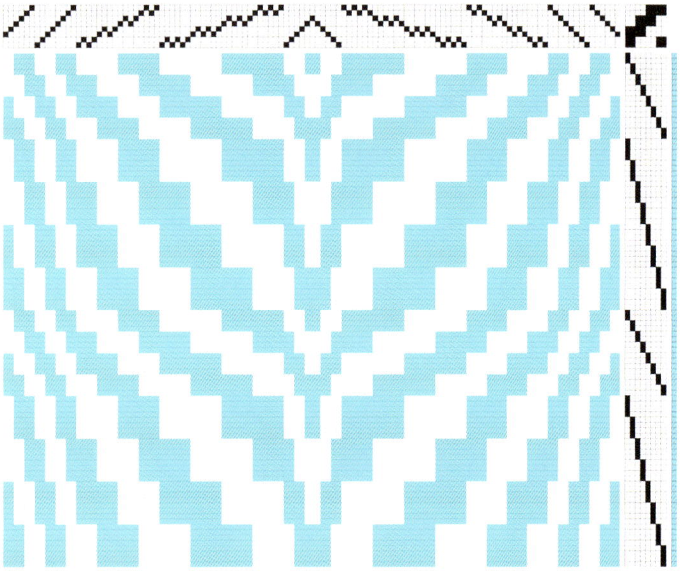

The threading of the Florentine star in overshot fashion is combined with a 2/2 block tie-up, which means clean blocks when applying the weft shibori. Note that each step in the twill has been assigned two columns. This can be rearranged to use only one column, and the treadling would then need to be adapted in order to give the same information in the drawdown. It is important to note that these and following profile treadling drafts require the ground plain weave to be inserted between each shibori pick in a ratio that is decided by the weaver prior to weaving, in order for the resultant fabric to be a woven shibori.

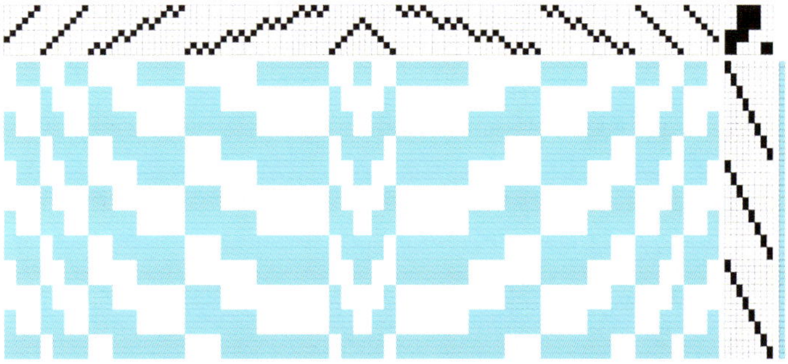

The same threading has been used in this draft but with a different tie-up combination showing the effects.

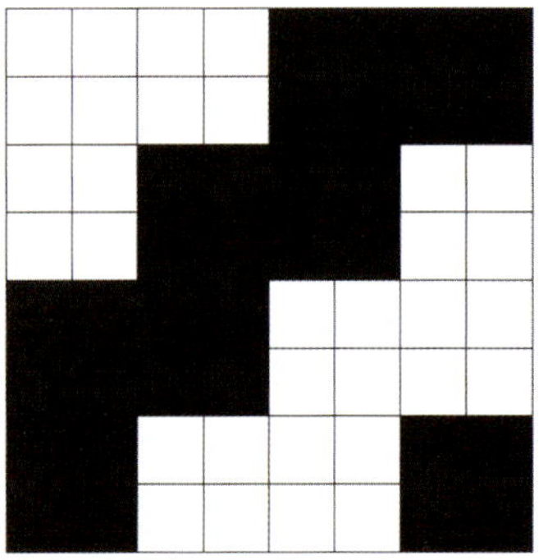

The tie-up shown in detail.

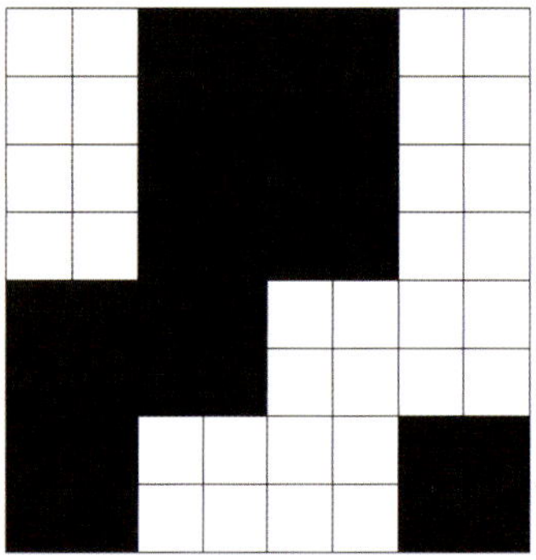

This new tie-up is shown in detail.

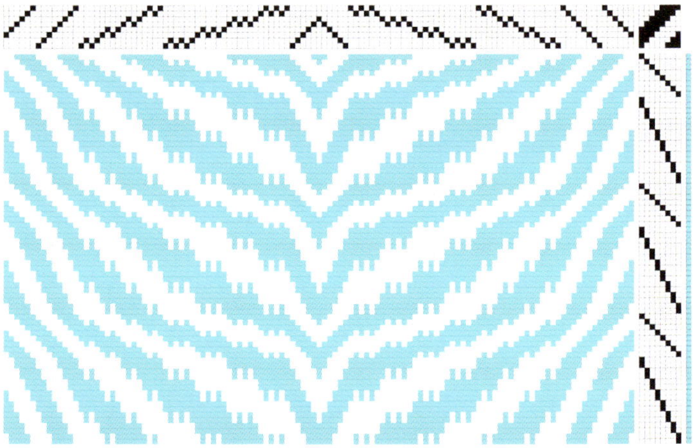

The same threading now employs a 4/4 twill progression in the tie-up and a profile treadling using different angles for the weft blocks by repeating the straight draft but doubling the number of picks for the second repeat. Many variations can be tried.

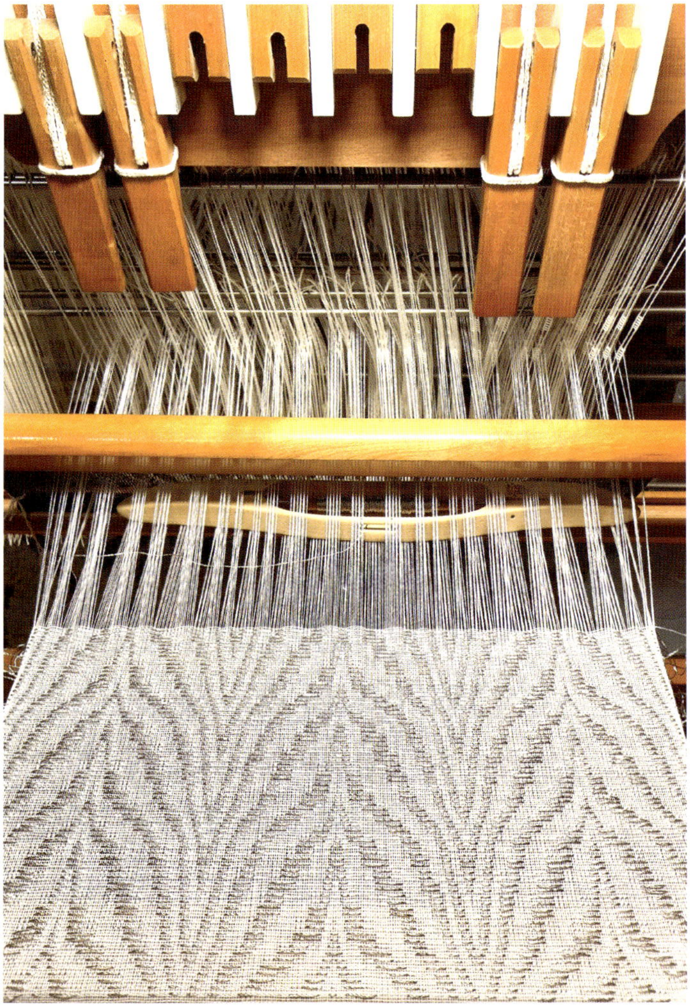

The Florentine Star draft was woven with block shibori rather than twill fashion to give clean blocks.

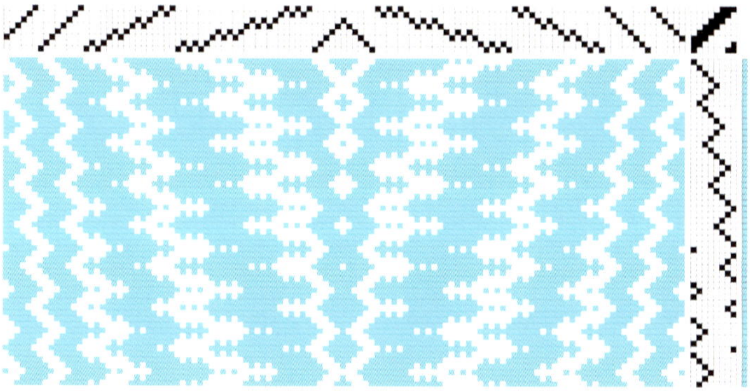

A tie-up of 3/5 twill progression combined with a point advancing treadling gives a completely different appearance.

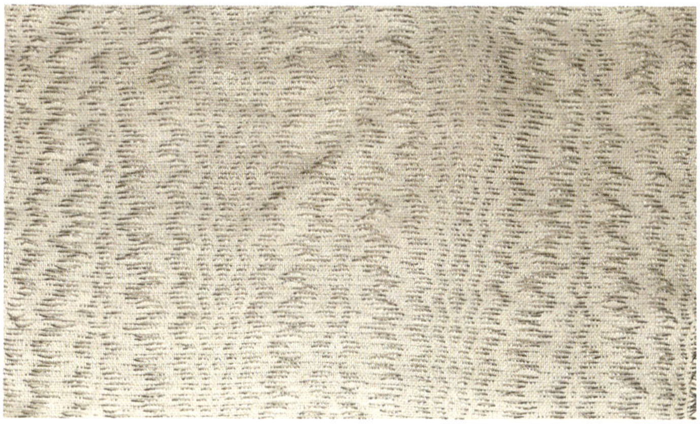

Block shibori was also used for the advancing treading.

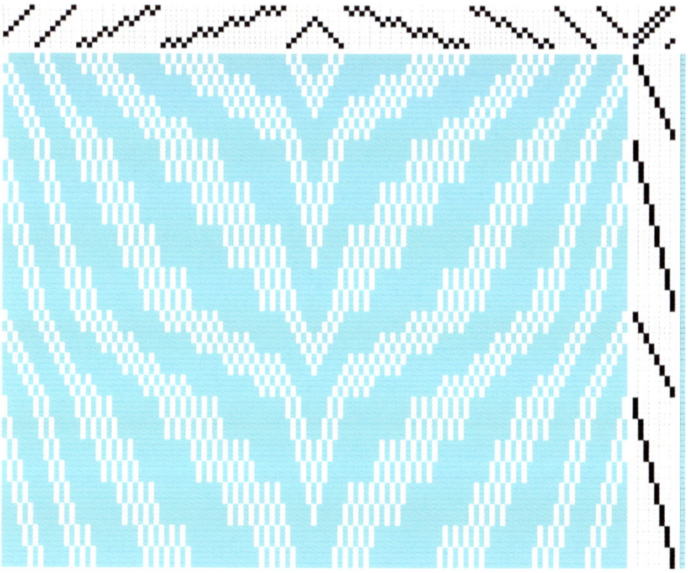

The tie-up here has taken the 3/5 twill and made it a plain weave progression in a twill fashion – a 1/1/1/5 tie-up. This will give a deeper pleat where the turquoise floats push the ground cloth to the other side of the shibori weft.

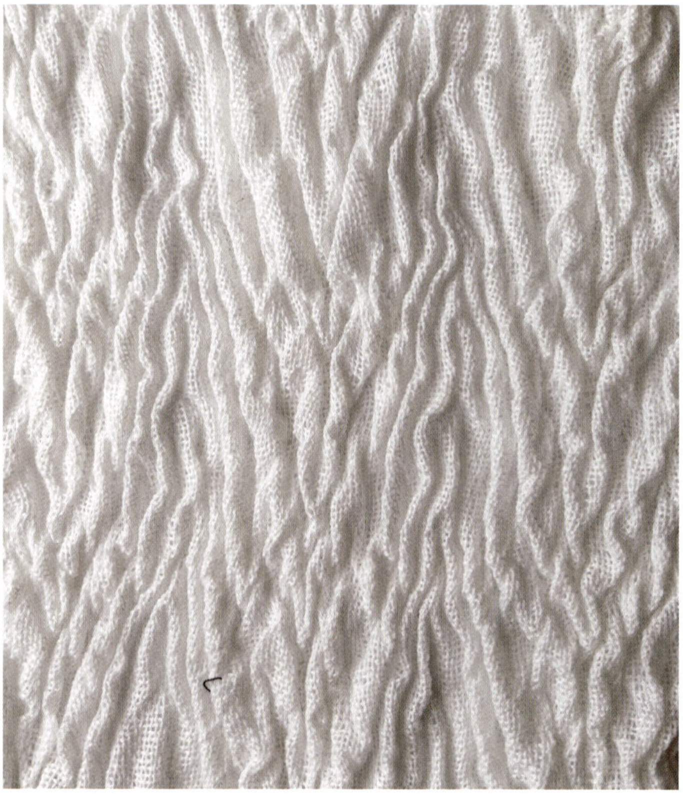

The straight and extended straight design shows the V-shaped folds.

The traditional overshot option gives a more literal translation of the overshot but spread across the eight shafts in the tie-up.

Different tie-ups will give different effects and alternative treadling patterns can be explored.

Overshot Designs for Warp Shibori

Six shafts will allow for overshot designs to be created in warp shibori, although the pleats will be horizontal in nature. They do not have to be pulled up tightly to create the desired effects.

Using warp shibori tie-up and treadling conventions, many variations can be created. For the curious weaver, both warp and weft shibori could be applied to adapted overshot designs.

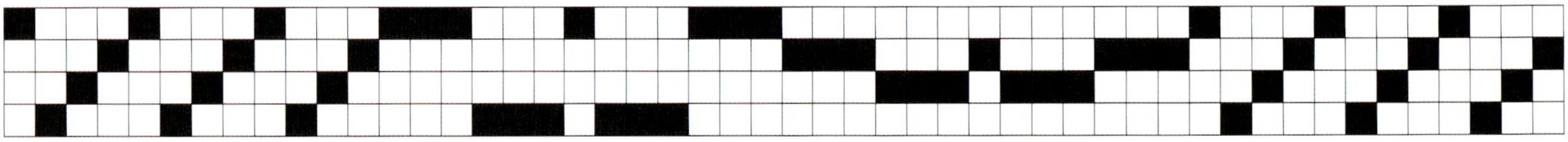

The overshot profile threading can be adapted for warp shibori. Wandering Vine (Cat Track and Snail Trail) has been shortened a little in order to be inserted into the threading.

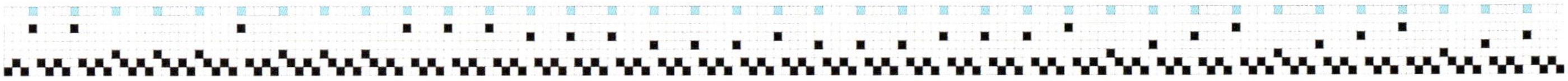

A detail from the threading draft shows two shafts being used for the plain weave ground and the remaining four-shaft profile inserted on shafts 3–6.

Twill and Point Designs

Straight and point threadings can create curves and angles in pleated lines through shifting the shibori one or more ends incrementally. The more shafts available, the more this aspect can be explored, but good results can be achieved with eight shafts.

Varied threading groups can also be sampled to compare how each affects the cloth.

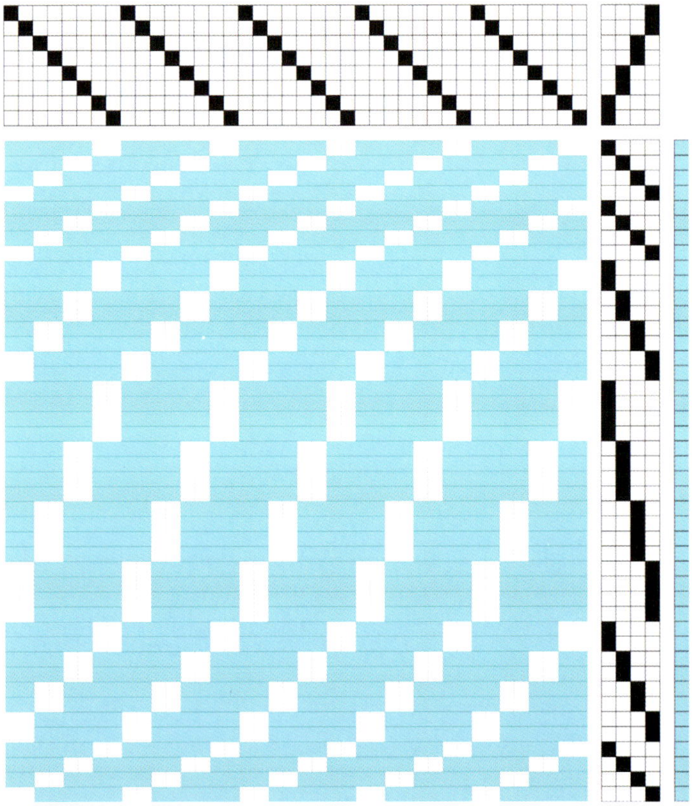

Using a straight entry threading and a profile tie-up and treadling plan, this could be woven on eight shafts. Using the threading as a profile draft, with ten shafts, this could be converted to a warp shibori. In addition, translating the profile to 16 shafts and a weft shibori, this could be expanded to allow for wider threading blocks leading to more variation in the design angles.

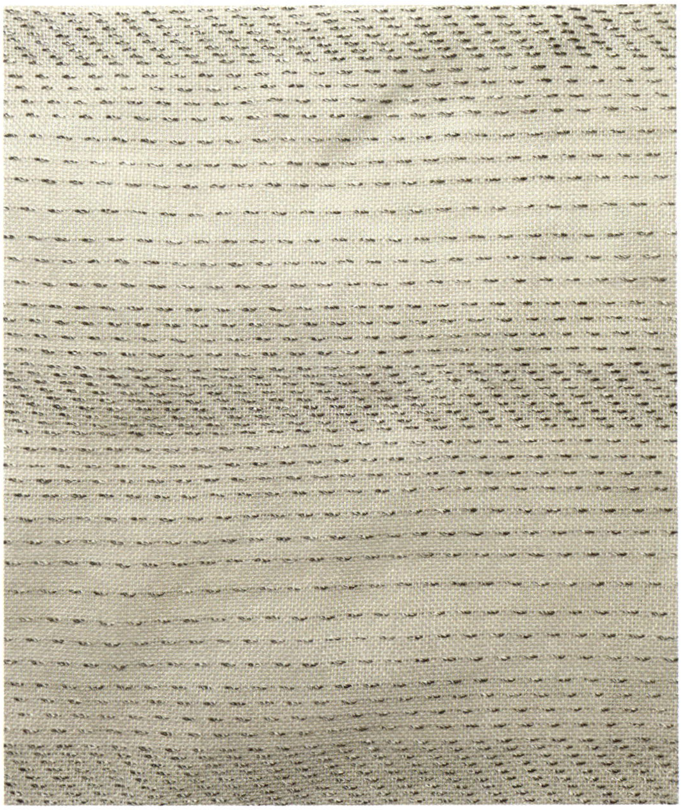

Using a straight entry threading to create diagonals with movement.

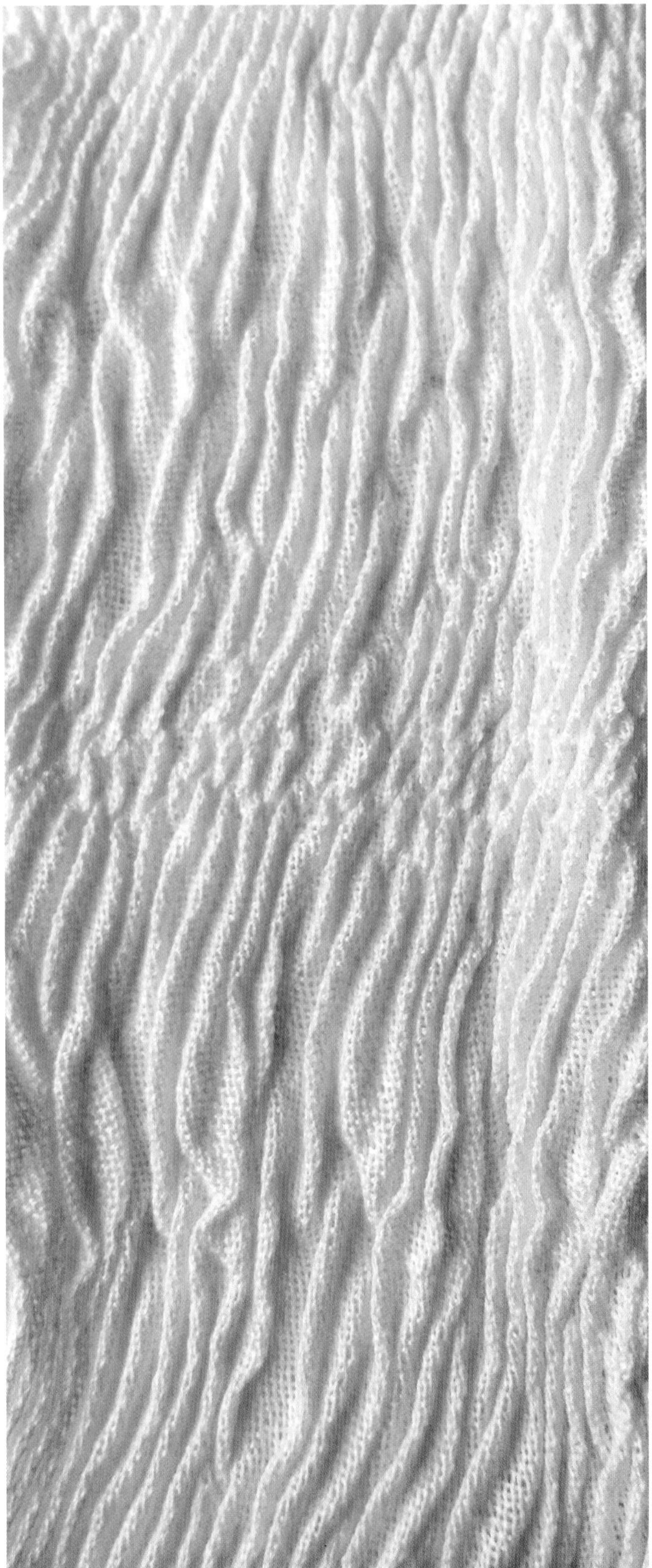

After wet-finishing, the organic nature of the movement is revealed.

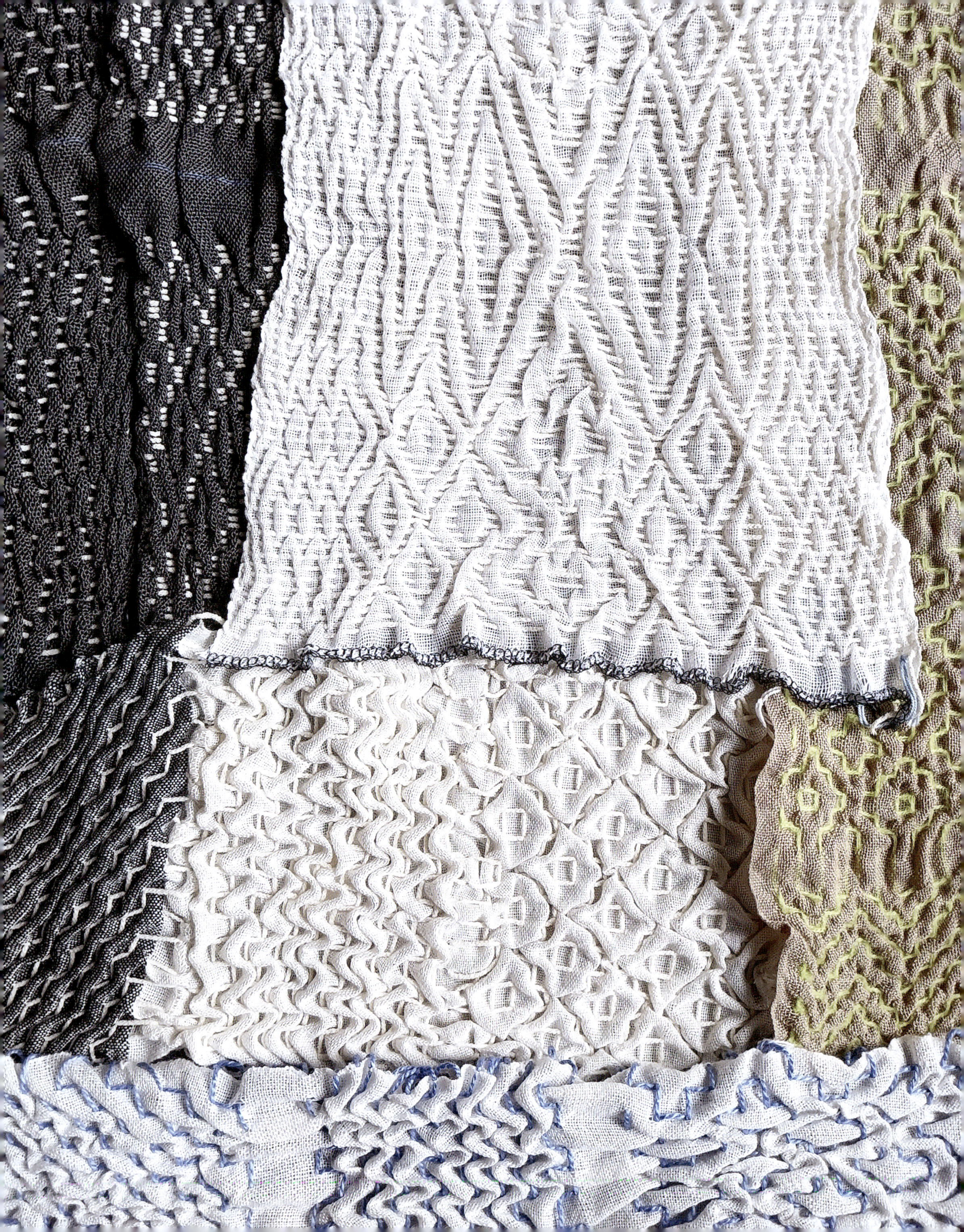

CHAPTER 7

SASHIKO

'Sashiko' is a Japanese word for the many styles of repairing, reinforcing and embellishing of folk textiles that originated in poor farming lands of northern Japan. The design style of a basic running stitch was creatively used for strengthening cloth and adding warmth, as a way of recycling and lengthening the life of everyday textiles. When every textile is precious no matter what state it is in, and every scrap needs to be used for as long as possible, this technique can be both decorative and functional.

From these inauspicious beginnings, sashiko embroidery has become a distinct style for patterning. Sashiko in weaving is usually a decorative addition creating integral designs in warp and weft and is known as *sashiko ori*. But with a dimensional surface hat on, it also has other suggestions for use – as supplementary shibori wefts and warps and also in deflected double weave.

SASHIKO TERMS

To avoid confusion, the following terms are used:

Sashiko shibori – Traditional sashiko designs pulled up and finished, and the shibori threads removed after finishing.

Sashiko ori shibori – Traditional sashiko designs woven with shrinking yarns (elastane or wool), or non-shrinking yarns pulled up loosely, which remain in place after finishing.

Sashiko ori style – Non-traditional designs (such as from overshot, deflected double weave or other threading conventions) in which the design yarns remain in place after finishing.

SASHIKO SHIBORI

'Sashiko' in Japanese means 'to stab'. In shibori this means that the sashiko yarns go completely from one side to the other with no interweaving. Therefore, whole threading blocks are impacted together. When used in combination with the traditional designs of sashiko, *Sashiko shibori* uses the traditional stitch designs as supplementary warp and/or wefts that are then pulled up, exactly as in traditional woven shibori. After wet-finishing, the gathering stitches are removed, leaving no evidence of the original design, only the resulting texture.

Weft-sashiko Shibori

Like regular shibori, weft-sashiko shibori uses the gathering pattern thread in the weft only. Different ground weft yarns will give different results. As well as polyester, try linen, paper and other kinds of yarns to see how well they hold the shaping after wet-finishing.

Not all traditional sashiko patterns are useful for texture, but there are quite a few that have potential. Four-shaft designs are Ishi datami and Yoko gushi.

Collection of Sashiko images using shibori and deflected double weave.

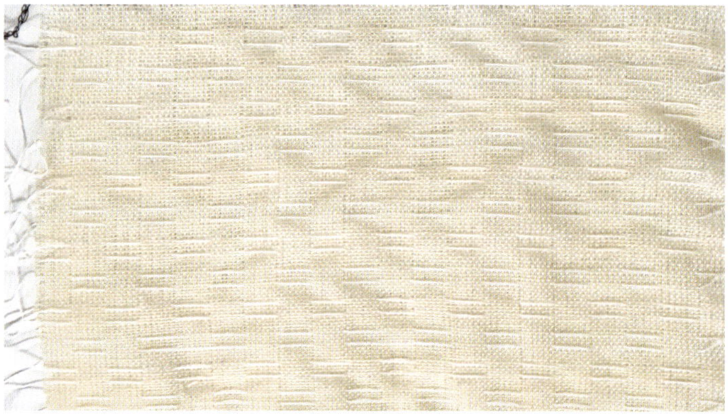

Four-shaft Ishi datami woven in linen before pulling up.

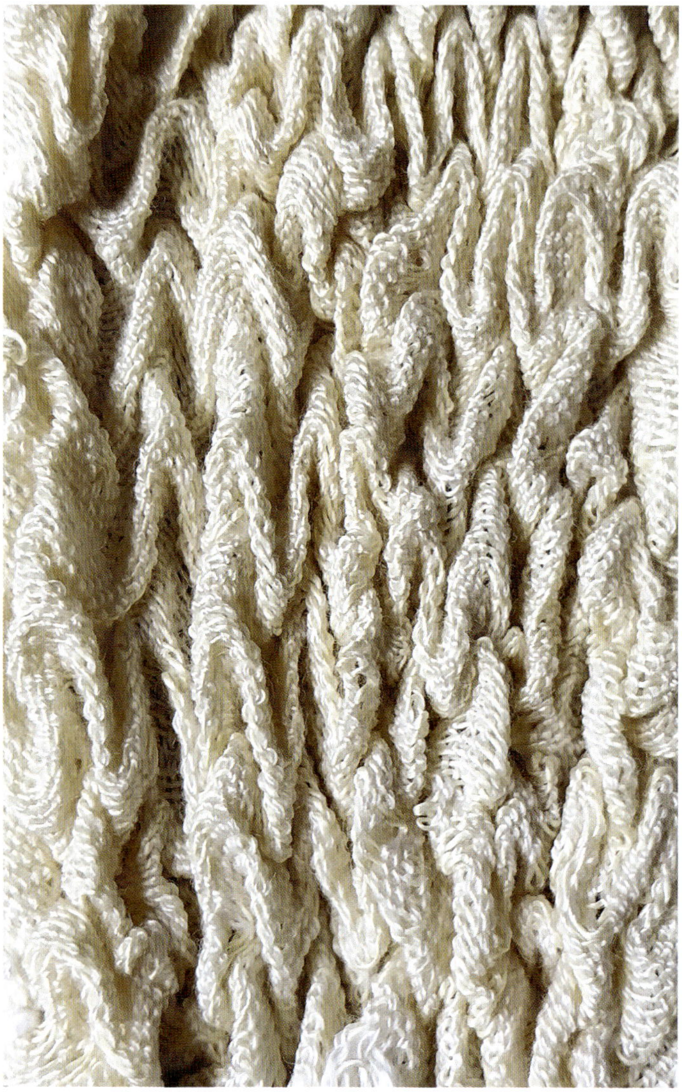

After steaming.

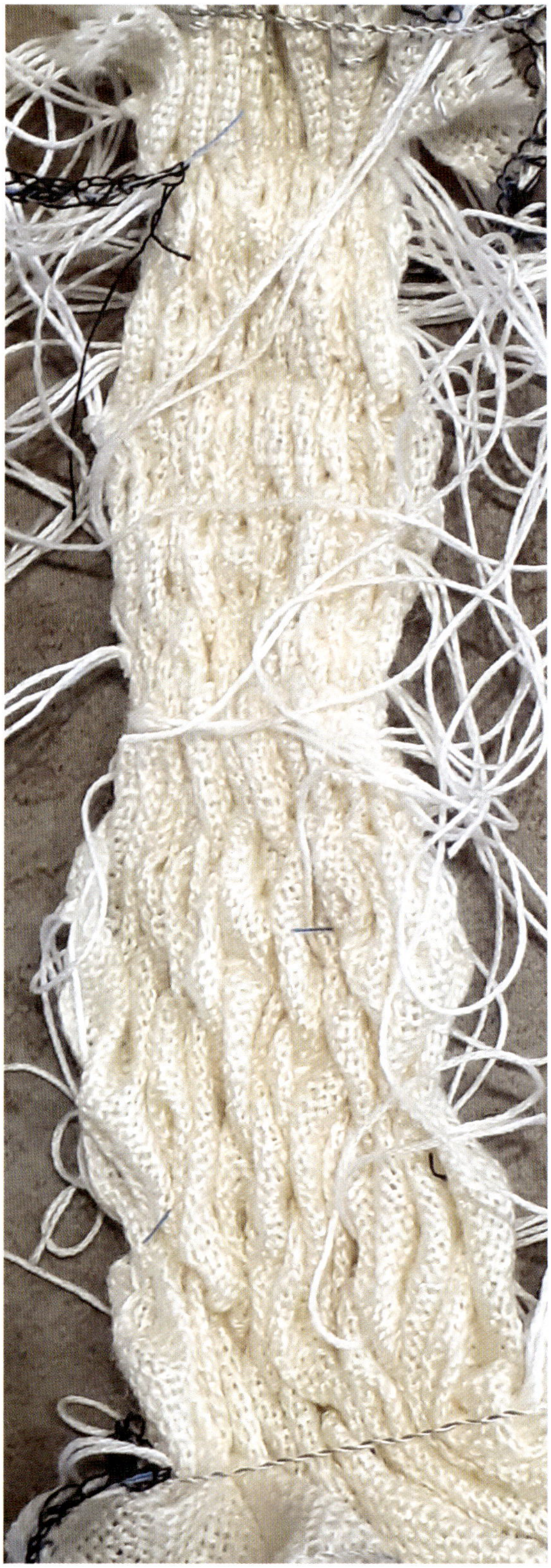

Lambswool weft tightly pulled up before steaming.

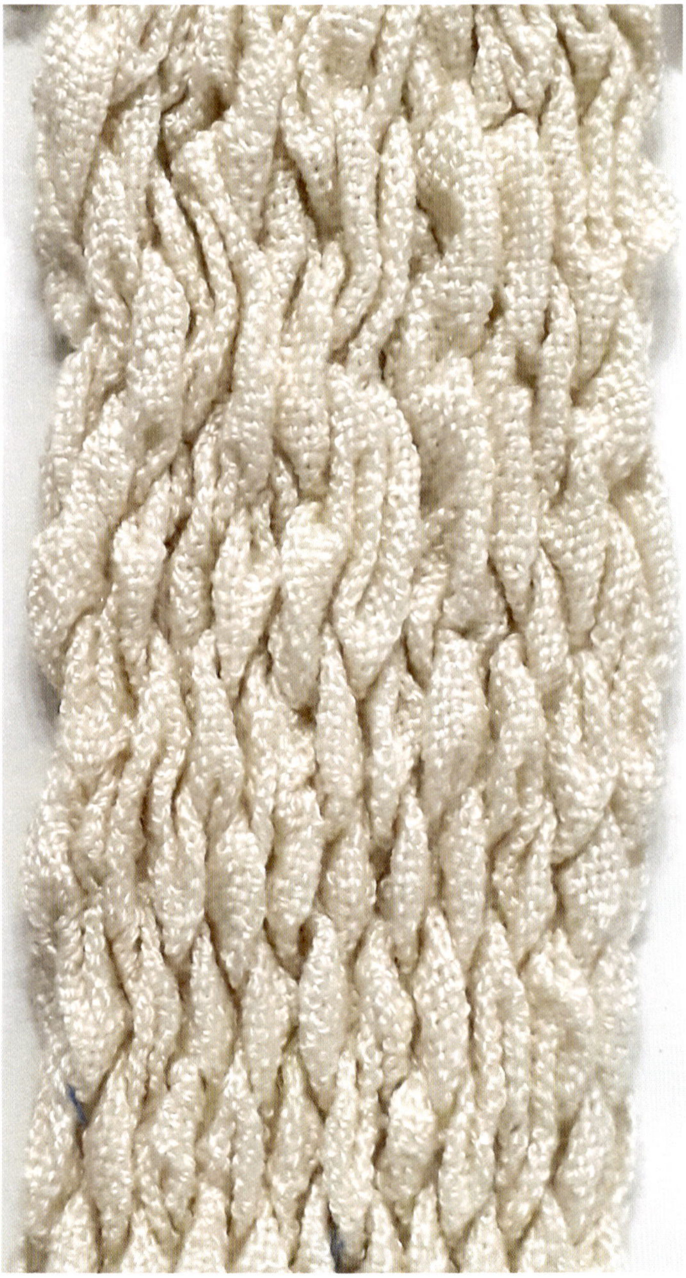

Lambswool tightly pulled sample after steaming.

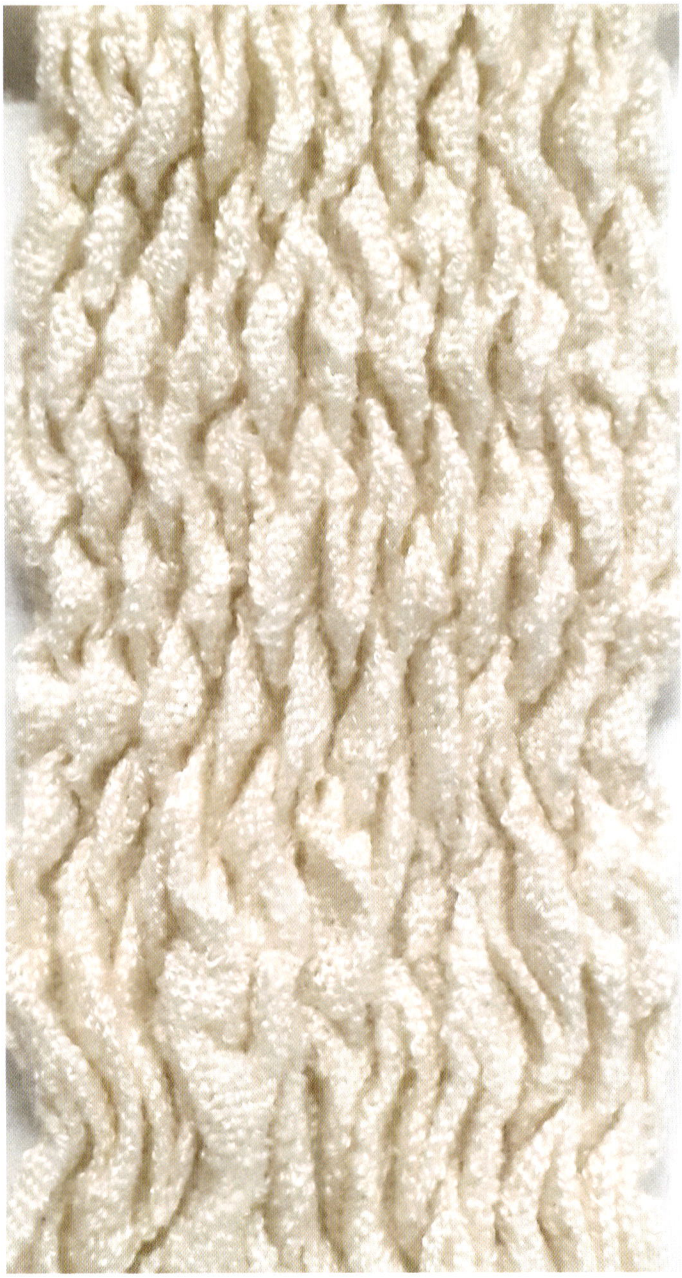

Lambswool tightly pulled sample after fulling.

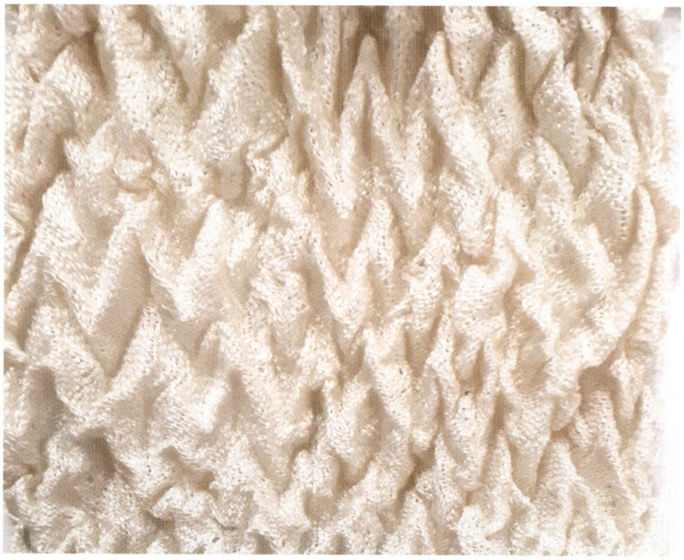

Fine Japanese paper tightly pulled sample after steaming.

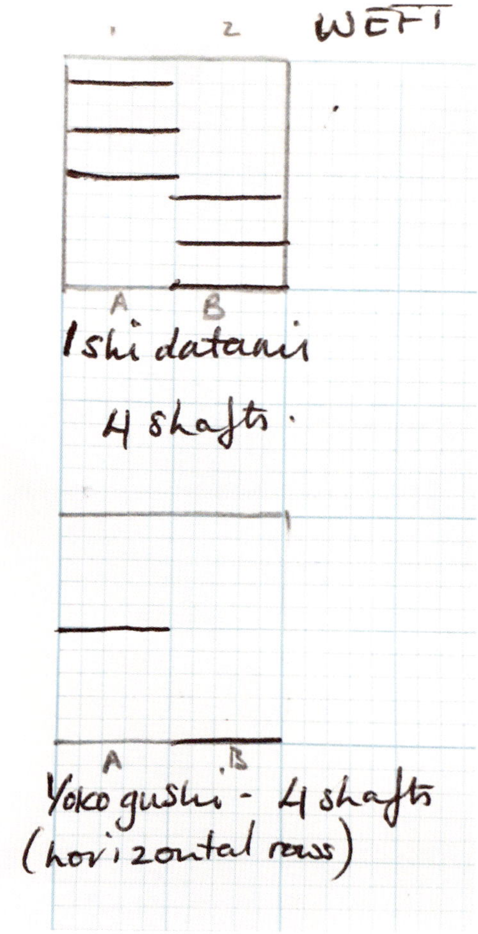

It is a useful exercise to check whether designs are likely to be translatable for weaving by drawing them out by hand. Ishi datami and Yoko gushi only required two blocks of plain weave each for weft-sashiko shibori.

Once translated from the paper sketch into weaving drafts, the similarity with shibori can easily be seen.

A six-shaft design is called Masugata. This can also be woven in an eight-shaft version.

Another design in eight shafts is Kasuri Koshi.

These samples explore material properties. Steaming for one hour and fulling were the wet-finishes of choice. The warp for these is a fine lambswool.

These horizontal sashiko designs are easy to use for *sashiko ori shibori* and can be a great introduction to using shibori wefts with elastane or overtwist if these yarns are being explored for the first time. *Sashiko ori shibori* uses the traditional designs with the pattern threads remaining in the finished fabric, whether non-shrinking pattern threads, elastane or wool are used. With this method, there is the added impact of having the decorative element of the *sashiko ori* patterns visible with a contrasting colour to the ground, for instance.

Ground wefts can be anything, especially if no heat-setting is planned. The pattern wefts can be singles yarn, overtwisted (which will coil up on wet-finishing), elastane or woollen yarns.

Variations on the theme can be increased picks of the same block in the shibori wefts.

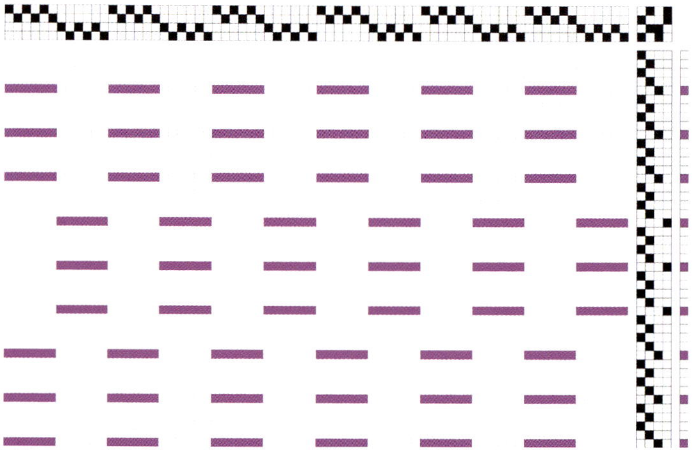

A four-shaft simple supplementary weft design floating over one block of two shafts and under the other in a repeat before switching over is called Ishi datami. Purple has been used in the weft to indicate that these sashiko picks are not removed.

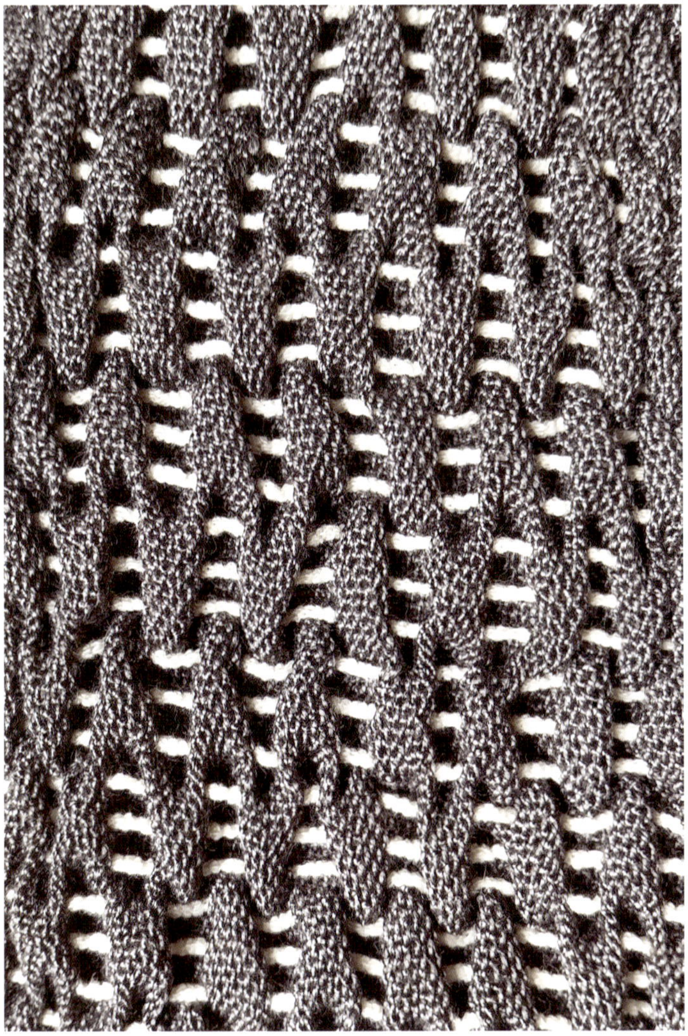

Ishi datami is woven here with an elastane sashiko weft and cotton warp and weft.

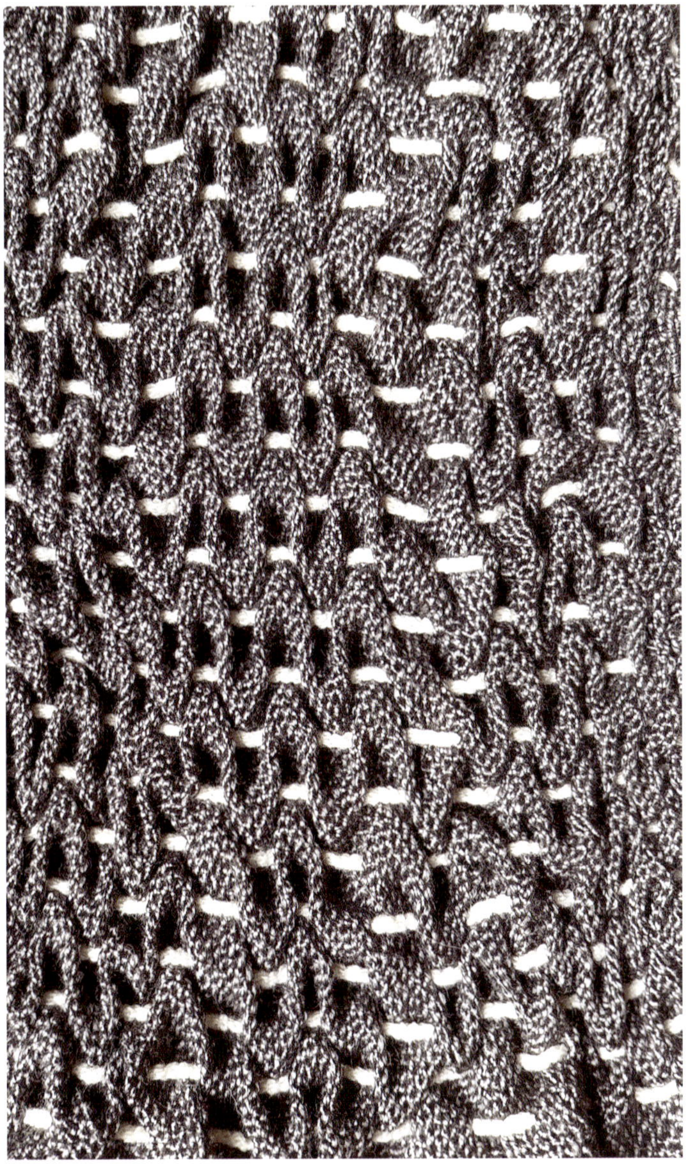

On the same warp and threading, Yoko gushi can also be woven.

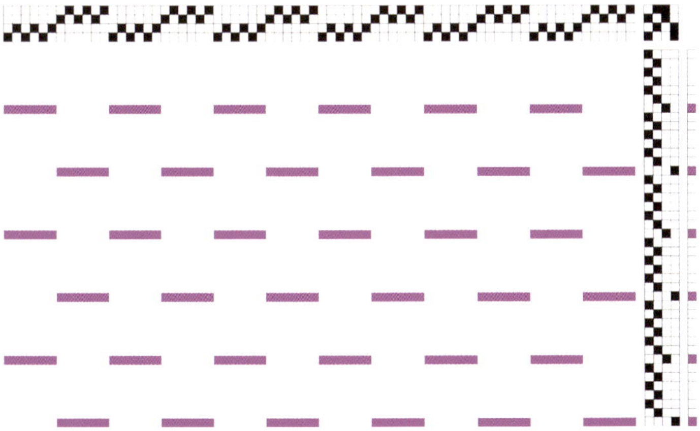

Changing block floats for each pattern weft pick gives a design called Yoko gushi.

For *sashiko ori style*, overshot-style threadings can be adapted. A contrasting colour can be effective for the pattern ends and picks. If the ground warp is light, then a dark or bright colour can be used for the pattern warps and wefts.

Using a point threading, extending the blocks in an overshot fashion, a design can be created and woven with a plain weave ground and two blocks lifted at a time in a 'woven as drawn in' for the elastane weft.

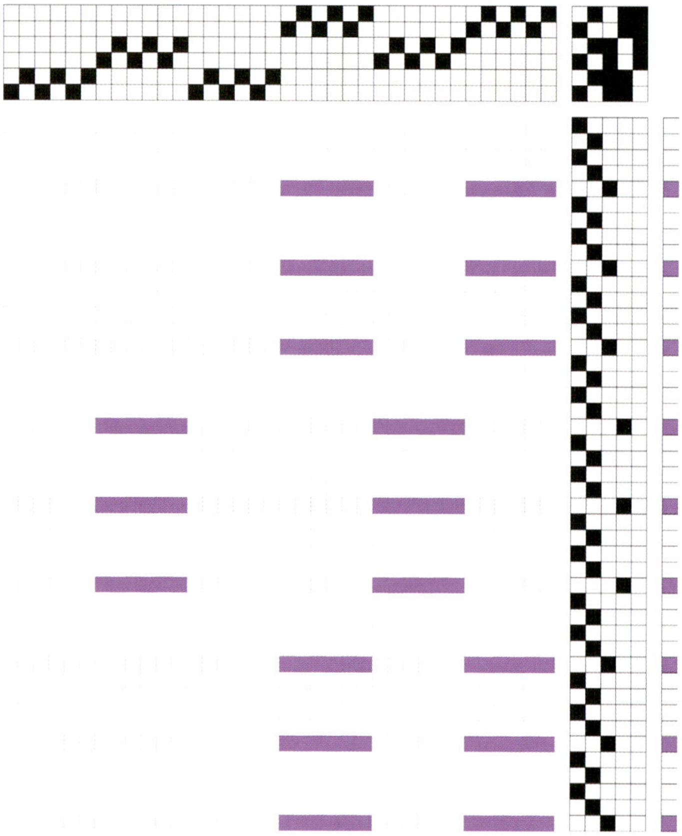

Masugata can be woven on six shafts as in this draft. Each block pattern is repeated three times before changing to the next group.

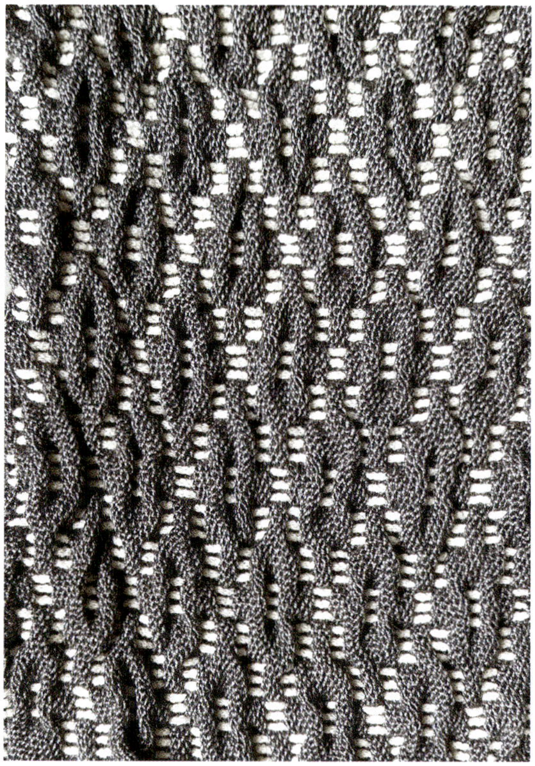

Here, the eight-shaft version Masugata is woven.

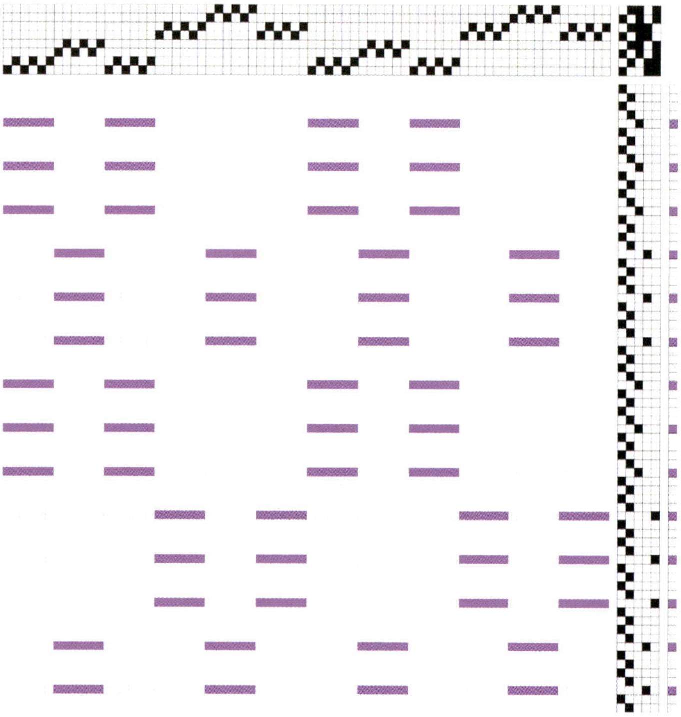

Eight shafts can give a larger version of the same rhythmically repeating design.

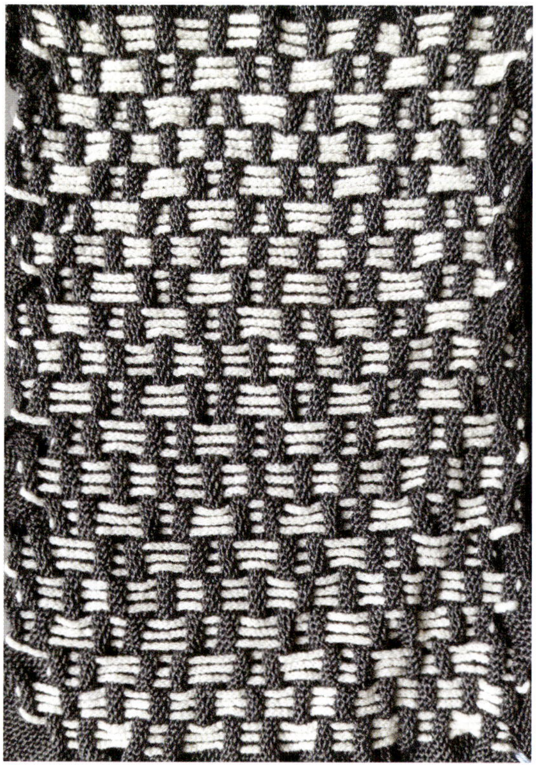

It has a different design on the reverse.

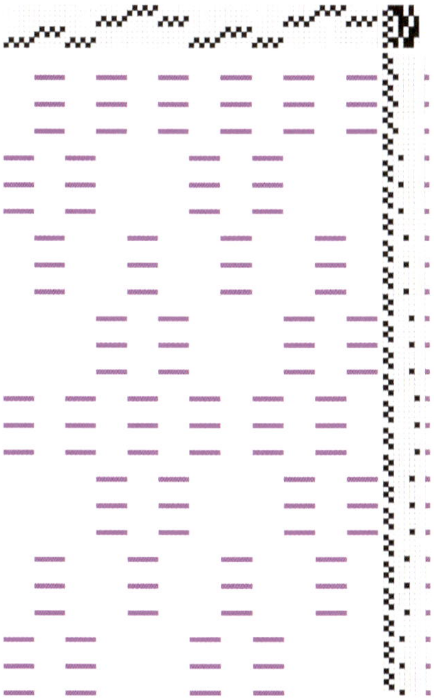

A variation on the theme is called Kasuri Koshi.

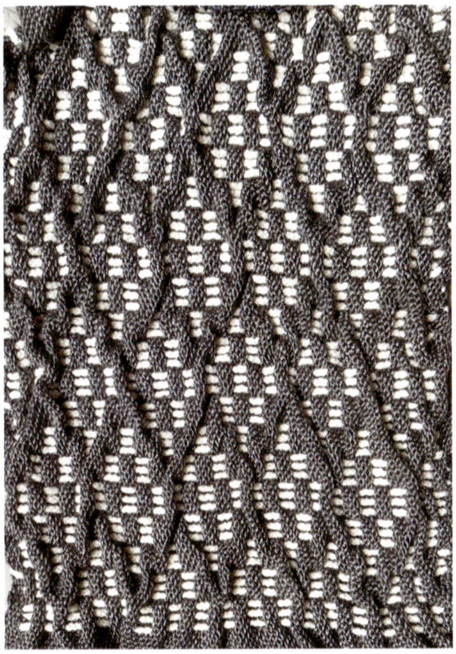

The same threading allows for Kasuri Koshi.

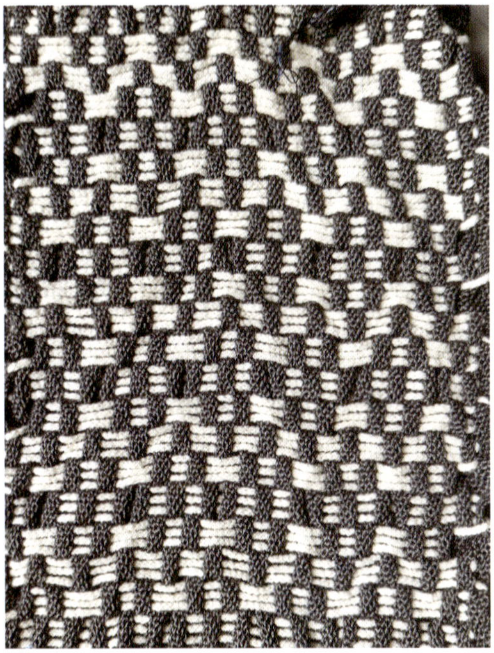

This also has a different design on the reverse.

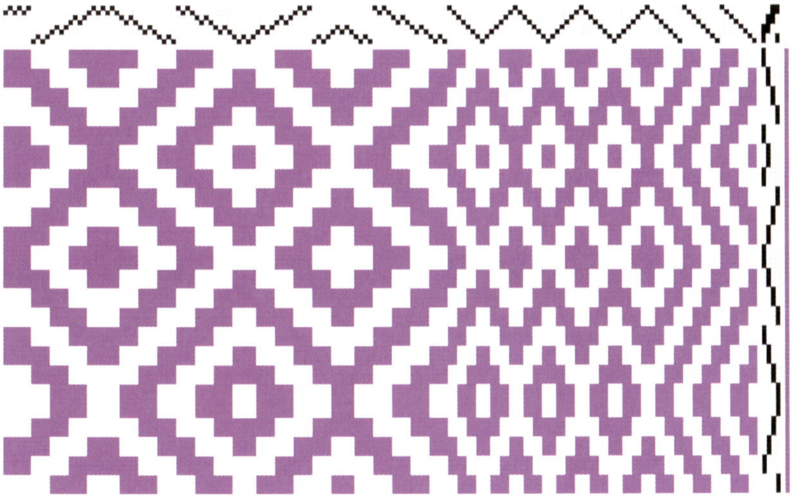

Varied threading allows experimentation for this *sashiko ori* study. Four blocks of two shafts each are used with a straight threading, a point threading and an extended block rosepath variation. This profile draft does not include the ground weave.

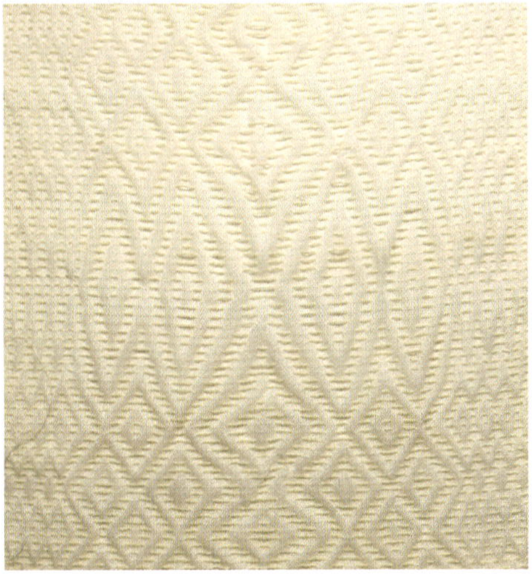

An eight-shaft shibori study warp with a mix of point-based threading and block threading led to this optical dimensional and textural effect.

Warp- and Weft-sashiko Shibori

To my mind, it is in the warp and weft combinations that the beauty of *sashiko ori* for shibori really comes out. The designs are traditionally named and can be applied for up to eight or more shafts.

The yarns and method of weaving is the same as for regular shibori.

As the sashiko warp threads are not integrated into the ground cloth, take-up variation between the ground cloth and the sashiko warp ends can be considerable. A second beam is useful but individual sashiko warp ends can be successfully hung over the back beam with a small weight to give tension. (*See* Appendix I for using a second loom.)

Using elastane-based pattern ends gives flexibility to the fabric and so is very useful for garments. However, one design element to be aware of is the float lengths for the shibori warps and wefts, which need careful consideration depending on the end use of the cloth.

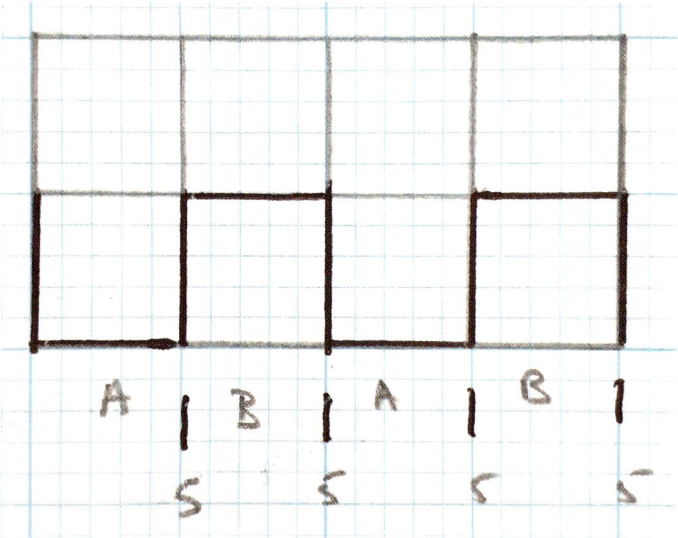

Sketches are useful to allow you to work out whether to spend time on developing a design and then a warp.

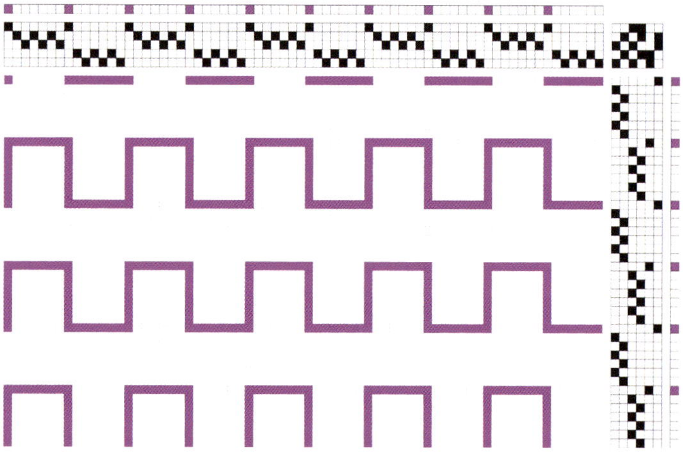

Warp and weft sashiko gives more interesting designs. A simple five-shaft version is Hira yama michi with its crenellated forms. The vertical design lines are created by using a supplementary warp end on shaft 5.

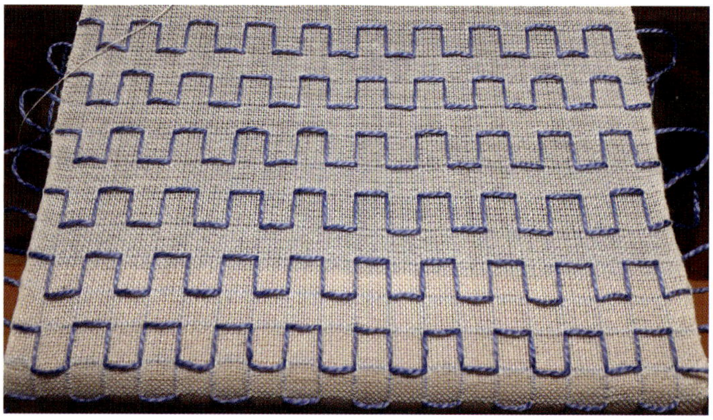

The Hira yama michi design on the loom for a cotton warp- and weft-sashiko shibori.

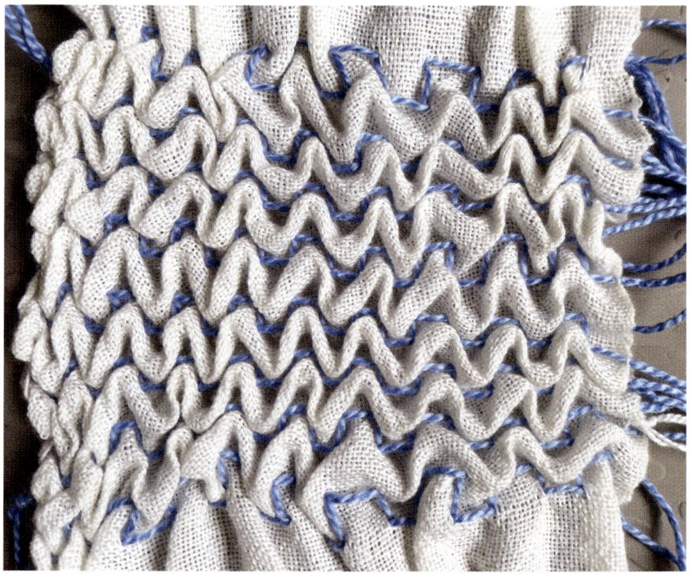

Once off the loom, pulling up can commence.

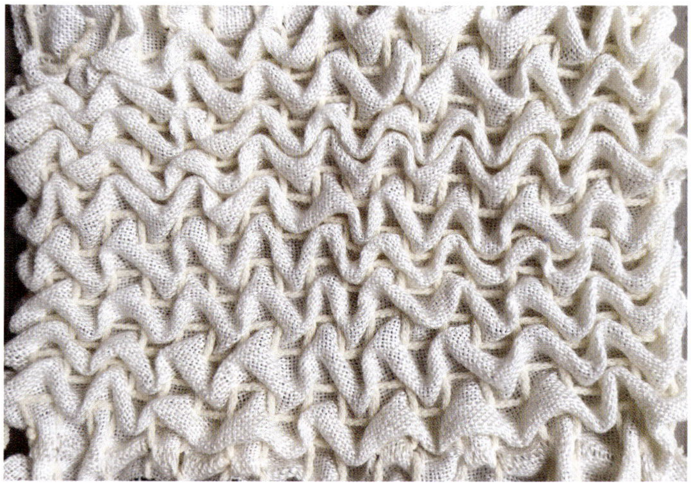

The elastane sashiko shibori warp and weft does the pulling up instantly.

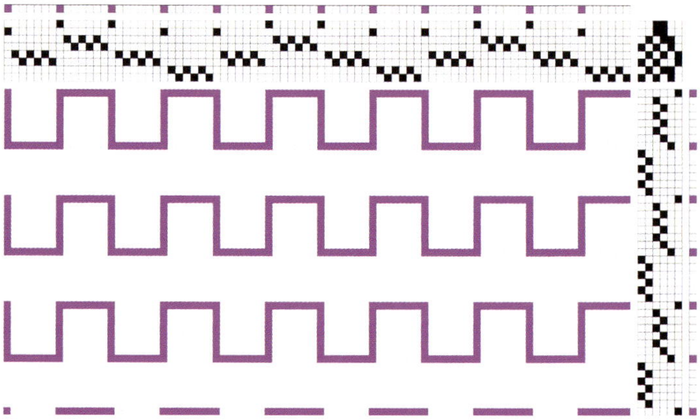

An eight-shaft version of Hira yama michi puts the warp ends on shafts 7 and 8. The main threading is a three-block point threading, which is not necessary for this draft but is versatile to be able to create other designs on the same threading.

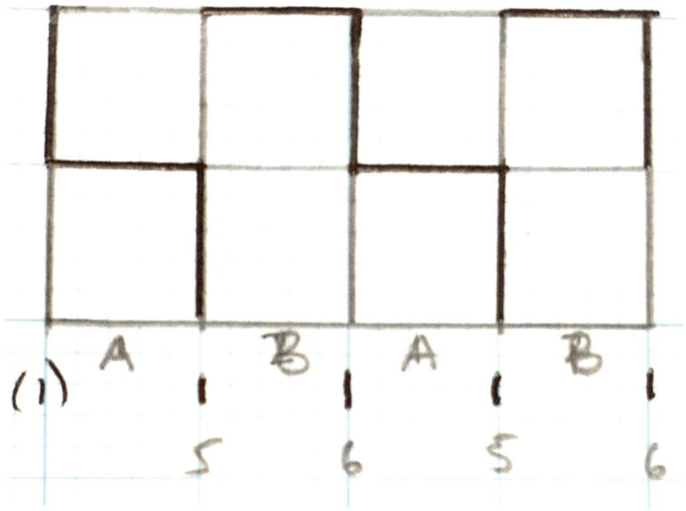

The sketch of Dan tsunagi shows that only six shafts are required.

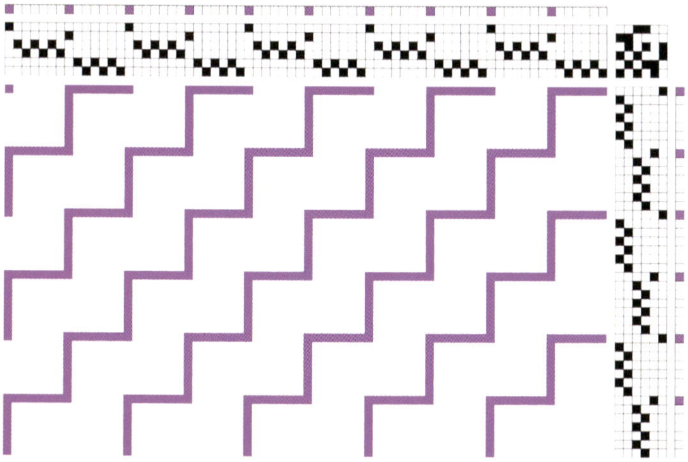

Six shafts using four for the ground weave and two warp shafts on shafts 5 & 6 allow for the stair effect of Dan tsugani.

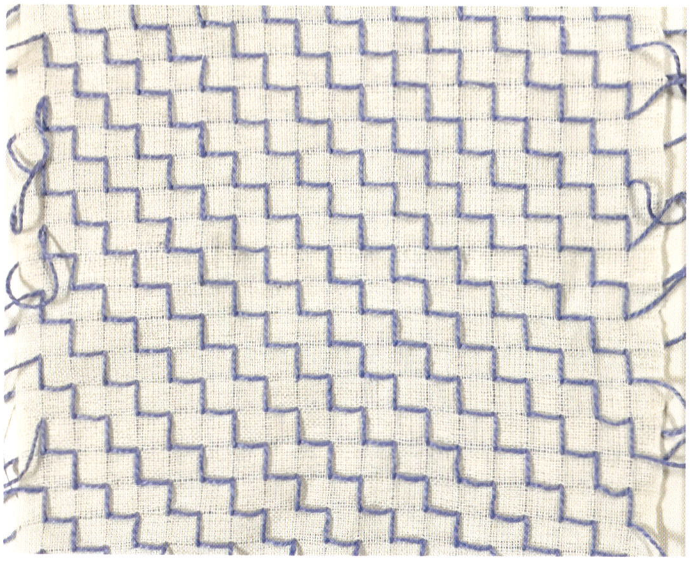

The sample prior to pulling up.

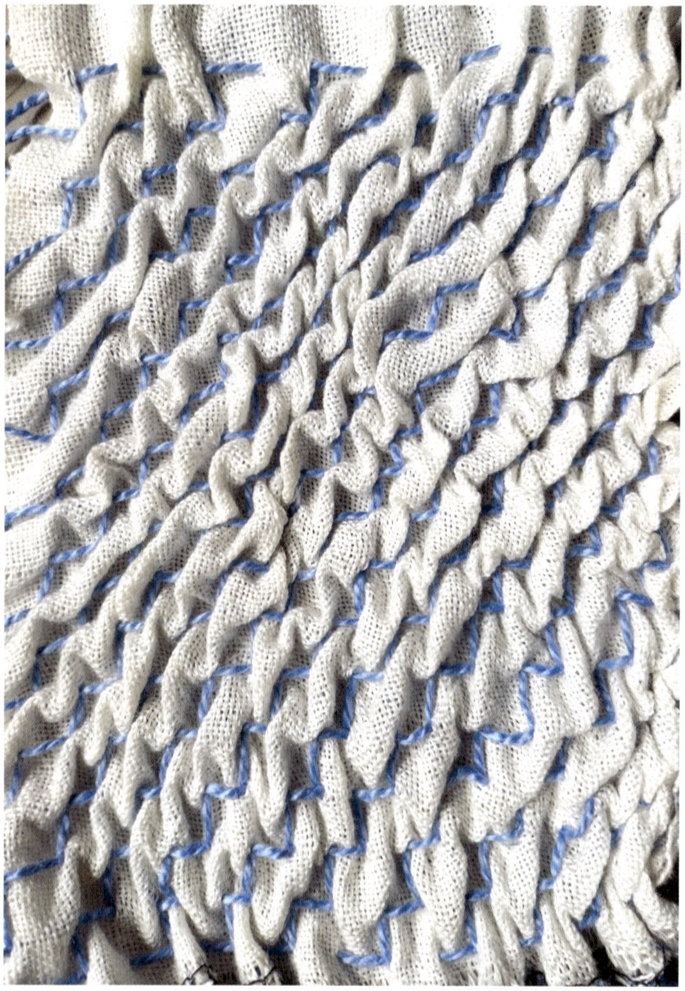

After pulling up.

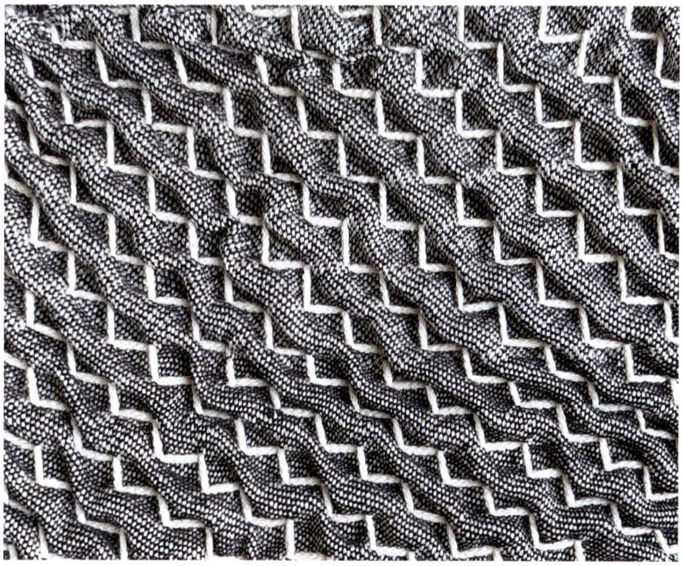

The elastane version. The design has an impact on how this sample reacts. The elastane pulls the fabric onto the bias and has to be stretched out to be photographed.

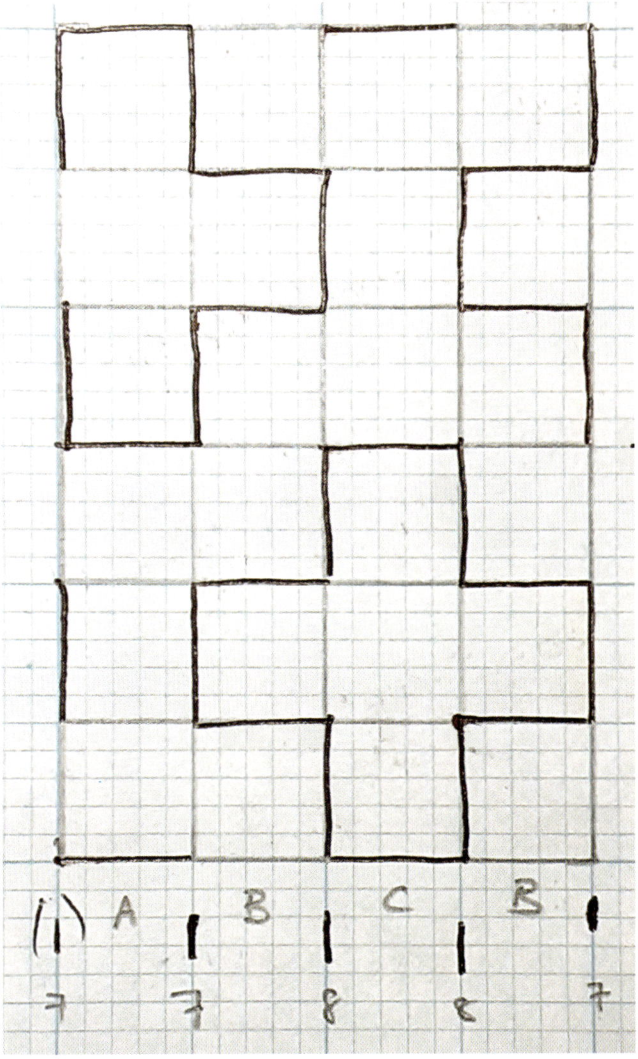

Jūjizashi on eight shafts is an interesting design.

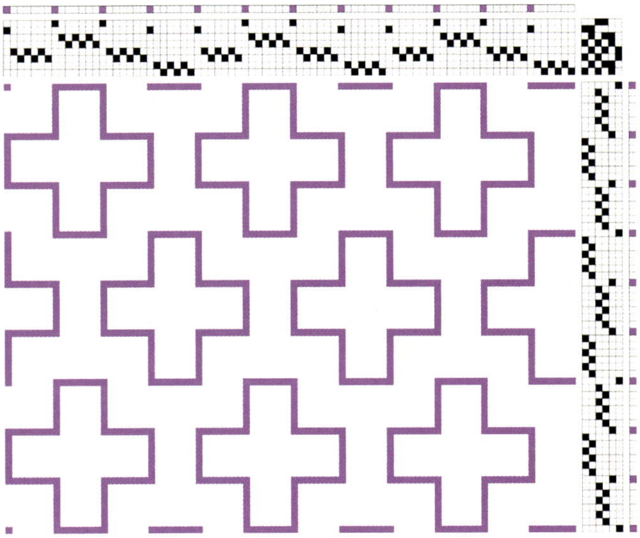

Eight shafts are needed for the Jūjizashi design with its crosses.

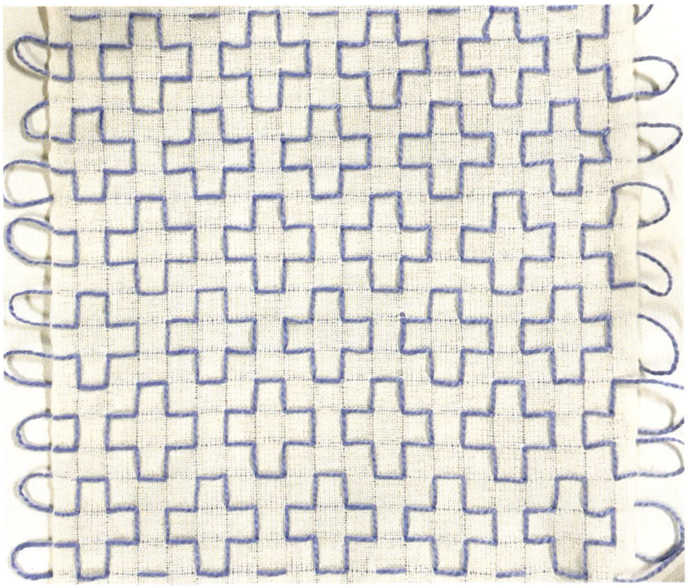

This is the side that reflects the sketch.

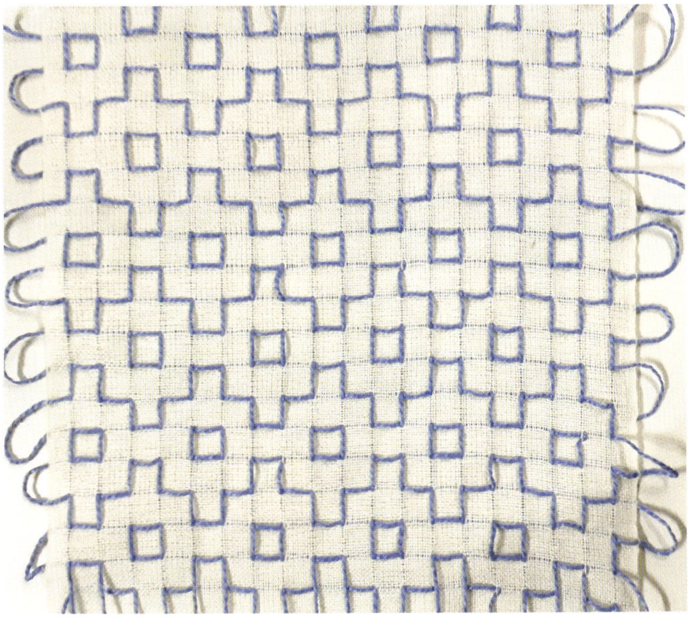

However, something completely different happens on the other side.

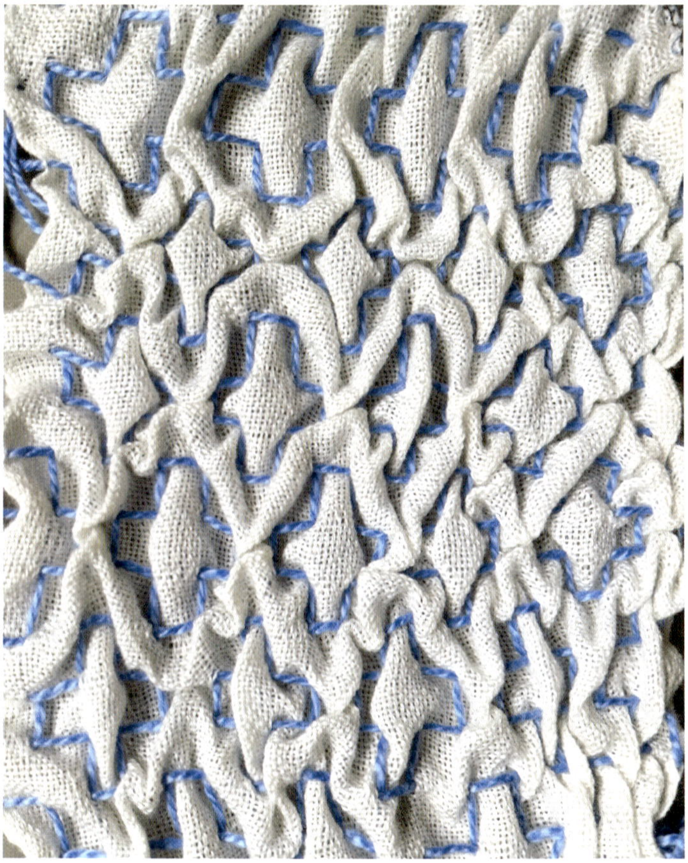
Side A pulled up.

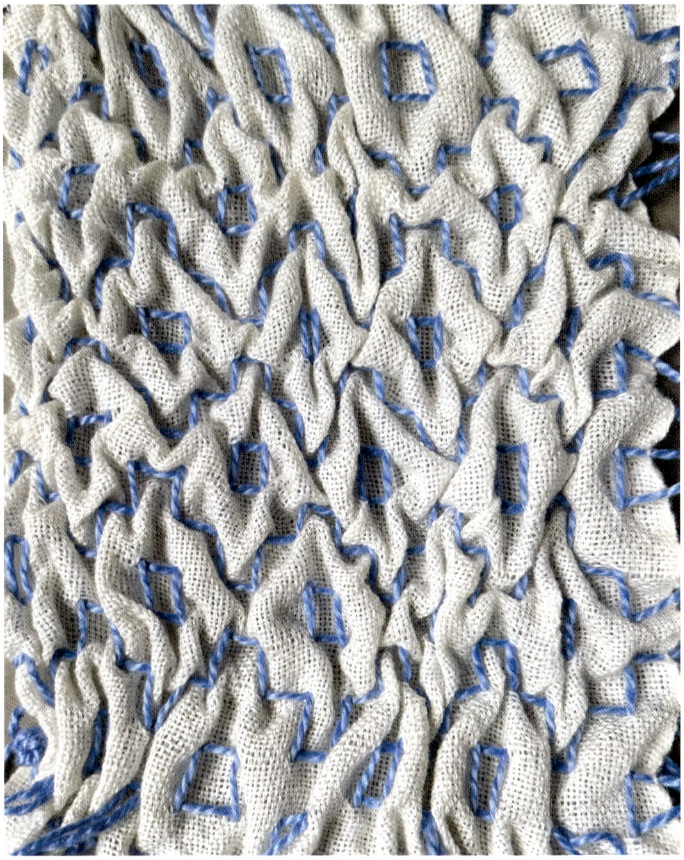
Side B after pulling up.

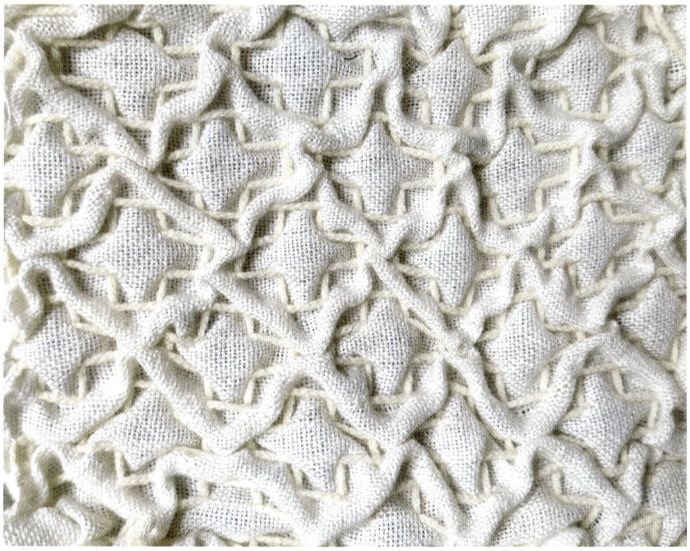
The elastane Side A.

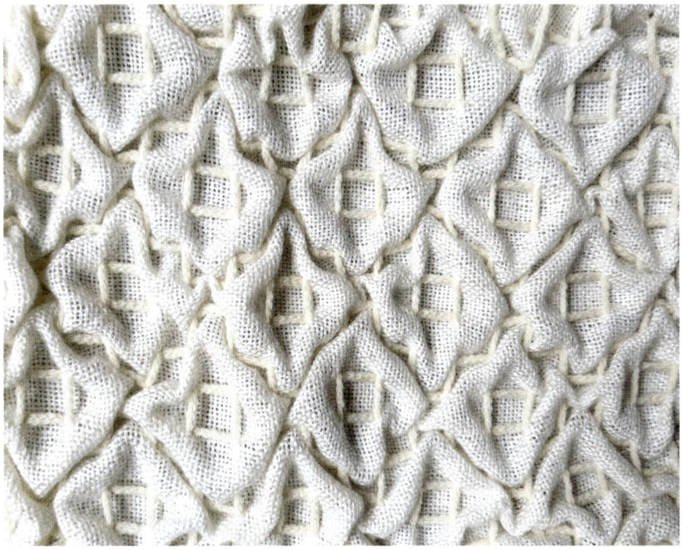
The elastane Side B.

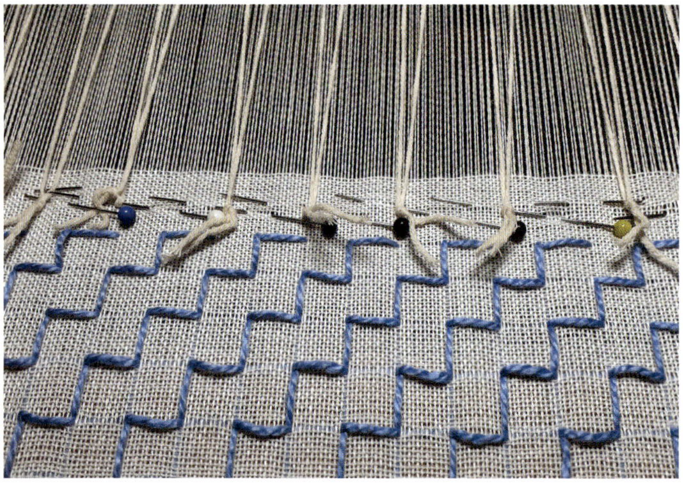

In order to attach elastane sashiko shibori warp ends to the cloth, first knot the warp ends in pairs. This will allow for ease of securing to the fabric with long-shanked pins.

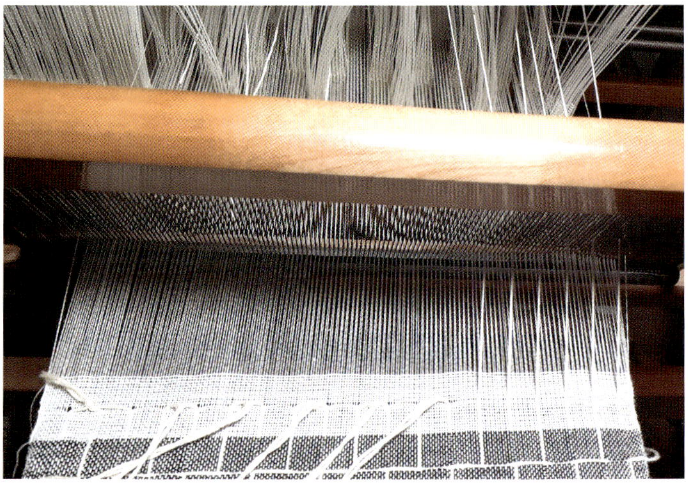

At the end of the warp shibori, this is one way to ensure that the warp ends keep their elastane stretch when released from the loom. Knot them in pairs, being careful to ensure that just enough stretch is applied to get the desired effect prior to knotting.

USING A STICK SHUTTLE

If weaving samples or multiple pieces on the same warp, it is helpful to use a stick shuttle to pull some extra warp shibori through between samples. When the samples are separated, both ends of the warp can be knotted to ensure that the elastic warp doesn't pull through the fabric once the tension is released.

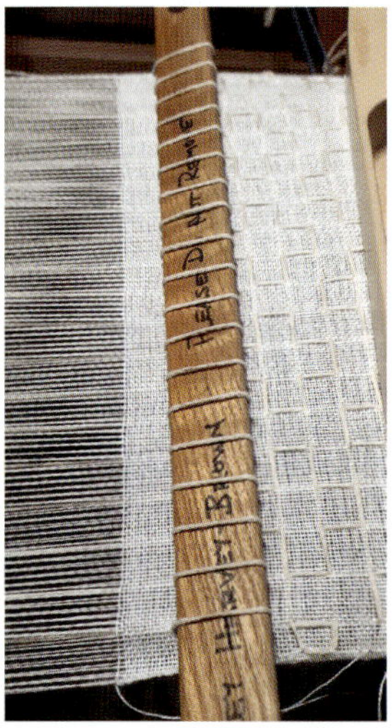

It can be challenging to ensure that there is enough elastane warp available to be able to tie-off each sample. Here a stick shuttle is used to give some extra elastane warp between samples.

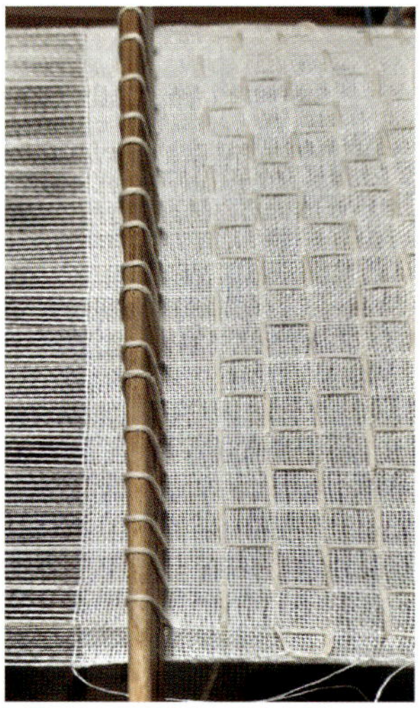

Turning the shuttle on its side ensures that enough elastane is available after weaving.

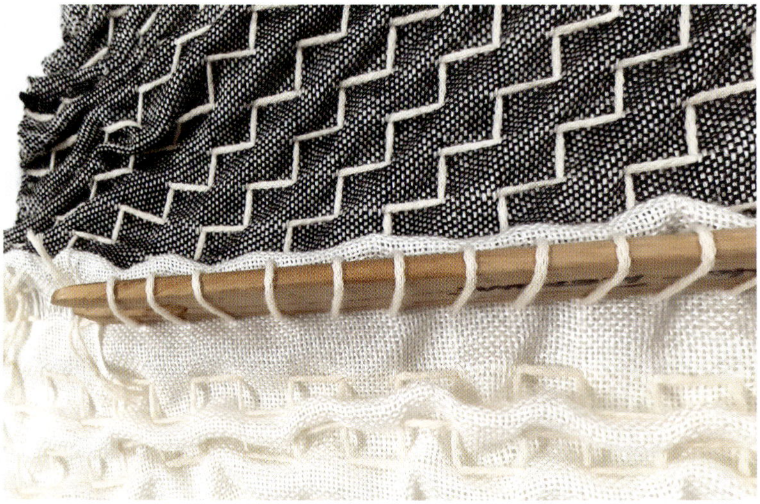

Once the cloth is removed from the loom, the shuttle can be removed from the cloth as each pair of ends is tied for both samples.

Elastane gives great effects but needs a certain amount of attention when weaving. Elastane *sashiko ori* warps can be placed on a separate beam and put under slightly more tension, or extra weights can be added to the specific ends in order to create a little more drama when the tension is released. Sampling is always required!

The second method is to pull up the elastane ends by hand after completing weaving, and knot or otherwise secure the ends.

There are two methods for creating the texture with the elastane weft as well. Usually, some kind of temple is required. This can be homemade. (*See* Appendix I for details.)

If a small to medium amount of texture is the aim, the elastane weft can be placed (i.e. no pulling), then beaten in with the first pick of the next block of ground weave. Each of the surface floats can be pulled up by hand so as to maintain an even tension across the width of the warp, gripping the yarn at the selvedge so that it doesn't pull the selvedge in. With the ground cloth already woven, ensure the tension remains and then place in the next elastane pick. Moving on fairly regularly helps, but not too often. A regular temple will be positioned just below the fell as usual. If using a homemade system, positioning it about 1in (2.5cm) below the fell seems to work well, but this is down to personal preference.

If a centre-feed boat or roller shuttle is used for elastane wefts and the weft spool is getting low and possibly catching a little, always pull out enough yarn for the pick that is about to be woven, plus half as much again to ensure that the bobbin does not pull to unwind as the shuttle is thrown. If the weft pulls hard, this causes selvedge issues.

Using elastane yarn eliminates the need for wet-finishing as decisions on the amount the fabric is pulled up to create the desired designs are made during weaving. All that is required is to tie-off the shibori ends. Steaming a polyester ground weft will certainly hold the pleating in shape if you should ever wish to remove the sashiko designs, but for this method, the shibori ends are part of the pattern.

More than eight shafts are required for a few designs that come from a style called *Hitomezashi*. In embroidery, they are worked as a grid of straight lines where stitches meet or cross to make the design. The designs featured here meet but do not cross, using vertical and horizontal rows only. Some of them have a striking resemblance to deflected double weave designs.

For weavers with more than eight shafts, taking some time to study the drafts associated with the four- to eight-shaft designs will greatly enhance understanding of how many shafts these designs will require and how to weave them, if desired.

Hand-drafting with a pencil, an eraser, a ruler and a squared paper pad, begin with the horizontal lines and then turn to the vertical lines. While it is tempting to do it on the computer, physically drawing the lines by hand with pencil onto paper makes the actual structure of the design clear in both mind and body in a more fundamental way than inputting it onto the computer. It helps to understand and figure out the blocks, the shibori warp shafts that are required, and how they function together or separately so as to work out how to weave the design. This will additionally assist in the understanding of how blocks work in other techniques too. Once this is done, it is easy to enter the elements into a weave software programme.

Sashiko patterning encourages exploration with how much or how little the designs are pulled up until a style emerges that suits the individual weaver. If the ground weft and/or warp is a heat-set yarn or wool, that particular design can be impressed into the cloth permanently with wet-finishing or steaming. Alternatively, the *sashiko ori* threads can be tied at whichever point desired, and the textural patterning can be arranged at will.

Beth Ross Johnson has created a Sashiko Design Generator in collaboration with forresto using algorithmic binary indicators to create the designs. (*See* Artists' Links.)

SASHIKO DESIGNS FOR DEFLECTED DOUBLE WEAVE

Some designs migrate across different sections of the book, and sashiko designs lend themselves to other weaving conventions. In addition to being a pull-up thread such as a supplementary warp/weft, it can also be designed into deflected double cloth. For further information on how to create this, *see* Chapter 8.

Especially using unbalanced ratios, step patterns resembling traditional sashiko designs are often used in deflected double weave. Using more than eight shafts gives many more options to bring this purposefully into the design.

The simple Jūjizashi and Yamagata forms explain the principles.

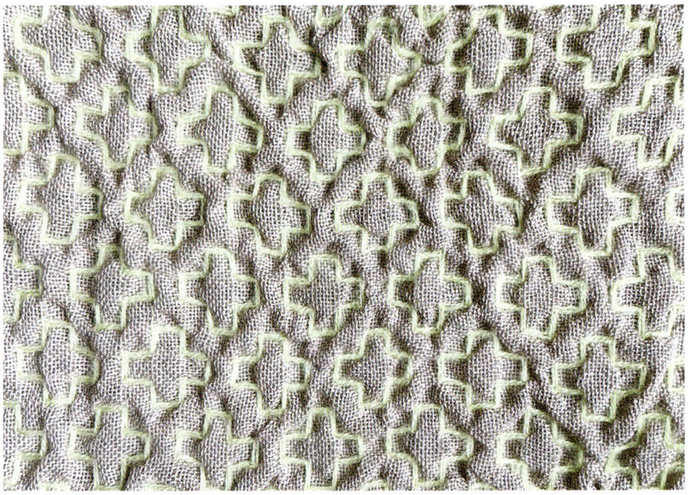

Deflected double weave works really well for sashiko. As seen with the shibori designs, there are different effects on both sides of this Jūjizashi eight-shaft design. Just two ground blocks are needed, but a further four shafts are required for each of the two wool warps providing the textural element of the deflected double weave.

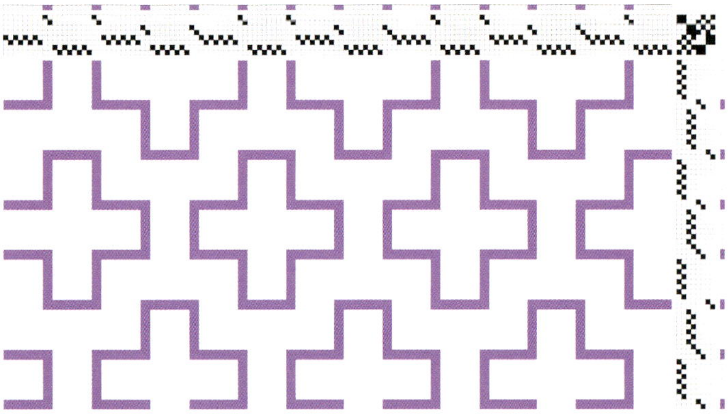

Jūjizashi can be woven as a deflected double weave using eight shafts.

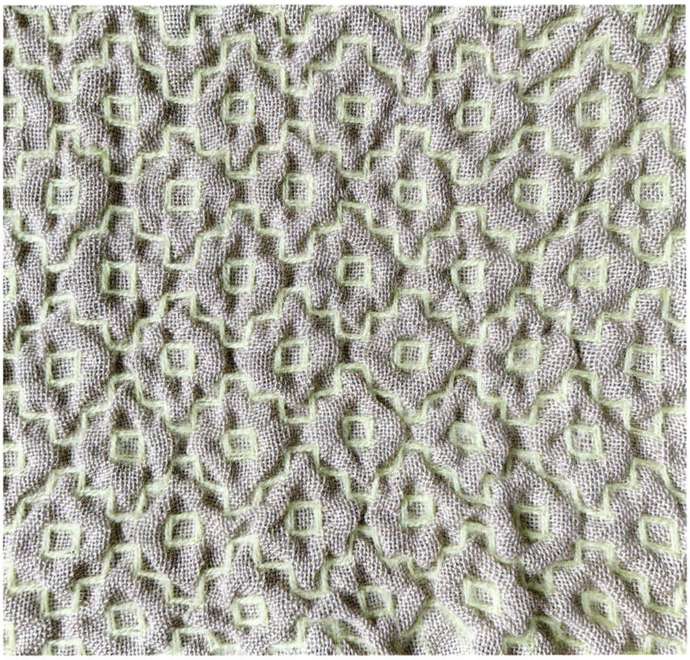

Side B.

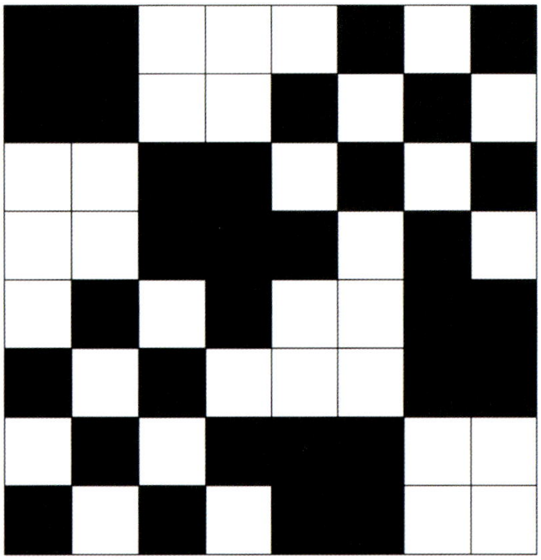

The quadrant tie-up shows which pattern blocks are being used for each element of the design.

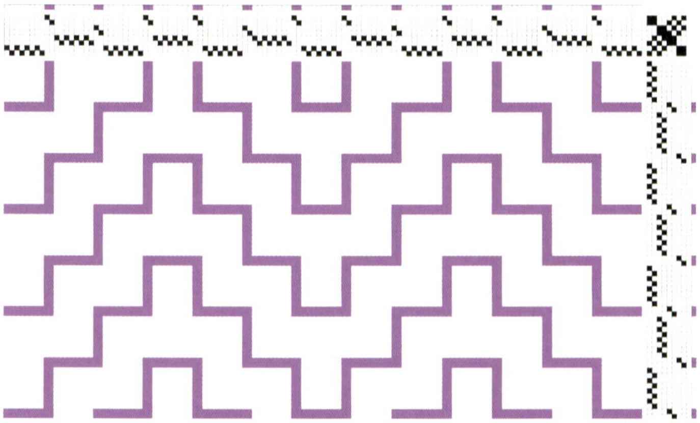

Yamagata shows the impact of a different threading pattern on shafts 5 & 6, 7 & 8.

There is not much difference between the threadings of Jūjizashi and Yamagata, but the bottom-right quadrant in the tie-up has switched the blocks around.

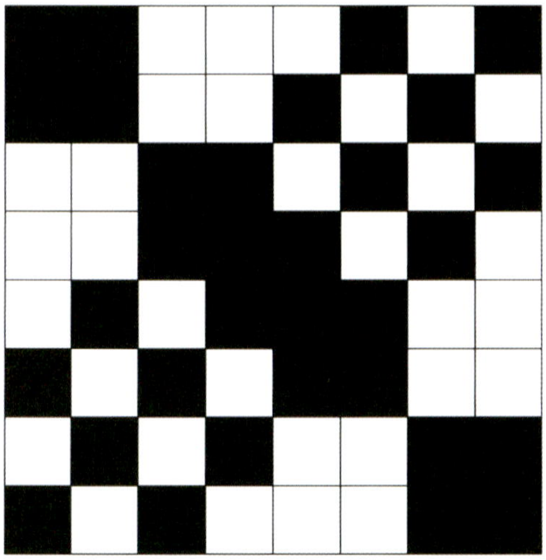

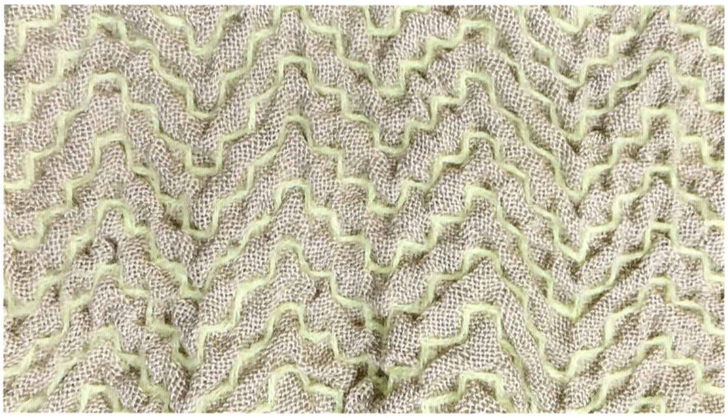

Yamagata is a variation of Dan tsunagi. It is the same on both sides of the fabric.

With the same threading as for Yamagata, variations on the persimmon flower stitch – Kakinohanazashi – are possible.

Igetazashi – the 'well curb' stitch – has a dramatic impact but would require 22 shafts in a divided threading.

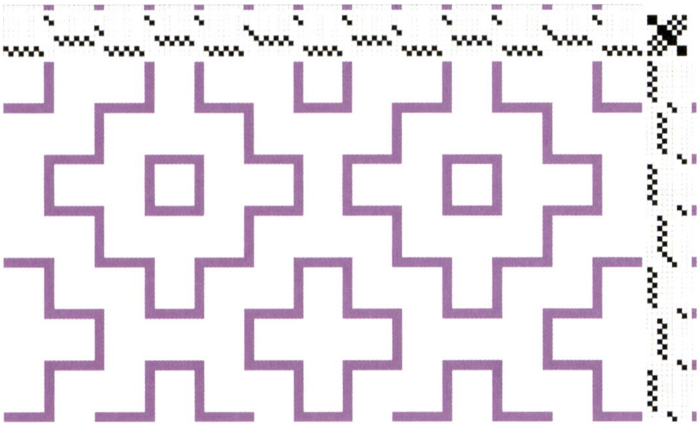

Kakinohanazashi can use the same threading and tie-up as Yamagata but with variations in the treadling.

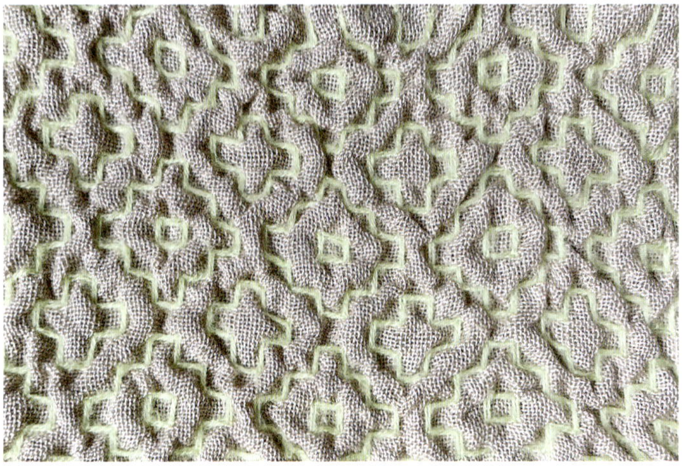

Kakinohanazashi (the persimmon flower stitch) is also the same on both sides.

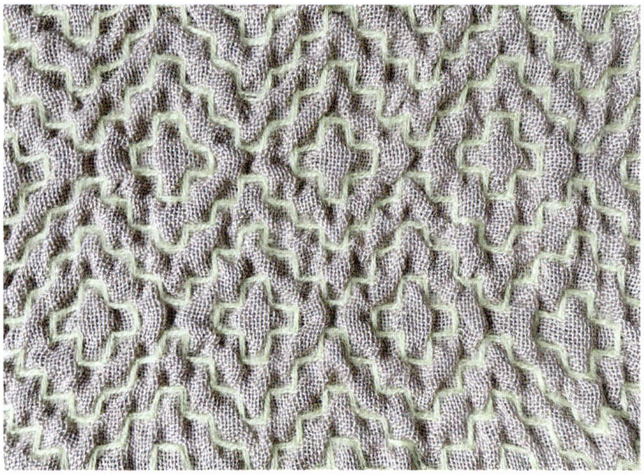

Sanjū Kakinohanazashi is a mix of Yamagata and Kakinohanazashi but has different surfaces on each side.

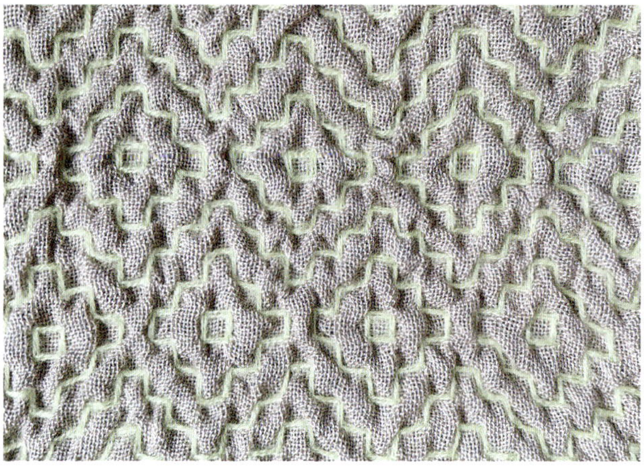

Side B.

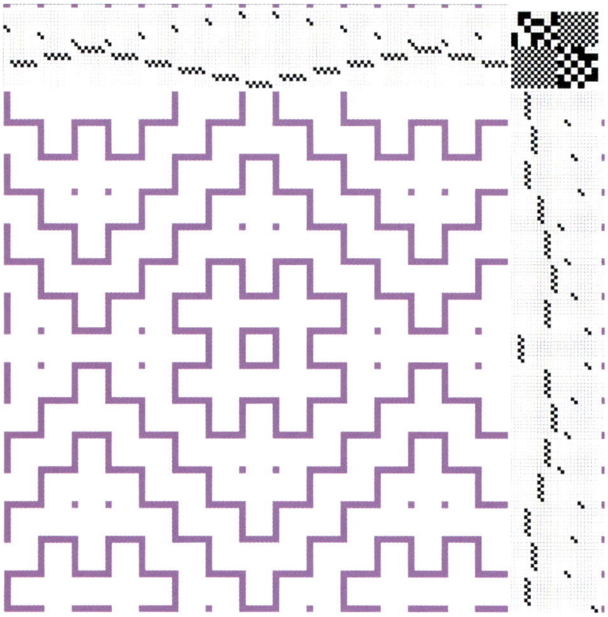

The Igetazashi – 'well curb' stitch – is a design that would require quite a few more shafts than many weavers have available.

Wet-finishing

For wet-finishing, non-shrinking pattern yarns will need to be pulled up a little to create the dimensional patterning and knotted off to keep the patterning consistent. With wool, wet-finishing is still required as this is the method that will allow the gathering effect to occur as the wool yarns full in hot and sudsy water.

Sashiko as Design in Stitched Double Cloth

Different forms of sashiko designs can also be used in stitched double cloth. Single line forms can be effectively adopted for that (*see* Chapter 10).

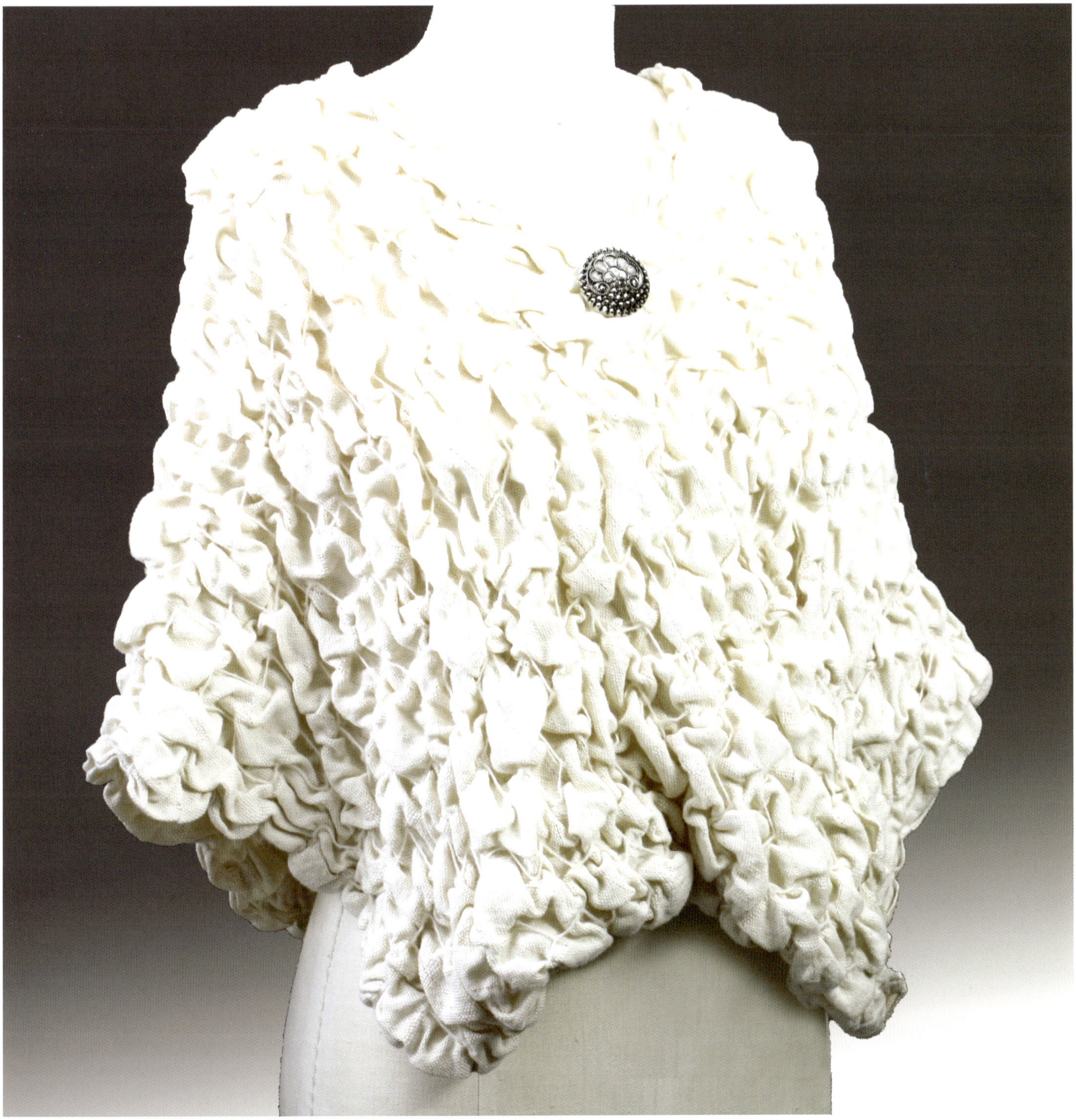

Karen Donde's original 'Bubble Wrap' draft uses organic cotton, worsted wool and metallic rayon. The ends are sewn together with a twist in the shawl. (Photo credit: Karen Donde)

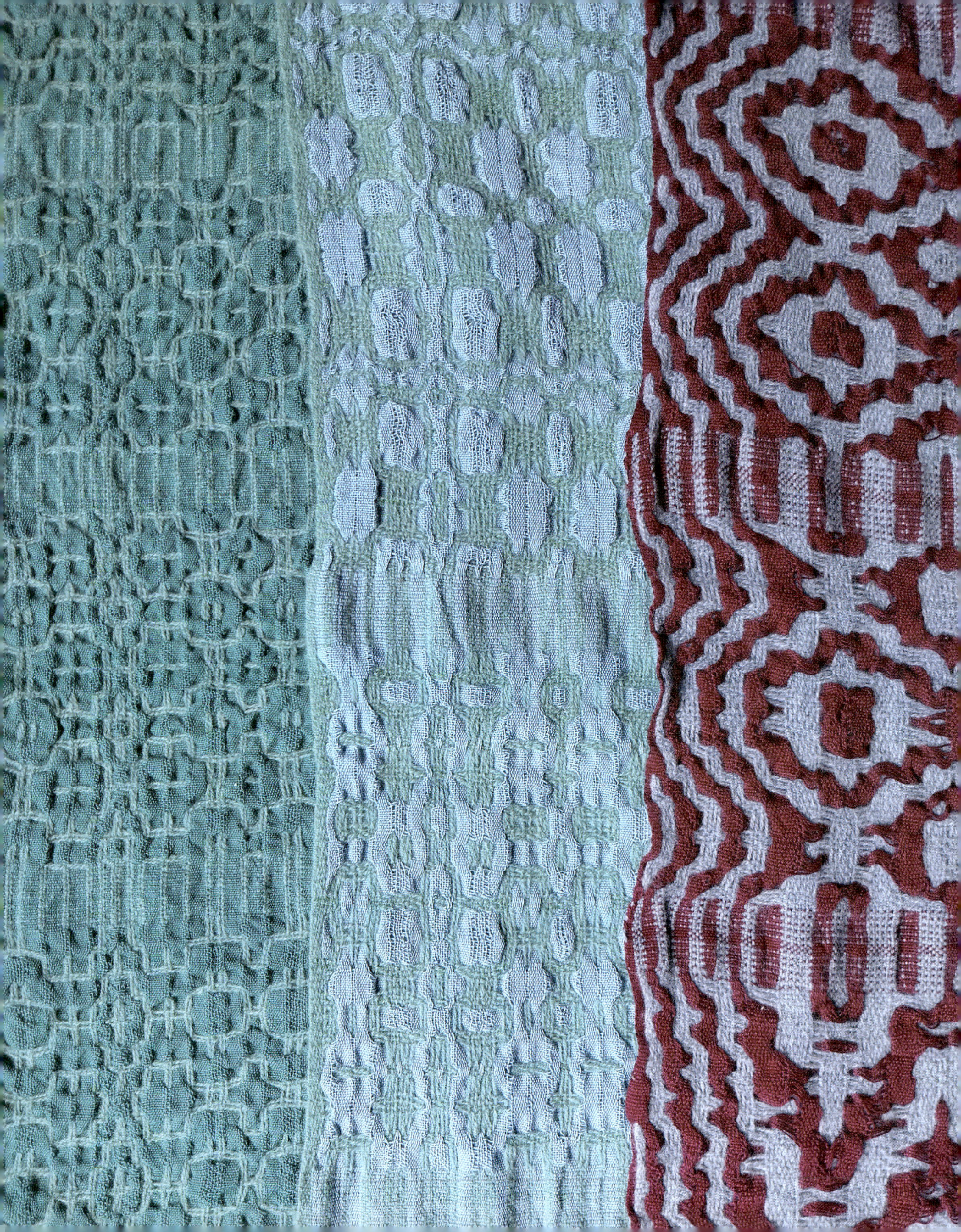

CHAPTER 8

DEFLECTED DOUBLE WEAVE

Deflected double weave can be thought of as a blend of double weave and honeycomb (sometimes known as deflected or distorted weft in the UK), which is maybe not an association weavers would normally make. In one sense, it is not what is normally understood as a double weave. It uses two warps and two wefts as in double weave, with a structure of plain weave cells and floats in warp and weft, as in honeycomb. Unlike double weave, the two warps are placed side by side rather than one on top of the other, and active cells are woven in opposition to each other. Unlike honeycomb, it doesn't include outline picks in plain weave – although that is a variation that can be adopted.

Two wefts are used to interact with the two warps, with one warp being woven with its own weft, and the second warp with the second weft, creating individual woven cells surrounded by warp and weft floats. The warp floats are selected either to be raised above the current weft being used or to remain down to lie as floats underneath the weft. The longer the active floats in warp and weft, the bigger the dimensional result.

The double layered nature of the final fabric shows up mostly once the warp tension has been relaxed and the floats and cells can move about. With the interaction of the warp floats being either above or below the plane of the adjacent cell, the two separate warps are intertwined intimately and can move to lie partially (or wholly) one above or underneath the other, depending on the orientation of the floats and cells. This becomes more emphatic after wet-finishing, and the two sides of the fabric can look totally different, especially if one of the warps uses shrinking yarn and the design is asymmetrical.

Deflected double weave is incredibly versatile as it can be adapted in many ways. For example, it can also be woven with double weave pockets and lacy interactions, as Janney Simpson does (*see* Bibliography). Varying ratios play a big part in this weave for texture.

Many intriguingly complex patterns can be created through the selection of colours. Dimensional textures can also be created through using one warp and its associated weft in an active yarn, with the other warp and weft in a passive yarn. With our eye to dimensional weaving, this latter is what we are exploring in this chapter. Different colours in the drafts have been employed specifically to highlight the different yarns, but if the aim is for texture only, using contrasting tones for the active and passive yarns in weaving, i.e. black for active and white for passive gives the maximum impact.

Wool or elastane are often the materials of choice for the active yarn. For our purposes, the active yarn will often be referred to as wool and the passive as cotton.

Samples exploring various ratios of active to passive yarns in deflected double weave.

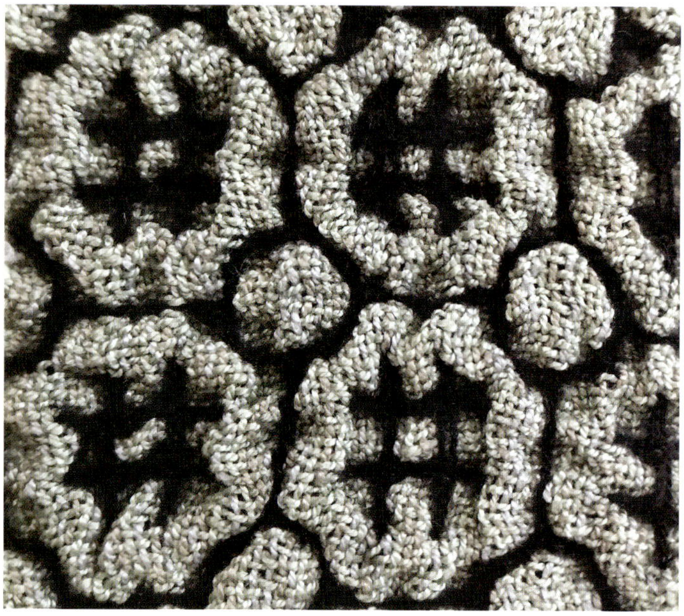

Many deflected double weave designs can be converted easily into textural effects. Barbara Herbster's sample shows two distinct faces with contrasting amounts of ends and picks between the two elements of thicker cotton and thinner wool.

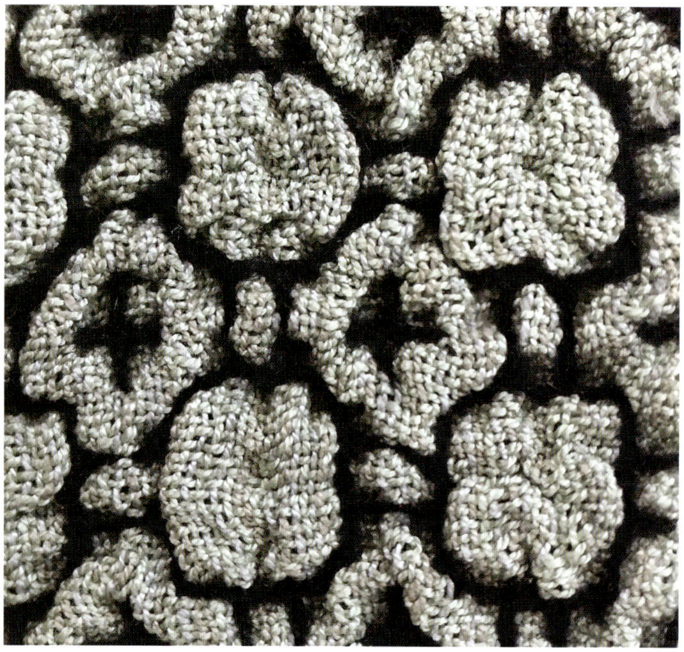

The reverse side gives a different effect. (Photos: Barbara Herbster)

PRINCIPLES

A minimum of two cells of plain weave, side by side in the warp, are woven alternately, first one cell (A) weaving plain weave for several picks, then the second cell (B) weaving plain weave for several picks. Only one of the two cells is woven at a time, while the weft yarn floats either under or over the cell not being woven. This is possible on four shafts and is easily extended to eight.

It is often designed with one warp being slightly wider than the other. There are a couple of reasons for this:

1. Symmetry in visual design
2. Ease of weaving

With deflected double weave, because the two warps are independent of each other and only connected through the interaction of the floats, moving from top to bottom and bottom to top, each warp has its own selvedge. A consistent and neat selvedge to the inner warp is required so that it doesn't have odd floating ends trapped on the wrong side of the fabric and having to travel up to the next segment separately from its colleagues. The same principle is needed, whether one warp is extended beyond the other, or both have one outer edge each.

An interesting effect can be created in, say, a scarf where the central area is a fairly narrow deflected double weave with wool and cotton, and extended cotton

WEAVING THE TWO WEFTS

For ease of weaving, start the two wefts on opposite sides so that they remain separated after each segment. Whichever is the inner warp on the selvedge, check to see the next action that block is due to take.

If it is to be raised while the following weft block is being woven, the resting weft needs to be on the surface of the fabric with its weft coming up between the last two warp blocks.

If it is to be lowered, ensure that the resting weft passes between the two outer blocks to the underside of the fabric so that it lies under the outermost selvedge block of the other warp.

selvedges that ruffle gently after the wool has shrunk during wet-finishing.

Ratio

The ratio of the two yarns has often been discussed before, but it is being reiterated here because it can make a big difference with this structure. Experimentation will reward the curious weaver with very marked variations in textural and visual appearance. A ratio of 1:2 (one active yarn for every two passive yarns) is a good place to start, but other ratios such as 1:3 and 1:4 and so on are possible, even down to just two ends of active yarn in a block against many finer ends in passive blocks. The odd–even threading ensures that plain weave continues to be woven.

Sett

Normally a deflected double weave is sett between a twill and a plain weave, depending on yarn choice. For shinier yarns such as mercerised cotton, the need for controlling the slippery nature of the yarn would tend to lean towards the twill sett. When using unmercerised cotton, cottolin or linens, a sett closer to plain weave would be more appropriate as these yarns have more body to them. When the selected yarns have different thicknesses, it is often an average that is taken for the sett. However, the two yarns can be sett differently across the same warp.

For dimensional texture, the passive areas will be larger than the active areas, which means longer floats on the active yarns. The selected ratio will also have a bearing. If the active yarn is used sparingly, sett only for the passive yarn. If the two are closer together in ratio, sett them according to their yarn properties. If the active yarn is wool, a slightly open sett allows for the woven areas to full as well as for the floats to shrink on wet-finishing. If the passive yarn is a firm or thicker yarn, such as a cottolin, perhaps have a slightly more open sett than for regular plain weave so that it is not too stiff a fabric for the active yarn to affect.

It also depends on how the individual weaver likes to weave – a firm fabric or a more pliable one. Sampling will help to determine the best sett for individual preference.

DESIGNING

Four Shafts

Deflected double weave can be created on four shafts with two blocks. A surprising number of variations can be achieved with only two blocks of threading as there are four different blocks of treadling that can be combined in various ways. (*See* Bibliography – *Heddlecraft*, April 2020, for full details)

One block uses a passive yarn and the other an active yarn. During wet-finishing, the active yarn shrinks, creating surface texture in the passive fabric. To obtain more texture, increase the widths of the passive blocks in both threading and treadling. It could be interesting to vary the ratio of the active to passive yarn blocks across the width of the same warp to create gradations of texture.

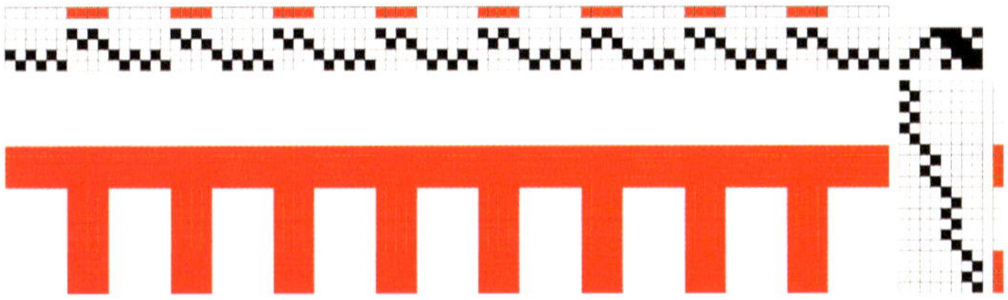

These drafts show the front and back of deflected double weave for four shafts. There are four different elements to the tie-up. The first two columns show a cell on shafts 1 & 2 weaving plain weave while shafts 3 & 4 remain down. Columns 3 & 4 show shafts 3 & 4 weaving plain weave while shafts 1 & 2 remain down. Columns 5 & 6 show shafts 1 & 2 weaving plain weave while shafts 3 & 4 are lifted, so above the weaving cell. Columns 7 & 8 show shafts 3 & 4 weaving plain weave while shafts 1 & 2 are lifted above the weaving cell.

The reverse view.

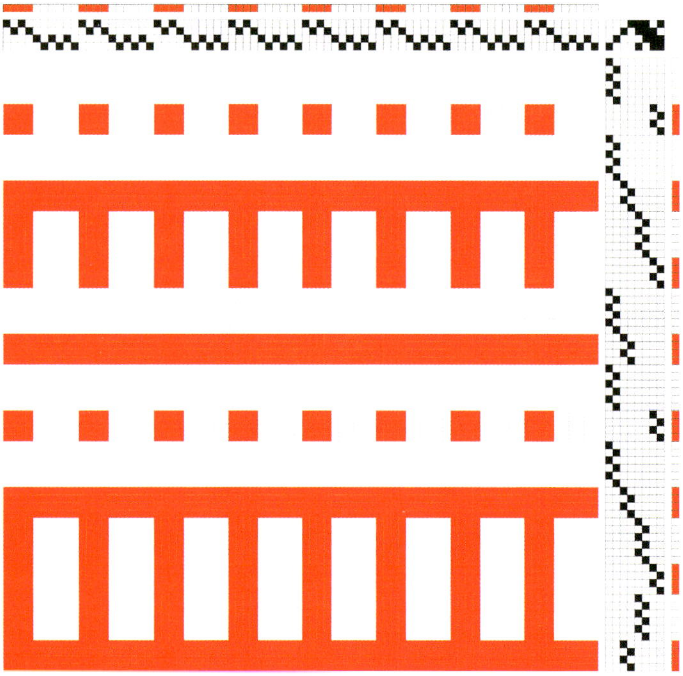

The four different elements lead to many combinations. The draft shows one selection.

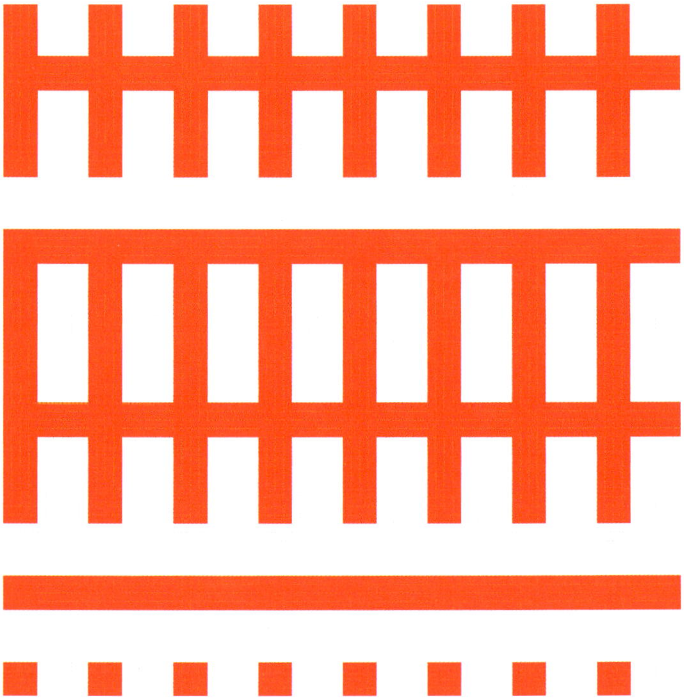

The same draft is now viewed from the reverse.

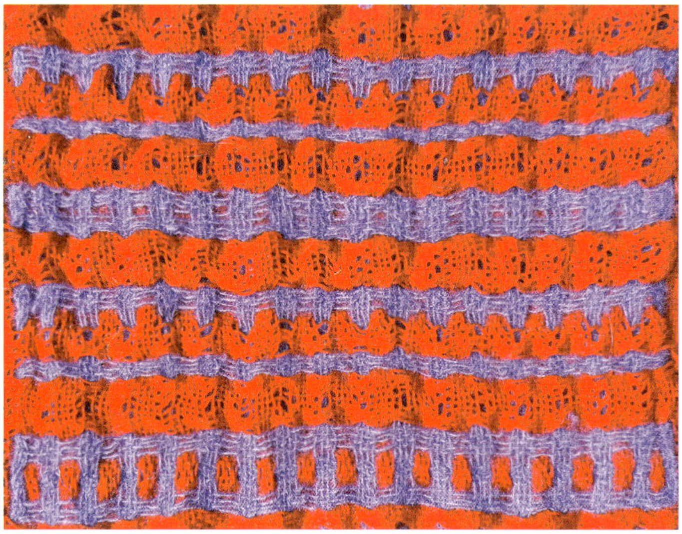

With wool and cotton as the two warps, there is the potential for texture. The wet-finishing has been done lightly so only a little textural effect is created.

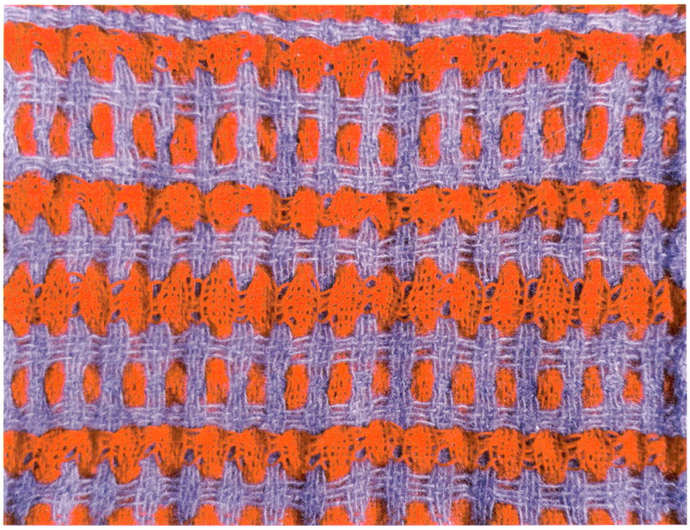

The corresponding reverse side of the fabric shows the variations between sides.

Eight Shafts

There are several ways of designing deflected double weave drafts for eight shafts.

Regular Threading Blocks Profiles

The first method uses a regular deployment of the threading blocks. This is very familiar to most weavers as the threading, although in blocks, resembles many threading drafts found in publications and online that can be used as profile drafts.

For our purposes, warp I (arbitrarily cotton) is threaded on shafts 1 & 2 and 5 & 6, Warp II (say wool) is threaded on shafts 3 & 4 and 7 & 8. If we assign letters to each block – A (cotton), B (wool), C (cotton), D(wool) – we can thread those blocks in any adjacent order we wish, so A can be followed by B or D; B by C or A; C by B or D; D by A or C. Many block variations are possible.

The tie-up for this regular order of threading blocks has a distinctive appearance. (The tie-up describes whether a block is being woven in plain weave or whether it is floating.) If the floats are up, then that warp block is on the upper layer. If the floats are down, then that warp block is on the underside. It is the interaction of the floats with the woven cells that denote whether the woven cells will appear on the face or the reverse of the fabric and also dictates where the shrinkage will occur when using a combination of active and passive blocks.

For the first two treadles, Blocks A and C weave plain weave with the same cotton weft, while Block B remains down and Block D floats above. In the next two treadles, Blocks B and D weave plain with their weft (wool), Block C is down and Block A is up. For the next two treadles, the sequence moves up once more so that Blocks A and C are weaving plain again with the cotton weft, but this time block D is down and Block B is up. The sequence concludes with treadles 7 and 8 weaving Blocks B and D in plain weave with the wool weft, Block A remaining down and Block C being lifted. The tie-up can switch over which warp blocks are floating and which stay down.

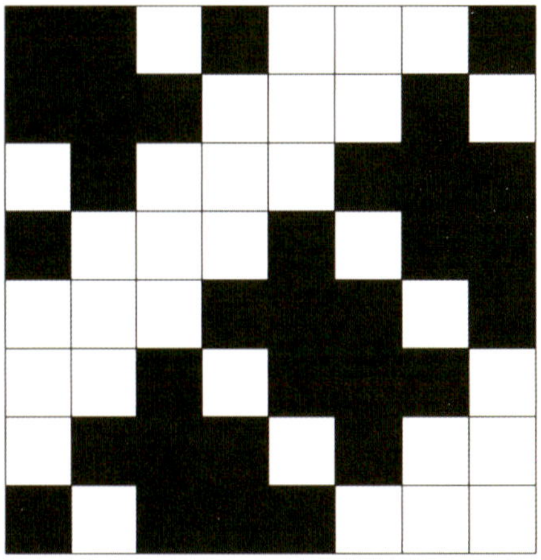

The regular deflected double weave tie-up for eight shafts has a distinctive appearance created through the use of plain weave on two sets of shafts, accompanied by blocks of warps up (black) and down (white). Blocks A and C weave plain together with the first weft and Blocks B and D weave plain together with the second weft. Each weft only weaves with its own warp.

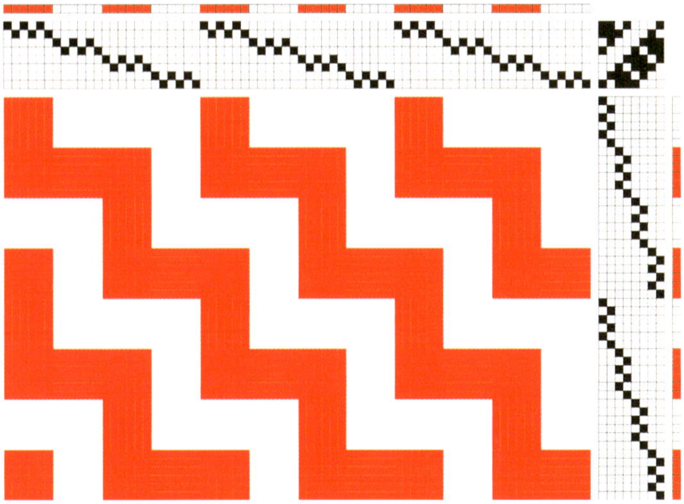

An example with straight block threading and treadling. The threading blocks are remaining fairly even in these examples, although more texture will be obtained through reducing the ends and picks in the wool warps and weft blocks. Even designs like this are the same on the front and back.

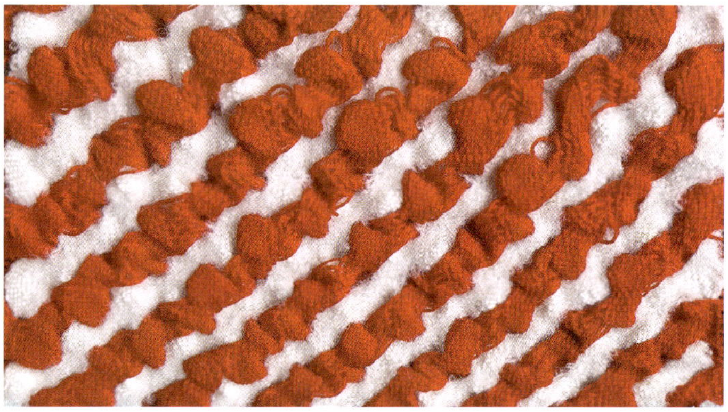

The wet-finishing of the white merino results more in a diagonal effect in comparison to the stair-step effect of the draft.

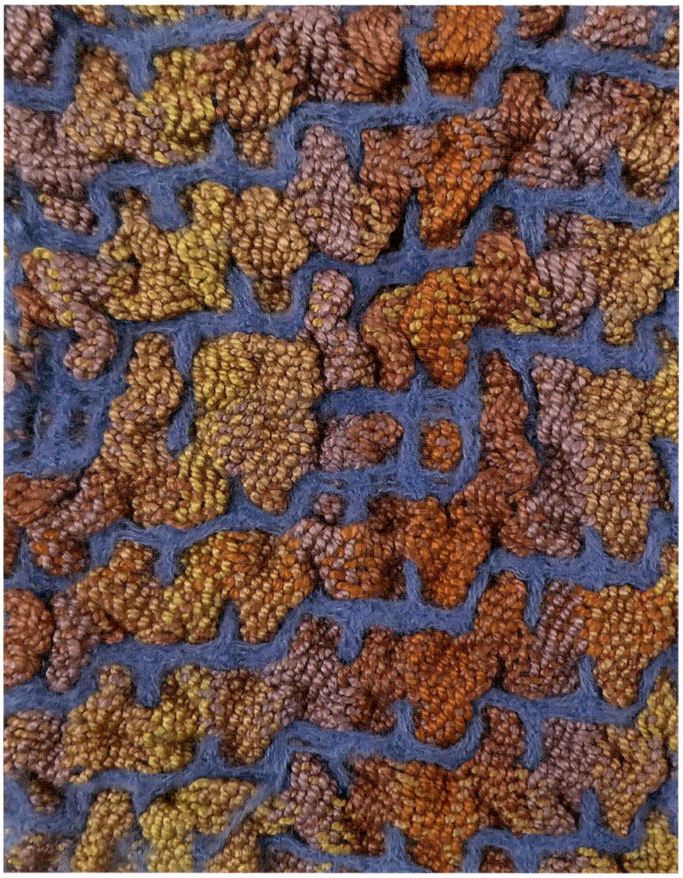

Blocks irregularly threaded and woven as drawn in give the exaggerated and irregular steps in this sample (from a workshop by Ruby Leslie).

For weavers who like to use skeleton tie-ups on their floor looms, there is a 10S version and a countermarch 12S version. This can be useful in designing directly on the loom, especially if the orientation of the floats is to be changed at any point without having to retie pedals. Both require two pedals to be used together in order to raise the required shafts.

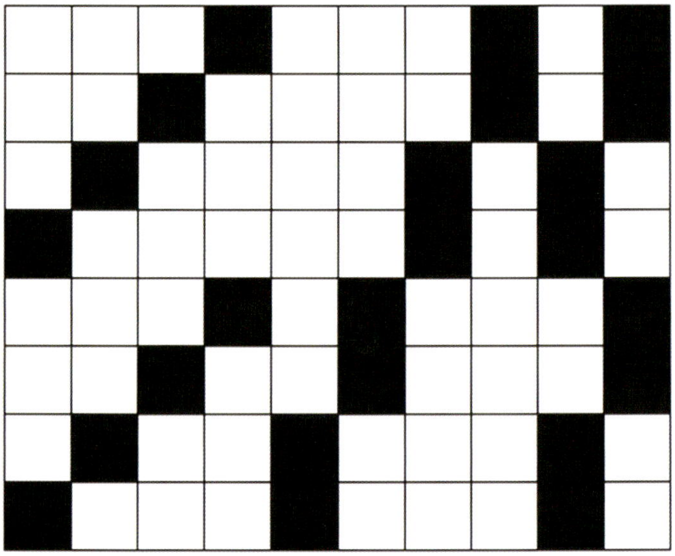

Skeleton tie-ups can be useful for some floor loom users. This one is for ten treadles and shows only rising shafts.

1	2	3	4	5	6	7	8	9	10	11	12
		X	O		X		O		O		X
		O	X		X		O		O		X
X	O			X		O		O		X	
O	X			X		O		O		X	
		X	O		O		X		O		X
		O	X		O		X		O		X
X	O			O		X		O		X	
O	X			O		X		O		X	

This 12-treadle countermarch skeleton tie-up has two distinct areas to it. The wider squares for treadles 1–4 give the plain weaves for Blocks A/C and B/D. The other treadles give the lifting options for each block. Treadles 1 & 2 (A/C) will only be used in conjunction with treadles 6, 8, 10 and 12, which dictate what is happening with the floats of Blocks B & D. Treadles 3 & 4 (B/D) will only be used in conjunction with treadles 5, 7, 9 and 11, which dictate what is happening with the floats of Blocks A & C. Note: The dark grey denotes where no shafts are tied. O denotes lifting shafts and X denotes lowering shafts. This is contrary to many tie-ups, where X denotes a rising shed.

With four-block profile drafts and assigning two shafts for each block, direct translations can be made with interesting pattern results of even the simplest two-block repeats on each warp. To enhance the dimensional aspect, increase the threading repeat in the passive warp and weft, and reduce the active threading repeat to one unit. Another option is to grade the amounts of passive to active warps/wefts across the warp.

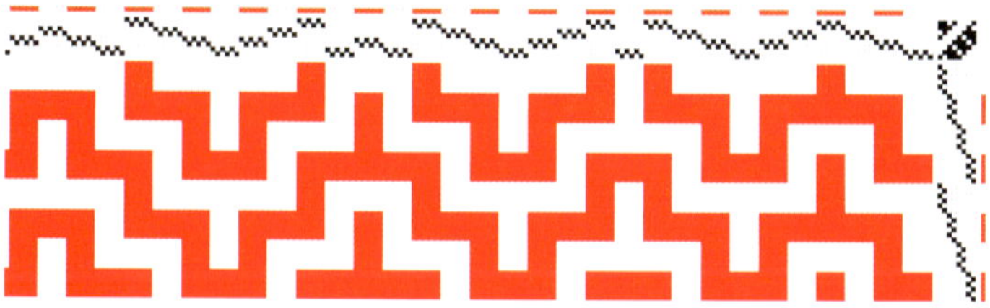

Graphic images of weaving software can only show the theoretical layout of the weaving for deflected double weave. This blocky ziggurat line will change upon wet-finishing.

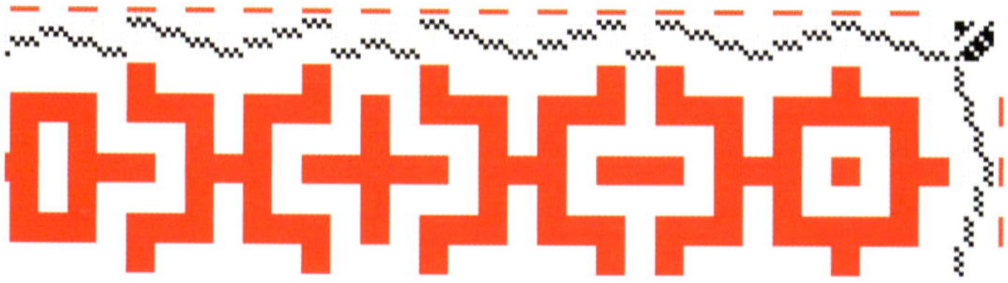

A point design contains cross, box and square designs in the draft.

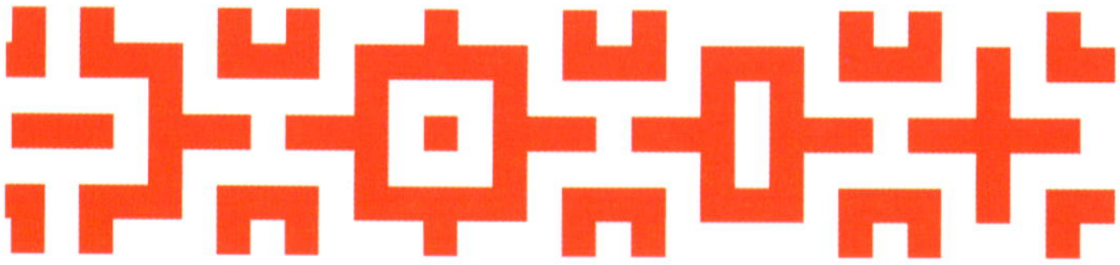

The reverse of many deflected double weave cloths are very interesting because of the orientation of the floats that are not being woven.

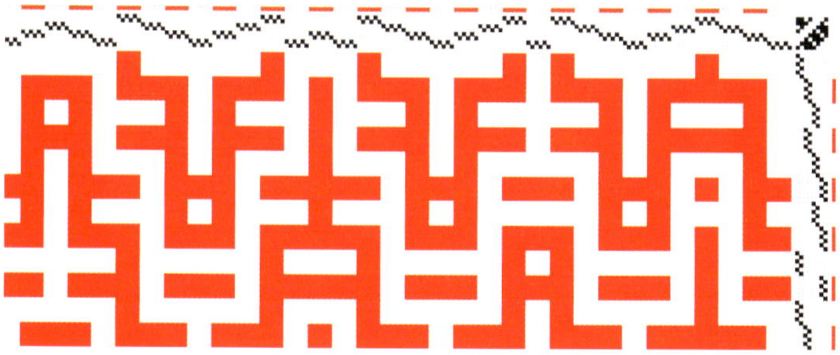

An advancing draft, however, has the same effect on both sides, although the design is shifted slightly.

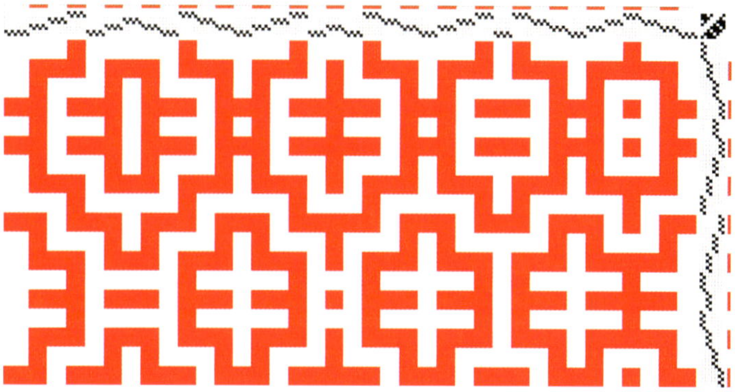

M&W is a design that varies on the two sides. The name comes from the graphic shape that the letters 'M' and 'W' have when turned sideways to fit on the treadling plan.

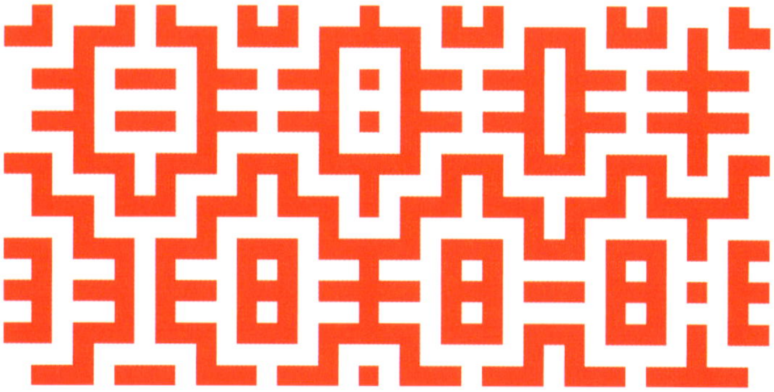

Especially when using different ratios or active versus passive warps and wefts, different effects will result after wet-finishing.

Overshot Profiles

A typical four-shaft overshot design can be translated into eight shafts quite easily. Instead of using overlapping blocks as in traditional overshot (1,2; 2,3; 3,4; 1,4), eight shafts are employed (1,2; 3,4; 5,6; 7,8).

As mentioned before, reducing the amount of ends and picks for the active blocks gives a more effective textural result.

Usual treadling patterns, such as straight, point block, M&W and woven as drawn in, give interesting results. There are even more possibilities when the reverse side is seen, especially if using an asymmetric design. While balanced designs show the same effect on both sides, an unbalanced design creates a reverse side that is completely different from the front, so resulting in a more interesting cloth.

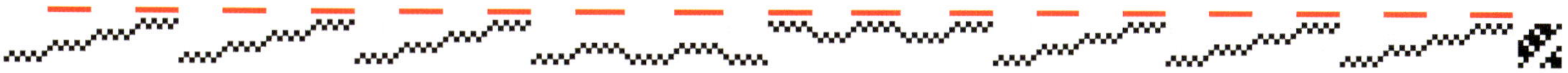

A four-shaft overshot threading of Wandering Vine, also known as Cat Track and Snail Trail, is combined with the alternative version of the deflected double weave tie-up. This tie-up gives the opposite effect of the tie-up used previously, which, when used with even numbers of ends and picks in similar yarns, has very little impact on the appearance of the fabric. However, when used in conjunction with varied ratios of warp and weft blocks, and with active and passive yarns, it can make a considerable difference if the tie-ups are swapped over.

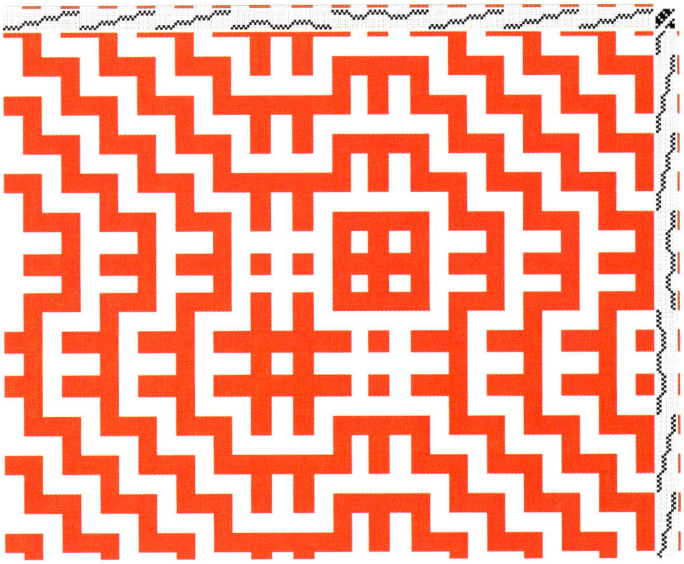

Woven as drawn in, where the same pattern is used in the treadling as in the threading, is a good place to start when designing deflected double weave from overshot designs.

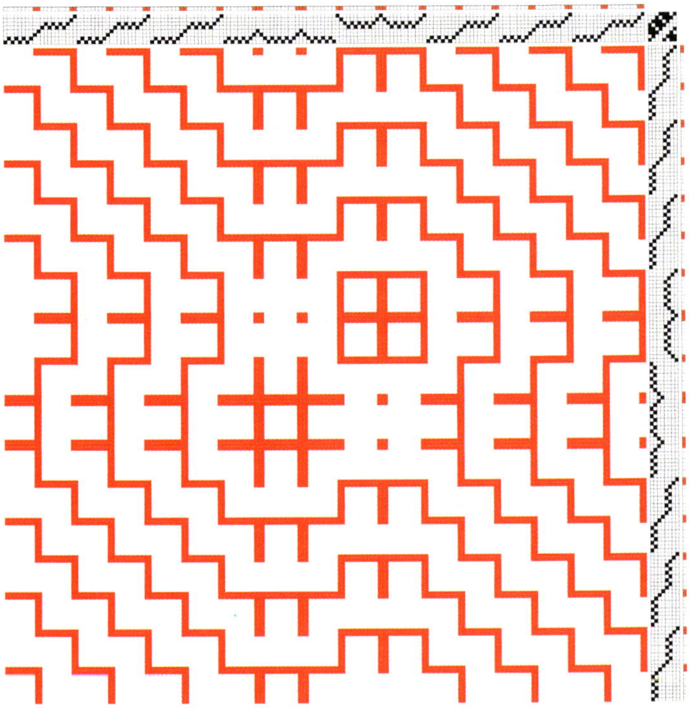

Changing the ratios between threading and treadling blocks can make a distinctive difference in the appearance of the design. Here, just two ends and picks have been used for an active yarn block and eight ends and picks for the passive yarn block.

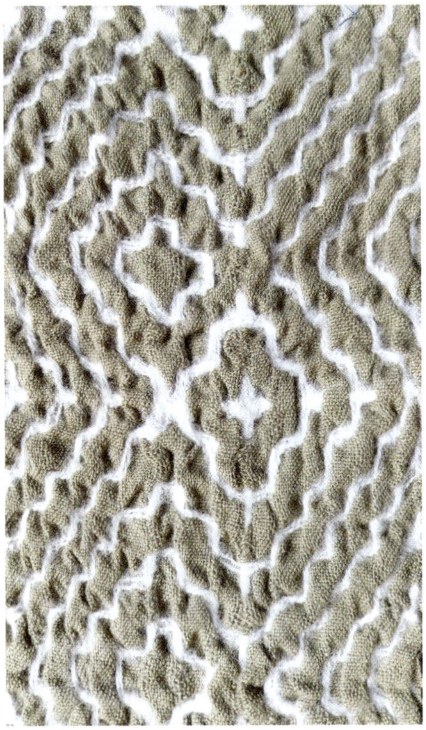

The sample shows what happens when two picks per unit (three at the reverse points) are used for the white merino warp and weft in this sample. The cotton warp and weft are able to pucker up.

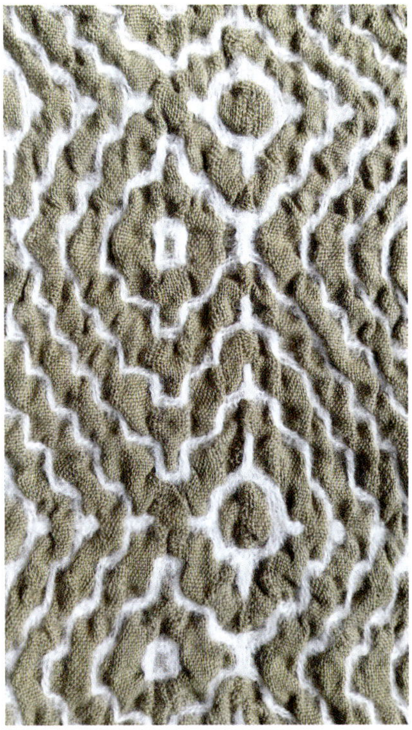

The two faces show different patterns in the cats paw section of the draft.

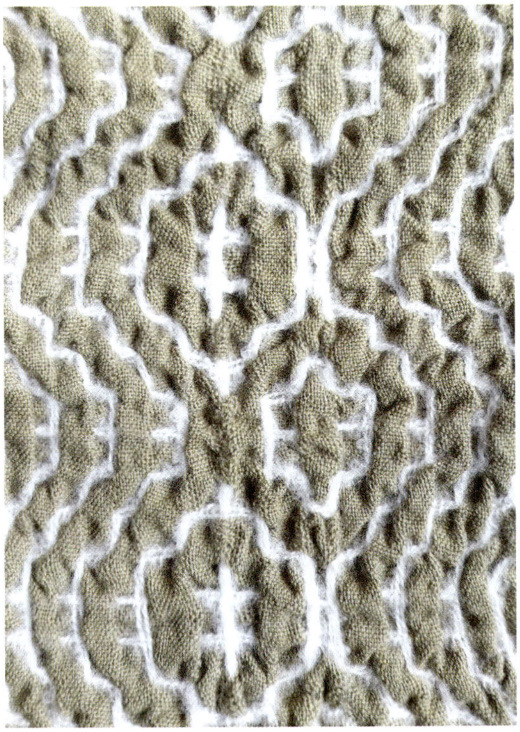

M&W, as a treadling block pattern, usually gives interesting results.

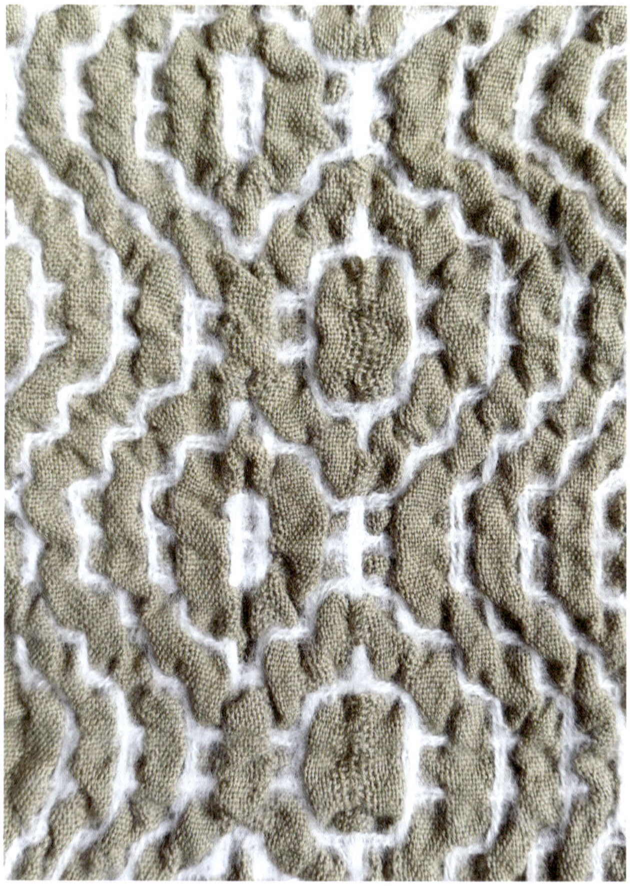
The reverse gives another design.

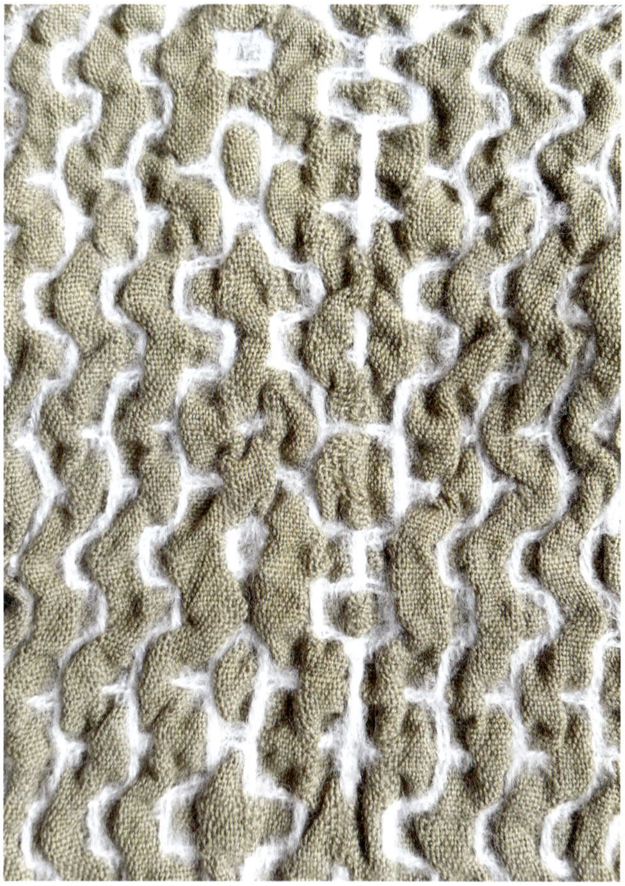
An advancing block design gives an elongated design line. The progression is: ABCDC BCDAD CDABA DABCB.

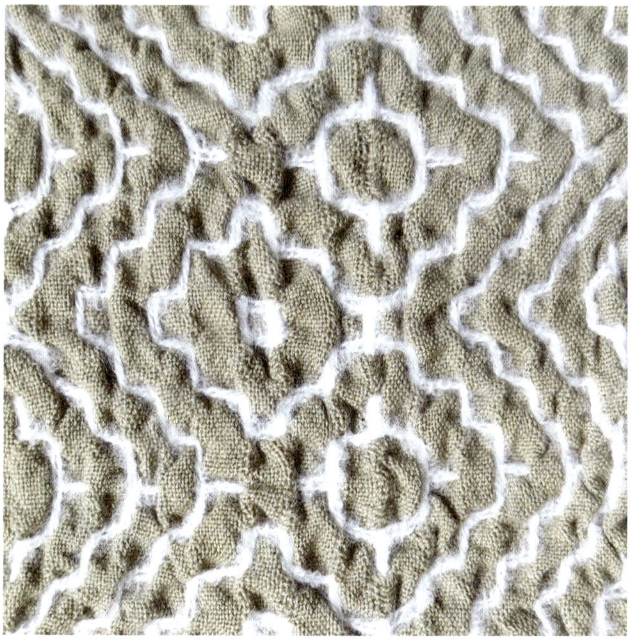
A diamond block treadling pattern shows the two elements of the cat's paw effectively.

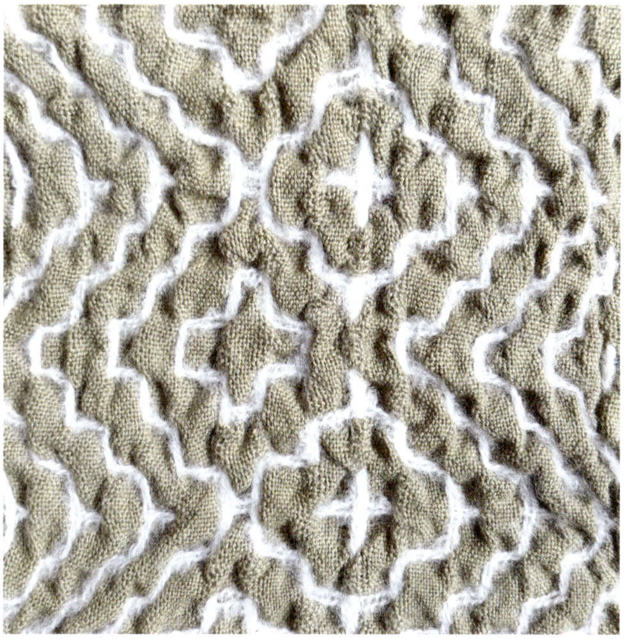
The diamond in reverse.

Designs that have a lot of symmetry will not offer great variation from the front to the back of the cloth. However, where designs use blocks in opposition to each other, i.e. blocks C and D used together and opposing blocks A and B, as in Johann Speck #33 from Marguerite Porter Davison's *A Handweaver's Pattern Book*, two very different faces show on front and back. Proportions of active to passive blocks can be varied to give more or less texture.

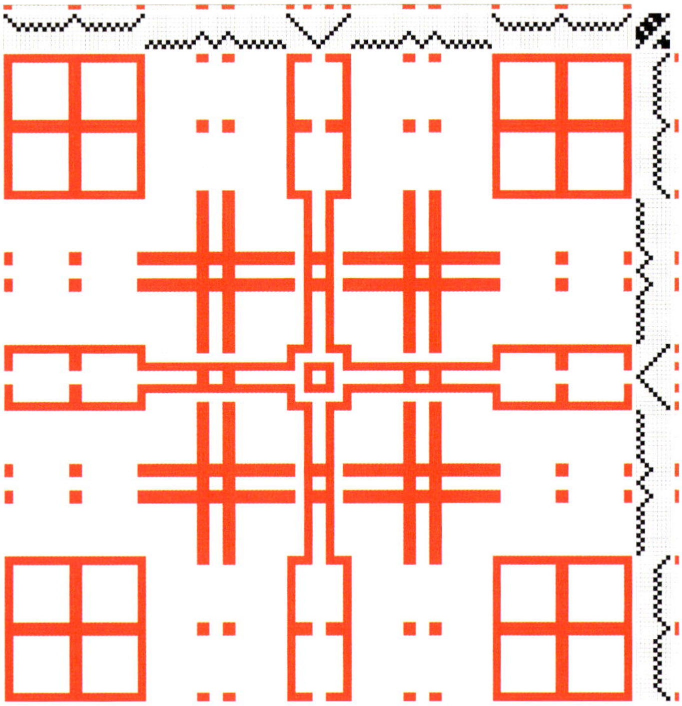

This design, taken from Johann Speck #33 overshot pattern, is a good example of an irregular draft that gives two distinct faces on either side.

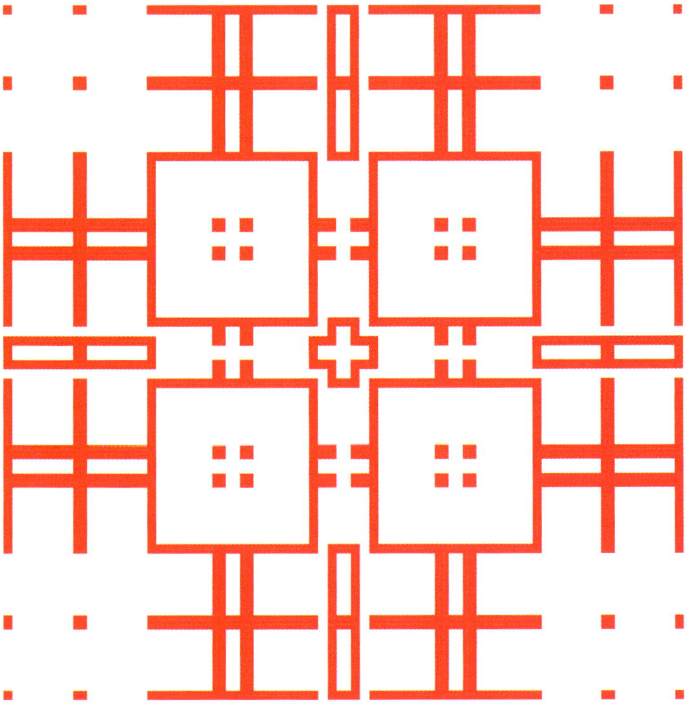

This design works well in regular deflected double weave as well as when using different ratios and active and passive yarns.

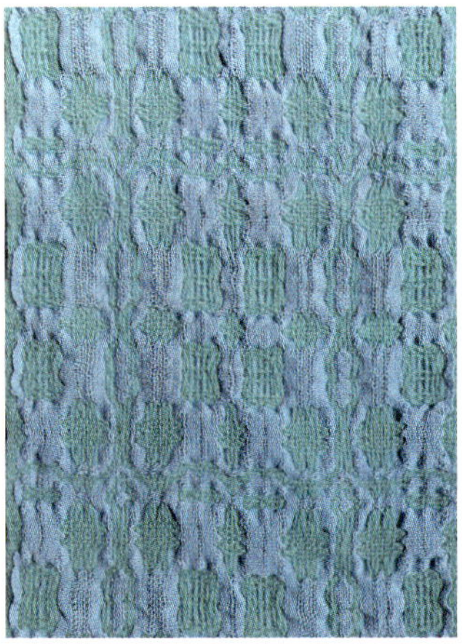

Johann Speck #33 was explored with uneven ratios. In this sample, 12 ends of cotton per threading block was contrasted with four ends of wool, a ratio of 3:1. At midpoints, two ends of wool were used.

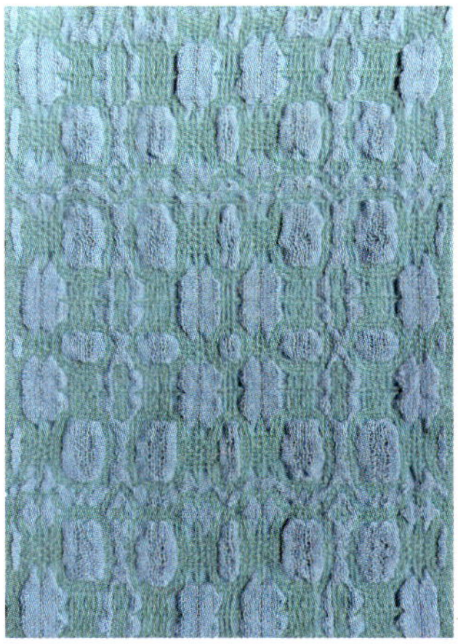

The front and reverse of this design give very different effects.

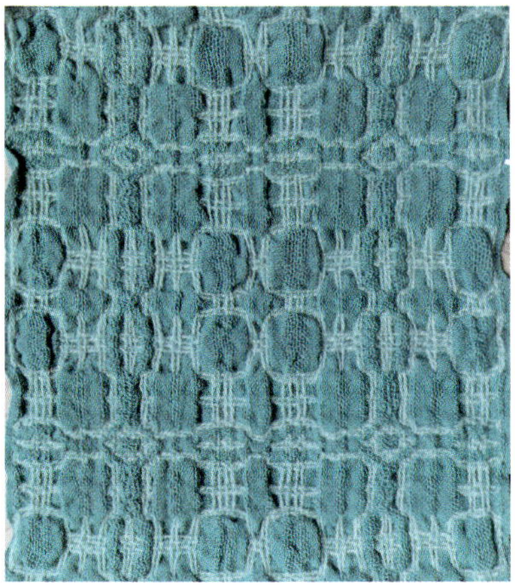

In the second sample of the same draft, only two wool ends were used throughout to give a more deeply textured result.

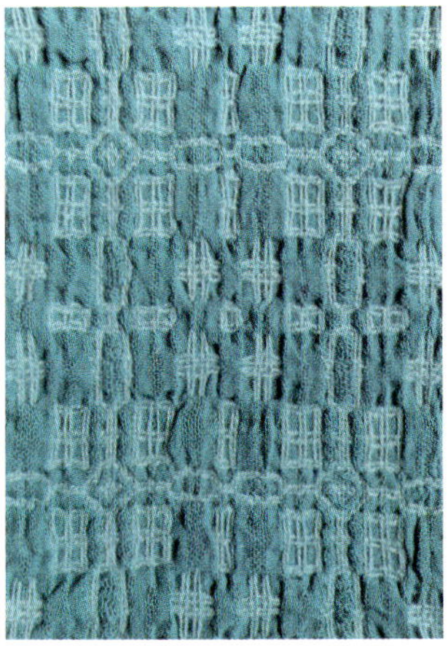

The window-pane element of this design becomes more visible here.

Any profile overshot design can be converted, and treadling variations explored. To turn a four-shaft overshot threading into a four-block profile, take each threading block – 1,2; 2,3; 3,4; 1,4 – and reduce it to just one shaft – 1; 2; 3; 4. A certain amount of interpretation is required from the weaver as to exactly how best to interpret the threading blocks. That is good because it allows for small design decisions which encourage the weaver to begin developing their own variations and therefore gaining confidence to break out and design their own profiles. Having reduced the overshot threading into a four-block profile, two shafts per block can now be assigned for an eight-shaft deflected double weave – 1,2; 3,4; 5,6; 7,8.

After that, reductions in proportions can be assigned as desired. This exact method of translation was used for the overshot designs already illustrated.

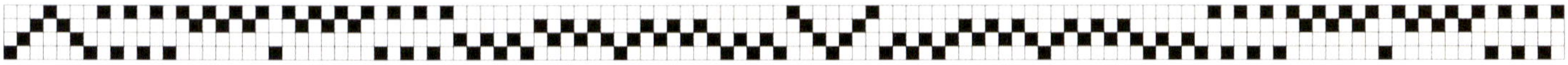
The original four-shaft overshot threading before being converted to a deflected double weave design.

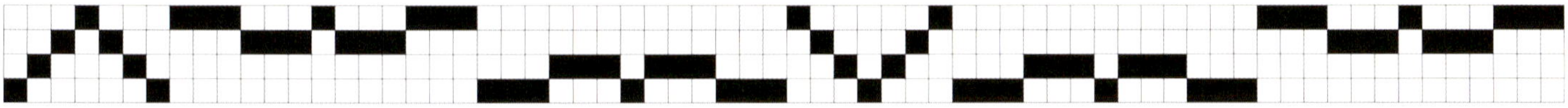
The four-shaft profile draft created from the overshot threading.

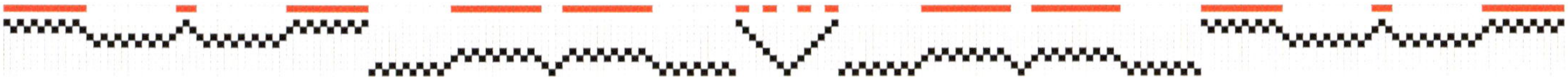
The eight-shaft threading developed from the four-shaft profile draft. Block A has been assigned shafts 1 & 2; Block B has shafts 3 & 4; Block C has shafts 5 & 6; Block D has shafts 7 & 8.

Other Profile Designs

Using an advancing unit block profile gives a more jagged edge to designs, which can also give interesting texture.

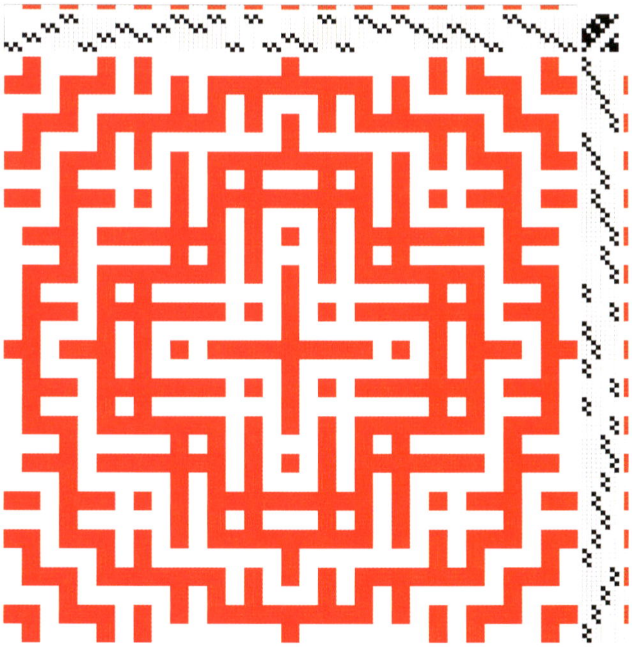
An advancing unit block profile in warp and weft has been used to create the woven-as-drawn-in design here.

The two sides are different.

An optical effect of a bulge can be adapted for extra dimensional effects by using an active yarn for two of the blocks. The passive blocks have been made a little larger and the active ones a little smaller to create the additional textural element.

Weaving the bulge with the treadling line flipped horizontally but altering the proportions of weft picks, a similar result can be achieved but giving a 'fish-eye' appearance.

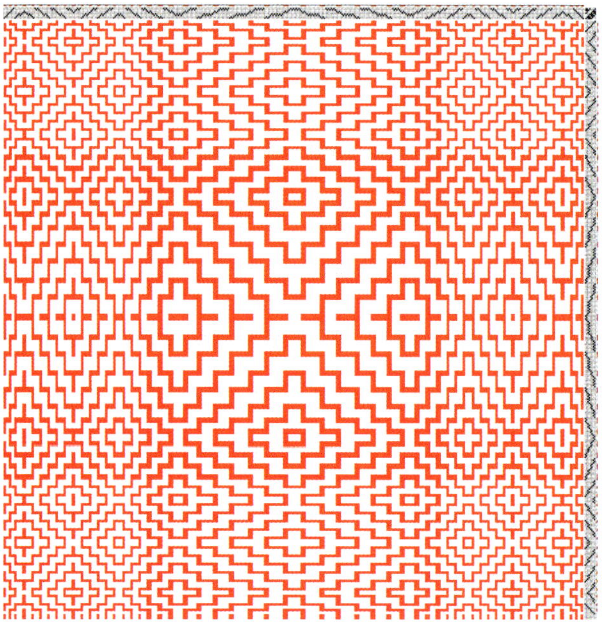

A design that increases the block sizes incrementally in both warp and weft can give a bulge effect. This uses woven as drawn in directly the same as the threading order, giving a quadrant look to the design in the centre.

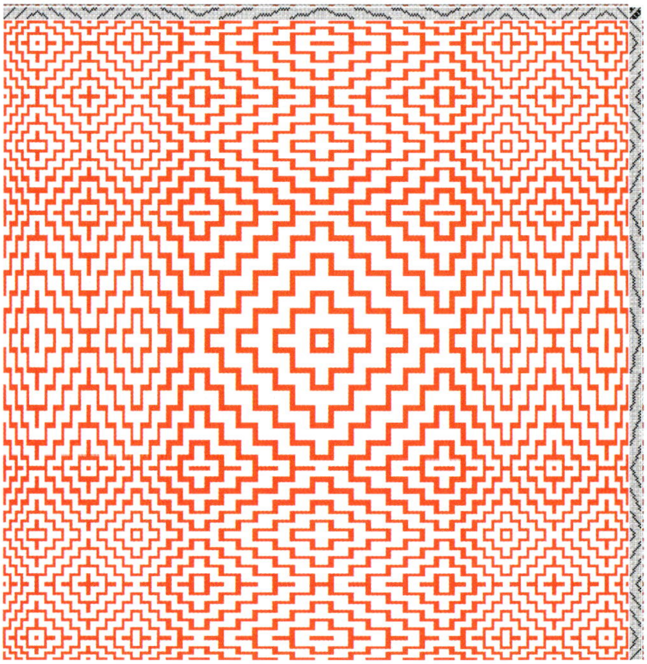

A fish-eye look can be obtained from the same draft if weaving starts from the centre of the quadrant but weaving the opposite proportions.

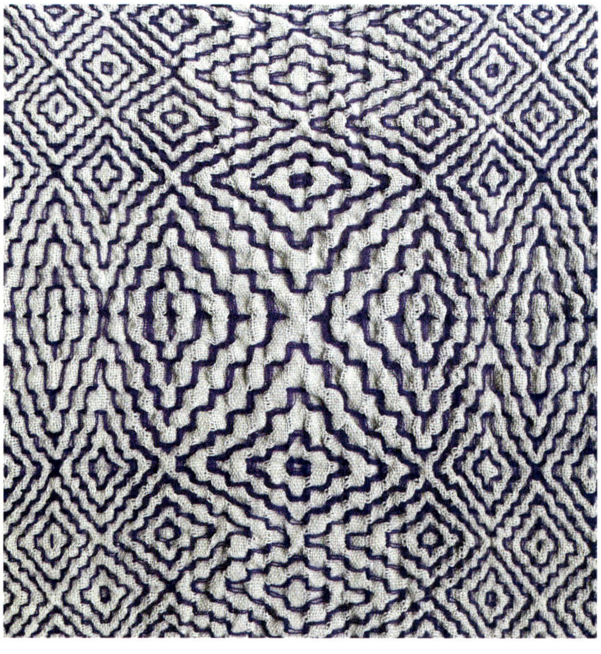

Block widths can be varied to give an optical effect to dimensional texture. Here the four-quadrants effect is seen.

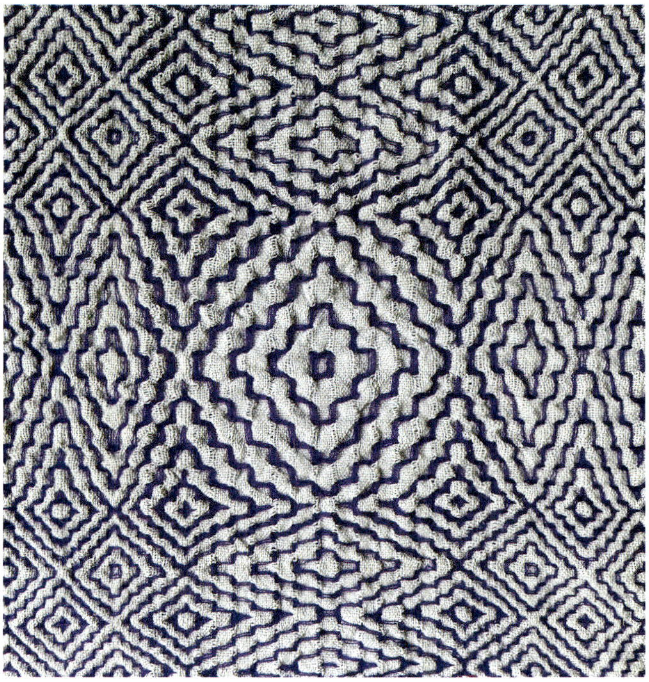

The opposite 'fish-eye' version can be generated from the same warp.

The same warp can deliver other effects.

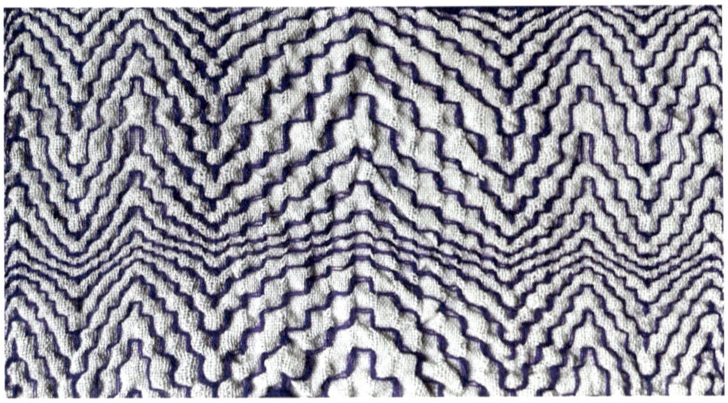

The effects of the block widths can be seen here with a straight block treadling order.

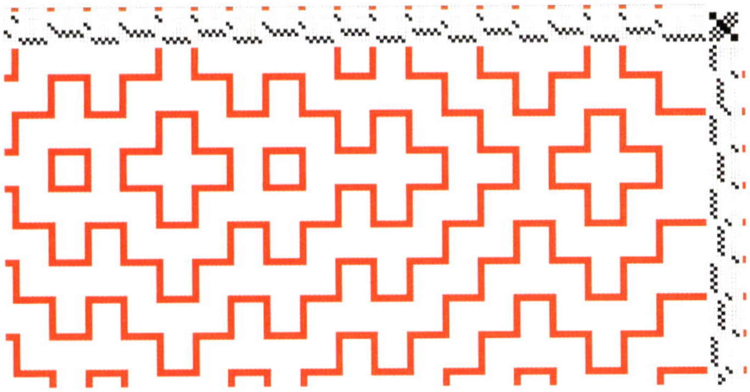

The draft shows two blocks (A and C) weaving one layer – shafts 1 & 2 and 3 & 4. There are two pattern blocks (B and D) weaving the other layer on shafts 5–8. The tie-up shows that each of the two blocks for each layer can be independently lifted or remain down when the other layer is being woven.

The sashiko style of this two-block ground deflected double weave follows the profile treadling of ACBD × 2, ADBC × 2, ACBD ADBC.

Divided Threading Blocks Method

A second method of designing deflected double weave drafts is the divided method.

In this two-block ground model, the passive ground fabric uses two blocks alternating with two pattern blocks. On eight shafts, four shafts would be required for the ground. and the remaining four shafts would be available for the patterning. Block A is on shafts 1 & 2, Block B on shafts 5 & 6, Block C on 3 & 4, and Block D on 7 & 8. Blocks A and C are now on the four shafts closer to the weaver, and Blocks B and D are on the four shafts furthest away.

Although the ground blocks alternate continually, the pattern blocks can be used in any order to create many different effects, including repeating blocks. With more than eight shafts, more pattern blocks can be used in any order required, so long as they alternate with the ground blocks. This has a feel of a block version of double two-tie threading, especially when more than eight shafts are used. Blocks A & C would remain the 'ties' and pattern blocks would be B, D, E, F, etc. for as many pairs of shafts as are available on your loom.

As you can see, these designs have a visual comparison with sashiko-style designs but depending on the yarns used, the ratio of active to passive and how they are wet-finished, they can illustrate a completely different aesthetic.

Active to passive yarn ratios can be quite extreme: 1:4 or 1:6 or more are quite feasible as the long floats created by larger passive blocks allow for more dramatic shrinkage during wet-finishing.

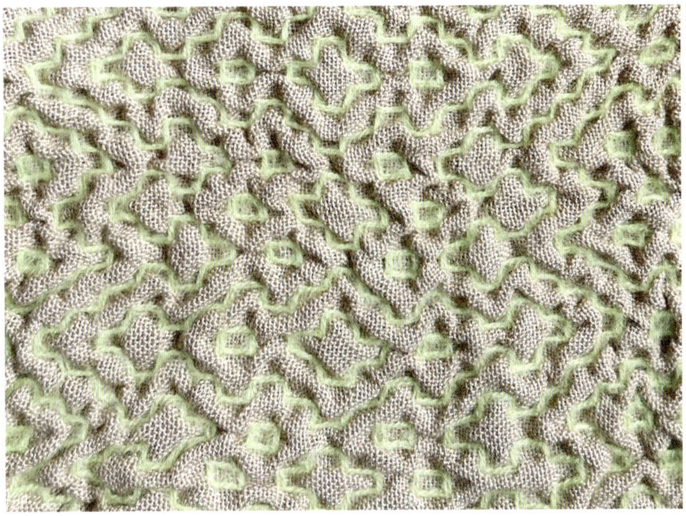

After wet-finishing, it is interesting to look at these samples in two ways. Firstly through the wool patterning that has contracted during the finishing process. Secondly, there is a different pattern emerging of the contours of the passive yarn.

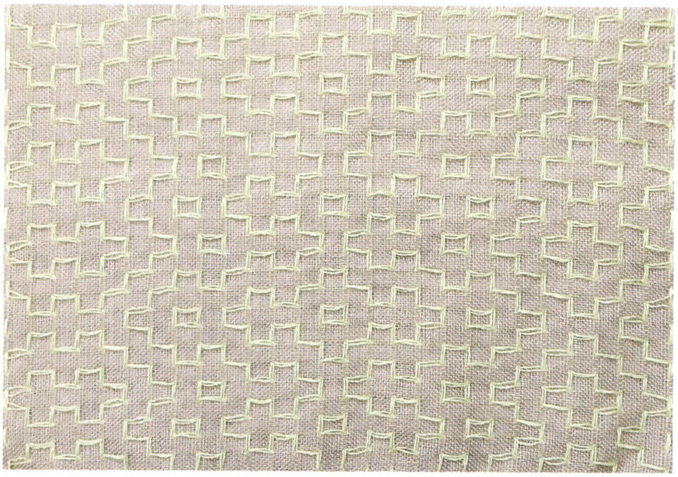

The reverse, prior to wet-finishing. The warp and weft are cotton and lambswool.

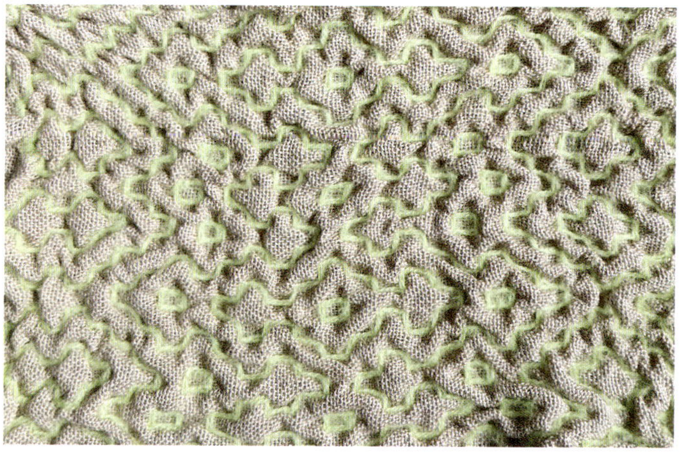

The reverse side shows a different meandering of the contours.

This sample was woven as drawn in.

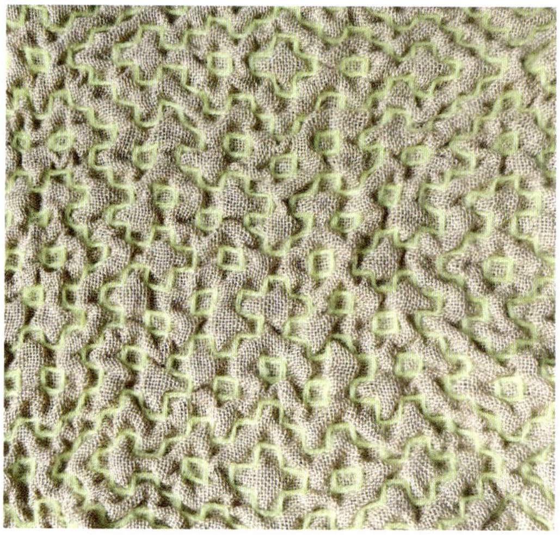

If these were woven in different colours, the effects might stand out more effectively, or conversely disappear. It would be interesting to weave this all in white to see which would dominate – the wool design or the textured surface.

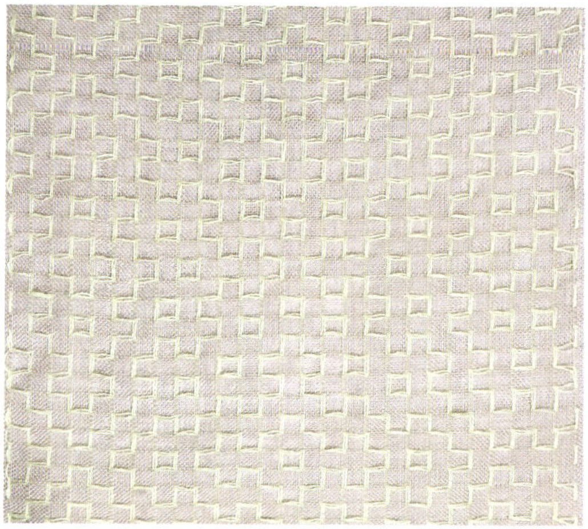

The reverse, fresh off the loom.

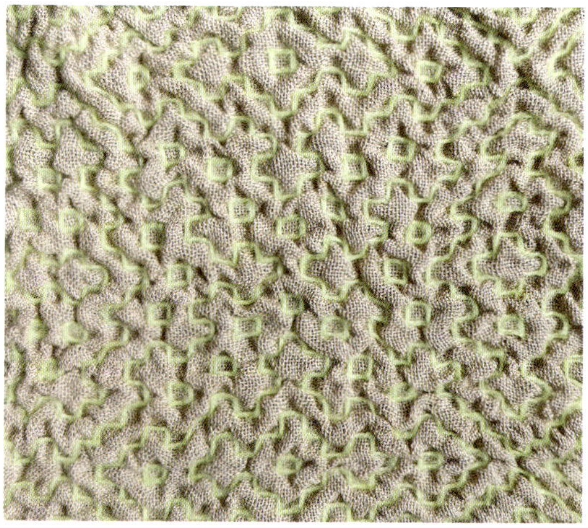

Perhaps a bold colour like red for the passive yarn would give the raised element more prominence.

Marian Stubenitsky, in her book *Double with a Twist,* also uses a telescoped profile, reducing an eight-shaft profile design down to four shafts (taking the top four shafts and shifting them down onto the first four shafts). Shafts 1 & 3 of the profile are assigned one colour, and shafts 2 & 4 are given another. Now the process moves from profile to threading and a mind-shift needs to occur.

Block A retains its eight-shaft threading position on shafts 1 & 2, but Block C is now going to shift down to shafts 3 & 4. In between these two blocks are going to be Blocks B and D on shafts 5 & 6 and 7 & 8, respectively. However, Blocks B and D can be repeated independently, according to the telescoped profile design.

Regardless of which of the various threading methods are employed, each warp group only interacts with its own weft, meaning that active blocks are woven with the active weft, and passive blocks are woven with the passive weft.

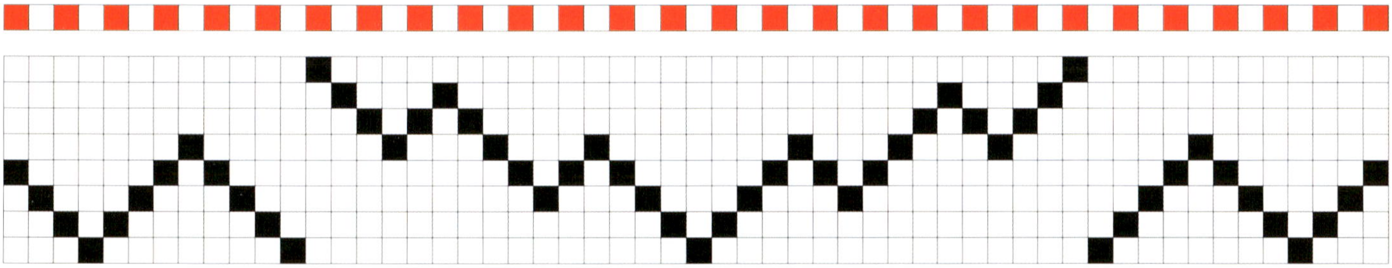

Marian Stubenitsky's eight-shaft profile threading before telescoping to four shafts.

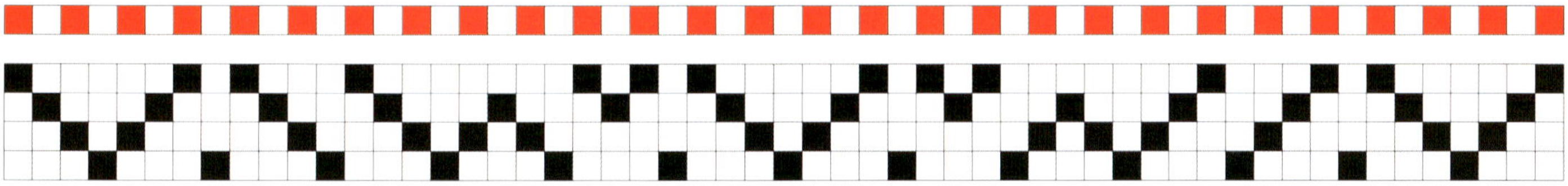

The same design with the top four shafts cut and pasted over the first four shafts. Shafts 5–8 literally move down to shafts 1–4 en masse. This is the new profile draft.

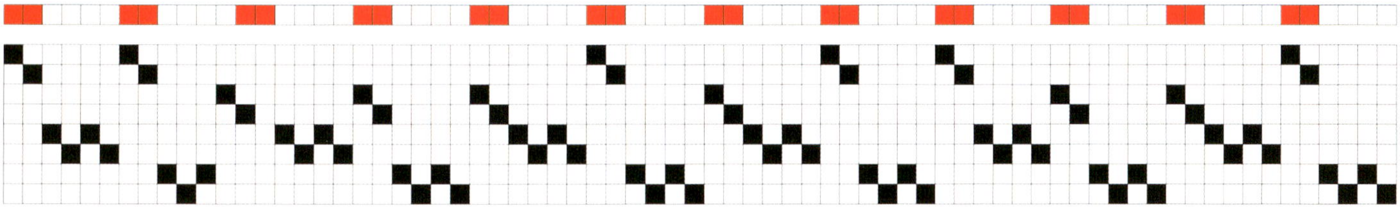

In the threading draft, shafts 1–4 are at a higher ratio (2:1) than shafts 5–8. There are four ends for each block on shafts 1 & 2 and 3 & 4, the passive yarns. Two ends per design block are given to shafts 5 & 6 and 7 & 8. These are the active yarns.

Tie-up and Treadling

The double-block ground method resembles the quadrant tie-up seen before for eight shafts as it shares many of the same principles. There are four possible tie-ups for textured fabrics.

With treadling, there are two main combinations of treadling patterns:

1. A followed by B, with C followed by D.
2. A followed by D, with C followed by B.

These can be switched around between the two groups as desired, with the ground always alternating with the pattern. Blocks can be switched at the end of a repeat of four blocks or midway through the sequence. With the two main treadling groups used in these ways – in combination with the four tie-ups – there are many different designs that can be created.

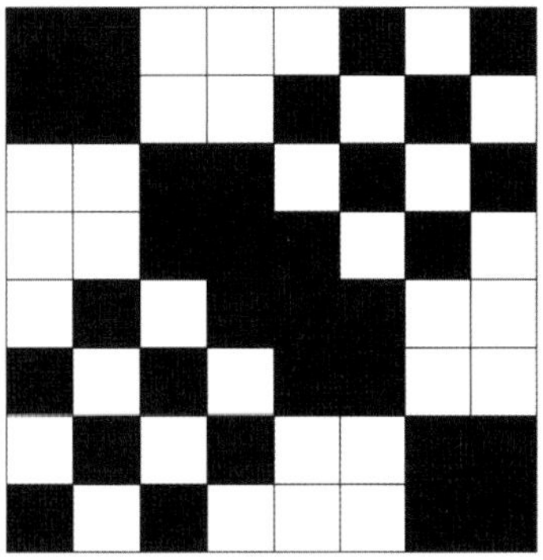

Version 1 tie-up here is the one used earlier, showing individual elements being lifted in specific combinations. The following tie-ups show the same process, but with each block acting in a different position. This makes a difference when using the same treadling sequences for each.

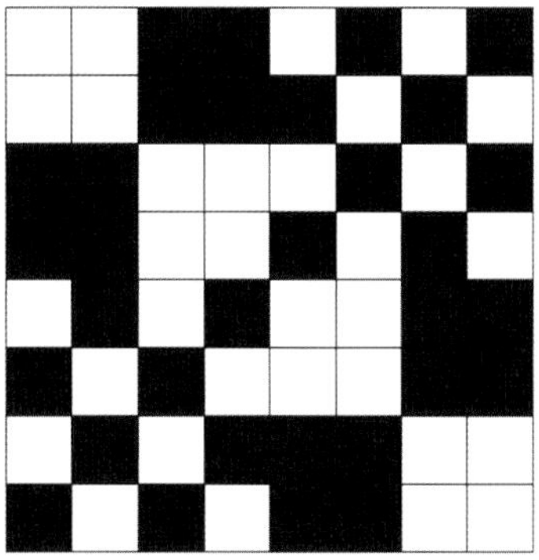

Version 2.

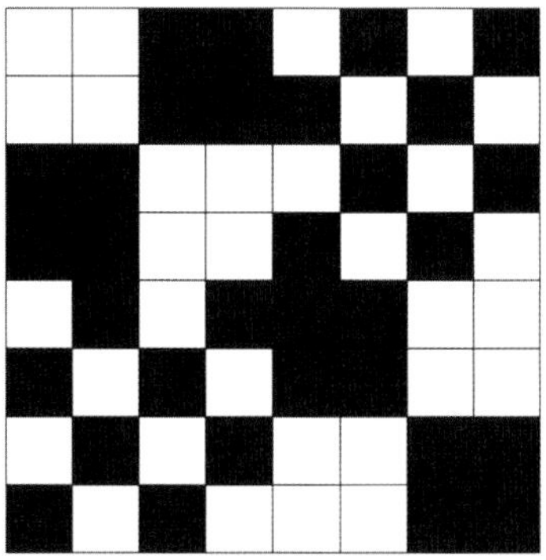

Version 3.

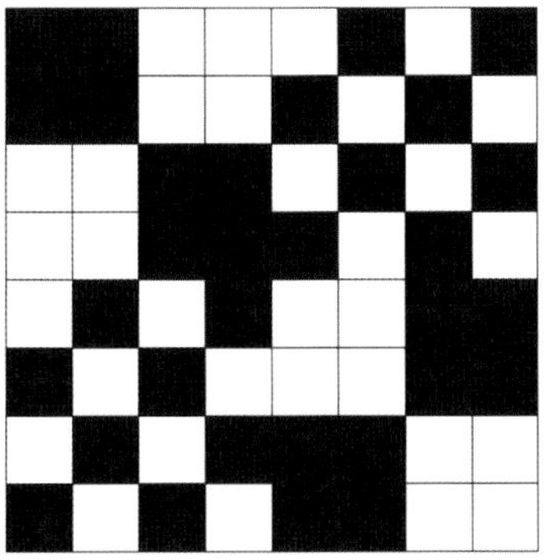

Version 4.

More Than Eight Shafts

With more than eight shafts, many more designs are possible using most of the methods suggested for eight shafts and expanded to as many shafts as are available.

Regular Threading Blocks Method

The regular threading blocks method can be used regardless of how many shafts are available, so long as each block uses two shafts.

Divided Threading Method

The divided threading method allows for the ground and the pattern blocks to be split, putting the ground weave on two blocks on four shafts, leaving all the remaining shafts available in pairs for design blocks. The tie-up is an uneven quadrant with up and down choices for the blocks.

For the adventurous, extra layers can be added for additional complexity.

Deflected double weave is a branch of dimensional weaving (and colour-and-weave) that has great potential and room for exploration. There is so much to experiment with – mixing materials, ratios and different threading conventions – to give a huge diversity of approaches.

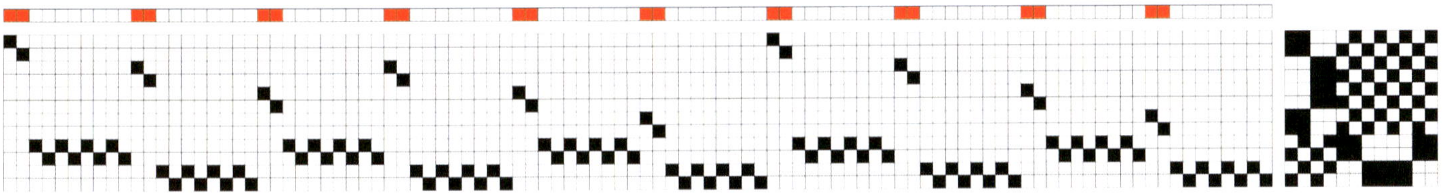

A 12-shaft design with two blocks (four shafts) for the ground weave, and the remaining eight shafts available for four blocks of patterning. The tie-up uses one set of opposing lifts for the floats of the pattern blocks while the ground layer is being woven. Other options could include the pattern blocks on shafts 5 & 6, 7 & 8 being used together versus shafts 9 & 10, 11 & 12. Alternatively, shafts 5 & 6 and 9 & 10 could be used together against shafts 7 & 8, 11 & 12. The ground weave floats could also be adapted as well as treadling plans.

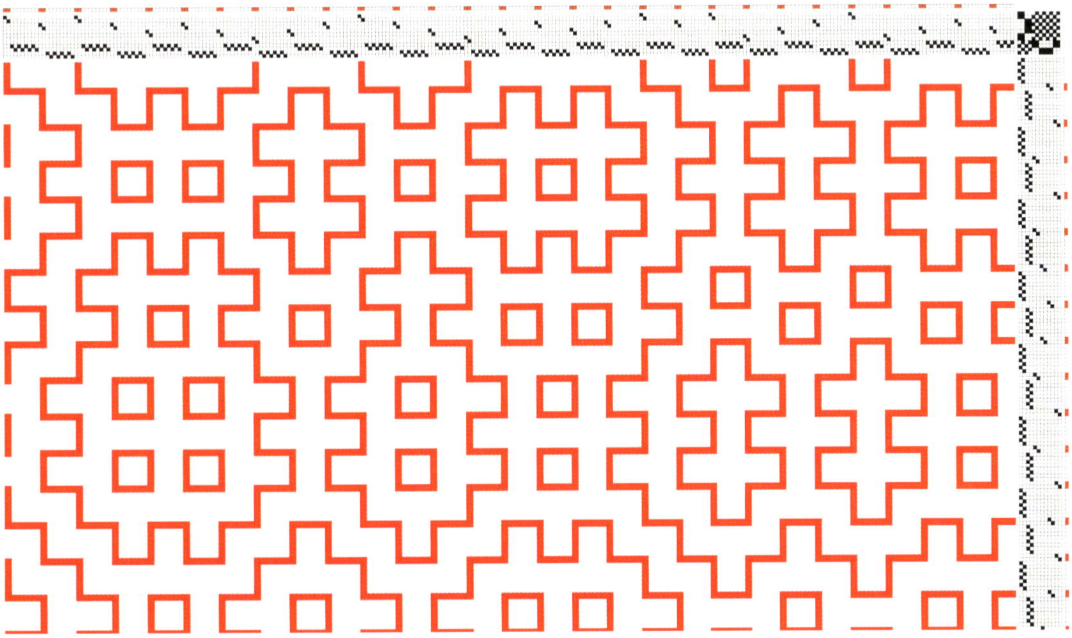

A detail of a woven-as-drawn-in draft shows some of the variety of forms

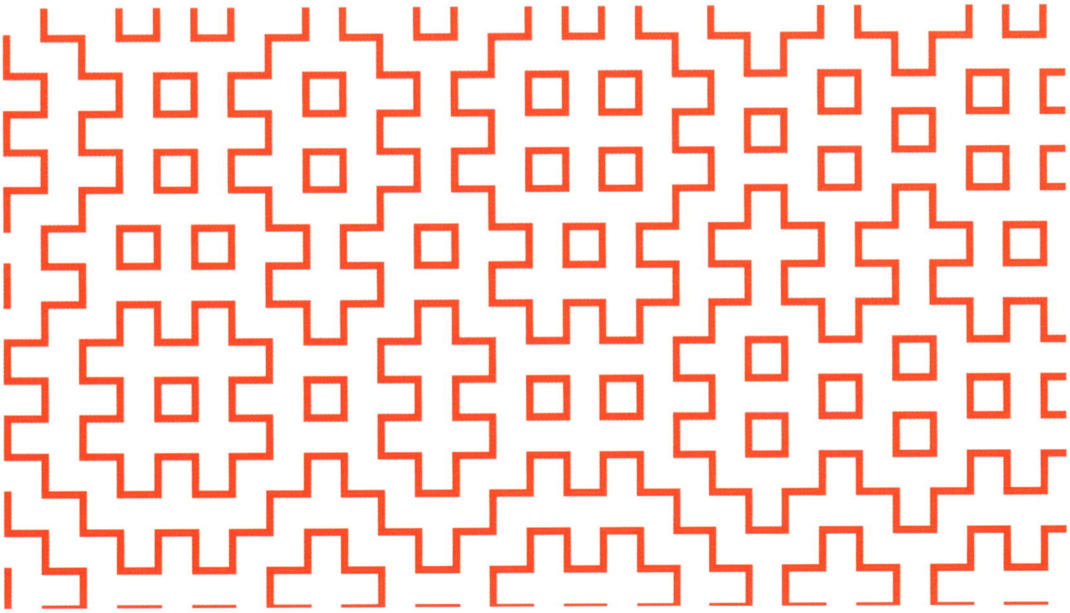

The reverse draft view shows the variation between front and reverse.

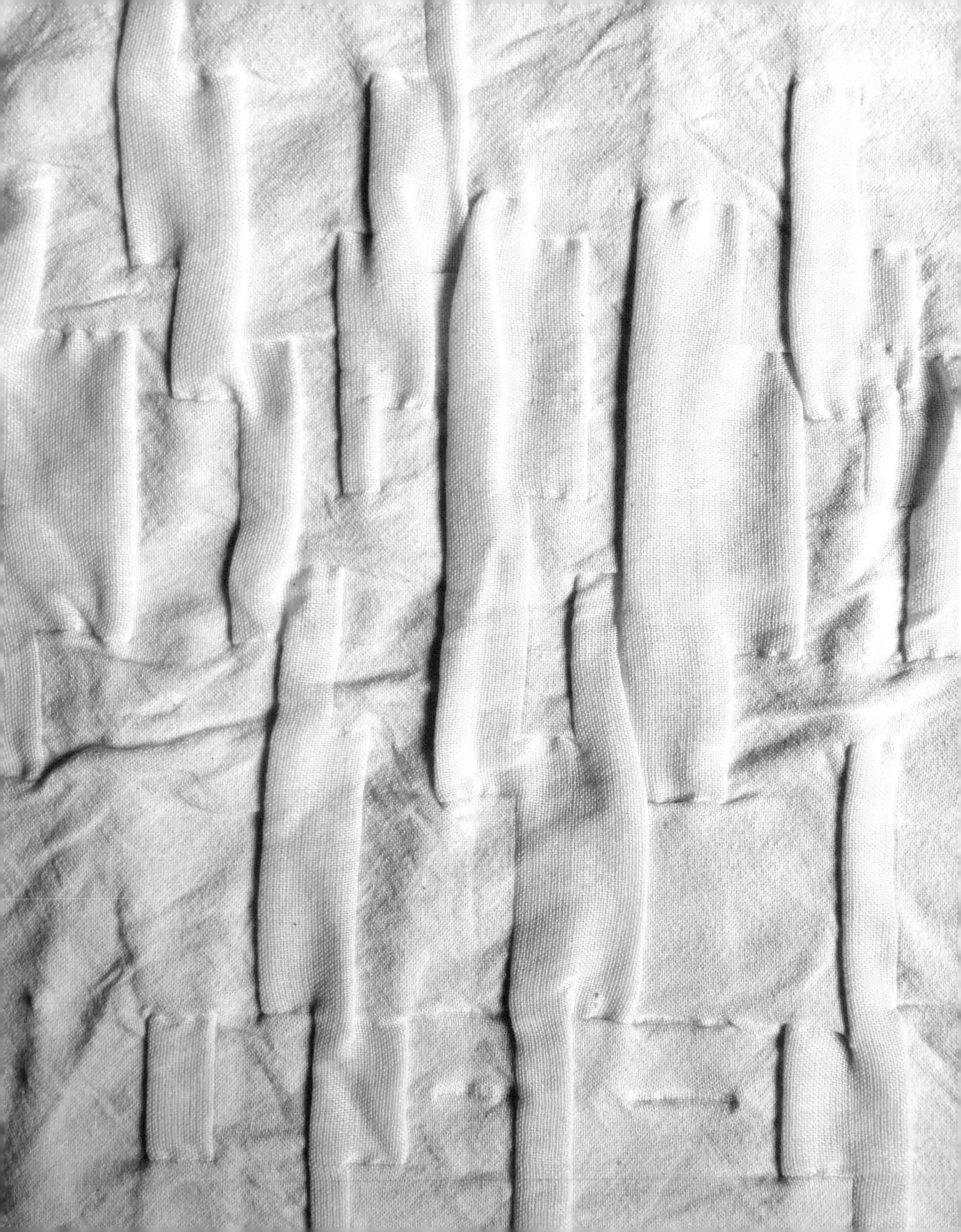

CHAPTER 9

DOUBLE CLOTH

Double cloth can be used for dimensional effects in many different ways. In this chapter we are looking specifically at interchanging layers, often incorporating differential shrinkage. Other methods of connectivity between layers are covered in their own chapters (*see* Chapters 2, 3, 8, 10, 11, 12 and 14). This chapter also touches on integration of layers, which is explored further in the other chapters.

Double cloth for texture is no different from regular double cloth in structure. Two layers of fabric are woven simultaneously on the loom and are connected to each other by various means. The difference between regular double cloth and textural double cloth is in the use of materials with the effects often being created through the dynamic reaction of active versus passive yarns, which have different rates of shrinkage during wet-finishing. The French word *cloqué* describes the blistering or puckering effects that result from these techniques.

WARP

For the non-shrinking layer, use 'passive' yarns such as cotton, linen, silk, bamboo viscose, superwash wool or polyester. In general, non-mercerised cotton gives a more effective result for dimensional texture than mercerised cotton, as there is a bit more surface texture (also known as 'tooth') to non-mercerised cotton, although high-shine yarns can be used, depending on the desired end result.

Most of the techniques use plain weave in the non-shrinking passive layer. Plain weave generally gives the best textural results after wet-finishing and twills reduce the number of shafts available for designing the textural results. However, if sufficient shafts are available and appropriate setts are used, then twills and satins can be variations.

Solid pale colours often give the most visual dimensional results, but colour is an area for personal experimentation. Bear in mind that dark colours might not show the texture as clearly, and solid colours usually show the dimensional texture more clearly than variegated colours as the eye is drawn to colour variations before texture. However, this is only general advice and a variety of colours have been used in the woven images. Black texture can also be effective. Stripes, especially in a very close range of tones or tints, can greatly enhance a piece, depending on the results you want to achieve.

The second layer is of a shrinking or 'active' yarn. Recommended yarns for this layer are merino, quality lambswool, wool crepe or elastomeric yarn. High-twist or overtwist yarns have not generally been used in this book. However, if using these yarns, do bear in mind that the weave structure is usually plain weave, and a high-twist warp needs to be sett a little more openly to allow the yarn room to move. Any colours can be used in the active layer, especially for contrast effects.

The two warps can be wound together onto the same warp beam if the project is not long, or too dense, but for a longer warp it is advisable to use two warp beams, if available.

Ratio

Changing ratios in either warp or weft, or both, is a practical way of increasing dimensional shrinkage. Regular

The interchange between two layers of cotton warp on a multi-shaft loom gives many blocks to play with. The wefts were Puma cotton, slightly elastic, and polyester.

double cloth usually has a 1:1 ratio, meaning one warp end of one cloth is followed by one warp end of the other, alternating end on end, although the sett for double plain weave with a 1:1 ratio if the two warp yarns are different thicknesses may often not be the best sett for textural results. If the active yarn chosen is thinner than the passive yarn, the two warps may be threaded in the traditional 1:1 ratio for double cloth if the sett uses a double plain with the passive yarn as the sett guide.

The easiest way to alter the ratio is to reduce the amount of active yarn used in the weft. For example, just use one active (i.e. wool) pick for every two passive (i.e. cotton) picks. The same idea can also be adopted in the warp, only threading one wool end to every two cotton ends. This gives a looser weave in the active (wool) layer, which allows for greater shrinkage potential.

This 1:2 ratio of active to passive (i.e. wool to cotton) is a good place to start. Using a four-shaft draft to illustrate the principles, cotton is threaded on shafts 1 & 2, and wool on shafts 3 & 4. The drafts begin with cotton on 1, followed by a wool pattern end on 3, then another cotton on 2. Sley these three as a group. The next group will be cotton on 1, wool pattern end on 4, then cotton on 2. Continue in the same way.

For an even more dimensional result, use the same or a higher ratio in both warp and weft.

The samples all need to be wet-finished before their true nature is revealed, with the exception of elastane yarns.

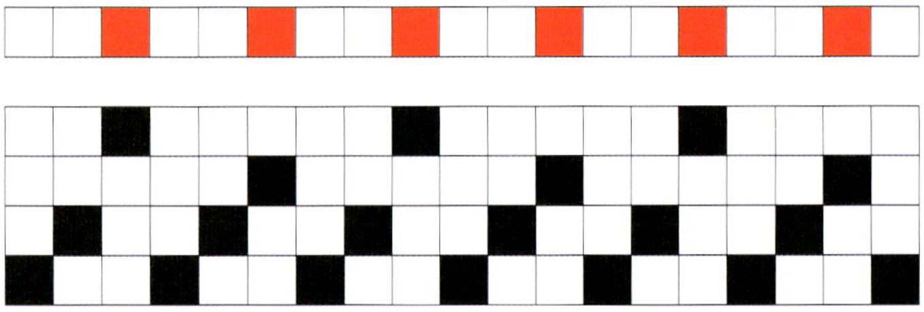

A ratio of 2:1 passive to active (also written as 1:2 active to passive) has two ends of one warp (white) followed by one end of a second warp (red). In this four-shaft draft, shafts 1 & 2 are for the passive white warp, and shafts 3 & 4 are for the active red warp.

RATIOS

If using a 1:2 ratio of wool to cotton and, as an example, a plain weave sett of 20 ends per inch for the cotton warp, the wool will be 10 epi, making a combined epi of 30. The yarns will be sleyed together. A 10 dents per inch reed can be used in order to sley two cotton and one wool end together with three ends per dent.

PRINCIPLES

The different systems we are looking at in this chapter are:

1. Interchanging layers (in other words, swapping the layer that is on the top to the bottom, and vice versa)
2. Interchanging warp and weft blocks
3. Combined single and double cloth

Four Shafts

With four shafts, there are two plain weave layers available. The only methods possible are through switching the two layers over (interchanging) so that the top layer becomes the bottom layer and vice versa, or by integrating the two layers into a single layer and contrasting that with the two separate layers. The design potential is all down to how much to weave the two layers separately, when to swap them over, or when to integrate them, and for how long.

Interchanging Layers

This is a two-shuttle weave – one weft in the active yarn, one in the passive – here weaving with a 1:1 ratio of active to passive. In our examples, the cotton weft weaves with the cotton warp, the wool weft with the wool warp. The two separate layers interchange – switching from one side to the other.

- **Pick 1:** Raise shaft 1. Weave with cotton weft.
- **Pick 2:** Raise shafts 1 & 2, plus shaft 3. Weave with wool weft.
- **Pick 3:** Raise shaft 2. Weave with cotton weft.
- **Pick 4:** Raise shafts 1 & 2, plus shaft 4. Weave with wool weft.

That is the basis of the weave, although picks 3 and 4 could be switched over in the order of progression so that one shuttle can be used for two picks before switching shuttles. However, it is generally a good idea not to weave more than two picks of any one layer at one time before weaving the other layer because of the difficulty in maintaining an even fell on both layers.

It is important to maintain a regular beat on both the layers at once. Looms with a sliding beater will have no issues with this as the reed remains perpendicular to the warp at all times. Looms with overhung or underslung

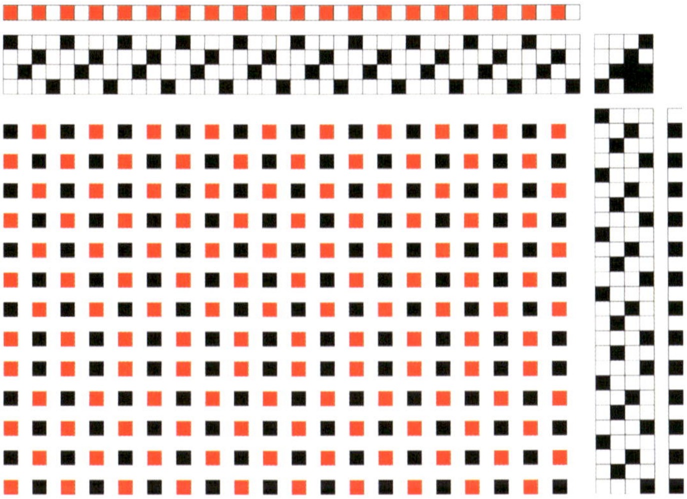

This draft shows a double cloth in a 1:1 ratio with the white cloth on the surface. Note the tie-up, which shows that shaft 1 (white) only is raised in column 1, followed by the whole of the white layer on shafts 1 & 2, plus shaft 3 (the first shaft for the red layer) in column 3 so that the lower cloth can be woven. The red/black cloth is hidden underneath the white one. In column 2, the other part of the plain weave for the white cloth is woven, namely shaft 2. In column 4, shafts 1 & 2 are raised again so that the white layer stays above the red layer and the second half of the plain weave for the red layer, shaft 4, is also raised.

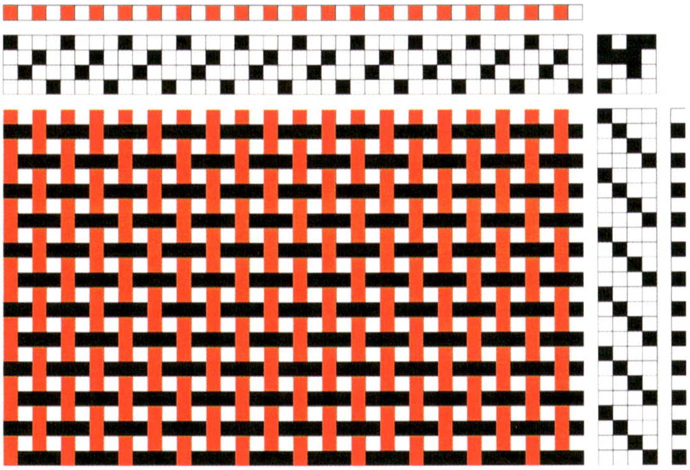

This draft shows the complete opposite. The red/black layer is now on the surface and the white layer underneath. This draft shows the reverse lifts, keeping the order of the wefts the same, firstly white, then black. Column 1 now shows that shafts 3 & 4 – the red layer – are raised along with shaft 1 for the white weft to weave with the white warp underneath the red warp. Column 2 shows shaft 3 only lifted as the red warp is on top. Column 3 shows the red warp up (3 & 4) while the plain weave on the white warp and weft is woven with shaft 2, and column 4 gives the final plain weave pick for the red warp on top with shaft 4.

beaters, however, necessitate frequent winding on of the woven cloth to allow the reed to stay in the 'sweet spot' for weaving where the reed connects with only a shallow angle to the fell or perpendicular. With regular interchanging of layers, this problem is reduced but good practice will help alleviate any incidence of irregular beating due to an angled beater.

If you are using a 1:2 active to passive weft ratio, and assuming everything else is the same as above, the picking order is as follows:

- **Pick 1:** Raise shaft 1. Weave with cotton weft.
- **Pick 2:** Raise shaft 2. Weave with cotton weft.
- **Pick 3:** Raise shafts 1 & 2, plus shaft 3. Weave with wool weft.
- **Pick 4:** Raise shaft 1. Weave with cotton weft.
- **Pick 5:** Raise shaft 2. Weave with cotton weft.
- **Pick 6:** Raise shafts 1 & 2, plus shaft 4. Weave with wool weft.

With other pick ratios, increase the number of cotton picks to wool picks in a similar fashion (i.e. with a treadling ratio of 1 wool: 3 cotton, three cotton picks will be woven to each wool pick).

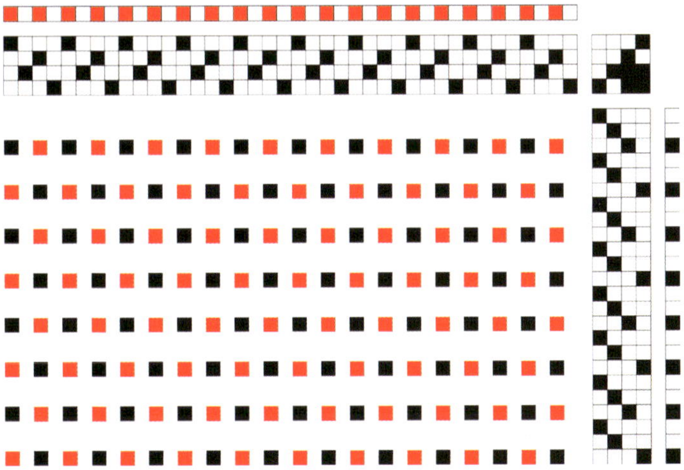

Even with a different ratio in the weft, the threading and tie-up can remain the same. Here we have a 2:1 passive to active treadling and a regular 1:1 ratio in the warp.

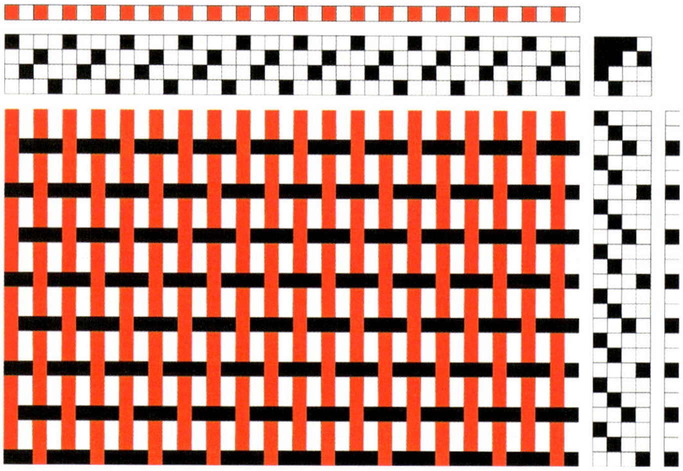

The difference between the ratios in the weft is now apparent with the red warp and black weft.

ALTERNATIVE WEAVE

Some weavers find it preferable to weave as follows: Pick 1 (cotton), pick 3 (wool), pick 2 (cotton), pick 4 (cotton), pick 6 (wool), pick 5 (cotton). This follows the same order as the threading and ensures that the wool is spaced evenly between the two cotton picks in each half of the repeat.

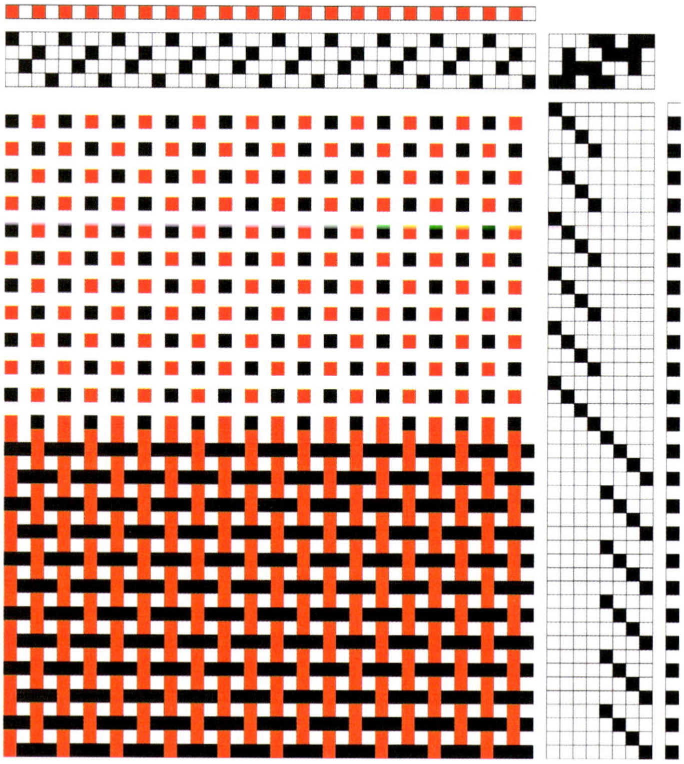

Interchanging layers with a 1:1 ratio brings the two tie-ups for the different layers together in one tie-up. The layers are switched completely so what was on top moves to the underneath and the layer on the bottom moves to the top.

Switching/Interchanging Layers

One of the easiest methods for adding texture is simply to bring the bottom layer up to the top and move the top layer down to the bottom.

Differing amounts of texture can be created through varying when the layers interchange.

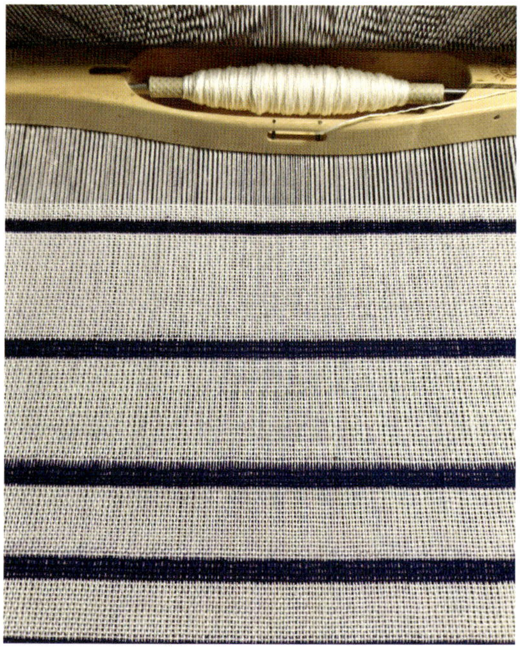

Varying the length of separate layers being woven gives tighter or looser contraction in the passive layer after wet-finishing. The sample here uses from 4 to 32 picks in increasing then decreasing amounts on the passive layer in cotton.

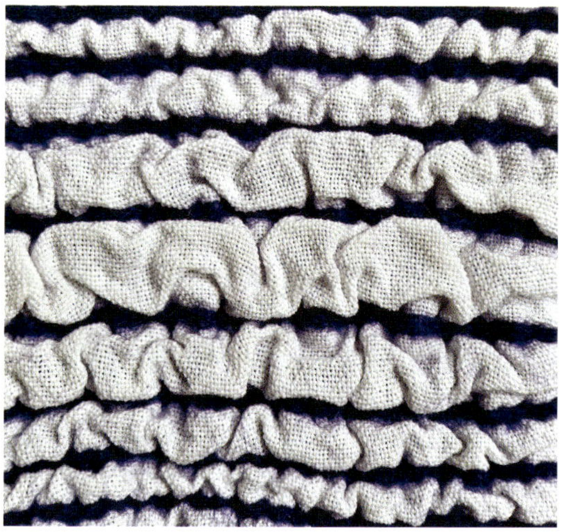

The shrinkage during wet-finishing affects the type of contraction seen in the top layer.

Integrating Layers

Layers can also be woven together as one – integrated.

The integration of just two picks is achieved by weaving pick 1 with shafts 1 & 3 and pick 2 with shafts 2 & 4, thereby treating the two fabrics as one single dense layer.

This single line (of two picks) which joins both layers together will give puckered areas interrupted by an indentation line, especially if the two layers are using a ratio of 1:2 or more wool to cotton. Weft yarns can be explored and twills and basket weave can be used in the integrated single cloth areas. This element will be explored more when using more than four shafts.

Simple integration can be achieved by simply weaving plain weave on shafts 1 & 3 versus 2 & 4.

Ruffles

This is a double cloth that has one or two single-cloth edges. If the wool side is on top during the weaving it is easy to see what the shrinking layer is doing. Ruffles are formed in the cotton area during wet-finishing as the wool shrinks. With four shafts, only two shafts are available per layer, so each layer is plain weave. The same principle is used as previously described.

If you decide to try this, be aware that because the passive layer is wider, when the active layer is woven underneath in a separate layer, it is not possible to see whether you are pulling the weft too tight. Alternatively, you can change the layers so that you are weaving face down with the narrower layer on top.

If the active layer is to one selvedge only, shaping of the fabric can be achieved.

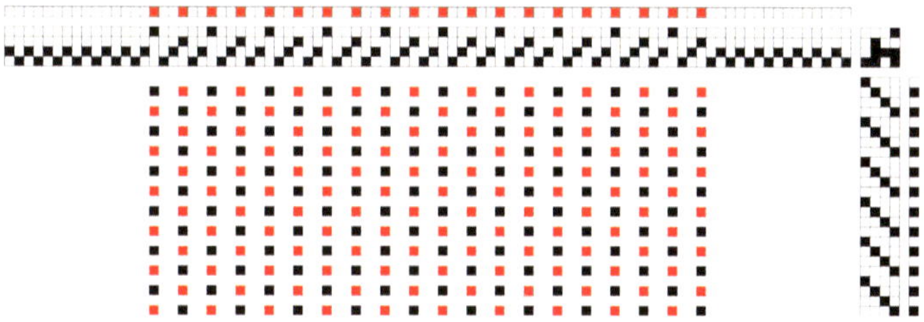

Ruffles can be created by using one layer only on the edges of the fabric. If the passive warp is continued past the active warp, any movement from the active yarns contracting will create soft ripple or ruffle effects on the extended passive cloth areas.

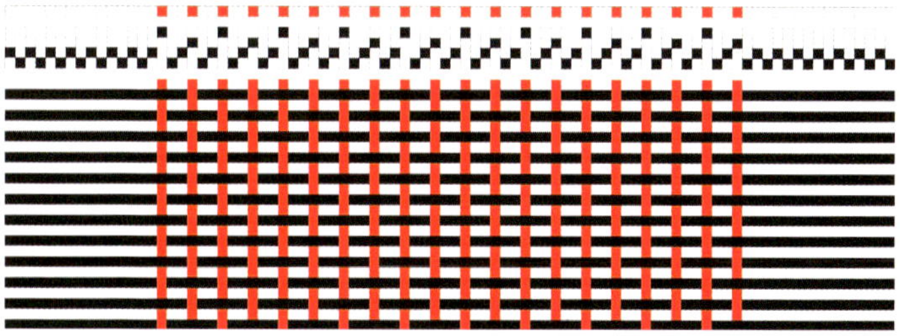

With a 2:1 passive to active ratio in the threading, and a 1:1 ratio in the treadling, only the central area will be impacted by the contracting of the active yarns.

WOOL WEFT FLOATS

In the weaving software used here, you will notice that there are long wool weft floats across the ruffling selvedges of cotton. It is not possible to remove those from the draft, but in practice, the central wool area weft does not carry to the selvedges. It is only woven where it interacts with the wool warps, so it becomes self-contained in the central area, allowing the cotton to pucker during wet-finishing without any wool weft interacting in the selvedge areas.

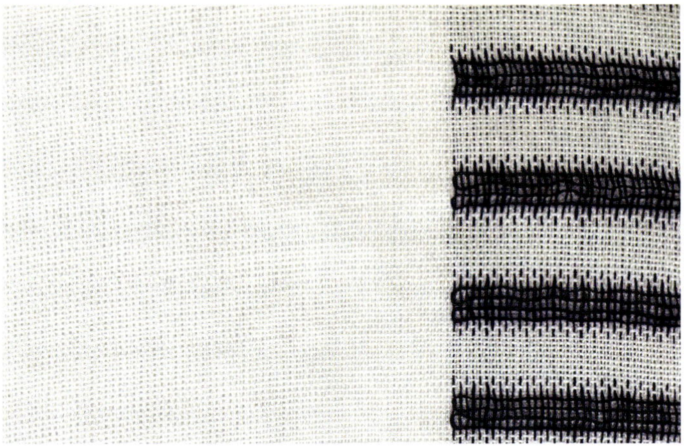

Placing the second layer in a small segment of the warp will give ruffled or shaping effects. Here the shrinking warp takes approximately one-third of the width of the warp and the double cloth is woven.

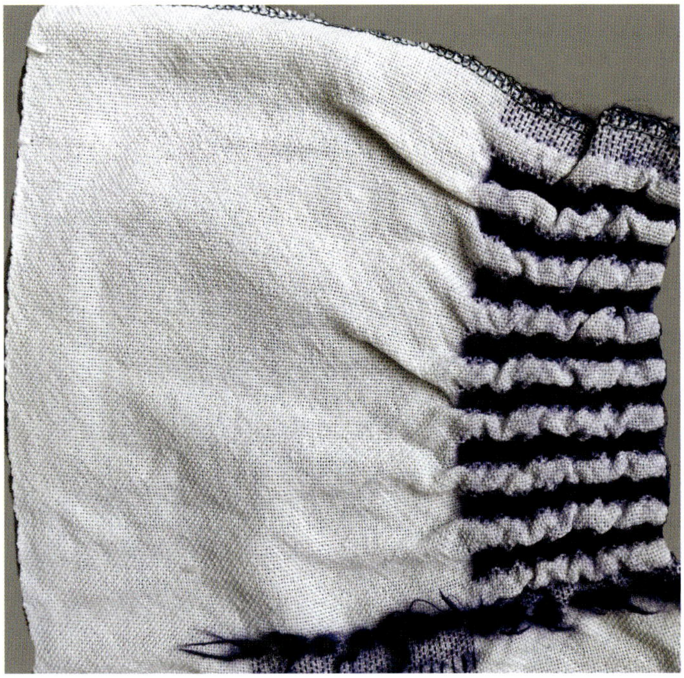

On wet-finishing, the shrinkage at the selvedge is more as there is less resistance of the passive layer, resulting in shaping of the cloth.

Six Shafts

As more shafts are introduced, there other options are possible.

With six shafts, two sets of three-end threadings can be used.

You can also use four shafts for the shrinking layer and two shafts for plain weave layer or vice versa, allowing for four-end twills to be used on the active layer.

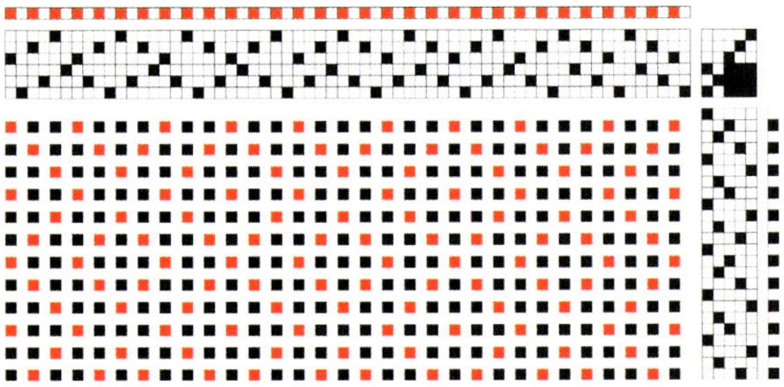

Six shafts allow for more options. This draft shows plain weave on the top white layer on three shafts with a 1/2 twill on the red/black layer underneath.

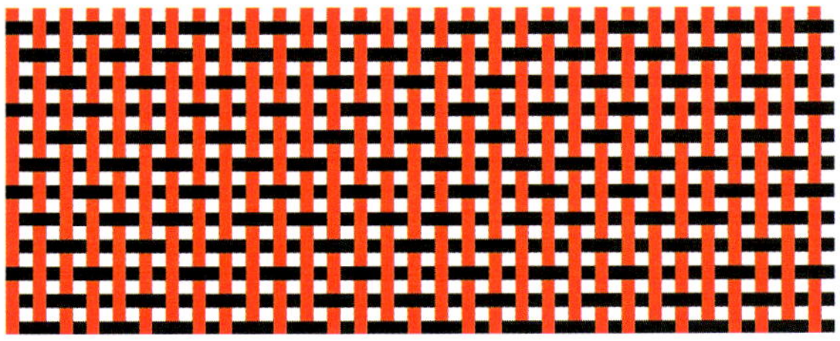

The twill can be seen through looking at the floats. The effect during wet-finishing is more apparent due to the extra length of the floats in a twill structure allowing for greater shrinkage.

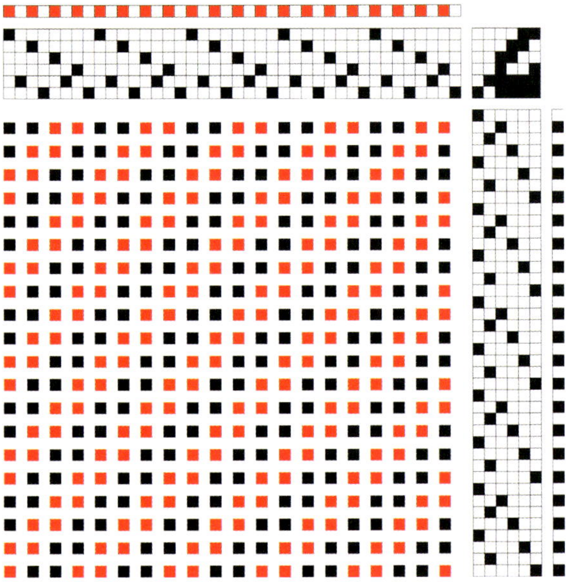

This variation shows two shafts for the plain weave top layer and a 2/2 twill on the underneath layer.

Interchanging and Integrating Blocks

As for four shafts, the two layers can produce horizontal weft stripes, especially when used with increased picks of the non-shrinking layer to those for the shrinking layer.

With six shafts, there are additional choices. Using plain weave for all blocks, three blocks of two shafts become possible, which can be divided up to create different effects.

Two Blocks on the Passive Layer

Choosing two blocks for the passive layer, there is the option for one of those blocks to be above or below the active layer and for the other to integrate with the active layer.

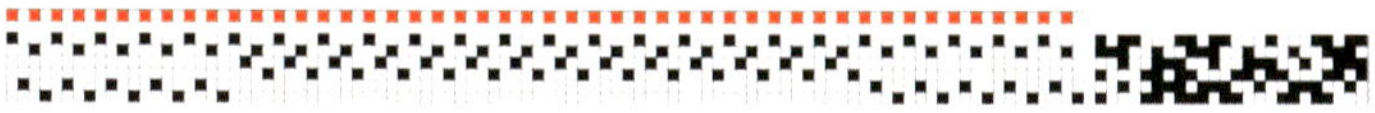

The threading shows two blocks (shafts 1 & 2 and 3 & 4) for one layer, with the second layer on shafts 5 & 6. The extended tie-up gives all six possibilities for combining and keeping separate the two layers of the six-shaft double cloth.

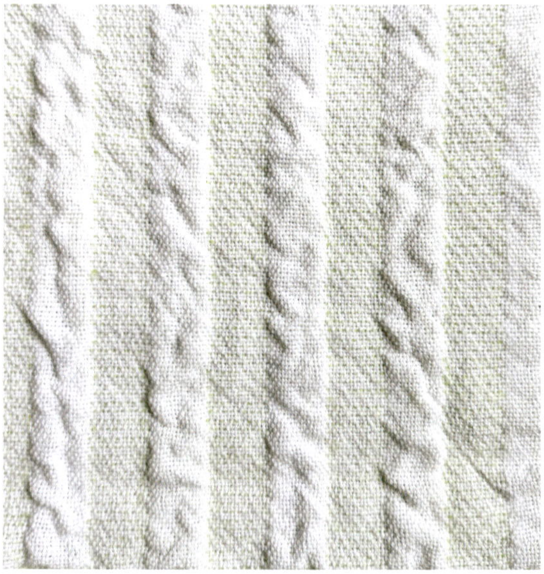

In this sample, vertical textural stripes alternate with integrated stripes. Because the floats behind are not too long in either direction, the texture is subtle.

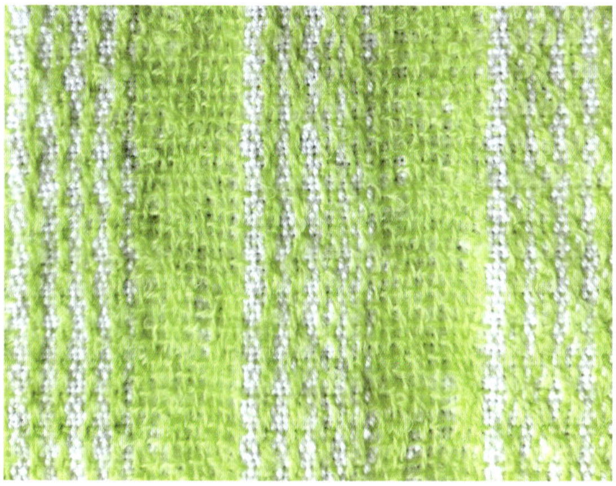

The reverse shows how the wool layer weaves on its own and then is integrated with the cotton layer in the warp stripes.

In these drafts, a 1:1 ratio of wool to cotton has been used, but other ratios can also be adopted.

Horizontal stripes, vertical stripes and chequerboard effects can be designed through separating out the layers, combining the two passive blocks into one versus the active block, integrating one passive block while leaving the other to weave separate layers for a vertical stripe, and alternating the integrating blocks for a chequerboard effect.

Six shafts can also be used to weave three layers, which is covered in Chapter 12.

The layers can be interchanged or integrated. Here is a horizontal stripe layer exchange.

The different warp blocks as seen in the threading can be independently combined or kept separate and interchanged. This is one variation, integrating shafts 1 & 2 in two different ways with the black layer, but keeping the central block of shafts 3 & 4 as a separate layer both on the top and underneath.

This gives the second variation for the same threading draft. This time, shafts 3 & 4 are integrated with the black layer and shafts 1 & 2 are playing an independent role both above and underneath on the edges of the draft.

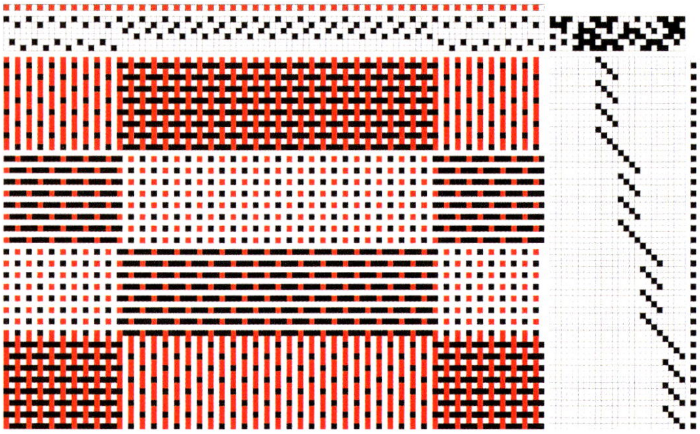

Both the previous drafts can be amalgamated with the blocks made equal to create chequerboard effects. With these six tie-up possibilities and different weft materials, various looks can be achieved.

A chequerboard effect is created by a small area of alternating vertical stripe texture.

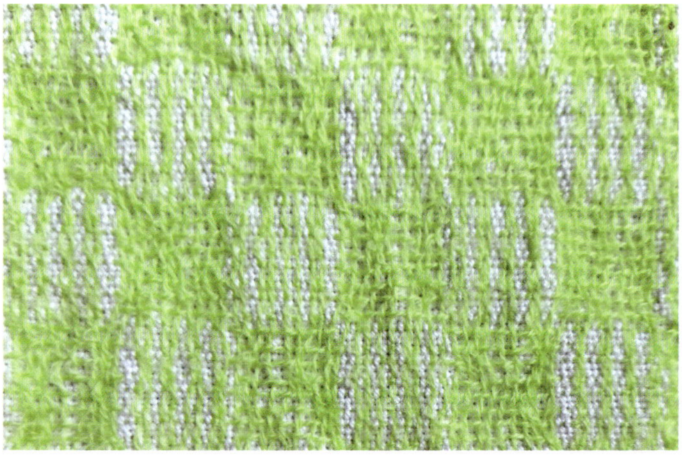

The reverse shows the principles.

A grid design can also be created by using both horizontal and vertical textural elements.

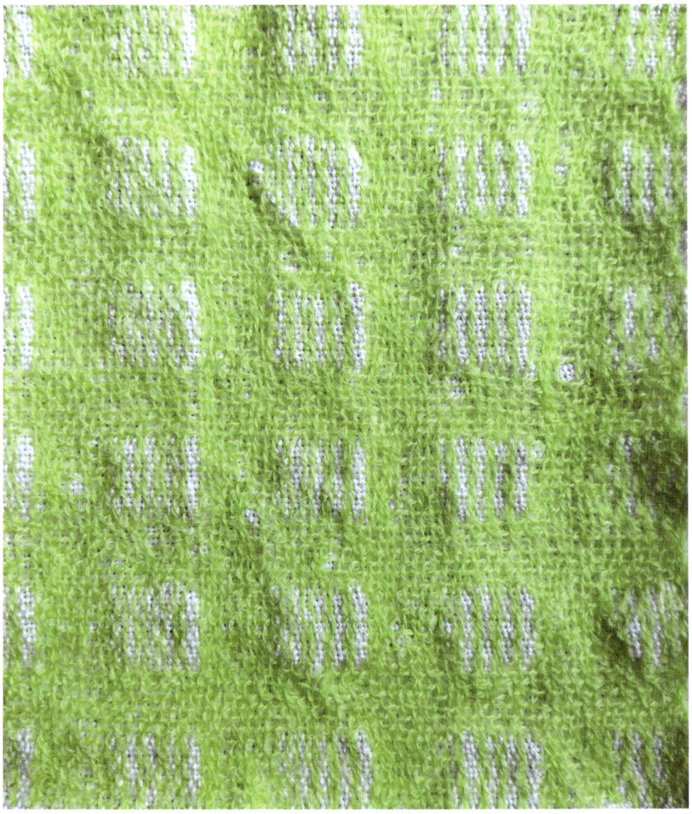

The reverse shows the islands of integrated squares surrounded by the two separate layers.

Eight Shafts

The same block design principles used for six shafts can be applied to eight or more shafts but with extra options.

One Block

One block per layer can be exchanged independently.

One block can be integrated into single cloth in several different ways.

One horizontal band of plain weave in the active yarn contrasting with small horizontal bands of 1/3 then 3/1 pleats on the passive layer, tied into together after the two twill bands have been woven, can give very effective pleats (*see* Chapter 3).

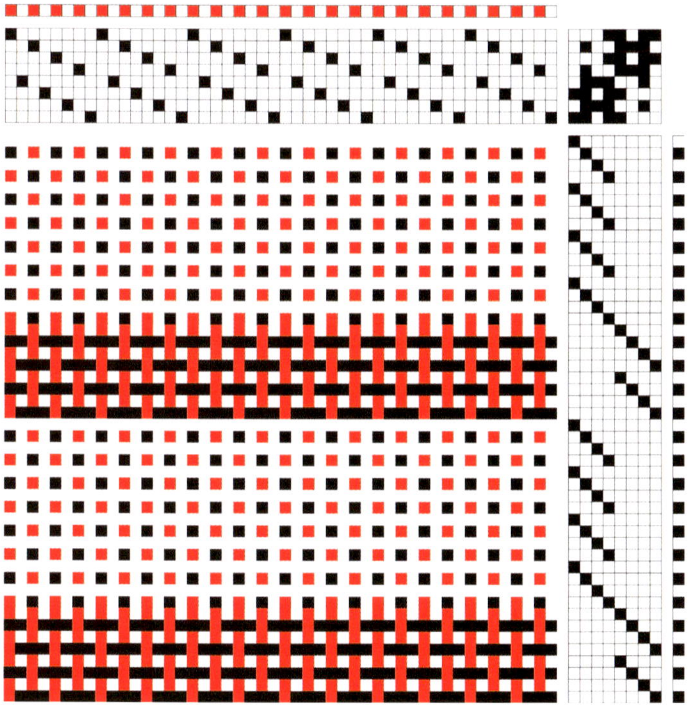

Eight shafts can give the same result with interchanging plain weave layers as the four-shaft version. The tie-up is necessarily a little more complicated, but the same principles apply. The threading is a divided parallel threading. Shafts 1–4 are for the first cloth, and shafts 5–8 are for the second cloth.

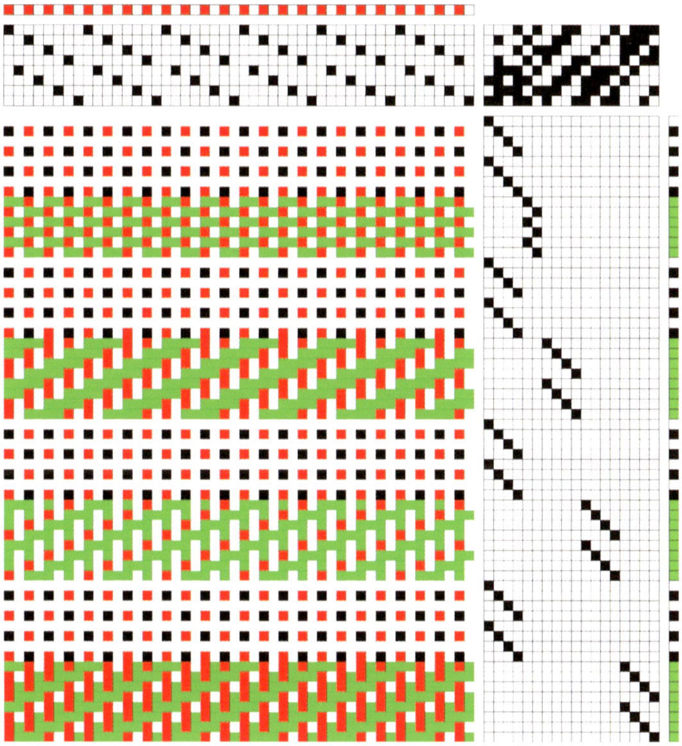

Integration into one cloth can be achieved using twills and plain weave. The tie-up shows regular double plain (first four columns); plain weave on 1,3,5,7 v 2,4,6,8; columns 7–10 show 2/2 twill, which will combine the two layers; columns 11–14 shows 3/1 twill on shafts 1–4 and 1/3 twill on shafts 5–8; columns 15–18 show the reverse – a 1/3 twill on shafts 1–4 and a 3/1 twill on shafts 5–8. The draft shows each variation plus the double plain between each example.

Two Blocks Per Layer

Two threading blocks per layer can be swapped around so that they create alternating opposing blocks of wool and cotton, or one layer of cotton versus a wool layer, and switched over. They can also work as integrated twills. Chequerboards are also feasible, both as double plain, or double plain and integrated twills.

Note: Threading blocks have to work in opposition to each other.

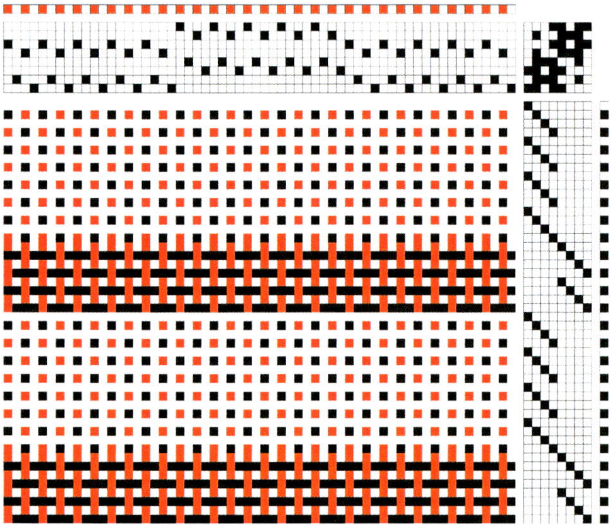

The threading here shows two blocks per layer. They are threaded in parallel to each other. With layer exchange to happen for each block, the threading blocks have to work in pairs, one set for each layer. The draft shows the blocks working together as complete layers to interchange, which gives horizontal banding effects.

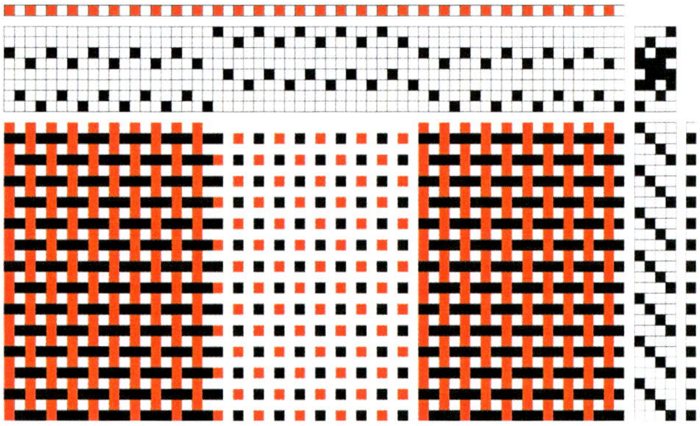

Vertical exchanges use one block from each of the layers to switch positions, so that both sides of the cloth show vertical bands.

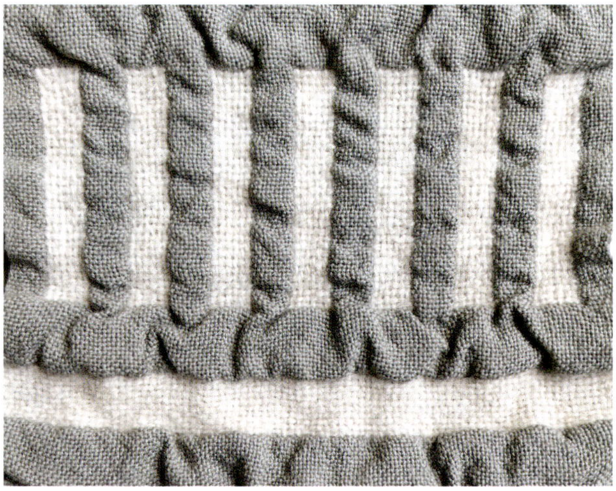

Both horizontal and vertical stripes are easily obtainable with eight shafts switching alternating blocks of active versus passive layers.

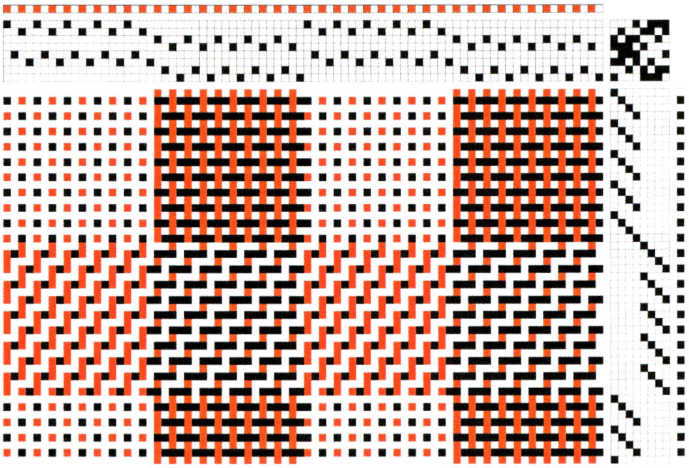

Blocks of single twills and double plain are shown from both sides in this draft. Compare the first half of the tie-up to the second half, which shows how the blocks and layers work together to ensure total amalgamation for the twills.

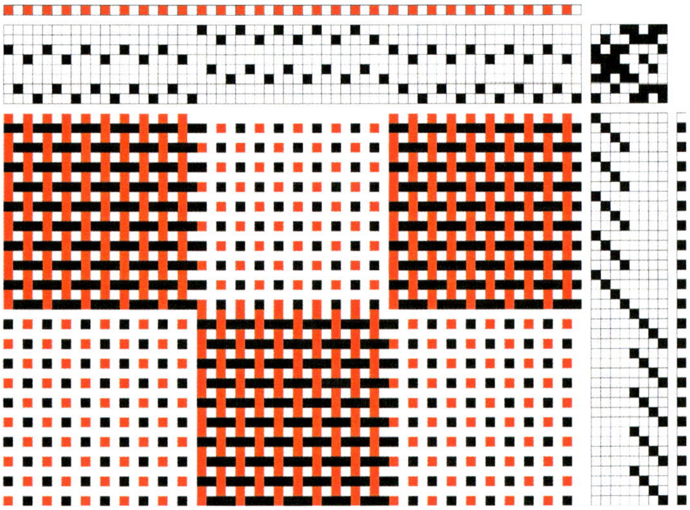

Chequerboards using both layers at the same time are possible. This draft has both layers weaving separately but interchanging in the chequerboard fashion.

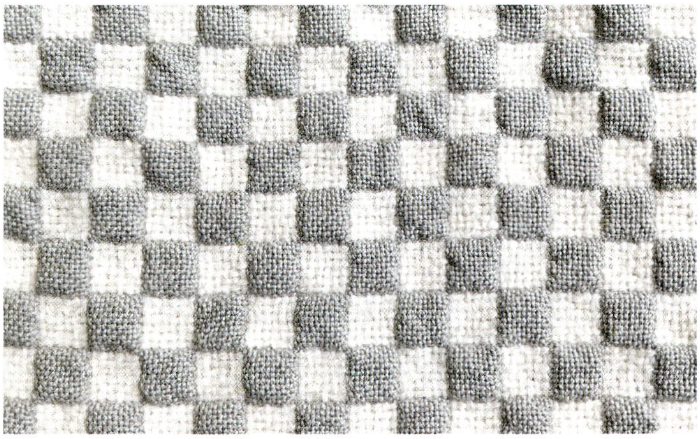

A chequerboard on eight shafts with cotton and wool warp and weft.

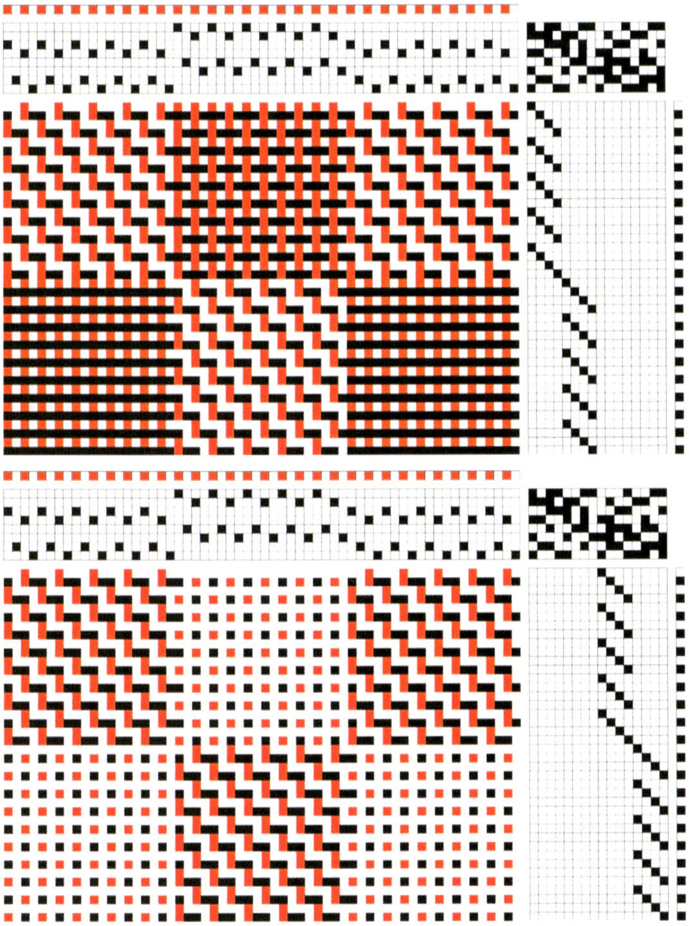

Chequerboards can also be woven integrating one of the squares as a single cloth while the other square retains its double layer. Both faces are shown here.

The same threading will give grids.

In addition, consider ratios of active and passive warps, which might not necessarily be the same in each of the blocks. For instance, a 1:2 wool to cotton ratio can be used in the first block of both layers, then a 1:1 ratio in the alternating block to give added variety and surface interest. Other ratios could be 1:3, 1:4 or even 2:3. Ratios can also be explored in the wefts.

WARP AND WEFT INTERCHANGE

Warp interchange is when one warp block changes from being the bottom layer to being the top layer.

Weft interchange is when one weft weaves one block on the top layer and the next block on the bottom layer, regardless of which warp is woven in either block.

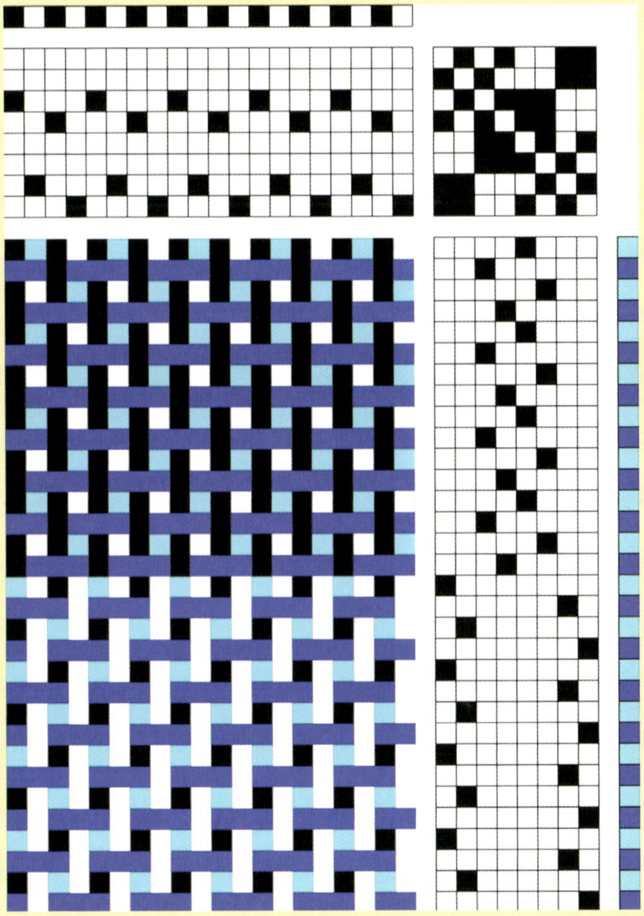

Warp interchange.

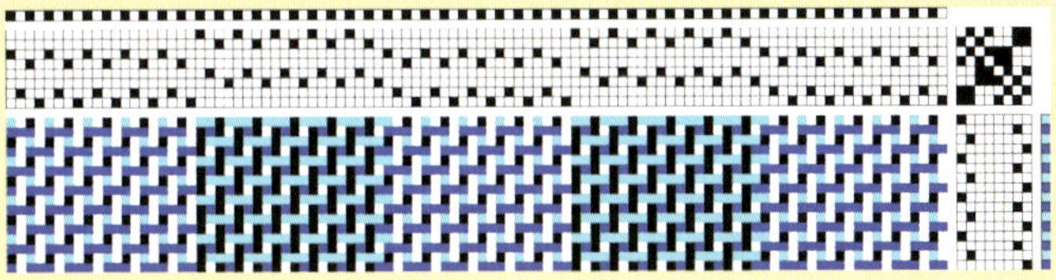

Weft interchange.

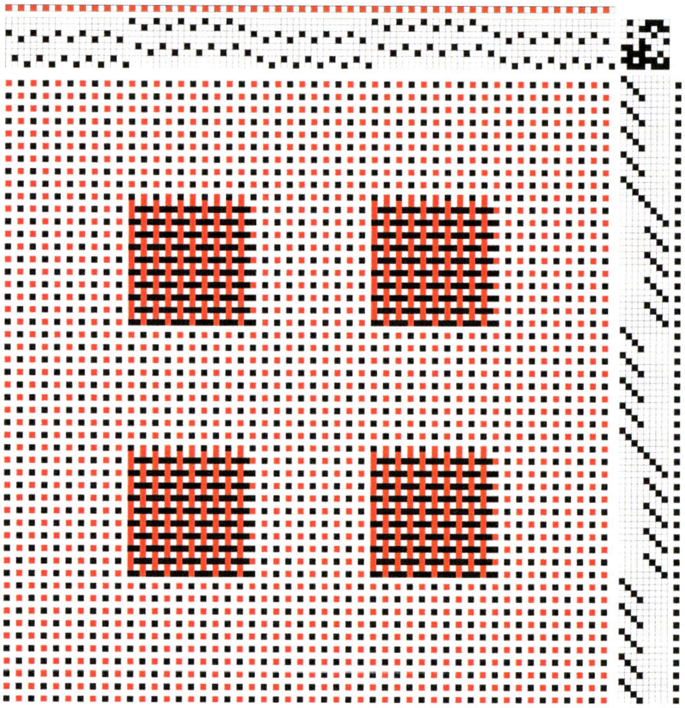

Using the same threading and combining vertical stripes, horizontal stripes and interchanging layers, a grid can be formed.

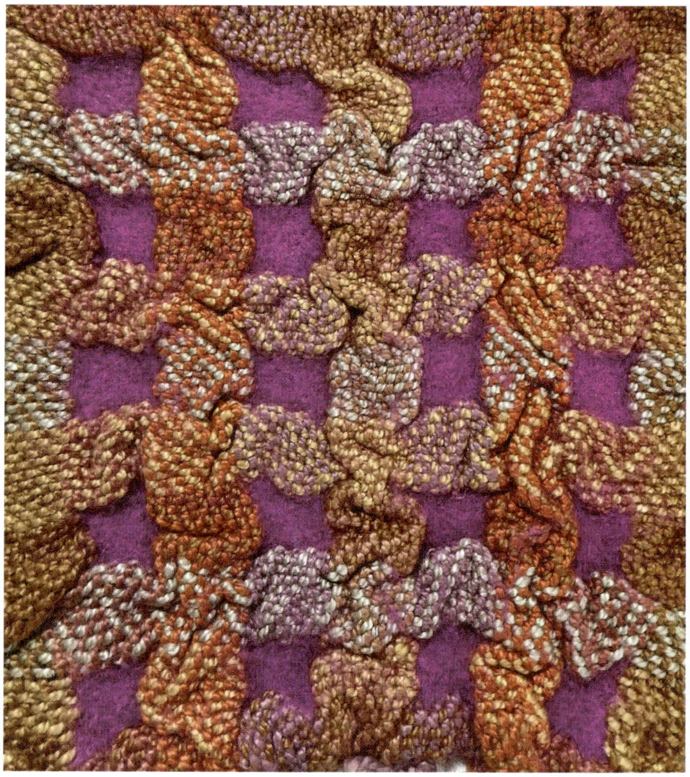

On one side of this grid fabric, the puffs from the passive layer surround small squares of wool. (Samples from a workshop by Ruby Leslie.)

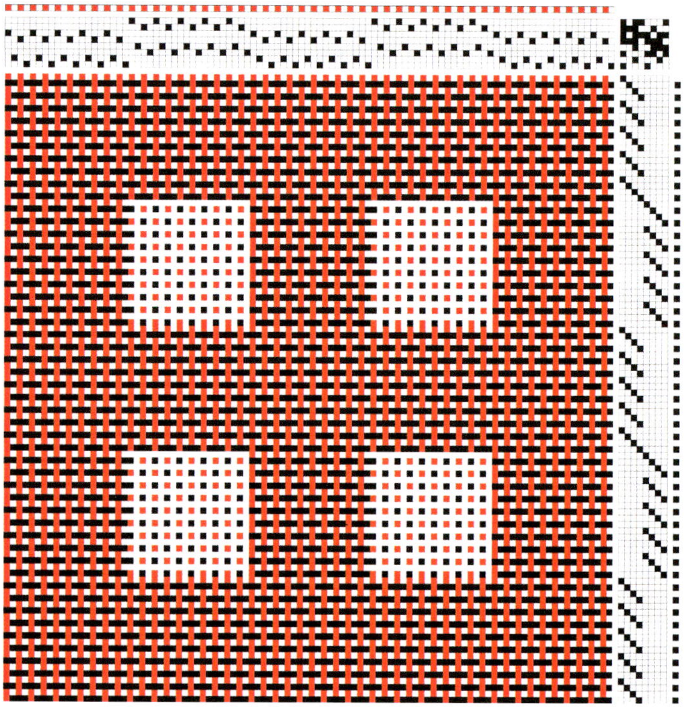

The other side changes the perspective.

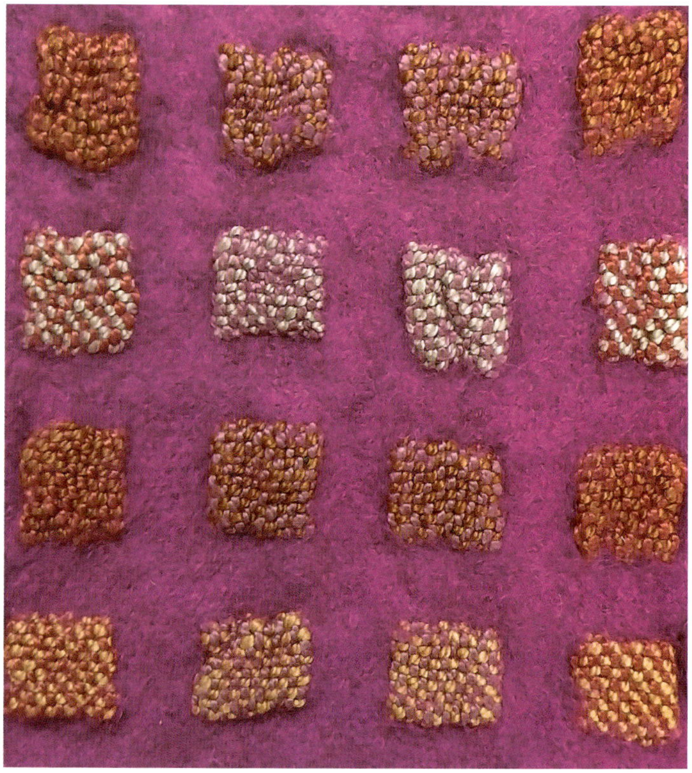

On the other side, little islands of passive squares float above a base of wool.

Three Blocks on One Layer

Three wool threading blocks on one layer can be used opposite a single cotton layer on two shafts. These could integrate with the cotton layer independently, in pairs or act together as a complete layer giving several permutations. Depending on how the blocks are threaded on the active layer, many different versions can be created.

With three blocks, there are different options for integration.

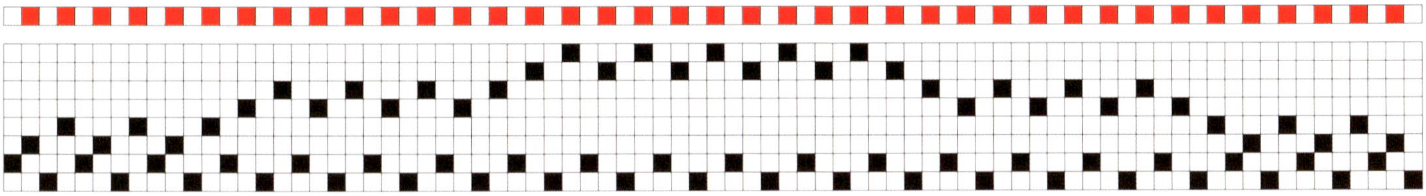

Three threading blocks on the active layer and one threading block for the passive layer can give variations of amalgamation in a cloth. This draft uses a block extended point for the active layer threading blocks.

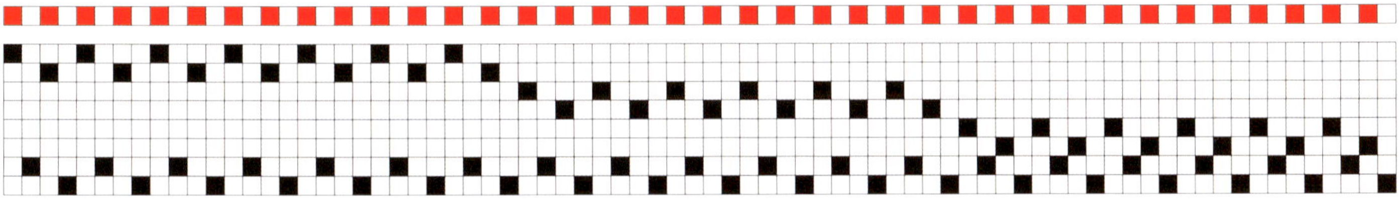

This threading shows a straight block threading alternative. This is the basis for many of the samples that illustrate this section.

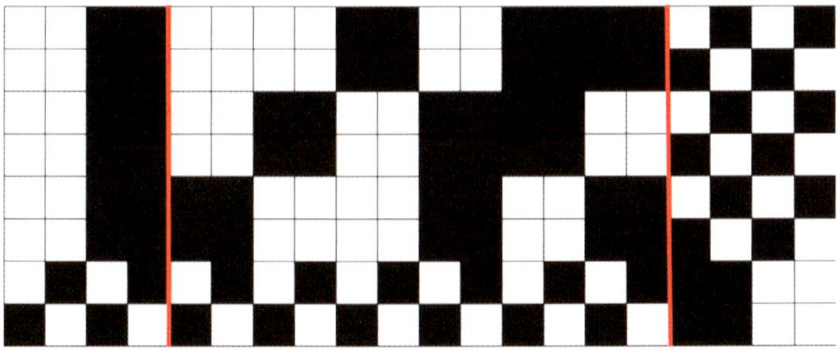

The tie-up for the various combinations can be divided into three segments. The first four columns in the tie-up denote whether the active warp (shafts 3–8) is up or down, affecting whether the passive layer is above or below the active layer. The next 12 columns denote which of the active warp blocks is integrating with the passive layer. The final four columns are the active layer weaving together and denoting whether the passive warp is above or below the active warp.

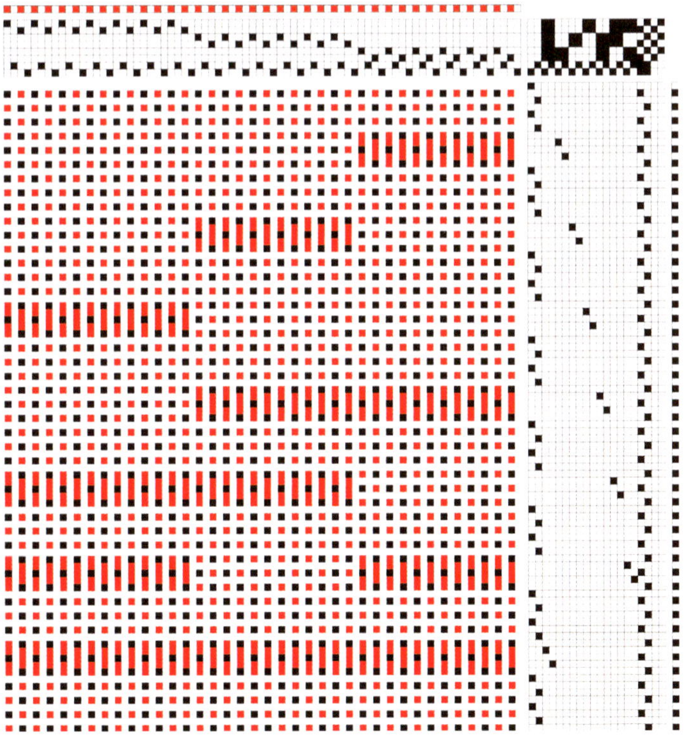

The treadling in this draft shows the variations possible using just two picks per amalgamation.

Integrating the active blocks in with the passive layer in full blocks also gives different effects, as we saw with the six-shaft version earlier.

Similarly, the reverse can be designed, with three passive blocks working opposite a single active layer.

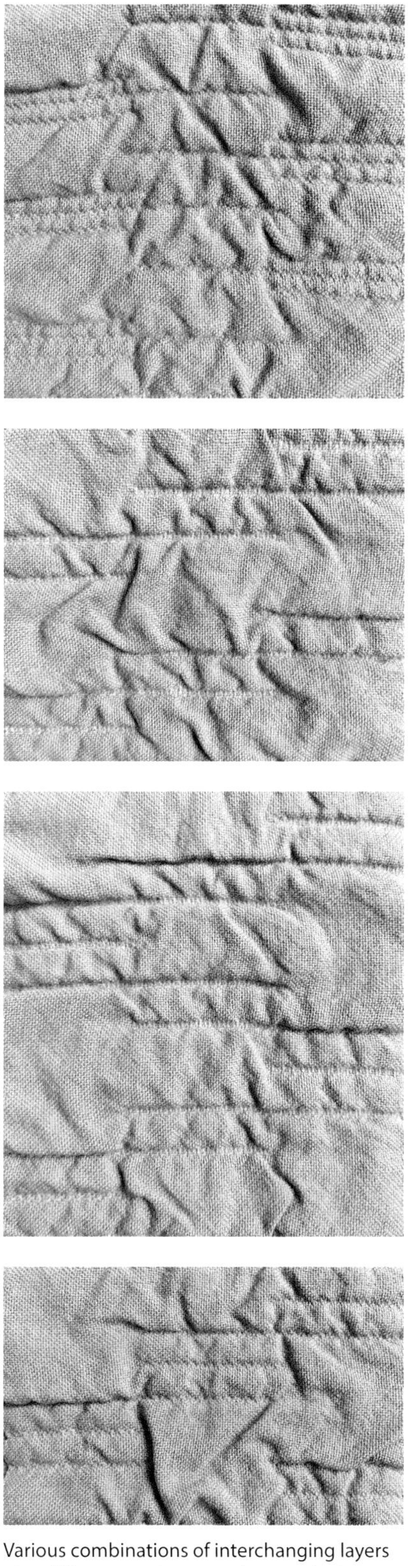

Various combinations of interchanging layers give different results as can be seen in these four sets of images.

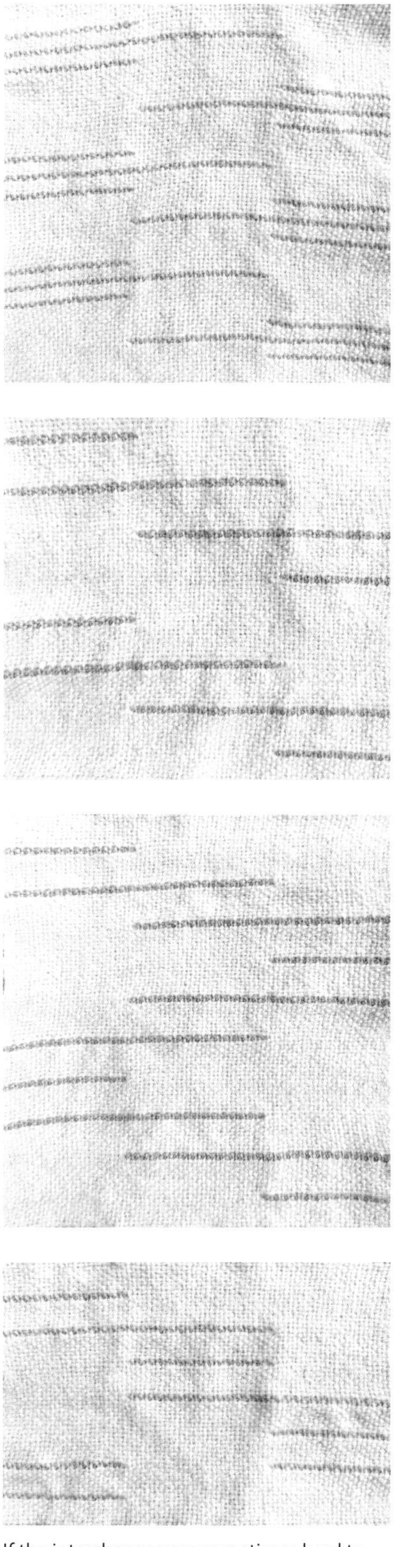

If the interchanges are sometimes hard to see on the passive layer, their construction can be seen clearly on the active underlying wool layer.

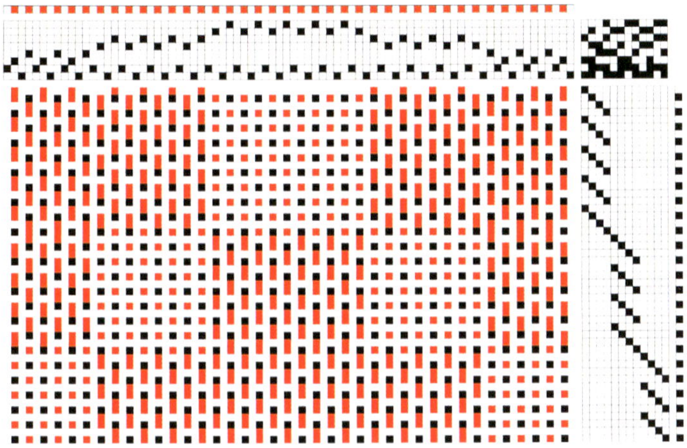

The blocks can be fully integrated or separate.

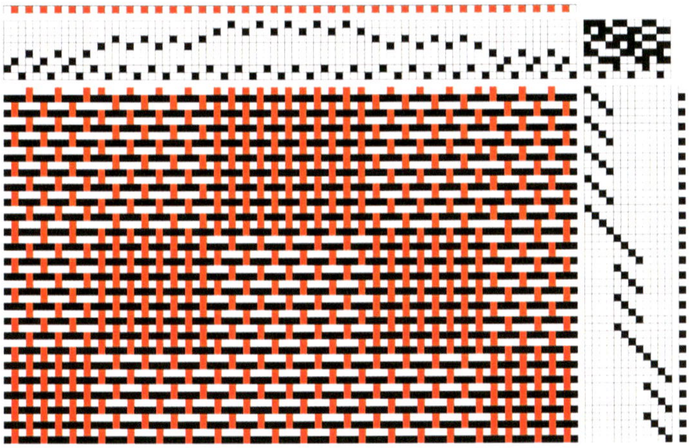

These drafts show both sides of one double cloth block while the other two threading blocks are integrated.

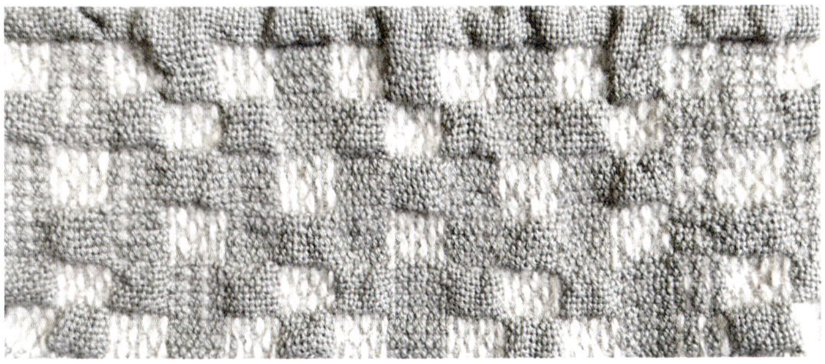

This sample explores the integrated blocks in cycles.

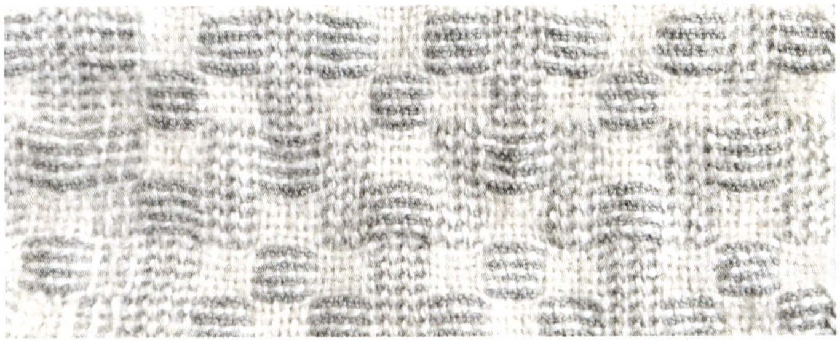

Different integrations show their structure on the reverse view.

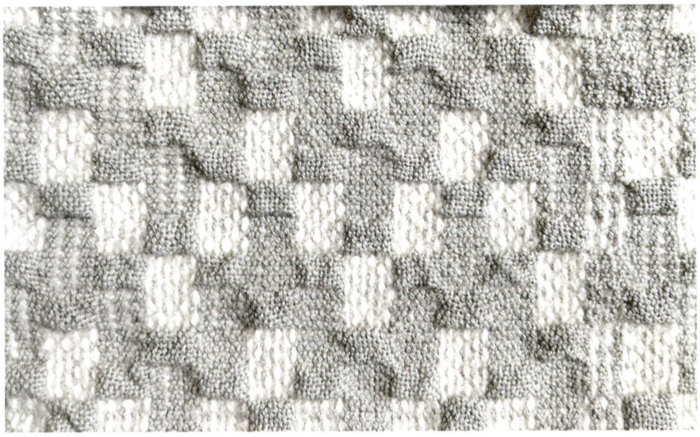

A different combination of the various blocks, both integrated and double.

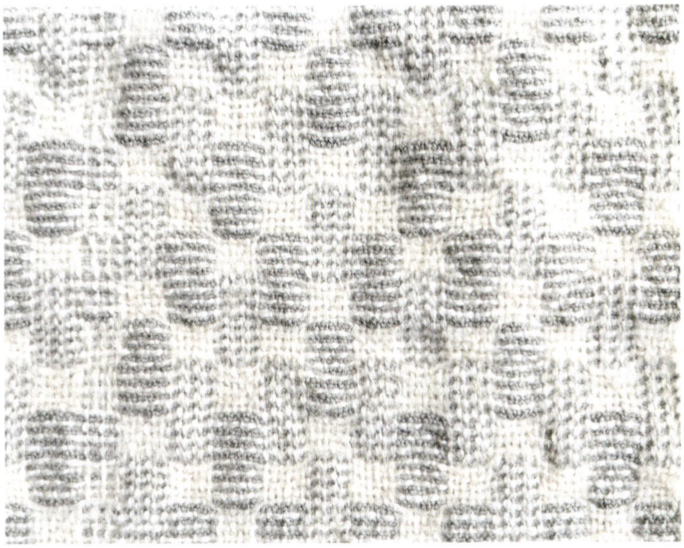

The reverse view showing the structure.

Additionally, blocks can be woven with areas of weft floats, which, if using an active weft, would give vertical shrinkage to the cloth.

Three or four layers can be woven with an eight-shaft loom (this is explored in Chapter 12).

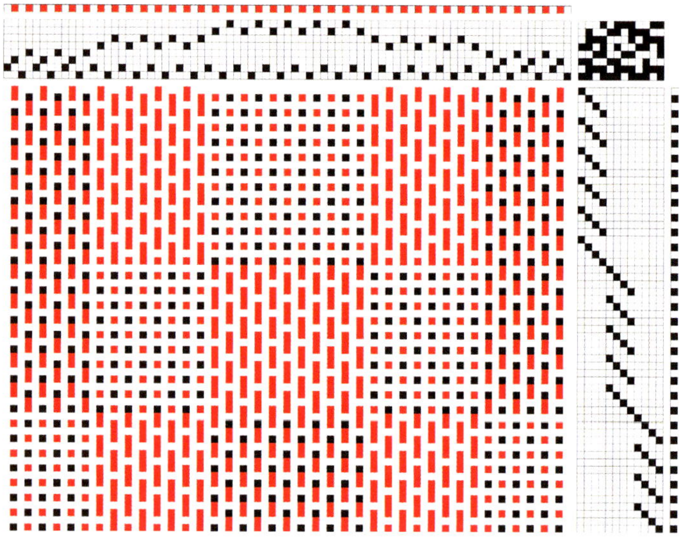

Another variation allows for weft floats on one threading block, which integrate with a second block and weave a separate layer in the third block.

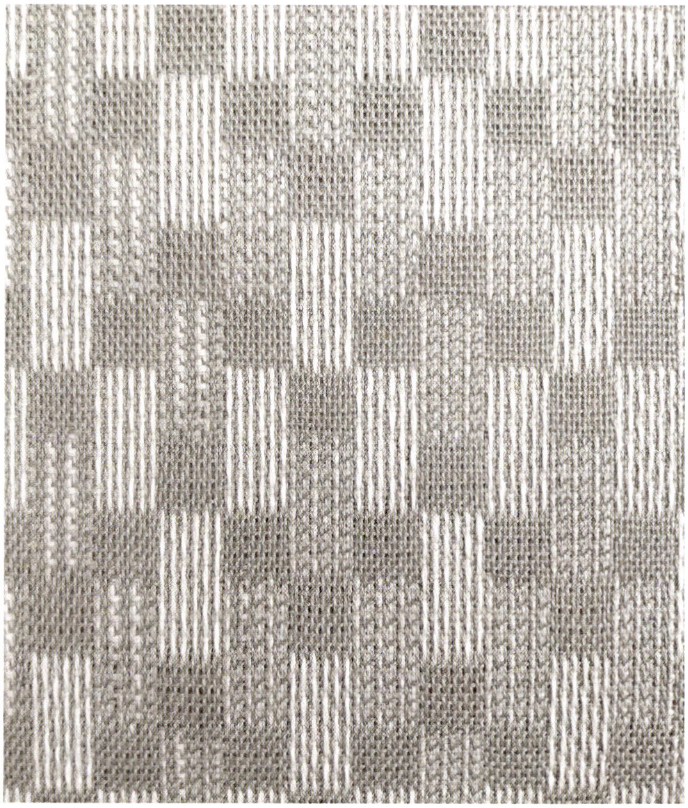

This sample has one active block (B), two integrated blocks (A & C) incorporating weft floats in one block to give a more textured passive layer surface. The on-loom image shows the patterning prior to wet-finishing.

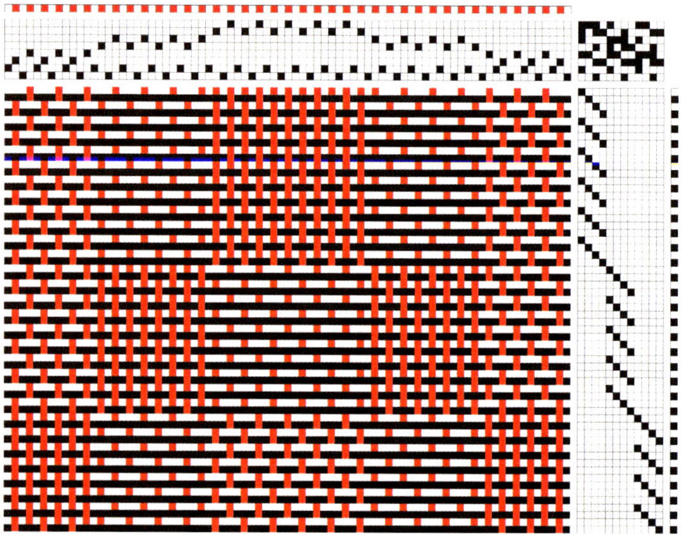

The reverse view shows the long black floats in one area, the integrated area and the double cloth layers.

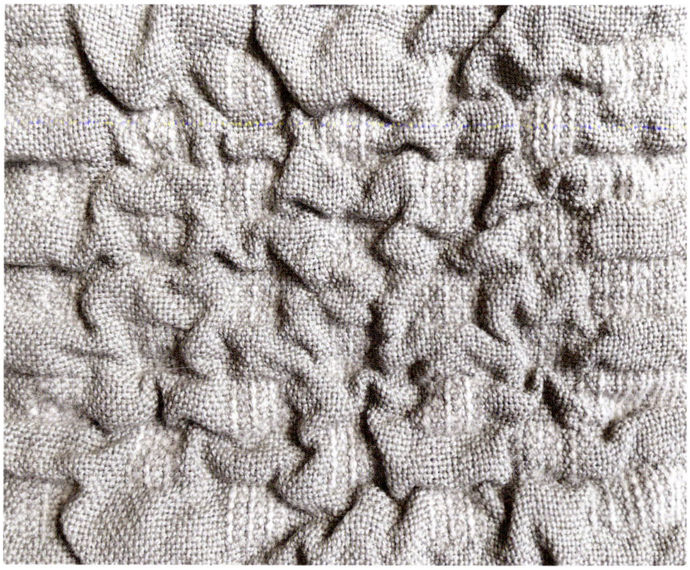

Wet-finishing gives effective texture.

More Than Eight Shafts

With more than eight shafts, there are more possibilities. Using the same principles as for integrated blocks on eight shafts, with 12 shafts you could create grids of puckered passive cloth surrounding integrated areas with the active cloth. Using active warp floats and weft floats, the integrated areas retract into the fabric and the surrounding passive layer puffs up.

If you have 12 or more shafts available, different weave structures that promote contraction, such as waffles, could be used against plain weave. The automatic dimensional shrinkage, which occurs once the warp is released from tension, will give instant surface texture on the plain weave surface.

There are other options available for using waffle in double cloth. These can be found in Chapter 2.

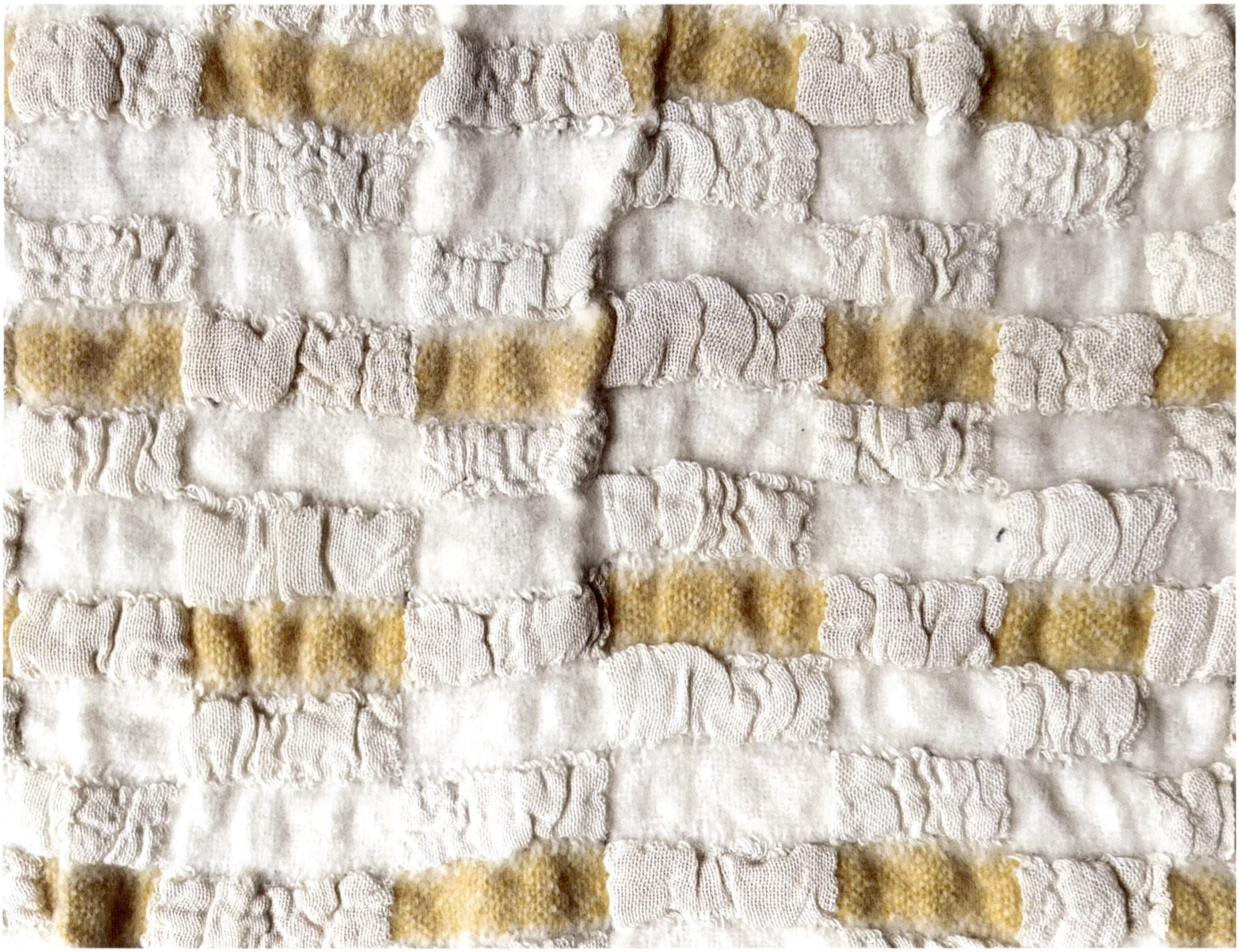

Extra interest is gained by mixing sizes of yarn, types of yarn and colour contrasts. A different coloured wool weft every third block has been introduced while alternating interchanging layers and contrasting the wool layer with a fine cotton.

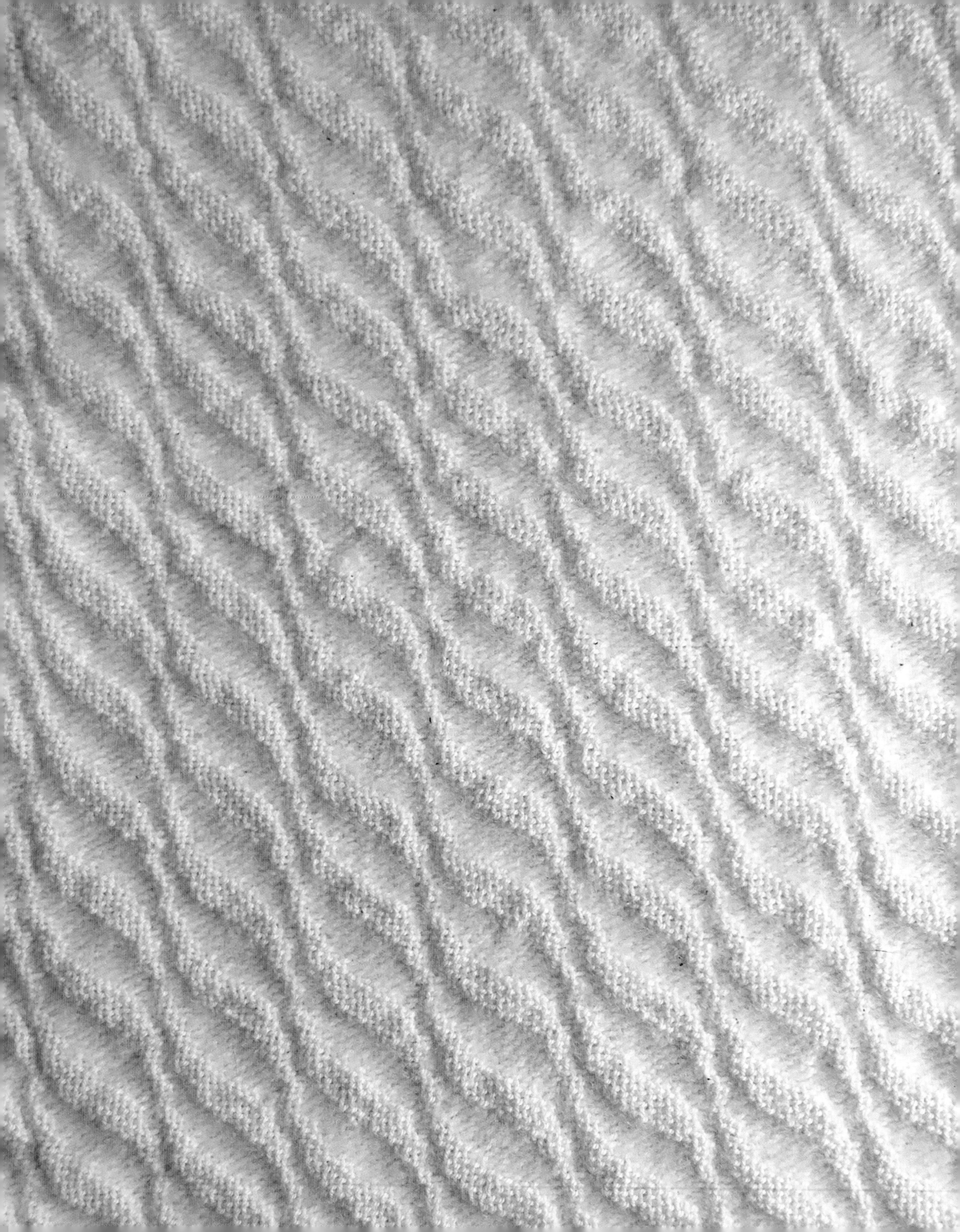

CHAPTER 10

STITCHED DOUBLE CLOTH

In addition to double weave blocks, there is also the possibility to create textural 'stitching' of individual or groups of ends from one layer into the other.

The texture is on one side only. The name tells you that two layers are required. The two layers of fabric are woven simultaneously on the loom, as for double cloth texture, with the effects being created through integrated elements and the dynamic reaction of the two layers, which have different rates of shrinkage during wet-finishing.

Often, stitching was used as a form of stabilising two layers of fabric. The stitches were usually hidden from view under a float. It would be classed as an error should the stitches become visible. However, for our purposes, this is a technique where a complete contrast of colour between top and bottom layers can be used, and the stitches highlighted.

CLOQUÉ, MATELASSÉ AND PIQUÉ

Stitched double cloth is another form of cloqué (blistering or puckering) and other techniques you might have heard of are piqué and matelassé. Piqué and matelassé use two warp beams and have one of the warps at a higher tension. They both also can utilise a wadding weft, which acts as a stuffing (*see* Chapter 3).

The verb *matelasser* means 'to quilt' in French. Often in traditional matelassé, the two layers are of the same fibre, with one warp held under much higher tension on the second beam. In this book, we are looking at the use of an active warp for one layer, which gives shrinkage during wet-finishing, so a second beam is not necessarily required for shorter warps, although very useful if available. Matelassé can be woven with different weave structures in the non-shrinking cloth or with combinations of structures.

Piqué has two versions: one where the tight second layer is only woven where it is stitched into the top layer (loose-backed), leaving the non-woven area as floats, and the other where the tight second layer is woven (fast-backed). The non-shrinking layer is nearly always in plain weave. Loose-backed piqué can give dramatic results if wool is used for the floats.

The two terms matelassé and piqué were often interchangeable in industry, so there is considerable confusion as to what each distinctly means. Both of these terms seem to apply more to stitched cloths rather than block effects.

Two shafts, usually shafts 1 & 2 provide the passive plain weave layer. The active yarn in this book is woven as a fabric underneath, but various elements from the threading are included in the passive layer for one or two picks to provide the 'stitching' textural element. During wet-finishing, dimensional texture appears when the shrinking layer, with its occasional connections to the top layer, contracts, pulling the non-shrinking layer into various puckers and folds, depending on the pattern of connections (stitches) between the two layers.

Four Shafts

The principle behind stitching is to integrate one or more ends from the shrinking (active) layer into the non-shrinking (passive) layer, using the weft for the layer being woven. Having a different ratio for one of the layers is often

A regular undulating twill design has been converted into stitched double cloth by joining two layers – one active (wool), one passive (cotton) – together in some areas while leaving them separate in others. The areas in which they are not 'stitched' leads to contraction in the wool when wet-finished, giving a dimensional texture.

recommended. If the active layer is sett more openly with fewer picks, when wet-finished it will shrink more, forcing the passive layer to buckle and pucker.

With a four-shaft loom, pick-up techniques can be used to create effects. However, if loom-controlled techniques are preferred, horizontal bands can be formed. This is not hugely different from integrating layers in a double cloth with differential shrinkage for a couple of picks (*see* Chapter 9) but it does give an interruption to the top layer and can be varied by how often one shaft of the active layer is brought up to join the passive layer. The opposite can also be woven – one shaft from the passive layer is woven in with the active layer, using the active weft.

Dramatic differences in appearance can be experienced by switching out materials used for the passive weft. Different twist amounts of the yarn used will also have a bearing on the resultant texture.

Six Shafts

Stitched double cloth on six shafts is far more varied if two shafts are used for the non-shrinking (passive) layer. Other

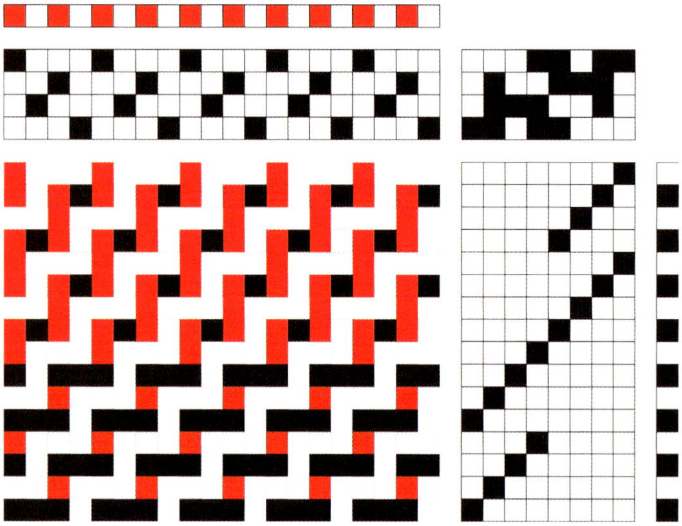

The four-shaft tie-up shows the regular double cloth tie-up giving plain weave on both layers, with one layer weaving white and the other layer weaving red and black. Both sides are shown with an interchange of layers.

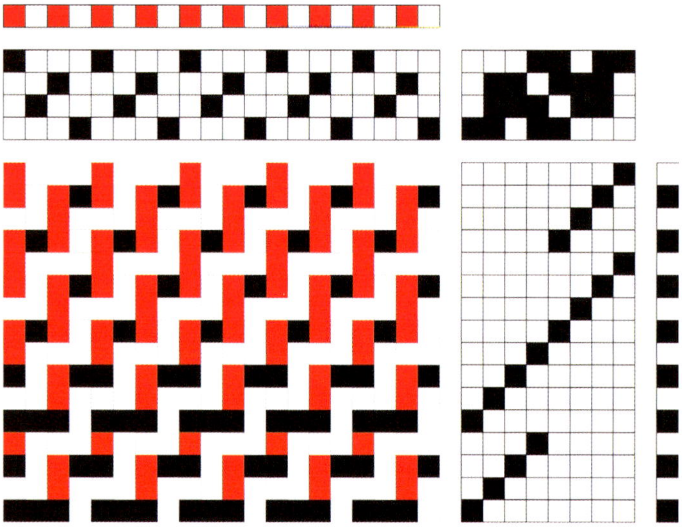

There is a slight change in the tie-up to create a stitching point, bringing the one shaft of the lower warp up to join the white warp. The drawdown shows the slight change. In column 3 of the tie-up, two shafts are lifted instead of just one. Shaft 3 joins the top layer's shaft 2. The same change has been made in the interchanged layer, shown in column 6. This time, it is the white shaft 2 that has been raised to join the top black layer. Compare the two drafts.

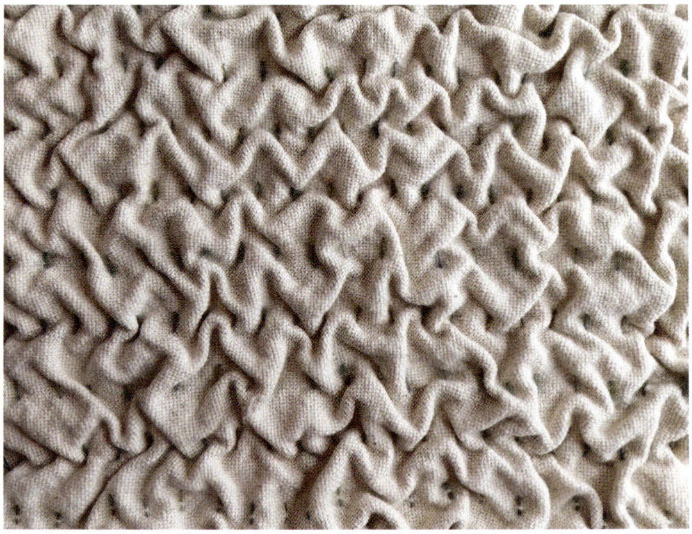

Simple alternating stitches can lead to quite considerable texture. There are 16 plain weave picks between each stitching element, which allows for the increased texture.

threading conventions, such as point threading or extended point, can be adopted for the remaining four shafts with the shrinking yarn. This will enable different parts of the threading to connect the two layers together and allow for patterning in the stitching.

Even very simple stitching designs can give effective texture.

Repeating the same pattern shaft for two or three ends can expand or enlarge a draft and create different scale effects in one threading. If a contrasting colour is used for the active layer, the stitched design becomes subtly visible in colour as well as texture.

Take some squared paper or open a weaving programme and create some design lines on a grid that is four squares high and as many squares wide as desired. This becomes the threading for the active layer.

Insert blank spaces at the beginning of the draft and between each of the design ends. Add alternating ends on shafts 1 & 2 into the spaces.

With stitched double cloth, individual shafts of the active layer are woven together with the passive layer, effectively 'stitching' specific points together.

Designs can be created directly in the liftplan, or, if preferred, in the tie-up. The weaving sequence for six shafts always remains the same.

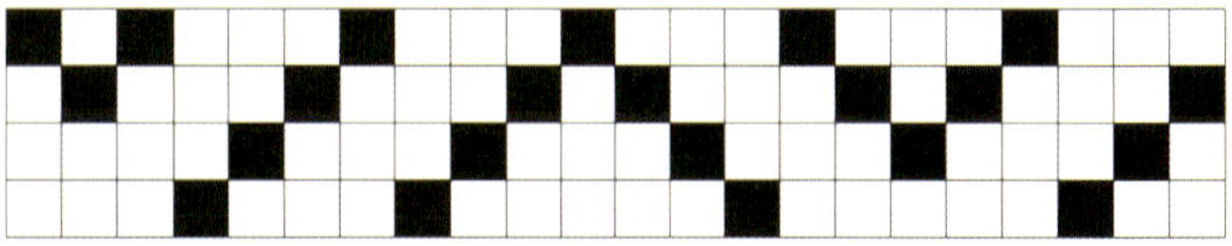

A four-block profile threading draft is the basis for a design for one layer of a double cloth.

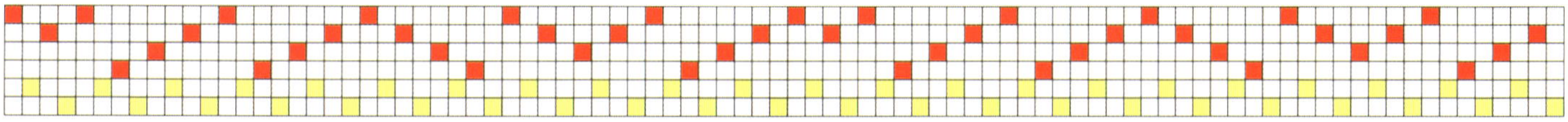

The next stage is to insert a space before every design end. Now add two more shafts – we're choosing shafts 1 & 2. The spaces will be filled in with alternating ends on shafts 1 & 2. In this illustration, shafts 1 & 2 in yellow will be our top layer – our passive layer. Shafts 3–6 in red will be the lower layer with active yarns.

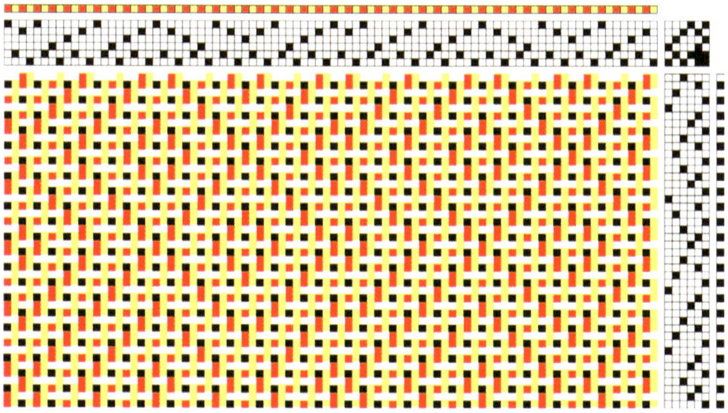

The tie-up shows that the lower layer weaves plain weave on columns 5 & 6, with shafts 1 & 2 being raised. The top layer weaves with one shaft of the lower layer joining it for every pick. This means the bottom layer is being stitched into the top layer in every top layer pick. The active lower layer will contract on finishing and pull the top layer into a puckered or puffed pattern. The drawdown shows this, especially if you half-close your eyes while looking at it. The red (active warp) will become clearer where it is stitched into the top layer.

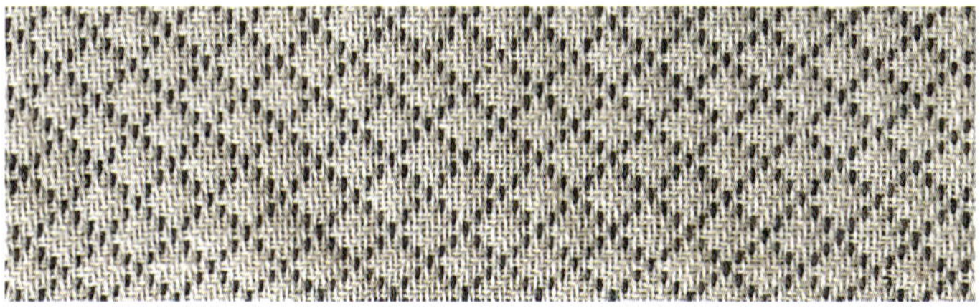

Stitches are using one shaft only on this point threading but keeping the active warp shaft up for two picks, as the ratio of active to passive yarns is 1:2.

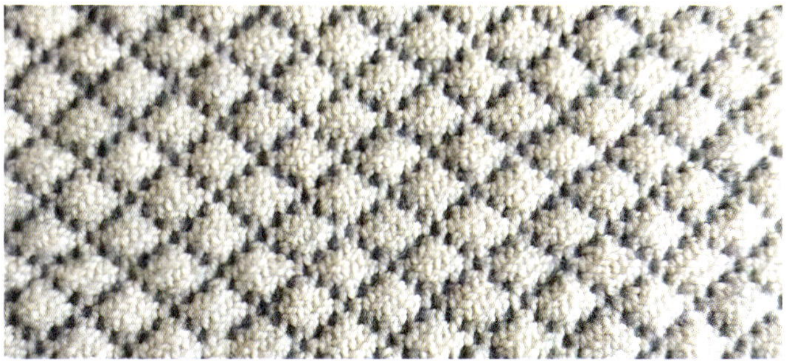

Photographed directly from above, the sample has a slight raised appearance.

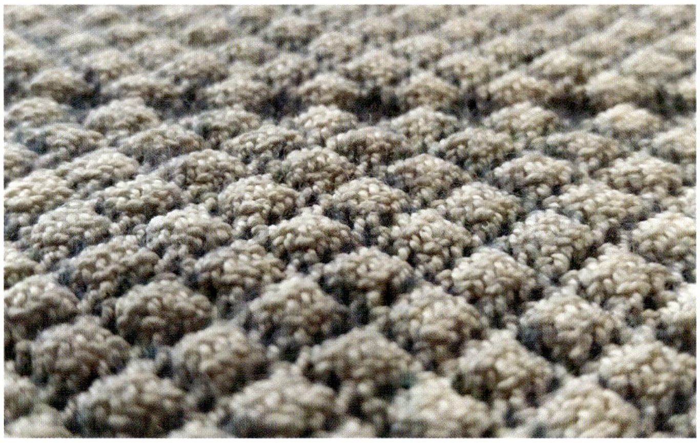

Photographed from an angle, it is possible to see the amount of texture on this sample.

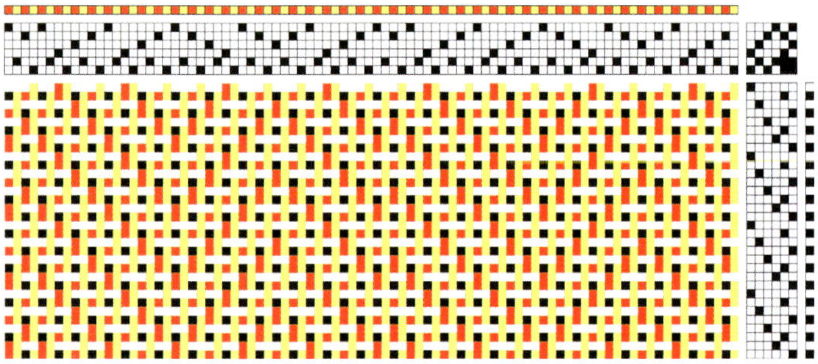

A point twill has been stitched in this draft.

If just one shaft from the active (red) warp is included with the plain weave of the passive (white) warp, then distinct textural patterns can be created with minimal stitching and maximum textural impact. The resulting pattern can be seen on both sides of the cloth, especially if you half-close your eyes, although the texture will only appear on one side after wet-finishing.

Stitches can be incorporated as and when desired. Simply lift the selected pattern shaft(s) on one or more picks to change the results.

OVERSHOT DESIGNS

Designs adapted from overshot threadings can be used to create stitched double cloth on six or eight shafts in both threading and liftplan. The simplest method is to use two shafts for the passive top cloth and the next four shafts to adapt a four-shaft overshot design into a threading to create stitching based on that design. The pattern is created by lifting the required shaft(s) along with the two plain weave top layer picks, then weaving plain weave on the active cloth underneath.

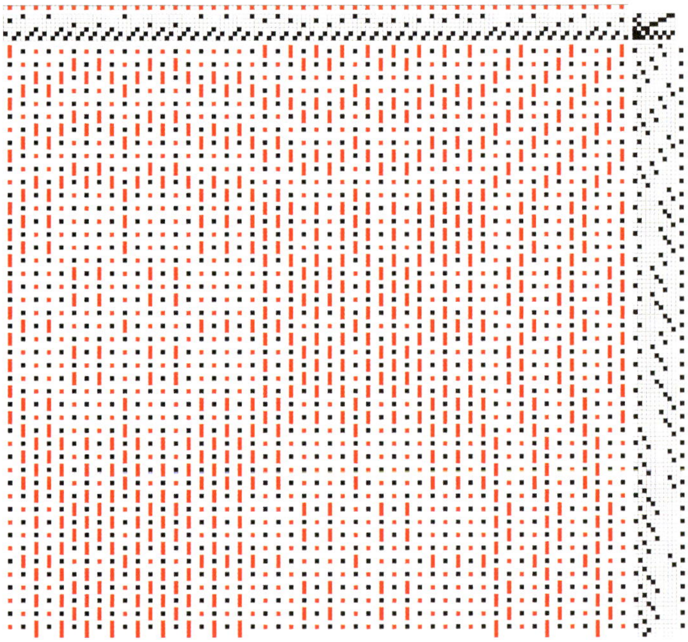

The ratio of passive to active warp and weft can be changed for greater effect. This draft shows a 2:1 ratio with two passive ends to one active end. The Wandering Vine (Cat Track and Snail Trail) overshot design has been adapted and used for the stitching.

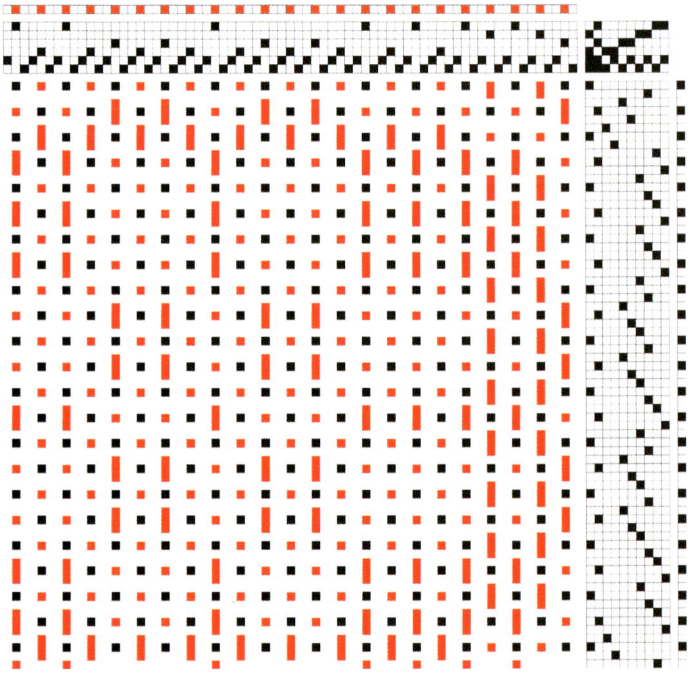

A detail from the overview gives greater visibility to the stitching.

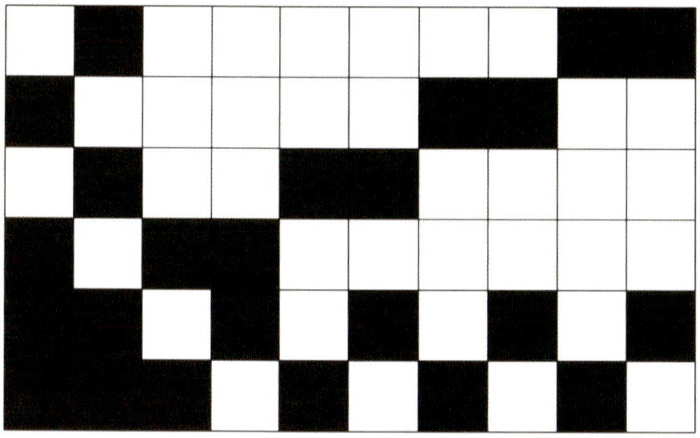

The tie-up is shown in a larger size so it is easy to see what is going on. Columns 1 & 2 show the lower cloth plain weave lifts. Columns 3–10 show that just one of the lower warp shafts is raised for two of the top layer picks because of the 2:1 ratio in the weft.

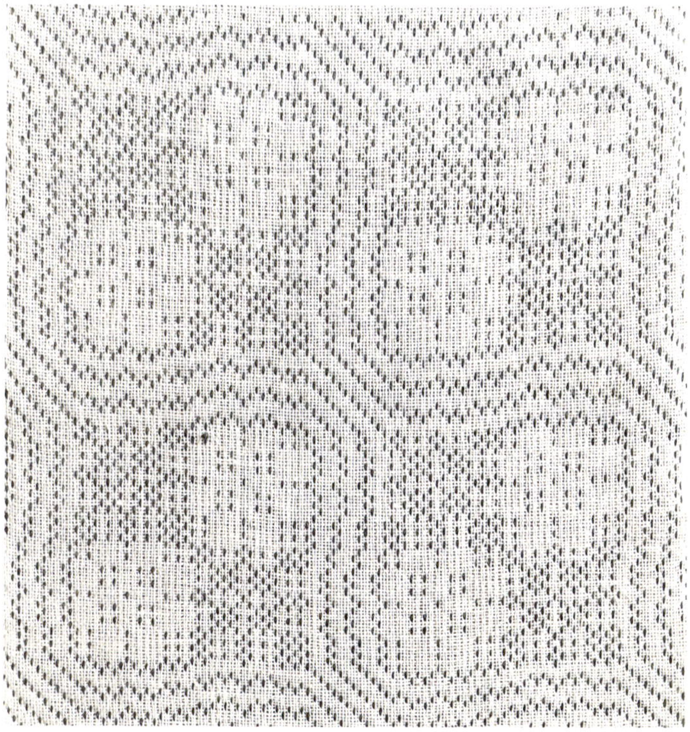

The Wandering Vine overshot pattern prior to wet-finishing has been turned into a stitched double cloth by weaving just one or two shafts from the active warp in with the passive warp. As before, each stitch is for two picks.

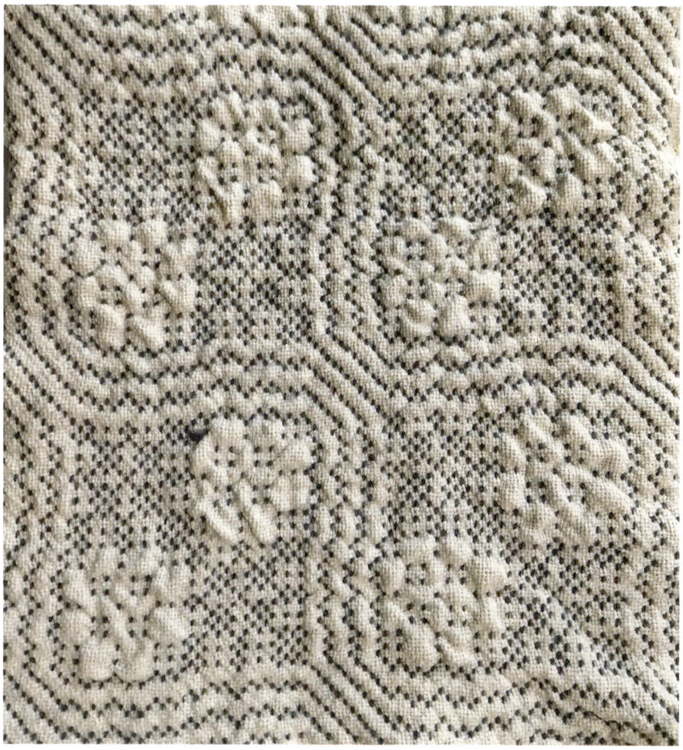

After wet-finishing, the cat's paws element of the design really pops out from the flat plain, outlined by the Snail Trail. The Snail Trail is not as prominent, as the stitches are closer together on the passive cloth. Larger plain weave areas in the top cloth allow for greater texture.

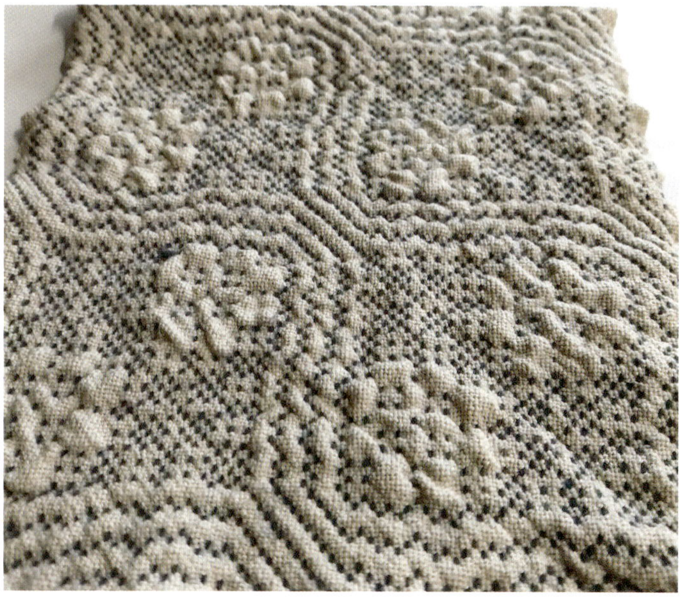

An angled view shows the amount of texture created.

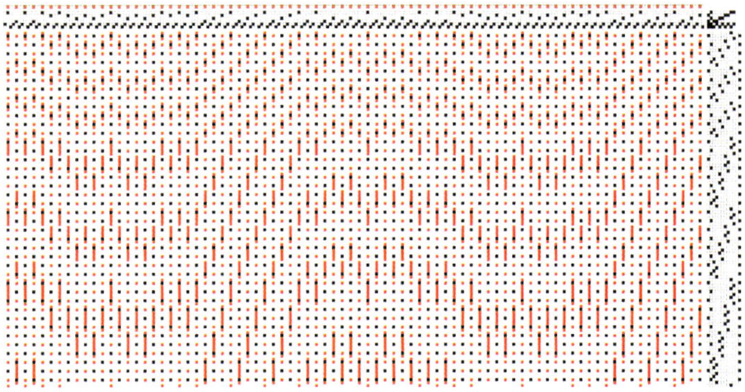

The same threading and tie-up has been modified by a straight treadling sequence that doubles then trebles the number of picks that the stitches are incorporated into, giving variations in the scale of the design.

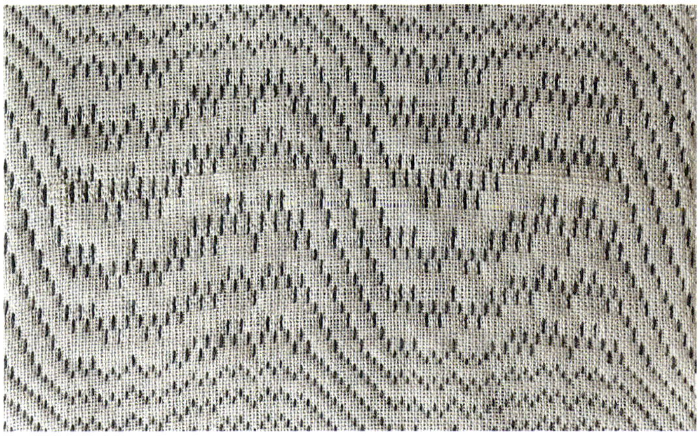

The same warp incorporating this new treadling plan gives varied amounts of stitching and corresponding variations in increases in the plain weave to create scale.

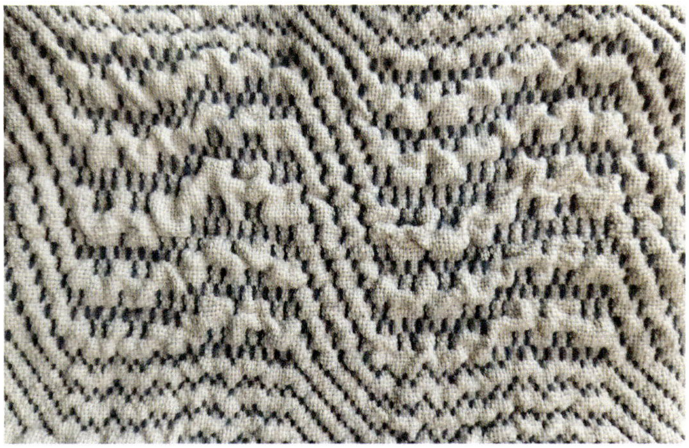

After wet-finishing, these variations become interesting.

The drafts may look fairly complicated, but once weaving has begun, it is quite intuitive to follow what the design shows you on the cloth, rather than slavishly following a treadling pattern. If you allow yourself that freedom, many more ideas can be generated as confidence in the process grows.

Eight Shafts

With eight shafts, there is much more design potential for taking this method of stitching further, using the active warp yarns over six shafts (shafts 3–8) for more intricate stitching points. A larger-width design can be created using a ratio of 1:2 wool to cotton and an extended advancing threading (*see* Glossary for further information) on shafts 3–8.

If your floor loom allows, skeleton tie-ups can be used.

With a 1:2 ratio in weft as well as warp, both the picks of the non-shrinking layer can be woven one after the other or split so that the picks follow the threading convention, whichever is easiest.

- **Pick 1:** Raise shaft 1 and a selected pattern shaft and weave with cotton.
- **Pick 2:** Raise shaft 2 and the same selected pattern shaft, and weave with cotton.
- **Pick 3:** Raise shafts 1 & 2, and 3, 5, 7 and weave with wool.
- **Pick 4:** As Pick 1, and weave with cotton.
- **Pick 5:** As Pick 2, and weave with cotton.
- **Pick 6:** Raise shafts 1 & 2, and 4, 6, 8, and weave with wool.

The basic double cloth remains.

TOP TIP

A floor loom with tie-up and treadling is useful for regular lifting, but for more variety and added stitching points, a table loom or dobby loom gives greater flexibility.

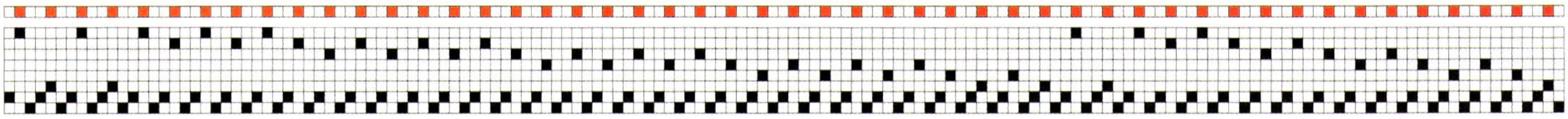

With eight shafts, two shafts can be used for the top layer, allowing for six pattern shafts in the lower active layer. The threading in this draft shows an extended advancing threading on shafts 3–8.

Apart from the two plain weave shafts, any of the shafts on the active layer of a loom with more than four shafts are potential pattern shafts and can be used in whatever order and combination is desired to create stitching patterns. However, the more pattern shafts woven in one pick with the passive layer, the less the fabric will pucker as the active yarn is integrated more firmly into the passive layer, thereby not allowing it as much room to shrink when wet-finished.

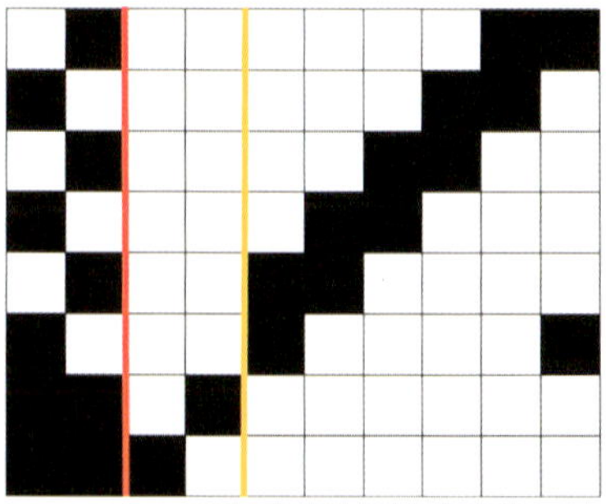

A skeleton tie-up can be used for floor looms with limited treadles, so long as two-pedal treadling is possible. The first two columns give the full tie-up for the lower layer to weave plain weave. The second two columns give the basic plain weave for the top layer, separated from the remaining six columns by a yellow line. One pattern shaft is pressed at the same time as one or other of the top layer plain weave pedals in the two columns to the left of the yellow line. The weaver has the choice of which two shafts to integrate with the top layer.

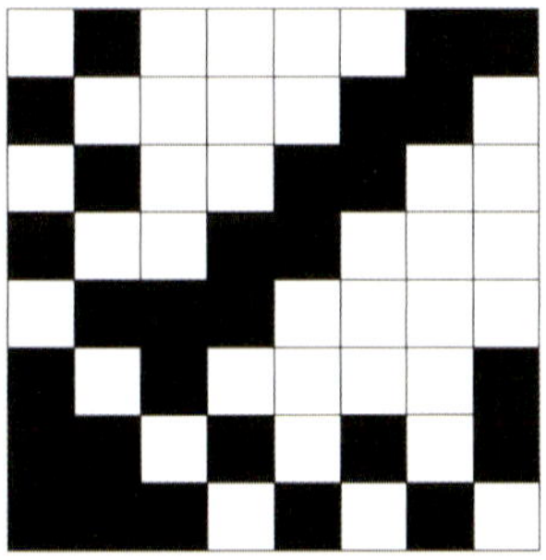

An eight-shaft skeleton tie-up creates the two layers and the stitching points.

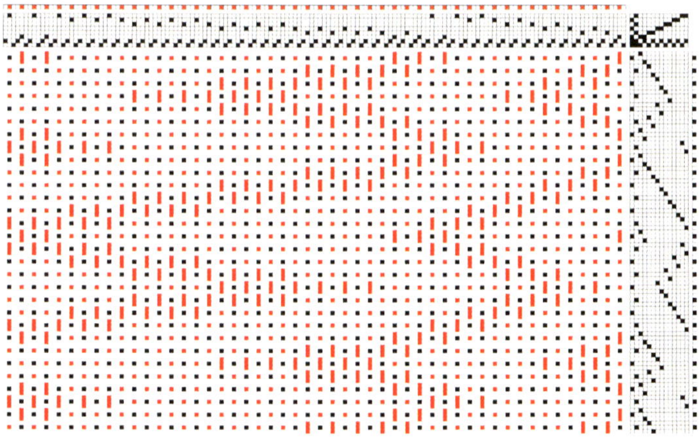

A meandering stitching line has been designed using multi-treadling in this draft, which could be converted using the first skeleton tie-up. Note that each plain weave pick on the top layer has one of the pattern shafts weaving with it. The lower active layer remains consistently weaving plain weave on shafts 3–8 and raises shafts 1 & 2 so that it can weave below.

Using a 1:1 ratio for threading can still be effective. For weavers used to tied threadings for single cloth, this will look like a double two-tie threading system. However, the tie-up is the deciding factor.

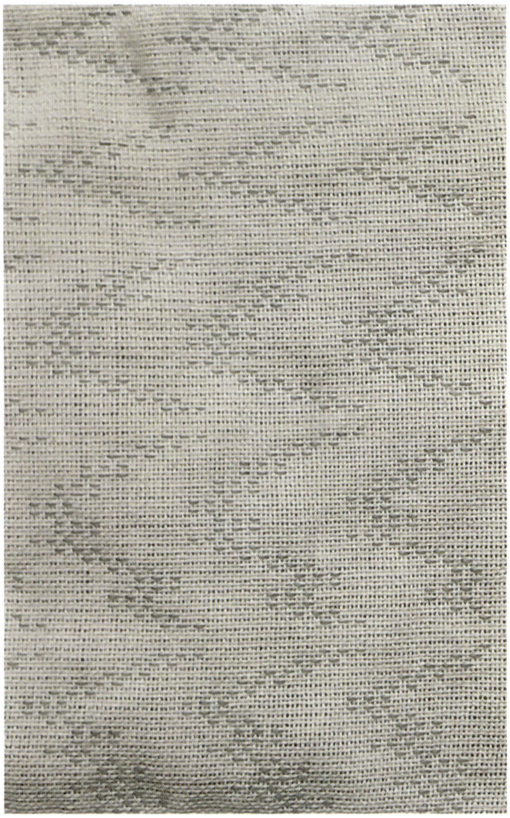

The point and extended point threading gives variations in the design line.

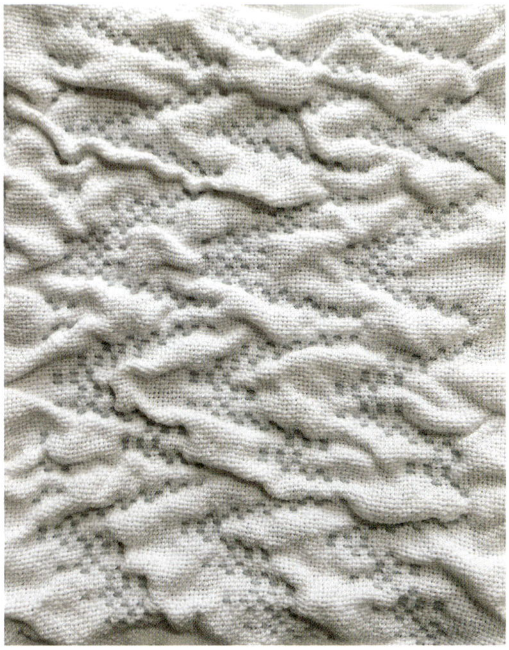

The wet-finished sample shows considerable texture.

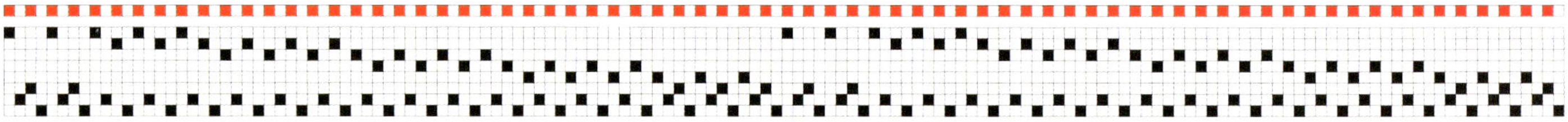

A 1:1 ratio in the threading has the same appearance as a double two-tie threading single cloth. However, the tie-up dictates the structure of the cloth.

Another possibility is to put a twill on the non-shrinking layer, although that reduces the number of shafts available for the stitching layer.

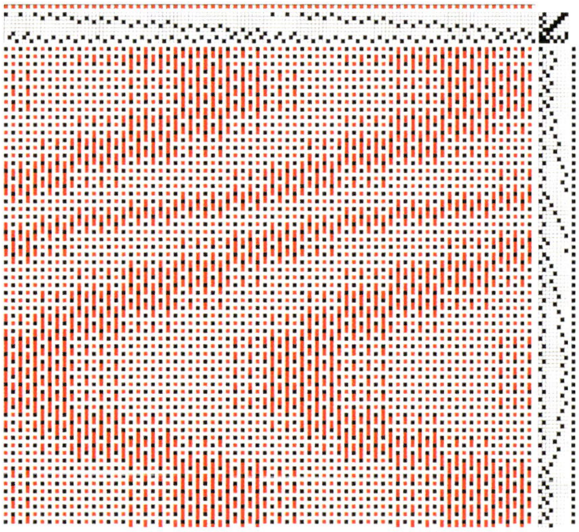

An excerpt from the draft used with kind permission of Bonnie Inouye.

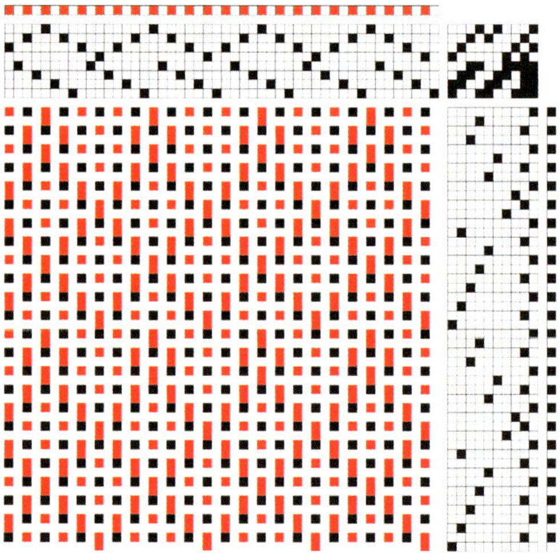

The passive top layer has been placed on shafts 1–4 so that a twill can be woven. The active lower layer is on shafts 5–8 with a point threading and stitching a single shaft into the twill of the top layer, while maintaining its own plain weave layer underneath.

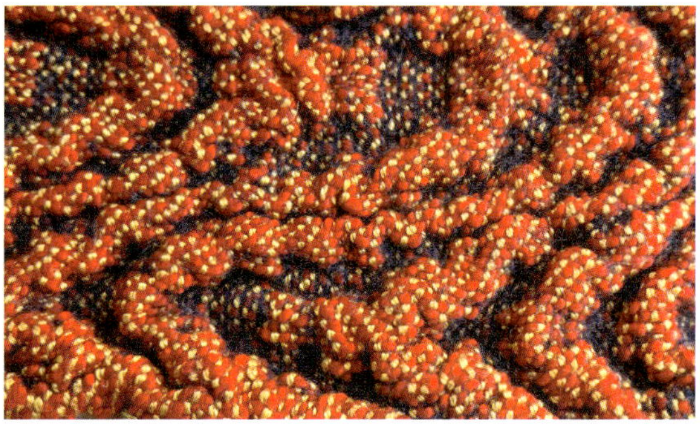

A double two-tie threading for this sample uses a 1:1 ratio.

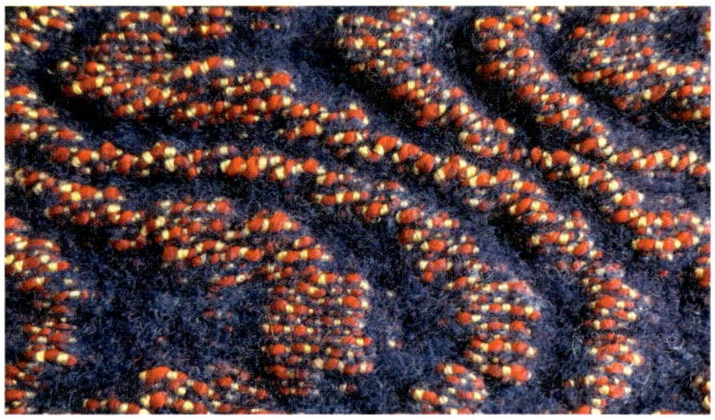

The reverse shows the amount of fulling that has occurred on the active layer.

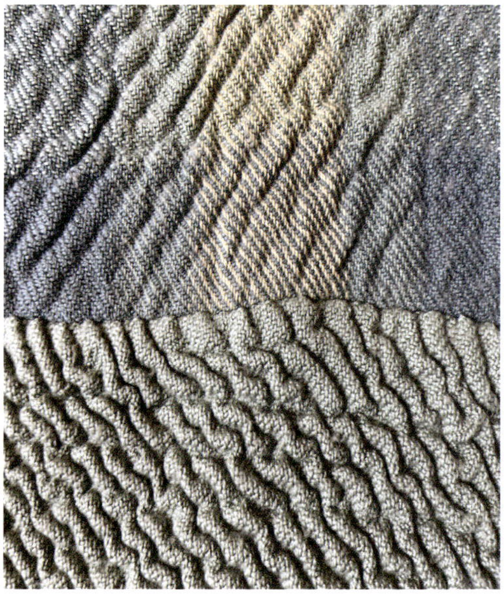

Jennifer Verrall wove this sample on eight shafts using a 2/2 twill for the cotton ground cloth, with a ratio of four ground weave ends/picks to one merino wool end/pick. The wool was woven in plain weave with a straight entry in both warp and weft.

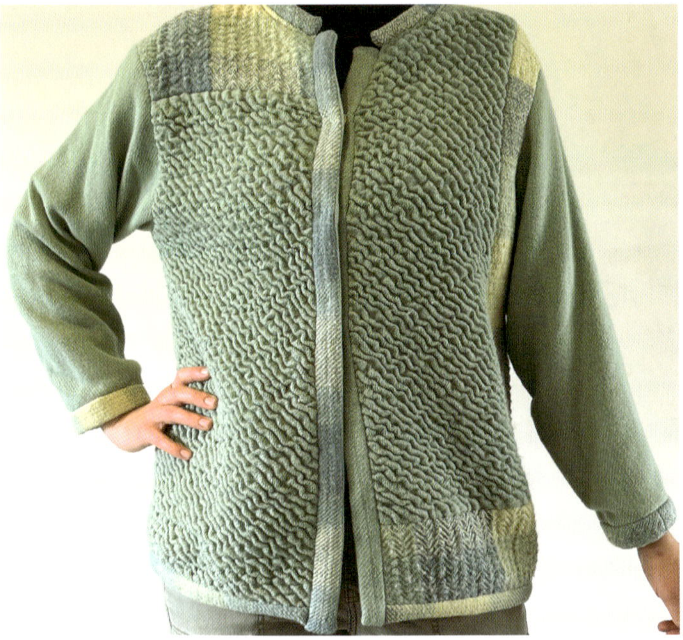

The sample was then woven up, contrasted with a plain cotton twill from the same warp for the sleeves plus some additional chequered preliminary samples, and pieced together to create this effective jacket.

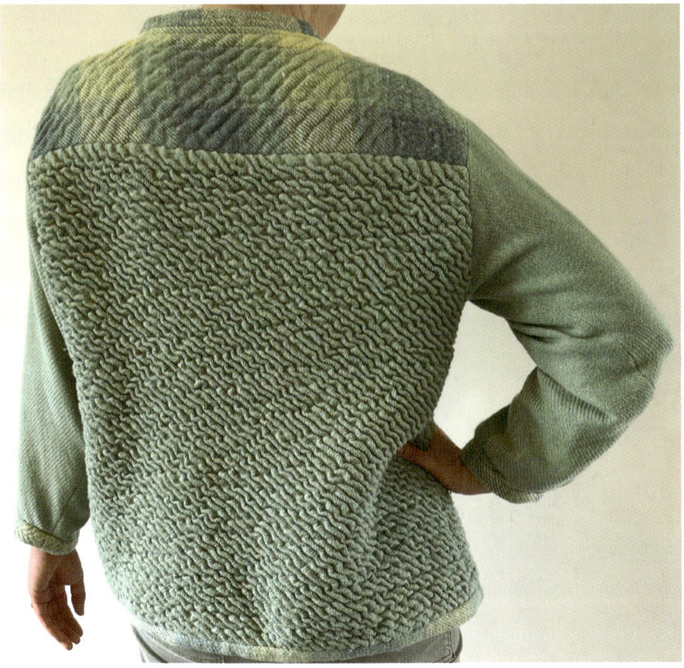

The reverse view.

MOTIFS

Various motifs can be generated, especially when using a point threading on the active layer. Of course, the more shafts available, the greater the variety of motifs that can be designed.

Sashiko

Sashiko motifs can be adopted for stitched double cloth, using stitching in simple straight lines often on point threadings. Other ratios can also be used.

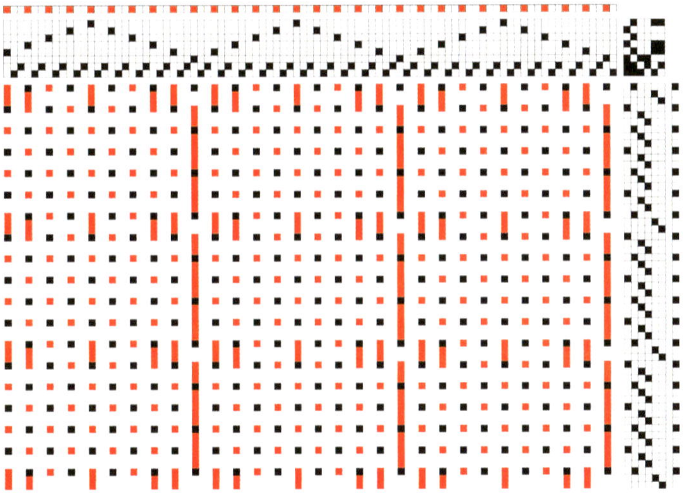

Sashiko designs are well suited to stitched double cloth. This eight-shaft draft has the top layer on shafts 1 & 2, with a point threading for the lower active warp. The design is called Hanashijushi.

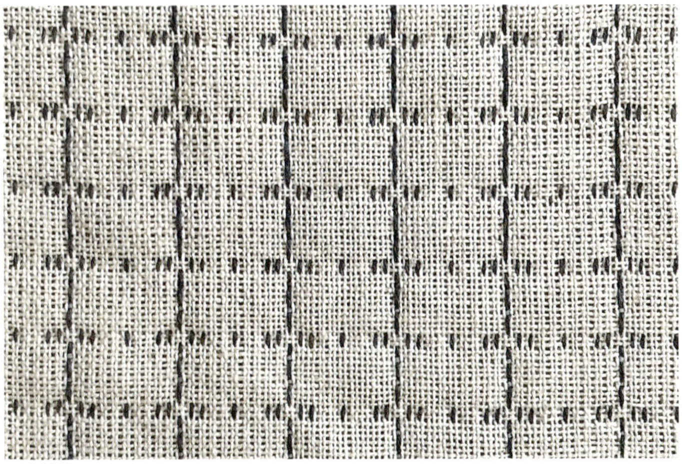

Here, the simple verticals and interrupted horizontal lines of Hanashijushi are shown straight from the loom, before wet-finishing.

Simple cross effects (Jūjizoshi), line and cross effects (Hanashijushi), diamond motifs (Nagarebishi) and more elaborate designs (Kasuri tsunagi) can easily be created on eight shafts, with six shafts for the design lines and two shafts for the plain weave passive layer.

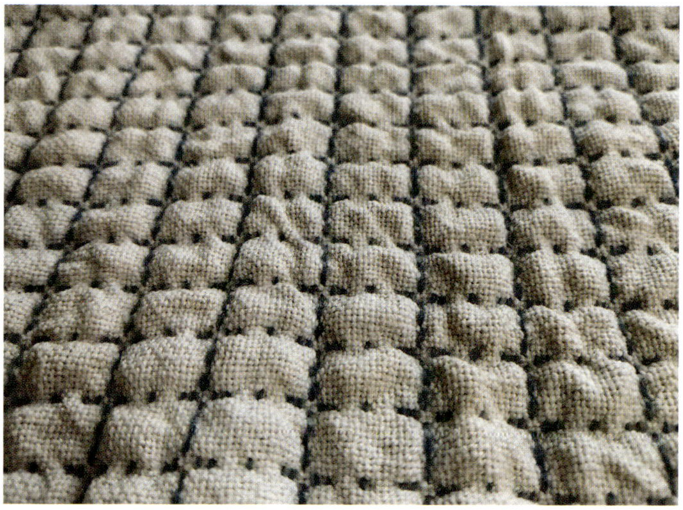

The effective result after wet-finishing shows up well in this angled image.

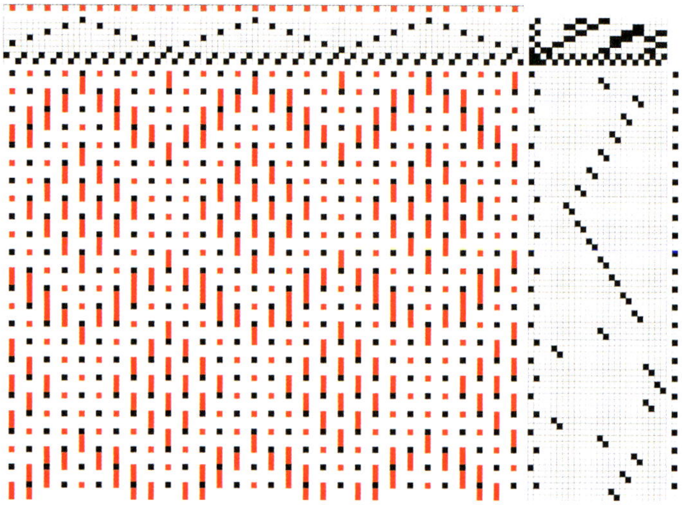

The same threading can give the design of Nagarebishi, although 24 treadles are needed.

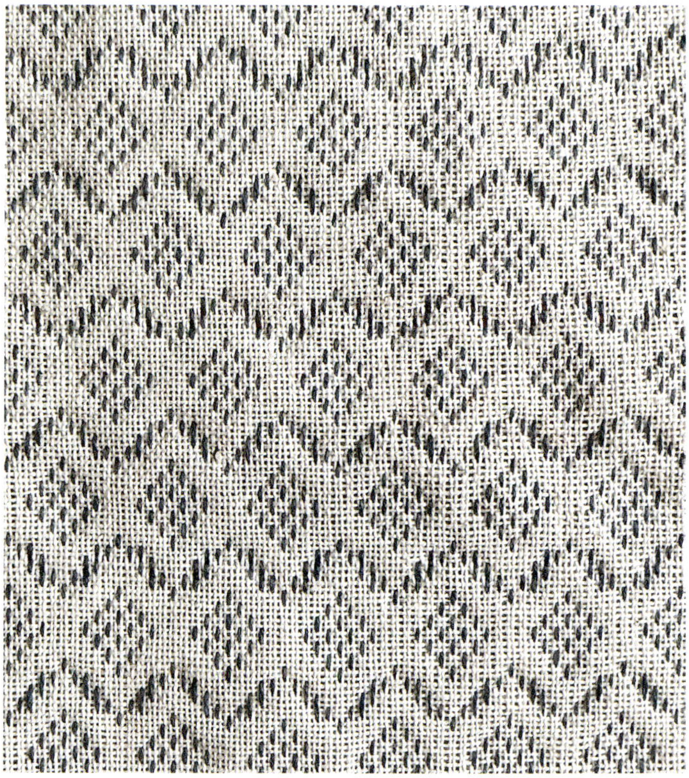

Nagarebishi is a little more complex, but works on a point threading, with two shafts for the passive top layer (ecru) and six shafts for the point threading on the lower active warp.

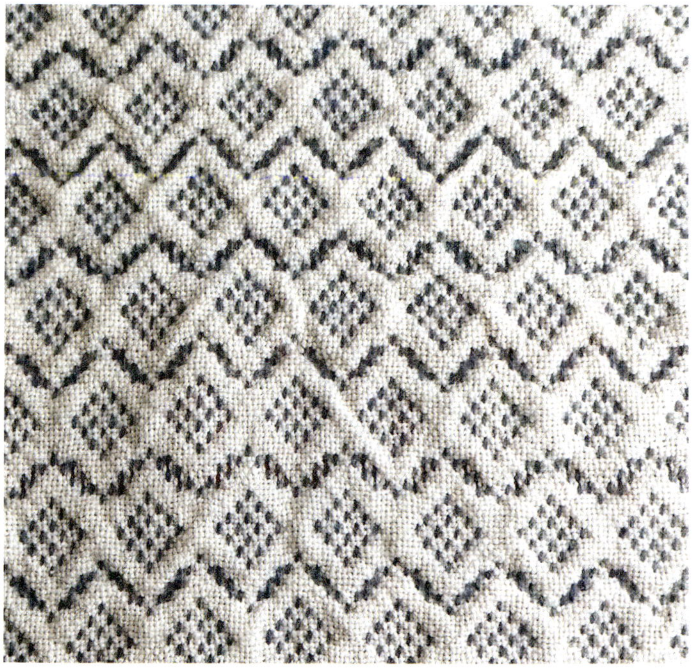

The texture is not as pronounced as for Hanashijushi as there is more stitching connecting the two layers together, but it is still dimensional.

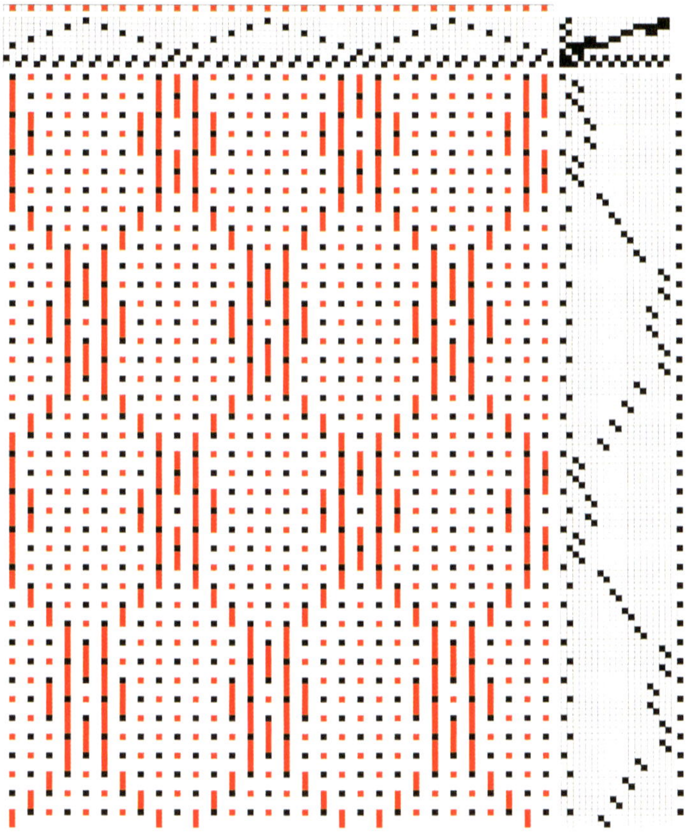

Kasuri tsunagi also uses the same threading, with 18 treadles.

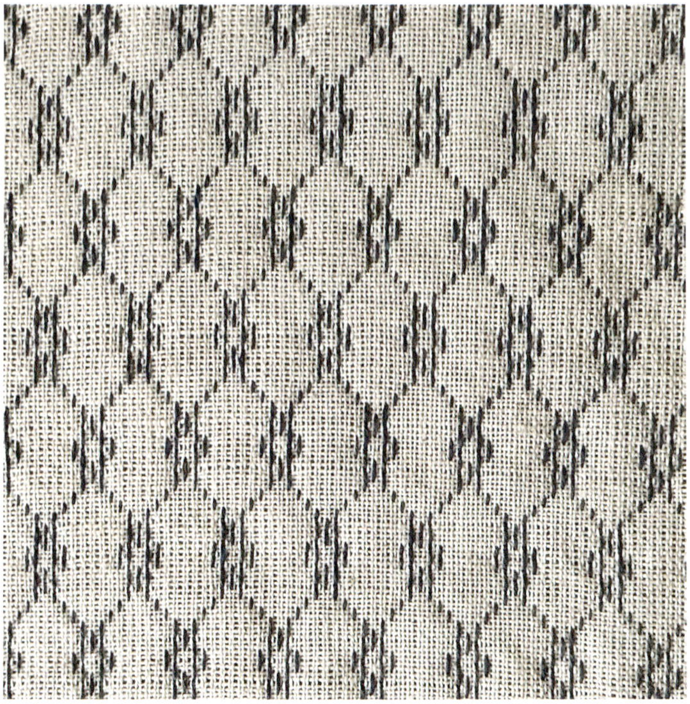

Kasuri tsunagi is a more sophisticated design, again possible on the six-shaft point threading for the active warp.

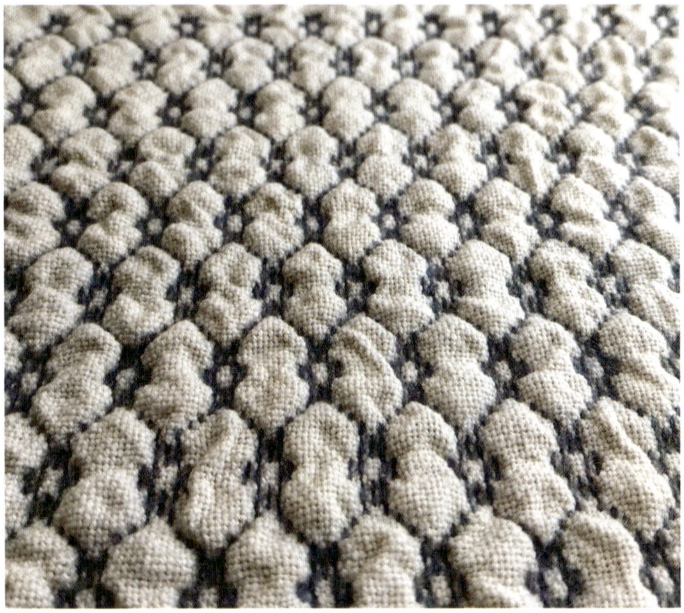

The texture is quite pronounced in the larger unstitched areas. The stitching design gives an interesting twist to what is principally an enlarged diamond.

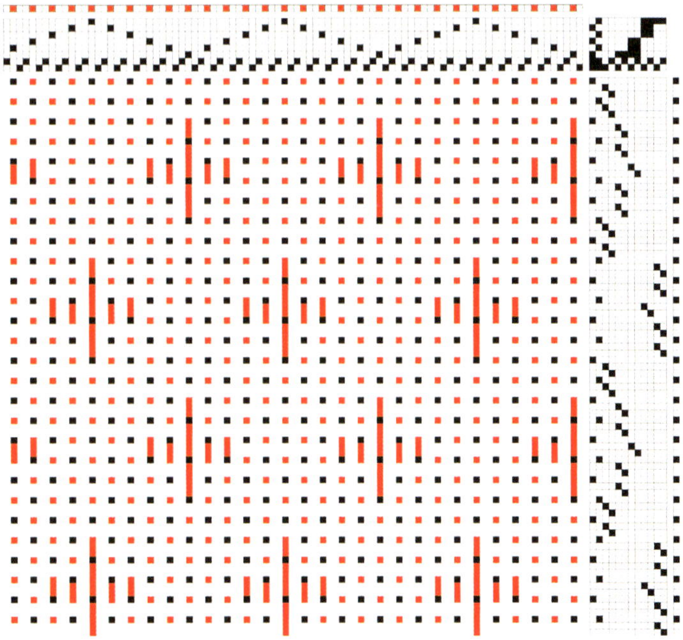

Jūjizashi can be woven with the same threading and 12 treadles.

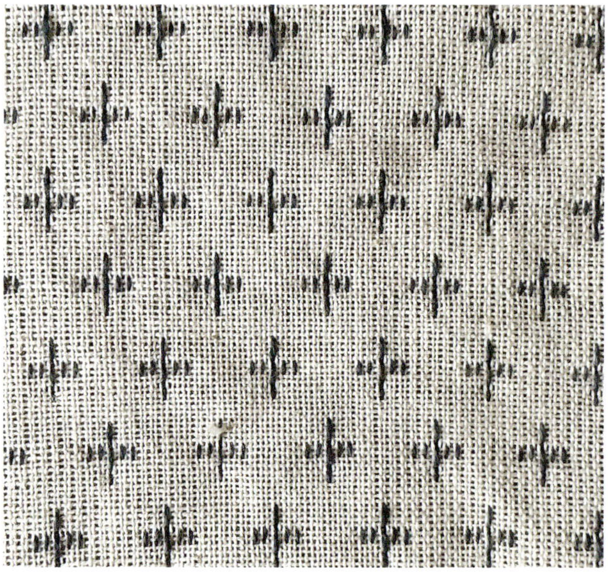

Jūjizashi is a very simple cross design.

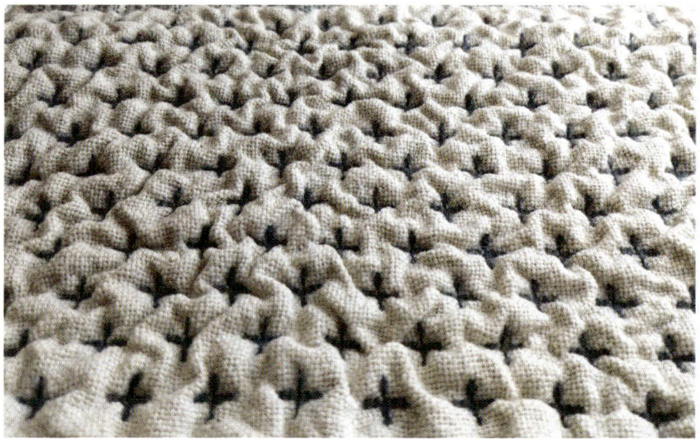

Because of the small amount of stitching, the texture is pronounced.

Other Structures for the Active Layer

One incredible textural effect is created by confining the passive layers to two shafts (or four if you have lots of extra shafts) and using the active layer with a completely different weave structure that has lots of floats. This is even more effective using a ratio of *at least* 1:2 active to passive ends and picks. The float length will affect the amount of shrinkage, along with the choice of yarns used and sett.

Probably one of the most effective and dramatic textural results using this approach is created by weaving a waffle (UK honeycomb) in the active yarn and stitching the two layers together at the central point of each waffle. Upon wet-finishing, the waffle shrinks a lot, giving rise to what to a brain-like texture.

With 12 extra shafts in addition to the two for the passive layer plain weave, at least two different sizes of waffles could be used, allowing for varying coruscations of the fabric. Combine that with various passive layer materials and many interesting iterations are possible. Add varying ratios to the mix and you have extreme biology/geology in the making!

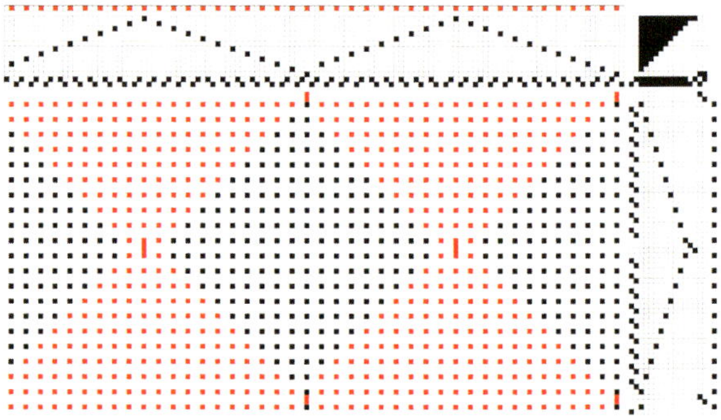

Waffle is a wonderful generator of 'brains' effects in stitched double cloth. This draft uses 14 shafts, but smaller-sized effects can be created with fewer shafts. The stitching point is relegated to just two shafts – the points – on shafts 3 and 14.

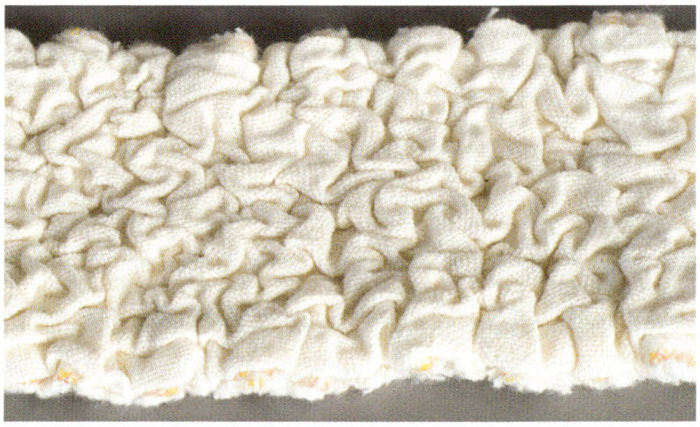

Waffle weave was used as the active warp's weave structure instead of plain weave, with the stitching points only at the extremes of the waffle. One size of waffle created this 'brains' sample.

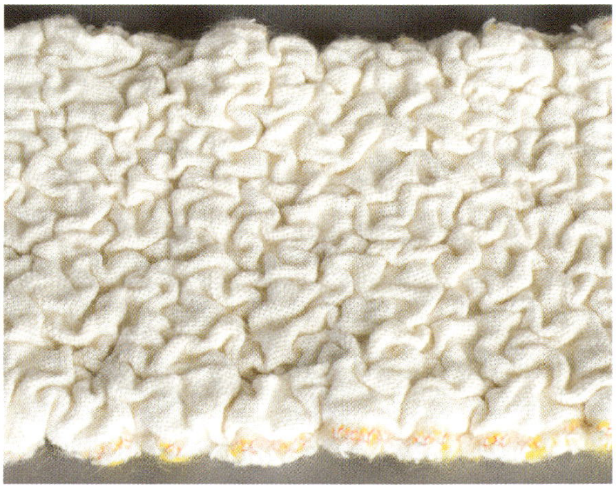

The waffle used here is a smaller version of the previous one, which creates more compact and regular 'brains'. (Photos: Colin Usher)

STITCHED DOUBLE CLOTH FOR SHAPING

One more unusual method for using stitched double cloth is for shaping. If the active warp is restricted to one side of a warp, a curve can be created on wet-finishing, which could be useful for items like scarves or neck wraps. Reducing the ratio of the active to passive warps to 1:3 or 1:4 would give even more curvature on wet-finishing.

Wet-finishing

As you would expect by now, these fabrics need to be wet-finished to bring their full potential to life, unless they are woven with elastomeric yarns (*see* Chapter 1). If wool is used as the shrinking yarn, and it has gone through the fulling process, the effects will be permanent. If elastomeric yarns have been employed, they can be stretched out after weaving, but they will always spring back to their restful state once the tension is released.

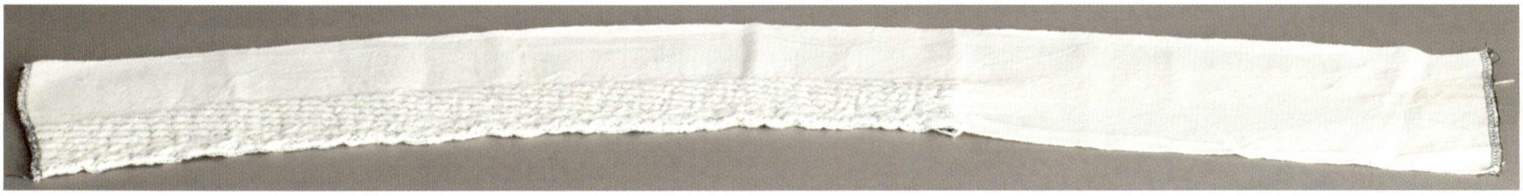

Shaping can be useful for garments or accessories when stitched double cloth is kept to one side of the fabric.

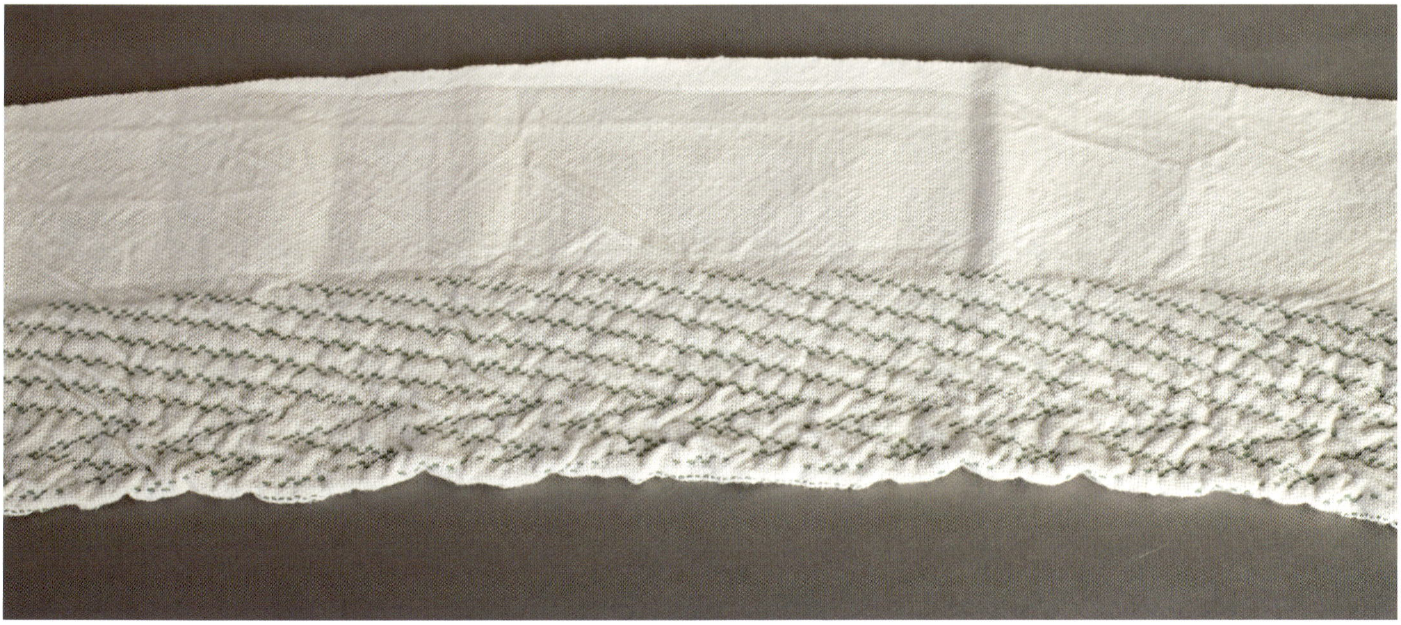

A close-up view shows the method, although this sample was created for proof of concept and not for extreme shaping. (Photos: Colin Usher)

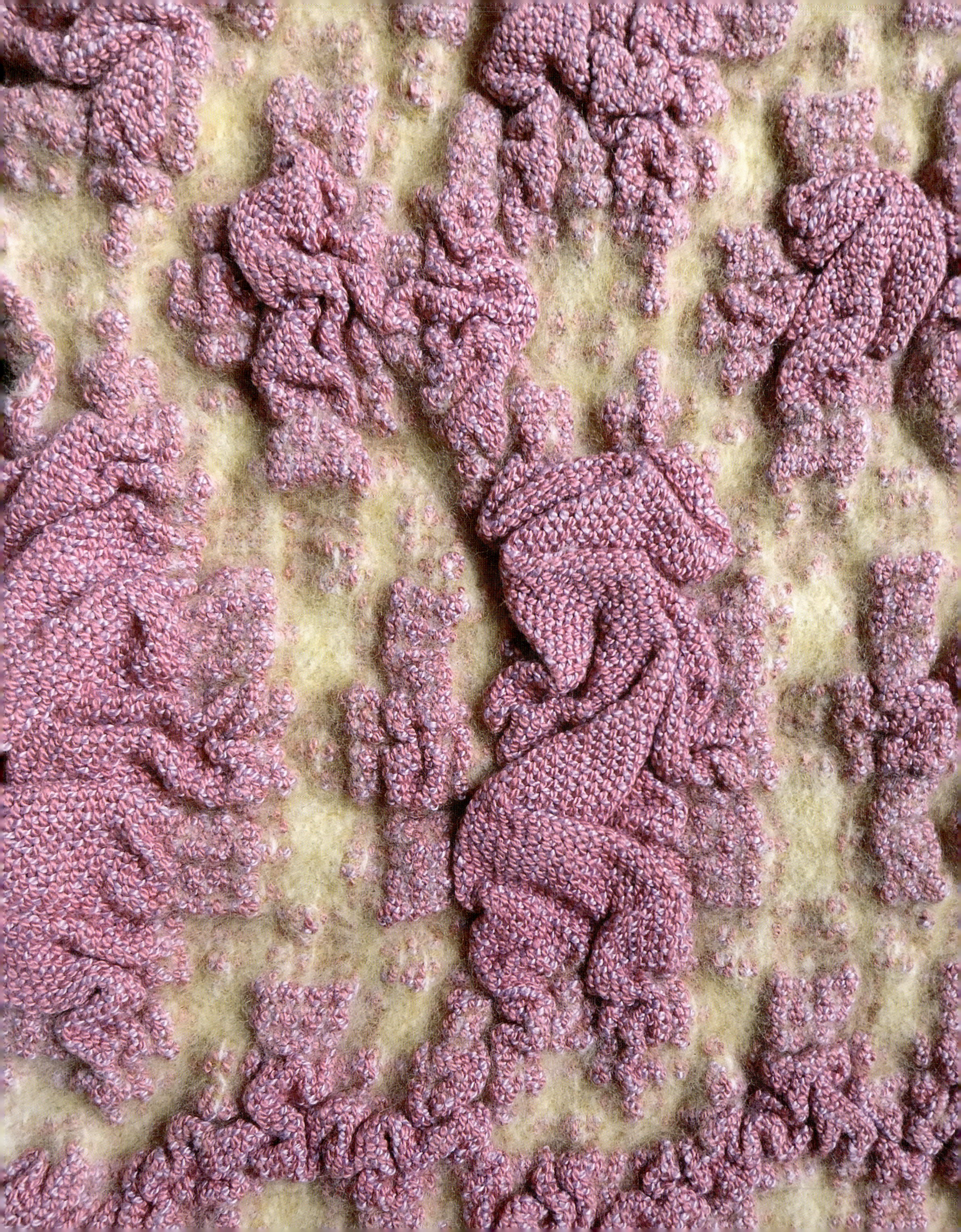

CHAPTER 11

FOUR-COLOUR DOUBLE WEAVE (AND FRIENDS)

Before we move on to four-colour double weave (4cDW), there are some threading conventions that are useful to introduce here as they are related to 4cDW in principle – all use combinations of single and double cloth areas, although designed in a different way. They use threadings that look to be single cloth, although the tie-up shows us otherwise. These threadings are:

1. Advancing
2. Network drafted

Please note that these usually require eight or more shafts for the designs to be large enough to be effective. They also require more treadles, so table looms with eight or more shafts or dobby looms are often best suited for these designs.

ADVANCING AND EXPANDED ADVANCING THREADINGS

This uses a more conventional single cloth 'twill' advancing threading approach, with alternating warps and wefts of active and passive yarns. In effect, the odd-numbered shafts are for one cloth, the even-numbered shafts are for the other. The two warps are not divided into clearly defined units repeated to create a visual block. Each layer is created by moving through its shafts in a more fluid way. Therefore, the two layers are much more nuanced in their relationship to each other, and the edges are not as clearly defined as in the previous chapters.

The basic principle behind this is that two shafts per layer are required at all times for creating a double cloth area. When using adjacent shafts, for instance, 1, 2, 3, 4, shafts 1 and 3 will create plain weave on the first layer, while shafts 2 and 4 will create plain weave on the second layer. When the threading advances by five steps, it is possible to create an advancing area of double cloth in each progression through applying twill-like elements within the tie-up. If the opposite face is to be brought to the top in any area, then the tie-up must reflect this.

A 1:1 active to passive ratio is suggested for this particular mode of designing, although using a finer active yarn (i.e. wool) than the passive while keeping the sett at double plain weave or slightly more open (less ends per inch/cm) will give the effect of a more open ratio. Be aware that if the active yarn is wool, it needs to have enough shrinkage potential to compel the passive area to pucker so sampling is highly recommended. Alternatively, another active yarn such as elastane-based warp and wefts can be used to encourage the passive yarns to form the dimensional surface. The elastane element does not need to be put under much tension to create an effect.

Threading Options

Several threading options are available to create the effects:

1. Straight
2. Repeated sequences
3. Advancing
4. Expanded advancing

A 4cDW sample developed after a workshop run by Bonnie Inouye, using pink (warp) and lavender (weft) cotton, white merino wool warp and gold wool weft. Woven on a 16-shaft table loom.

These allow for a variety of scales and more or less definition, according to taste. Straight threadings are most often used when using graphics programmes to design weave structures (*see* Bibliography – Alice Schlein, *The Liftplan Connection*).

Advancing twill threading or treadling is made up of sequences of straight runs. In order to ensure that the design continues uninterrupted, the sequence needs to be longer than the twill block that is being featured. For instance, using four-end twills, the advancing run is of five or more ends.

Expanded advancing twill threading or treadling allows a run to be expanded by repeating the four-end twill repeat one or more times. A five-end run is extended by a four-end repeat before moving on to the next five-end run.

Point threading and treadlings cannot be used directly in a mirror effect as that would lead to a repeated end or pick in the fabric, which could appear as a fault. Instead, the impression of a point can be created by reversing the order of the returning section.

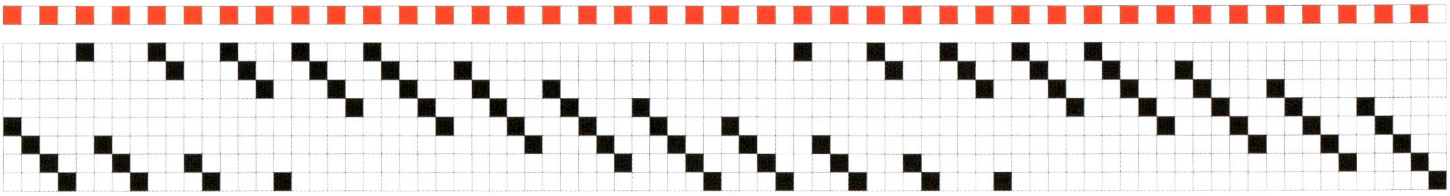

This advancing threading shows the repeated sequences of runs of straight threading over five shafts at a time. Each sequence begins on the next shaft up from the original starting point of the previous sequence. When the sequence runs over shaft 8, It wraps around to shaft 1 to allow the pattern to continue uninterrupted.

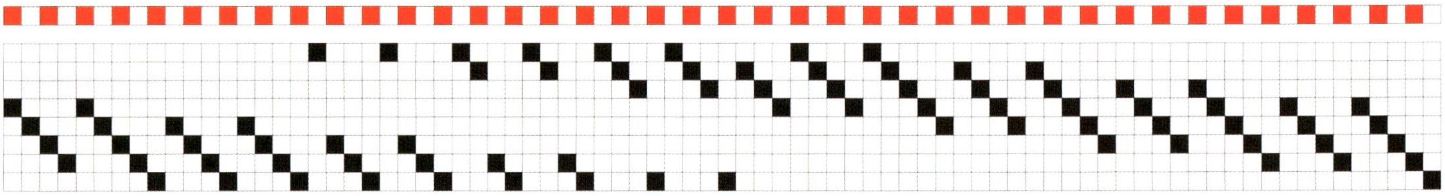

Using the same basic advancing threading, expanding it takes an element from the five-end sequence and repeats it. With a five-end run, the last four ends are repeated before the five-end sequence starts again, as before, on the next shaft up from the original starting point of the previous sequence. This sequence too repeats the last four ends before the pattern carries on. As before, the threading wraps around from shaft 8 to shaft 1.

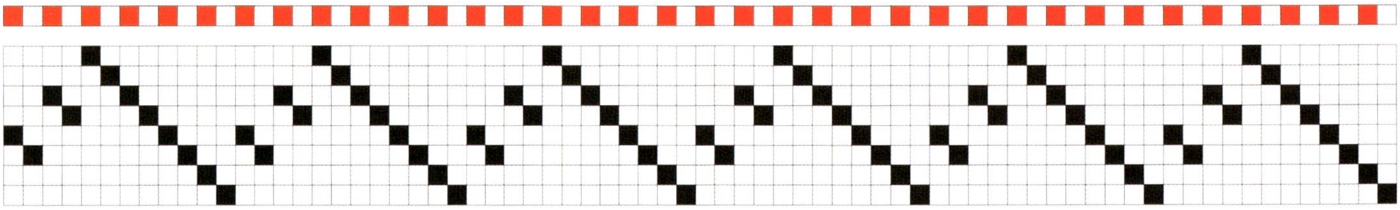

Point-effect threadings are useful when a point effect is not possible due to a repeated end or pick that can look like a fault in the cloth. Instead, the shafts are grouped in pairs and placed to maintain the odd/even threading order to create the impression of a point in the fabric.

The tie-up begins with the diagonal stair formation of a traditional double cloth tie-up, which gives the two separate layers on face and reverse.

Step one is the basic double cloth tie-up; step two adds the integration.

The tie-up does not have to be symmetrical. Every group of four shafts (which is the smallest unit of plain weave for both layers) can be adapted, either individually or in groups.

Three areas are created:

1. Where cloth A is on top
2. Where the two are integrated
3. Where cloth B is on top

These three aspects are what gives the design. In her book, *Exploring Multishaft Design*, Bonnie Inouye gives many variations of designing in the tie-up for double weave when using similar threading conventions. For weavers with multiple shafts, there is a lot of potential for designing greater or lesser amounts of surface dimension through the tie-up by varying the areas of which layer is uppermost, or integrated.

Tie-ups can also be rearranged into a more familiar parallel two segment side-by-side tie-up, if this is preferred. This gives the two sides separately.

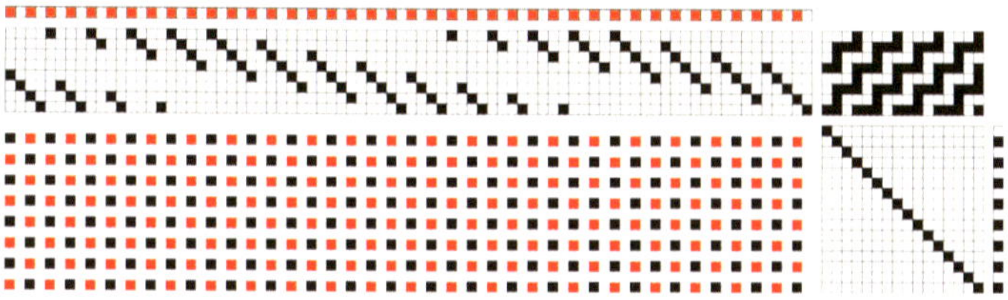

Step 1. To begin the compilation of a tie-up that is both double cloth and single cloth patterning, start with the staircase tie-up that is usually associated with double cloth. The cloth shows the white layer on top and the red/black layer is being woven in plain weave underneath.

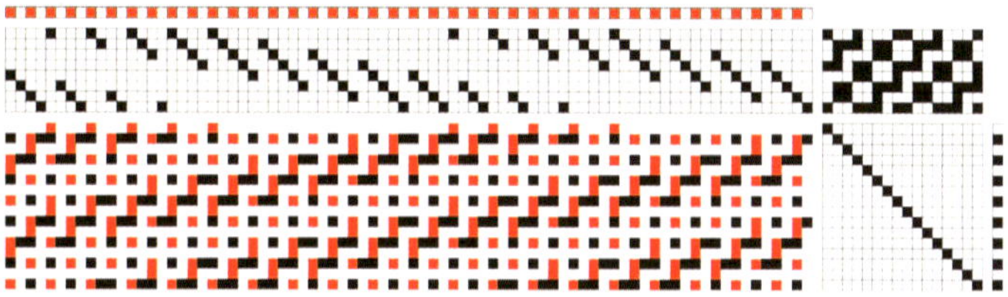

Step 2. Adapt one of the staircases in the tie-up to show square blocks in both black and white. Here the first staircase has been modified. Larger square blocks containing either four white or four black squares show which areas have been adapted to lower (white) or raise (black) shafts. This wraps around from shaft 8 to shaft 1. The basic double cloth remains in one section of the warp.

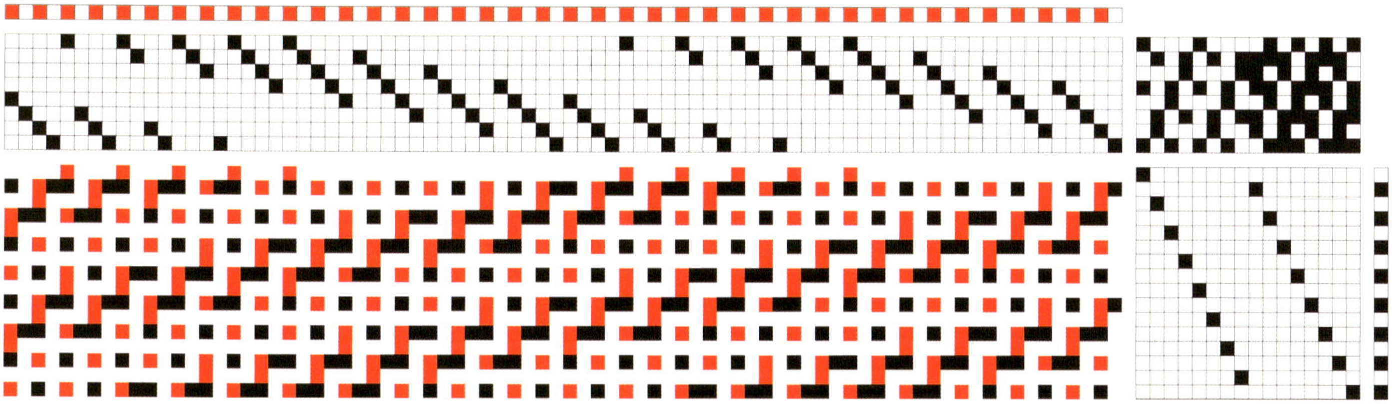

This tie-up shows the same result as the previous draft but has been divided to show the two separate layers. The first half, with the lighter appearance, is actually the lower side of the cloth. The second half, with the darker appearance, is the top layer. Some weavers prefer to see the two sides separately like this to understand what is happening in the weaving. The treadling is in parallel, with one layer being woven with one weft, then the other layer being woven with the other weft.

Treadling

Just as in the threading, treadling can also use advancing and expanded advancing sequences to create curves and larger design areas. Treadling can use either the single tie-up or follow a parallel line using the side-by-side tie-up, whichever is preferred as seen in the two drafts.

It is important to understand the principles behind the tie-up and treadling.

Bear in mind that for the passive layer (white) in our example, every passive weft will weave either shafts 1 & 5, or 3 & 7, in order to create the plain weave across the passive warp, which is threaded on shafts 1, 3, 5 and 7. Conversely, the active layer requires the active weft to weave shafts 2 & 6 or 4 & 8 to achieve a plain weave on the active warp threaded on shafts 2, 4, 6 and 8. That creates the ground web of the fabric.

The next step is to decide which layer is to be dominant in which area and whether on the surface or underneath. Remember that if the active warp is dominant on the surface, the passive warp will be dominant underneath. The balance must be maintained to achieve a good cloth.

Looking at the table, you will see that there are two triangular patterns, one occurring in the red (wool) shafts interacting with the cotton warp and one in the blue (cotton) shafts interacting with the wool warp. The movement of shafts between the two layers shows how the emphasis changes from wool to cotton for each layer and how the two separate layers interact with the interlaced areas.

So, using the table, with wool as the active yarn and cotton as the passive yarn, the first cotton pick (appearing on the bottom layer) will be showing mostly active warps (wool) on the surface. Shafts 2, 4 and 6 are lifted to allow for this. Shaft 8 will be integrating in with the cotton layer. Then the cotton plain weave shafts of 3 & 7 are also raised, and the cotton weft thrown. You can see this as pick 1 in the table.

For the wool (upper) layer, the entire cotton warp is on the reverse side of the cloth, so only the wool layer plain weave is woven, which is 4 & 8 in our example, ensuring that all the cotton shafts are down so that they will show on the reverse. See pick 2 on the table.

Pick 3 shows that the opposite of pick 2 is required for the bottom layer so the whole of the wool layer using shafts 2, 4, 6 & 8 will be lifted, along with the other plain weave cotton shafts 1 & 5. The cotton weft is thrown.

The fourth pick is the wool weft weaving the top layer, so 2 & 6 are required but this time, shaft 1 (cotton shaft) is included as the cotton shafts begin their ascendency to the top layer. Continue progressing through the table with each pick.

TOP TIP

If you want to create your own designs, it is imperative to know what is happening. Take the time to study the table carefully to appreciate how the interchanging works and then play with designing new drafts using these principles.

	Passive Warp			Active Warp	
	Passive warp plain weave	Active warp selected shafts		Active warp plain weave	Passive warp selected shafts
Pick			Pick		
1	3, 7	2, 4, 6	2	4, 8	-
3	1, 5	2, 4, 6, 8	4	2, 6	1
5	3, 7	4, 6, 8	6	4, 8	1, 3
7	1, 5	6, 8	8	2, 6	1, 3, 5
9	3, 7	8	10	4, 8	1, 3, 5, 7
11	1, 5	-	12	2, 6	3, 5, 7
13	3, 7	2	14	4, 8	5, 7
15	1, 5	2, 4	16	2, 6	7

The table shows the interaction of shafts per pick, denoting which shafts are doing the patterning and which the plain weave. This table is not specific to any particular draft but shows the process for moving the dominance of each warp from one side of the fabric to the other. It can be adapted as required.

Straight and reverse treadling (similar to the point-effect threading) is used for this highly-finished sample.

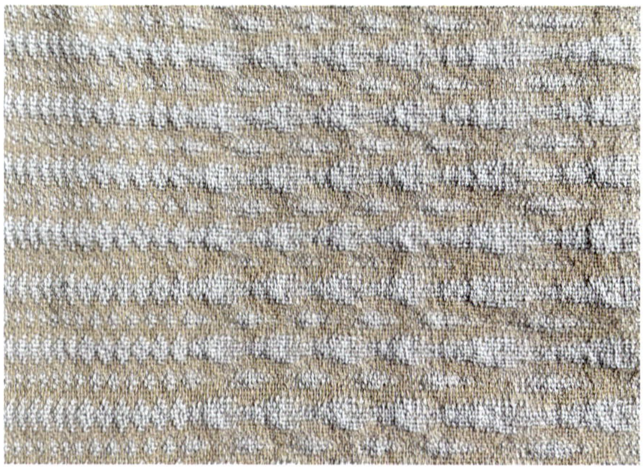

The design has clarity in this sample.

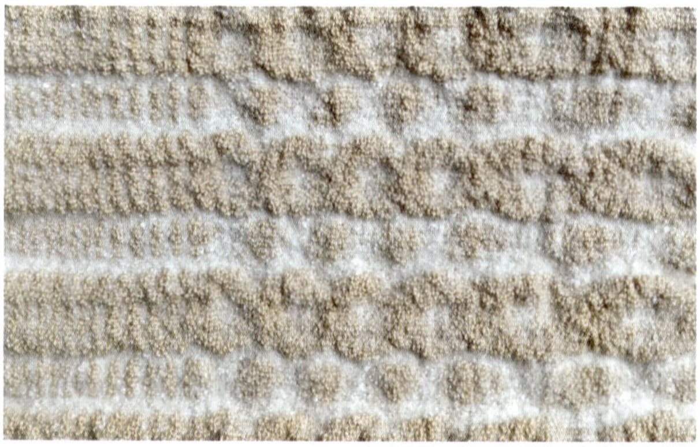

An advancing and return treadling pattern gives a more organic design and more dramatic texture.

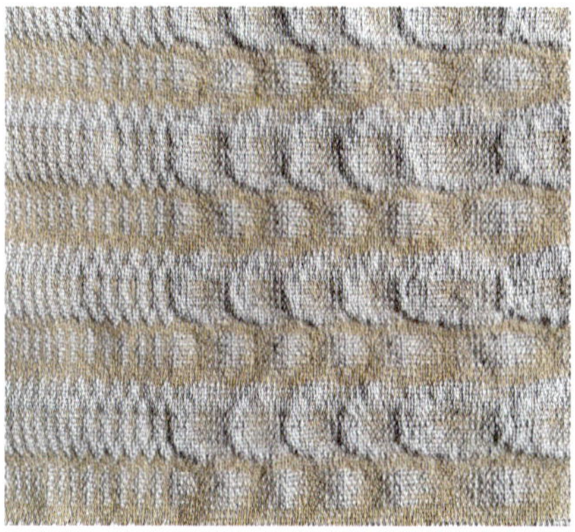

The second set shows gentle texture.

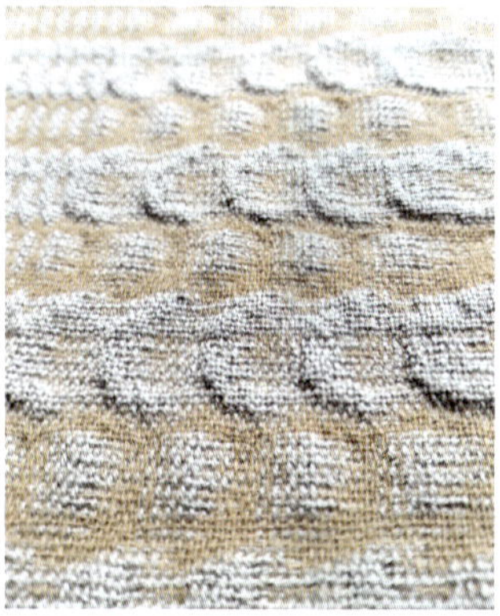

The angle on this image shows the depth of texture with the gently finished sample.

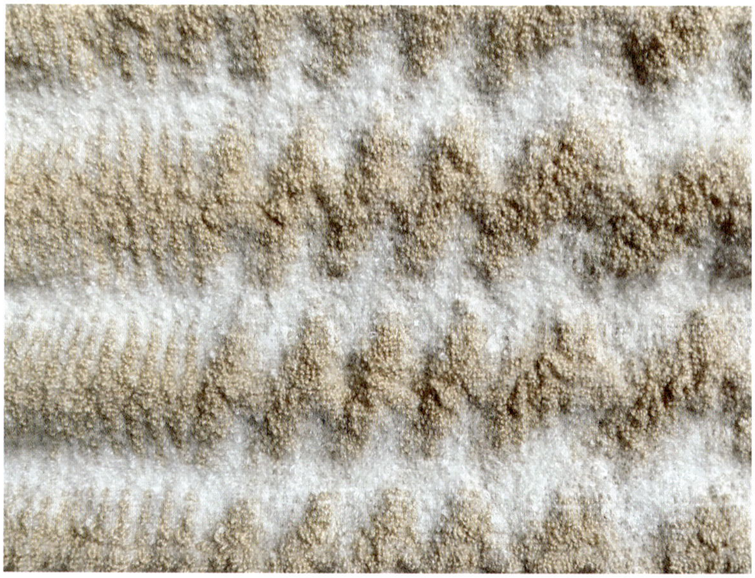

Here, the advancing treadling was used in conjunction with the advancing threading.

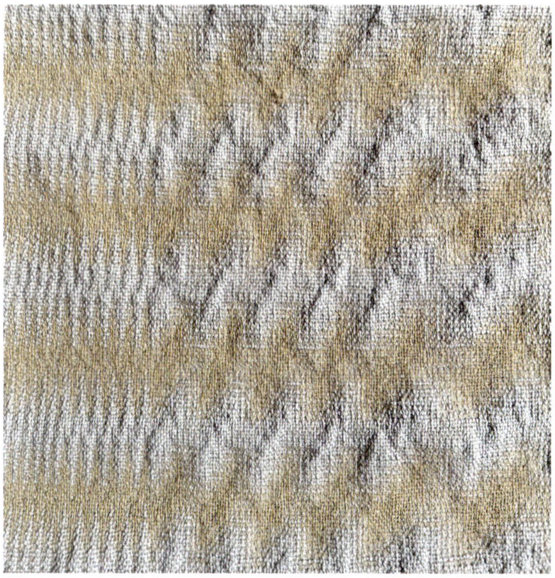

The second set shows a reduced textural result.

NETWORK-DRAFTED THREADINGS

Network-drafted threadings can also be used for dimensional double cloth. They belong to an underlying network that allows for 'legal' moves to ensure that tie-ups and treadling plans will create the underlying structure, with a four-end initial. All the principles can be studied in Alice Schlein's book, *Network Drafting*. It is possible to design for eight shafts, but more shafts allow for greater design possibilities.

The first example is a 'turtle'* design, with the design starting and finishing on the same shaft.

Another way to think of it is like a variation on a regular block threading so that there are defined areas of one dominant cloth contrasting with opposing areas. Using network drafting for this kind of designing allows bordering areas to intermingle the layers. It uses a tie-up similar to the advancing draft above. The treadling is woven as drawn in.

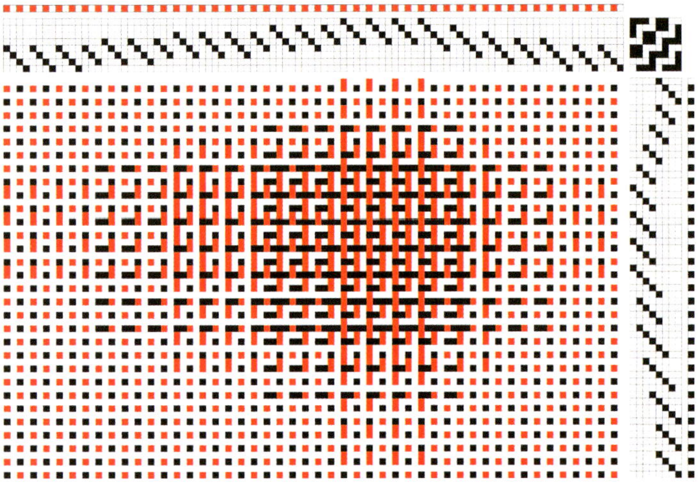

The draft shows the networked threading, a tie-up related to the tie-up in the previous samples and a woven-as-drawn-in treadling plan. It gives areas of double cloth and amalgamated areas.

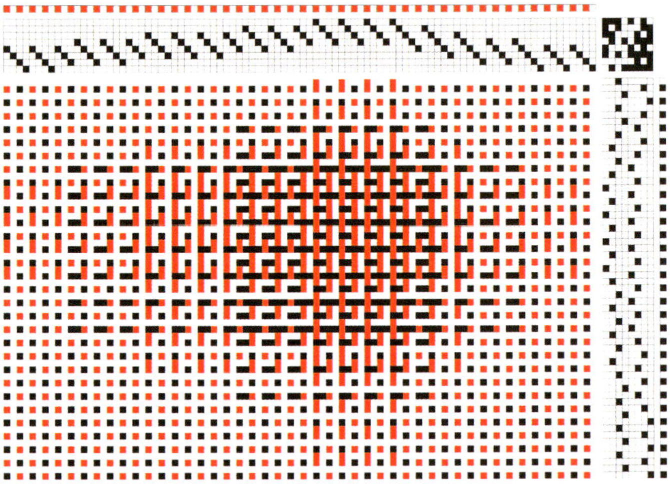

This draft shows the same information but with a divided tie-up showing the two sides of the cloth and the associated parallel treadling plan.

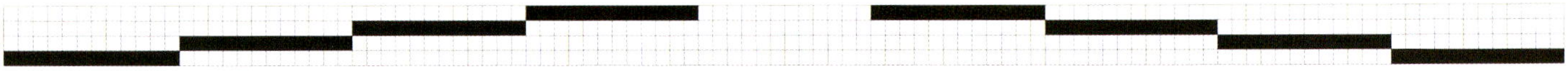

This profile threading draft, from Eva Stoessel, is called a 'turtle' design, starting and finishing on the same shaft. This is the starting point for creating network drafted patterns. Reproduced with kind permission.

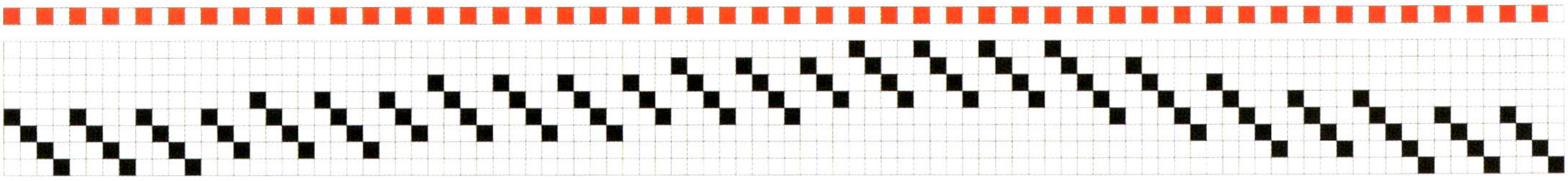

This threading draft is the result of the software programme turning the profile draft into a networked threading. The threading is contained within the eight-shaft height and not wrapped around to shaft 1. Most weaving software will create this kind of threading, whether digitised or telescoped. Further details as to how to create networked drafts are to be found in Alice Schlein's book.

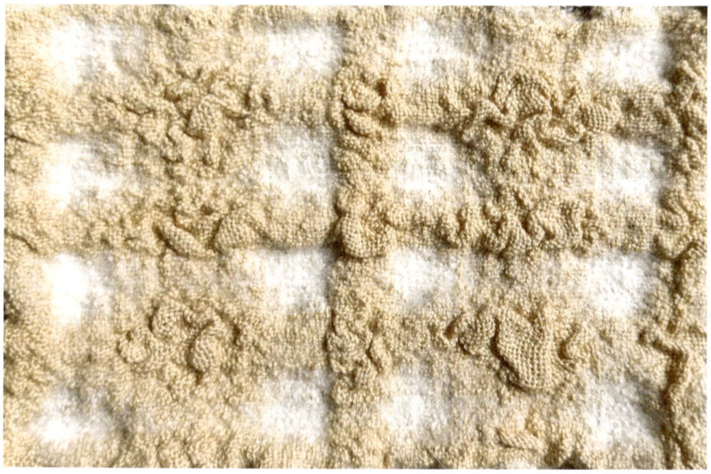

Eva Stoessel's 'turtle' design line was used to create this sample, which was subject to strong wet-finishing.

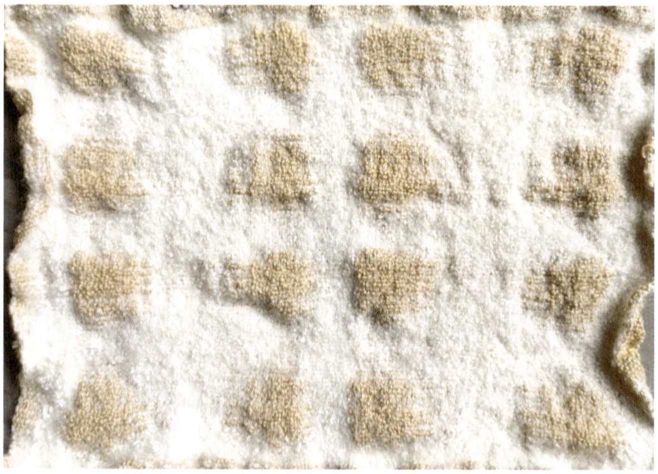

The reverse side after strong wet-finishing. The white merino has practically felted and shrunk by approximately one-third in length and width.

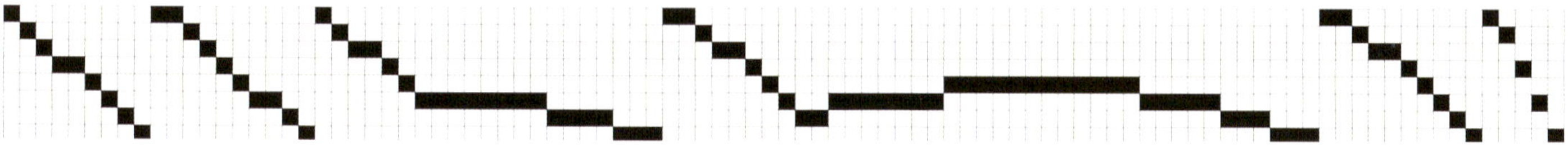

This profile draft, from Alice Schlein's book, shows an example of a 'snail' design, where the design does not start and finish on the same shaft. Reproduced with kind permission.

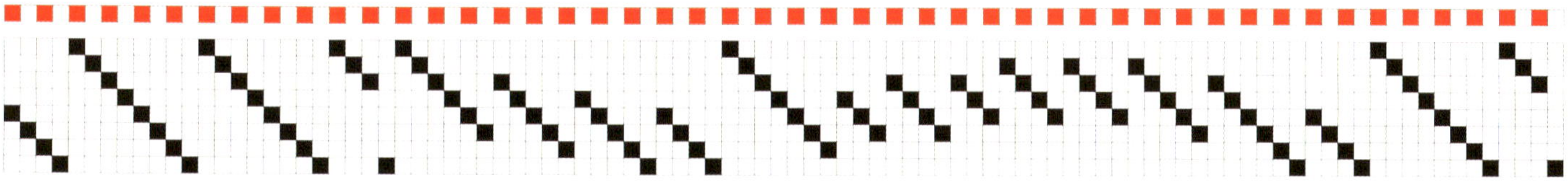

This is the weaving software's conversion of the profile into a threading draft.

The second example uses a 'snail'* design line from *Network Drafting* (p20), which wraps around the threading plan area. It has been telescoped to eight shafts.

(*These are terms used to describe design lines in *Network Drafting*.)

Tie-up

This is a method better suited to multi-shaft looms of 12 shafts or more to allow for larger areas of double cloth and greater textural results using higher ratios of passive to active warps/wefts. However, these are used in conjunction with parallel threading, which is described under 4cDW later in this chapter.

Table or dobby looms are often the looms of choice for networked designs as many more treadles are required than are possible with treadle looms. The examples shown here were woven on an eight-shaft table loom. The liftplan shows how the double weave stair pattern can be seen combined with the squares that indicate raised or lowered pockets. The tie-up would require 25 treadles.

As before, if one of the warps and wefts is an active yarn, this will give textural effects on wet-finishing.

TOP TIP

As these examples show, careful attention is required during wet-finishing not to 'overcook' the samples, unless that is the desired intention.

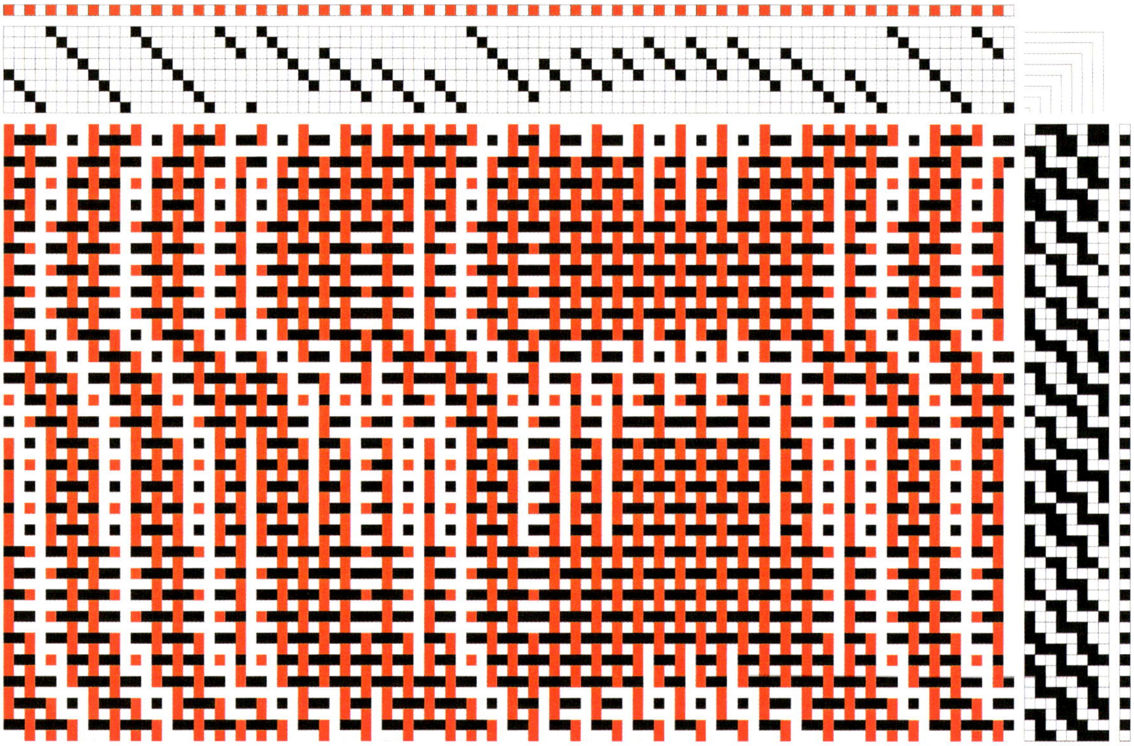

A liftplan is shown here, as the tie-up would be very long and confusing to read. This kind of design requires either a table loom or a dobby loom to weave because the number of combinations of shafts raised within the tie-up would be too many for treadle looms.

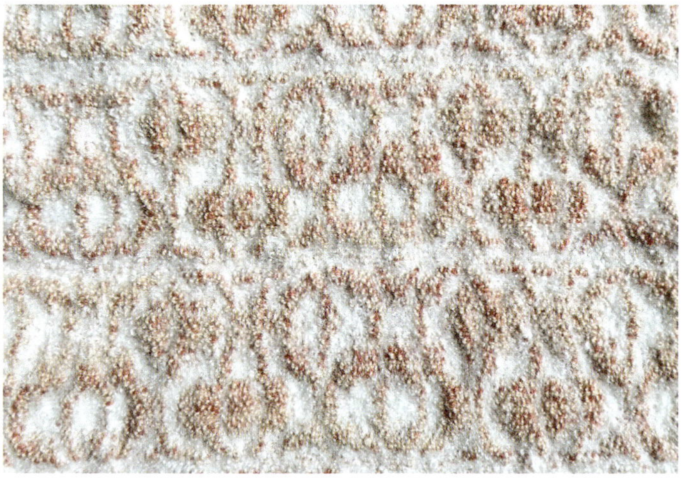

The threading and treadling use an adaptation of the draft, and the weft is a variegated cotton.

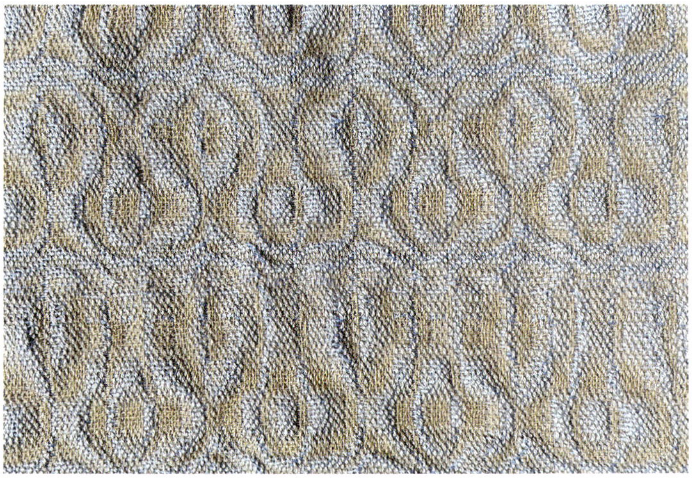

The second warp shows a more defined texture and clearer patterning.

FOUR-COLOUR DOUBLE WEAVE

Four-colour double weave (4cDW) has similar principles in that the two layers integrate in a complex and subtle way. It is another method of using integrated and separate layers organically, but this time using parallel threadings.

It was named because of the various colour effects generated by using two colours in the warp and two colours in the weft, which give four different colour blends in the weaving. Rather than thinking in colour terms, if we think in terms of four different *weave effects*, we get the essence of how to use this method of drafting and weaving for textural impact.

For instance, imagine that there are two colours in the warp: A and B. There are also two different colours in the weft: C and D. These four colours can be combined in different ways: A with C, A with D; B with C, B with D.

If one warp and one weft (say A and C) are replaced with active yarns, the combinations are:

- **A (active) with C (active):** Overall shrinkage will occur;
- **A (active) with D (passive):** Horizontal texture will occur;
- **B (passive) with C (active):** Vertical texture will occur;
- **B (passive) with D (passive):** Balanced fabric will allow for both stable fabric and horizontal/vertical texture when opposed by A and C.

The same or different active and passive yarns can be used in both warp and weft, so the combinations can be varied at will. Using a ratio that reduces the amount of warp and weft of the active yarns or increases the amount of warp and weft of finer passive yarns will enhance the textural effects generated.

The principle behind this particular method of double cloth drafting is to integrate the layers into each other in a progressive way, rather than using blocks (*see* Chapter 9) or individual stitching ends (*see* Chapter 10).

The technique of 4cDW was first devised by Marguerite Gringas (Canada) in 2000, using extended parallel threadings along with divided parallel treadlings derived from shadow weave terminology (the Atwater method). Both Marguerite and Bonnie Inouye (US) were very interested in using alternating warp colours in various ways; Bonnie also developed it for textured fabrics in both warp and weft. Both weavers have written about it in various publications (*see* Bibliography).

Using four colours when creating textural variations can be visually confusing, especially if the combined colours do not create distinct tonal variations between the different effects. Therefore, it can be helpful to reduce the colours used to three. As colour tends to draw attention away from textural effects, using the same active weft as in the warp, in the same colour, helps to reduce this distraction. Using a different colour in the passive weft gives an added depth to the visual appearance, although using the same colour as the warp will create a visual accentuation of the texture as the eye is not distracted by the colour. As usual, it's down to personal choice and there are no hard and fast rules.

Parallel Threading

A parallel threading is one that takes a design line and duplicates itself. The copy is sliced into the first threading, alternating between the original and the copy, starting the copy halfway up the total number of shafts that are being used. The term 'echo weave' is also applied to this threading strategy as the second design line creates an 'echo' of the original. It is a useful strategy to use when you have two or more warp colours in an alternating or consecutive order.

Parallel threadings can be used for many different structures.

DIVIDED PARALLEL THREADING

Often the threading of the original design line is contained within half the number of the total shafts used for a design. The original design line might be using shafts 1–4 and the copy shafts 5–8. This is a divided parallel threading. These are used to show the individual layers more clearly in the draft, using the tie-up to denote specific areas.

The tie-ups are often arranged in a quadrant so that it is very clear what each group of four shafts are doing at any one time, depending on the treadling pattern. For a visual learner, using a tie-up and treadling is the most useful way to design and absorb this method. (A detailed description will be given a little later.)

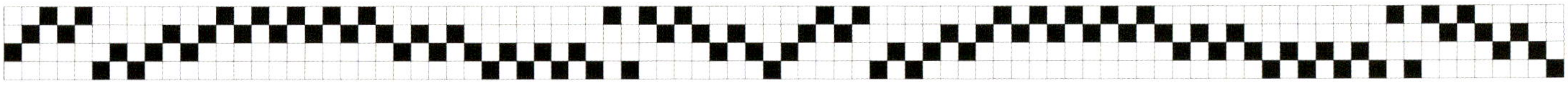

A four-shaft overshot-style original threading draft is the basis for the following 4cDW divided parallel threading draft.

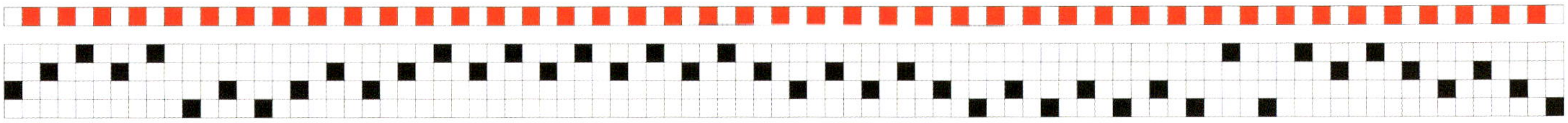

Step 1. To convert the original threading into a divided parallel threading, add a space after every end.

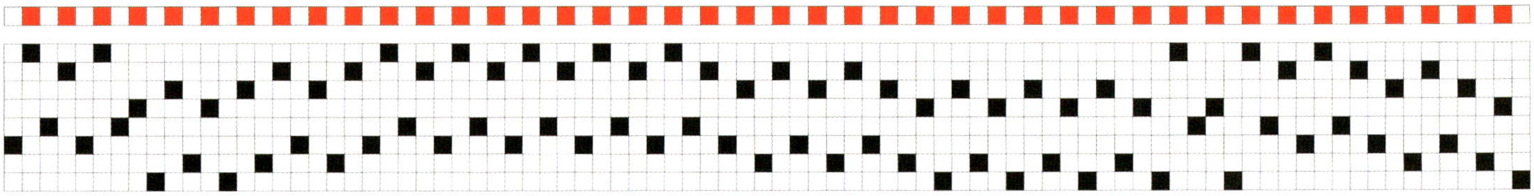

Step 2. Add another four shafts to the threading draft (eight shafts in total) and copy each thread from the original draft into the adjacent blank space exactly four shafts higher. The original four-shaft design remains on its original shafts of 1–4, and the copy is placed onto shafts 5–8.

EXTENDED PARALLEL THREADING

The extended parallel threading design line uses *all* of the shafts available. This means that the copy does too, but starting from halfway up the shafts. So, for an eight-shaft version, the original may start with shaft 1 and the copy would then start on shaft 5, but thereafter the parallel echoes the original line four shafts apart, regardless of where the original design line wanders. The particular use for parallel threadings in 4cDW is that one colour is assigned to the original design line (first layer) and a second colour to the second design line (second layer).

There are a few other options derived from this.

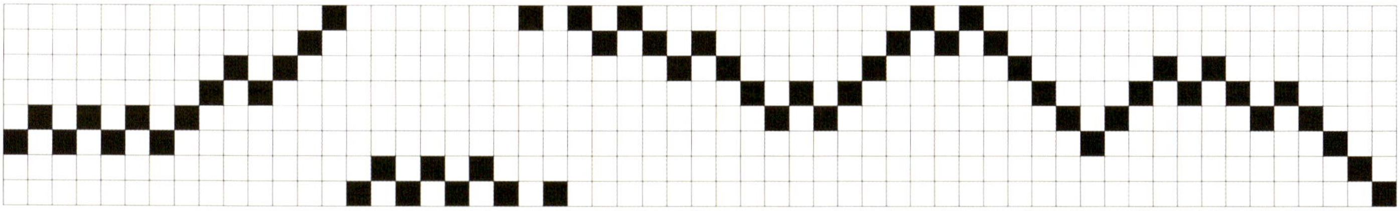

The extended parallel threading starts with a design on the full eight shafts.

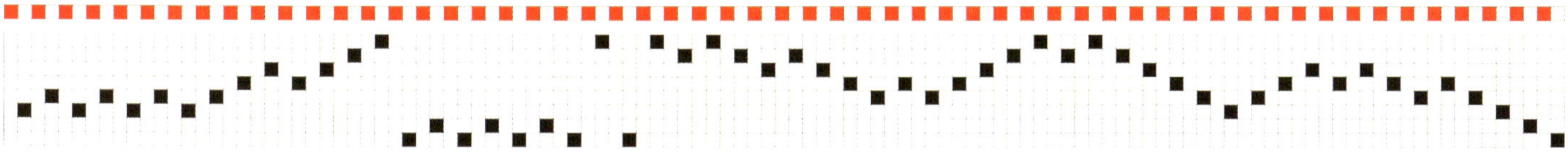

Step 1. Add a space after every end.

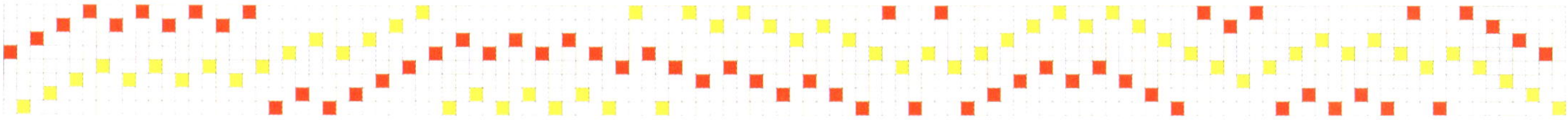

Step 2. Copy each thread from the original draft into the adjacent blank space exactly four shafts higher. When the design reaches above shaft 8 in the copy, wrap around to shaft 1. Both the original line and its copy use all eight shafts. To show this more clearly, the original design line is shown in yellow, and the copy in red.

Tie-ups

Tie-up for Divided Parallel: Quadrant Fashion

This method uses one quadrant for each part of the warp for each layer. It is very easy to see what is happening.

The tie-up is divided into equal quadrants both vertically and horizontally, giving four shafts and four treadles to each quadrant.

One way to think about the tie-up for a divided parallel threading is essentially to regard it as stitched double cloth in both layers. Each layer weaves plain weave but includes (or stitches) elements from the other layer in a 1/3, 2/2 or 3/1 twill. Varying the proportions and the position of the twill line gives different effects.

If you choose to connect the two layers in a twill fashion, the red and green quadrants (solid white or solid black in the basic illustration) is where the twill will be placed. The yellow and blue quadrants will generally be in a plain weave for structure. A general starting point is that the corresponding diagonal quadrant of the tie-up has the connections in the same opposing way, so what is black in one twill quadrant is white in the other.

Creating the tie-up starts with straightforward double cloth layers. For this exercise, we're using a 2/2 twill for designing and a plain weave for structure.

All three twill tie-up variations can be placed alongside each other in an extended tie-up, and the emphasis of both layers gradually changed by moving the treadling line across the three variations.

TOP TIP

Switch the shafts around and use the front shafts for the active yarn if it is one that might cling to itself while weaving, so that the action is easily visible.

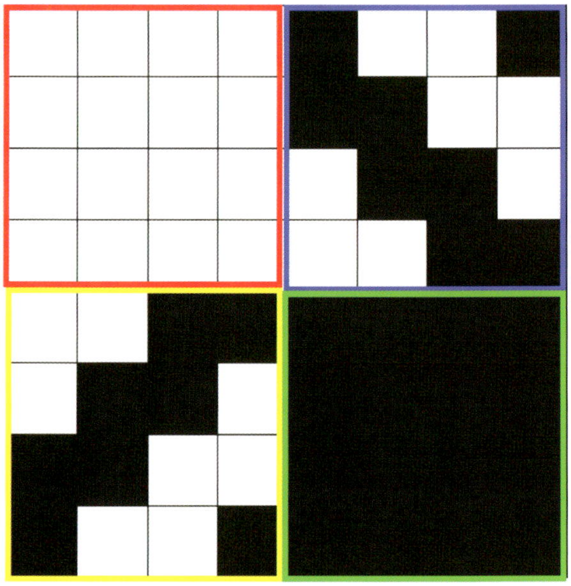

A basic quadrant tie-up is divided into four segments, not necessarily all equal in size. In this demonstration example, the bottom-left segment (yellow outline) gives the weave structure for the original line and its weft (2/2 twill) on shafts 1–4. The top-left segment (red outline) on shafts 5–8 denotes how the second design line is going to interact with the first – all white means it's a bottom layer, not interacting. The top-right segment (blue outline) shows the weave for second design line and its weft (2/2 twill inverted because it's weaving underneath) and the bottom-right segment (green outline) gives the interaction of shafts 1–4 with the second design line – all black means all lifted so it's the top layer, not interacting. A double cloth with this tie-up would be weaving 2/2 twill on two separate layers, not interacting in any way.

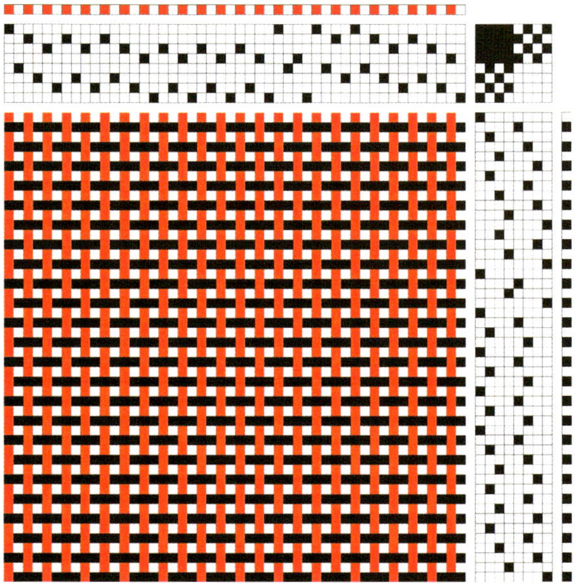

This draft includes a quadrant tie-up showing plain weave on shafts 1–4 (lower layer) and shafts 5–8 (upper layer).

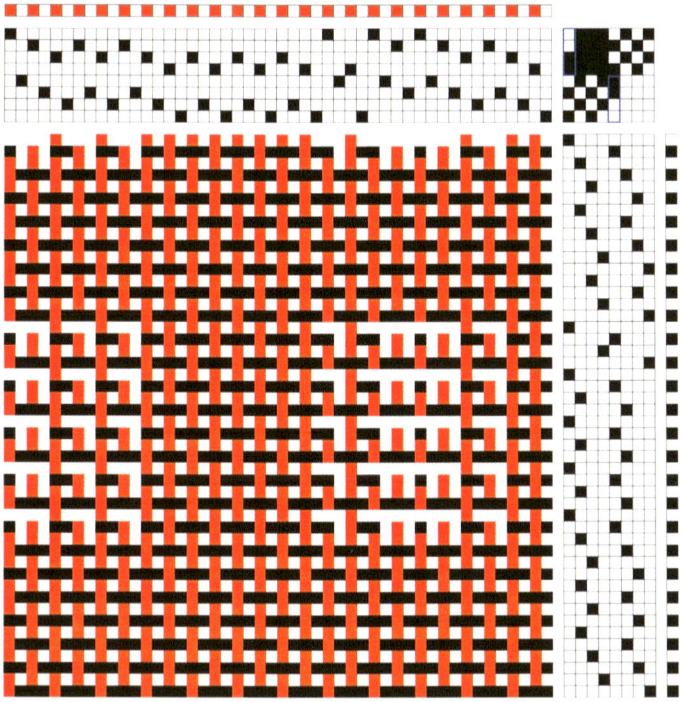

Step 1. To switch elements from one layer to the other, two moves are necessary. Here in column 1, shafts 7 & 8 have been dropped from the top layer (i.e. made white). The opposite action is to raise shafts 3 & 4 from the bottom layer in column 5 (i.e. made black). Both are outlined in blue.

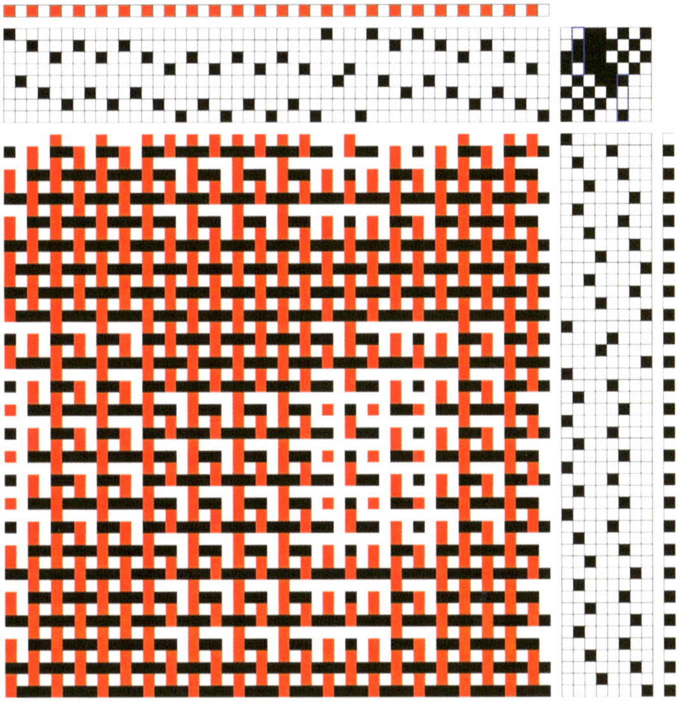

Step 2. In column 2, shafts 5 & 8 have been dropped from the top layer with the opposite effect in column 6 of shafts 1 & 4 being raised.

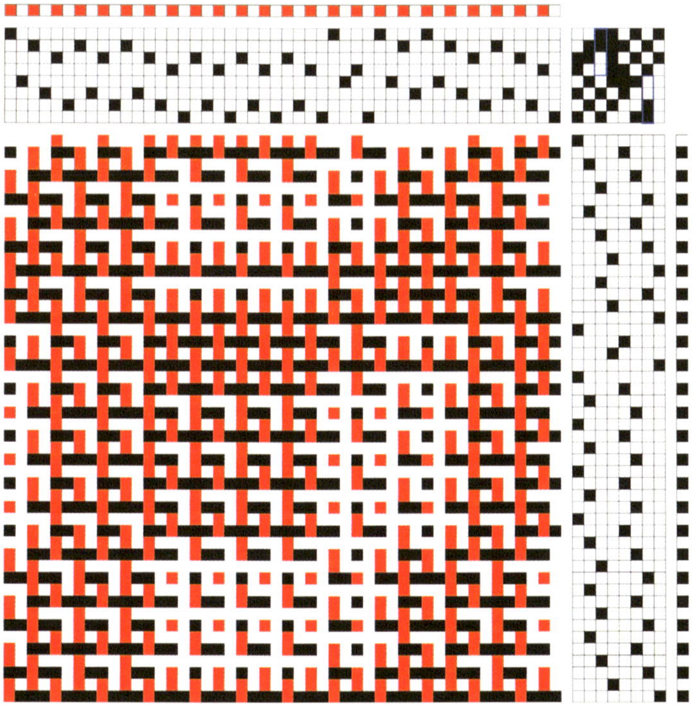

Step 3. In column 3, shafts 5 & 6 have been dropped and shafts 1 & 2 have been raised in column 7.

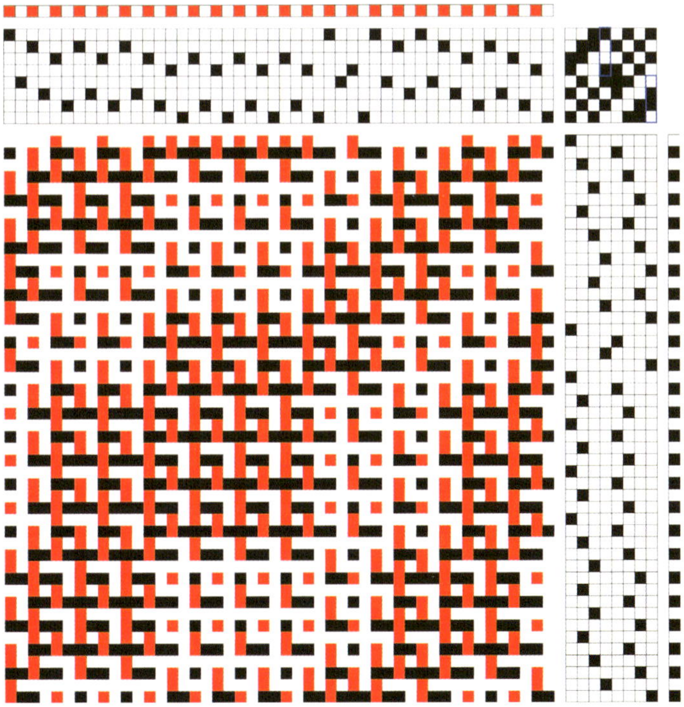

Step 4. In column 4, shafts 6 & 7 have been lowered from the top layer and shafts 2 & 3 have been lifted from the bottom layer in column 8.

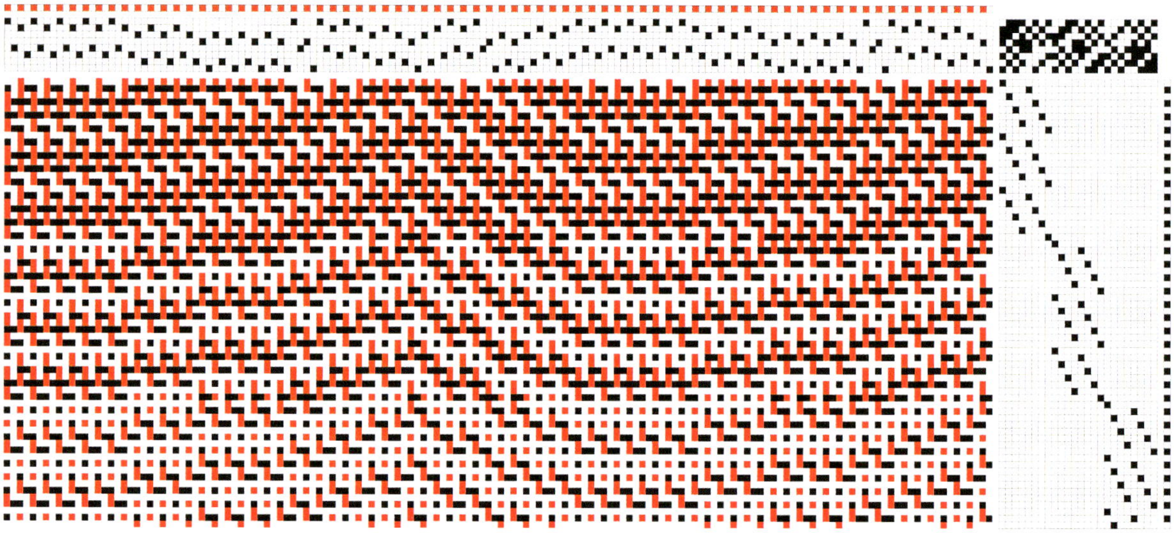

All three twill variations (3/1 1/3; 2/2 2/2; 1/3 3/1) have been placed alongside each other in the tie-up and the treadling moves across all three tie-ups, changing the amount of weft versus warp on each layer as it progresses.

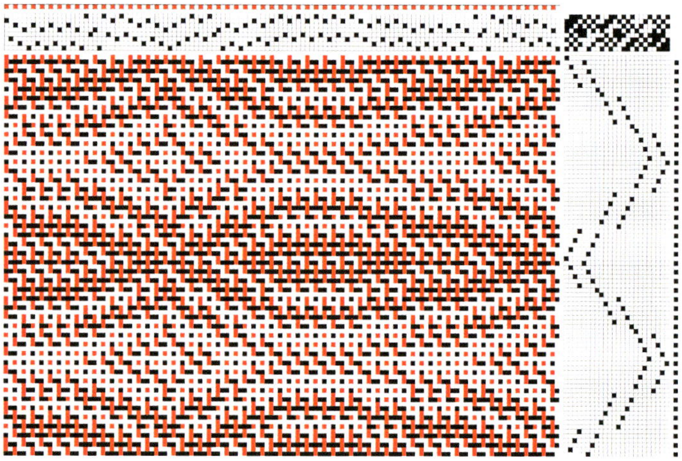

A mirrored treadling shows one example of how the patterning could be developed. Repeating each treadling segment would give a longer repeat and increase the potential for shrinkage.

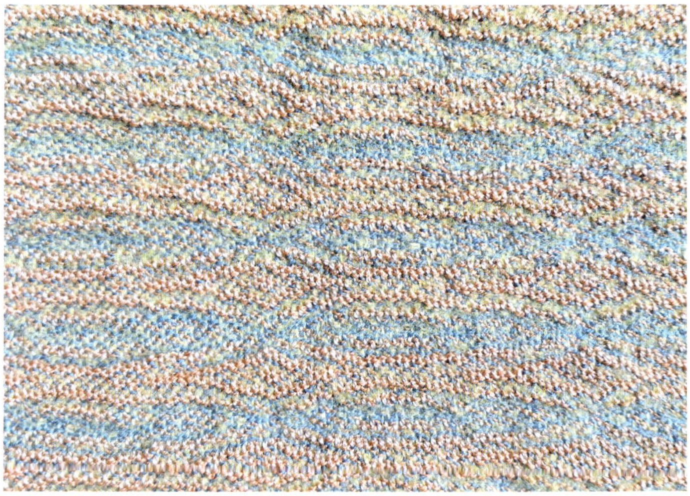

A slightly lighter silk (peach) was used in this mirrored cycling draft.

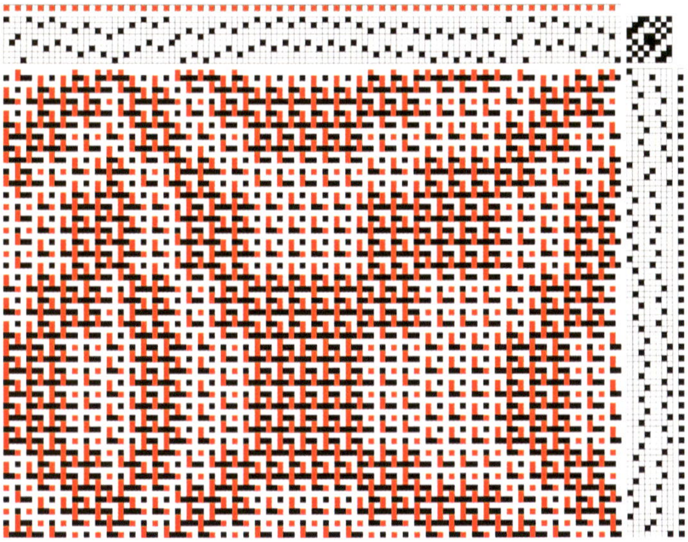

Further adaptations can be created if the same twill line in one segment only is moved or cycled up or down one square. This can be done in either the top-left or bottom-right quadrants. This example uses 2/2 twill in both segments.

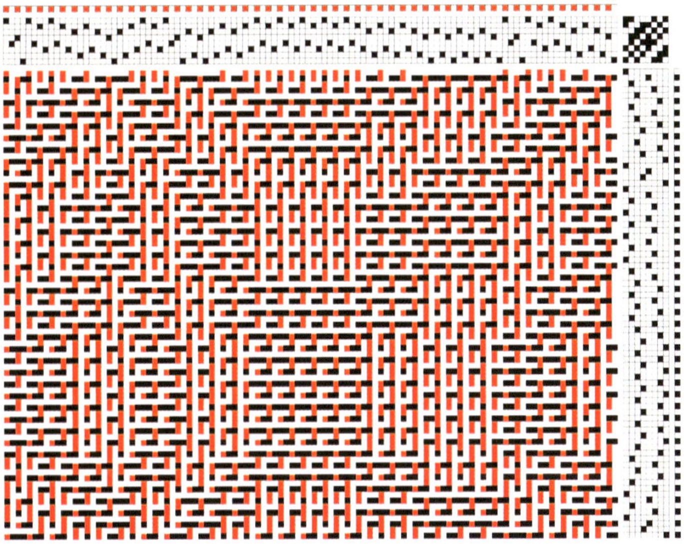

This tie-up moves the top-left segment one more square higher. The bottom-right segment is staying put.

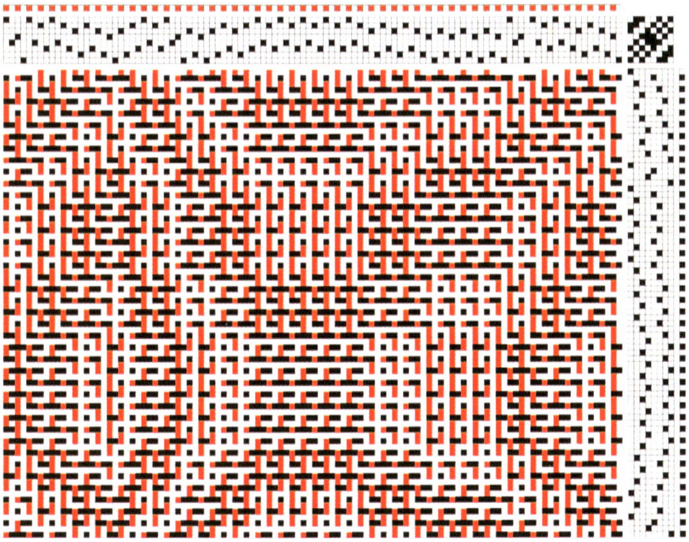

Moving the top-left segment up one square while keeping the bottom-right segment stationary gives a different effect.

The top-left segment of the tie-up has moved up one more square again. The bottom-right segment is still in its original position.

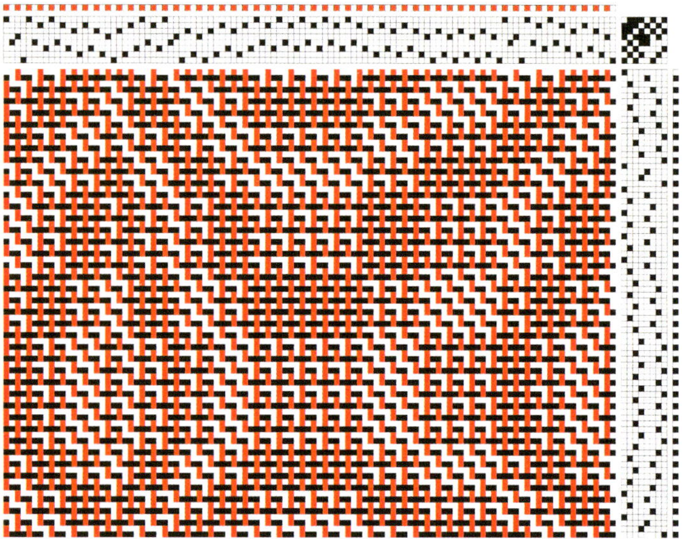

This draft shows the 3/1 1/3 tie-up in the top-left and bottom-right segments. This type of uneven tie-up gives the best effects for textural results.

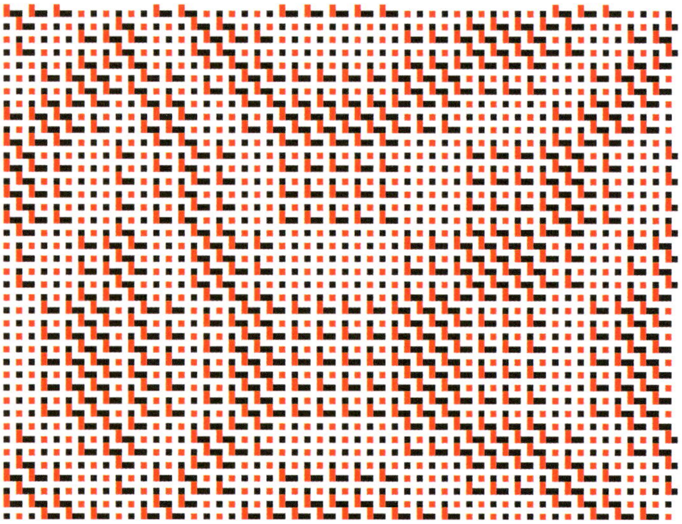

This is the underside, showing the opposite effect on the lower layer.

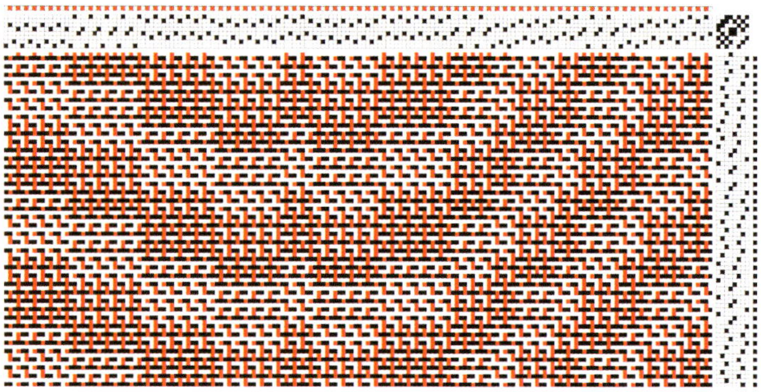

This shows a 2/2 1/3 tie-up in the amalgamating areas, demonstrating that the twills can be mixed.

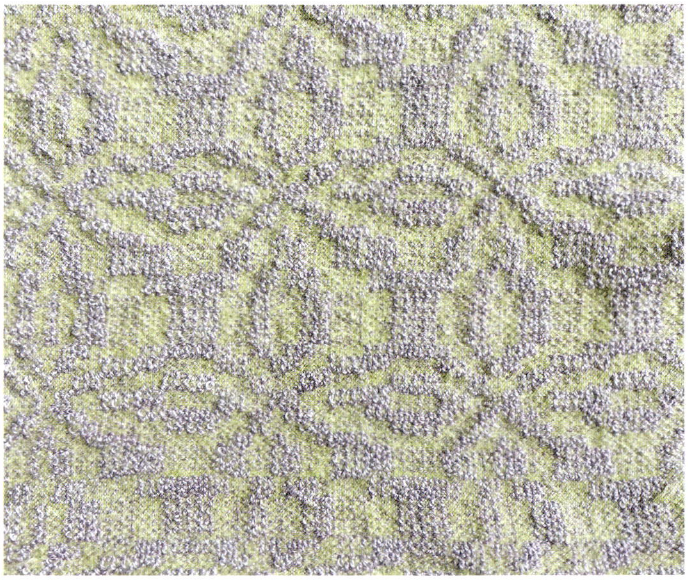

The warp for these samples is a grey Tencel™ and a lime-green merino. The weft for this sample is a lavender silk and the same lime-green merino as the warp. The tie-up is uneven, using plain and 2/2 on one side and plain and 1/3 on the other. This side shows the plain and 2/2 twill side.

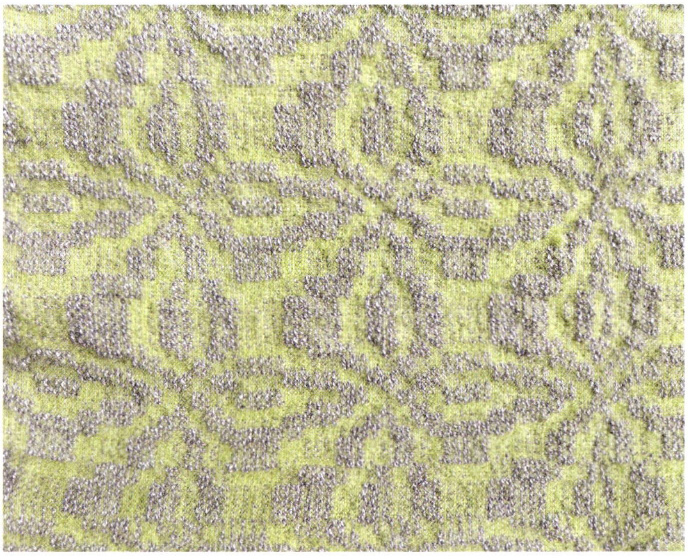

The plain and 1/3 twill emphasis allows the wool to be dominant on this side.

More effects are created if the same twill line is moved or cycled up or down one square in either the top-left or bottom-right quadrant. Variations depend on which section of the quadrant is changed.

An uneven ratio in the interacting portion of the tie-up allows for different emphasis on either side of the cloth. For example, a 1/3 twill with its opposite 3/1 will allow for the colour, or texture of the first weft yarn to be dominant on the front surface and the colour or texture of the second weft yarn to be dominant on the reverse (as seen from the top of the fabric).

For textural effects, more exaggerated texture is created when the active areas are larger. This is more effective when using 12 or more shafts.

Because one layer is woven on one set of shafts (even if they change affiliation as the design progresses), each side can be weaving a different four-shaft structure, so long as there are plain weave elements to create a viable fabric. For example, a 1/3 twill on one side could be combined with a 2/2 on the other.

Tie-up for Extended Parallel Threading

In extended parallel, the plain weave will always impact both 'layers' as the shafts are shared between the two layers. Two shafts of plain weave usually oppose the other two shafts: one set for one layer, the other set for the opposite layer. However, different amounts of plain weave can be used, which affects the handling and firmness of the fabric as it integrates the two layers to a greater or lesser extent. Nonetheless, two shafts per layer are required as a minimum for each side. To bring a design into the fabric, areas of twills are required in the tie-up alongside the elements of plain weave.

Tie-ups for extended parallel warps in 4cDW are usually written out in a side-by-side parallel format. Many weavers prefer this method as you are more aware of which side of the cloth is being woven and how the structures interact.

It is easiest to demonstrate this initially for more than eight shafts as what is happening is clearer. Bear in mind that with one active warp and one active weft plus one passive warp and one passive weft, there are various combinations of texture that can be achieved.

In the example here, a point design is used over 16 shafts in an extended parallel threading. Half of the 16S tie-up is a plain weave. The rest is the selected twill structure, in this case a 4/4 twill. A twill will give warp and weft floats, which controls how much of each warp and first weft appears on one side. This is in a twill step progression, just like a regular twill tie-up. This gives one surface of the fabric. The first 'treadle' has the first weft weaving plain weave on shafts 1–8/ The second set of shafts (9–16) are weaving the 4/4 twill.

The reverse side tie-up is obtained by 'changing the face' so that what was black becomes white and what was white is now black. Then this new tie-up is cycled up by half the number of the total shafts. This 'new' tie-up will provide the reverse of the fabric, meaning that the first treadle of this part of the tie-up is now weaving the twill on shafts 1–8 and the plain weave on shafts 9–16 which gives the opposite effect from the first tie-up.

Add the second tie-up to the first, and you have the complete plan. Treadling alternates between the first tie-up with weft C, and the second tie-up with weft D. Two picks make a complete sequence.

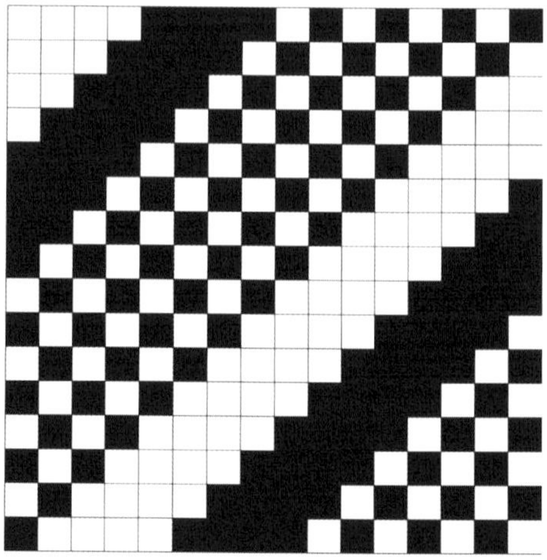

Sixteen-shaft tie-up showing plain weave over eight shafts, and 4/4 twill over the other eight shafts, in a twill progression.

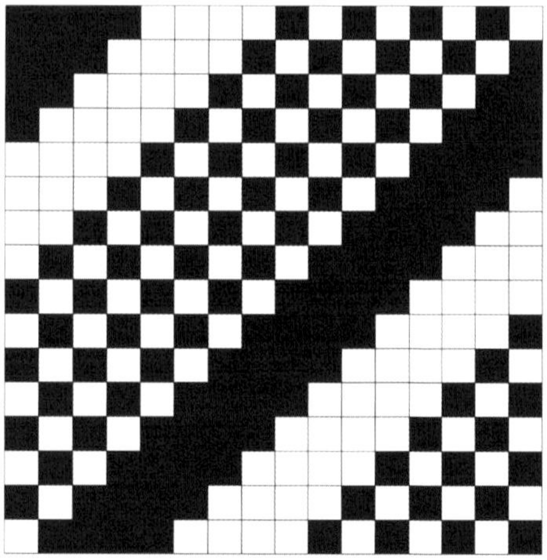

The second half of the tie-up is created by first changing the face of the tie-up. What was black now becomes white and what was white now becomes black.

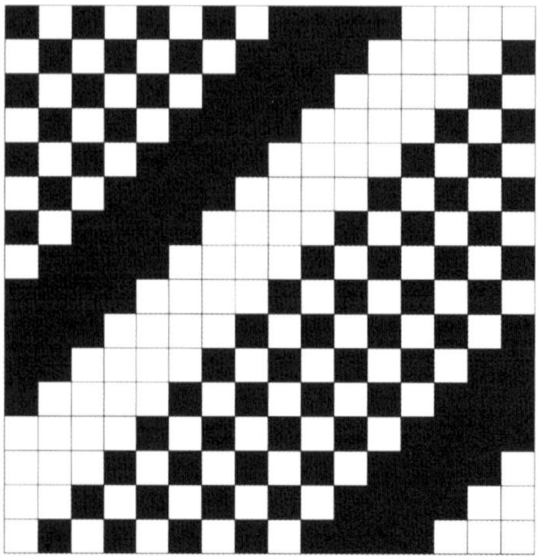

The second stage involves cycling, or shifting, the whole tie-up eight shafts higher (or lower – the result is the same).

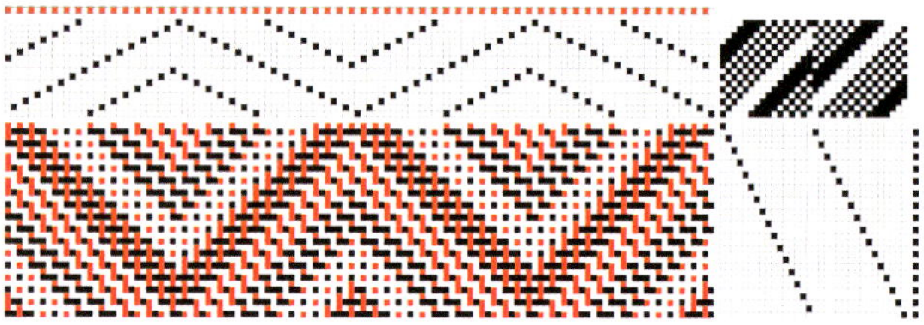

The draft shows a parallel point threading over 16 shafts, the two tie-ups for the different sides, and the parallel treadling to weave the two different sides.

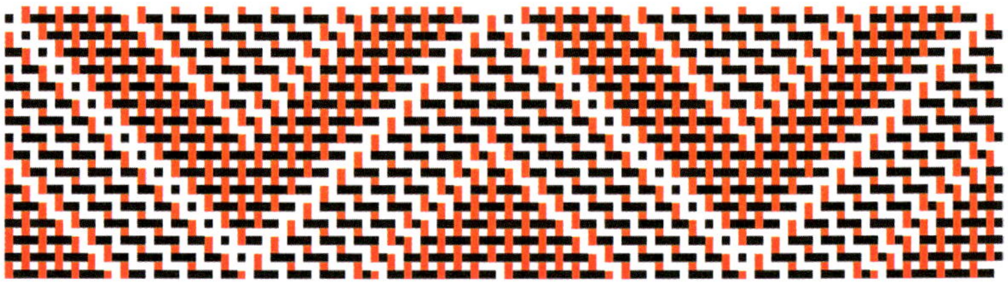

This is the opposite side of the draft.

Introducing additional texture into the mix can be effected by changing the proportions of the twill section, and therefore the emphasis of the two wefts are correspondingly changed. With a 2/6 twill for the twill section of the first side tie-up, for example, only 25 per cent of the warp will appear on the surface, leaving that side's weft to be dominant with 75 per cent coverage. The opposite effect will occur on the reverse side, as the second warp will be taking the major role with 75 per cent, and the second weft with only 25 per cent. This starts to give some texture because the shrinking weft and the shrinking warp (if both are used) will lead to texture being forced into the passive warp and weft.

Various twill tie-ups can be explored. What happens if further areas of plain are introduced between the warp and weft twill sections? As with the divided parallel tie-ups, it is possible to use different twills on front and back.

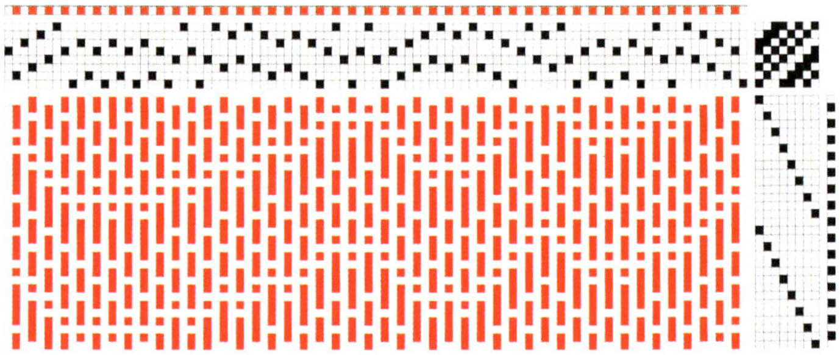

The same principle is used for the eight-shaft design with a 2/2 twill on one set of four shafts, and a plain weave on four shafts following a twill progression.

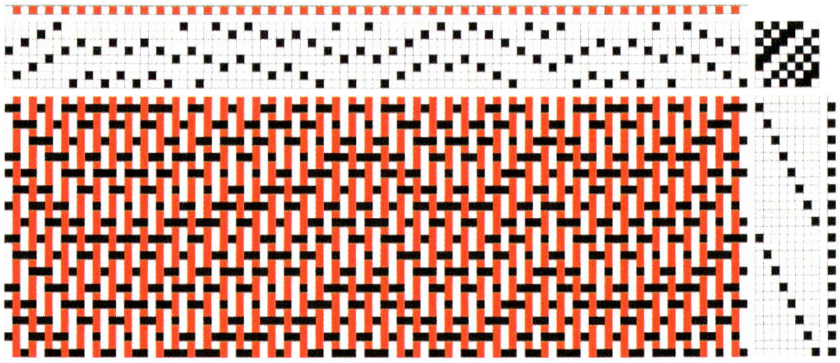

The tie-up changes face and is shifted up by four shafts for this version.

Eight-shaft Tie-ups

For eight shafts, we have fewer tie-up choices, but some variations are possible.

The regular method again has half plain weave and half even twill. Again, the tie-up needs twice as many treadles as shafts.

The same effects are happening on the front and reverse of the fabric.

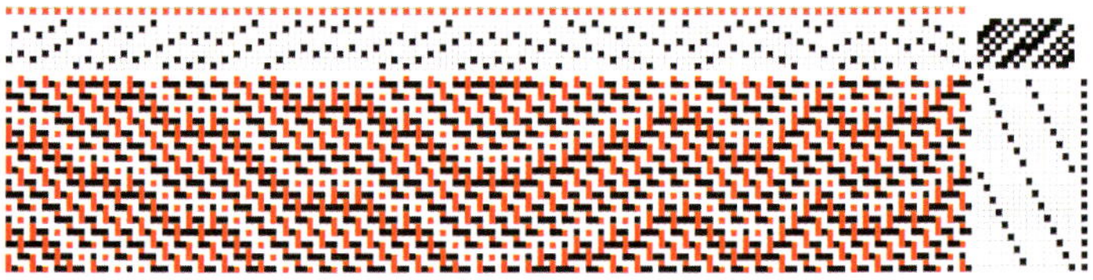

The two tie-ups are now placed side-by-side with parallel threading and treadling.

The twill tie-up element gives each warp and weft equal prominence, and four distinct areas are created. A 1/3 or 3/1 twill tie-up creates a larger area of longer floats. The twill sections tie both warps and wefts together in a single bound area. Wefts can be switched, so what was weaving the back switches to weaving the front, and vice versa.

For a more textured effect, the first half of the next tie-up increases the plain weave onto three-quarters of the shafts, progressing in a diagonal lift progression until it comes to the beginning again, wrapping around the shafts when the line demands, as is usual in twill tie-ups. The other half of the tie-up changes face and cycles up four shafts. You will notice that there is only a weft-dominant and a warp-dominant face. They do not share both. However, it still needs a lot of treadles – 16.

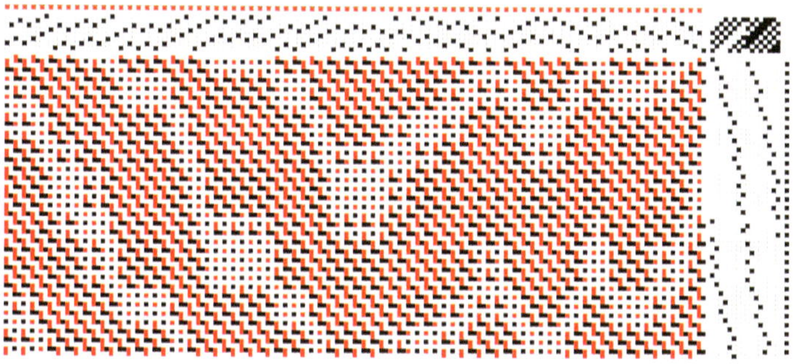

The tie-up has been changed now to a plain weave on six out of the eight shafts following a twill progression. This view is from the top – the view that the weaver sees.

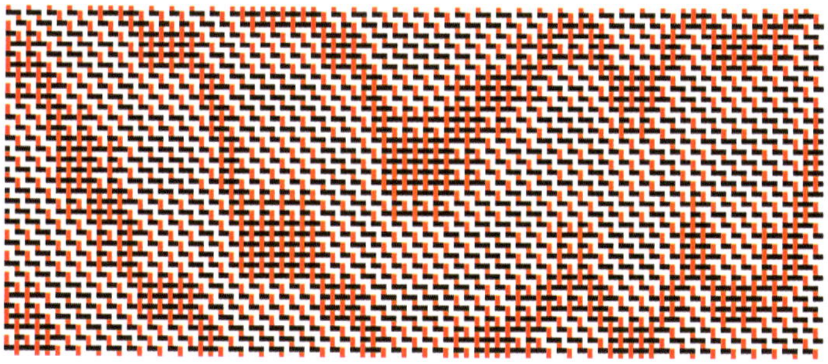

This is the view from under the cloth.

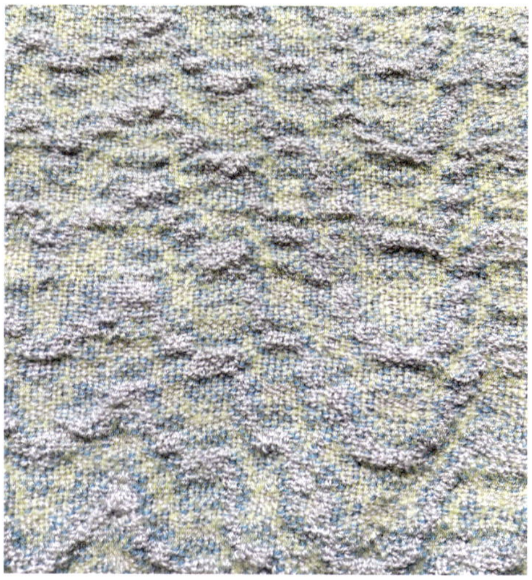

Weaving an advancing treadling plan plus changing the wool weft to the blue merino/silk gives a very different result on both sides of the cloth. This truly is becoming 4cDW.

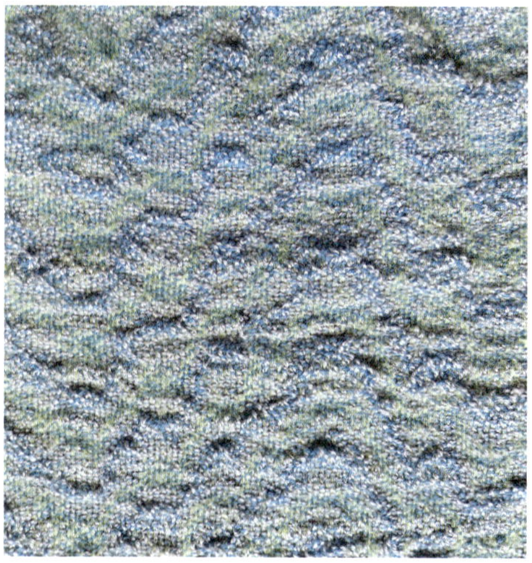

This sample uses a plain weave in conjunction with 2/2 twill. The twill moves in block repeats of two picks. The plain advances irregularly. Written out in full, the tie-up requires 32 treadles. This is not a problem if weaving on a dobby or a table loom but would not be achievable on a treadle loom without the use of a different system of tie-up.

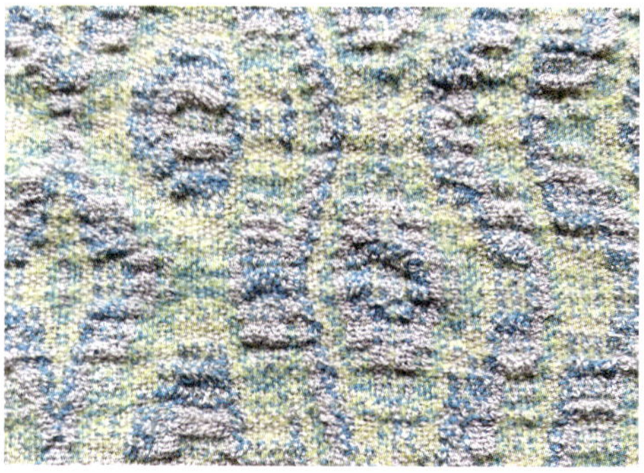

The reverse side features the floats of the blue weft whereas the front side is more lavender.

In her book *Weaving with Echo & Iris* (*see* Bibliography), Marian Stubenitsky has a chapter on 4cDW, utilising a variety of approaches. One uses block threadings, as seen in overshot, then put into a parallel threading system. Using active and passive yarns in the warp and weft and varying the ratios of weave structures in the tie-ups as we have already explored, different types of surfaces are generated.

The warps for this set of samples are a green cotton and a white merino with a ratio of 1:1. The block threading gives a feel of overshot half-tone either side of a feature. The wefts for this sample are a cinnamon brown cotton and a brown worsted yarn.

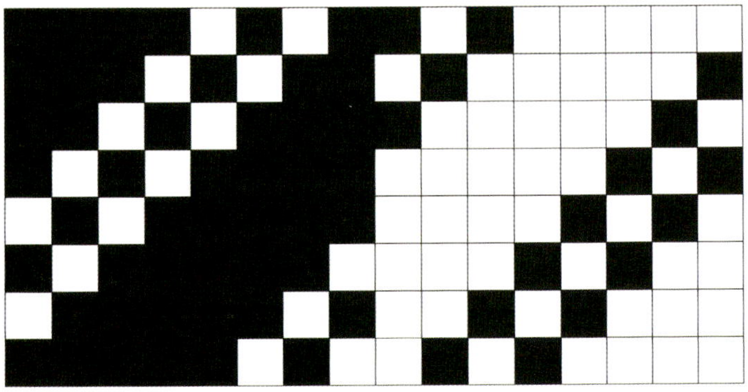

The tie-up shows a twill line of plain weave with warp-dominant twill to lift the entire top layer of four shafts (called a 4-0 ratio by Marian) so that the first half of the tie-up weaves the bottom layer and its opposite side with plain weave in a twill fashion only weaves the upper layer.

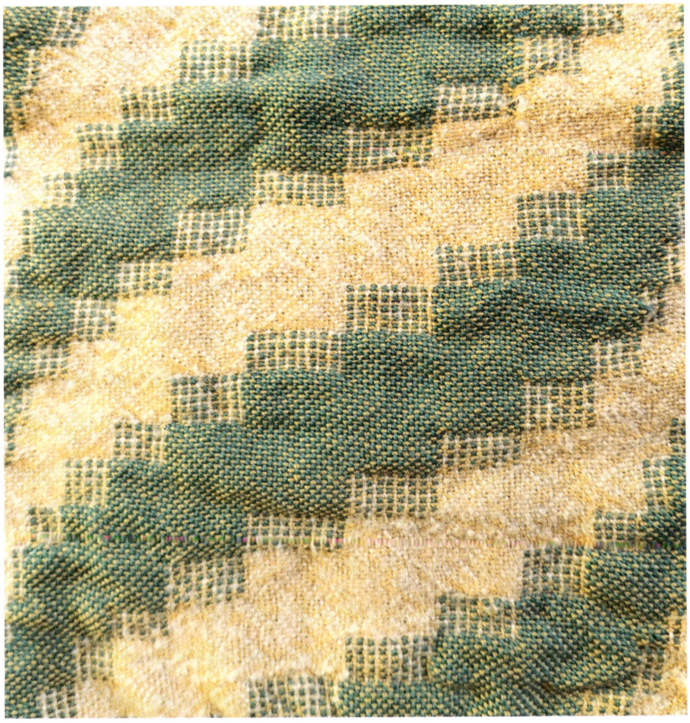

The cinnamon cotton weaves the plain on the top layer.

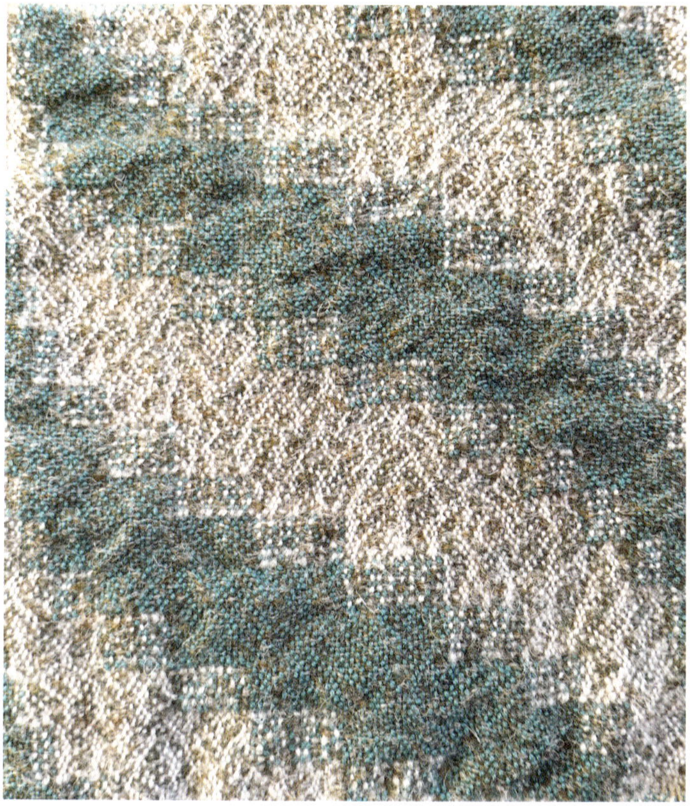

The reverse shows the brown wool's interaction with the underneath layer. There is additional interest caused by the 'tracking' of the two wool yarns weaving plain weave. The amount of shrinkage is slight.

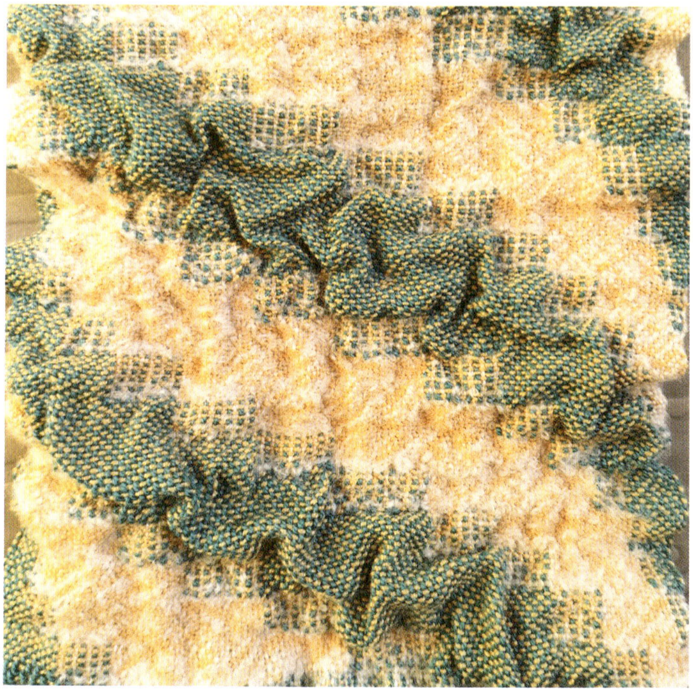

The wool weft is switched out for the same merino as used in the warp. The shrinkage is considerably more and the cotton-only areas are dramatically textured.

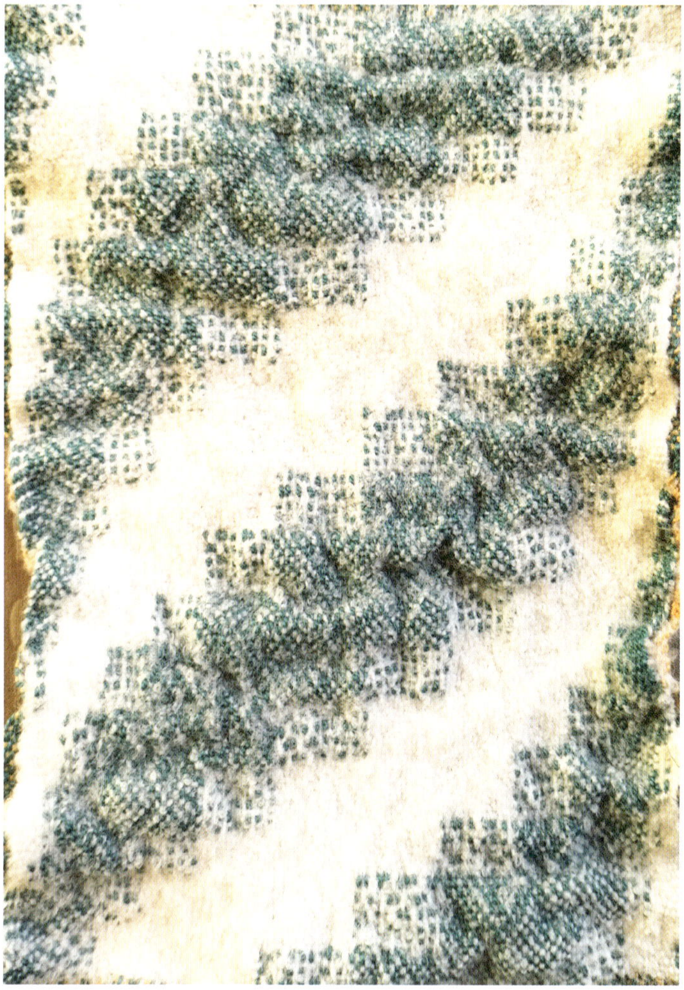

The merino shrinkage with itself has caused horizontal puckers where it interacts in plain weave with the cotton weft.

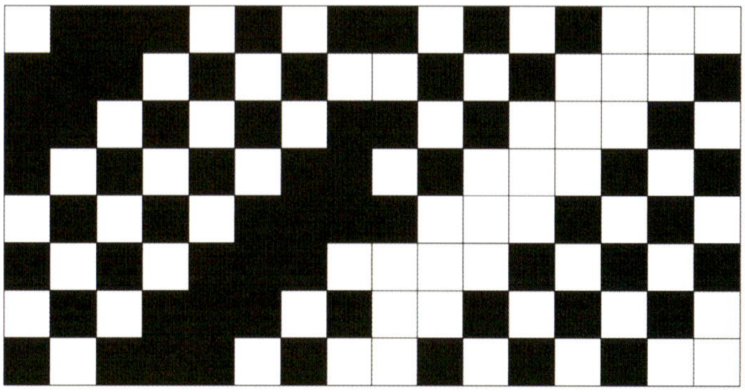

The tie-up here puts more plain weave into both layers, leaving one less shaft to be raised when weaving the bottom layer (a 3-1 ratio line).

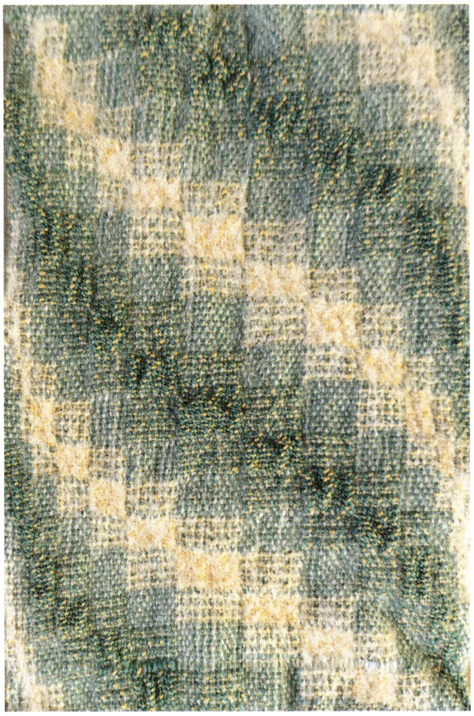

With only a little texture in the cotton-only block, it has a surprisingly different look. A thicker wool weft is used instead of the merino.

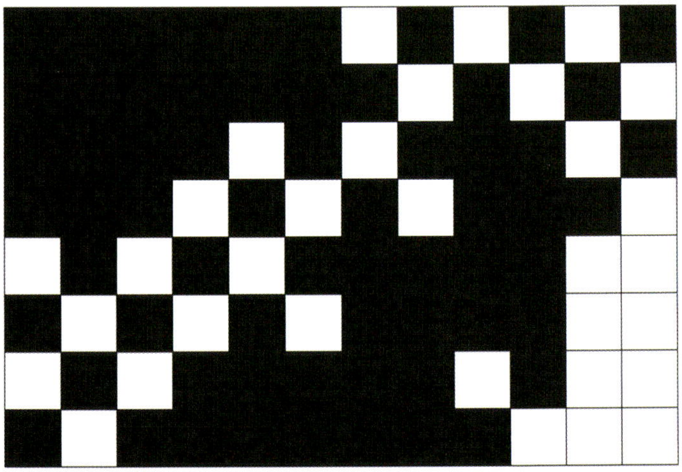

This tie-up switches the twill tie-up to a block one, and the block treadling to an advancing form. The progression of plain weave in the tie-up is not linear. The same plain weave belongs to two blocks. This gives a less blocky look to the sample. Because of the separation of the wefts which only weave with their own layer, this has a 4-0 ratio.

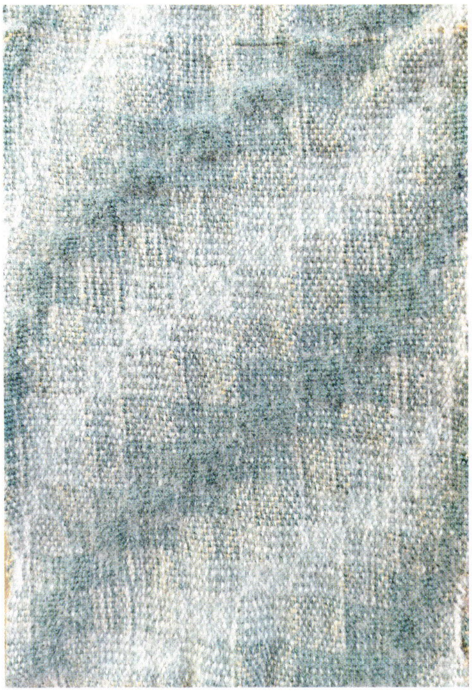

The reverse side shows the interaction of the green weft.

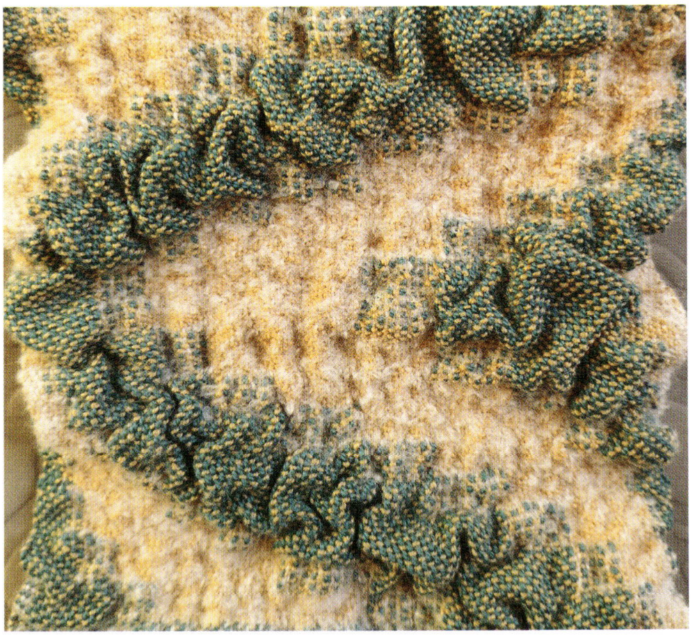

The active weft is the white merino. The changing blocks in the wool layer and the accompanying but varied change in the plain weave give higher shrinkage in small segments. This creates the strong puckering seen in the cotton mix. The cotton weft only appears on this side but weaves with both warps.

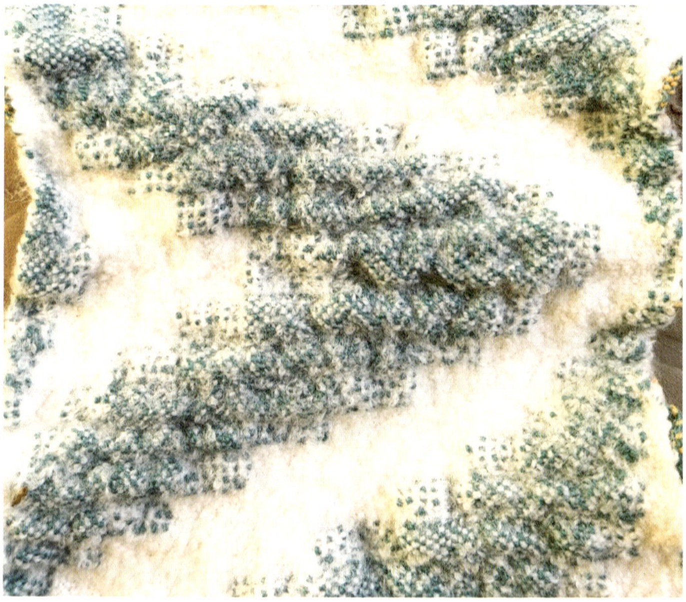

The reverse side shows horizontal puckering where the cotton warp is woven with the wool weft. The wool weft only weaves on this side.

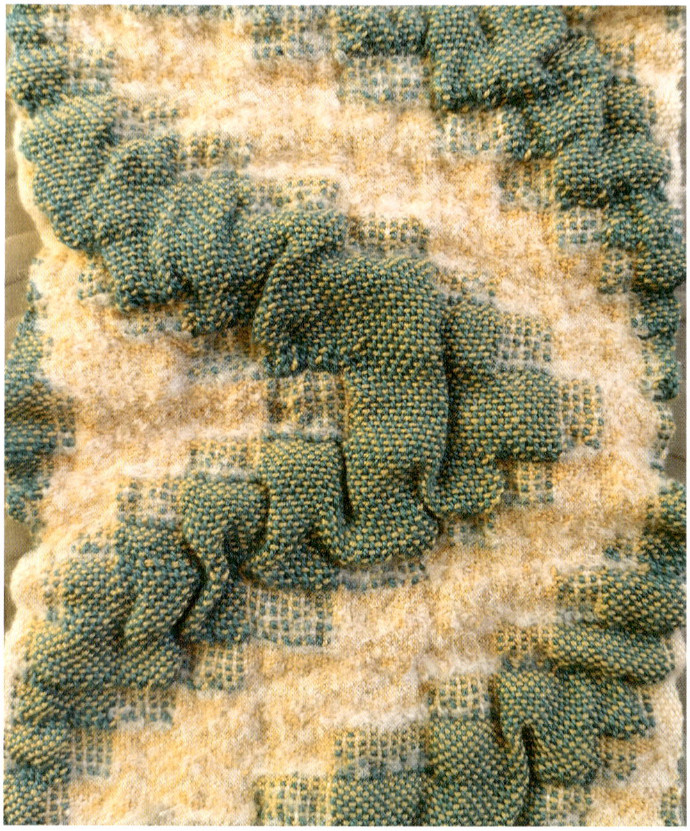

A thicker green wool is used for the active weft in this sample, which otherwise is the same as the previous one. The size of the wool weft on the lower layer makes the sample longer, giving the cotton a chance to pucker without being too contracted. The half-tone block threading effect is quite apparent on this side.

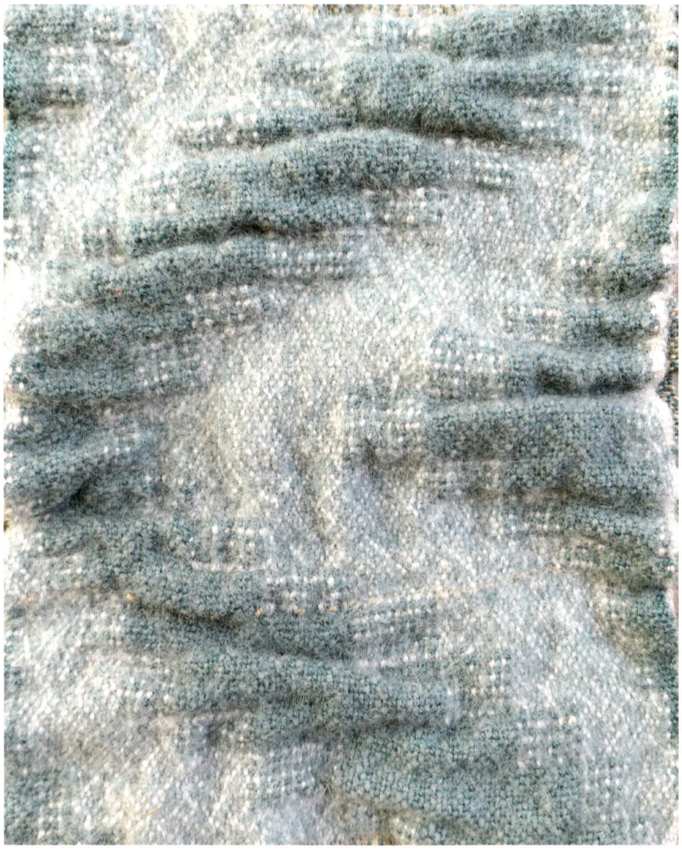

The comparative thickness of the wool, which is about twice as thick as the merino in the warp, has given merino more room to effect its shrinkage. This is why there are wider horizontal pleat effects on this surface.

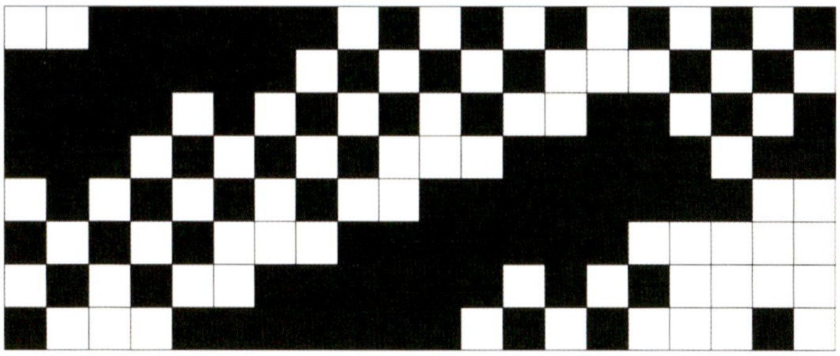

In a similar way to the previous sample, the plain weave and the blocks of 3/1 twill no longer move in a twill fashion. While the blocks progress in an orderly fashion, the plain weave meanders around in the space between the 3/1 blocks.

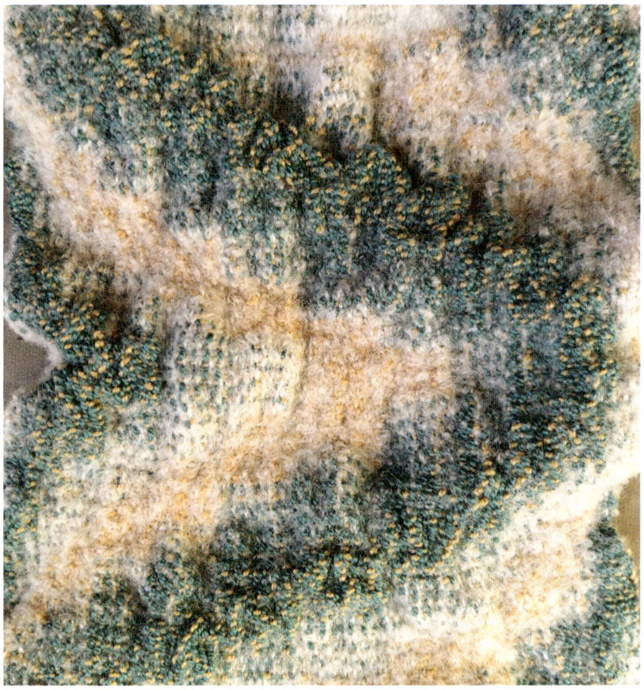

In comparison to the previous two samples, the two layers are tied together all the way through as one upper layer shaft remains integrated with the lower layer and vice versa for each pick.

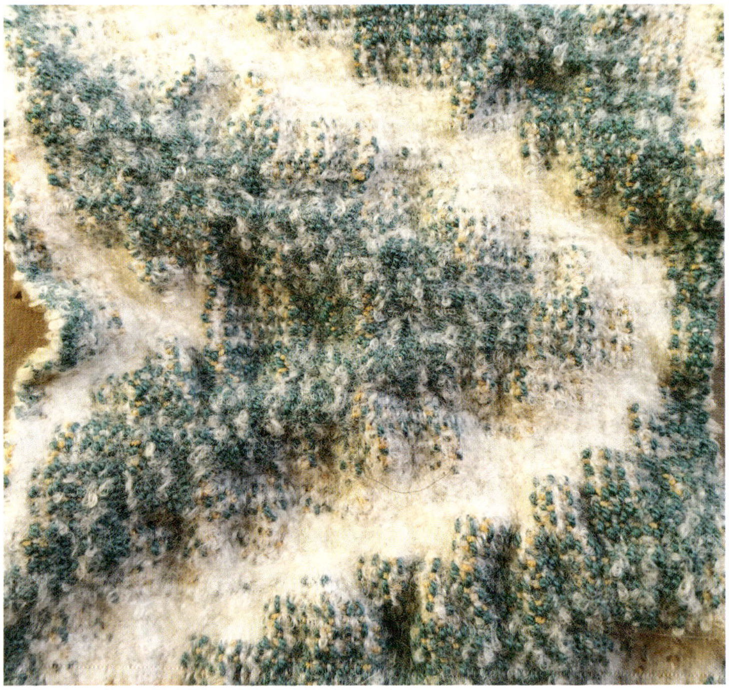

The reverse side, showing the use of the white merino in the weft.

Multi-treadle Tie-ups

Multi-treadling is a shorthand way of writing out tie-ups that can be easier to read than either full tie-ups or a liftplan.

One example shows a plain weave on the first half of the tie-up, with the twill element of the draft for the second half. This combines the two areas.

In this case, every *odd*-numbered pick will be weaving one side of the fabric, with the plain weave for that side. Every *even*-numbered pick will be weaving the other part of the plain weave for the reverse of the fabric, using the equivalent shafts for that side but read from the same section of the tie-up four shafts away to create the plain weave layer for that side. The twill is added to the plain weave on *both* picks to tie the two layers in the desired weave. In this case, it is a 3/5 twill.

Two treadles are indicated on the draft: one for the plain weave element and one for the twill element for each pick. The twills are not four shafts apart, which gives different effects on either side of the cloth. In effect, the even picks amalgamate one of the plain weave shafts within them. Again, this is a tie-up method that is most suitable for table and dobby looms as you would still need 16 treadles on your floor loom, which most do not have.

A liftplan view helps to see how the two layers interact in the weaving.

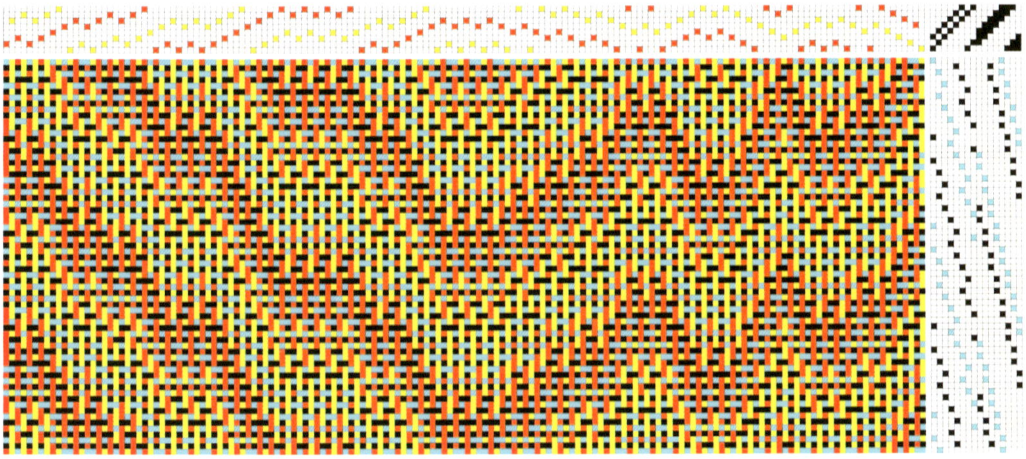

Multi-treadling is a method for treadle looms that can use treadles individually or together, depending on the number of pedals/treadles available. It is also a method for writing drafts that can be easier to read for the table or dobby loom user. Instead of having all the shafts being used in one column, they can be spread out into their constituent parts. In this case, there is a plain weave on four shafts and a 3/5 twill. In this draft, a light blue has been substituted for the white in the weft so that the treadling can easily be viewed. Each pick contains a plain weave and a twill selection. When combined together, all the lifts can be created with the progressions of each structure being easy to see.

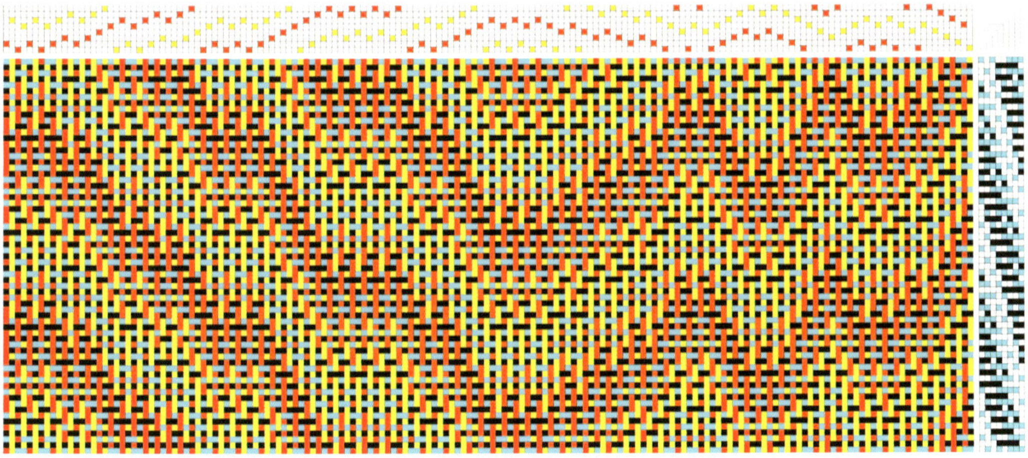

The same information is given here for table and dobby loom users. Some weavers prefer to see all the information in the liftplan format, while others find the multi-treadle option easier to read.

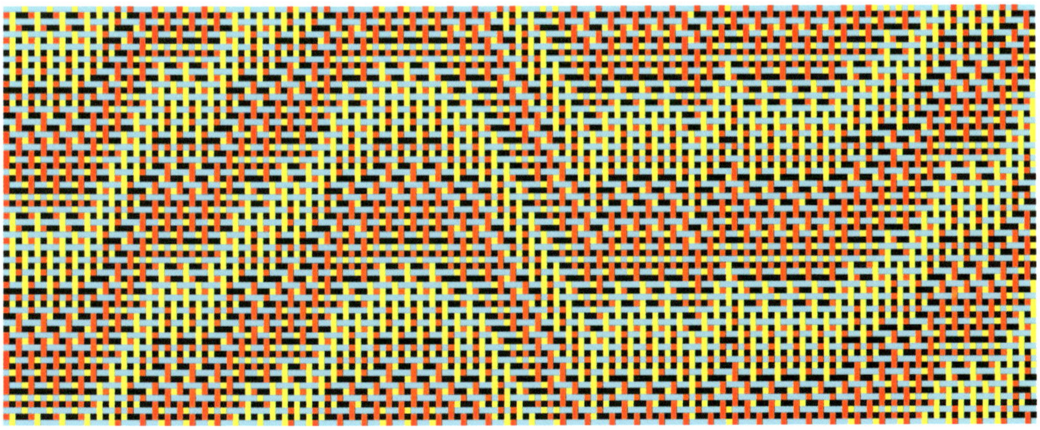

This is the underside of the cloth.

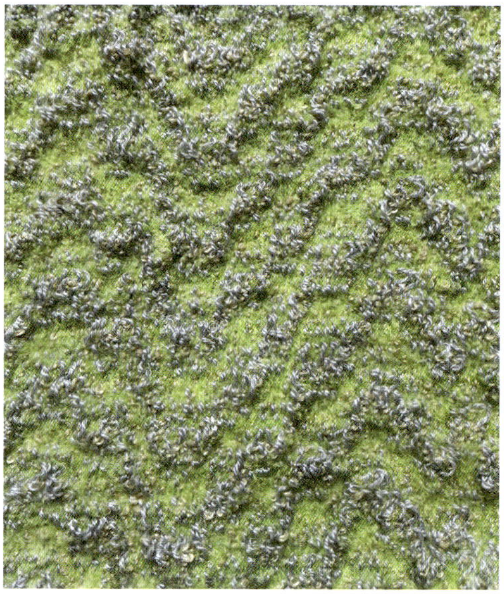

The warp for the extended parallel samples uses the same grey Tencel™ and lime-green merino as the divided parallel warp. The weft is a gold silk noil alongside the lime-green merino.

The next example of multi-treadling for eight-shaft looms can be expressed in several different ways. It combines both single treadle and double treadling.

Only one treadle is required for the second and alternating picks. This particular design has plain weave combined with weft twill on one layer, and plain weave with warp twill on the other. The first pick is weaving the bottom layer, lifting specific warp threads and also weaving plain. The second pick is weaving the top layer and only weaving plain weave, so only needing one treadle. This gives two distinctive faces.

You can also write tie-ups as a single tie-up rather than a parallel. One reason some weavers prefer the tie-up like this is that treadling can be written in a straight or advancing pattern with no parallel treadling.

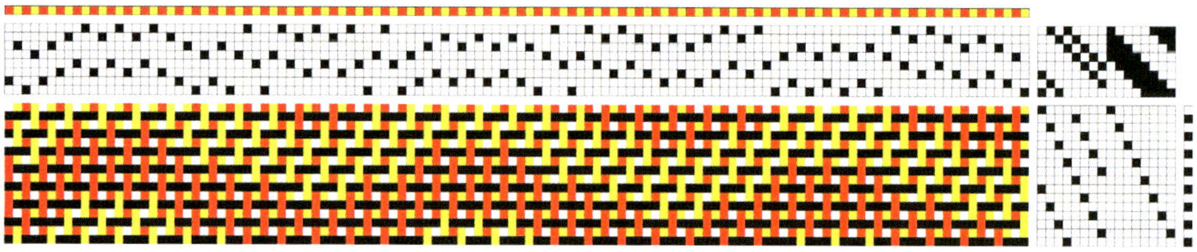

This tie-up uses a parallel tie-up for plain weave and twill. The draft is different from the previous one because only one treadle is required for the top layer, leading to two very distinct faces of the cloth. Where the plain weave works in conjunction with the twill in this draft, it is in the areas that are not involved in the twill.

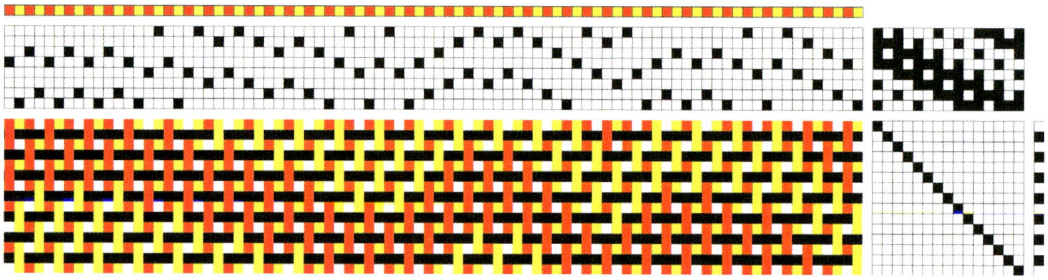

The same information is shown here in a different format.

Skeleton Tie-up

The third method is for treadle-loom users with ten or more treadles. This skeleton tie-up is from Bonnie Inouye (reproduced with kind permission).

Skeleton tie-ups are often not possible, but sometimes a slight adaptation to the weave structures might allow for one. Depending on the design, a skeleton tie-up can give plain weave across the full warp, but also used with another treadle will create the pattern, depending on which other shafts are raised in conjunction.

JACK AND COUNTERMARCH LOOMS

Skeleton tie-ups are useful for jack looms and some countermarch users, depending on the type of loom. Treadle looms have a limited number of treadles available to tie-up for these designs and sometimes it is possible to reduce the number of treadles required by stripping down a tie-up to a few constituent parts. Countermarch looms usually are required to tie all shafts to all treadles, including rising and sinking shafts in order to create a large shed, which assists in weaving. However, some looms can also be tied up just to the rising shafts, which allows for one or two treadles to be used together, so long as there is enough shed for the shuttle to pass through.

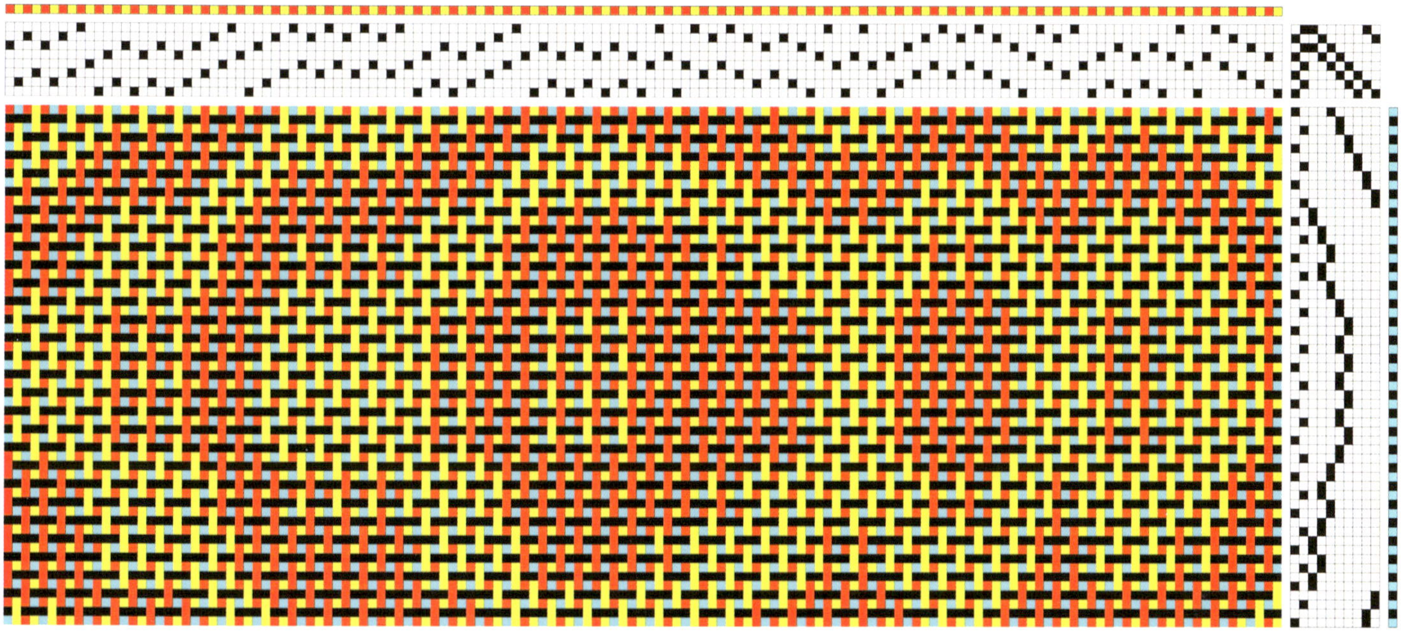

This skeleton tie-up uses only ten treadles with light blue shown for the two treadles of plain weave of 1,3,5,7 v 2,4,6,8. The selected plain weave for the bottom layer is woven using two shafts plus a combined lift of four shafts to raise the top cloth. The difference between this tie-up and a regular double cloth tie-up is that the layer being lifted moves through the eight shafts according to the design line. To weave the top layer, only the two plain weave shafts denoted in the pattern part of the tie-up are used, which move according to the design.

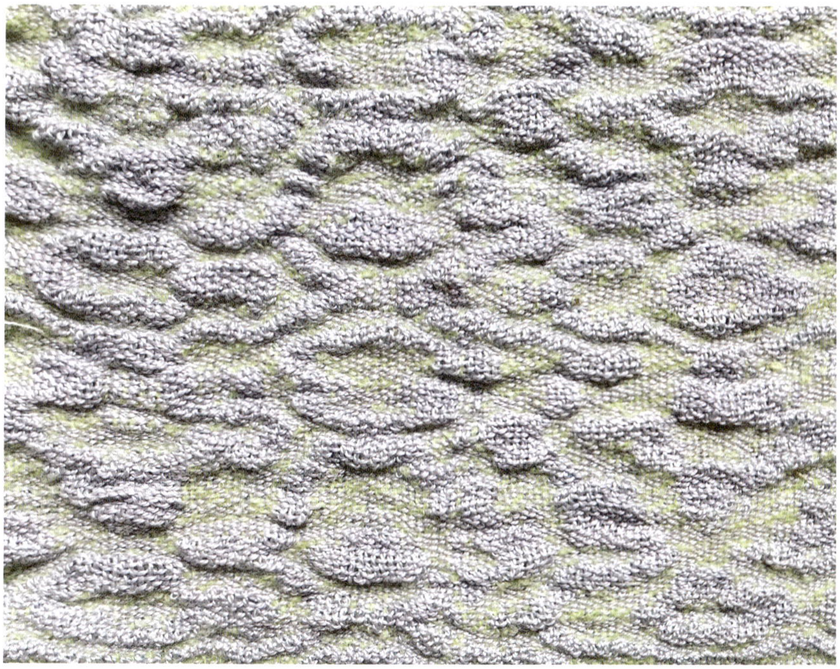

This sample has two distinct faces: one side shows the passive (lavender cotton) weft face, the other the active (blue merino) weft face.

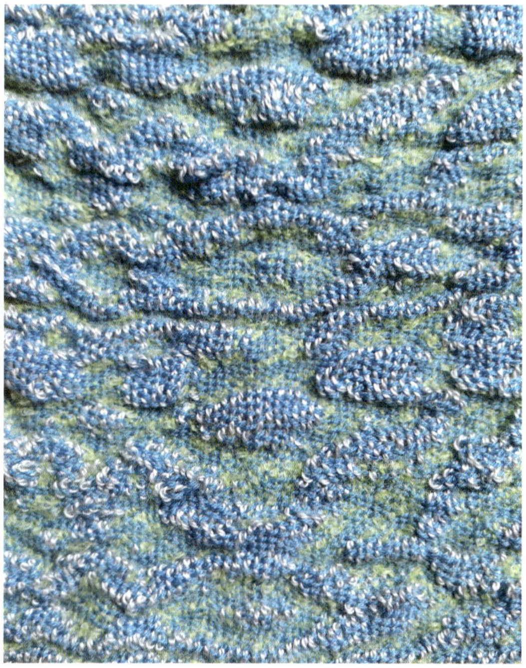

The tie-up gives plain weave on one side of the fabric, followed by plain on the opposite of the fabric with the first layer lifted. This is a close-up of one portion of the reverse side.

Wet-finishing

As ever, wet-finishing also needs to be sampled to ensure that just the right amount of shrinkage is obtained for the desired result.

Because of the relative openness of the sett, simple soaking of woollen yarns in hot sudsy water (to remove any spinning oils or size applied to the yarns) followed by plunging into cold water and then between 10 and 20 minutes of tumble-drying on a regular heat with a wet towel is often enough to create distinct shrinkage effects. Depending on the proportions of active to passive yarns – especially if a higher ratio of passive yarn is used – plus taking into account the shrinkage potential of the active yarn, more or less time will need to be given to the amount of manipulation during wet-finishing and whether tumble-drying will be required.

TOP TIP

Careful record keeping is essential for future guidance.

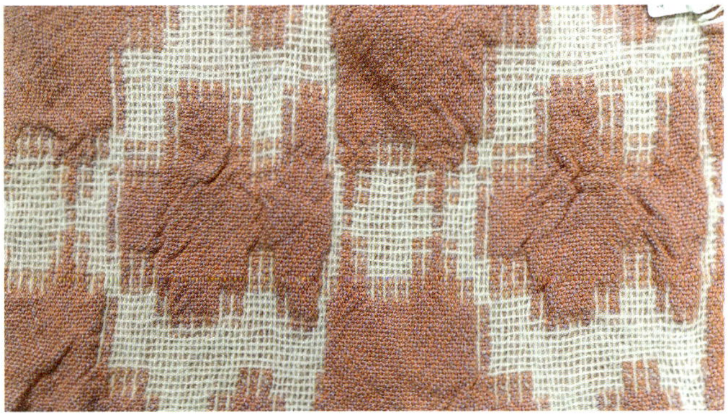

The ratio for these samples is 2:1 passive to active in warp and weft. The white warp is a fine wool, the peach a 6/2 ne cotton. The unwashed sample shows the interaction with the same weft for the wool and a lavender 6/2 ne cotton. The lavender colour of the weft influences the overall cotton hue towards a pink.

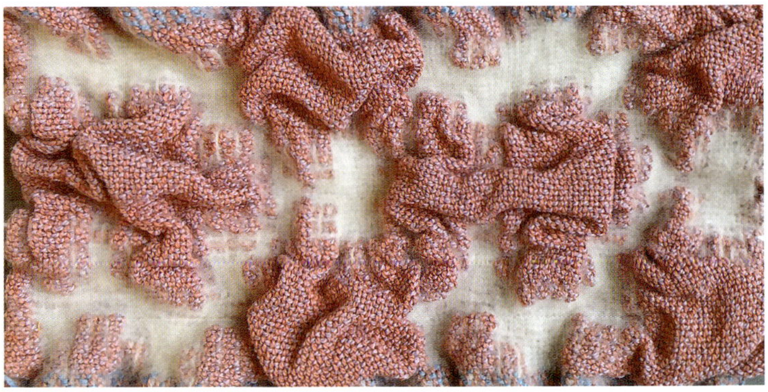

After wet-finishing, this is the same side as the unwashed sample. When wet-finishing, all kinds of shrinkage can take place, depending on the positioning of the areas of wool versus cotton.

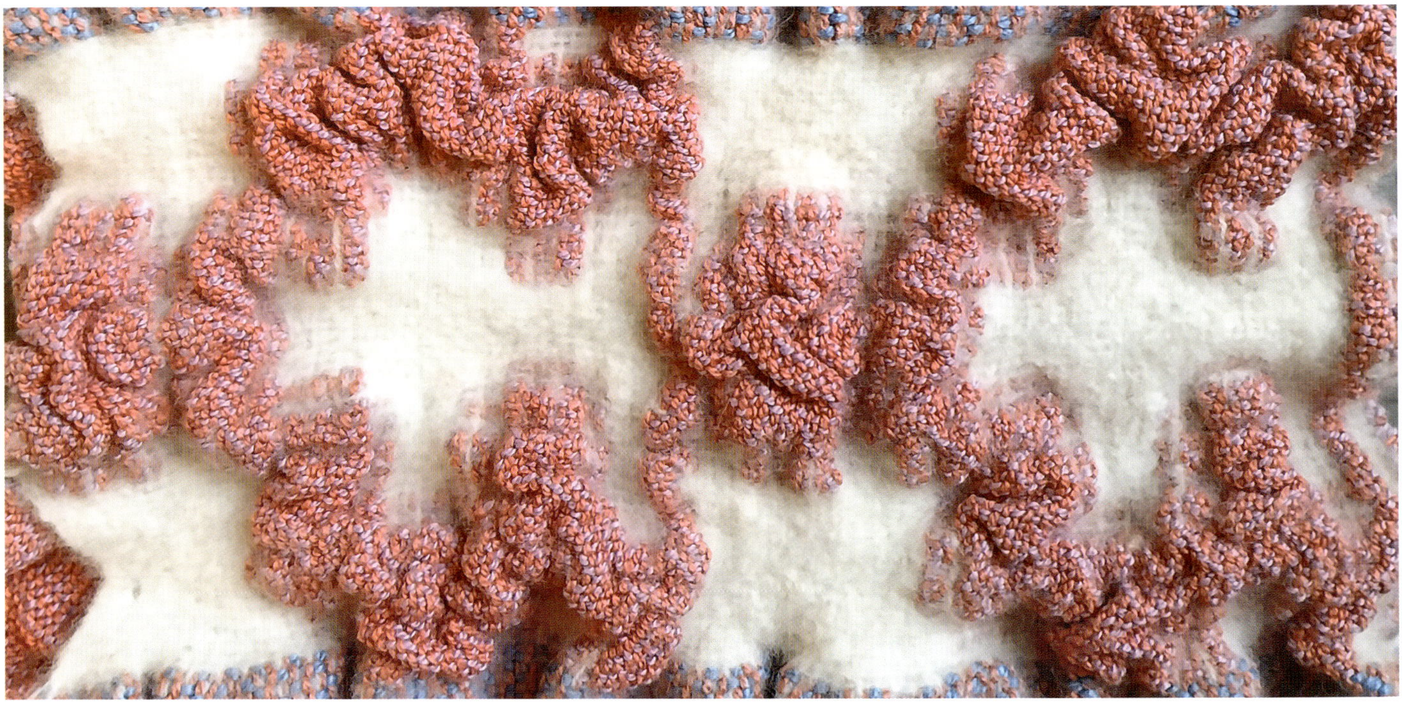

This is the opposite side.

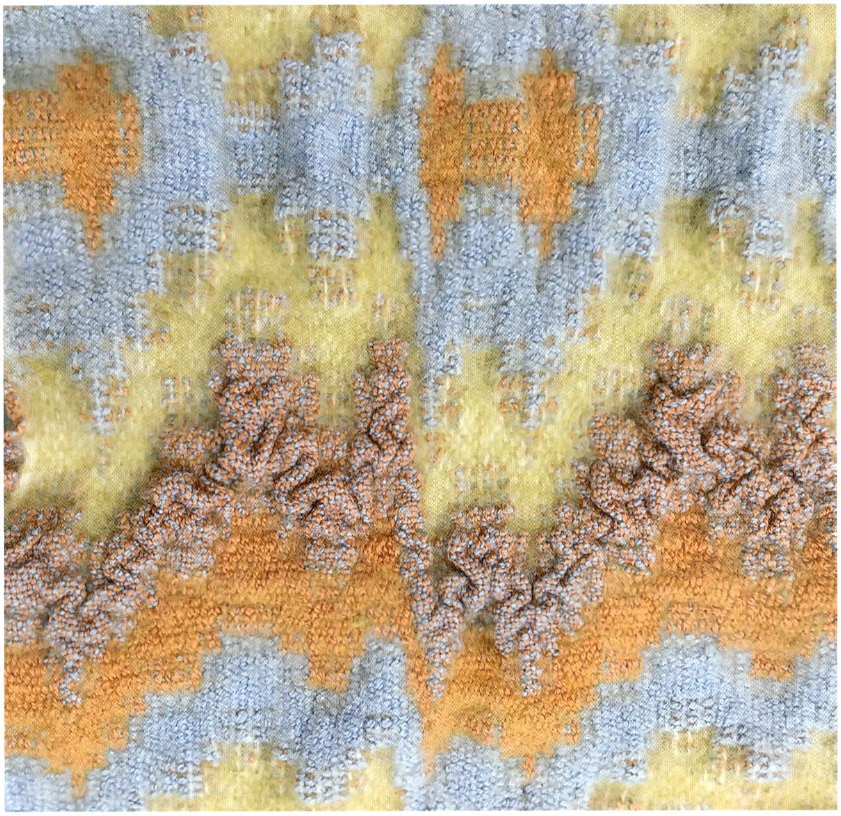

The combination of strong colours in the cotton in warp and weft together with the 2:1 ratio of passive to active (cotton to wool) in both warp and weft bring four different elements out in this sample. The warp-dominant peach contrasts with the weft-dominant blue. The interaction of the two passive yarns gives a melange which is opposed by the mix of white and yellow wool at a looser ratio. The wet-finished result shows the reaction of the totally passive area – the mix of the two cottons – to the shrinking of the woollen yarns at the looser ratio underneath.

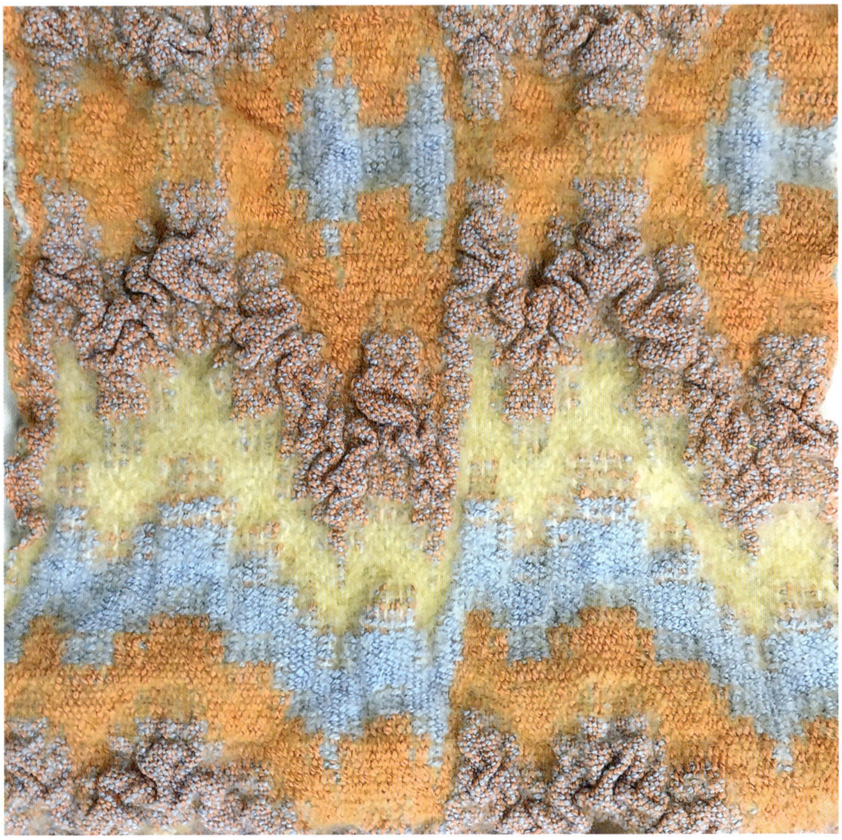

The opposite side. It is possible to see where the weft-dominant blue section 'bleeds' into the more open woollen area through an intermediary stage.

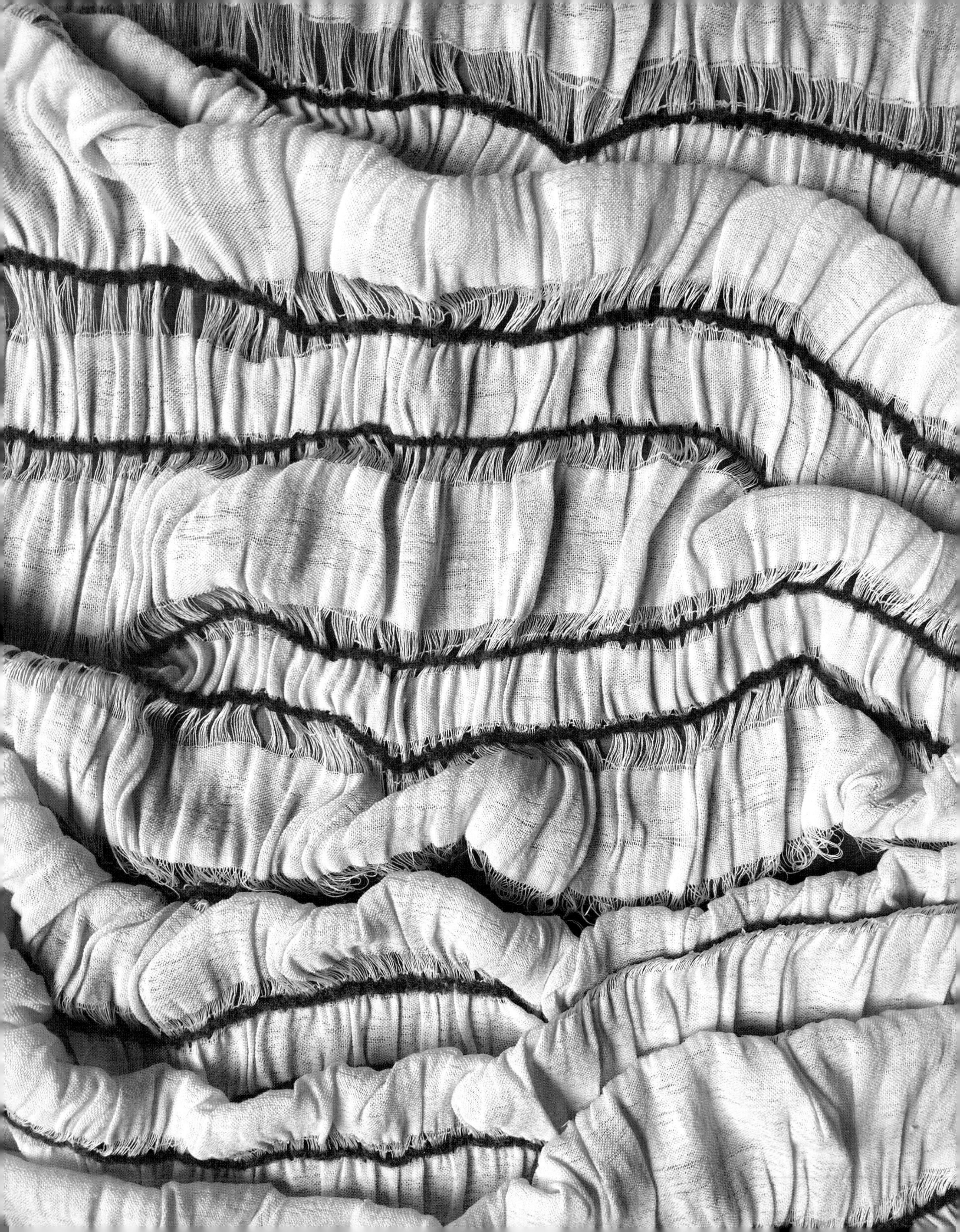

PART TWO: SCULPTURE

So far, you have learned different methods for creating dimensional cloth using regular weaving structures. Some of these, such as shibori, distort the flat plane. Others, such as overshot for texture and some double cloth variants, grow out of the flat plane.

This section of the book moves into further dimensionality through thinking in a sculptural way. There are ways of shaping your work into three dimensions once off the loom. There are also methods you can use to create the sculptural effect on the loom.

Materiality also has a major role to play here. There is soft sculpture, which allows for a piece to be worn as a garment or accessory or as art, displayed in a horizontal position or suspended. There is hard sculpture, which creates self-standing or wall-based artwork. This book is not covering the use of metals in the warp. Christine K. Miller's *Weaving With Wire* is an excellent resource if you wish to use wire in the warp. However, metal and paper have been used in the weft to explore sculptural elements where appropriate.

For hard sculpture, higher density of sett will often be a factor to increase rigidity in the piece. Multi-layer and tubular weaving also require quite high-density setts. When using higher setts, extra care needs to be taken when tying on to the cloth beam to ensure that *all* the warp ends in each dent have the correct tension. It is so easy to count the dents and tie on without checking that every dent has been tensioned evenly. Just a little extra attention at the preliminary tying-on stage pays dividends in the ease of weaving later on.

Dimensional effects can be exaggerated through the use of tensioning devices. Sally Eyring's book *3-D Hand Loom Weaving* delves deeply into how to adapt and create tensioning devices for your loom for specific results. This approach uses the loom as a tool to be modified for extreme shaping on the loom in order to weave garments, in addition to weaving for art.

In this part of the book we are focusing on multi-layer sculptural effects, tubular weaving and incorporating some tapestry techniques into shaft-loom weaving in order to create truly three-dimensional results. Skills learned here will give you the tools to be used in your own design process so that you can develop your unique sculptural style. Wet-finishing and other methods of finishing will be given by chapter.

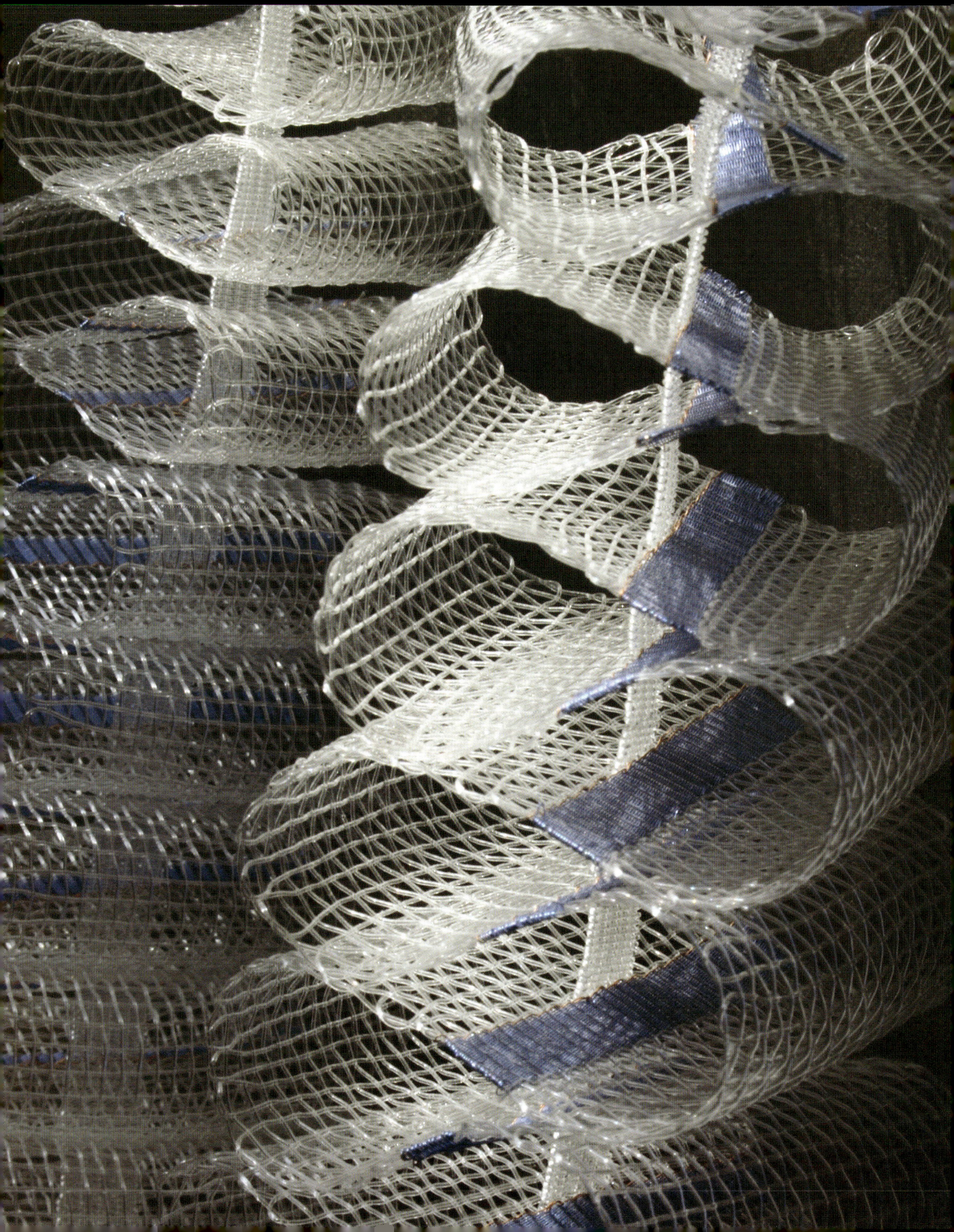

CHAPTER 12

MULTI-LAYERS

In Chapter 9, we looked at how different threading conventions can be used for four, six or eight shafts to create the two layers that will interact. However, there are lots of ways to create more sculptural effects with two or more layers.

Eight Shafts: X-formation and More

As well as four separate layers, with eight shafts and double cloth, it is possible to weave an X-formation. Rethreading is required as one-half of the warp will need to have four shafts (two for the upper layer, two for the lower layer), and the other half of the warp will need to use the other four shafts (two for the upper layer, and two for the lower layer).

This time, the weft travels from the top layer of one side to the bottom layer of the other side (same colour in weft and warp) and the second weft travels from the lower layer of the first side to the top layer of the second side (again, same colour in weft and warp). In effect, the centre of the warp becomes a vertical hinge, and when you change which horizontal layer is on the top, that becomes a horizontal hinge. Each vertical side of the warp can be woven independently to create different angles, hinged in either direction.

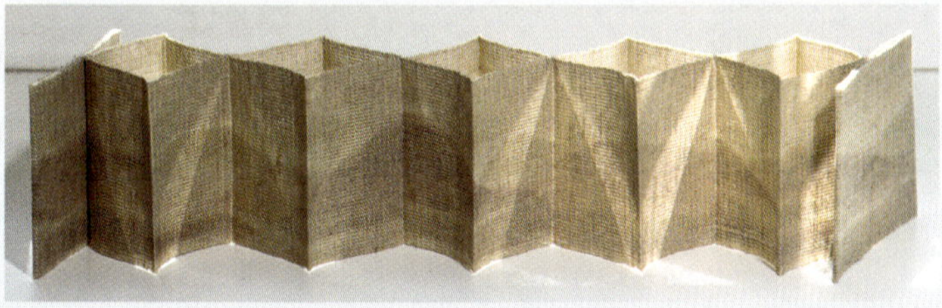

In addition to transparent and airy works, Kay Sekimachi also uses double cloth and multiple layers to form sculptural folded work. (Photo: Tom Grotta)

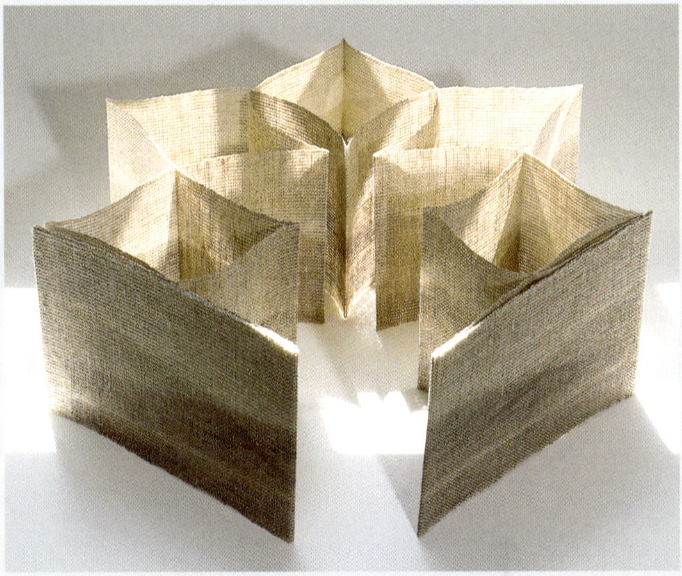

Another version of the interchanging double cloth form creates a floral impression in 3D. (Photo: Tom Grotta)

Once this is mastered, colour variations can be used in the weft. Firmer yarns will allow the different elements to stand, or alternately the different elements can be stiffened with diluted PVC or similar, or incorporate some interior stiffening through inclusions.

Paul R. O'Connor created fascinating origami-like geometrical forms which have inspired many weavers over the years. Lucy Smyth follows this tradition.

Paul also created sculptural effects by using multiple layers and shaping them through structure and inclusions with the top of the fold acting as a hinge and the four layers hinged in various ways to make different formations, a method that Susie Taylor has also explored.

Sue Hiley Harris's *Hidden Wave* detail in nylon monofilament and enamelled copper wire. Technically, this piece uses two layers only, but its sculptural format fits the multi-layering ethos and foretastes the work of Kay Sekimachi and Melanie Olde (seen later in the chapter). (Photo: Sue Hiley Harris)

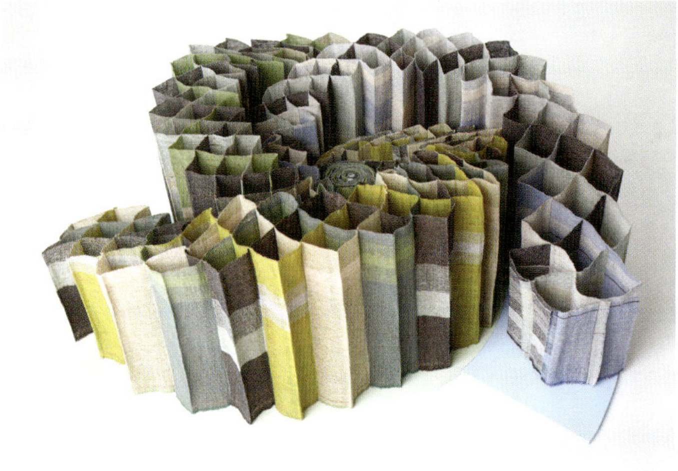

Maelstrom, created by Lucy Smyth (formerly Lucy McMullen) not only interchanges layers but is comprised of many blends of colour in its three components. It can be refigured into many different iterations. (Photos: Lucy McMullen)

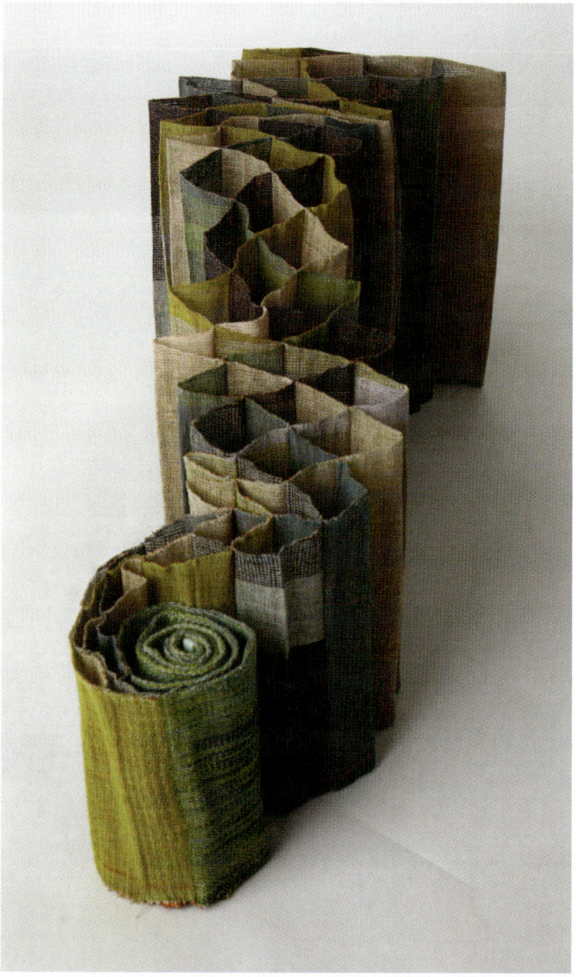

One of the three components (Green + Blue) being unrolled.

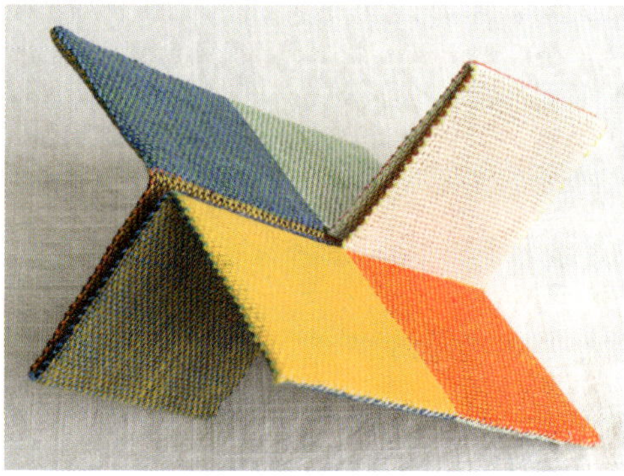

Susie Taylor has woven these geometric forms in double cloth. They can take on different guises thanks to the inclusions inside that stiffen them. This is *Origami Sculpture 1*. (Photos: James Dewrance)

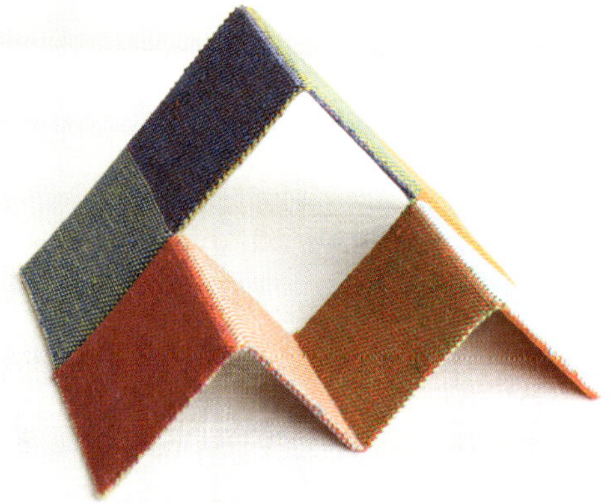

Origami Sculpture 2

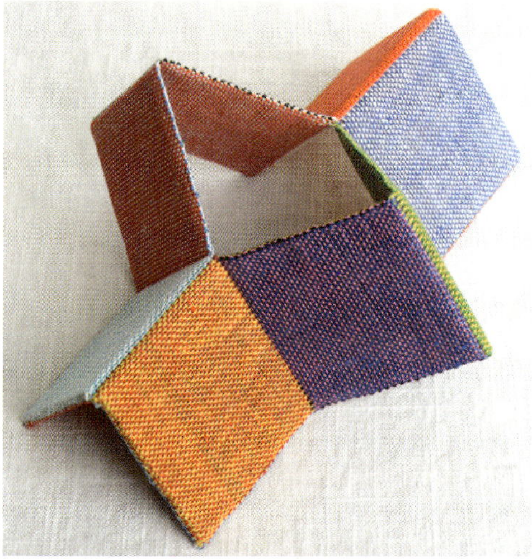

Origami Sculpture 3

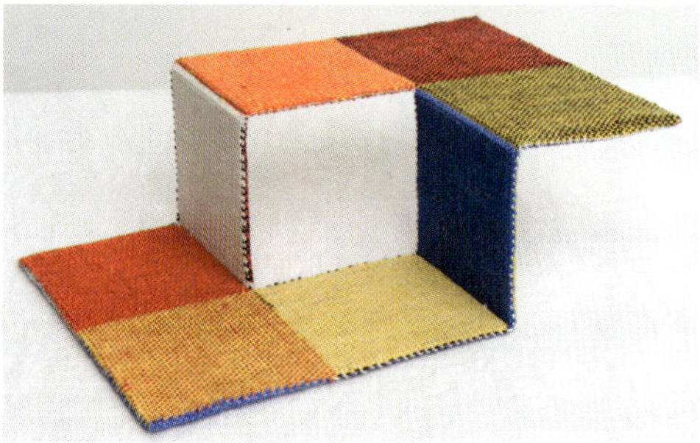

Origami Sculpture 4

Different Widths

As seen earlier, narrower layers can be contrasted with wider layers. Larger layer exchanges between wider layers and several shorter layer exchanges between the narrower ones are effective. With more shafts available, a wider layer could be divided into two or more potentially narrower segments that could be woven independently with a tapestry-type butterfly to create separate segments that could then exchange.

With two warp beams used for the separate halves of the warp, different tensions between the two halves would give a ruffled effect on one side versus the other, which could be swapped over. Or double weave pleats could be woven in one-half for a while, then the full width woven once more to create the pleats in one-half.

Your imagination is the limit!

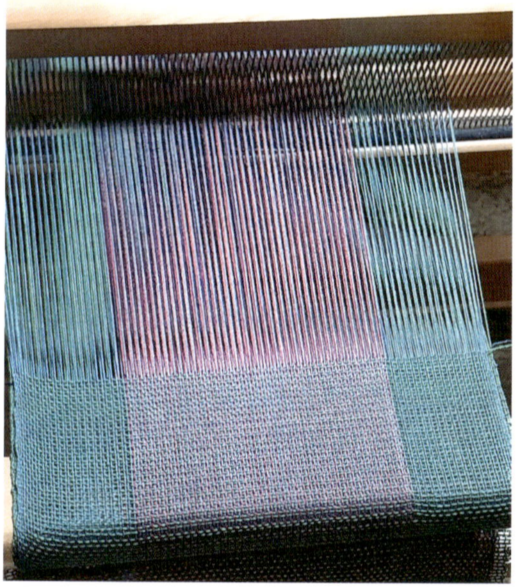

Ruffle effects can be achieved with two layers weaving separately at the selvedges and the remaining layers combined in the central tube section as seen on the loom in this sample by Frances Stevens.

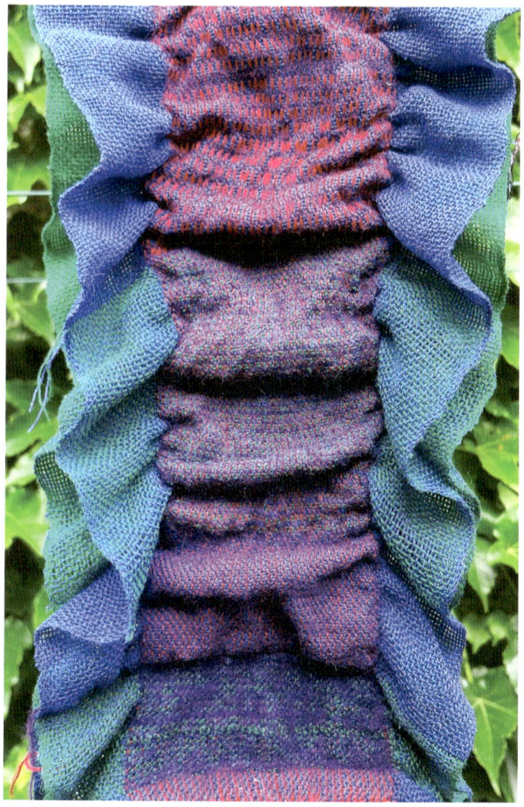

The finished piece shows how much shrinkage can affect the surface texture.

MULTIPLE LAYERS

As only two shafts are needed to weave one layer in plain weave, any loom of four or more shafts can technically weave layers, adding up to half the number of shafts that that loom possesses. There are, however, a few practical considerations to work through before preparing a warp of multiple layers, the main ones being sett and yarn selection.

Practical Considerations

Sett

As each layer adds its own sett to the mix, depending on the ends per inch/cm for plain weave, the combined sett gets higher very quickly.

The practical limits of the loom construction come into play here. If you are using a loom with a long distance between the back beam and the back of the shafts (usually found on floor looms), it is possible to have a higher combined sett than on a loom with just a short distance from the back beam to the back of the shafts. Physics dictates that the shorter the distance between these two points, the more acute the angle of the warp when the shed is made, putting more stress on the warp. The longer the distance, the greater the ease in creating a shed and the higher the tension that can be applied to the warp to enable closer setts.

TOP TIP

Table looms can be useful to try proof of concept, but sculpture is not always easy to create on these smaller looms.

Yarn Selection

Yarn selection adds its own complications. Wool and matt cotton, for instance, often create lint, as do some silk and other bast fibres such as ramie. They are also more likely to catch on adjacent warp threads as the surface of the yarn is rougher than those that have been through mercerisation processes, for example. This largely depends on how the yarns have been spun and whether they have been sized prior to sale or if you decide to size your warp before beaming. The tighter the spin, the less the propensity for shedding lint but the more rigid the yarn. It is always a trade-off between the yarn's integrity for what you wish to do, and the flexibility or otherwise that you want for the end result. For sculpture, rigidity can be a valuable asset for free-standing or shaped pieces.

Metal yarns and nylon monofilament (often known as 'fishing line') are other options for warps. (For warping methods with these particular yarns please refer to the Bibliography – Wilson/Osterkamp). These are particularly effective for sculptural effects, with metal yarns giving body and monofilament translucency.

Weaving in multiple layers means tightly bunched warp ends. Fuzz balls can readily appear with more traditional yarns as the warp yarns are in such close proximity to each other. When changing sheds, the yarns rub against each other continually, gently abrading each other and setting the scene for the fuzz balls to occur. These little balls effectively wrap around two or more ends, physically binding them together and creating shedding problems. To help alleviate this, a useful strategy is to thread adjacent ends on shafts as far from each other as possible so that the angles of the shed for those ends are different to each other. The usual method for double weave is to put the second layer half the total number of shafts away from the first layer. Weavers of warp rep will be aware of this practice.

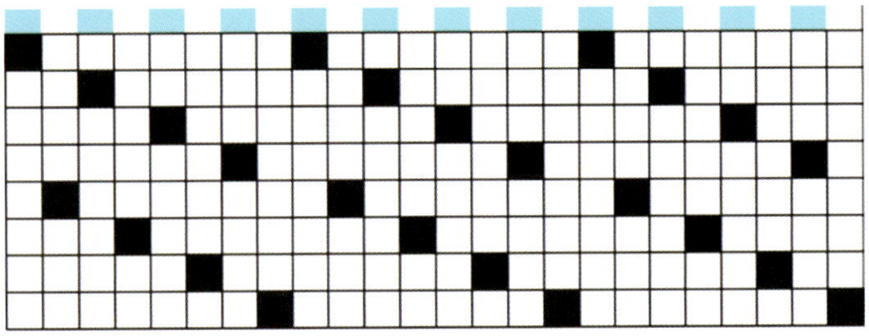

Regular double cloth in parallel threading shows shafts 1–4 being for one layer and shafts 5–8 for the other, using a standard 1:1 ratio between the layers.

If a loom has 16 shafts, and you wish to weave a quadruple cloth on eight shafts, you would be able to spread the layers apart more because of the facility of having spare shafts available. However, on regular eight-shaft looms, this is not possible and closer attention to yarn choices becomes more important.

Humidity

Highly mercerised yarns are often a good choice as they have a slipperiness that allows for easier crowding. However, humidity can also play a big role in warps with high setts. Some yarns, such as cotton, gain in strength and elasticity with higher humidity; others, such as silk, lose strength and elasticity.

Low humidity can lead to the build-up of static created through the shedding action operating on warp ends that are constantly rubbing against each other. Silk threads have a propensity to 'fly away' from each other in conditions of low humidity. This can be reduced with a light spritz of water across the warp to dampen down the yarn.

Sleying

Sleying is another area to think about. Should you sley with all the first ends of plain weave in each layer grouped together in one dent or should you separate them out a bit more? Will the reed action create abrasion on the crowded ends? Do you need to separate out more sticky yarns such as Shetlands (which often have a slightly oily size on them to guard against abrasion during warping and weaving)?

This decision could be resolved if you have several reeds to choose from. Fewer dents per inch/cm will allow for more ends to be sleyed together, but the metal is thicker in more open reeds and can lead to reed marks – gaps left in the fabric after finishing – depending on the process and amount of fulling. Largely it is down to sampling and your own assessments for the results you want.

The regular threading conventions for multiple layers of plain weave is to have one of the following:

1. Straight entry threading where the front group of shafts are the first ends of each layer (Group A) alternating with the second group of shafts for the second end of each layer (Group B).
2. Parallel threading where each group of two shafts creates one layer, i.e. shafts 1 & 2, 3 & 4, 5 & 6 and 7 & 8 for four layers, with 1,3,5,7 as Group A and 2,4,6,8 as Group B.

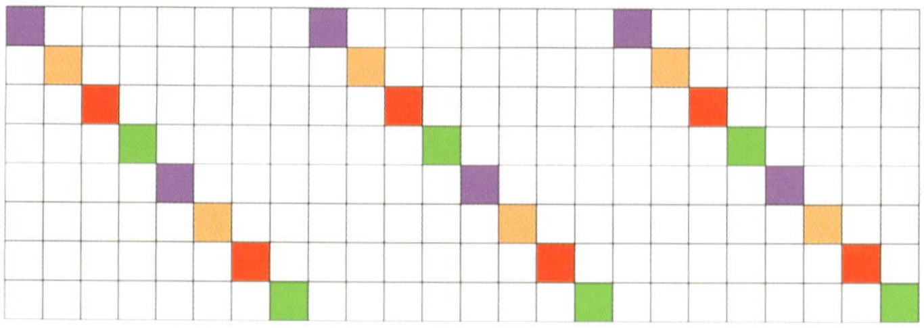

Four-layer threading using a straight entry threading system. Note that Layer A (green warps) are threaded on shafts 1 & 5; Layer B (red warps) are on shafts 2 & 6; Layer C (orange warps) on shafts 3 & 7; Layer D (purple warps) on shafts 4 & 8. This is easy to thread but it can be more complex to plan weaves. This draft shows the colour order in the threading in a direct way.

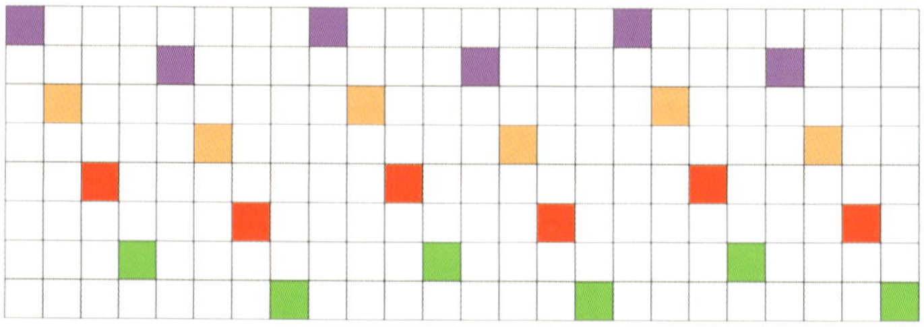

Parallel threading can be easier for some weavers. Shafts 1 & 2 are now devoted to Layer A (green warps); shafts 3 & 4 are for Layer B (red warps); shafts 5 & 6 are for Layer C (orange warps) and shafts 7 & 8 are for Layer D (purple warps).

It is important to note that in this book we are selecting in advance the shafts that work together to form one layer for demonstration purposes. However, once the main principles are absorbed, it is totally viable to select different combinations of shafts and layers. Whichever threading convention is followed, once weaving, there is a choice of changing layer partners. Any ends from Group A can be paired up with any ends from Group B. This particularly has an impact when using colour but also with texture. Different effects can be created if both active and passive yarns are combined in both warp and weft and mixing the shafts used for each layer at different times in the weaving. This is a ripe area for exploration.

Six Shafts: Triple Cloth

With six shafts, three layers can be woven. For textural considerations, elements to consider are: ratios between the different layers, different widths for each layer and different material properties in your warp and weft yarns for varying effects.

Another possible element is tension variation between layers through differential shrinkage, using a second back beam or adding tensioning devices to selected areas of warp. (*See* Bibliography – Sally Eyring, for various loom

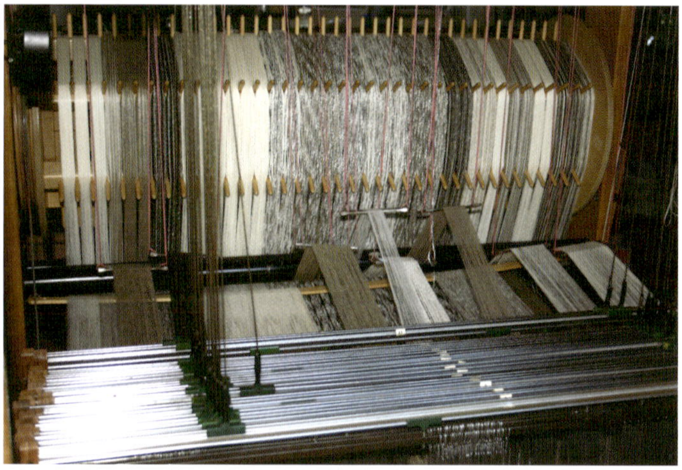

Additional tensioning devices can be created with a little ingenuity. This image shows the use of small reeds suspended from the castle of the loom which can be altered at will to ensure smooth weaving when using multiple warps of differing take-up. This could easily be small lengths of wooden dowels which are thick enough not to bend under tension.

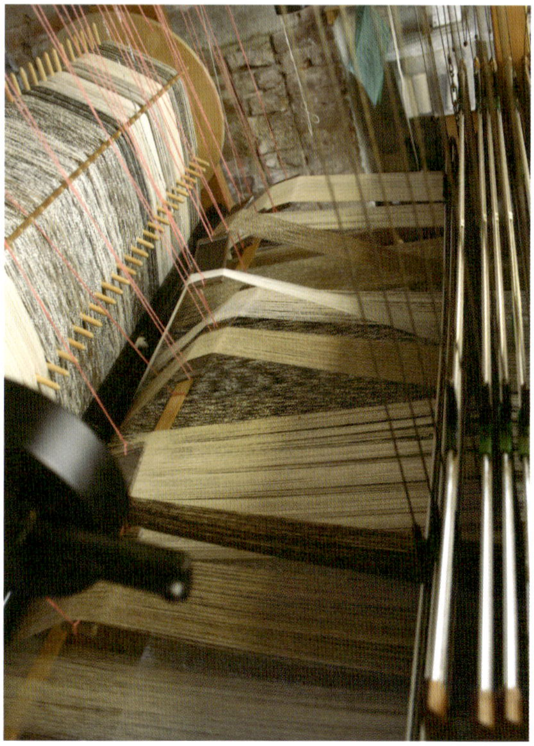

The detailed view gives an indication of the various requirements of each warp stripe.

adaptations for differential tensioning, and Appendix I for second back beam suggestions.)

Differential shrinkage and one back beam have been used to create the examples that follow to accompany this section, but it is important to stress that an active yarn does not have to be an element in this area of sculptural weaving.

Using a double back beam loom allows for differing take-up in weaving, and also gives the opportunity for different warp lengths so that one warp can be deliberately designed to be longer and weave more than the other(s), interacting in various ways to create sculptural effects.

Regular Triple Cloth

The instructions that follow are for general triple cloth. If the bottom layer is woven first and the layers are worked upwards, it is easier to see what is going on in each layer as it is inserted. For this reason, these drafts mostly use a liftplan mode rather than a tie-up and treadling.

- **Pick 1, Bottom layer:** Raise the top two layers – shafts 1–4. Now raise shaft 5 for the first pick of the bottom layer. Weave with the purple weft.
- **Pick 2, Middle layer:** Raise the top layer – shafts 1&2. Now raise shaft 3 for the first pick of the middle layer. Weave with the red weft.
- **Pick 3, Top layer:** Raise shaft 1. Weave with the green weft.
- **Pick 4, Bottom layer:** Raise the top two layers – shafts 1–4. Now raise shaft 6 for the second pick of the bottom layer. Weave with the purple weft.
- **Pick 5, Middle layer:** Raise the top layer – shafts 1&2. Now raise shaft 4 for the second pick of the middle layer. Weave with the red weft.
- **Pick 6, Top layer:** Raise shaft 2. Weave with the green weft.

Each layer can change position in the stack. Using different colours for each layer helps to see which layer is doing what and which shafts to raise for the desired result.

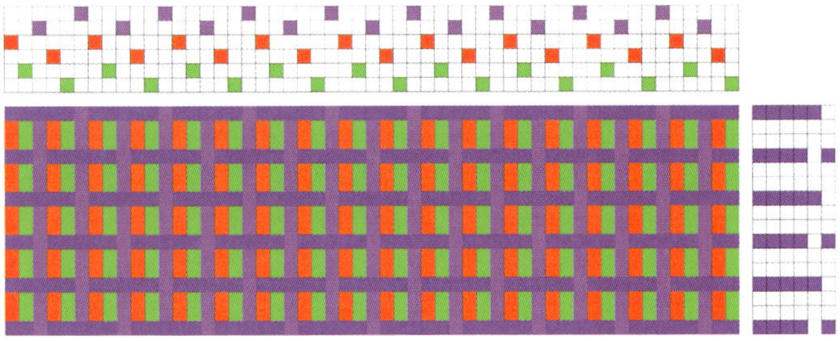

This triple cloth on six shafts has a bottom purple warp layer woven with picks 1 and 4 with the dark purple weft. The draft shows the view from underneath the loom. While the draft shows each layer's wefts both woven at the same time, this will in practice usually be split into the separate pick order listed in the text.

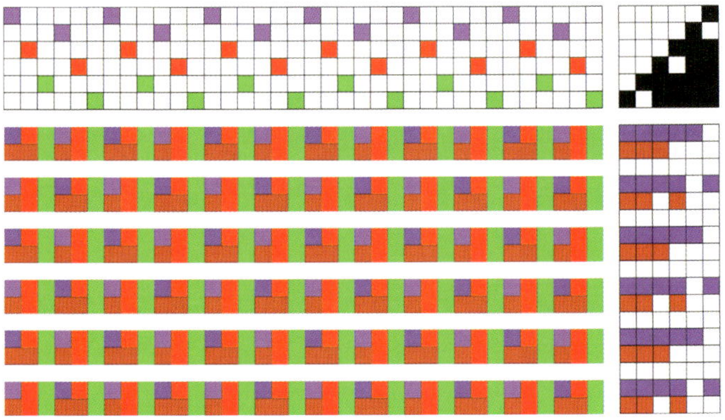

The middle layer draft is viewed from the top of the loom and shows picks 2 and 5 creating the middle layer. The top warp can be seen floating on the surface. (The 'white' weft does not actually exist but the draft has to show it.)

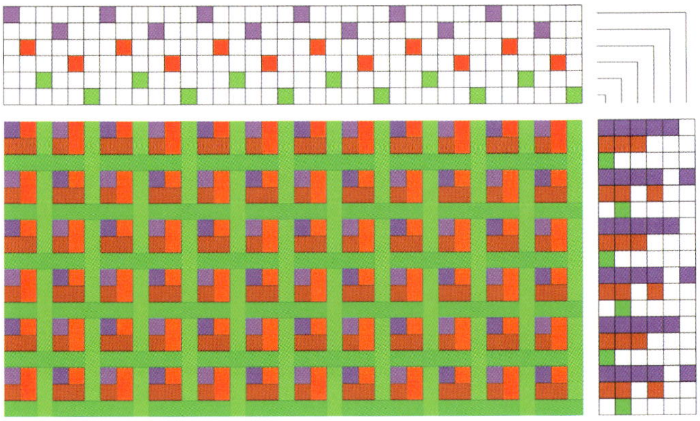

The top layer draft shows the final stage, weaving the top layer in green.

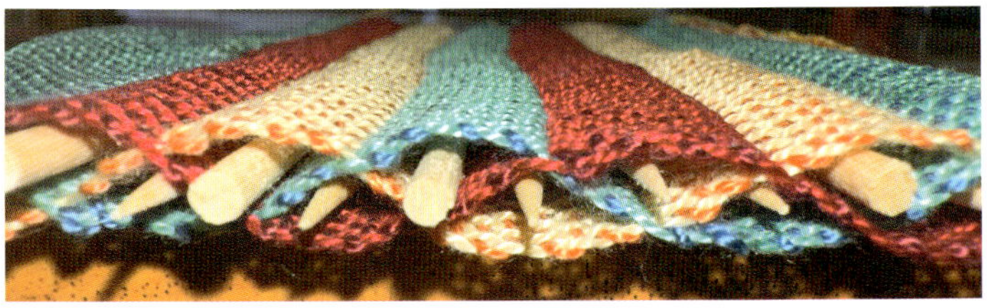

Jennifer Verrall used dowels to show the combinations of layers in this piece. (Photo: Jennifer Verrall)

Once these principles are understood, different integrations or interchanges can be made:

- Bring two or all three layers together for a few picks for an integrated weave.
- Have the middle layer in an active yarn and the outer layers in passive yarns and bring them all together for one or two picks before separating out again – this is especially effective when the active layer uses fewer ends, i.e. a ratio of 1:2 or 1:3 active to passive.

- Alternate two passive layers against an active layer.

Work in Progress

The following four images help to explain how different width layers can be woven.

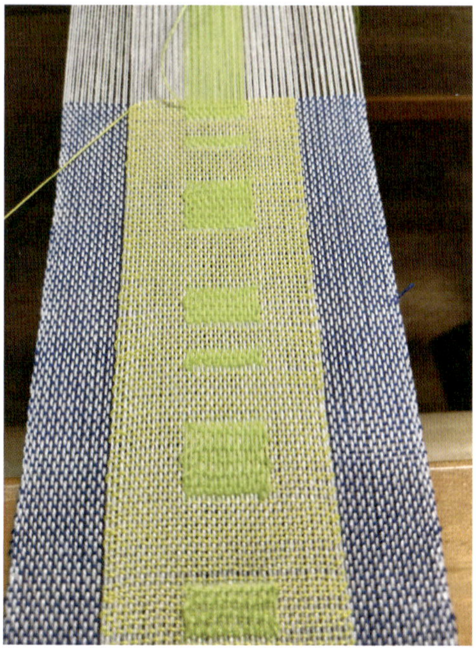

This image shows the independent wefts for the yellow cotton and the green wool. The blue cotton is there but cannot be seen in this photo. Each shuttle has its own place to sit when it is not being used to ensure that it does not get entangled with the other wefts. A mirror rests on the knees and a loom support so that the bottom layer can be seen to ensure that no stray warps or errant wefts are caught up underneath.

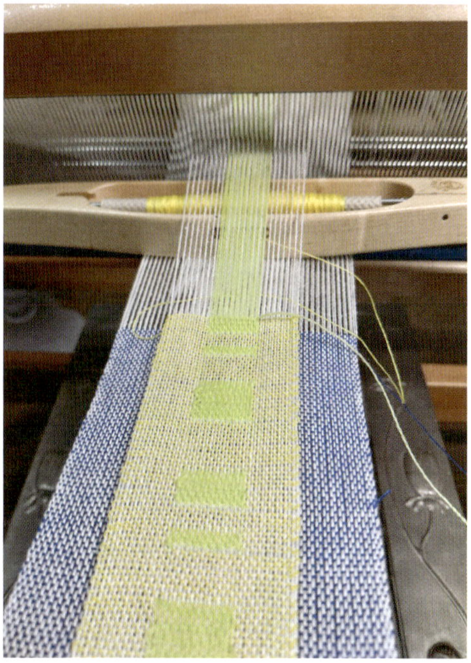

The green layer in its entirety is raised, and the first of the yellow layer is being woven with the yellow weft.

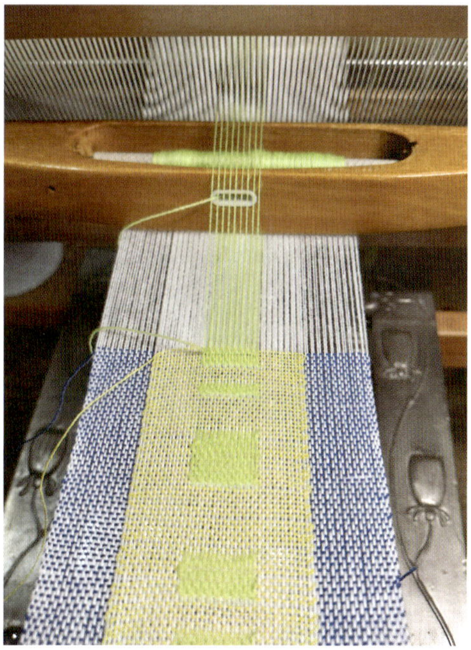

The green wool layer is being woven on the surface with its own weft.

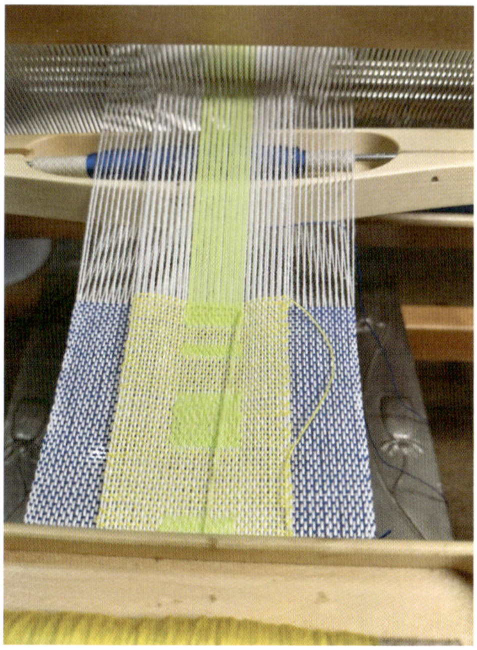

The whole of the green and yellow layers are now lifted, and the first pick of the bottom blue cotton layer is being woven with its blue weft.

There are many options to consider and lots of material properties to discover.

As before, different combinations of shafts can be assigned to the different layers of the same width so that the warps are visually intermingled in different combinations while retaining three separate layers at a time.

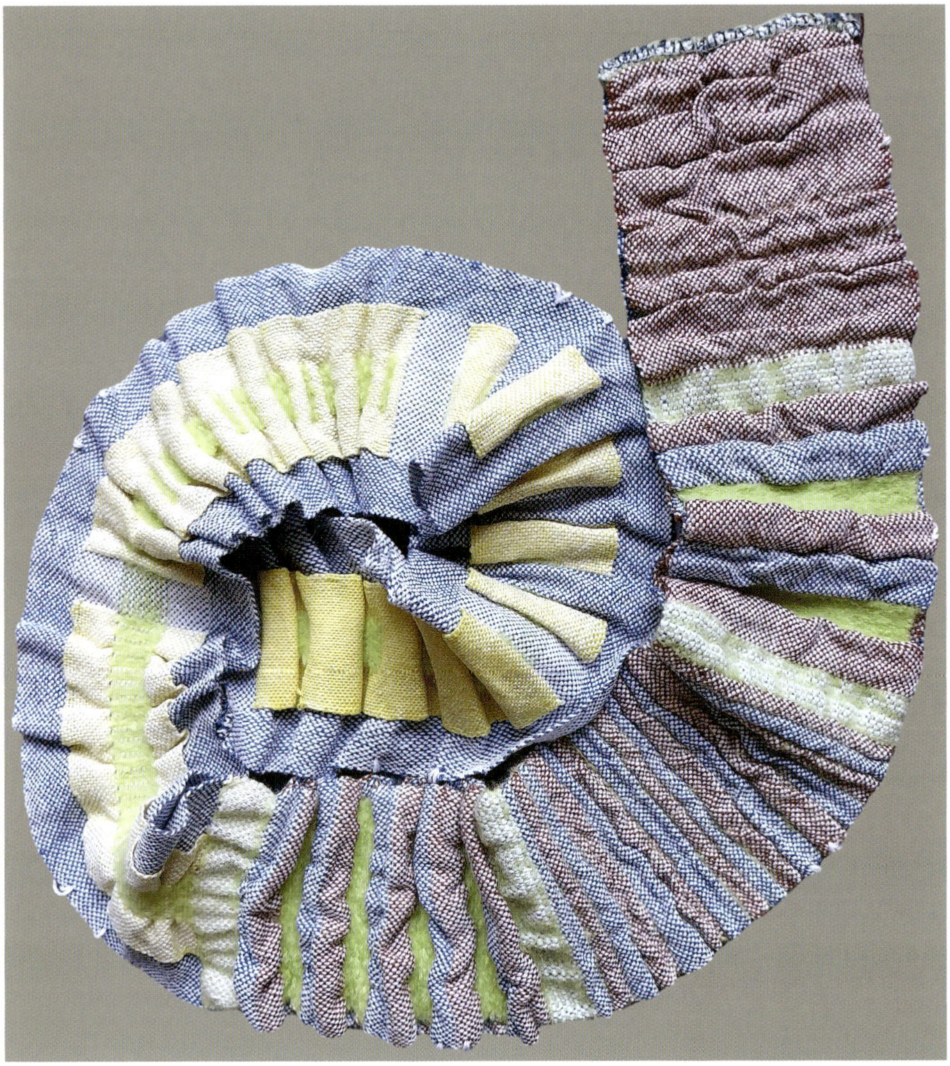

Eight samples exploring texture on three layers using six shafts.

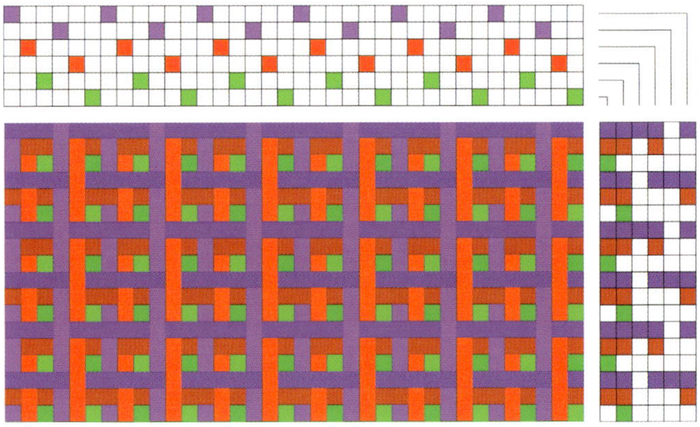

This draft shows different combinations of shafts being used to create different layers. This draft shows the bottom view where one of the bottom purple warps (shaft 5) and one of the middle red warps (shaft 3) are weaving with the bottom layer weft. Shafts 4 (red) & 6 (purple) are weaving the middle layer. Shafts 1 & 2 (green) are weaving the top layer.

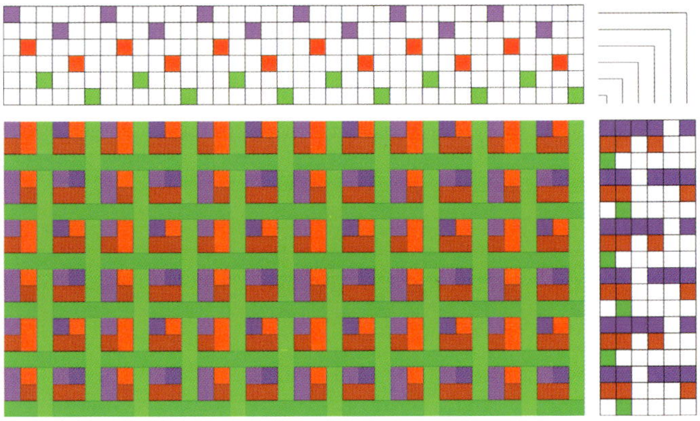

The top view shows the green on the very top but the purple and red warps on shafts 4 and 6 can be seen weaving on the middle layer with the dark red weft.

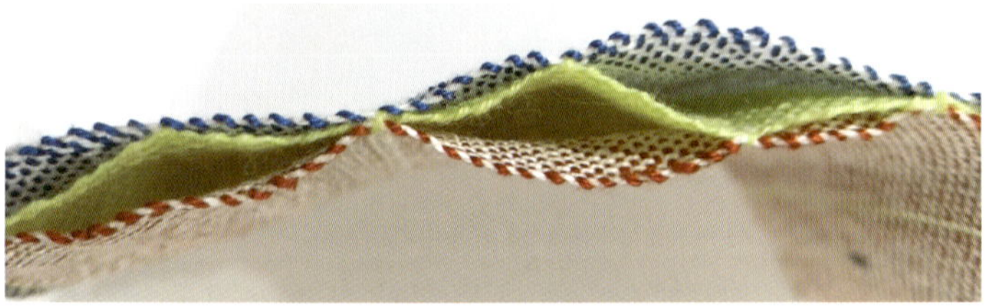

Three layers with top layer blue cotton, middle layer green wool, bottom layer brown cotton. Looking at the side, the middle layer joins with either the top or the bottom layer at different intervals. This is before finishing.

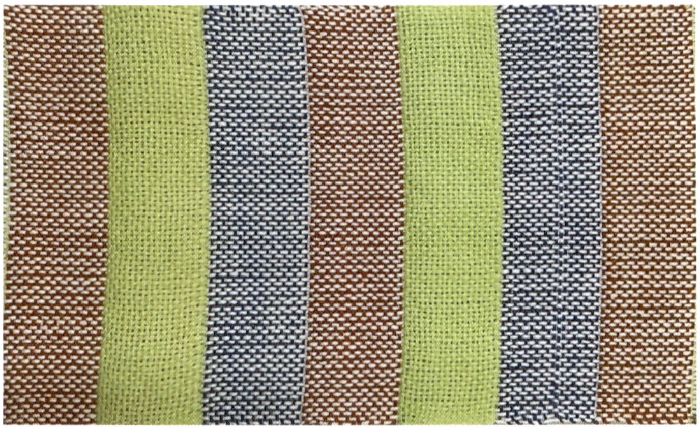

The same three layers but alternating and stacking in a different order. Here the blue and brown cotton layers work as a pair with the green wool layer switching from top to bottom for three interchanges, before the two cotton layers separate and the wool is in between. This view shows one side before finishing.

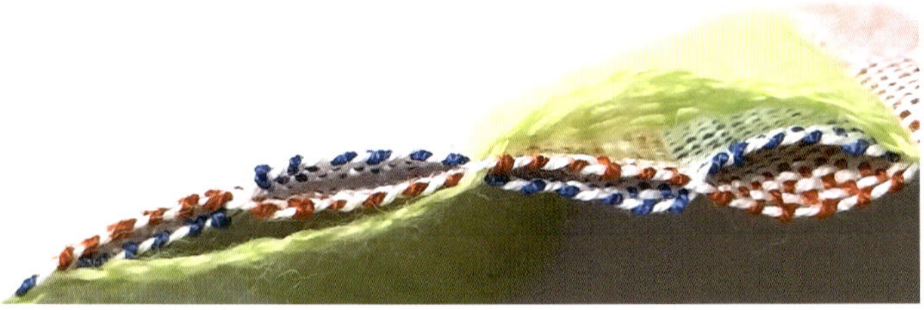

Keeping the two cotton layers to one side of the wool layer, the two cotton layers interchange. The next repeat has the two cotton layers switching sides with the wool.

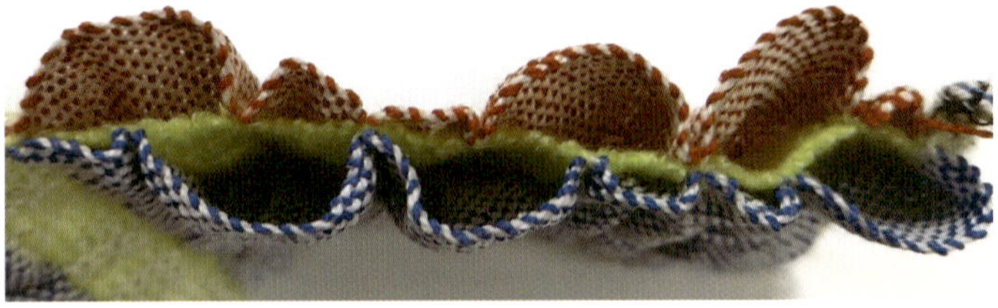

Looking at the side, the three layers after wet-finishing. The brown and blue cotton layers are joined to the wool layer in different places to give different effects on wet-finishing.

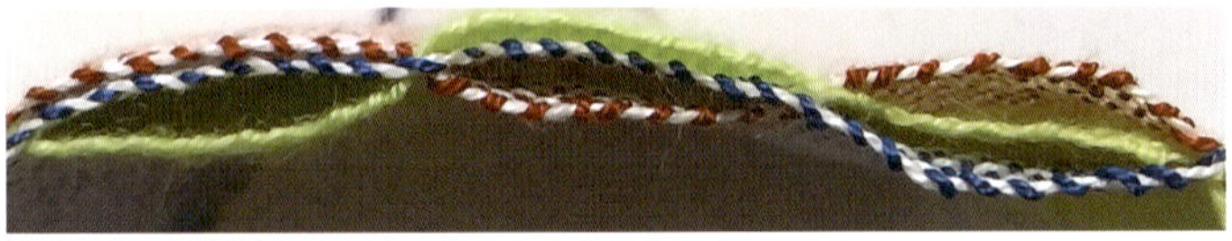

The side view shows the switching of layers.

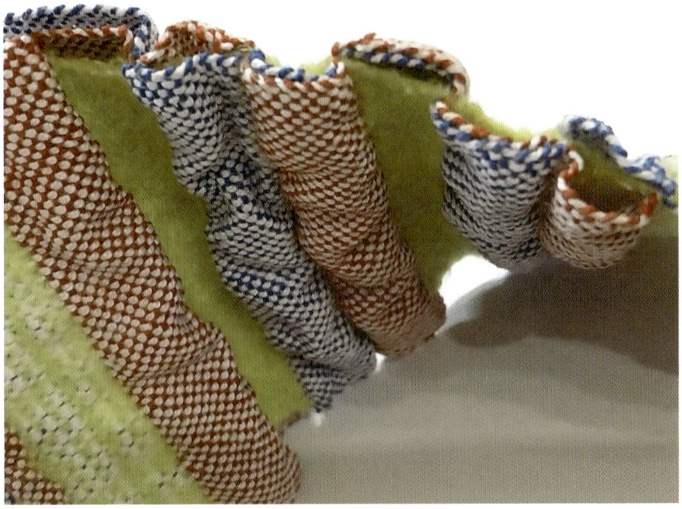

After finishing – the side view.

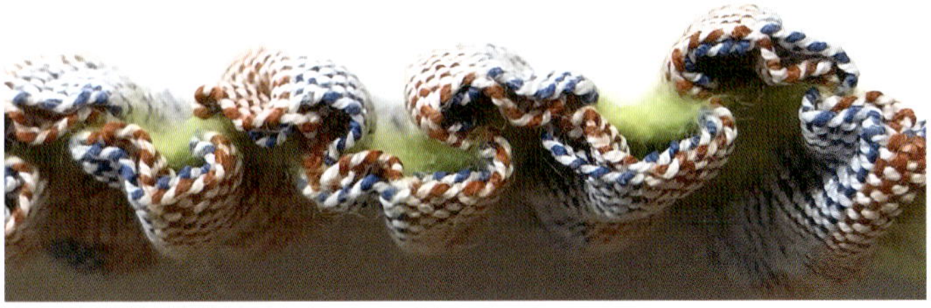

The side view after finishing.

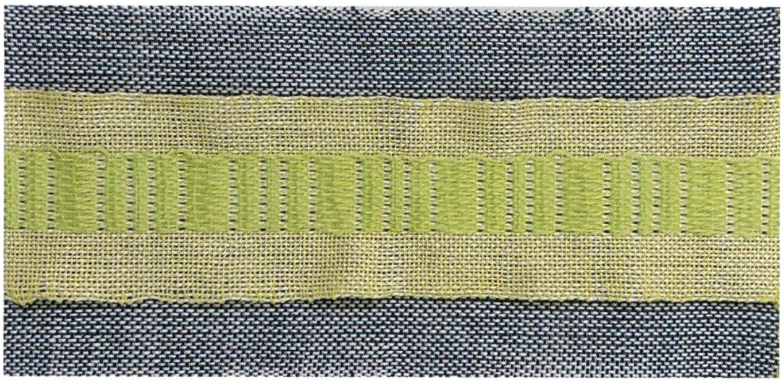

The three layers now have three distinct widths of cloth: the blue cotton being the widest, the yellow cotton narrower, and the green wool a warp stripe of 1in (2.5cm). The wool layer is interwoven with both cotton layers every four picks. It weaves with itself for two picks.

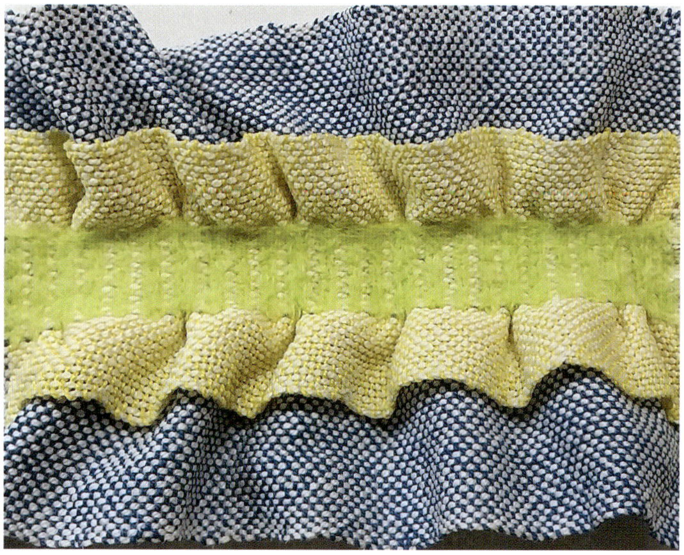

The front side after finishing.

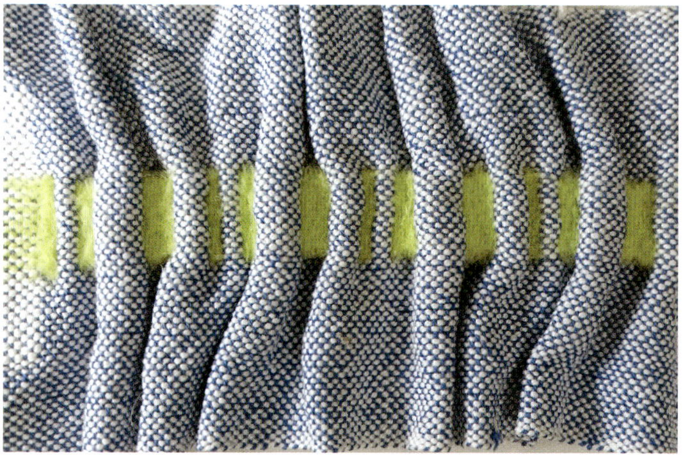

The reverse side after finishing.

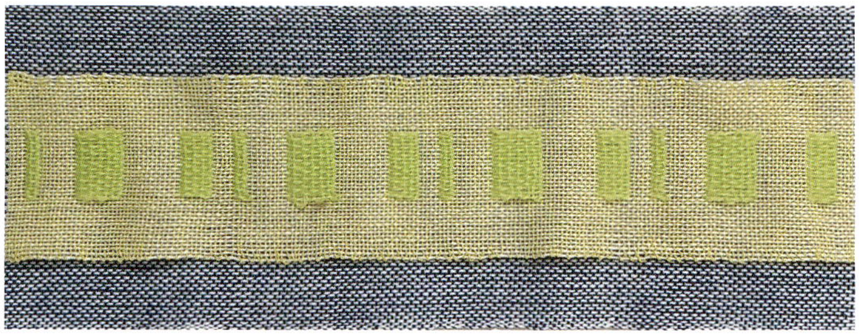

The wool has now been used to switch between weaving above or below the cotton layers. It does not interact them in any other way other than interchanging positions.

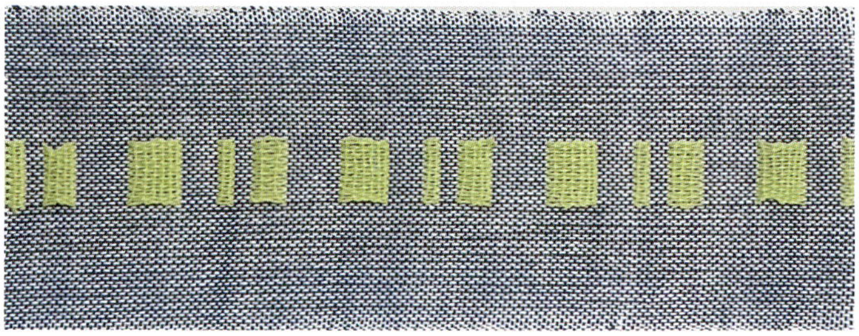

The reverse side is shown before finishing.

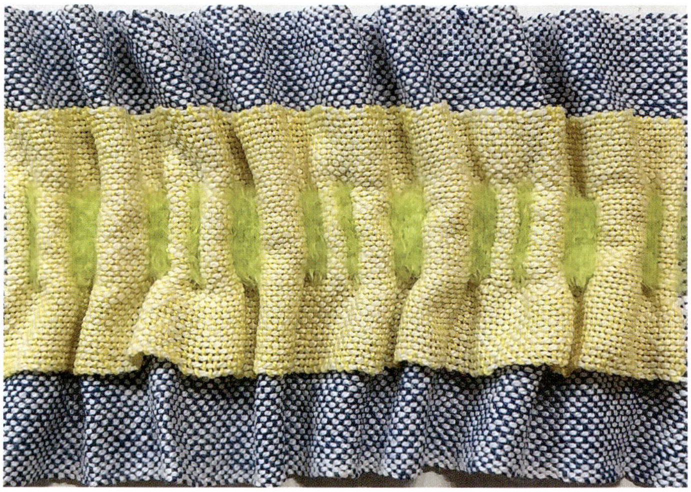

Here the wet-finishing has been done. This view is from the front side.

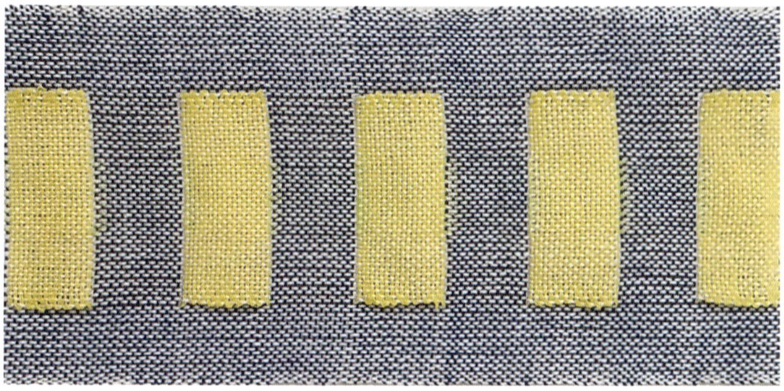

This time both sides mirror each other. The wool layer runs through the middle, regardless of which side the yellow warp is weaving.

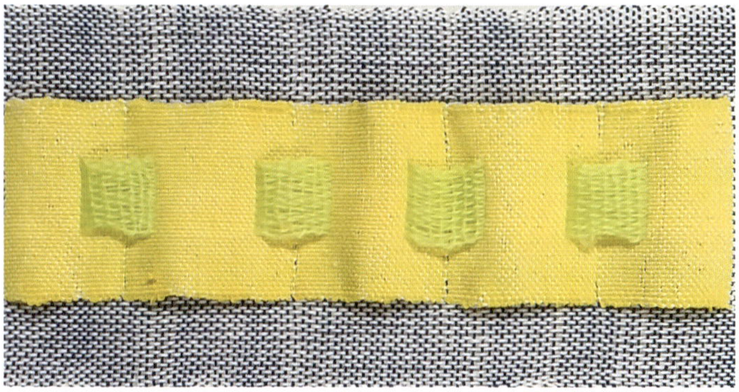

The wool layer interacts only with the yellow cotton layer, switching positions so that it weaves above or below the yellow layer. The yellow cotton stitches itself to the blue layer at the midpoint when the wool layer is floating above it.

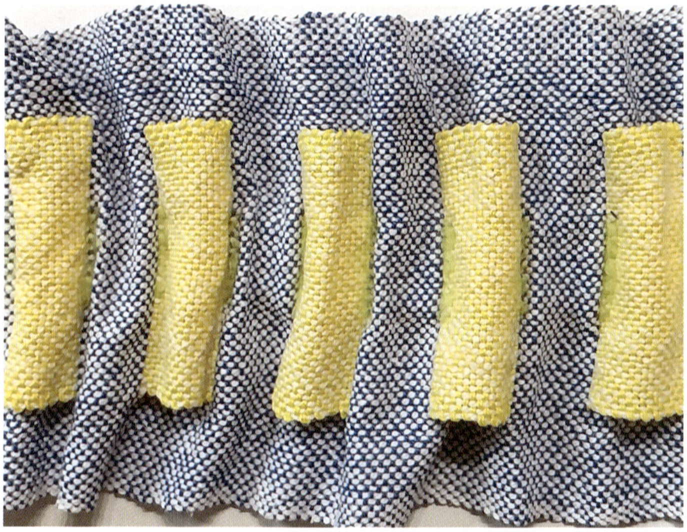

This is the result after finishing.

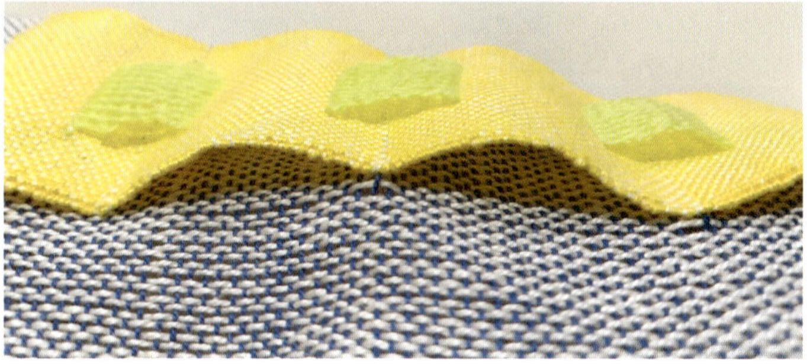

Before finishing, the side view shows the stitching (directly below the middle of the green wool layer when it is on the top) and the interaction of the wool layer with the yellow cotton layer.

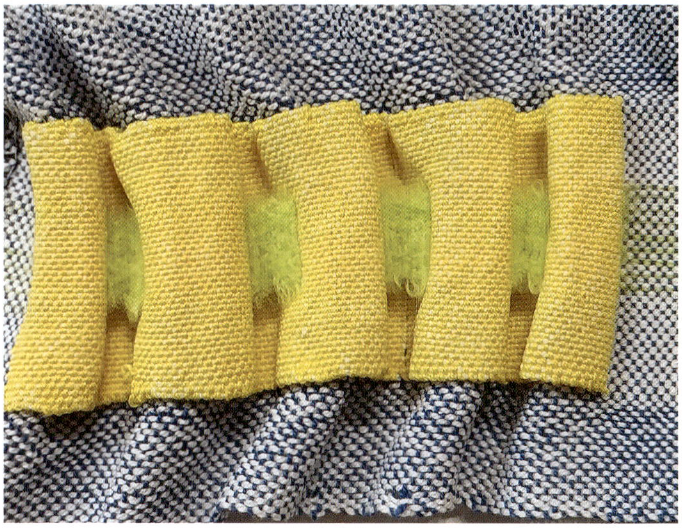

Here we see the result of wet-finishing.

Finishing

If using differential shrinkage with wool, then it is important to full well with lots of soap, heat and friction, especially if a wool layer is hidden between the outer passive layers.

However, if you are using firm yarns to create a sculptural effect that will be displayed and not worn, then depending on how you wish to display it, it might not require any wet-finishing at all. It might, however, require a little extra stiffening (*see* Chapter 14).

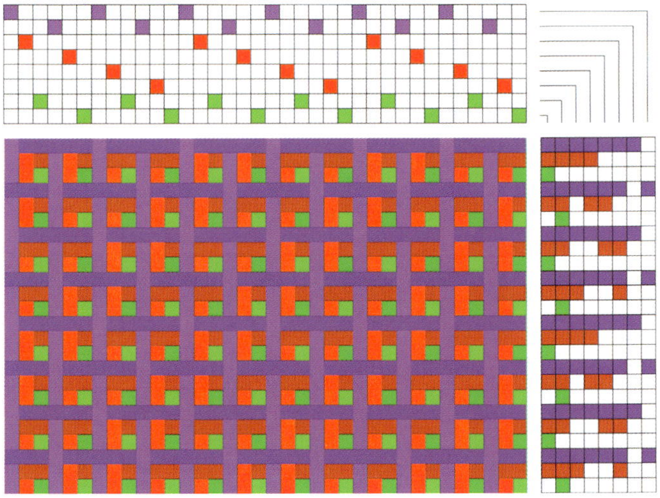

Triple cloth on eight shafts with shafts 1 & 2 for the top layer, shafts 3–6 for the middle layer and shafts 7 & 8 for the bottom layer. The first draft shows the liftplan for the back layer.

Eight Shafts

With eight shafts, triple or even quadruple layers are available. Using eight shafts for triple cloth, one layer could be a four-shaft twill weave, while the other two layers are plain weave.

Triple Cloth

These drafts again use wool in the triple cloth, with the wool layer being threaded on four shafts in the centre and two cotton layers of plain weave on either side.

Here the wool shafts are shown in red and the cotton layers in green and purple, but the shaft selection can be changed according to personal preferences.

As before, the weaving starts with the bottom layer, then the middle layer, then the top layer, so that each layer can be seen as it is woven. Four shafts have been selected for the active layer so that twills can be used. This will allow for greater shrinkage potential of the inner layer.

If a floating selvedge is used for all yarns, the yarns will interact at the selvages. Using differential shrinkage, this will allow for weft-wise shrinkage for all layers in the cloth as well as warp-wise shrinkage. If the separate layers are completely self-contained by eliminating any floating selvage and the layers only woven with their respective wefts, then only the woollen element will shrink. This will generate some ruffling in the warp direction.

One or more of the internal shafts can also connect with the two outer layers – a technique known as stitching, which is discussed in detail in Chapter 10.

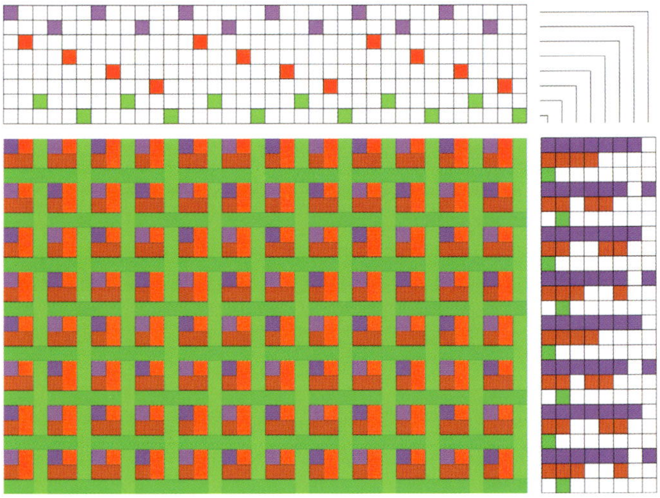

This draft shows the top view. The inner layer cannot be seen separately in the draft, but with the draft exploded, all three layers can be visualised.

TOP TIP

Multi-layer fabrics do not have to use differential shrinkage.

Another triple layer effect uses two outer layers with three-end weave structures, while the middle layer weaves plain weave.

The shaft arrangement can be rearranged as desired, as we saw for six shafts.

Again, if differential shrinkage is required in both directions for all layers, this is only possible if a floating selvage is employed for all wefts or at least one shuttle is used for two layers.

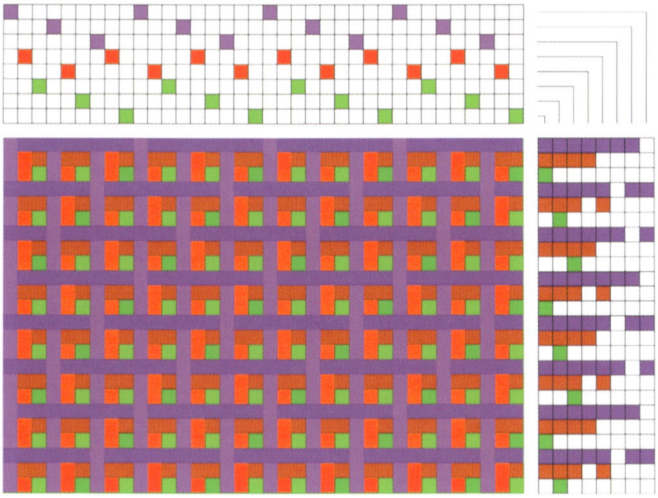

In this version, the two outer layers use three shafts each and the inner layer weaves plain weave on two shafts, showing both sides of the cloth. The first draft shows the underneath layer.

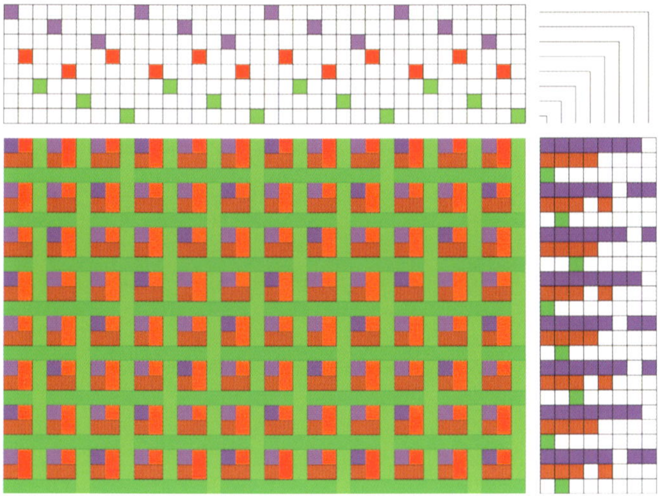

The top layer is shown here.

Triple layers can be woven with multiple shafts, and many effects created. Paulien van Asperen takes the op-art world of Yaacov Agam's three-dimensional *Polymorph* series, and Carlos Cruz-Diez's *Physichromie* work as inspiration and turns it into multi-shaft dimensional wall pieces.

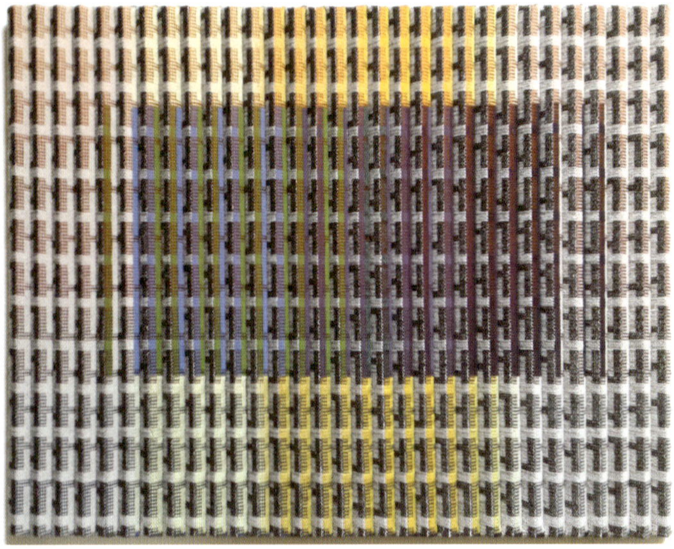

Agam-O-Weave by Paulien van Asperen was inspired by Yaacov Agam's dimensional painted pieces, which are comprised of painted slats set in Λ on a board. Two designs are created: slices of one design on one side of the angled slat, slices of the other on the opposing angle of the slat. When viewed head-on as a normal art piece, the two works combine at an angle to give a melange – neither one thing nor the other, but hints of both. (Photos: Paulien van Asperen)

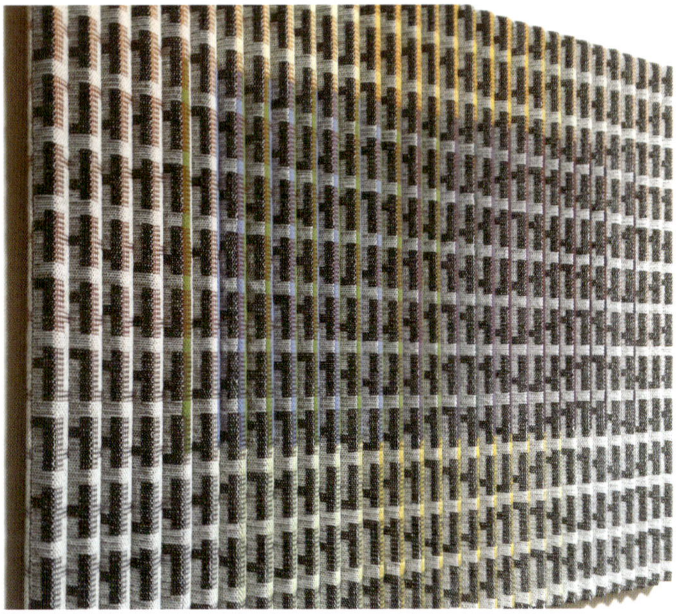

When viewed from one side of the work, one image appears.

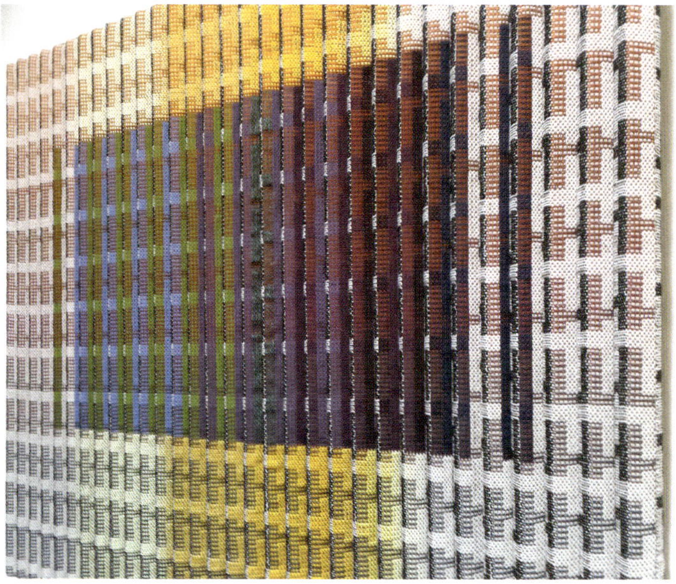

Viewing from the other side of the work reveals the second image.

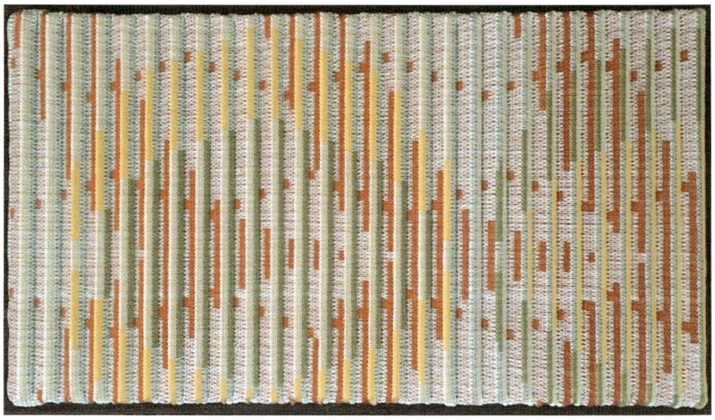

A more recent piece is *Point of View*. (Photos: Paulien van Asperen)

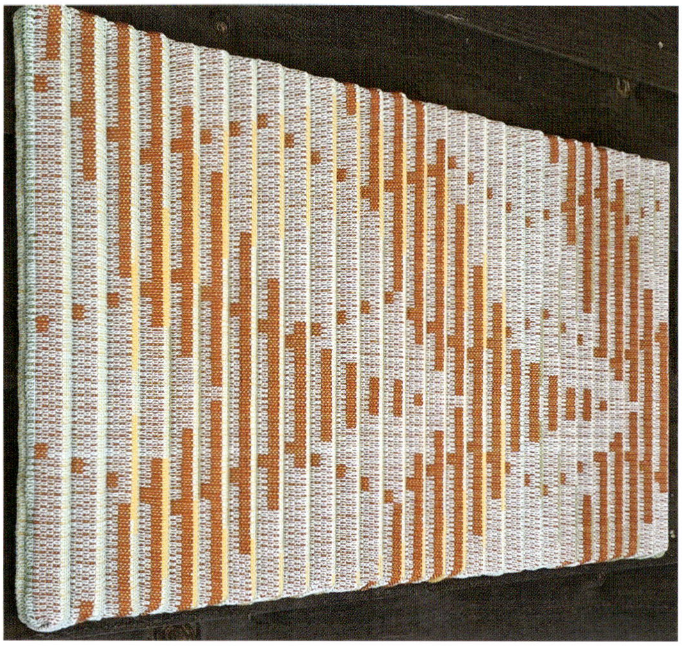

Side view from the left.

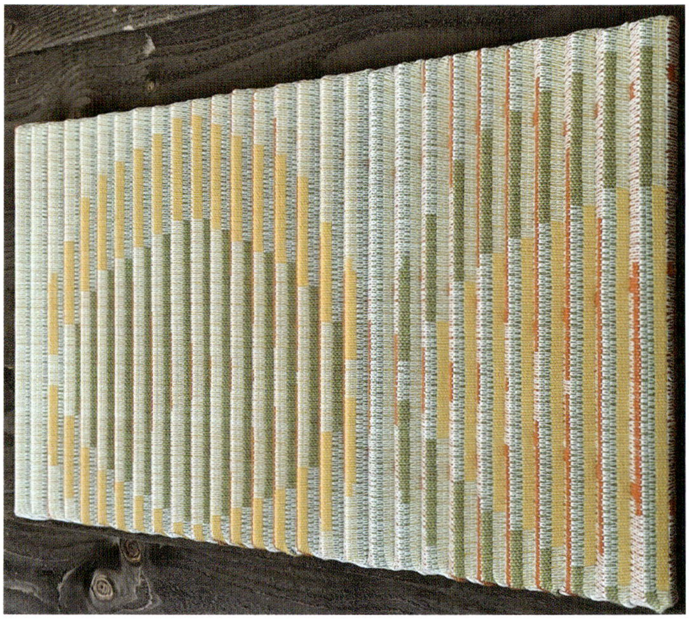

Side view from the right.

Four Layer Weaving: Quadruple (Quad) Cloth

With quadruple cloth, plain weave is used for each of the four layers, using the same process as described for three layers, swapping the four wefts around between the different warps but also switching the four layers into different positions in the stack, changing which one is top, upper middle, lower middle or bottom.

The main thing to remember is which layer order you want. It is helpful to start weaving with the bottom layer so that you can see what you are doing there, then weave the next layer up, and the next and finally the top layer. This way you will be removing shafts for each layer, and it becomes easier to think about. But it does not matter if you choose to start with the top layer and work down, adding

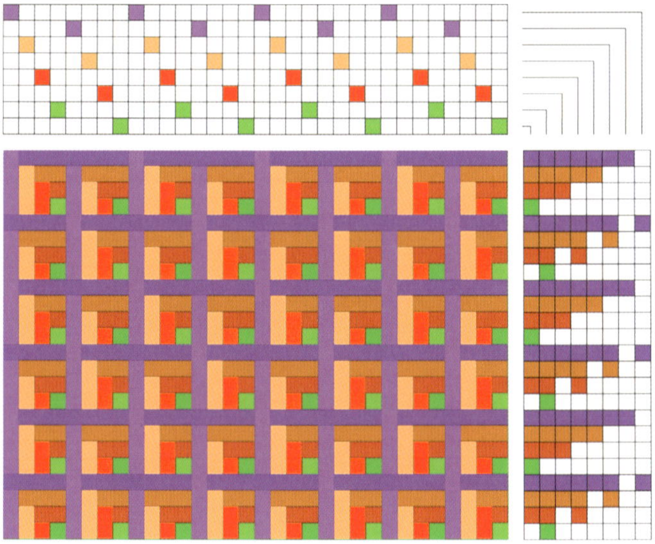

Quadruple cloth on eight shafts with shafts 1 & 2 as the top layer, 3 & 4 as layer two, 5 & 6 as layer three, and 7 & 8 as the bottom layer. As before, we start weaving with the bottom layer. The bottom of the two middle layers (orange warp/ brown weft) can be seen just below the purple layer.

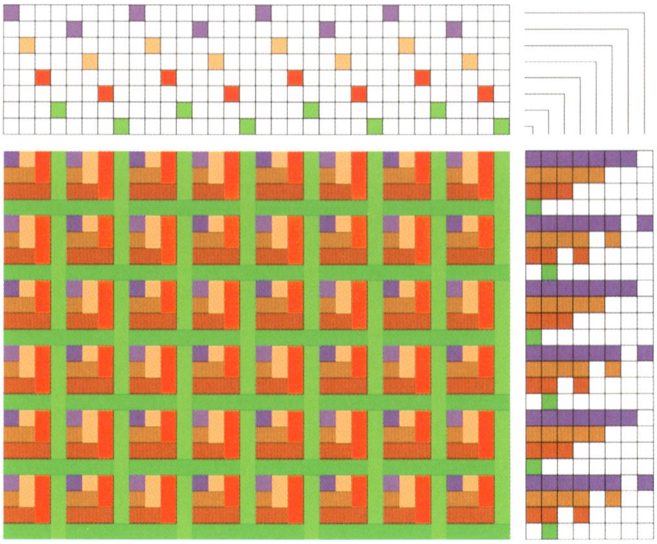

The top view shows the green layer on the top. Just below that is the red second layer.

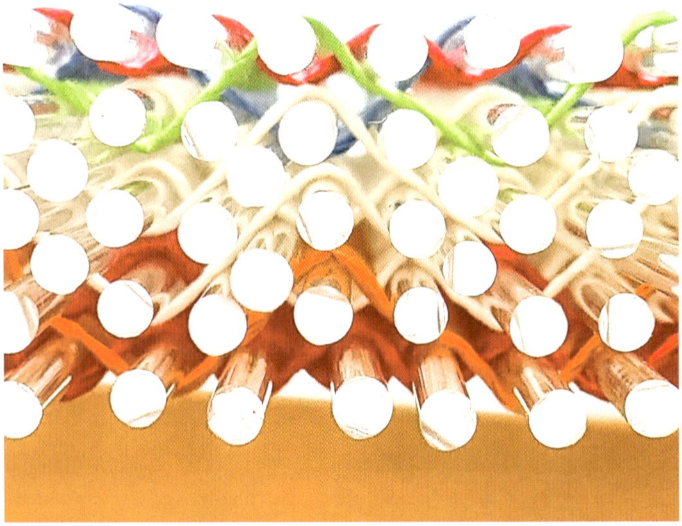

Melanie Olde uses acrylic rods as wefts to show how the different warps move from one layer to another in multiple layers. (Photos: Melanie Olde)

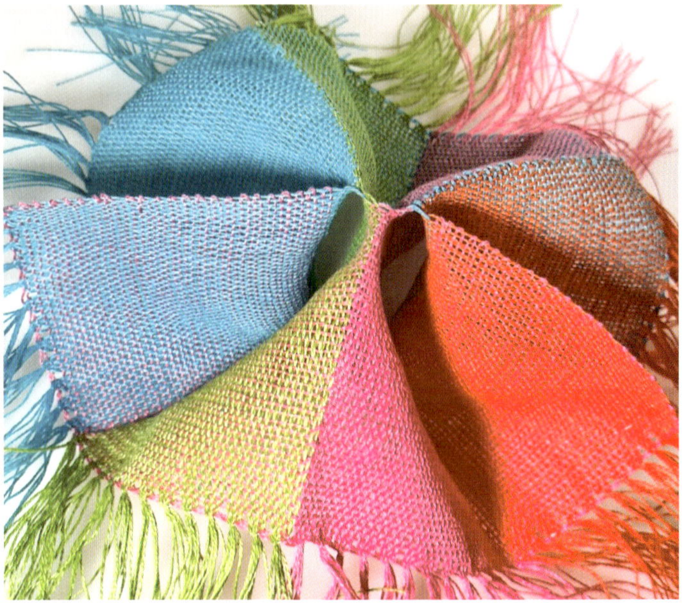

This sample shows four layers on eight shafts designed for a workshop on 3D by Melanie.

shafts to the mix. Whatever works for you is the method to use.

Once the principles behind the layer switching are understood, many variations on the theme are possible, creating interesting artwork. Material properties can be brought into the mix to give incredibly varied results.

Active yarns can be used for any of the layers, creating differential shrinkage elements.

Alternatively, all layers can be passive yarns.

Using translucent and semi-opaque yarns, shadow play can be introduced, as illustrated by the amazing ephemeral hanging sculptures of Kay Sekimachi. This body

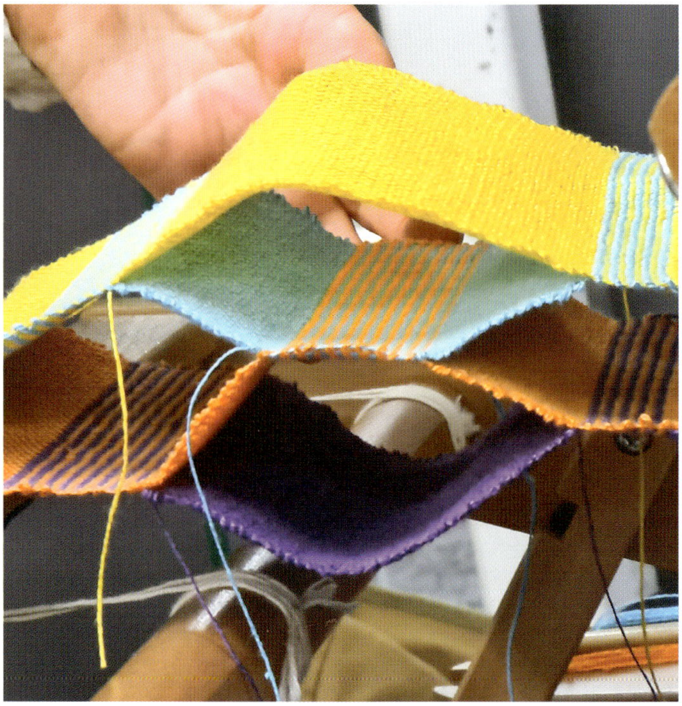

Student work in one of Melanie's workshops, showing how different layers meet, combine and separate.

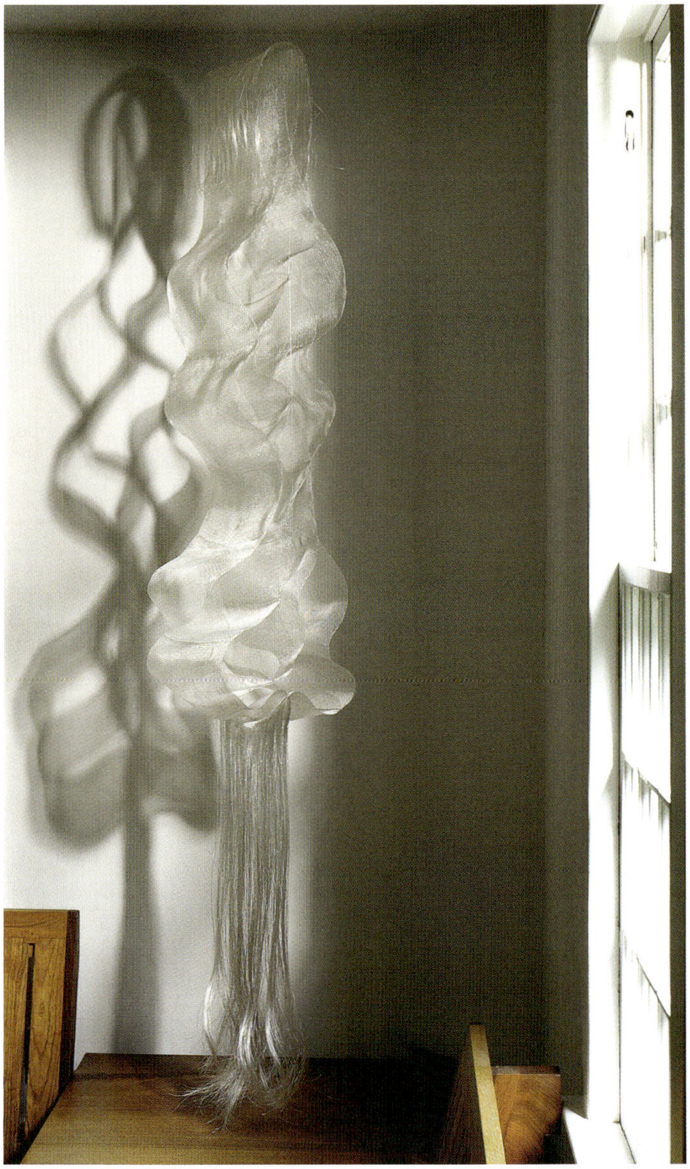

The shadow effects created by *Ogawa II* in this image show the play of light and shade, transparency and translucence. (Photo: Tom Grotta)

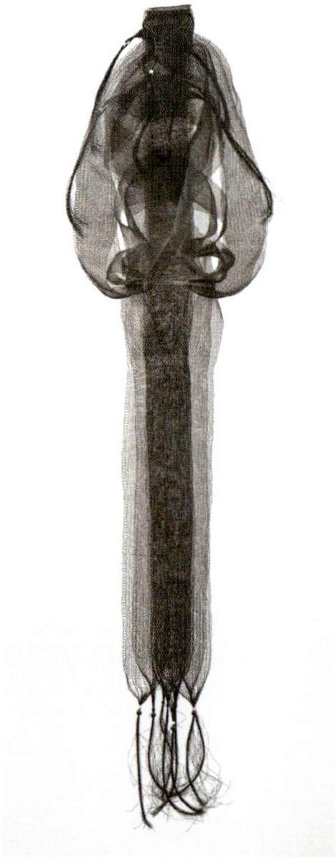

Kay Sekimachi has woven many wonderful multi-layer pieces like this and was a pioneer in developing weaving as a sculptural form in this way. Monofilament is the yarn of her choice for these diaphanous works. *Untitled Monofilament*. (Photo: Tom Grotta)

of work influenced many weavers in the 1970s and beyond as it brought a completely different aspect of woven art to the public eye. The finished work can be pulled up to give drape on the multi-layers to achieve the Kay Sekimachi look.

Melanie Olde is inspired by plant growth patterns to create very interesting pieces, branching and morphing into different sculptural forms with monofilament.

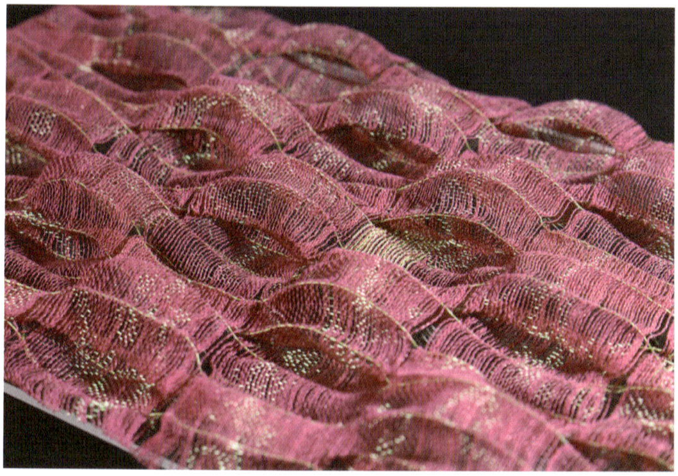

Melanie Olde explores the algorithms of growth in plants in this piece called *Hexagon Cellular Symmetry 1*, investigating continuous hexagonal structures within the weft-wise depth of the fabric. Materials are silk, stainless steel and nylon monofilament. (Photos: Melanie Olde)

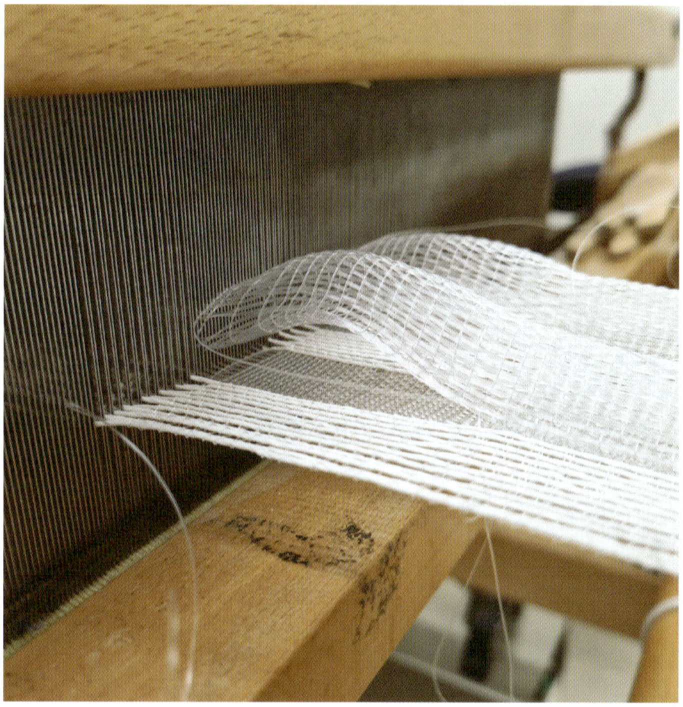

The materials are nylon monofilament, paper and silicon tubing.

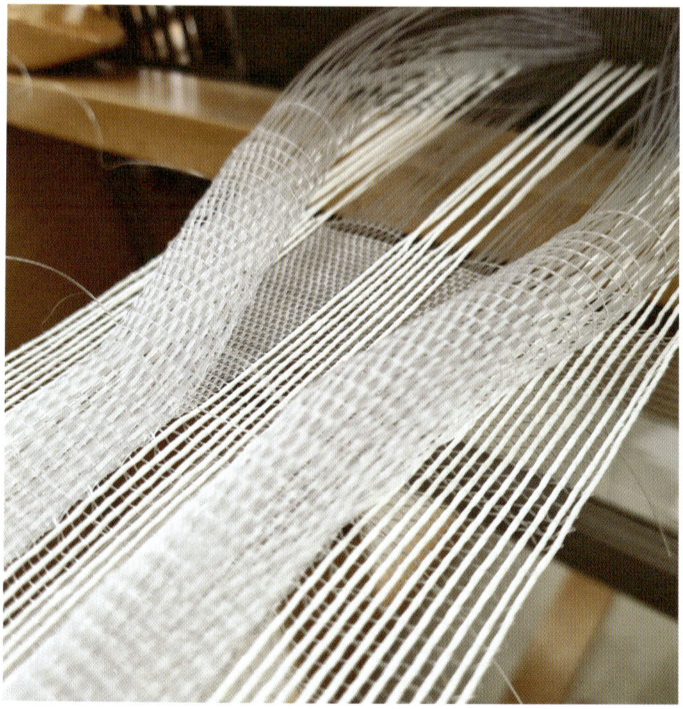

Recent work on Melanie's loom includes these multi-layer pieces that incorporate tubular monofilament forms in conjunction with paper warp, which seem to have a life of their own even while on the loom. These experiments investigate different ways to create warp-wise tubes that can be used as a gripping mechanism. Tests for their active potential involve integrating a pneumatic system in woven tubes that are connected and disconnected from the ground fabric.

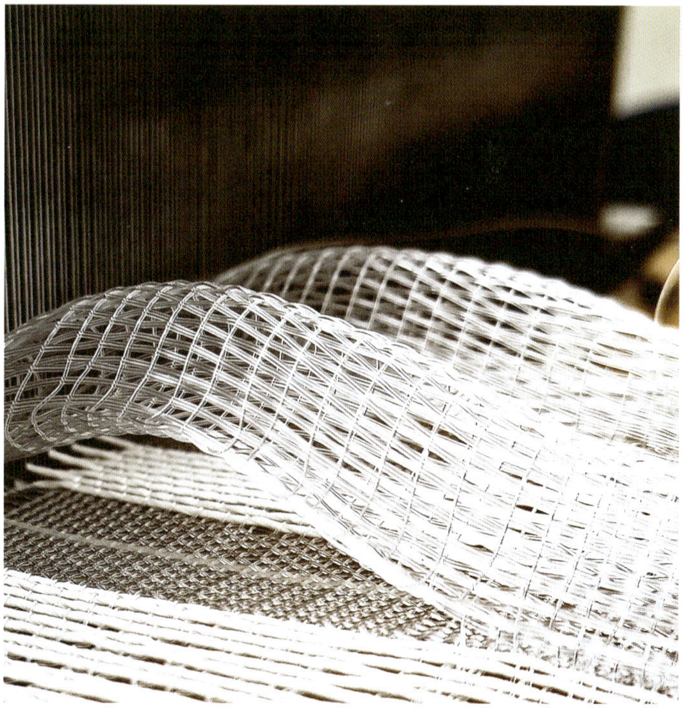

Detail.

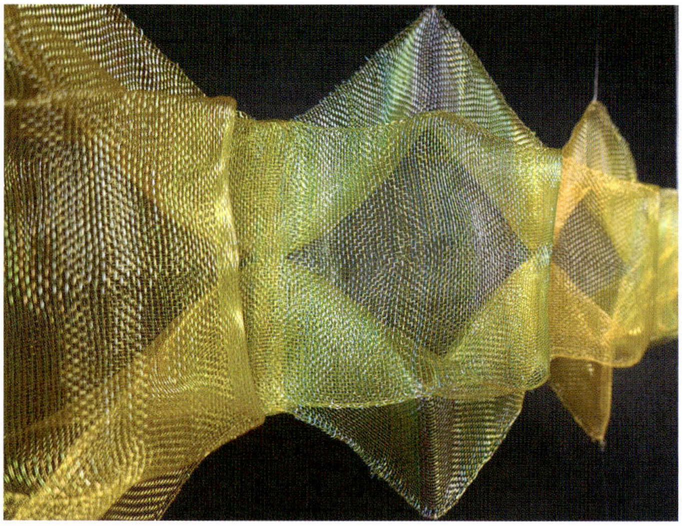

Morphology I, again by Melanie, is inspired by natural plant algorithms and auxetic geometries (shapes that expand in one axis when stretched in another). The colour changes are based on algal growth patterns and are woven in nylon monofilament. This complex piece includes the auxetic modules and concentric tubes, as well as golden ratios. The honeycomb structure must be woven in its collapsed form to activate correctly, which involves five layers controlled in two blocks.

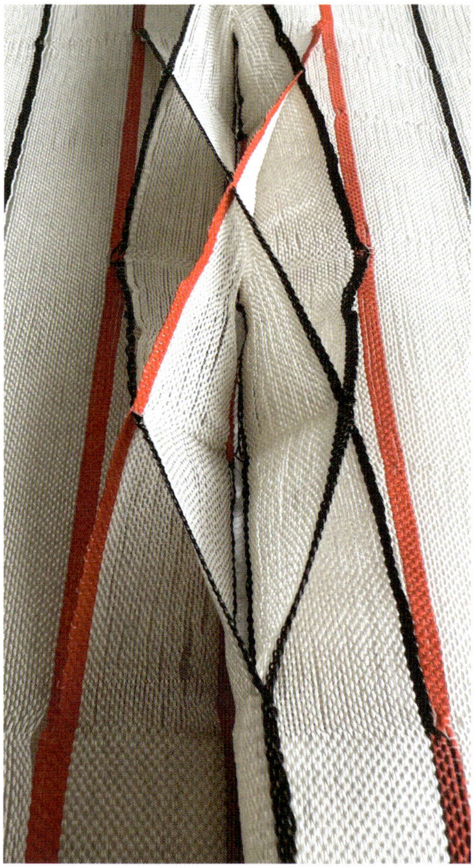

A different view of the piece helps visualise how the geometry was achieved.

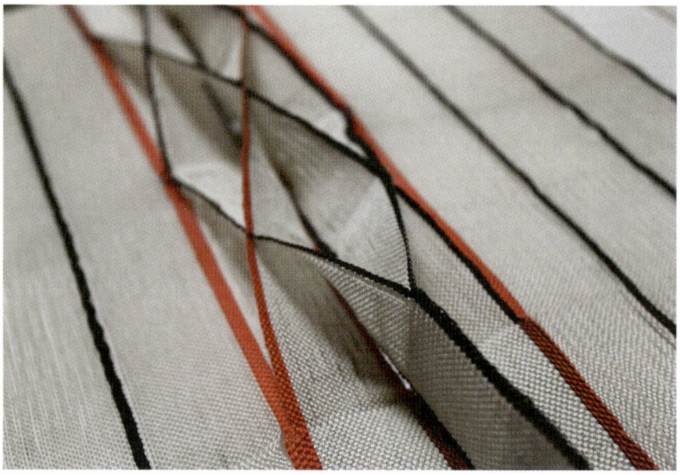

Pop Out, by Lucy Smyth, is woven on 24 shafts and is six layers in the central section. The warp is silk and the weft monofilament.

Monofilament and silk are the yarns of choice for a sample by Lucy Smyth that includes a central multi-layer section with single cloth on either side. Multi-layers give a smorgasbord of methods and combinations that can be explored.

Inclusions

With enough shafts and different double cloth elements, inclusions can be added. These are hard or more flexible additions that can be inserted into a double layer before the layer is closed in order to stiffen a particular area. They are often used to create a solid sculptural effect, as was demonstrated in Susie Taylor's work at the beginning of this chapter.

Thought has to be given as to if and how inclusions can traverse the front beam and go around the cloth beam, depending on the characteristics of both the choice of inclusion and also the loom being used. Solid plastic insertions may have to be fitted after the work is removed from the loom, resulting in weaving open sides to the area, which have to be hand-stitched closed after insertion.

For looms that have cloth storage to the rear, this might not be such an issue once the shaped fabric is safely round

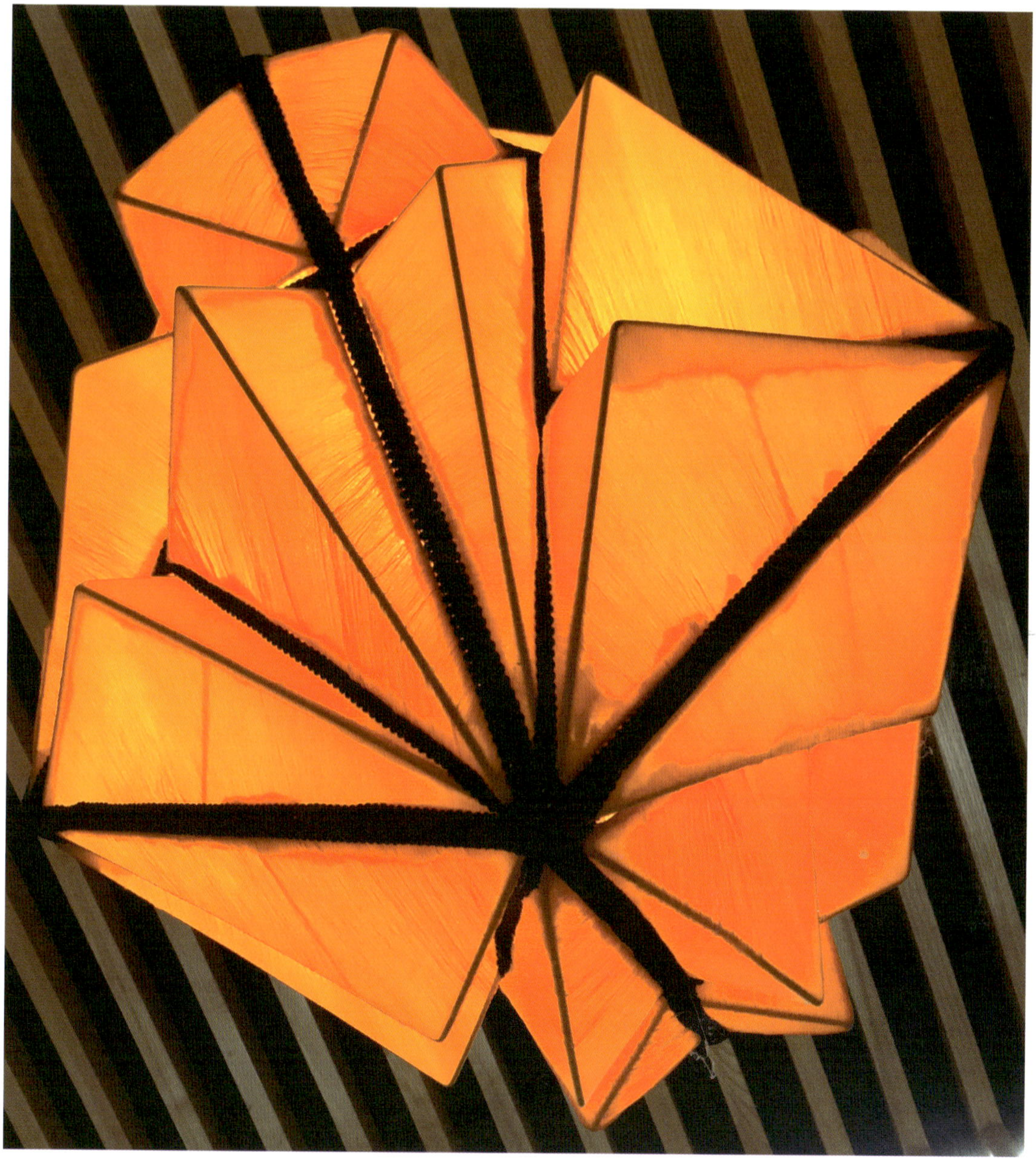

Inspiration for multi-faceted multi-layer weaving from a restaurant light-fitting.

the breast beam. However, if the cloth storage is at the front of the loom, a more experimental method has been suggested for shorter warps of suspending the woven cloth from the front of the loom using weights rather than being taken up by the cloth beam. The warp is attached to the cloth beam as usual through tying or lashing, but when a suitable length of fabric has been woven, the fabric can then be weighted at the front of the loom.

Soft and hard inclusions and coatings are discussed further in Chapter 14.

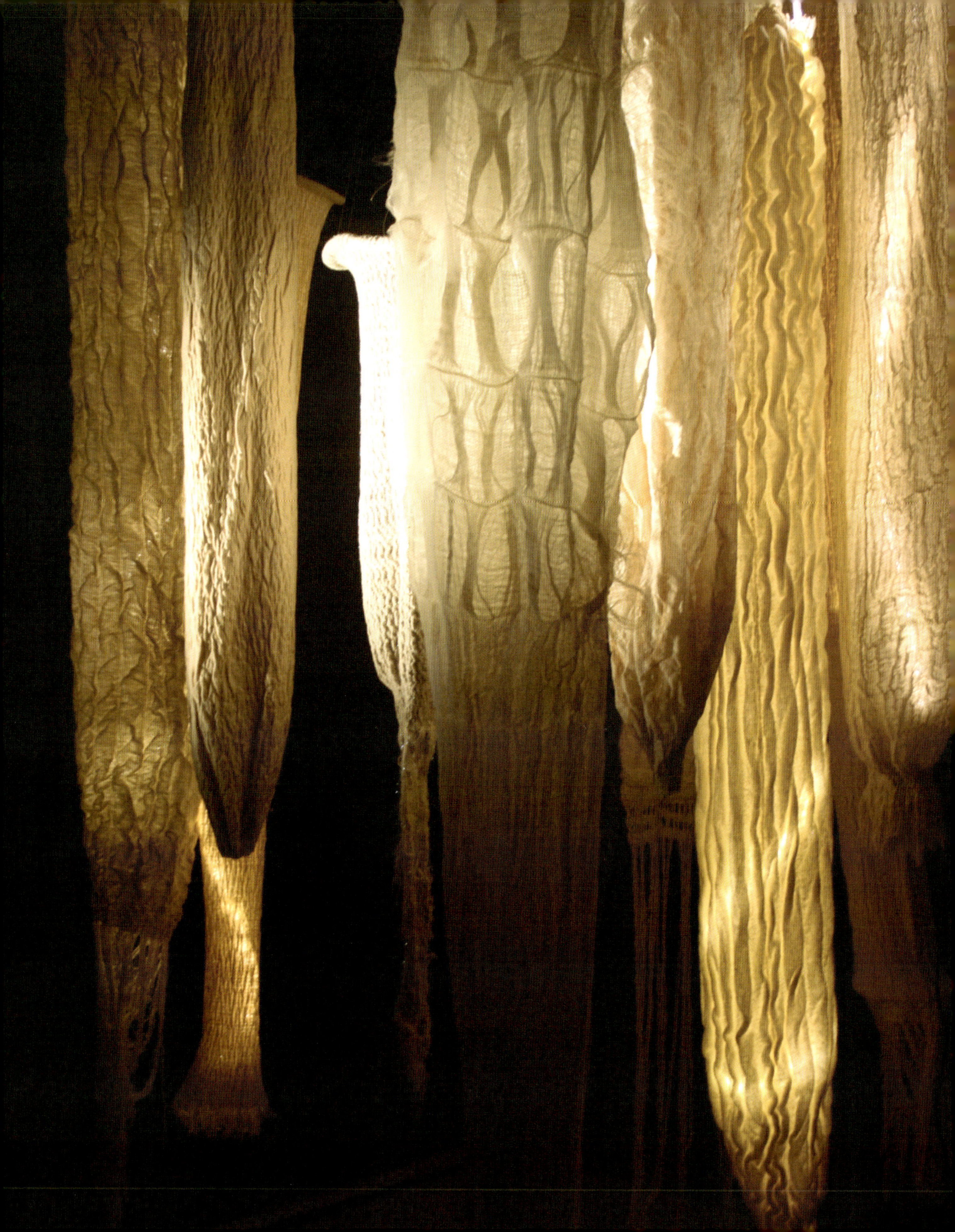

CHAPTER 13

TUBULAR

At first glance, tubular weaving might seem a rather odd thing to do, but there is a reason that this is the largest chapter in the book! The more you dive into it, the more possibilities emerge, and it takes on amazing forms and constructions. The principles are simple, but the variations are huge. It can be used for garments, accessories (collars, snoods, cowls, shrugs), lighting, cushions, hanging sculptures, standing sculptures, exploring geometries, moving from closed tubes to double width to separate layers, to multiple tubes alongside or on top of each other, and – as seen in the previous chapter with Melanie Olde's work – in combination with a ground layer.

Material properties play an integral and versatile role, changing the appearance and quality of a piece simply by the wefts chosen. Many tubular forms can be illuminated from within. With LEDs this is now possible without the fear of fire or overheating. This chapter cannot cover everything that tubular weaving offers, but it will provide solid principles to guide the curious weaver and a wealth of ideas to stimulate the creative mind.

Materials

Surface dimension can be introduced by varying the yarns selected. As we have seen, although plain weave is not the only weave structure available, depending on the number of available shafts, it is the most accessible and also one of the most effective for creating dimensional results.

Warp stripes in yarns that react differently during wet-finishing will give a rippled surface dimension to the tube. Wool and cotton or wool and silk warp stripes, for example, would give effective results. Weft rippling can be introduced by using weft stripes in the same active and passive yarns. Overtwisted yarns as opposed to fulling or elasticated yarns would give other variations. All can be explored, even with four shafts.

GENERAL PRINCIPLES

If you can weave two separate layers, then you can weave a tube. While a double width cloth is two layers woven with the weft progressing in a C-shape (i.e. top, bottom, bottom, top), tubular weaving is two layers woven with the weft progressing in an O shape. It doesn't even need two wefts.

The same main principles of sett and materials behind multi-layer weaving are applicable to tubular weaving, especially when going beyond simple tubes, but tubular weaving is not as difficult as it might sound. The most basic definition is a double cloth with joined selvedges. Therefore, the basic premise is that the sett is a double plain; in other words, twice the usual sett for a plain weave on a single cloth for the yarn being used. When weaving tubes, special care needs to be taken with the selvedges.

Draw-in

In essence, there are no selvedges on a tube. However, because they are woven in two layers, there are two edges to the warp. As is usual with weaving in general, selvedges tend to become a little closer when woven. To guard against that in tubular weaving, the last few threads on either side have to be spread out and fewer ends placed in each dent.

Illuminating tubular forms can work effectively, whether in a group or individually as a lamp or a lighting fixture.

This is usually done by halving the number of ends in each of the last few dents on either side of the warp, and possibly reducing that even more for the last two dents. Close attention to this is required while weaving to ensure the selvedges are not compressed, as that will lead to abrasion and broken ends on the selvedges and create a tight vertical line in two places in the tube, which is probably not what is desired.

One suggestion is to add floating selvedges on either side of the warp, leaving one empty dent between the fabric and the selvedge. The weft will have a little longer path to go around the edge of the tube, allowing room for the warp ends to spread after removing from the loom. Use a slightly thicker shiny yarn for the two floating selvedges. They are not required for the finished project and will fall away from the fabric after weaving, as they do not interact with the warp and their function is purely to help ensure that the edges are spaced accurately.

In addition to opening out the sleying three or four dents from the selvedge on either side, it is also useful to pull off enough weft from the shuttle prior to throwing the shuttle. This will ensure that the selvedge is not pulled in during the passage of the weft through the shed.

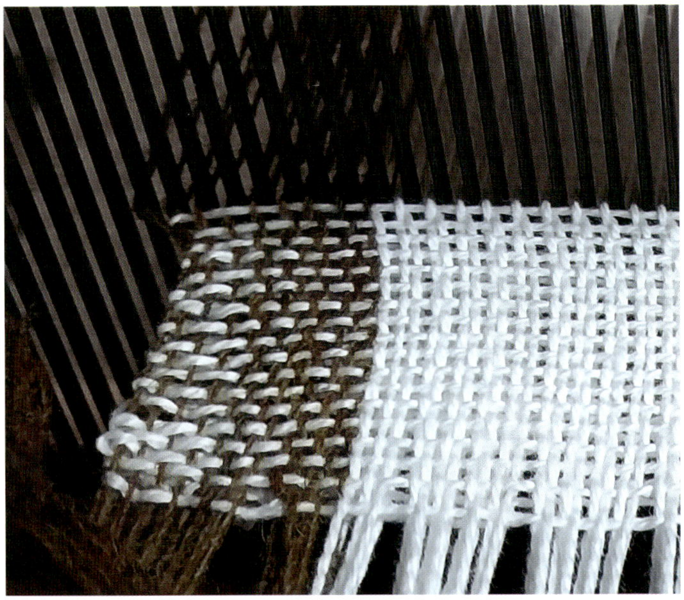

When sleying for tubular weaving, it is useful to spread the last few ends of the selvedge over more dents. Here the last four ends of the brown are spread out as one end per dent over four dents, rather than the two ends per dent of the rest of the warp. This is useful for the fold selvedge if you are weaving double width as well.

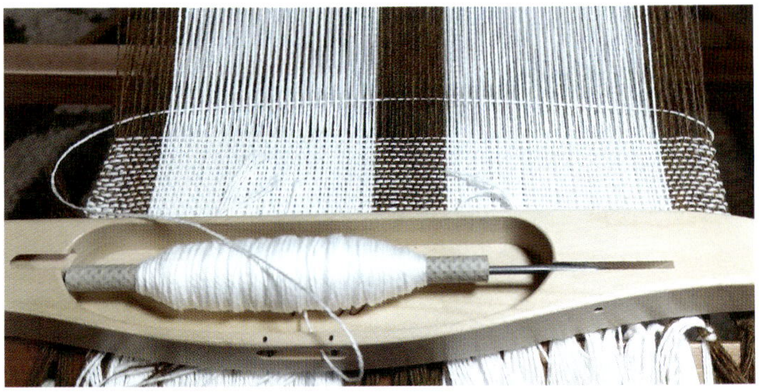

The first pick is woven (on the top layer here), but not beaten.

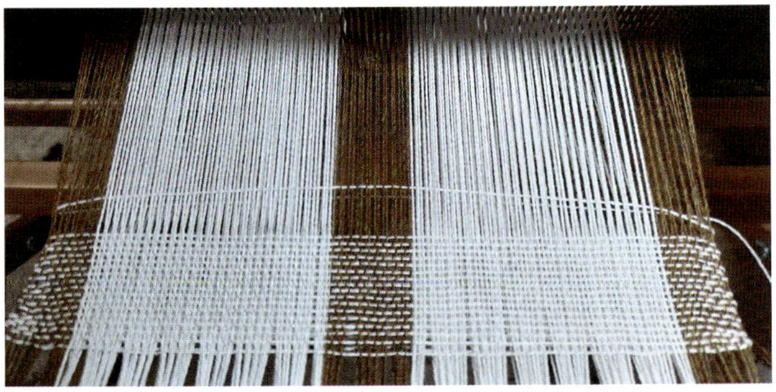

The second pick (on the bottom layer) is woven.

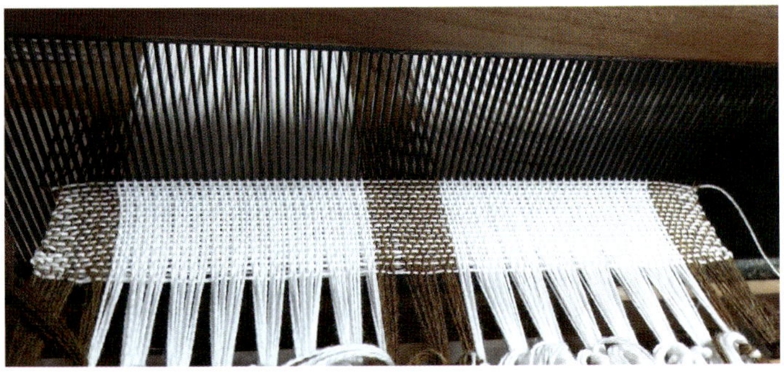

The beater brings both picks to the fell at the same time and with the same spacing. It is important to ensure that the beater is as close to perpendicular to the warp as possible for this to happen.

It can also be useful to weave both the top and its corresponding bottom layer picks before beating so that the two picks are beaten together in alignment, but this might impact the curvature around the selvedges.

A great deal depends on the weft yarn being used for the tube. The softer the yarn, the easier it is to pull too tightly at the selvedge and to lose evenness around the curve between layers.

Conversely, the stiffer the yarn, such as metals and some stiffer linens or paper, the more likely that the selvedges

TOP TIP

Careful observation is required in both weaving and wet-finishing to calculate the required amount of curvature for the weft yarn being used. Sample practice weaving is recommended.

TOP TIP

'Selfie' mode on a mobile phone can also be useful to check the underside of your weaving.

are going to be too loose. The aforementioned suggestions regarding spacing the selvedges might not be applicable as the yarn itself creates the curvature. Beating on the open shed might help with this as the selvedge can be watched closely as the new pick meets the fell to avoid the weft bulging out at the turn of the selvedge.

When weaving with medium or thick paper or metal yarns, the difficulty of bulging wefts is compounded as the weaving progresses. There is a tendency for the passage of the fabric over the front beam moving onto the cloth beam to squash the curve around the selvedges – something that has to be carefully reinstated after removing from the loom. It is possible to insert some padding between the layers of the tube to help reduce this, but it doesn't remove the problem entirely.

Metal wefts can also fold at the selvedge rather than gently curve, especially when finer gauges are used. This can be difficult to reinstate after removing from the loom.

Very shiny weft yarns, such as metal and monofilament, can lead to a shifting of the warp yarns during wet-finishing and a 'blooming' of the weft, especially at the selvedges, as the warps slide towards and away from each other across the slippery weft.

Beating Up

Much of the information that follows relates equally to double cloth weaving in general, but because a tube is seen from all sides, it has been included here.

When weaving a tube, rather than 'beating', it is more useful to think of 'placing' the beater against the fell, with more or less pressure depending on the desired result.

Applying even pressure on the beater is important, as well as good practice. Either use one hand in the middle of the beater if the piece is narrower, or both hands evenly spaced across the width of the weaving. This is especially important for lighter-built looms such as table looms, which may have a little flexibility in the beater top.

Be consistent with the pressure applied as the beater contacts the fell, unless you have specifically planned a crammed and spaced effect, or an irregular beat design.

Be aware of the angle of the beater when it comes into contact with the fell. It needs to be as close to upright – perpendicular to the warp – as possible. Sliding beaters are best for this. However, if the loom has an overhung or underslung beater, move the weaving on in small and regular increments so that variations in beat are minimised. This can vary from top to bottom of the fabric, depending on the action of the beater. Every loom has a 'sweet spot' where the weaving is as consistent as possible. Try to stay within this area when weaving. If the loom has a beater with several possible positions (a feature often found in overhung beaters on floor looms), then this is a good option if consistency in beat can be maintained.

Check the Underside of the Weaving

As you will be aware by now, the underside of the bottom layer is as important as the top of the top layer. Both will be seen by a viewer once the piece is off the loom. To that end, it is important to regularly check the quality of weaving on the underside of the piece. It is so difficult to be aware of all the interlacements when you cannot see what is happening, and errant warp or weft threads can easily occur, as can irregular beating. Therefore it is a good idea to have a mirror on the table (for a table loom) or on your lap (if that is feasible). Where it is not practical to have a mirror in situ, keep one close by so that you can keep checking on the accuracy of the weaving on the bottom layer. If you have difficulty in seeing what is going on, try covering the top layer with a cloth or a hand to cut out the light coming from above.

Moving the Warp On

As a double layer tube is wound on (in fact any multi-layer fabric that does not have regular interchanges of layers), the two layers will not take the same path around the breast beam. The one on top will move further than the one

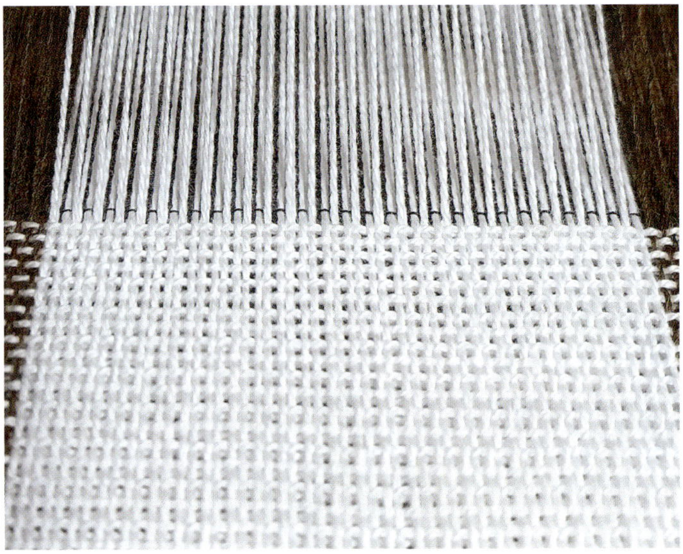

A connecting pick can be very useful to help alleviate any 'creeping' of one of the warps. A very fine supplementary weft can be used. Loops left between each connecting pick help with the removal of this weft after removing from the loom.

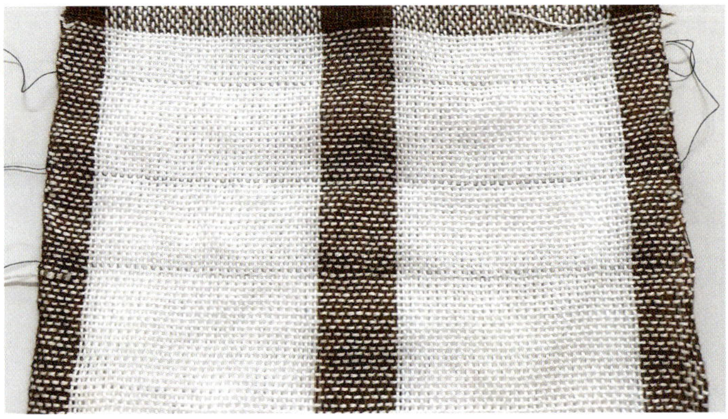

The finished sample shows the connecting picks ready to be removed.

underneath. The same principles apply as for car wheels when turning a corner – the wheel on the outer side of the corner travels a greater distance than the one on the inside of the curve.

There is a simple remedy when weaving – to insert an extra pick of really fine and slippery yarn at a regular interval, which combines the two layers together. For instance, on a warp where one layer is threaded on shafts 1 & 2, and the other on 3 & 4, after 1in (2.5cm) of weaving the two layers, add a very fine pick of silk or similar smooth yarn, lifting shafts 1 & 3 together. Then continue as normal with the main weft weaving the two layers in the tube. After another 1in (2.5cm), weave another very fine silk pick on shafts 2 & 4. Continue in this way for the length of the tube.

As the cloth is wound on around the breast beam, the two layers are linked as one and will not shift in relation to each other. The only drawback to this is that a separate weft occasionally joining the two layers makes it more difficult to ascertain if an errant end from one layer has got caught in with the other layer.

If padding is inserted to prevent squashing of the weft, it is worth considering that an occasional hand-stitched connection using a darning needle between top and bottom layers through the padding will help to keep the two sides of the tube parallel to each other.

DESIGNING TUBULAR CLOTH

The basic premise of designing tubular drafts is that the wrap-around edges of the two layers have to be carefully planned to ensure that one follows on from the other, which necessitates a bit of spatial thinking.

It also changes the direction of the threading on the reverse side. In regular double weave, you are viewing the two fabrics from either one side or the other.

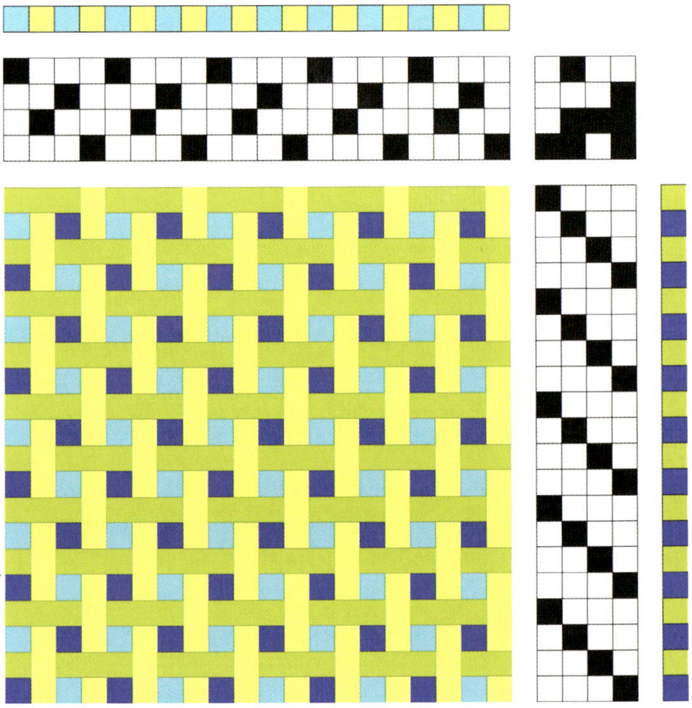

A regular double cloth on four shafts, front. Different colours have been used for both front and back warps and wefts for consistency throughout this chapter because of what needs to be done later in the tubular draft planning.

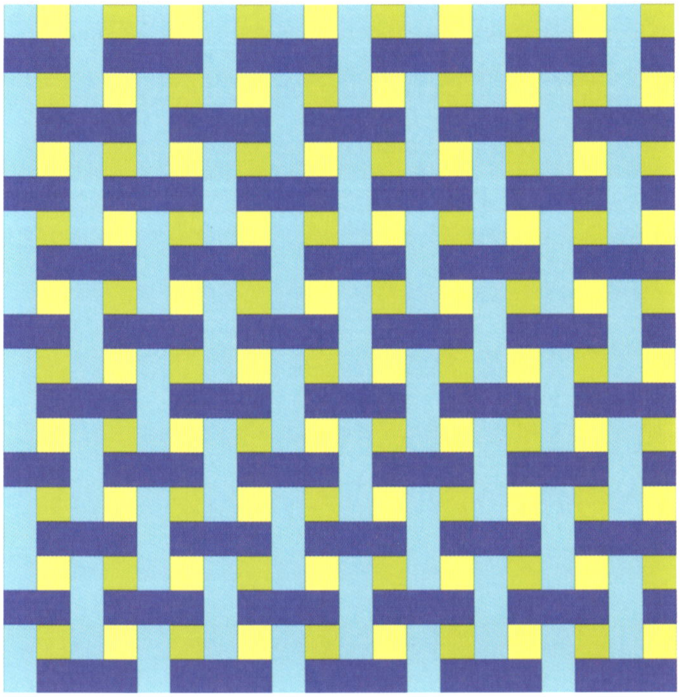

The reverse shows the darker blue weft weaving with the light blue layer on the back.

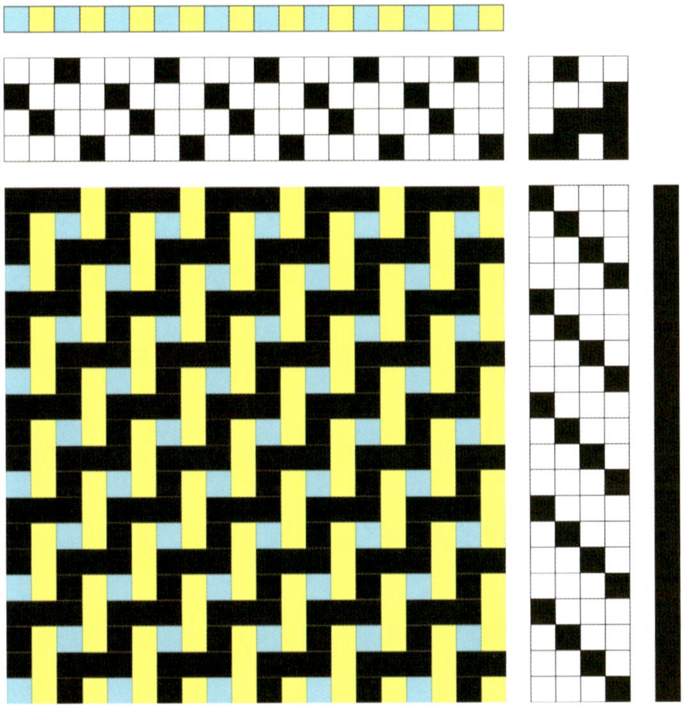

Look closely at the threading draft and the reverse side compared to the previous example. The second layer has switched its order. Think about walking around a tube hanging suspended. The surface should remain the same all the way round, so when viewing the reverse side, the threading order should continue as if there was no back. Therefore shaft 3 comes before shaft 4. On the threading draft, when viewing from the front, that means that shaft 3 reads first but in the opposite direction – from the left to the right.

Therefore, the threading only needs to make sense in one plane.

The two wefts required can either enter from the same or opposite sides. Each is completely separate and are only joined at the selvedge (if desired) by the intertwining of their respective wefts.

However, when thinking about this as a tube or double width, the order of the bottom layer threading has to be reversed to ensure that the weave structure continues in the same progression on the underside of the woven tube.

To see the whole tube correctly, a viewer would walk around the tube. Therefore, the weave structure needs to continue uninterrupted as you go around the selvedge of the fabric.

It takes a little practice to visualise this, but once you have realised that the outside of the fabric is on the top for the surface nearest you and underneath for the surface furthest away, you have grasped the fundamental principle required to weave anything in a tubular form. The interior of the tube is comprised of the inside (underside) of the top layer and the inside (uppermost surface) of the bottom layer.

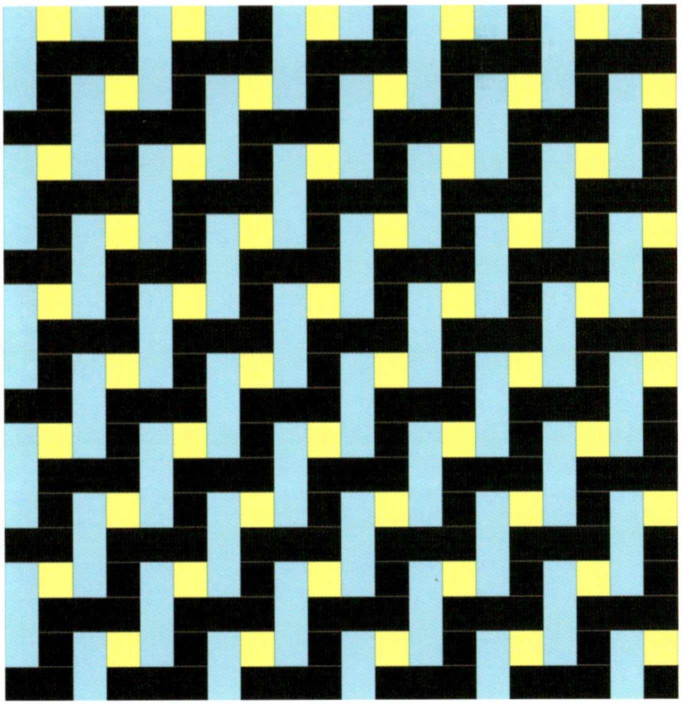

Only one weft is needed for a tube, weaving in an O shape (top, bottom, top, bottom).

Four Shafts

With four shafts, only plain weave or basket (hopsack) weave is possible. With only two shafts available for each layer, a hopsack would need to use two heddles on the same shaft adjacent to each other, alternating in pairs to create the effect.

An important point is to notice what is happening with the last end of the bottom layer and the first end of the top layer. If there is an even number of total warp ends, these two ends end up doing the same thing, so there is a doubled end on one selvedge. To eliminate this, remove either the first end of the top layer or the last end of the bottom layer (lying adjacent).

One more adaptation needs to be applied when weaving the tube. The tie-up changes from 1/123/2/124 to 1/124/2/123 to reflect that the underside of the fabric will be viewed from the other side of the warp.

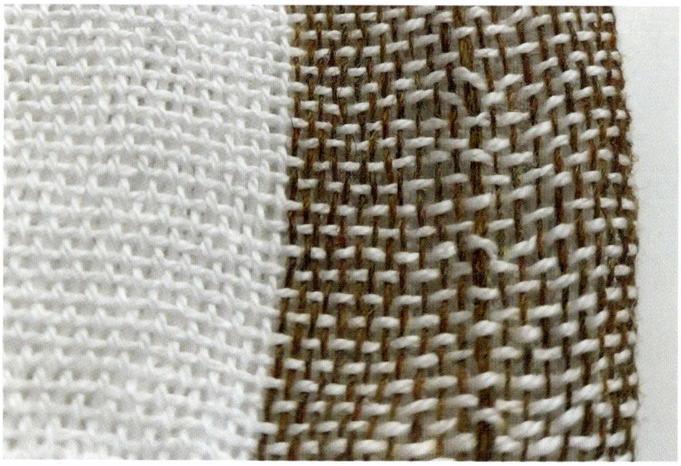

The doubled end here is the result of the first end of the top layer and the last end of the bottom layer (when in a tube) doing the same thing. Remove one of the doubled ends to solve the problem.

Combining a Four-Shaft Tube with Double Width

With four shafts, you can create more effects than just the simple tube. Combine the tube with double width weaving and you can weave a shawl with cuffs, which you can wear without it falling off your body and getting mislaid.

You can also weave two separate layers at the centre of the weaving and wear it more like a short poncho – no falling off the shoulders here either! With elastane or crepe yarns in the weft for the cuff area, you have elasticated cuffs. With silks for the remainder of the weft, you can have amazing iridescence.

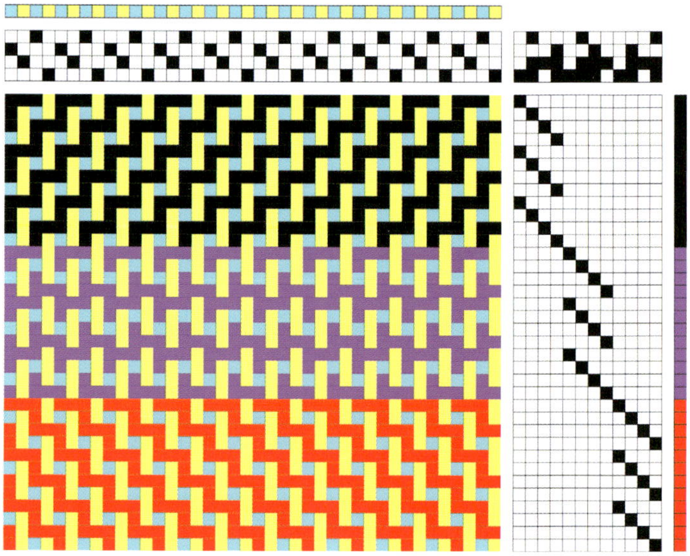

The tie-up shows three different ways of weaving the warp. The first four columns are for the single weft tubular weave. The next four columns are for weaving double width, again with one weft. Column 5 weaves the first part of the top layer, column 6 is the first part of the bottom layer. Now it changes format. Column 7 is the second part of the bottom layer on the return trip. Column 8 is the second part of the top layer. The single weft has woven in a C-shape then a reverse C. The final four columns are a regular double cloth with two wefts, which would be used for the separate layers forming the neck hole.

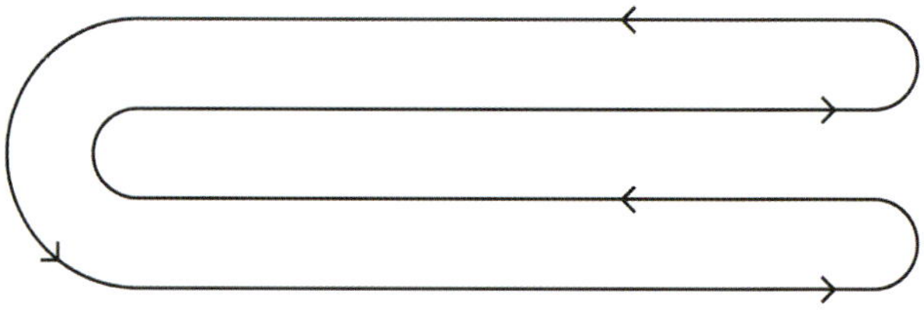

This image shows the path of the weft for double width weaving. Weave the first pick of one layer in one direction, then weave the first pick of the second layer in the opposite direction with the same shuttle. Then weave the second pick of the second layer in the reverse direction, followed by the second pick of the first layer. Repeat. If the start point is on the right, the fold is on the left selvedge. If the starting point is on the left, the fold is on the right selvedge.

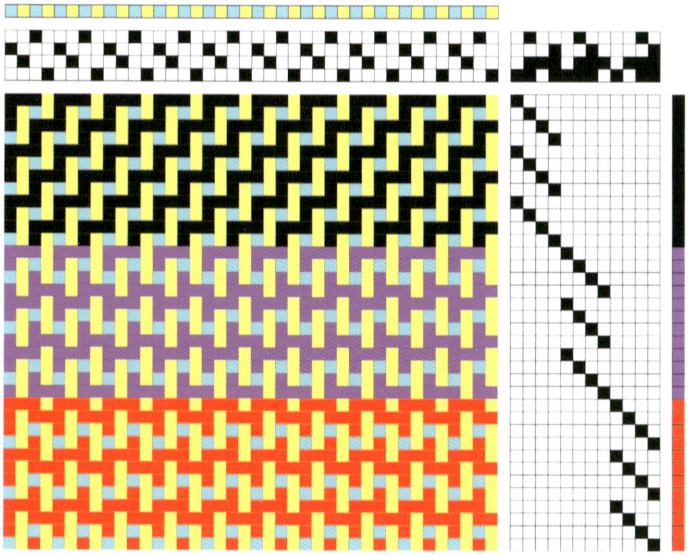

The three tie-ups here are the tube (black weft), the double width with the fold on one selvedge (purple weft), then the double width with the fold on the other selvedge (red weft). If starting with the weft on the same side each time, a different lifting order is required. A C-shape is still required for the second double width, but the two picks of plain weave of the top layer are woven before dropping down with the curve of the C to weave the two picks of the plain weave for the bottom layer, then curving back up to the top. If preferred, the layers can be switched, with the lower layer being woven before the upper layer.

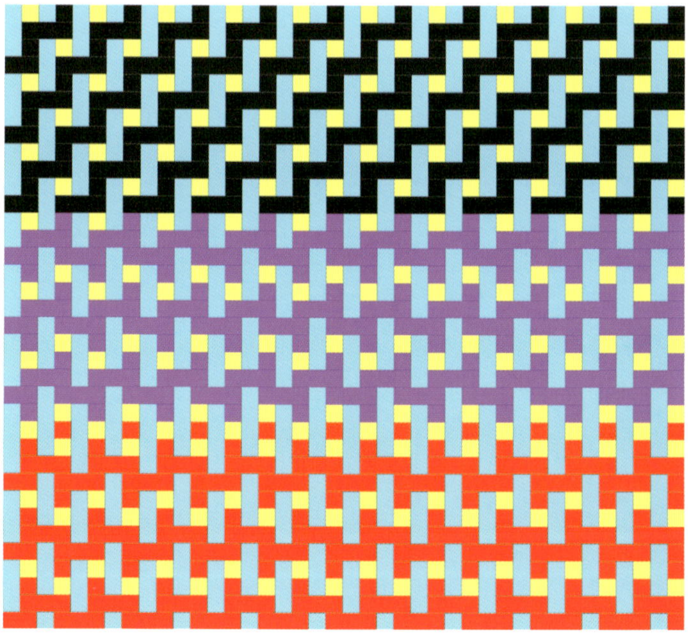

The other side.

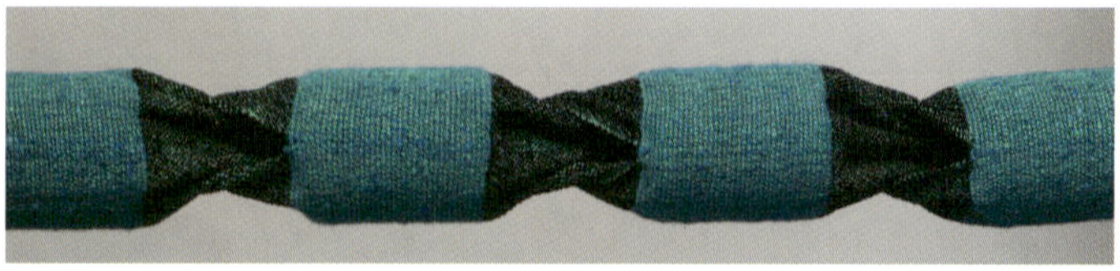

A sculptural piece is formed using the two different double width forms along with tubular weaving and pulling the work inside out through the open selvedge caused by the double width weaving. The piece was created to contain Christmas treats in the guise of an extended Christmas cracker. (Photo: Colin Usher)

With four shafts you can also weave scarves that flow in and out of themselves by weaving tubes interspersed with double width first open on one side of the warp, then after some more tubular weaving, changing the open side to the opposite selvedge. Once off the loom, the fabric can be turned through itself.

Multiple Tubes

If it is possible to weave one tube on four shafts, it is also possible to weave two or more in the same width. Individual shuttles or weft packages are required for each tube, as well as added patience, as the work takes twice as long to weave for two tubes than for one.

Multiple tubes can grow from earlier larger tubes or be absorbed back into a larger tube within the same piece. This could lead to loose trousers, for example, as a practical outcome. Equally valid is the artistic exploration of the potential inherent in changing scales of tubes. Plain weave is the only viable practical weave structure for four-shaft multiple tubes.

Eight Shafts

One of the first things to consider with eight shafts is if it is advantageous for you to spread a four-shaft threading over eight shafts. For 'sticky' or fibrous yarns, such as hairy, slub or noil yarns, this is a good thing to do to alleviate the catching of the closely sett warp yarns against each other and allows for higher densities to be woven with less warp frustration.

The most effective way to do this is to treat shafts 1–4 as one layer with its plain weave on shafts 1 & 3 v 2 & 4, with the second layer on shafts 5–8 using shafts 5 & 7 v 6 & 8. This expands the difference between each adjacent thread so that the angles of the two yarns next door to each other vary, making the shed easier to open.

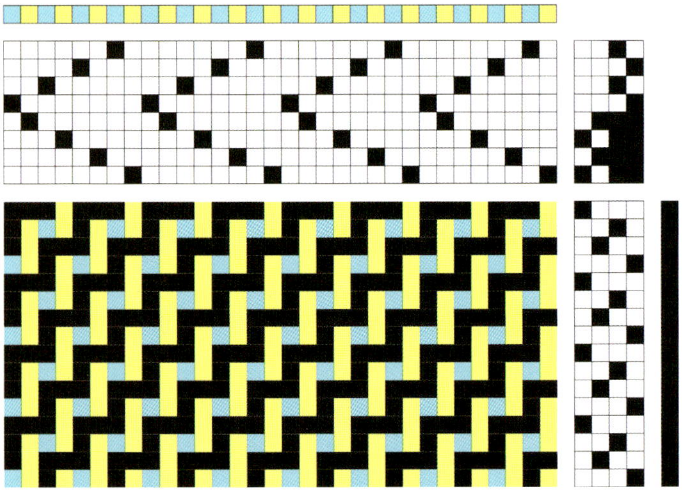

A regular single tube using two layers of four shafts each. Notice the change of threading direction for the underneath layer.

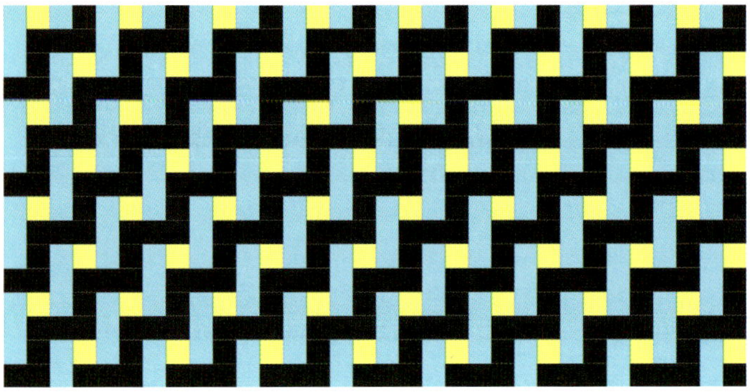

The reverse side.

Twills

Following on from four shafts, eight shafts will allow you to use four-shaft twills. Sett has a big impact here. Twill weaves require a higher density – more ends per dent – and certain yarns will impact even more on the weaving. If yarns are sticking together, especially when weaving the lower layer, lift the top layer out of the way first then add the respective shafts for the lower layer, either individually or together – whichever gives the cleaner shed.

Table looms will assist with lifting individual shafts; however, dobby looms will not allow individual shafts to be raised independently to create a multiple-shaft shed, unless programmed in specifically. Treadle looms with tie-ups that use two treadles in creating a shed might possibly cope with this situation, but even then, the action required could be too much for the warp yarns used.

Yarns that are more textured, like slubs and noils, are best used in the weft depending on the result desired.

With a twill, it becomes even more important to ensure that the weave continues unaltered around the selvedges. The twill order must be maintained while turning the corner. The only way to do that is to imagine yourself turning the corner with it and seeing the same order when viewed from the other side. This means that the threading

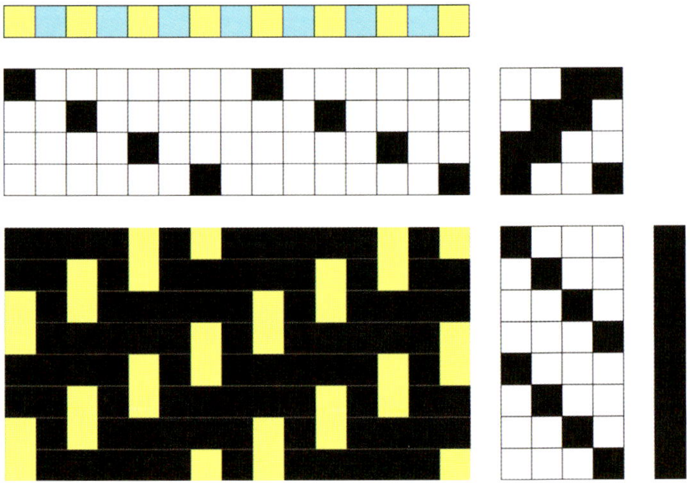

The eight-shaft tubular twill's upper layer is spread out over four shafts with a twill tie-up.

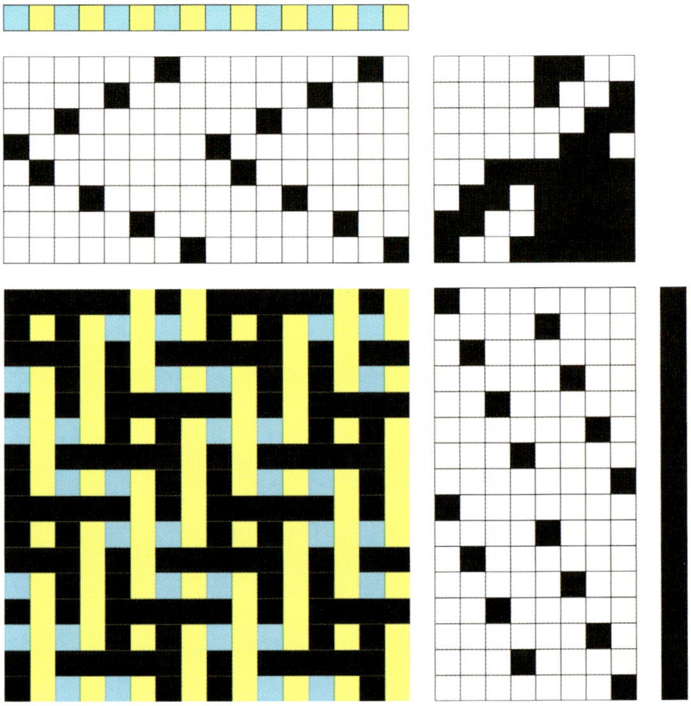

The return (bottom) layer is added with its (reversed) twill tie-up. The treadling is a divided parallel. The tie-up is now in quadrant form with the top-left and bottom-right quadrants dictating which layer is uppermost. The yellow warp shows a twill progression from top right to bottom left.

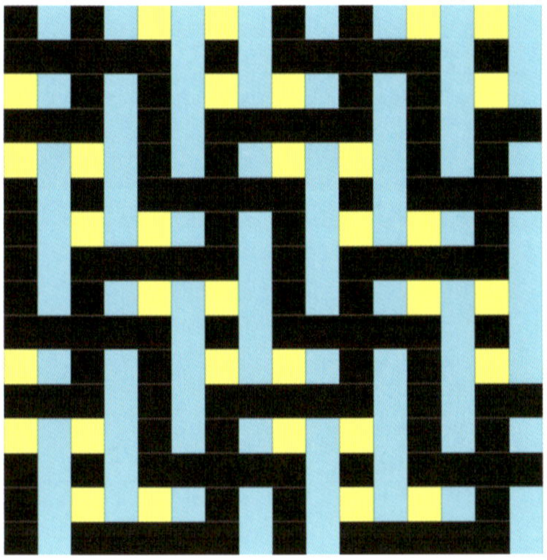

The reverse layer shows the light blue (reverse layer) warp with its twill progression from top right to bottom left. The twill line is continuing in the same direction around the tube.

is reversed for the underneath layer when seen from the top (and during threading).

The same method of weaving double width, then changing the sides and turning them inside each other after cutting from the loom, can also be done with twills to give beautifully draping scarves. For example, with a 3/1 twill all the way round, the warp-faced twill will be interspersed with the opposite 1/3 effect when the piece is pulled through itself.

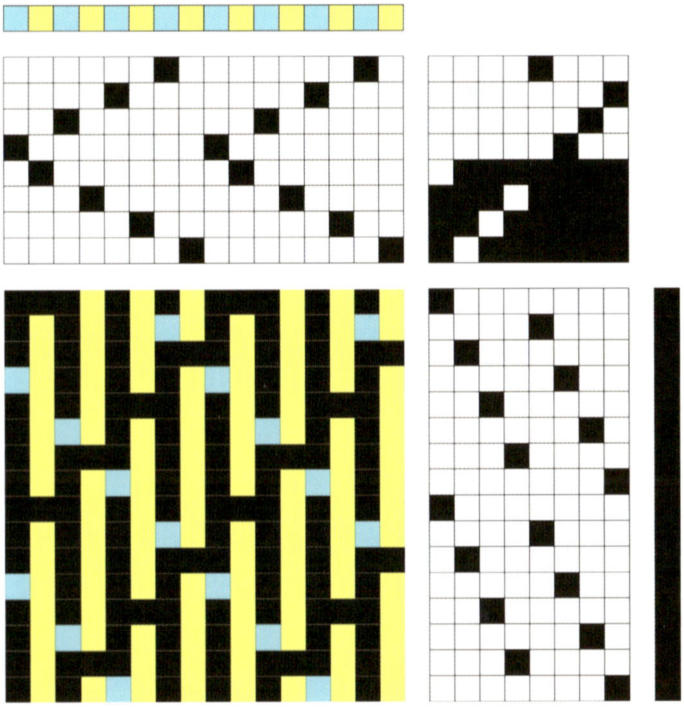

The reverse direction is inserted into the threading draft. The reverse tie-up is input and the quadrants of top left and bottom right completed to denote which layer is above during the weaving.

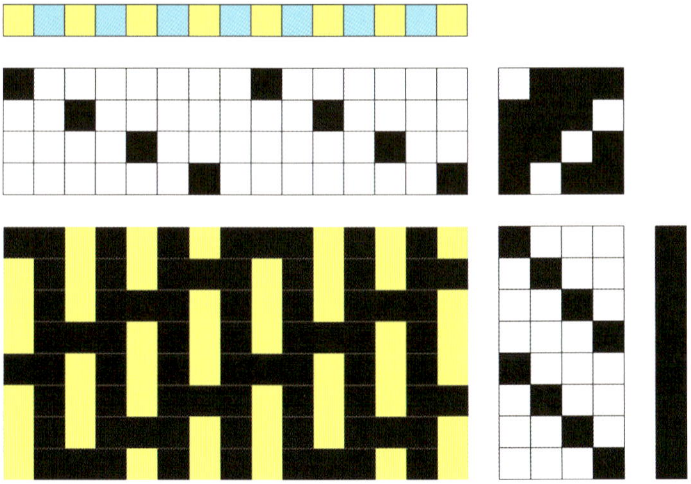

The same process can be followed with a 3/1 twill. First the threading is spread out for the top layer. The tie-up is applied.

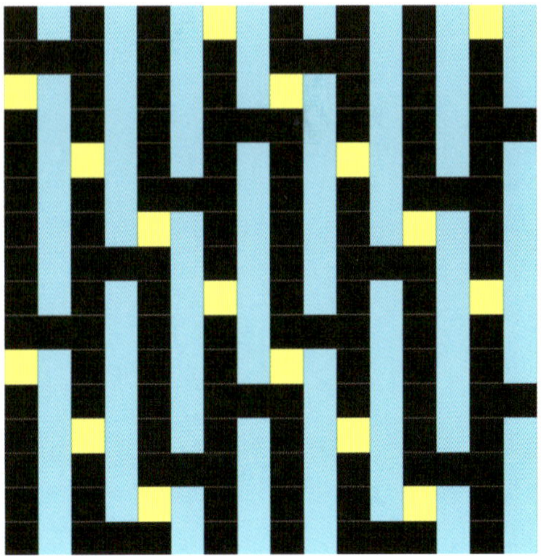

The reverse side can be used to check the flow of the twill. The long warp floats are running from top right to bottom left (yellow on the top layer, light blue on the bottom layer).

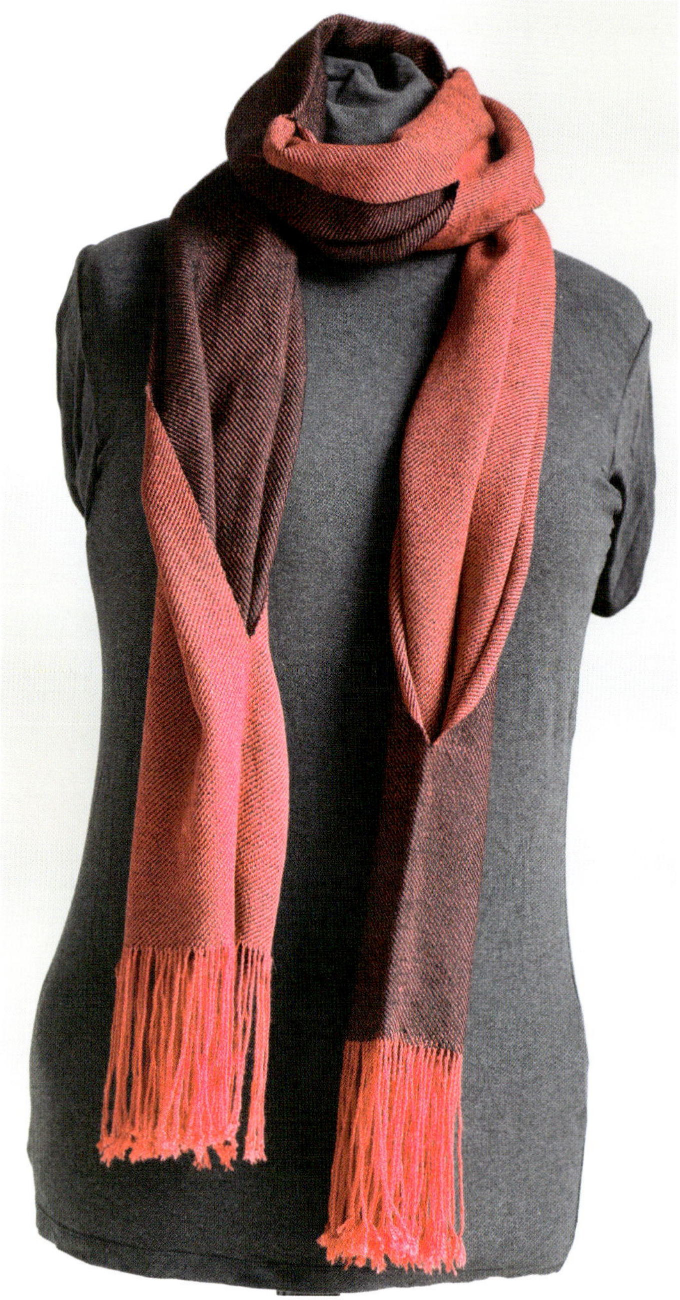

Alice van Duijnen wove this *Inside Out* scarf using a 1/3 3/1 twill effect to give distinctive colour contrast and extra warmth. (Photo: Alice van Duijnen)

You can also introduce advancing threading to the mix, so long as the draft remains true all the way round the fabric.

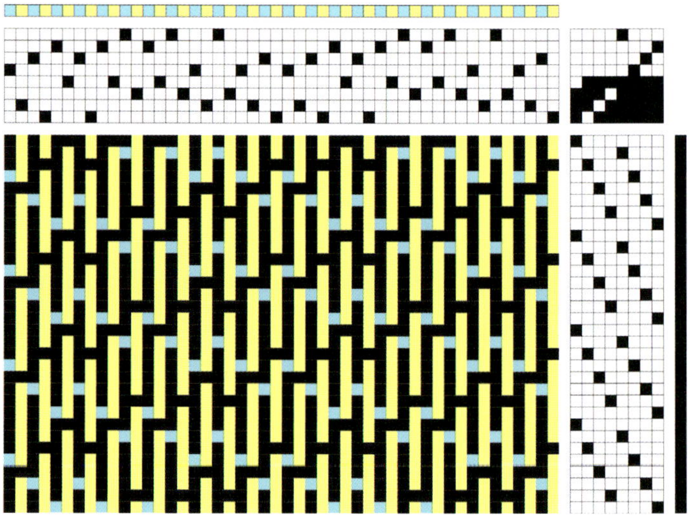

The advancing threading draft has been compiled in the same way.

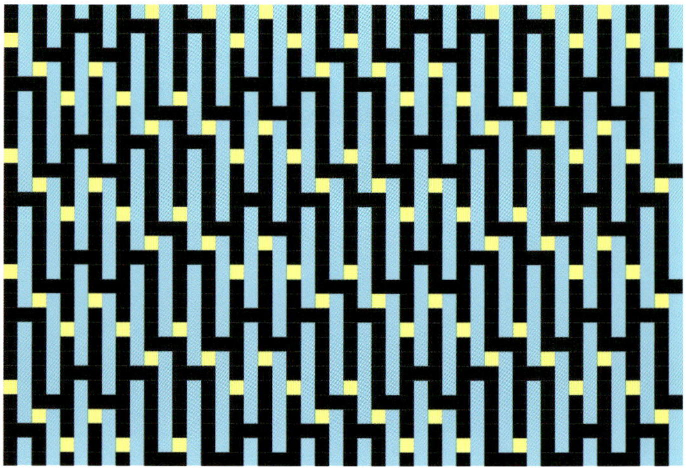

A view of the back of the fabric can show if the twill is flowing correctly.

One or More Tubes with Eight Shafts

With eight shafts there are several possibilities in tube sizes. A single tube can be woven using the regular two layers. It can also be woven with four layers, making a super-size tube. If the sett is for four layers, the density will be four times a regular plain weave sett. However, the main difference really lies in the order of the weaving of the layers. Extra attention needs to be paid at the selvedges of each of the layers unless a tighter density at each change of shed is desired.

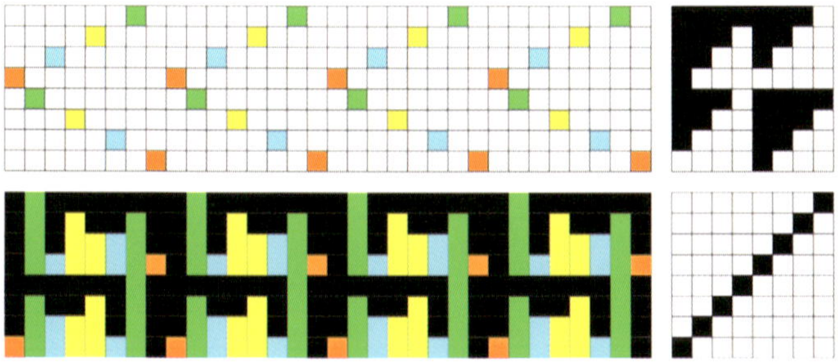

The view from the bottom layer follows the path of a single weft. Weave the bottom layer first pick; then follow it with the second to bottom layer first pick; followed by the second to top layer first pick; followed finally by the top layer first pick. Take the weft right back down to the bottom layer for the second half of the plain weave and follow the same trajectory using the second picks of plain weave for each of the layers.

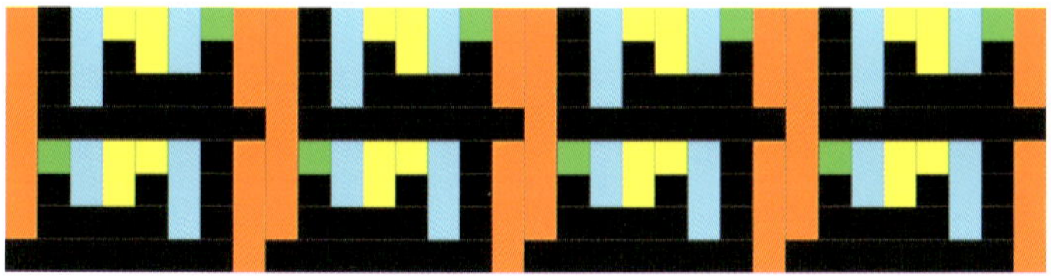

The front side. The inner layers can be seen.

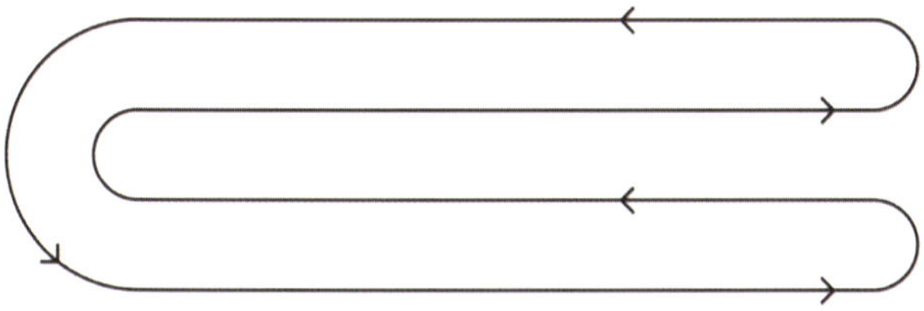

This line drawing of the single tube weaving direction may look a little familiar. It is the same as for the double width, but whereas for the double width there are just two layers, for the single tube using four layers each layer needs to be woven in turn. One complete circuit weaves the first pick of the enlarged tube. The same directional pattern is woven for the second pick of the enlarged tube.

Multiple Tubes: Adjacent Tubes

With two layers, it is possible to weave two or more tubes sitting beside each other simply by using two independent wefts and weaving each tube with its own dedicated weft. Separate mini-tubes can be woven with butterfly wefts, if you wish. With imagination and a little manipulation, inclusions can also be slotted inside these to make interesting jewellery or art pieces.

Multiple Tubes: Stacked Tubes

With four layers, you can weave two tubes – one on top of the other like a double-decker bus or train – with two separate wefts each weaving their own two layers in an O shape. Personal experience has shown that it helps to keep the two wefts on opposite sides of the loom so as not to get tangled in each other as each of the tubes needs to be separate unless specifically designed to join together in places.

Use shafts 1–4 for the upper tube and shafts 5–8 for the lower tube.

- Weaving from the bottom up – Weft 1: Pick 1 lifts shafts 1–4 up, 5 & 7 up, plus 8.
- Weft 1: Pick 2; shafts 1–4, plus 7.
- Weft 2: Pick 3; shaft 1 & 3, plus 2.
- Weft 2: Pick 4; shaft 1.
- Weft 1: Pick 5; shafts 1–4 up, 5 & 7 up, plus 6.
- Weft 1: Pick 6; shafts 1–4, plus 5.
- Weft 2: Pick 7; shafts 1,3, plus 4.
- Weft 2: Pick 8; shaft 3.

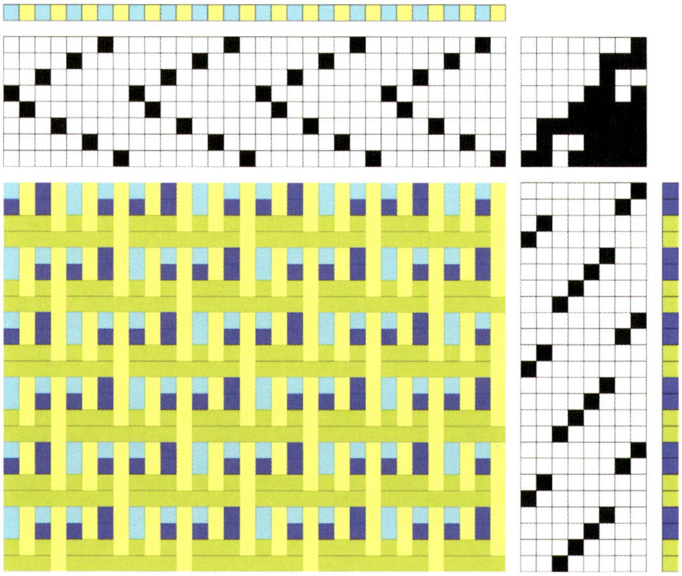

Double-decker tubes (one on top of the other) are woven in two-pick stages. Starting from the bottom layer, weave the complete circle (two picks) of the lower tube. Change wefts and weave the first complete circle (two picks) of the upper tube. Change weft, weave both second picks of the lower tube. Finally, change weft and weave both second picks of the upper tube.

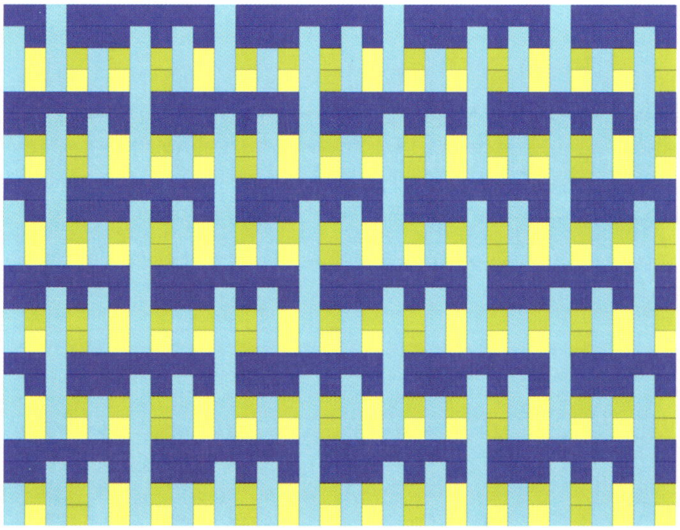

The reverse side.

The main limiting factor for this is the sett. If the single tube is sett at double plain weave, then it will have the regular plain weave for the whole tube. However, whenever another two layers are introduced, as in the double-decker tubes, the original sett is now going to be too open for each individual layer.

For the double-decker tubes, the sett will need to be quadruple the sett for a regular single layer cloth. If you are planning to add extra layers into the mix and change the orientation of the tubes in relation to each other, the sett will need to be planned and possibly weave structures changed to accommodate those changes according to your preference. For example, if the cloth is sett for double-decker tubes, weave structures such as twill or hopsack that use a tighter sett can be used for two horizontal tubes. With 16 or more shafts, satin structures could be considered for a single tube that is later to be divided up into double-decker (or more) tubes in twill or plain weave structures.

A double-decker sett will allow multiple vertical tubes to be woven adjacent to each other in two tubular layers. However, this does require multiple weft packages – one for each of the tubes.

Just imagine all the variations possible with single, double and quadruple tubes all available on the same warp and viable to be woven within the same piece! It all depends on the patience of the weaver and the physical and mental ability to juggle multiple shuttles or weft packages, keeping in mind exactly what is going on in three dimensions and with which weave structures. This is certainly a brain workout!

SEERSUCKER TUBES

In Chapter 4, six-shaft seersucker was discussed, which interspersed a double cloth band with a plain weave shrinking warp stripe. With eight shafts, seersucker can be adapted further into a tube. For each added effect requiring another two shafts in regular flat cloth, a tubular effect will require four shafts: two in each layer.

The shrinking stripes for seersucker can be added around the tube but threaded on another two shafts per layer to give a ribbing option in the tie-up, which increases the characteristic puckering effect.

The shrinking stripes are woven in a multiple rib, even while the ground plain weave in the non-shrinking areas continues. A second weft is not necessarily a requirement for this. The amount of repeated wefts going through the rib areas will impact on the results of the gathering when the tube is wet-finished. Repeats of 20 picks or more are perfectly acceptable as they will be assimilated in the rib as the active area shrinks, and are held in the plain weave segments causing the passive areas to pucker up in festoons and ripples.

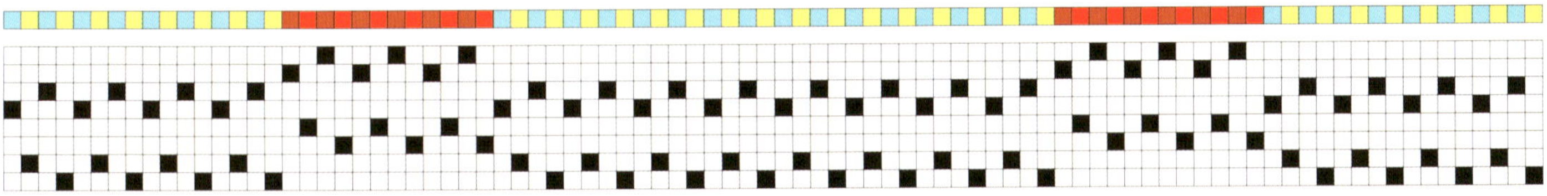

The eight-shaft seersucker threading follows the same convention as the other tubular threadings. The active warp bands are in red with darker red denoting the other underside of the tube.

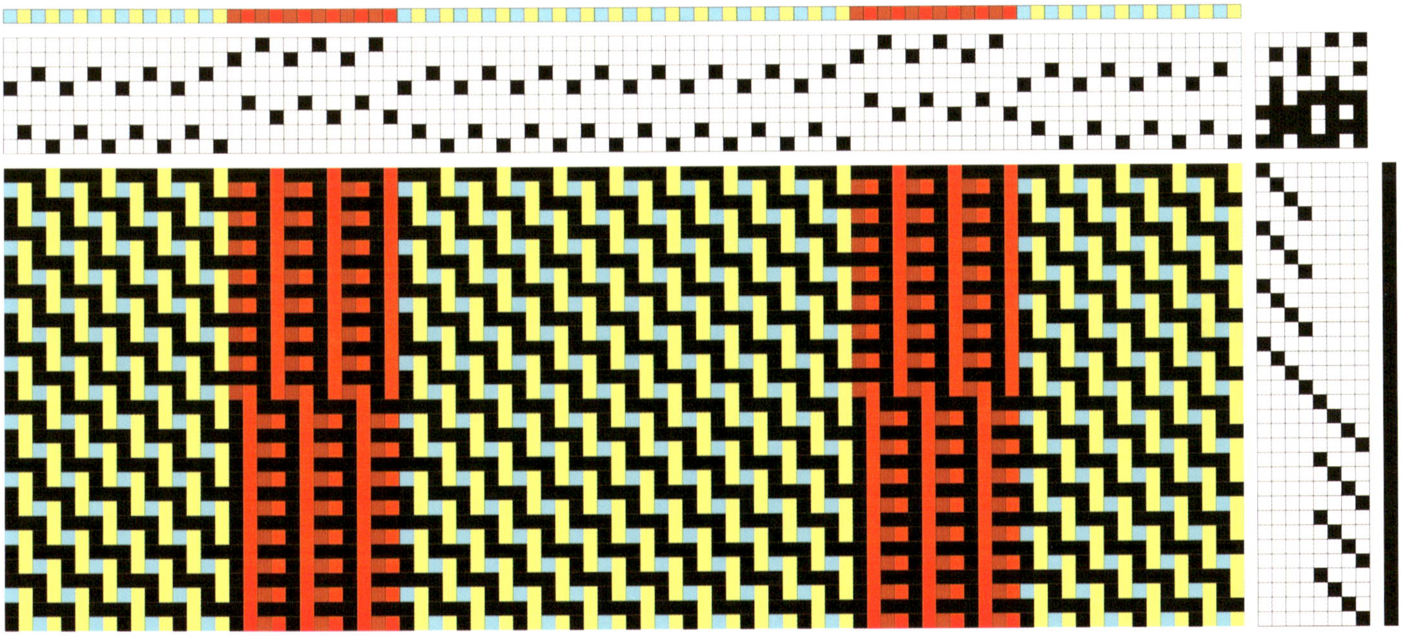

Seersucker with ribs and double plain.

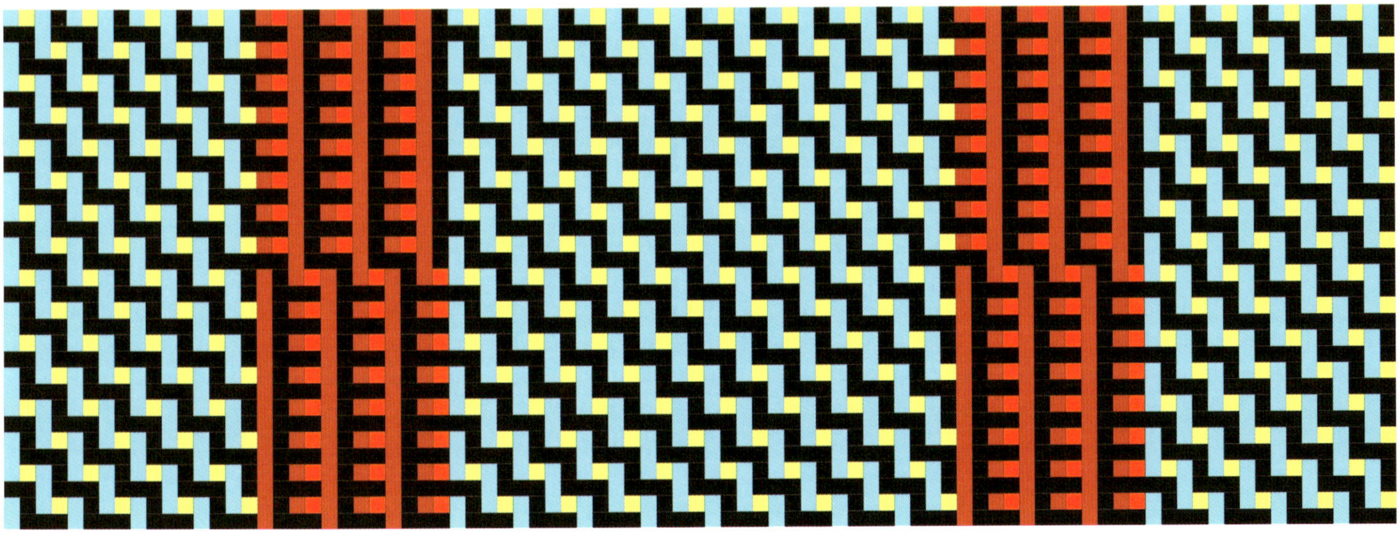

The reverse side.

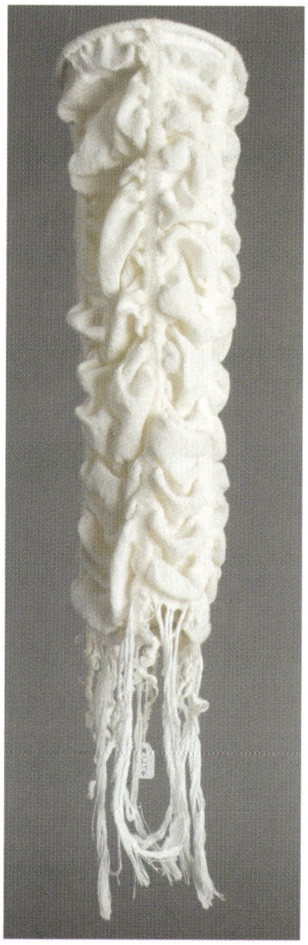

Three tubular forms in the *Growth Forms* series. The first is seersucker in cotton. (Photos: Colin Usher)

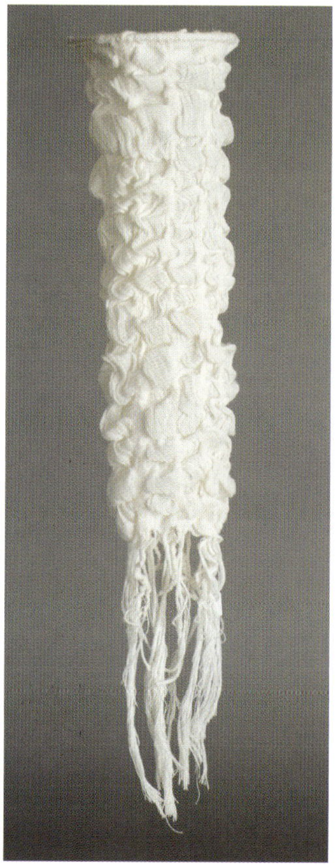

This is seersucker using a fine Japanese paper weft, giving the curl effect on immersion into hot water during wet-finishing.

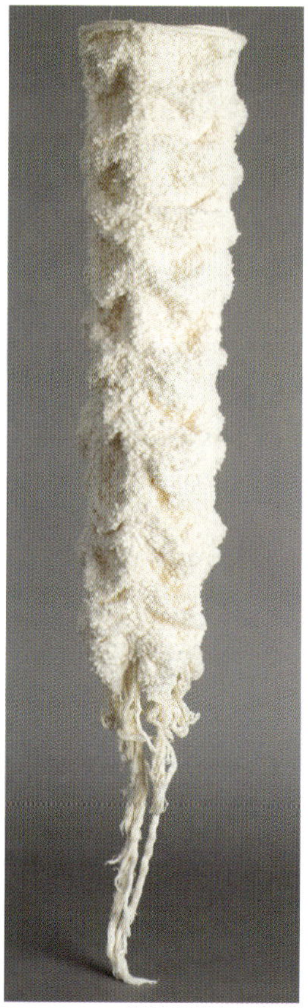

This is a seersucker using a highly textured novelty cotton yarn called 'Popcorn'.

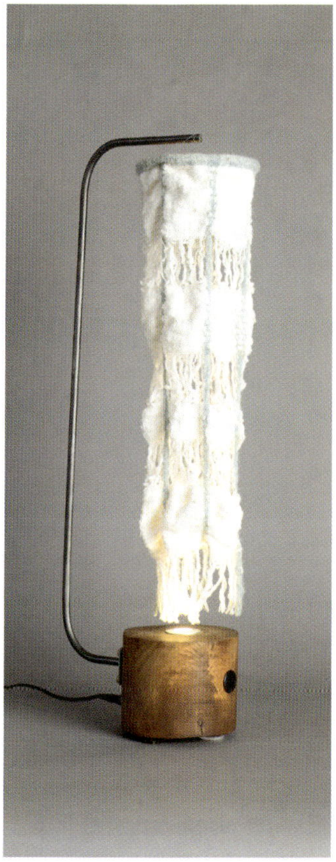

Illuminated tubular lamp with warps left unwoven. (Photo: Colin Usher)

Additional variety can be gained through the selection of interesting weft yarns. Fine paper yarns, which are often overtwisted singles, will release their tension on hitting the water in wet-finishing. This will create distinctive coruscations that are very different in appearance than the ripples and festoons of a cotton weft or a noil yarn.

Alternatively, bare warps can be left, especially useful for lamps and other light/shadow effects.

DOUBLE TUBES

Double tubes can be created – a quadruple layer fabric – with a little extra thought. In this instance, a double tube is woven using four layers with plain weave for each layer – two shafts for each. However, the two tubes are basically two Os: one nested inside the other.

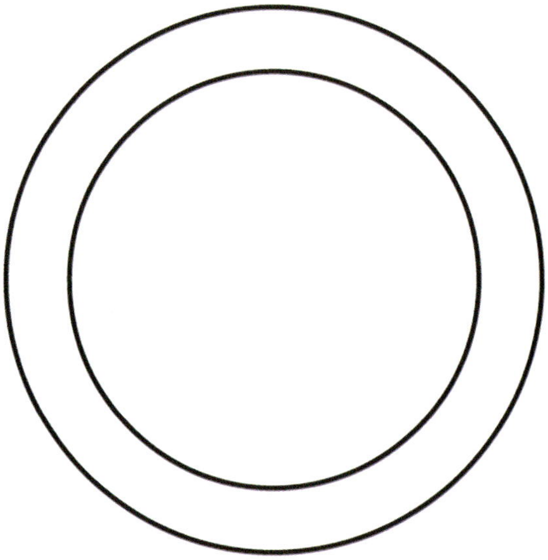

Two tubes, one inside the other, seen from above.

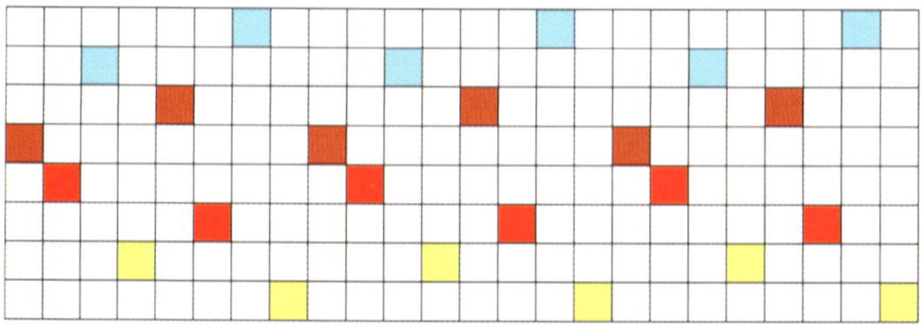

One tube inside another requires spatial thinking. The extreme outer layers, usually thought of as shafts 1 & 2 and 7 & 8, become one tube. The inner layers, shafts 3 & 4 and 5 & 6, become the inner tube. Colours have been used to help differentiate the layers here. The inner wool tube is in red and dark red for the warp (front and back of the inner tube respectively); the passive yarn is in yellow and light blue (front and back).

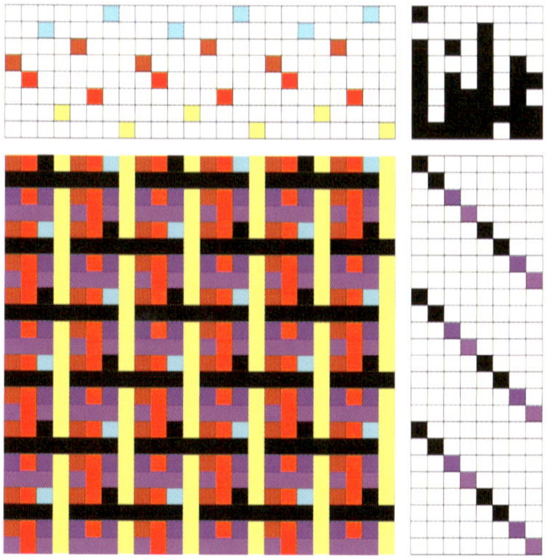

This shows tie-up and treadling. The wefts are kept as black for the top and bottom layers of the passive yarn and two shades of purple for the inner tube.

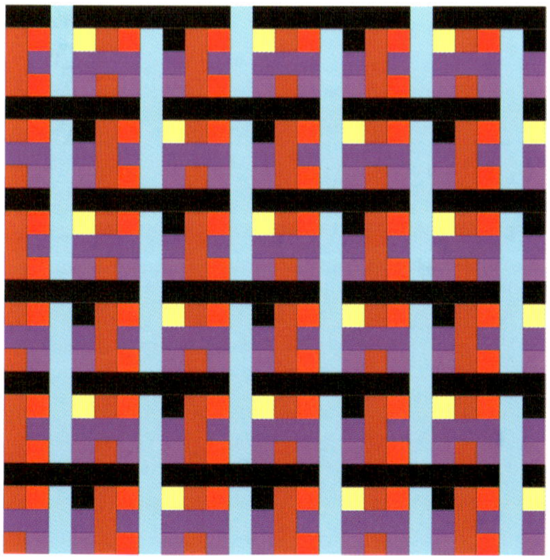

The reverse side of the tube. Note that the inner tube can never be seen directly.

INTERACTING WEFTS WITHIN THE TUBES

When weaving two tubes, one inside the other, attention must be paid to how the wefts of each tube interact with each other. *The inner tube weft needs to remain inside the outer tube at all times.* One suggestion is to affix one-half of a Velcro™ strip to the flat side of the shuttle being used and the other half of the Velcro™ to the front of the castle structure. Weave both picks of the inner tube as usual, starting with the bottom pick of the inner tube. Place the shuttle back onto the Velcro™ on the castle so that the weft rises from the web. Now weave the outer tube, again weaving both the bottom and top picks. Return that weft to the selvedge or to the woven web on the loom. This method should allow for the two tubes to remain separate.

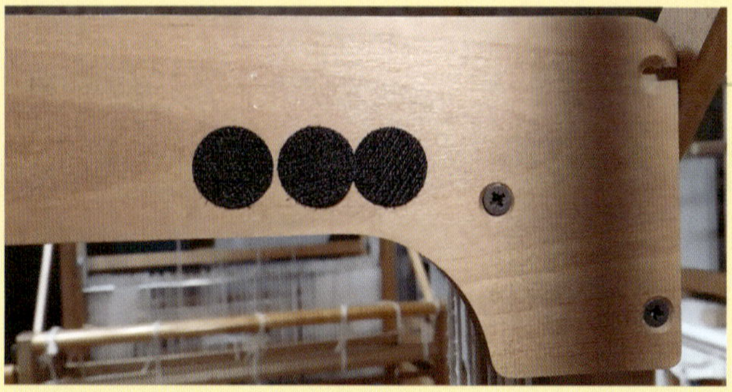

Circles of the 'hooked' side of Velcro™ have been stuck to the castle of a table loom for parking the shuttle of the inner tube when it is not being woven.

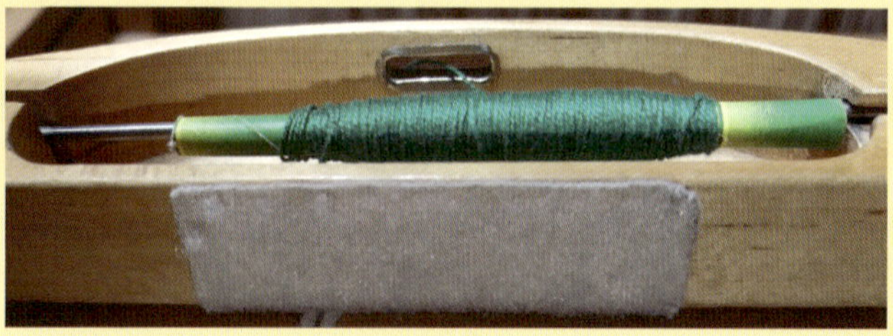

The soft side of the Velcro™ has been stuck to the outer flat edge of a roller shuttle.

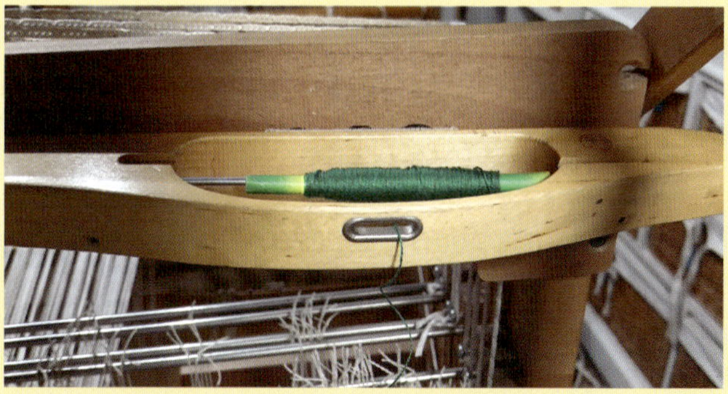

The two elements of Velcro™ stick the shuttle to the castle of the loom, so keeping the inner tube weft on the inside of the outer tube while the outer tube is being woven.

If the inner tube is of an active yarn that will shrink, interesting results can be obtained by weaving the two tubes separately for a while, then joining them together as one tube for a few picks, before separating them out again. Upon wet-finishing, the active yarn will shrink and cause the outer tube to pucker and gather in different ways, depending on the yarn composition of the outer tube weft. The eight shafts require two for each side of the two tubes.

It is not usually as necessary to be so vigilant of the selvedges on the inner tube. For one thing, they are not easily visible. However, too much tension on the selvedges will create warp breakages and care is still required to prevent this. Often, the inner tube is designed to be narrower than the outer tube.

If it is desired that the two tubes switch position so that the inner tube becomes the outer tube, any contraction of the selvedge of the original inner tube would become a point of warp strain.

Other suggestions for a tube within a tube can be using two warp beams with an elastane yarn for the inner tube. A high ratio of picks for the outer tube to inner tube and connecting them top and/or bottom will lead to various effects when releasing the work from the loom. The elastane interior tube will shorten dramatically, pulling the outer tube up into the interior, and causing drape. Monofilament or crammed-and-spaced in warp and/or weft could lead to effective lighting forms.

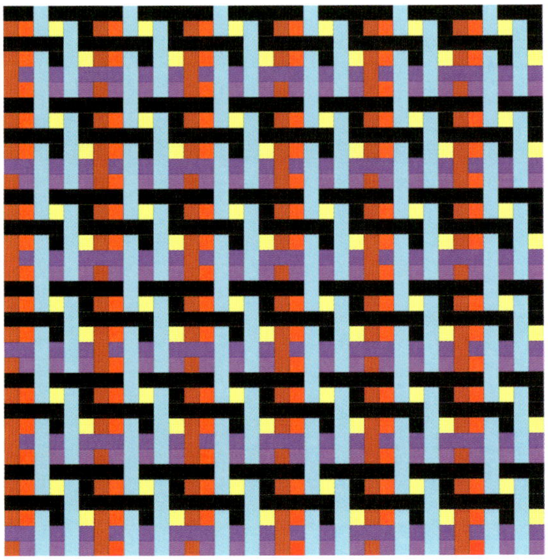

The reverse side.

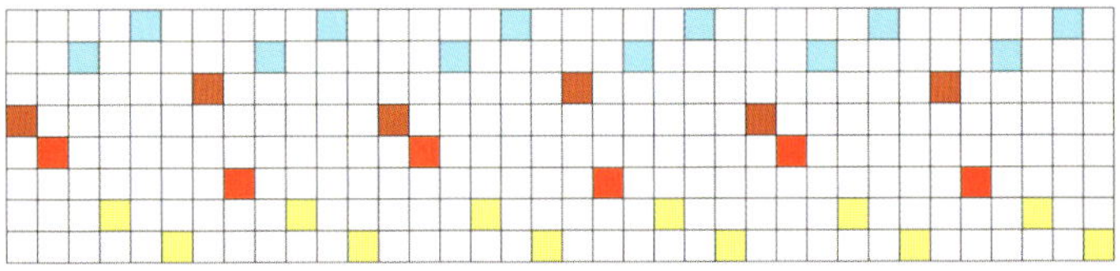

The 2:1 ratio of passive to active yarns gives this threading.

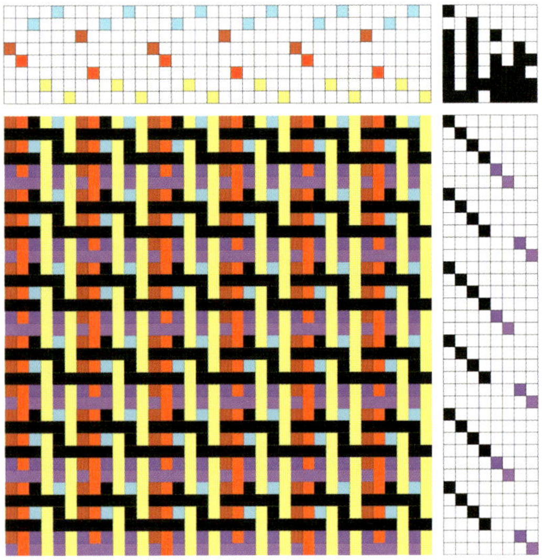

The same ratio is used in the weft.

Using woollen yarns for the interior tube will give similar but perhaps not such dramatic results, depending on the wet-finishing technique employed. Wool is a very useful medium because it will not give many problems when weaving, as elastane might. Often when using woollen yarns as the active element, a higher ratio of passive to active yarns is useful.

More Than Eight Shafts

Many of the techniques described in the previous section of this book can be adapted for tubular weaving, if enough shafts are available. One important point to remember when translating them into tubular form is how to imagine the threading and the tie-up for them.

Earlier in this chapter we envisioned how to view the tube in the round. This is even more important when patterning is involved.

Threading

One simple method to plan a more complex threading draft is to draft out the whole threading as if the cloth were a very wide single cloth, using translucent paper such as greaseproof or tracing paper. If the design has an even number of ends, make a vertical fold at the centre with the same number of ends on either side of the fold. If it has an uneven number of ends, make a vertical fold either to the immediate left or right of that centre end. Place the paper flat on a table. Now make the numbers of the threading that is folded underneath bold so that they can easily be seen through the translucent paper (although the numbers themselves will look as if they are being viewed in a mirror). This is the threading order to enter on the loom.

This process can easily be done with the click of a button on weaving software, but that does not explain what is happening. Through understanding how the threading is created in a physical form, three-dimensional spatial awareness is increased and the weaving is that much easier to plan and do. As stated for the four-shaft tube, ensure that you do not have a doubled end at the right-hand selvedge if you thread from right to left or the left-hand selvedge if you thread from left to right.

Tie-up

This is where things can get a little difficult to visualise, unless we have fully absorbed the fact that our tube has only one continuous outer surface and one (or more) continuous inner surface(s). This was mentioned earlier in the chapter, but it is imperative that this is understood at a fundamental level, especially when dealing with complex patterning in tubular form.

Even if we are creating a double cloth tube, the two layers actually contain four surfaces:

1. The outer upper layer (which we see when we are weaving)
2. The inner upper layer (the underside of the top layer's threads, which are not visible)
3. The inner lower layer (the topside of the bottom layer's threads, which are facing towards the weaver but hidden under the top layer)
4. The outer lower layer (the underside of the bottom layer, facing the floor/table which the viewer will also see once the piece is off the loom)

Strangely, having more layers doesn't make the visualisation harder, so long as the weaver knows which layer is doing what.

The main thing to remember is that the 'face' of the bottom layer is actually the surface looking down on to the floor. So when planning the lifts to create the pattern that the viewer will see, it is useful to imagine lying on your back on the floor under the cloth being woven on the loom. The next part is to ascertain which shafts are the ones showing the warp in your pattern from your position under the loom. That's what you want the viewer to see.

This is *not* the same as the shafts that are being lifted.

What is actually needed while weaving are the *opposite* lifts to the ones that you can see under the loom, because when weaving, you will be above and on the 'wrong' side of that layer. It may seem counterintuitive, but it is undeniably logical!

Another way to think about it is that a *rising* shed is needed when weaving the top visible layer so that the correct warp threads rise to create the desired pattern, but when weaving the lowest layer(s), a *sinking* shed is required. So to achieve the effect of a sinking shed on a rising shed loom, the lifts have to be reversed.

Using the extended parallel design from Chapter 11, let's put it into a tubular cloth.

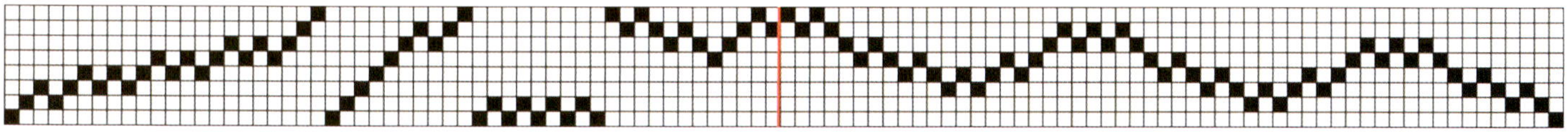

An eight-shaft extended threading draft is the starting point. The mid-point is marked in red. This is where the fabric will fold around to the underneath layer. For our purposes, anything to the right of this line is the top layer, while anything to the left of the red line will be the underneath layer.

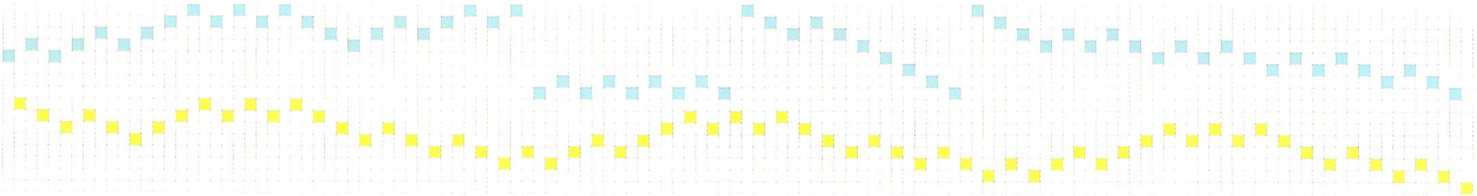

This is the resulting draft following the method outlined at the beginning of the chapter. Insert a space between each end of the draft. The second half of the threading (to the left of the red line) is flipped on the red line edge, so reversing the direction of the threading. Shift this flipped threading up eight shafts and insert into the spaces left between the ends of the first half of the threading. Here it is in light blue.

It is helpful to design the tie-up in steps if creating a design on a regular tube. Here are the step instructions for creating the tie-up for the extended parallel design.

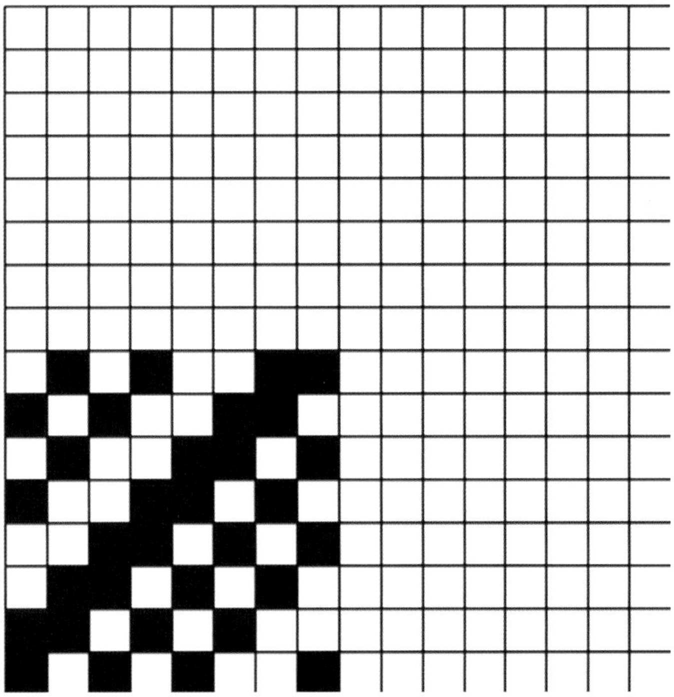

Step 1. Start by drafting the rising tie-up required for the top layer. This is placed in the bottom-left quadrant.

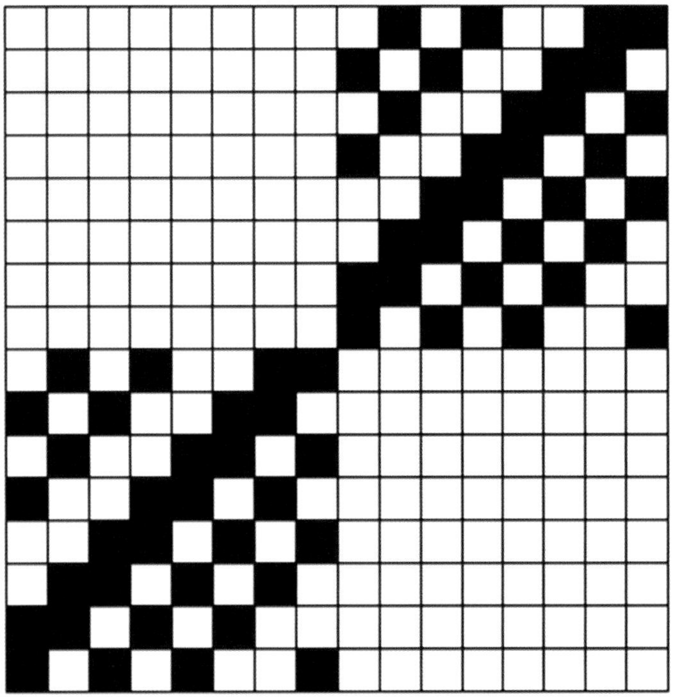

Step 2. Duplicate this or copy it on to squared paper.

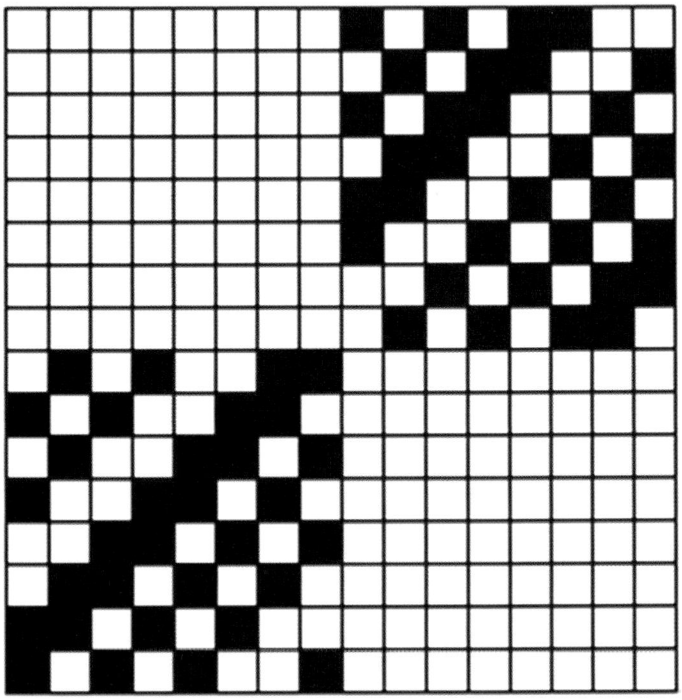

Step 3. Change the face in the top-right quadrant, changing all the black squares to white and all the white squares to black. This is now the opposite (sinking) tie-up for the bottom cloth.

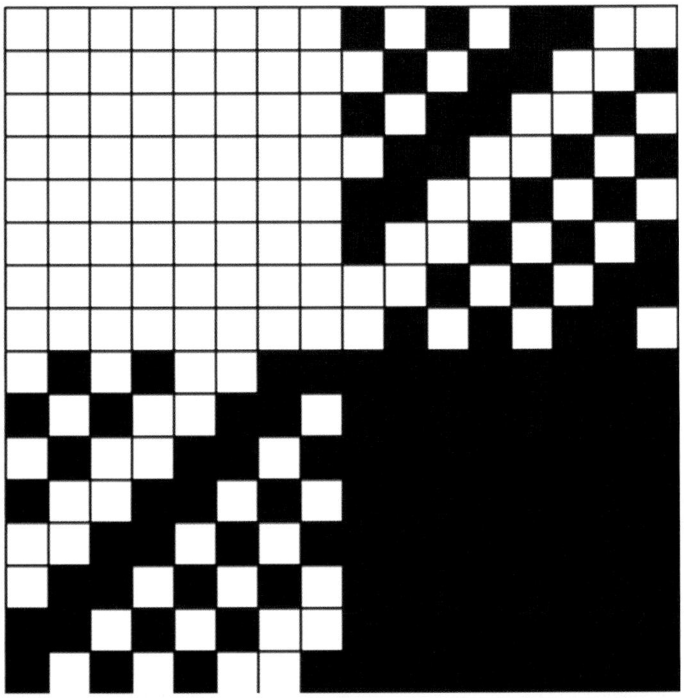

Step 4. To complete the tie-up, fill in *all* the shafts of the top layer in the bottom-right quadrant. These will be lifted out of the way so that the bottom layer can be woven.

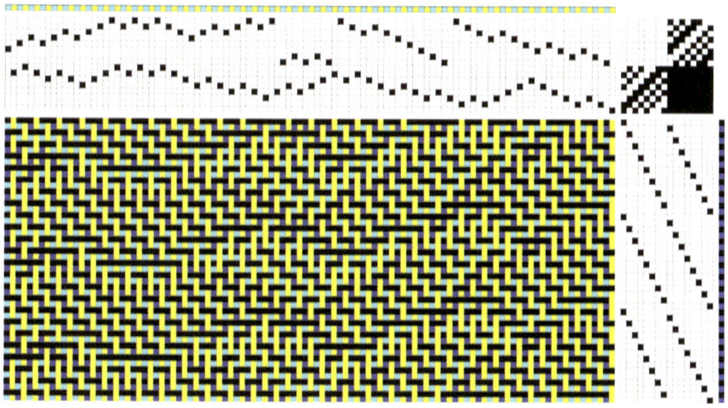

A detail of the complete draft.

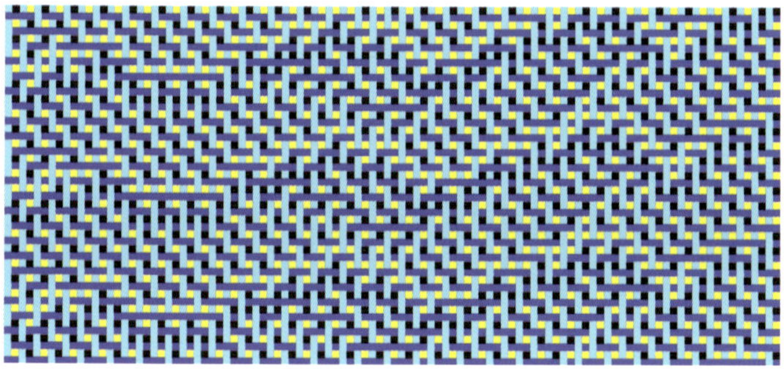

The reverse side of the detail.

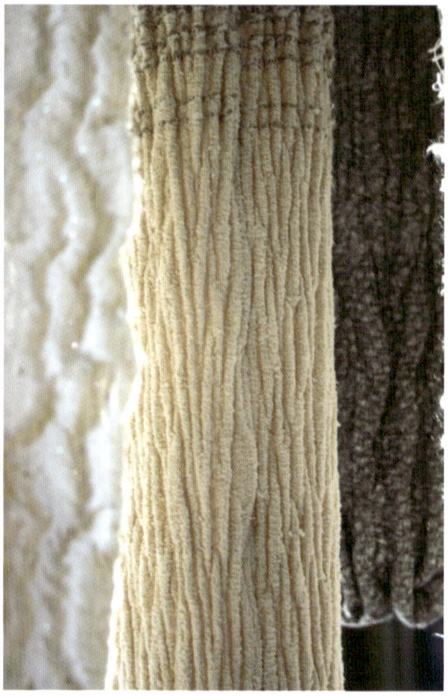

Silk noil has been used as the weft in this shibori tube. Note: If polyester, wool or elastane is not used for the ground weave, there could be a possibility that further washing after the shibori weft has been removed will lead to the texture completely disappearing. This is the case with silk noil and so it is not possible to wash this piece without losing the texture.

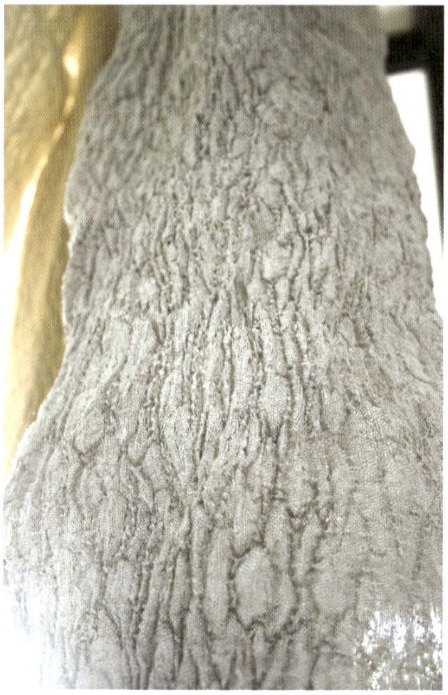

This *Growth Form* uses metal as its weft. The shibori pulls up the fabric tightly and the metal allows it to be pulled apart for less hard folds. However, once the fabric has been pulled out, it cannot be retightened, so prior thought is needed to ascertain how much manipulation is required for the end result. Too much repeated manipulation could result in breakages in the metal weft.

The weaving itself is quite straightforward. Weave in one direction for the top layer and weave in the opposite direction for the bottom layer, taking care not to pull in at the folds. As mentioned earlier, these edges should be spaced out more widely than the rest of the warp to minimise any pull-in, depending on the characteristics of your weft yarn.

OTHER TECHNIQUES FOR TUBULAR WEAVING

Shibori

Shibori used in textural weaving can involve the tube being woven in wool, which will hold its form after wet-finishing; polyester yarns, which will require heat-setting if used for wearable art; or perhaps immersing in, or painting on, a form of PVA glue or other craft sizing to enable the end result to be permanent and inflexible for sculptural forms. Metal wefts can also be used with the usual care around the selvedges. The shibori gathering thread itself will need an extra selvedge sleyed several dents away from the selvedge to ensure that there is sufficient shibori weft available to pull the design up after removing from the loom.

It is more effective on the overall appearance of the piece if the loops are pulled through to different locations on the tube prior to being gathered up. This ensures that the gathers are around the whole tube, not just at the selvedges (which otherwise would inevitably focus attention on the selvedges).

Stitched Double Cloth

In Chapter 10, we looked at how to use an active warp underneath the passive warp, weaving the two as separate layers with their own respective wefts but bringing elements from the lower layer into the top layer at selected points to create surface dimensional effects. Eight shafts there allowed for quite complex textural designs and patterns.

With tubular weaving, more than eight shafts are required for stitched double cloth patterning. In this case, the inner tube is threaded in the desired pattern, ensuring that the design line is reversed in direction for the lower part of the inner tube and the correct tie-up made to allow the design to flow around the whole tube. The outer tube is usually plain weave and the principles of stitched double cloth are followed as in Chapter 10, so that the stitched design appears on the outer tube.

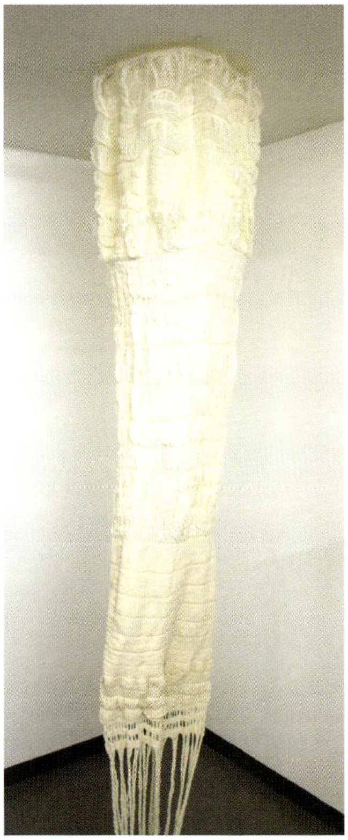

This large stitched double cloth tube uses a wool for the interior tube and a cotton for the exterior. There are three wefts that are woven on the exterior tube: monofilament (top section), Austrian paper (middle section) and cotton (bottom section). The stitched element was stitching the cotton top tube into the wool interior tube using the wool weft to give more shrinkage. The weave structure throughout the whole piece is plain weave so any variations in surface appearance are due to the yarns used.

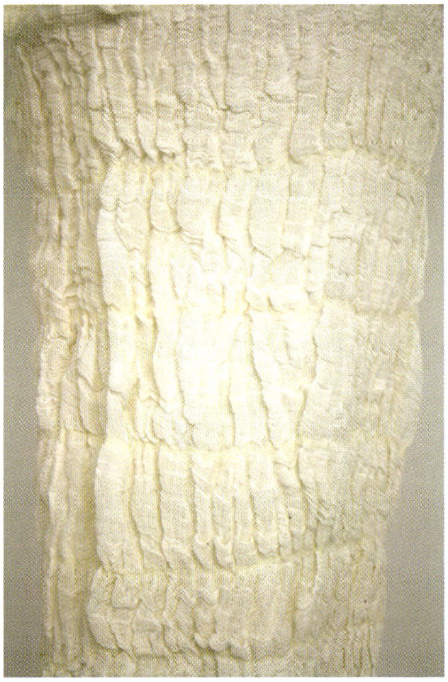

The Austrian paper yarn is thicker and more tightly twisted than the Japanese paper yarn used in the small *Growth Forms* and it has a different impact when wet-finished. The stitching remains the same throughout the whole piece, but the paper forms into columnar shapes.

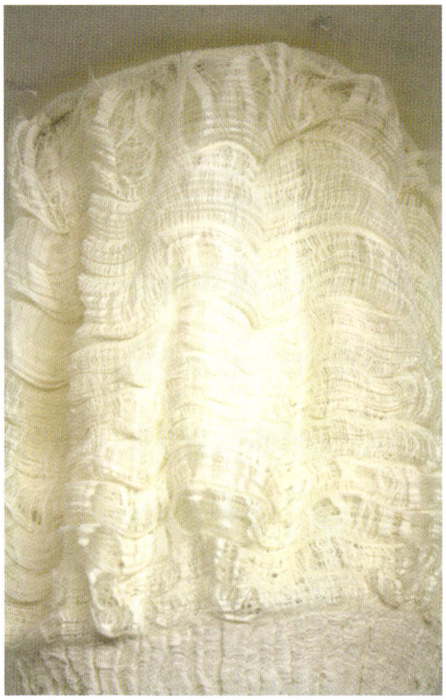

The monofilament (fishing line) is quite thick. Because of its relative rigidity as a fibre, it causes undulations in the surface of the tube. The extreme slipperiness of the monofilament can cause the cotton warp to slide along the weft and gather in areas, leaving gaps in the warp where the monofilament can push out of the surface of the cloth.

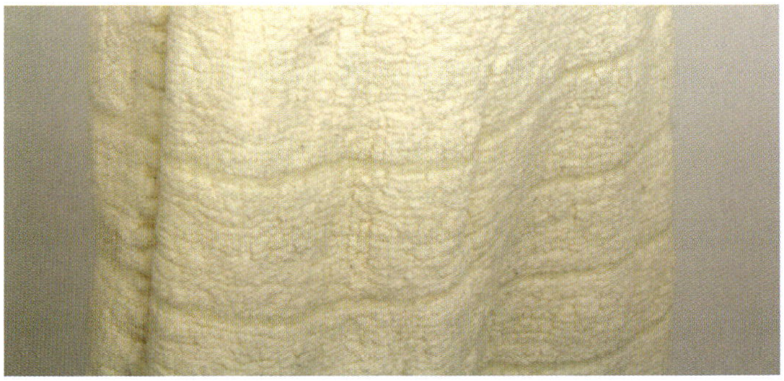

The cotton weft is the same used for the warp. The underlying wool tube impacted on the cotton tube during wet-finishing, which was done in a front-loading washing machine. Because of this, the cotton layer is integrated with the wool layer, leading to a very different texture.

If active yarns are used for the inner tube, extra dimensional impact will be obtained. Changing the ratio from 1:1 to 2:1 passive to active (i.e. twice as many outer tube threads than inner) will add extra dimensionality to the mix.

Honeycomb

Honeycomb (UK deflected/distorted weft) adds a very effective additional surface texture of a tube. The plain weave cell outlines can be used as a contrast, especially when using a fairly thick non-active weft yarn, which will provide a counter to the floats and increase the dynamism of the cells. A minimum of eight shafts will be required in order to have two blocks in each layer. Each additional cell will require a further four shafts (two per layer). It is useful to change block at the selvedges as the fold will tend to disappear, although attention has to be paid to the plain weave outline as it turns the curve.

Honeycomb can also be used with the double-tube configuration requiring additional shafts. The inner tube of an active yarn is interlinked with the outer layer for the plain weave outline of the honeycomb. The inner tube can

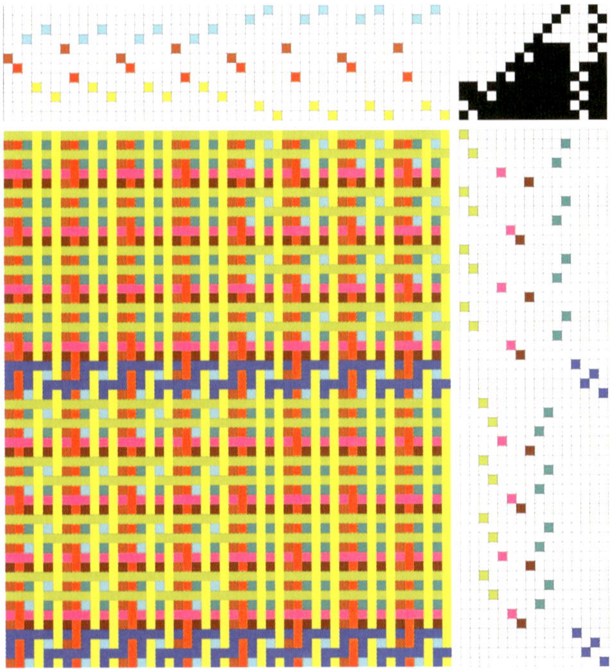

This 12-shaft draft gives all the information for the honeycomb to be used in tubular form. In this draft, the ratio of the outer passive tube to inner active tube is 2:1 in both warp and weft. The inner tube is weaving plain weave and combines with the honeycomb outer tube in the outline picks.

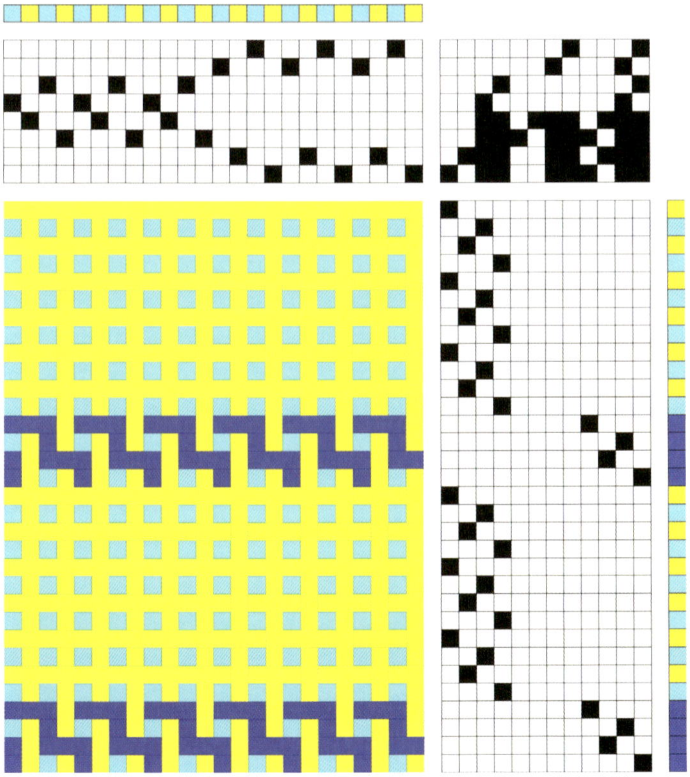

Honeycomb (deflected or distorted weft) can be woven in a tube with passive warps. The draft here shows a passive outline weft in blue.

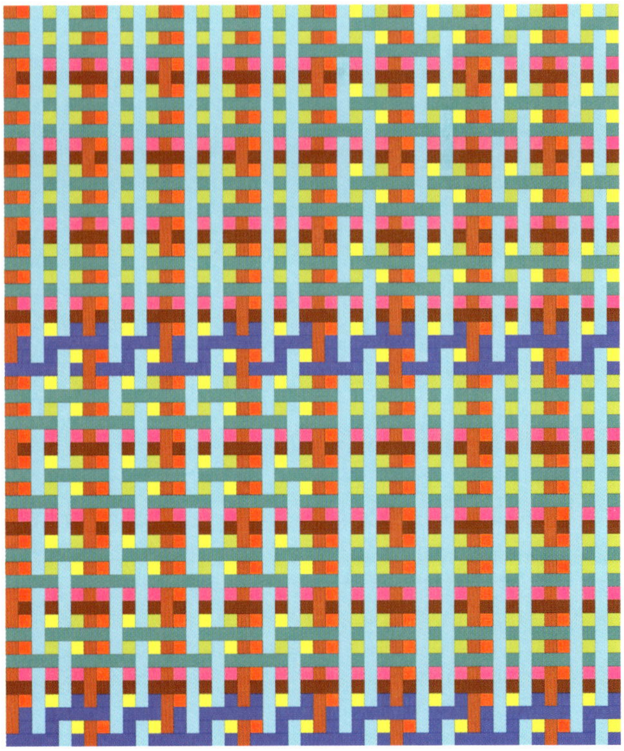

The interweaving of the honeycomb structure on the reverse side of the tube is shown here. As is usual with honeycomb, the block effect of the draft does not show the undulation of the outline weft that occurs when physically weaving the cloth and after wet-finishing.

be left as warp floats or woven in a plain weave at a lower ratio than that of the outer tube.

Alternatively, the two layers can work together to provide different blocks for the honeycomb with different warp yarns for each layer. If the blocks are interchanged through layer interchange, exploring different warp materials would give interesting variations to the external appearance of the tube.

FINISHING OFF

Cutting from the Loom: Woven Hems

The most effective way of creating a woven hem for the tube is to use a finer yarn to weave a tubular section of at least 2in (5cm) that will then be folded over twice to the inside of the tube, either before or after wet-finishing. If additional dimensional surface is being added to the tube through the use of differential shrinkage in the warp, it is advisable to leave the sewing of the hem until after wet-finishing.

Hand-stitching is the best way to sew a hem so that you can catch the inside threads of the back of the tube for an invisible effect. If a hanging system is being installed through plastic tubing or metal or wooden hoops, secure stitching is required, unless the finished weaving is very light in weight.

Cutting from the Loom: Hemstitch

If the tube is consistent throughout, then the cutting from the loom and knotting or hemming of the tube must be approached thoughtfully. Hemstitching on the loom is one of the most secure and well-finished ways. However, hemstitching a tube on the loom at the beginning of the weaving is not easy. It is important to proceed around the selvedge in an O formation, as the bottom layer will be seen from the underneath, and for the hemstitch to be the reverse on the lower layer so that it remains the same visually all the way around the outside of the tube. Some weavers prefer to wait until the fabric is removed from the loom, weight it to give warp tension, separate out the two layers and hemstitch at this point.

Hemstitching at the end of the work is considerably easier on the loom than the beginning and best begun with

USEFUL GUIDE FOR KNOTTING ON THE LOOM

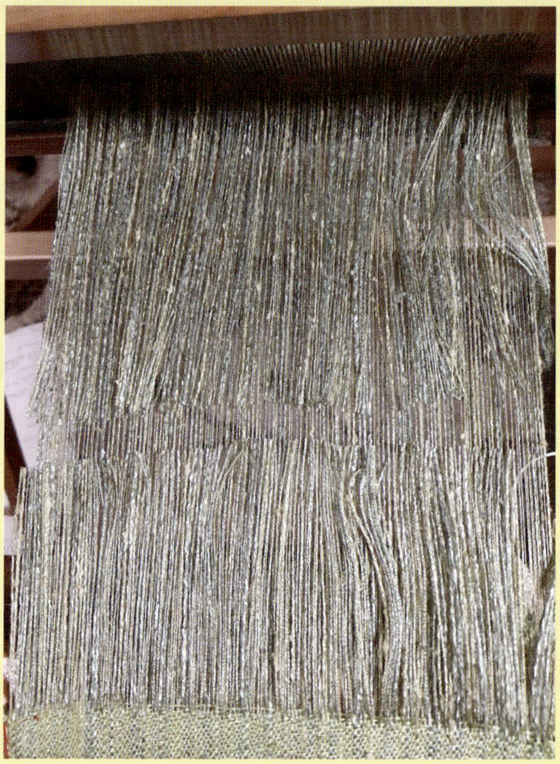

Wind on enough warp so that overhand knots can be created, then raise the top layer to separate the layers. Fix the batten so that it will not inadvertently swing back and accidentally remove the cut ends from the reed. Now cut the top layer, keeping the warp in its dents. It can be useful to tie a slip knot on the first warp group in front of the reed to ensure that any remaining warp will not slip through the reed if further weaving is planned.

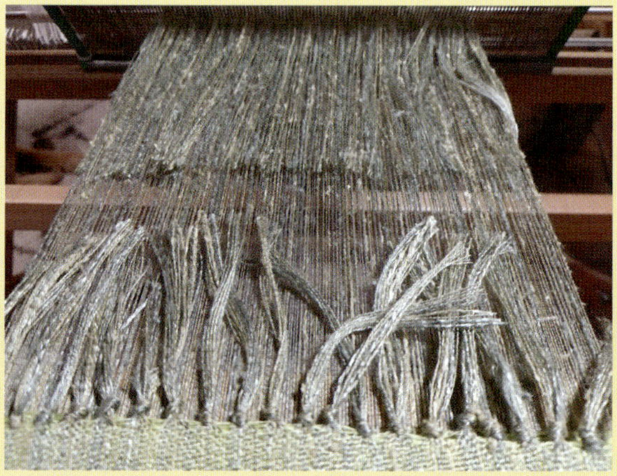

Collate the selvedge dents that are more open on both sides of the warp and cut the two layers for these dents only. Knot close to the first weft on both selvedges of the top layer before continuing across the whole top layer.

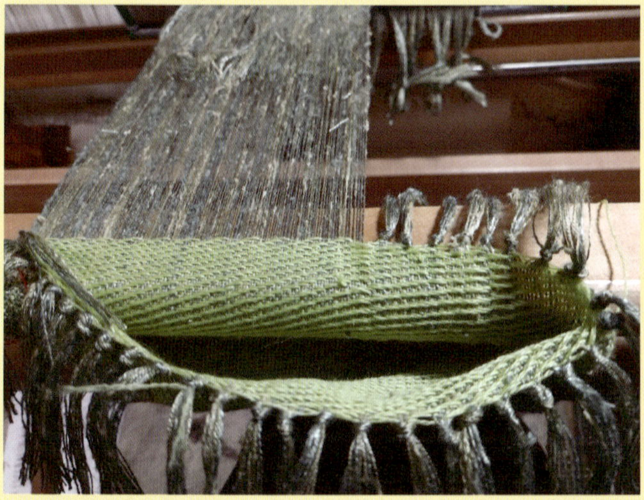

Once the top layer is complete, and using the same number of dents as for the top layer knots, cut each of the remaining warp groups to the required length. Again, use a slip knot to hold the combined warp layers in front of the reed, while using an overhand knot for the bottom layer of the tube to match the top layer.

the top layer lifted and working on the top layer from one side to the other. Then the top layer excess warp will need to be cut away and the hemstitch continued on the lower layer. Again, the lower layer hemstitch needs to appear the same all the way around the tube and the option remains to do this off-loom, as discussed above.

Cutting from the Loom: Overhand Knots

Overhand knotting can alleviate the complication of inverting the hemstitch.

When removing the fabric from the cloth beam, a similar operation for knotting is required. If the warp is knotted to the cloth beam, the initial knots will need to be undone and then separated into the two respective layers before the knots are tied to ensure that the tube remains a tube.

Wet-finishing

When wet-finishing tubular pieces, care must be taken to ensure that any active layers that are intended to be kept apart remain apart during the finishing, especially if a washing machine or tumble dryer is going to be used in the process.

TOP TIP

Alternating cold and hot rinses will encourage wool to contract after the initial hot wash. A washboard, manual manipulation, a washing machine cycle or tumble-drying will accelerate the process.

In addition, anything that is used as a separator must be capable of not being enmeshed with the active layer. Plastic bags knotted together, lightweight tarpaulin and old sheets have been used to keep layers apart. As usual, it all depends on how much shrinkage is required, the woven materials used and the size of the piece.

It can also be useful to turn the tube inside out prior to wet-finishing if there are interior sections that might full to each other.

It is a good idea to tie the interior separator together into a circle and then to stay-stitch the start and end of the fabric together so that shrinkage will be universal and to avoid the fabric bunching up along its length.

It is also advisable to check that nothing is fulling that is not intended to be fulling during the wet-finishing, so that any unscheduled areas that might be beginning to adhere to each other can be gently teased apart without any damage ensuing. Front-loading washing machines often do not allow for this.

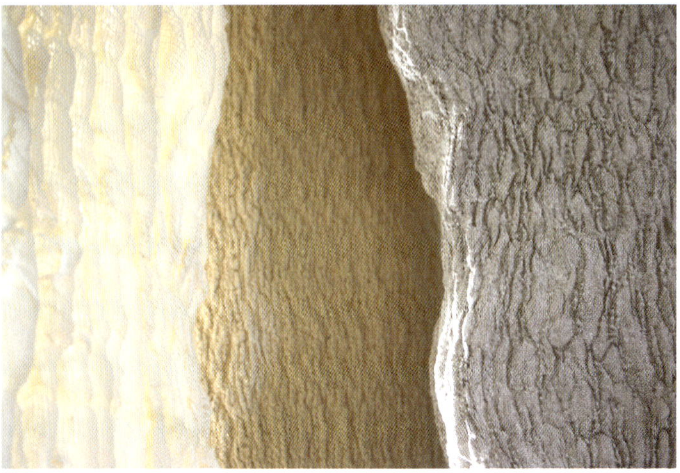

Left to right: stitched double cloth, overshot and shibori methods have been used in these pieces. Austrian paper, an acrylic noil and copper wire have been used as the wefts.

The usual process applies – heat, suds and manipulation (whether by hand or machine) will cause wool to full and eventually to felt. Hot water will cause overtwisted yarns to release their energy, and washing soap, shampoo or dishwashing liquid will remove any residual sizing on wool or other yarns if that has been applied during the spinning process.

Interesting effects can be created by concentrated manipulation in some areas but not others, causing an amalgamation of weaving, fulling and felting.

After Wet-finishing

It is possible to press the curves gently from inside and out with an iron once the work is removed from the loom to help smooth out the curvature of the selvedges, so long as your materials and methods of weaving allow it.

A Weaving Challenge...

If there are enough shafts on your loom, multiple tubes can be created that grow out of one tube; a form of branching like a tree. The various tubes can be side by side, on top of one another or a mix of both. Initial ideas inspired by trees and sea-life, such as certain coral forms, can lead to lots of ideas to explore.

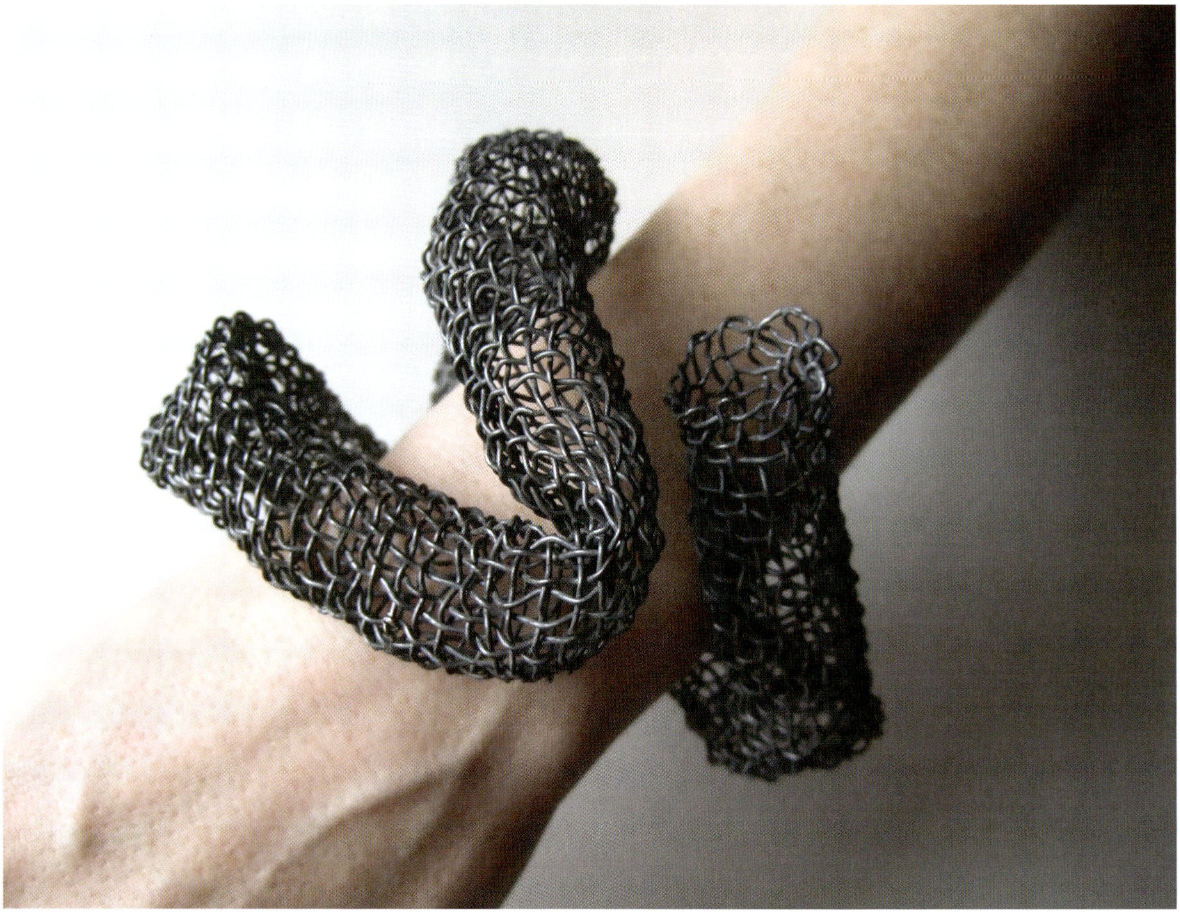

Sue Hiley Harris uses oxidised sterling silver wire (as here), copper and iron wire to weave sculptural pieces. Although not woven on a loom, this tubular piece can be used as jewellery, inspiring ideas of other ways to use tubular forms. *925 Folded #4*.

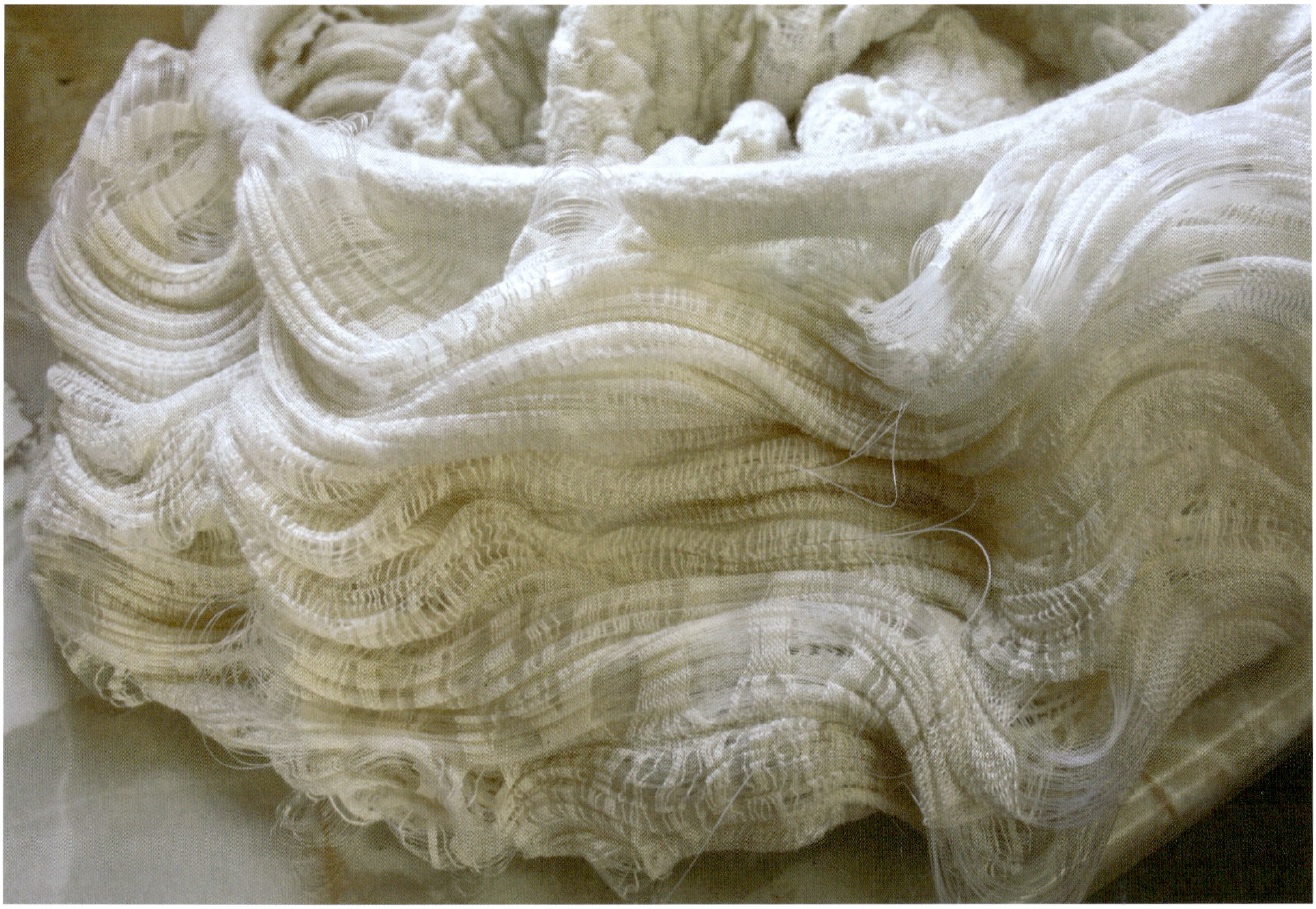

'Clam' - a double-tube (inner tube of wool, and outer tube cotton) woven with stitched double cloth and monofilament weft takes on another interpretation when presented in a different way.

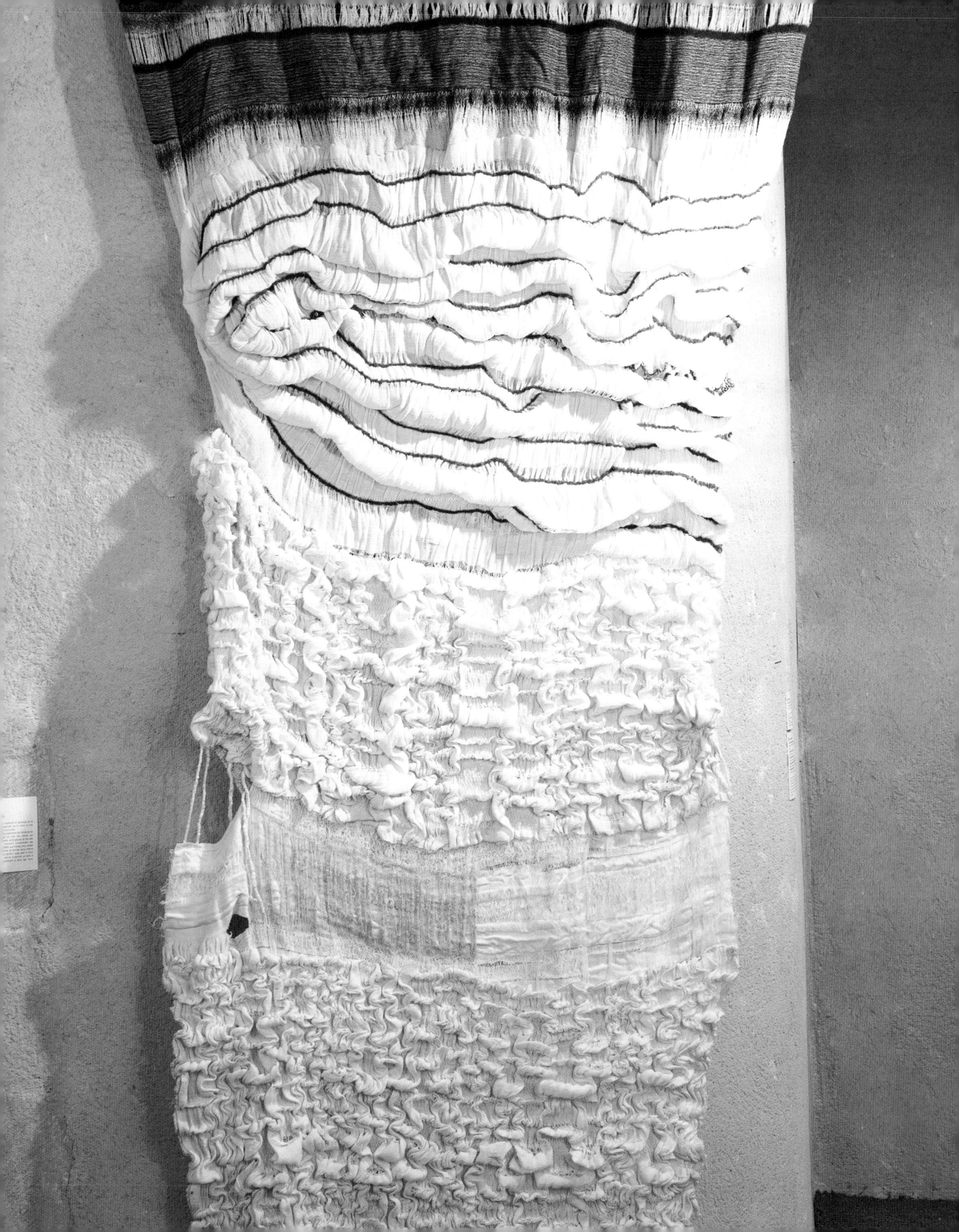

CHAPTER 14

SCULPTURAL SHAPING ON AND OFF THE LOOM

This final chapter describes some of the more extreme dimensional effects that can be created both during shaft-loom weaving, using several of the techniques already discussed, and some extreme wet-finishing. It also employs methods that can be adopted after the work is removed from the loom.

It encompasses both high-dimensional relief for wall pieces or flat-based artwork, and also sculptural assistance. This latter is probably the hardest area to demonstrate as it requires the ingenuity of the artist and the availability of more unusual supplies to create the desired artistic outcome for a project. It is hoped that some of these suggestions will spark an idea of how they could be applied to your own creations.

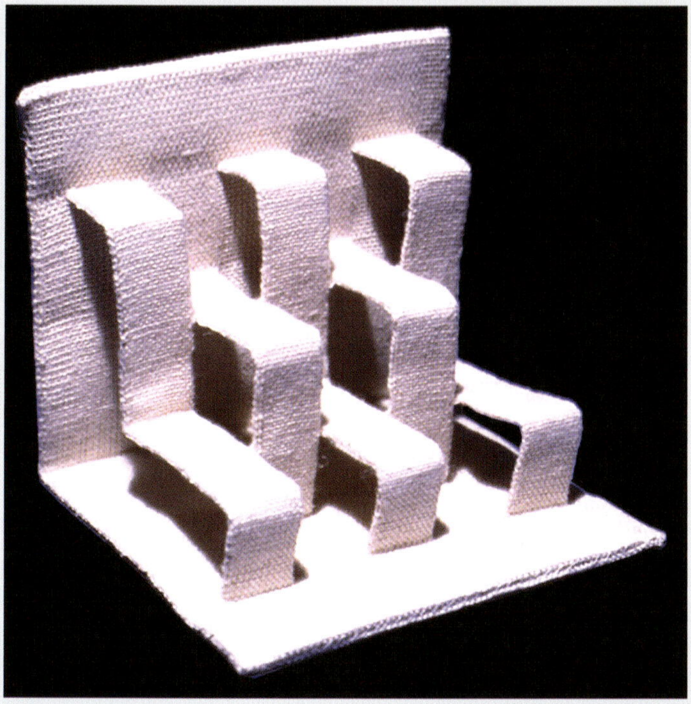

This sculptural piece by Paul O'Connor is woven in paper and uses various discontinuous weft techniques to achieve the dimensional relief.

Strata Wall II.

Using Handspun Yarns

Handspun yarns are especially useful for creating dimensional effects. Used independently, or as areas of weft attached to each other sporadically across the width of the warp, they can not only give a tactile quality but also dimensional shrinkage of varying intensities, depending on the methods used to spin them.

Woollen-spun yarns, with their greater loftiness and propensity for more shrinkage due to being spun from the rolag, can be contrasted with worsted-spun yarns. The latter are often heavier as they are prepared and spun so as to eliminate air. The fibre is combed from the middle of the staple to the tip, then turned around and combed again from the middle, this time to the cut base. They are spun in a parallel fashion, by drawing out a small triangle of fibre from the prepared staple, then allowing the twist into the drawn fibre – a short forward-draw method. They usually require more twist, and in the process of spinning, the scales are smoothed down so that they cannot overlap each other and cause felting.

There is a halfway house called semi-worsted. Basically, this uses a commercially carded (or carded on a drum carder) fibre, which is *not* formed into a rolag. The resulting long length of carded fibre, or roving, is then spun from one end in a worsted manner, keeping the carded fibres

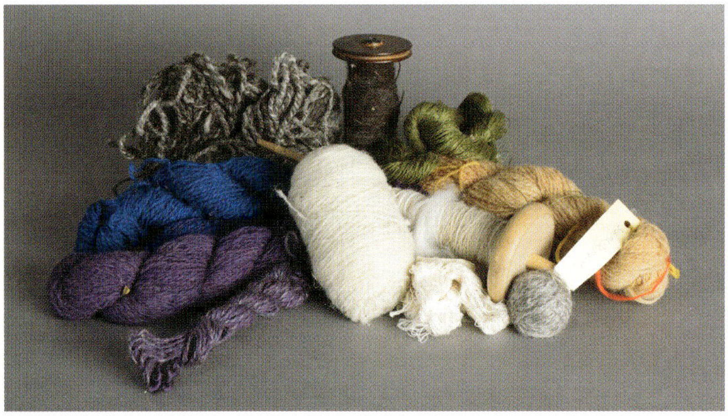

Handspun yarns spun in many techniques, such as thick/thin, slub and plying with different fibres. (Photo: Colin Usher)

parallel to each other. Semi-worsted often is spun in a short-draw or medium-draw, but with the same forward draft motion as worsted. It is also possible to spin it with the long-draw method, which traps a limited amount of air in the yarn.

TAPESTRY TECHNIQUES FOR INSPIRATION

There is considerable interest in three-dimensional shaping in tapestry weaving and books available for those whose passion is through tapestry. Even though this book is not about tapestry weaving, tapestry is a source of interesting techniques that can be applied to shaft-loom weaving, especially when allied to material properties and finishing techniques. Any of the following methods can be employed for your shaft-loom projects.

Tapestry is, by and large, a weft-faced fabric, with the potential for creating wonderful imagery with a very simple two- or four-shaft loom, vertically or horizontally mounted. Traditionally, it was woven sideways, i.e. the length of the warp became its width when hung on a wall.

All that is required is a shed on plain weave or a twill. The warp is spaced quite openly and is usually very strong. The weft is beaten in to cover the warp entirely using a weighted comb, fingers or a fork.

The simplicity of equipment allows for the maximum of design potential, with images or shapes able to be woven in segments, as opposed to having a single pick across the whole of the warp. Often, designs are created on paper – a cartoon – and attached to the warp in some way so as to allow the design to be followed closely during the weaving process. Other times, tapestry weavers prefer to follow what their instinct tells them to do.

There are different methods of weaving tapestry, sometimes building up a specific area of colour or shape independently of other areas, sometimes building up a pick of many different yarns, connecting the areas of colour through different joining techniques, or deliberately weaving adjacent areas separately with no connection, which create slits that can be left or sewn up after the work is finished.

Discontinuous Weft

Discontinuous weft, which is a very familiar method of tapestry weaving, does not often find itself in the shaft-loom weaver's lexicon. Discontinuous weft simply means that the weft yarn is used in one area only, similar in some ways to brocade. Whereas brocade is a supplementary weft effect used in small independent areas on top of a ground weave or replacing the ground weave only in that very small area, discontinuous weft forms part of the ground weave but is a specific yarn selected for that one area.

In order to create a full pick across the warp, several wefts are used in their own discrete areas to form the complete woven row. For shaft-loom weaving purposes, each weft is woven in order across the width of the warp so that one complete pick is made at a time. Often, small butterflies or bobbins of the individual yarns are used as it is generally easier to manipulate these rather than shuttles. The wefts can then be beaten up together for each complete pick. In tapestry, these are often woven in discrete blocks, with each block being woven at a time.

Different methods of discontinuous weft leave either vertical gaps in the fabric (meet and separate) or overlap in different ways.

Clasped weft in particular leads to spontaneity while weaving. For each pick, the clasping place of two weft yarns can be varied, giving even more creative choices. The choice of whether to return the two weft yarns in the same shed or to change shed before returning to the selvedges is entirely the weaver's.

Combine different fibres with different weave structures and many surface dimensions can be created. Uneveness in weaving in this situation – with a build-up of thicker

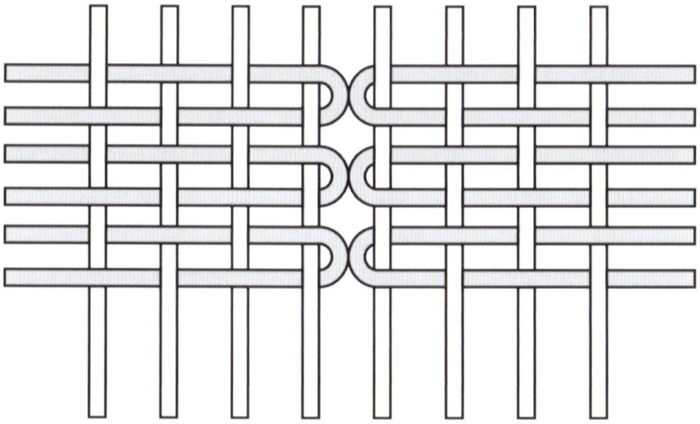

These line drawings show different tapestry techniques that can be used in shaft weaving for sculptural effects as well as for regular weaving. 'Meet and separate' has two weft yarns approaching from opposite directions. They meet but do not cross before returning to their respective sides on the next shed.

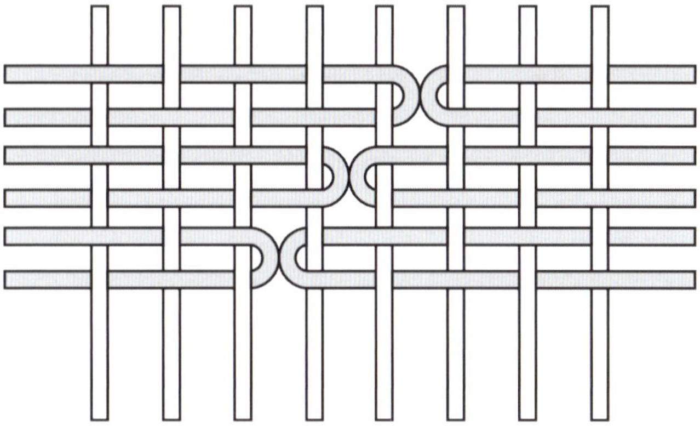

This is 'meet and separate' but moving across the warp end-by-end.

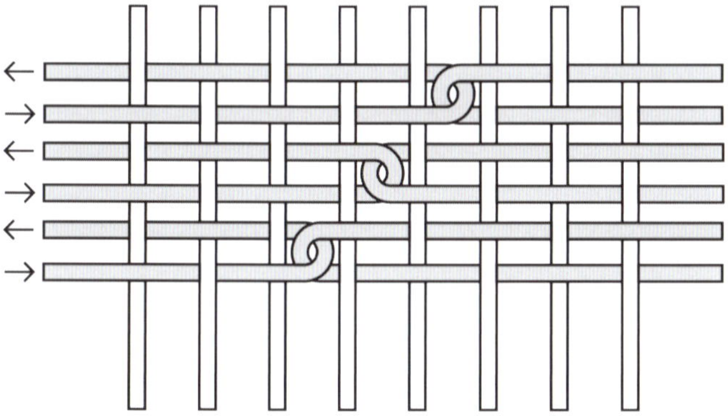

This is clasped weft and in this example, two weft yarns meet and interlock before returning to their respective sides in the next shed.

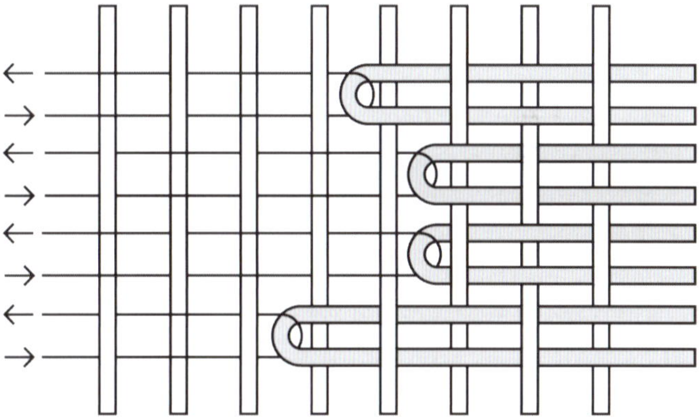

Here different thicknesses of yarn are meeting, interlocking then returning in the same shed to their respective sides, which allows the two wefts to be freely moved through the shed according to the weaver's intentions.

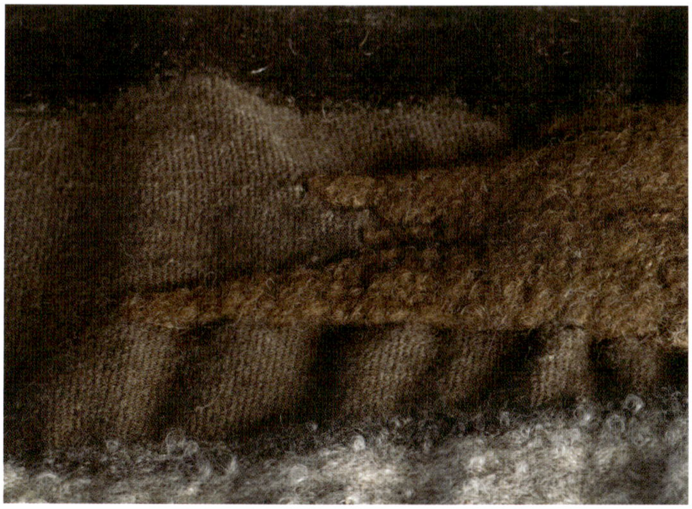

This image shows the 'meet and separate' method of abutting wefts. The thick wool on the left needed fewer picks than the thin wool on the right, so any other method would not have worked here. (Photos: Colin Usher)

This part of the work incorporates both 'meet and separate' and clasped weft, but using the two sheds.

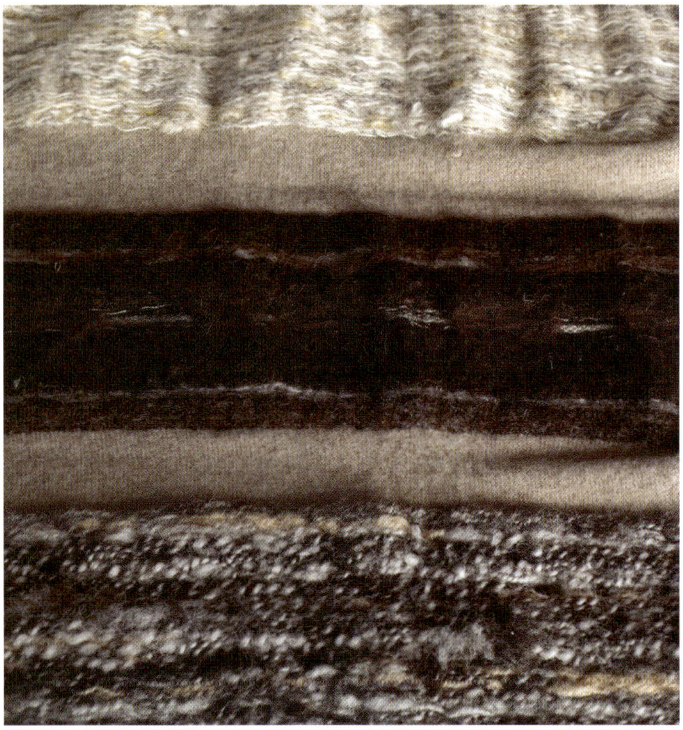

A combination of methods were used in the sections here, along with handspun yarns. When creating art pieces, anything goes, so long as it gives the desired effect and holds together as a fabric. (Photo: Colin Usher)

wefts in contrast to areas of finer wefts or wools in contrast to silks – will create ripples in the surface, especially if the fabric is wet-finished with heat and suds. If you have the patience, you can use a tapestry beater and build up different areas for yourself. However, with the loom's beater, you can beat as normal, including more picks for thinner wefts and fewer for thicker wefts.

Multiple Wefts

Other dimensional emphasis can be created using several wefts in one pick but using them in several places and allowing the weft to float between those particular woven areas. This specifically leads to long weft floats at the back of the fabric, but if these are of wool or other shrinking yarns, they will contract on wet-finishing and cause the areas on top of the floating yarns to pucker and be raised from the underlying floats. This is a method that can be employed in many different ways and to great effect. The weave structure can be whatever you please, but plain weave gives the most dimensional result on wet-finishing.

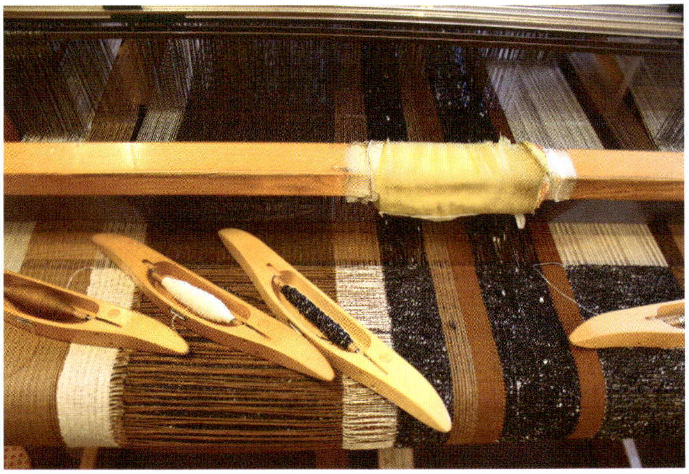

Multiple wefts can be used across the width of the fabric, weaving only where they are required, crossing the whole warp – unless an unwoven warp area is required. Where they do not weave, they float, sometimes on one side of the fabric and sometimes on the other. This is work in progress on *Strata Wall I*.

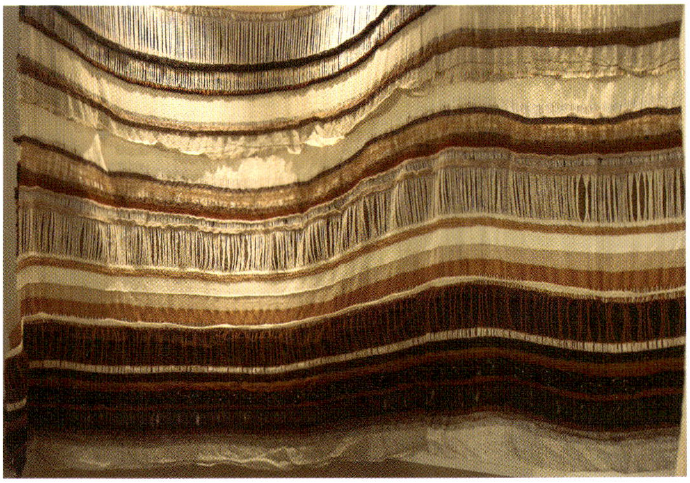

Strata Wall I is comprised of three lengths of the same warp sewn together but leaving small gaps. It is a double-sided piece using principally multiple-weft technique.

Sett

Varying the sett of the warp across the width of the work can also give surface ripples and undulations. The following methods are available to create effects.

Open-top Reed

The use of an open-top reed will allow for setts to be changed while the warp is on the loom and therefore during the weaving process of a particular piece, which can also be a fun way to explore sett variation and weft build-up. However, changing setts incrementally is advised to avoid undue stress on the warp. Experimentation is required.

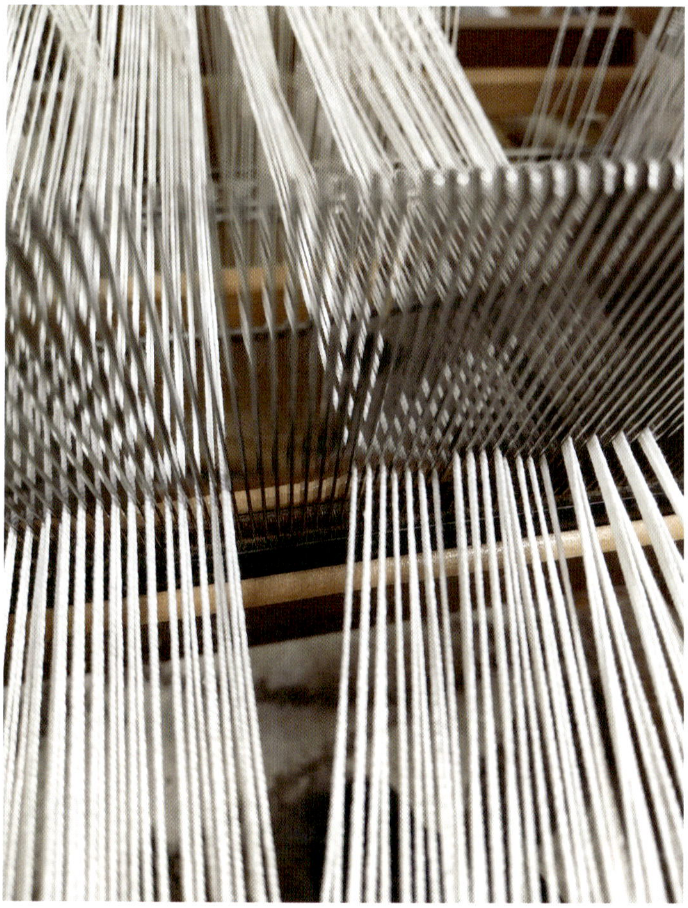

An open-top reed can be very useful for resleying in the middle of a piece without cutting the fabric off the loom. The reed cover has been taken off to show how simple it is to move the ends around. Different numbers of ends in each dent can be seen.

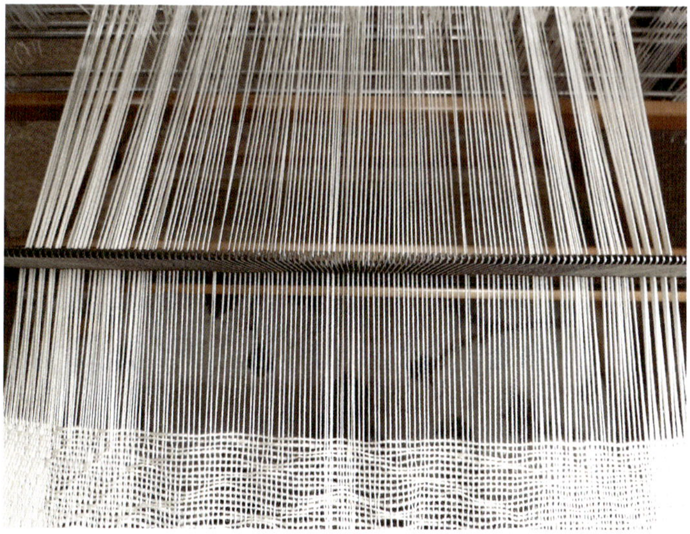

The same warp has been resleyed to smaller gaps but varied spacing. If using this on a table loom, it is useful to clamp the edges of the reed to the beater in order to be able to lift the top off the reed easily and still keep the reed stable in the beater. Large stationery bulldog clips can be helpful.

The Rail Reed™

This system allows you to change the density of sett as you weave without having to re-sley. Using hinged elements, individual reed modules can be changed from an open sett to a much tighter sett by squeezing the module sides and securing them with metal pins. Each module is independent of the others and can be at whatever density you wish.

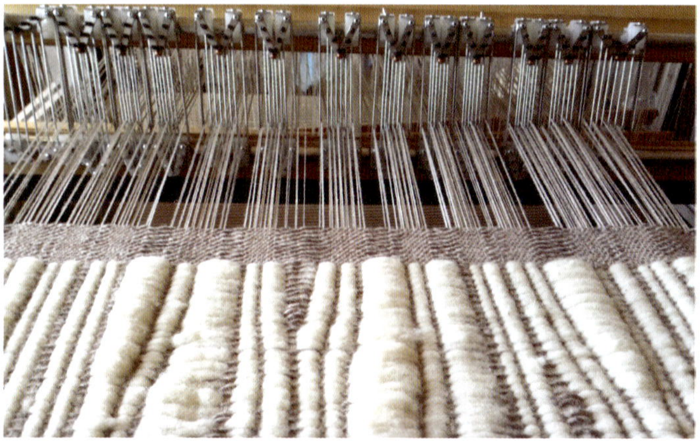

The Rail Reed™, designed and developed by Kadi Pajupuu, allows for contraction and expansion of specified sections of a warp according to the designer's intention. (Photo: Kadi Pajupuu)

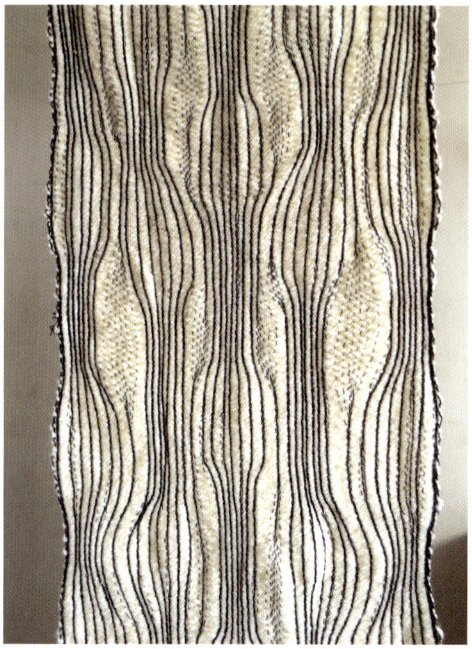

This piece, woven by Kadi, shows the effect of the undulation created. (Photo: Kadi Pajupuu)

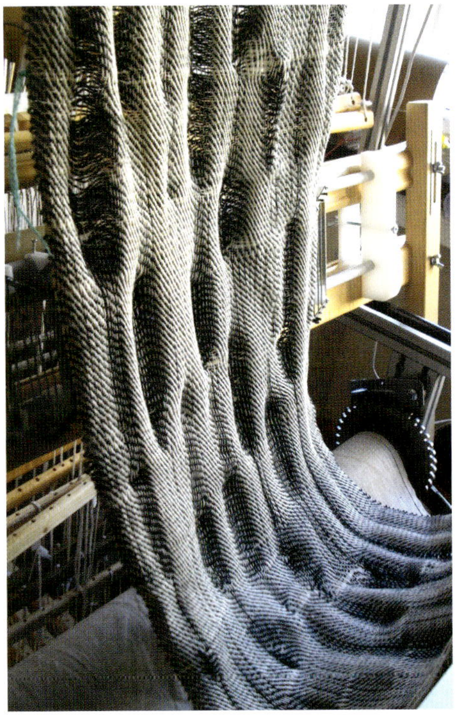

Juula Pärdi wove this beautifully dimensional cloth with the Rail Reed™ using a warp-faced twill. (Photo: Juula Pärdi)

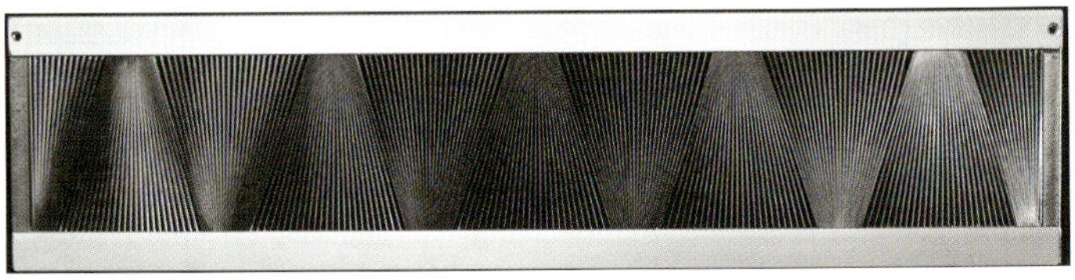

This Lars fan reed (also known as ondulé) is literally shaped in opposing fan shapes. They can be of different dentage and angles. (Photo: Nat Rea)

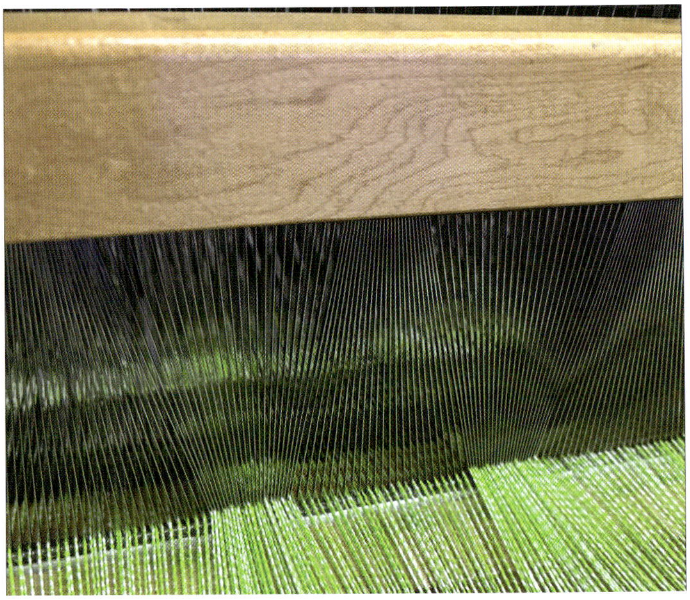

The fan reed in use at its lowest point. A system on the loom is required to raise the beater in increments so that the weaving can progress from the lower part of the fan reed through the mid-height (even dentage) to the other part at the top of the reed. Note: the physics of weaving does not allow for the two extremes at the very top and bottom of the reed.

Fan Reeds

Also known as ondulé reeds, this can also be a method of creating texture, depending on the materials used and the wet-finishing employed. They require adaptations to be made to the beater to allow the reed to be moved up and down in height at regular intervals. More information can be found in Norma Smayda's book *Ondulé Textiles* (*see* Bibliography).

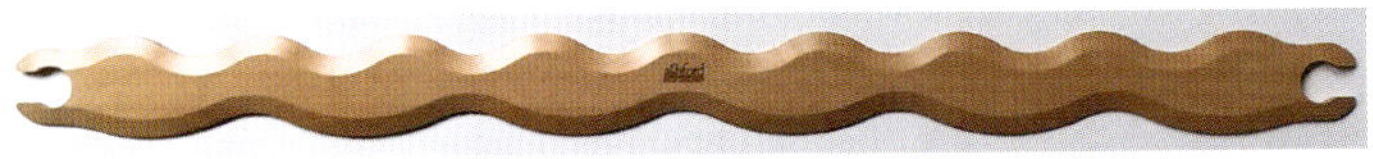

This wavy shuttle gives two different forms that can be used to create undulations in the weft through beating with this instead of a regular reed. Homemade devices can also be used. Gentle curves work best, and gradually shifting the shuttle across the width of the warp gives undulating wave effects.

Curved Edge Shuttles

Shuttles with curved edges can also be used to create undulations in the surface of the fabric by incrementally moving the shuttle a small amount each time the weft is placed in the shed.

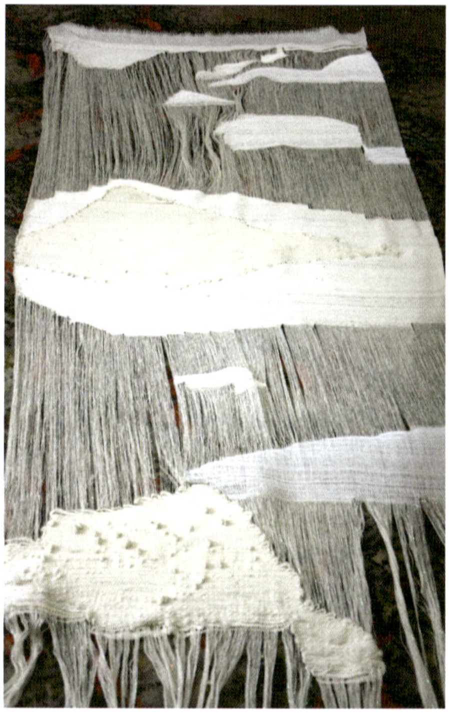

An artwork designed with large areas of unwoven warp, along with tapestry woven and fully woven areas highlighting different yarns and textural techniques is laid out prior to wrapping of the unwoven warps before wet-finishing.

The unwoven warps are tied together with small plastic strips cut from recyclable plastic bags. The tying is designed to allow small sections to full together as wool is one component in the warp.

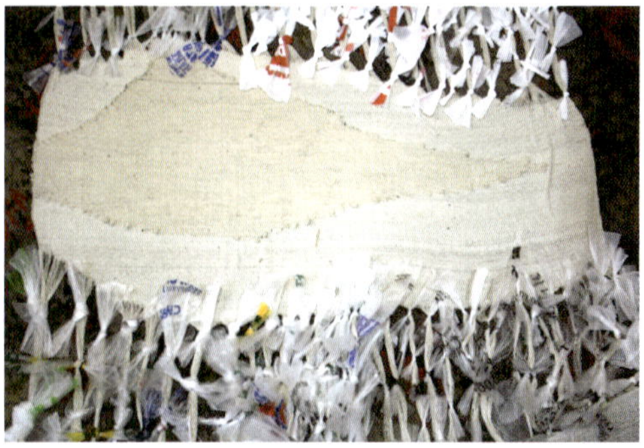

A detail showing the ties but also the deliberate looping of the thicker weft inlay where it changes shed.

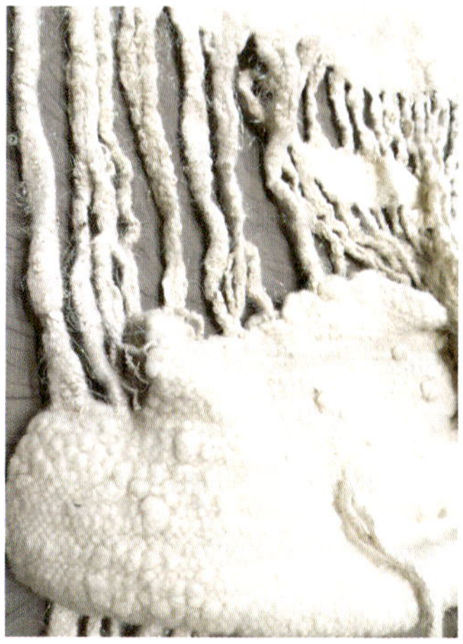

After wet-finishing, the unwoven warps have fulled together in their tied configurations.

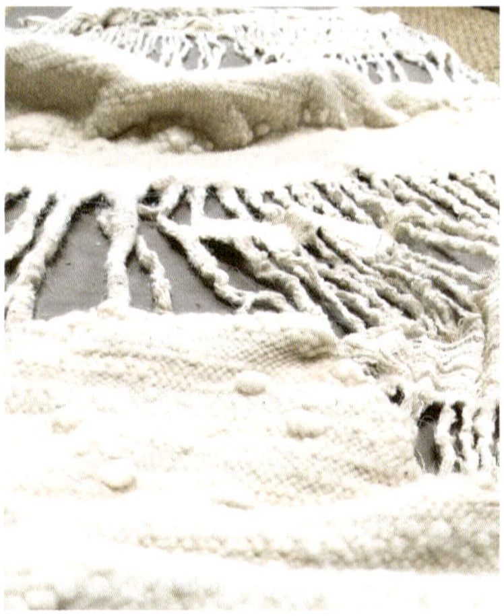

Dimensional texture has also appeared due to the unwoven warps behind selected areas.

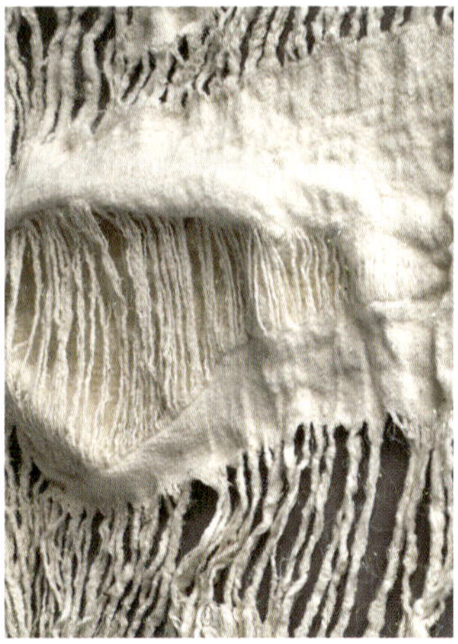

This shows the reverse of one of the selected areas where the warps have been left as floats to create a distinctive dimensional effect.

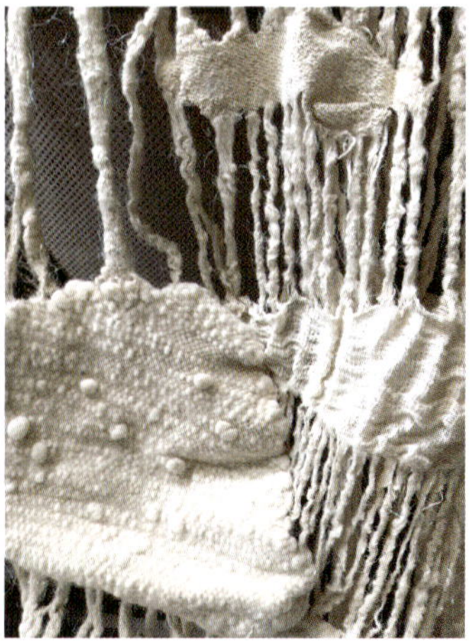

Differences in materials used for the woven sections can be seen, with the thicker wool complete with loops on the left, Austrian paper yarn on the right and a thick cotton rug warp yarn for the top section.

Unwoven Warps

In shaft-loom weaving, as well as in tapestries, translucent effects can be created through leaving warp threads unwoven. This can be taken to extremes for artistic endeavours. If the warps have elastomeric properties, or have shrinking potential, then many variations are possible. With single layer cloth, warp threads can be left unwoven, using discontinuous wefts in specific areas and leaving the bare warp scaffolding in place in others. Upon wet-finishing, wool warps will shrink, creating visually heavy areas where the weaving remains and causing puckering and distortion.

With two or more layers, shrinking warp floats can be left unwoven behind a woven section to cause the puckering effect. The variations of effects here are considerable, including:

- Bringing the warps to the front of the fabric and leaving unwoven;
- Using different weave structures with different take-up and shrinkage rates according to the lengths of warp and/or weft floats in the structure, and so on.

Your imagination is the limit here!

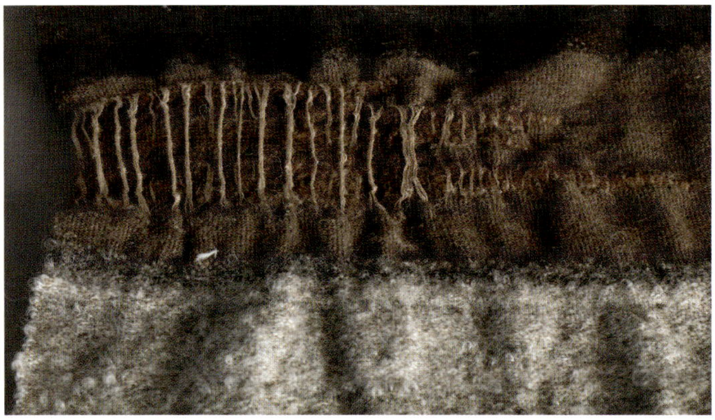

Warp floats left deliberately behind this piece enabled extra dimensionality on the surface to give the impression of tree boles. (Photos: Colin Usher)

Pulled Warps

We have covered one method of pulling threads – shibori – in both warp and weft in Chapter 6. This is not the same. Shibori warps and wefts are generally removed after their gathering purpose has been fulfilled. However, pulled warps as used in tapestry remain in situ as part of the framework of the fabric after pulling.

Susan Iverson's book *Tapestry with Pulled Warp* gives detailed examples of how to use this technique with tapestry, which has the density required to create stiff shaping, but the same techniques can be used, with caution and attention to the material qualities and weave structures in both warp and weft, for regular weft-faced fabric. A certain stiffness is required to hold the forms, or stiffness added after pulling, with the addition of resin, starch or PVA glue.

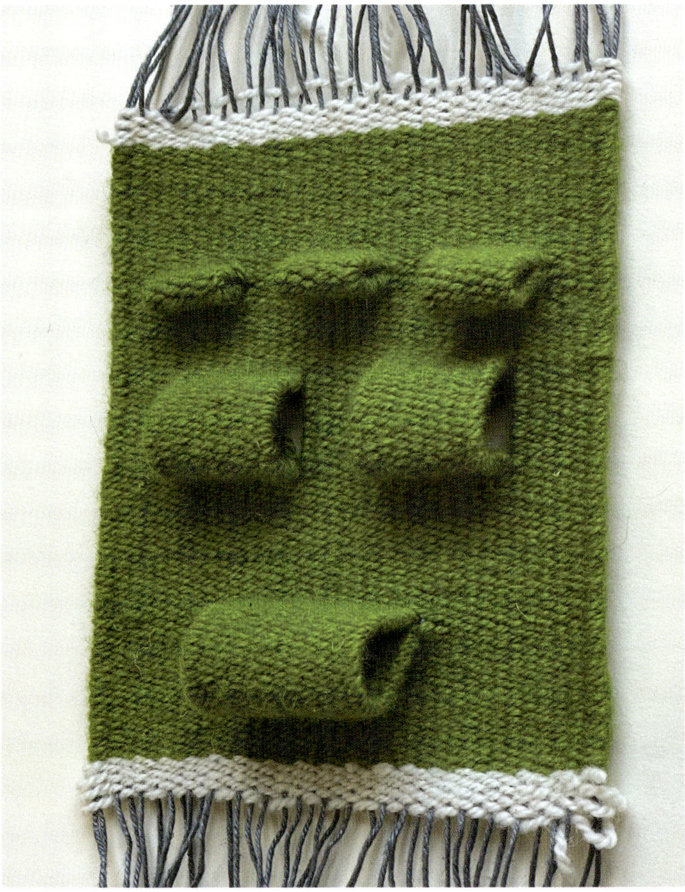

This graphic example of pulled warp tapestry in a sampler by Susan Iverson shows the possibilities of different sizes and methods of creating these dimensional forms. (Photo: Susan Iverson)

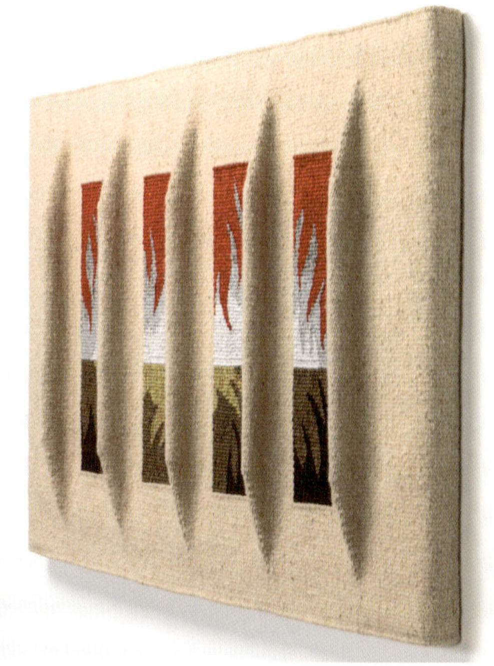

Horizon – Desert Fire was woven in wool, linen and silk on a linen warp, with the pulled warp technique used for the ridges in between the tapestry design areas. This piece has been hung sideways to allow for the dimensional ridges to run vertically. (Photo: Taylor Dabney)

The technique incorporates areas of pre-planned unwoven warp, but the unwoven areas are gently pulled through the weaving with great care after the work is removed from the loom prior to any finishing process. This creates the strong dimensional shaping that becomes integral to the work.

Multiple Techniques

Throughout this book we have been talking about specific separate techniques used to create different amounts and forms of dimensional texture in surfaces and sculpture. However, several of these can often be used together in the same piece. For instance, using woven shibori or overshot for texture in specific areas could be combined with double cloth. Interchanging layers and stitched double cloth used in the same piece can give many different effects. Sampling will give experience to know which ones are effective for combining to create the desired result, alongside material qualities and shrinkage potential.

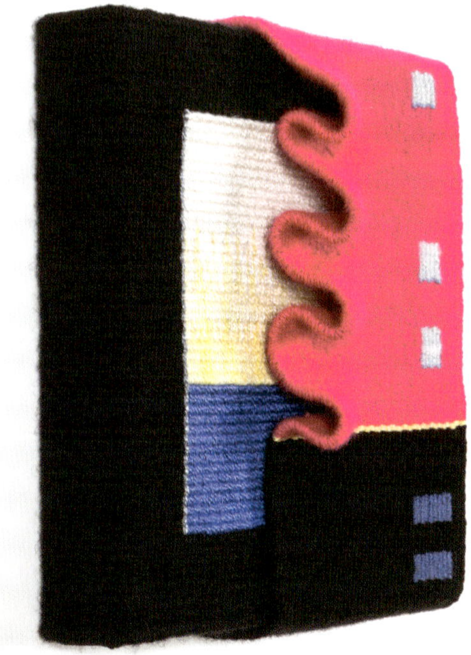

Magenta Morning uses the technique to create ruffled edges to the secondary layer. There is much to be explored in this technique. (Photo: Taylor Dabney)

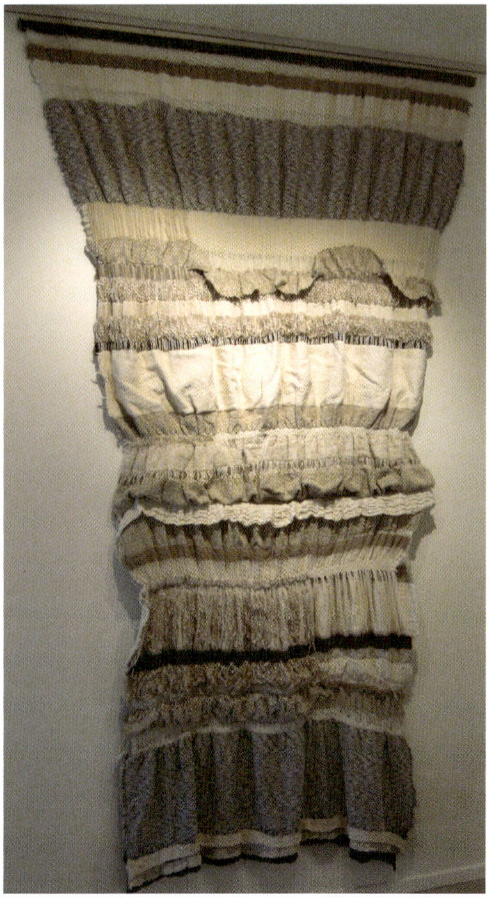

Strata Wall III is an example of using several techniques, including shibori, floating warps and multiple wefts. Materials choices were made to give contrasting effects. Colours were chosen to remain muted and natural so as not to detract from the textural and dimensional effects.

PHYSICAL PRODUCT METHODS OF SHAPING AFTER WEAVING

While many of us like to create pieces that are complete after wet-finishing, there is much to be said for continuing the creative process after we have finished the weaving, especially when creating sculptural pieces. This is an important area that should not be ignored, even if the bulk of this book is about creating the dimensional effects through weave itself using structure, materials and wet-finishing.

Inclusions

Inclusions were mentioned in Chapters 3 and 12 to aid in the final positioning of sculptural projects. Inclusions can be incorporated into any double or multi-layered fabric, whether the bottom layer is woven or unwoven. They are inserted during the weaving, after the work is removed from the loom, or after wet-finishing. Flat forms can include metal sheeting (copper, aluminium, stainless steel), wood or plastic-based forms. Perspex can be easily cut to specific shapes. More unusual but commercially available forms such as plastic right-angle lengths can also be used.

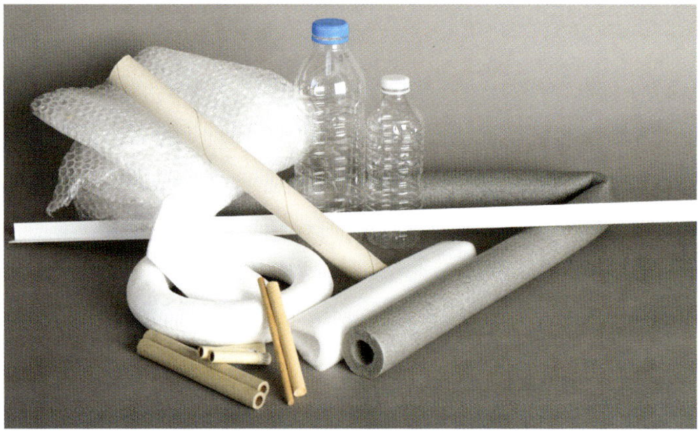

Some inserts are as simple as bubble wrap to add gentle volume after wet-finishing. Stiffer elements can include rolls from various kitchen and bathroom supplies, tubes cut from various bottle forms, foam tubes from parcel protection, swimming pool noodles, insulation for pipes, etc. (Photo: Colin Usher)

TOP TIP

Exploratory visits to home supplies, swimming pool supplies, outdoor supplies and hardware stores can lead to some very interesting discoveries.

Stiffening Products

These can be added to forms after finishing to hold them in the desired position. This includes PVA glue (polyvinyl alcohol), which is a biodegradable, non-toxic, water-soluble synthetic polymer that can be painted on, usually drying clear, or diluted for a softer result. Starches of various sorts can also be painted on in specific areas to aid with support and stiffening.

Resins can also be used, but research is advisable, as often certain resins may not remain translucent over long periods of time.

Softer forms such as buckram, interlinings and various polyester films (polyethylene terephthalate (PET) such as Mylar) might well be added during weaving, but this depends on the qualities of the materials being used and the design of the sculptural piece.

Other Methods

Other methods include special forms to hold work, such as the rods devised by Peter Collingwood for some of his sculptural *Macrogauzes*. The dimensional rods were cut into a V shape, then slotted into place between the chosen woven rods after the piece had been removed from the loom, being held in place by both the V shapes on either end and the weight of the macro, which provided enough tension to keep them in situ. Jason Collingwood, who assisted his father, mentioned that they also tied the rods in place for extra security for larger *Macros*. The V-shaped rods were an elegant and simple solution.

All additional supports for giving extra dimensional form to your work must be considered prior to the weaving commencing. Any feature of your work is important as to how it is created, interpreted and hung. If a piece is worth spending your time and energy on planning and executing, then the hanging or showing method is also worth equal consideration in advance.

Sometimes, of course, methods have to be adapted after the work is removed from the loom and wet-finishing done if required, but without prior thought and planning, the end result is not likely to be as effective as it could have been.

Closing Words

This is by no means an exhaustive book on dimensional weaving. Even during the writing process, more ideas came up that haven't yet found expression! For every question asked and answered, more surfaced. 'What if I used/tried/explored this?' was an everlasting question. But one has to draw the line somewhere or nothing would ever make it to the publisher.

I hope that this has given you a good start in your own investigations into dimensional weaving, or, if you are already experienced, at least that you have new avenues of exploration to take.

As ever, this is just a starting point.

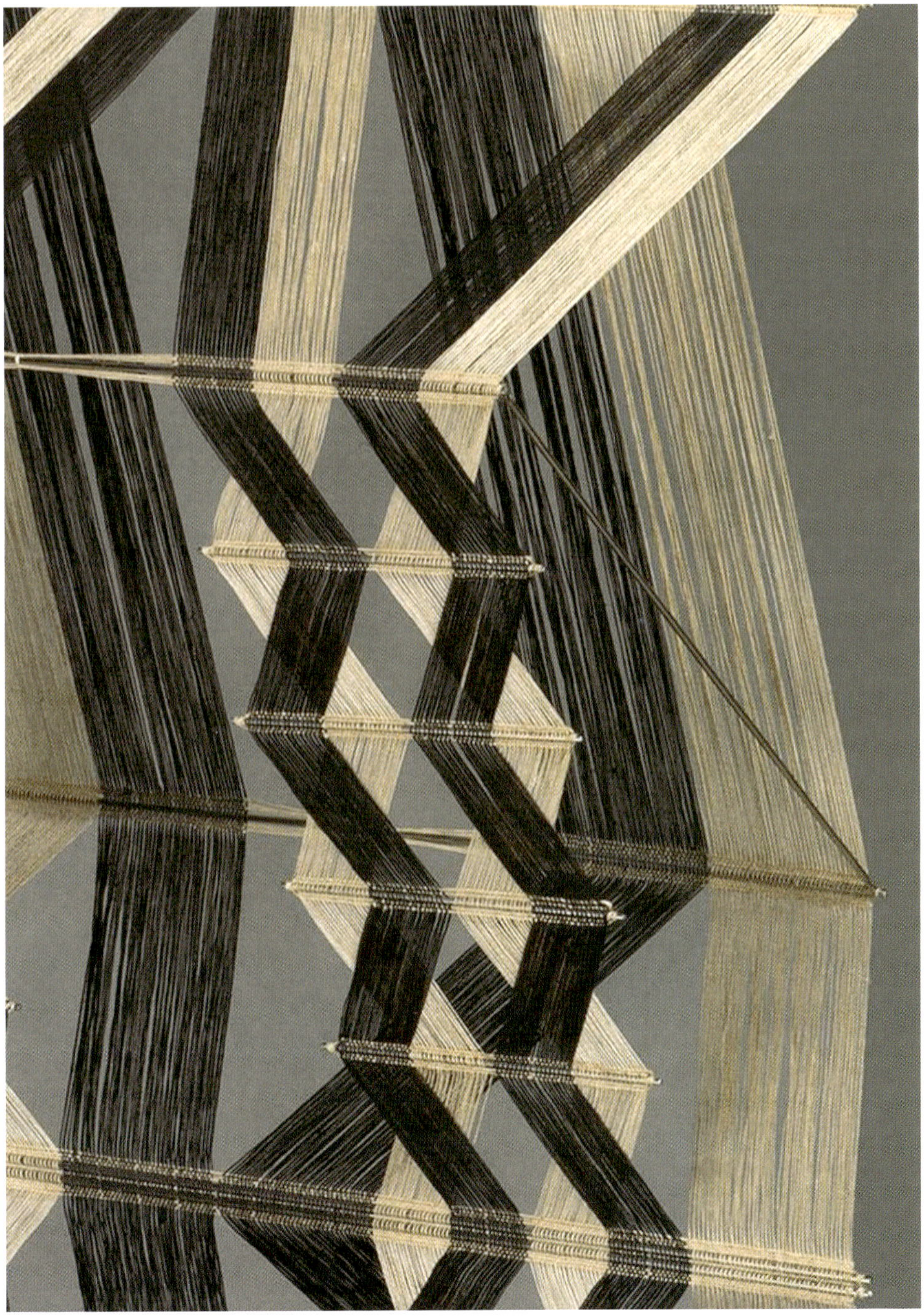

The V-end rods, shown in this detail of a *Macrogauze* by Peter Collingwood, are designed to keep different elements from the artwork at different distances, allowing the work to become sculptural. His inventions for weaving include the shaft-switching device for rug weavers. (Copyright Rose Uniake)

APPENDIX I: USEFUL TECHNIQUES

ADAPTATIONS FOR TEMPLES

Elastane wefts can be challenging for a small loom. If a temple of the required size is not available, one can be made with a little ingenuity from various implements around the home.

Weights can be added using yarn and various bottles, sized according to the amount of weight required. Water can easily be adjusted to give the best result. These are suspended over the side of the loom.

The weights have to be placed so that they are far enough away from the fell to allow for beating up properly because they overlap the sides of the fabric, unlike a regular temple, which only goes across the fabric and doesn't overlap the edges.

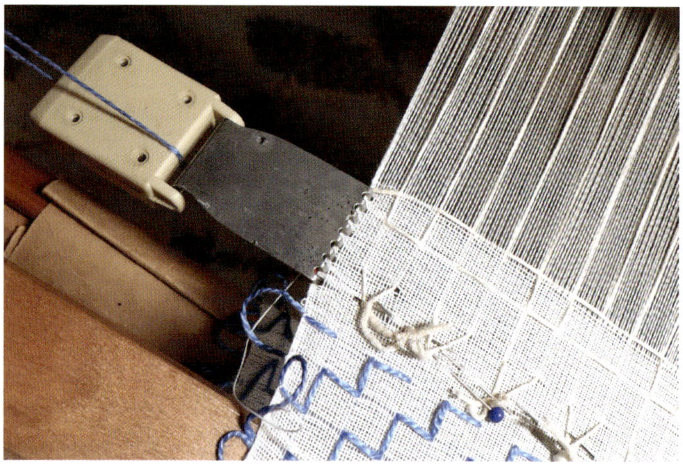

Here, knitting machine weights have been used to act as a temple as their teeth grip the fabric easily. Crimped clasps or anything that will grip and pull without sliding off can be used.

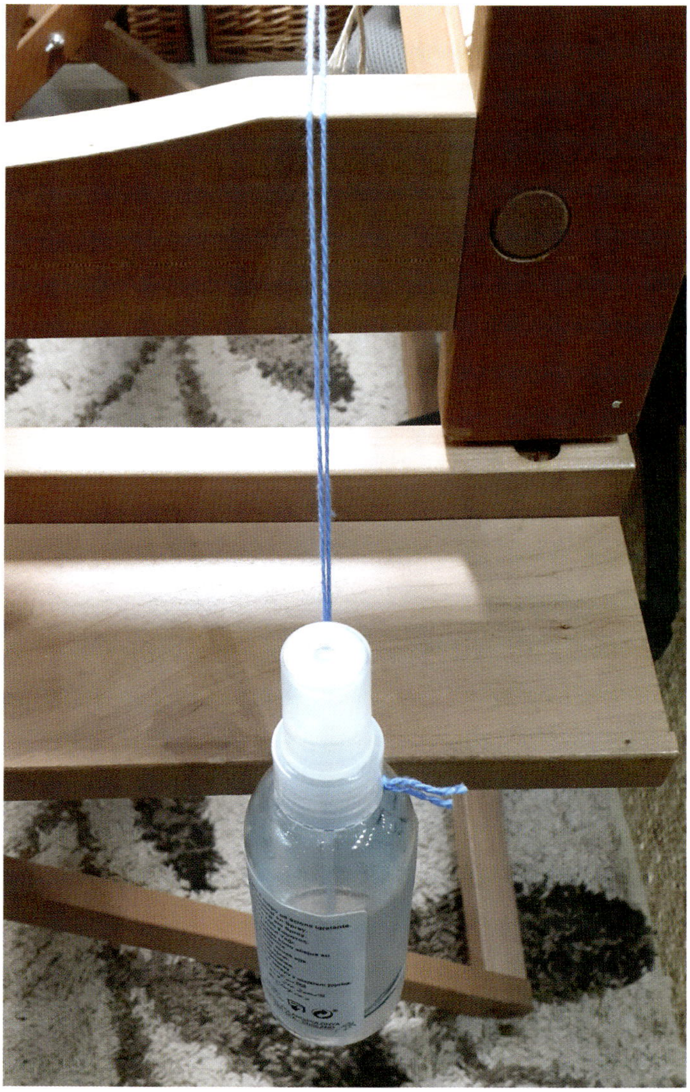

On a table loom with side panels to hold shuttles, it is better to extend the cord to allow for the weight to be free-hanging.

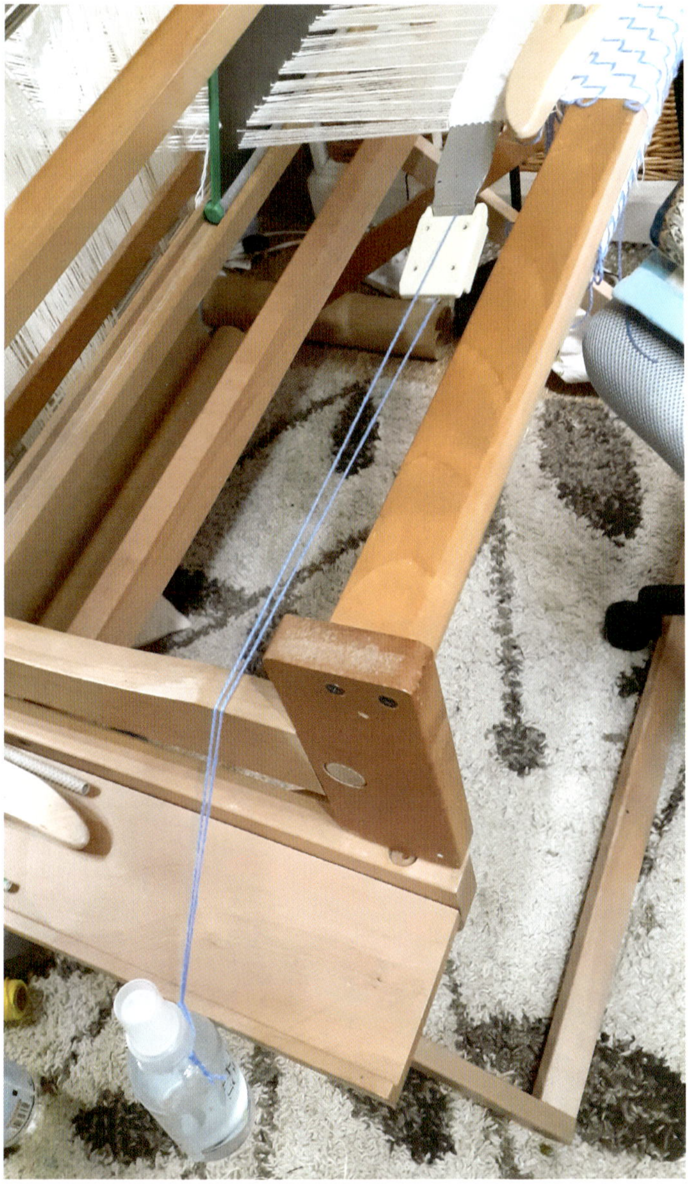

An overview helps to understand the principle.

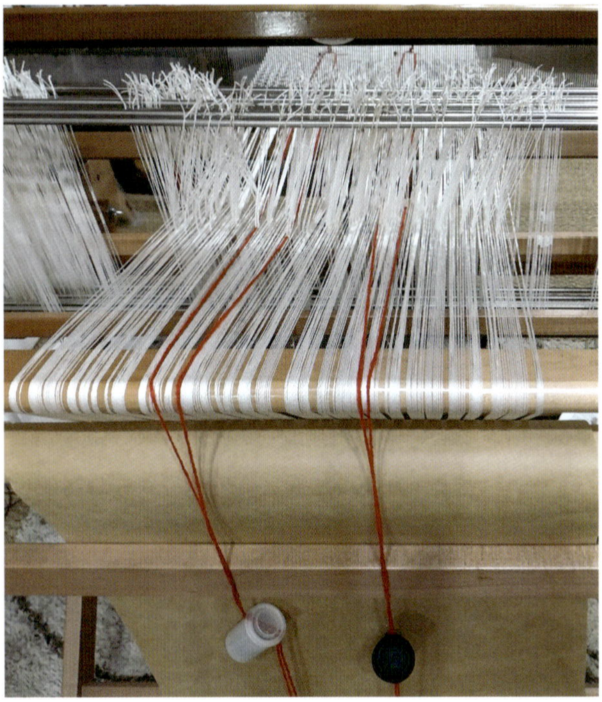

If the secondary warp is not very wide or only has a few ends, it is possible just to weight those ends, using whatever supplies are available, such as washers, small canisters (like the old film canisters) with old or foreign coins or metal nuts (to go with the washers).

ADAPTATIONS FOR ADDING A SECOND WARP TO A SINGLE WARP-BEAM LOOM

Double warp beams can be very useful in textural weaving, but if you don't have one, this is not necessarily a problem. The first suggestion is to suspend a secondary warp from the back beam.

For more ends or a complete width, one method is to have a set of cross- or lease-sticks about mid-way down the length of the hanging ends.

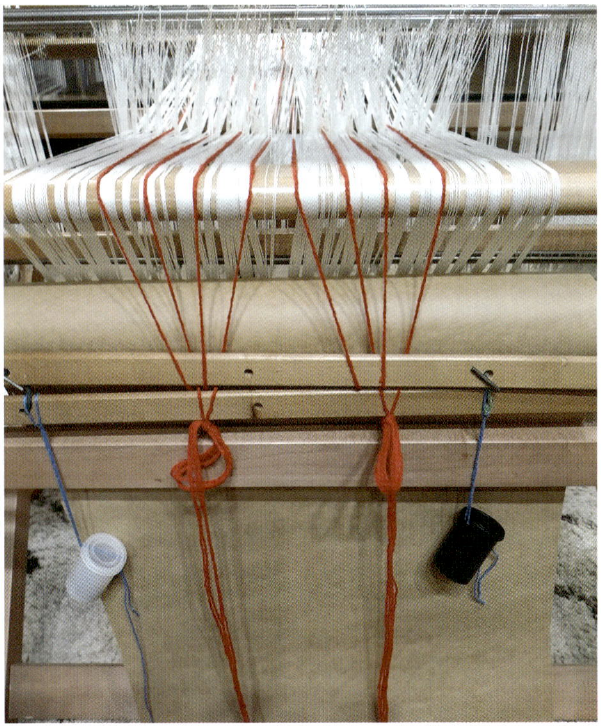

If the ends below are gathered into slip knots, weights can be suspended from the ends of the cross-sticks to balance the weight evenly across the width.

USING A SECOND LOOM'S WARP BEAM: INDIVIDUAL ENDS

A second loom can be the perfect solution, especially if it is a table loom or one that is easy to move about. Please note: These instructions are for dressing the loom from the back to the front.

Step 1. Prepare the first warp, including beaming, threading, sleying and tying on to the front stick.

Step 2. Wind the second warp. Beam it onto the second loom's warp beam, following your usual method. Winding is in the same direction as if you were going to weave on the second loom.

Step 3. Instead of bringing the warp in its usual path around the back of the back beam and towards the heddles, the warp comes over the front of the back beam (nearest the heddles) and towards the back. Double check to ensure that the locking mechanism will work by pulling gently away from the second loom when the warp brake or ratchet is locked in place. Note: If it is wound the wrong way, the brake ratchet will not be effective.

Step 4. Insert cross-sticks into the secondary warp.

Step 5. To help with threading, either secure the cross-sticks to the back beam of the second loom, or secure them to the main loom, whichever is most convenient.

Step 6. Thread and sley as usual and tie on to the front stick or pin to the fabric in pairs.

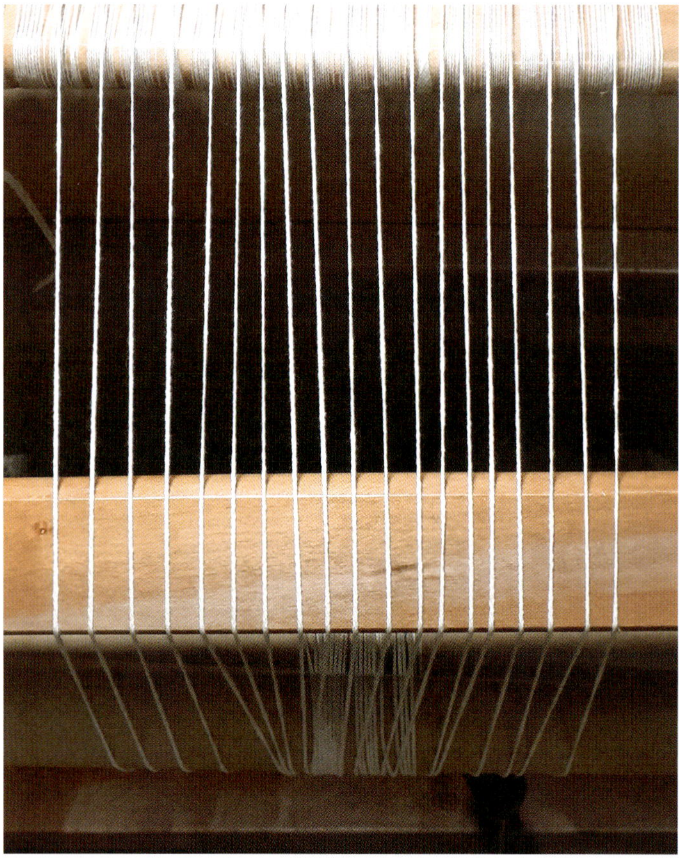

The second warp is wound onto the second warp beam and brought through to the main warp as in step 3.

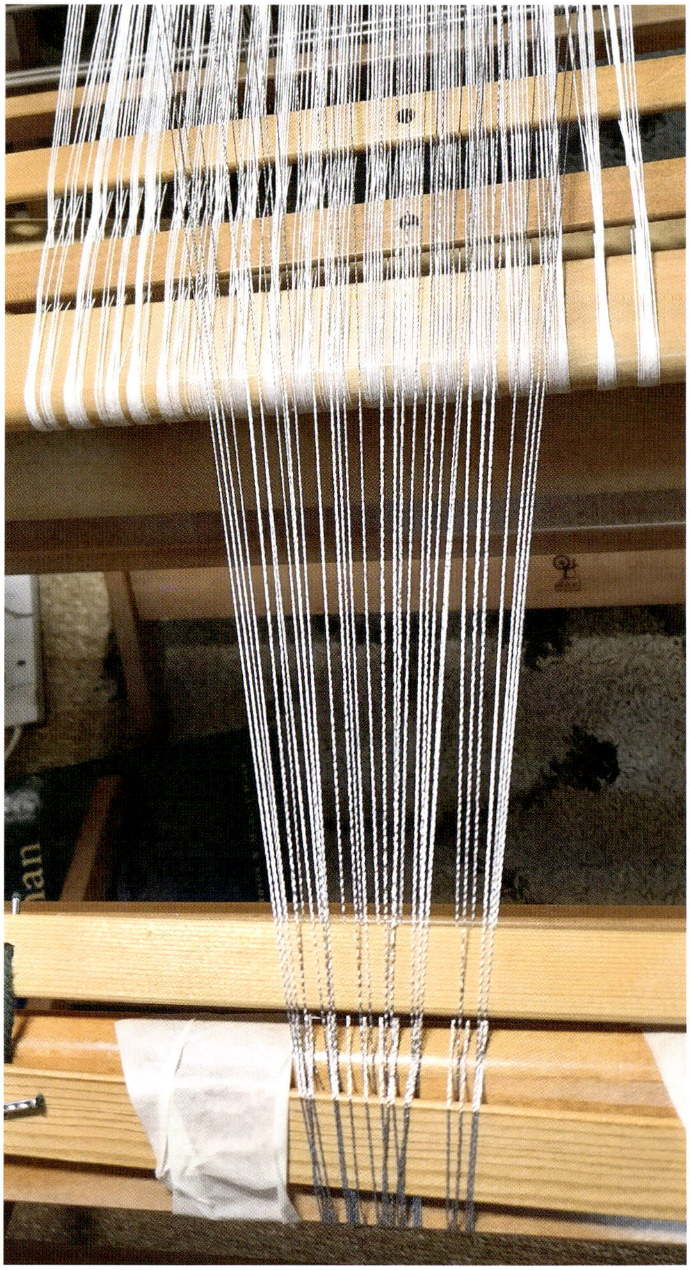

Steps 4 and 5: insert cross sticks and secure. Version 1.

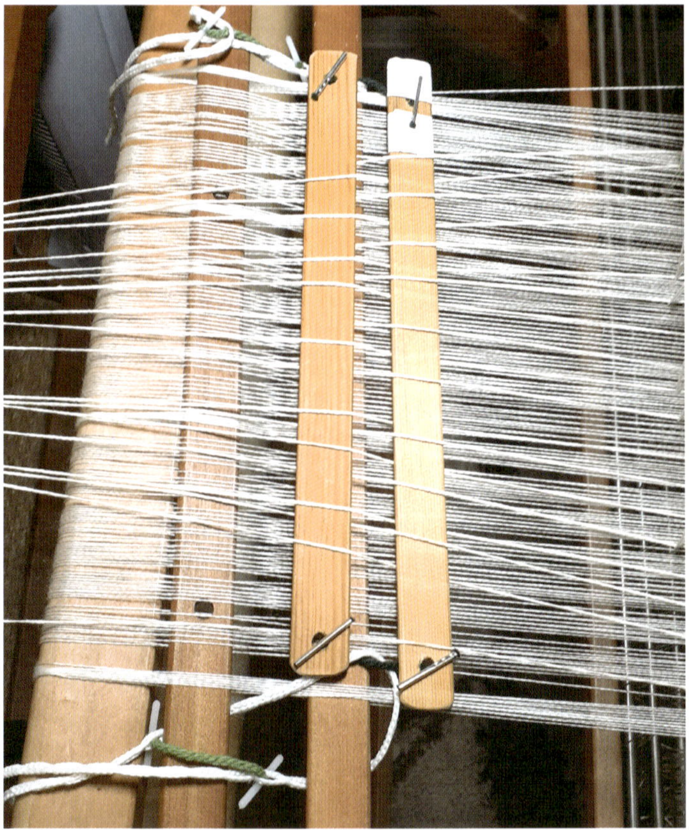

Step 5, version 2.

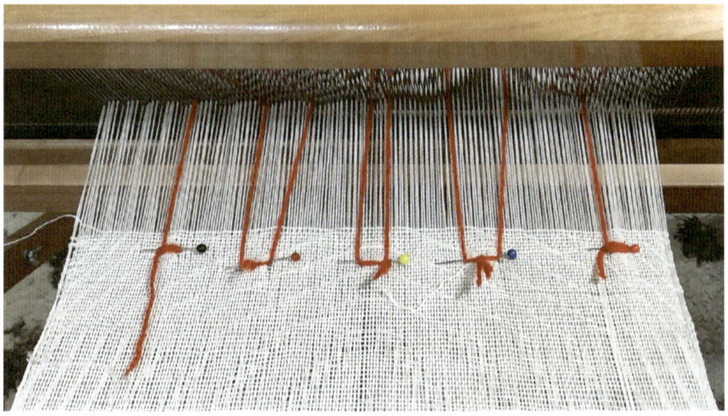

Step 6: attach to woven cloth.

USING A SECOND LOOM'S WARP BEAM – A FULL WIDTH WARP

There are modifications to this when using a full width second warp or double plain sett for double cloth. Please note that the system described here uses an independent

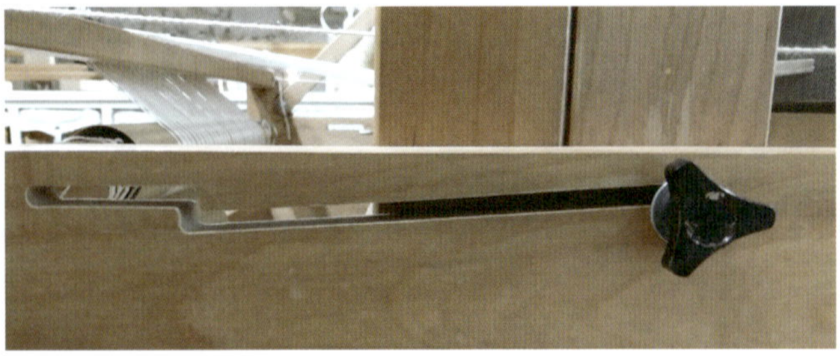

Ashford table looms have a slot which proves very useful for holding cross-sticks in place.

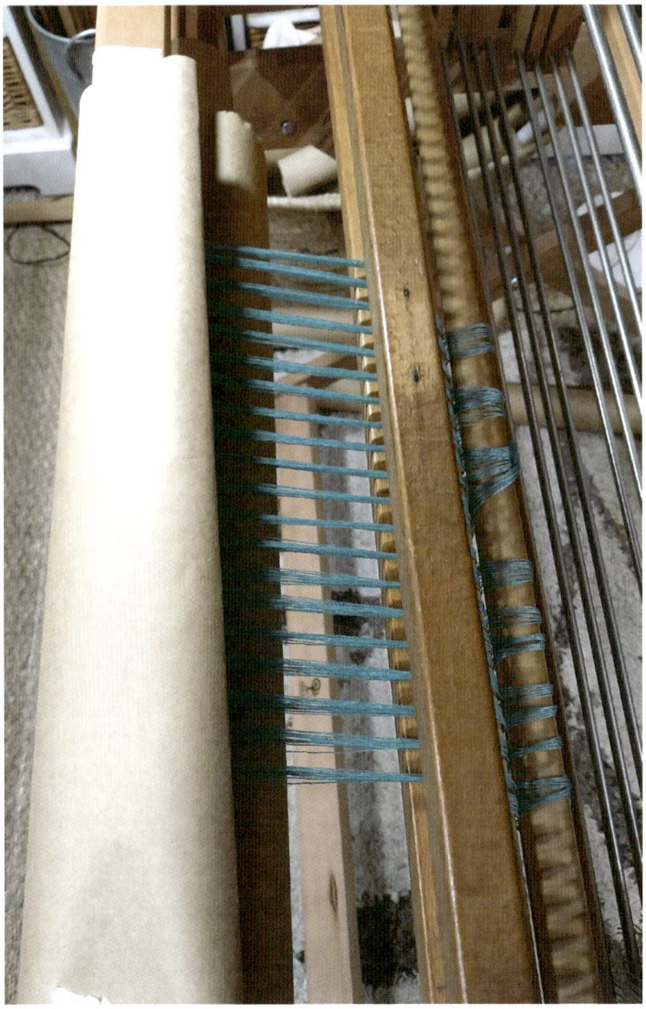

Thick paper between the two warps helps to separate them.

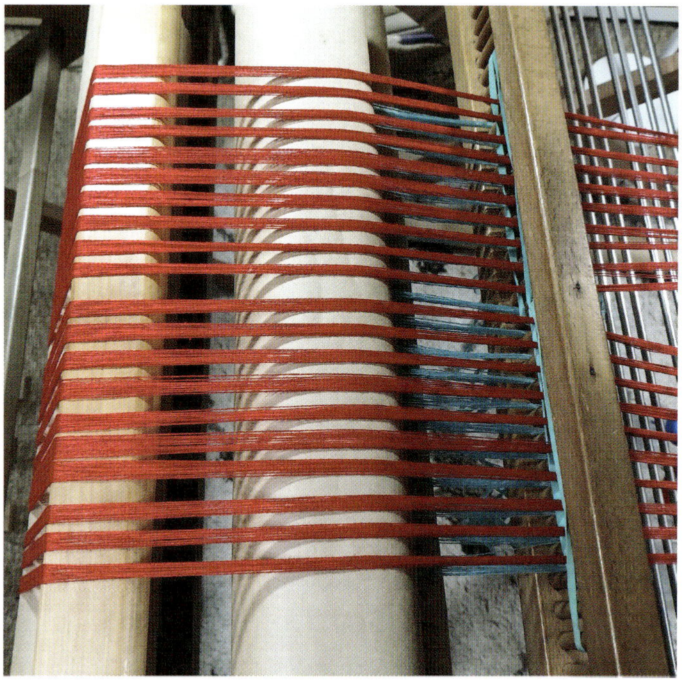

The second warp from the second loom is brought over the first warp (hidden underneath the paper), and placed in the raddle.

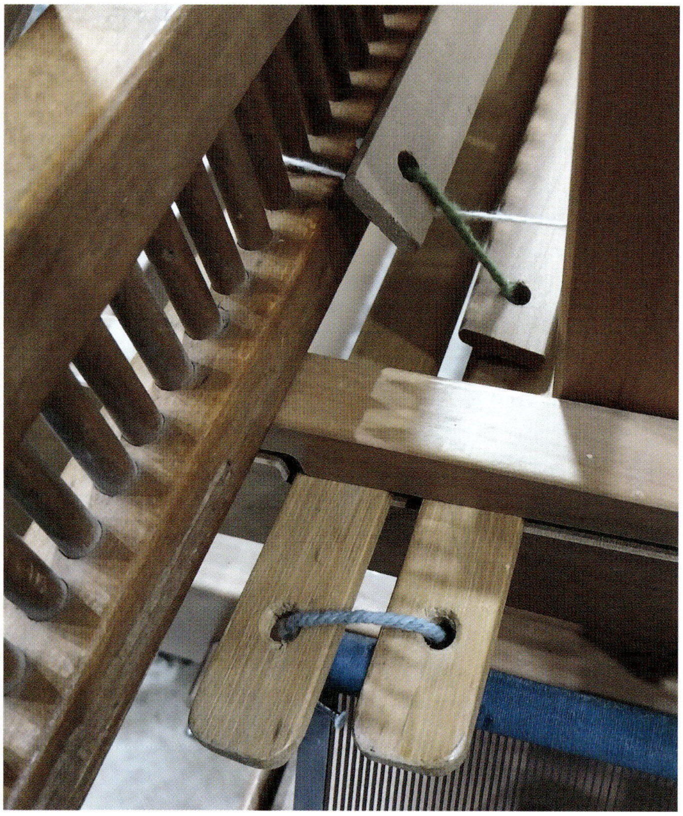

A second pair of cross-sticks is inserted to keep the two layers separate during threading.

raddle, which stays in place for warping, threading and sleying. This is a personal choice that works well to keep all threads in alignment throughout the whole of the warp preparation. Individual weavers might, or might not, find this useful.

Step 1. Warp, beam and raddle. If your loom allows, it is useful to secure the cross-sticks so that they do not move. In folding looms with open channels, such as the Ashford table looms, it is possible to slide long cross-sticks

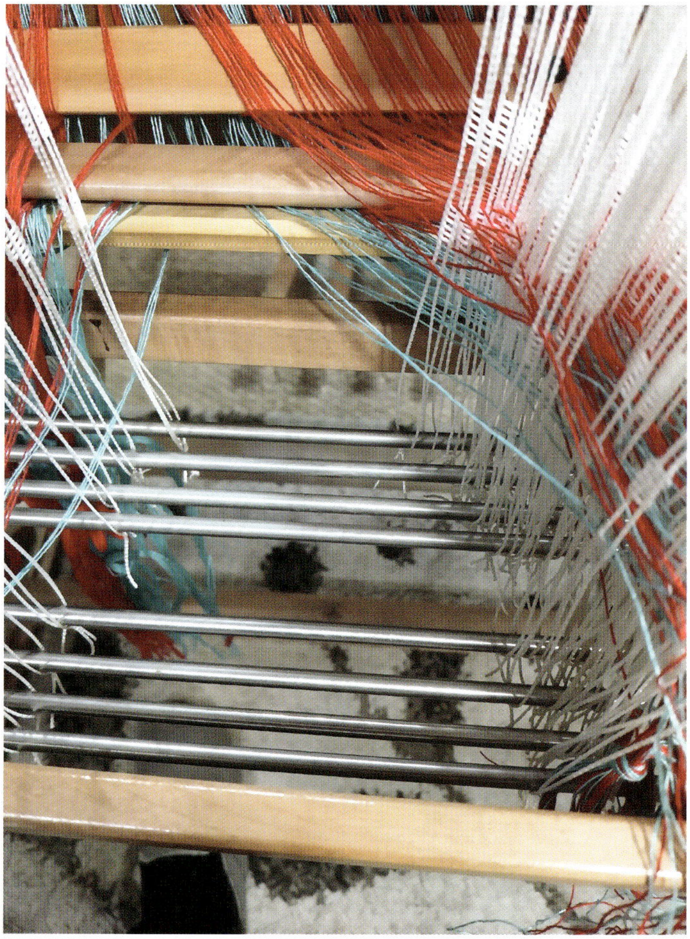

Threading proceeds as normal using both warps.

individually through the open channels on both sides of the loom, thus keeping them securely in place.

Step 2. Secure some thick paper or card over the back beam and the first warp.

Step 3. Make the second warp and put it on to the second loom's warp beam, ensuring that the path of the warp will go over the back beam before winding on to the second loom's warp beam. Place the warp bouts in the raddle above the first warp.

Step 4. Insert the cross-sticks for the second warp and suspend above the first set of cross-sticks.

Step 5. Thread and sley both warps as usual.

Step 6. Remove the raddle and cross-sticks of both warps prior to tying on.

Step 7. Secure an extra stick as a spacer on the top of the second back beam to keep the two layers slightly apart. This helps particularly when moving on just one of the warps, for instance when making pleats.

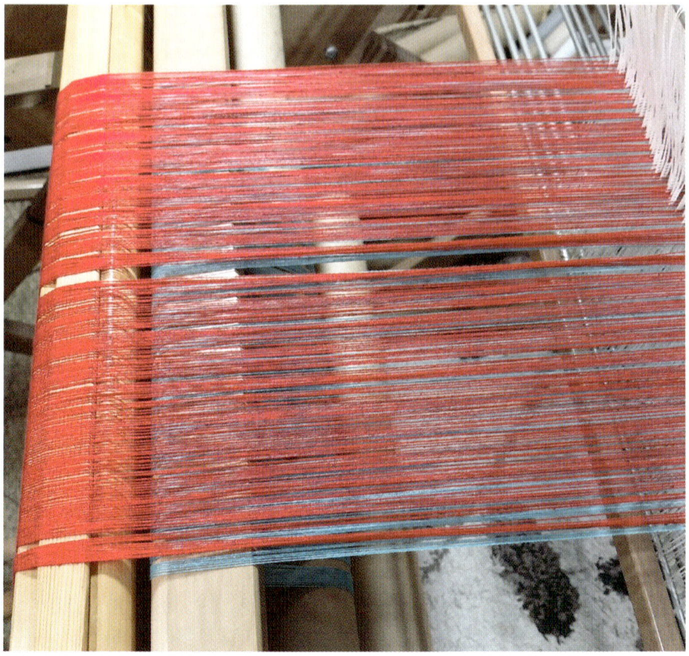

A thin stick has been placed underneath the red warp on top of the second loom's back beam to raise the warp a little above the green warp.

TIE-UP CONVERSION TO LIFTPLAN

Liftplans are a different way of interpreting the information of which shafts to raise or lower for each pick.

Many weavers find it just as easy to read a tie-up and treadling plan even when using a table loom. A dobby loom requires the liftplan conversion in order for the dobby pegs and lags (mechanical dobby) or the shaft selection box to select the correct shafts per pick.

Most weaving software has a conversion tool, which will do the translation automatically provided that the liftplan is requested. If you prefer to design in the tie-up/treadling mode, ensure that the design is initially saved in tie-up/treadling mode before the conversion to liftplan is done. Some programmes struggle with returning to the same tie-up/treadling plan if a conversion from a liftplan to tie-up mode is required for further alterations.

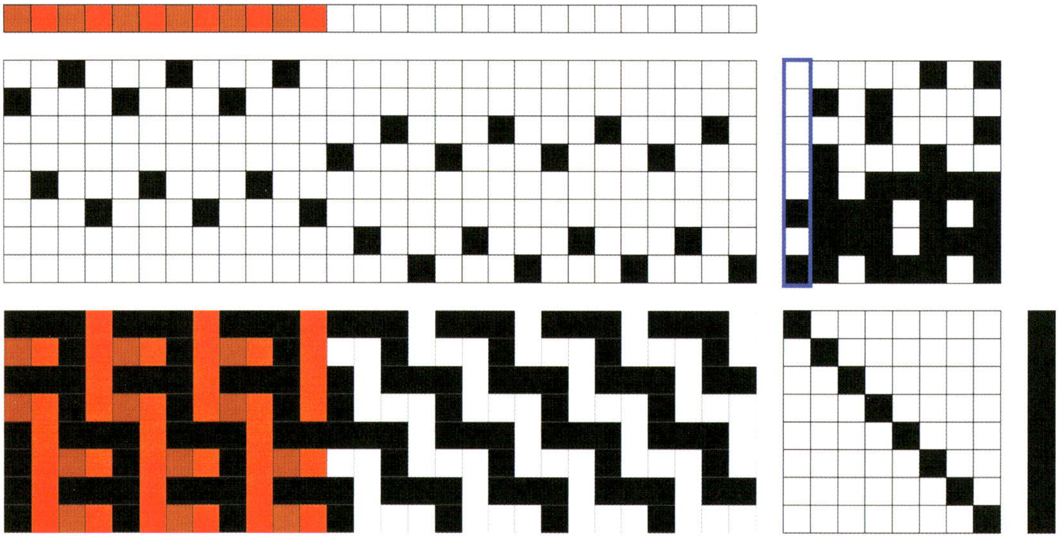

Tie-ups have a series of columns denoting treadles for a floor loom. Each column represents one treadle, which is shown with the shafts that are required to be raised or lowered or both (for countermarch looms). The treadling plan shows which treadle needs to be depressed for the required shaft selection for a specific pick.

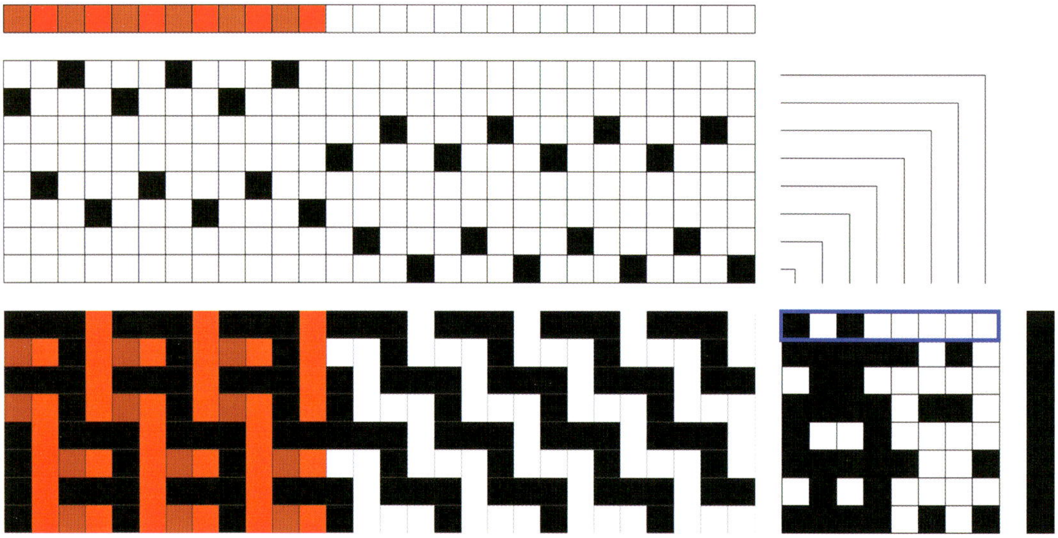

To translate it into a liftplan, you need a grid as many squares wide as the shafts that are to be used on your loom. Each pick requires that you look at the required treadle (reading vertically) and input the shafts to be used on the horizontal row of the liftplan, which now replaces the treadling plan. Each pick is translated in the same way

APPENDIX II: MATERIALS

BAMBOO VISCOSE

Bamboo viscose is a regenerated fibre – a man-made fibre artificially created using bamboo leaves and shoots. Most is made using a chemical process similar to the production of viscose rayon with sodium hydroxide and carbon disulfide solvents and then extruded directly into a chemical bath of sulfuric acid and then washed and bleached to create 'rayon from bamboo'. However, it is now increasingly possible to adapt the lyocell process to bamboo cellulose.

It can also be mechanically created through crushing the woody part of the plant and then using natural enzymes to break the bamboo cell walls, creating a mush that can then be mechanically combed out and spun into yarn.

https://fairware.com/bamboozled-getting-the-facts-on-bamboo-textiles (Accessed 28 April 2025).

BRASS

Brass is an alloy of copper and zinc and comes in tones from gold to pale yellow. It is quite malleable, especially the yellow brass as it has the greatest percentage of zinc in the alloy. It is not very strong at very fine gauges (36/40), although gauges such as 16, 18, 20 and 24 are flexible enough for weaving and are generally available in hardware and home-repair shops, picture framers, art supplies and specialist wire stockists.

COPPER

Copper is the most readily available, incredibly versatile and generally the least expensive wire for textile use. It is soft and extremely flexible and is wound on to spools, which are available in fine gauges (18–40 gauge) for weaving. It is readily available at plumbing and electricians' outlets, specialist shops, weaving and art supplies.

Coated wires have a permanent colour and polish. Many colours are available, such as black, purple and many shades of blue, green, red, pink and orange. The coating is very thin and well bonded to the metal so it does not crack or peel when manipulated.

COTTON

Cotton comes from a member of the hibiscus (Malvaceae) family of plants grown in warm, tropical regions. It is found in the seed 'boll', which contains soft, fluffy white filaments inside a husk protecting the small black seeds of the cotton plant. It is ginned to separate the fibres from the seeds before being cleaned to remove impurities, carded to align the fibres in the same direction, pulled into long strands called rovings, which are then spun into yarn.

Mercerisation

A further treatment to increase strength, lustre, facilitate easy dyeing and reduce fabric shrinkage is called mercerisation. The yarn is run through a 20–26 per cent caustic soda (sodium hydroxide) bath under tension before being washed. Much water is required in the growing of cotton and the mercerising process.

Gassed Cotton

Gassed cotton is further run swiftly over a gas burner to burn away the minute down hairs that remain on the surface of the yarn. This imparts even more lustre and smoothness to the yarn.

LINEN

Linen is a hard-wearing bast-fibre yarn processed from flax, traditionally using a mechanical process of pulling, rippling and winnowing, retting, scutching, heckling, then spinning. Faster methods of retting use chemicals to speed up the process of the separation of fibres from the plant stalk. Natural methods involve soaking the stalks in tanks or pools where natural bacteria decompose the pectin that binds the fibres together.

Its properties include coolness, durability, ability to quick-dry, resistance to stains and dirt, no lint or pilling, and it can withstand high temperatures. It also has hypoallergenic qualities, improves softness and drape with age and is easily biodegradable.

LYOCELL

Lyocell (also trademarked as Tencel™, Newcell™ and Seacell™) is a semi-synthetic fibre made by dissolving cellulose into pulp using the non-toxic solvent amine oxide (no hazardous waste). It is resistant to wear, tear and pilling and shares many properties with bast fibres such as cotton, linen, ramie, hemp but also silk and viscose rayon. It has minimal shrinkage, blends well with natural and synthetic fibres and is fully biodegradable.

https://en.wikipedia.org/wiki/Lyocell (Accessed 28 April 2025)

PAPER

Paper yarns for weaving are often made from natural materials such as flax, hemp or cotton. Historically, in Japan, bark from the mulberry tree was stripped, soaked to expose the cellulose, and beaten down into a pulp then mixed with water. When the water evaporated, paper remained. This dried paper was then cut into very narrow long strips from a sheet of handmade paper and twisted by hand, a process taken to a high level in Japan.

This process is still used today, and includes such fibres as bamboo, cotton, raffia and even recycled paper – although now industrial machines pulp the fibres and create the yarn. It is an ancient tradition still often used by crafters today using thicker strips and spun on a spindle or spinning wheel.

https://warpedfibers.com/paper-yarn-tutorial

https://orafabulousfibres.com/en-fr/blogs/lets-yarn-blog/paper-yarn-history-japan (Both accessed 28 April 2025)

POLYESTER

Polyester is a man-made filament fibre invented in the 1940s, derived from oil and made of ethylene glycol and terephthalic acid. Its molecular bonds (carbon, hydrogen and oxygen) can be broken by heat, allowing it to be shaped but also melted for recycling.

Melted polyester is extruded through tiny holes and stretched to many times its original length, a process that induces changes in the inner structure of the material that give it strength and stability. The stretched filament is heat set at a temperature just under the melting point (260°C/500°F), softening up between 238–240°C (460–464°F). When this degree of heat is applied to polyester fabric, it reverts to its unstretched state, shrinking drastically. Ideally, fabric should be held in its form and heated to around 200–220°C (392–428°F) for 20–30 minutes to set the three-dimensional texture, steam being most effective.

OVERSPUN OR HIGH-TWIST SPUN YARNS

Overspun or high-twist spun yarns (also known as crepe yarns) are usually of a singles ply. They capture a lot of kinetic energy during spinning, which can be seen when they are held in a gentle arc as they will endeavour to untwist, coiling up on themselves. This extra twist will seek to untwist itself from a cut end and needs to be restrained with sticky tape. Industrially, they are most often wound onto the cone in an S direction. When winding bobbins or warps, it is best to mount the cone horizontally so that the yarn is drawn from the cone without either removing twist (pulling off in a Z direction) or adding more twist (pulling off in an S direction). It is never recommended to wind these yarns into a ball or a yarn cake (cross-wound ball) as their energy will try to unravel within the ball or cake.

When used for weft, it is often necessary to use a temple and to only pull out just enough weft for the pick to avoid unwanted kinks at the selvedges. Overspun yarns are usually woven in an open sett to allow for the release of energy during wet-finishing, and used in a plain weave or small twill as longer floats will encourage spontaneous self-twisting of the floats on wet-finishing.

SILK

Silk is wound from cocoons produced by the Bombyx Mori silkworm, which is fed on mulberry leaves for around six weeks. Mulberry trees can be found worldwide, but today silk is produced mainly in tropical areas of India, China, other Asian countries and Brazil, where it grows in a continuous cycle. After six weeks, the worm then attaches itself to a branch and over the course of the next three to eight days, winds a figure-eight cocoon from a single filament around itself in order to pupate. The pupae are then usually asphyxiated so that the intact cocoons can be reeled by filament. Several cocoons are unwound together while in boiling water or steam and twisted to form a single strand of raw silk. The sericin gum, which the worm secretes to help glue the cocoon together, is usually retained to assist with protecting the fibre during processing and washed away later. If the silk moths have hatched from the cocoon, the broken cocoons can still be reeled but the filaments are shorter and can have 'noils' in them, small lumps that are attractive and used in their own right.

Tussah Silk

Wild silk is known as Tussah silk and is from silkworms that feed on a variety of trees, which give the resultant silk a range of natural earthy tones and a coarser texture. Silk has high lustre and is soft yet strong, delicate and durable.

STAINLESS STEEL YARN

Stainless steel yarn is usually a blended yarn, incorporating a small percentage (5–50 per cent) of fine strands of stainless steel into blends with polyester, cotton, viscose rayon, silk etc. It combines the attributes of the base fibre with the properties of conductivity and electromagnetic shielding, dissipating static charges throughout its life. It is highly resistant to corrosion and can withstand high temperatures. Molten stainless steel is extruded through a spinneret to form a continuous fibre. This can then be used as a yarn on its own or cut into required lengths, blended and spun using standard textile manufacturing processes. It can be dyed.

https://smartexyarn.com/blog/stainless-steel-yarn-benefits-and-applications

https://rondatex.com/knowledges/view_149.html

https://rondatex.com/knowledges/view_150.html (All accessed 28 April 2025)

VISCOSE RAYON

Viscose rayon is a regenerated yarn from a natural source, such as wood pulp, that is chemically treated in a solvent of caustic soda and carbon disulfide (environmentally toxic) to create a half-natural, half-synthetic fibre. The filaments are produced by extruding the liquid chemical through a spinneret for fibres or slits for cellophane. The yarn is absorbent, hard-wearing and can be blended with natural/synthetic fibres.

https://en.wikipedia.org/wiki/Rayon (Accessed 28 April 2025)

WOOL

Wool comes in many different qualities and counts from a wide range of sheep breeds. Generally speaking, fine count fibres from breeds such as merino, merino crosses, blue-faced Leicester, Shetland and other fine wools are usually preferred for fulling purposes. Methods of spinning have an impact.

Handspun Woollen-spun Yarns

These will full readily as they are spun from the carded and rolled tubular edge of a rolag, which traps air and mixes the yarns in a non-parallel fashion. They are also usually spun with a low to medium number of twists per inch.

Softly-spun Worsted Yarns

These also full readily as they have less twist than hard-twisted worsteds that are often used for men's jackets and outerwear. The softer twist allows the wool to bloom during the wet-finishing process.

Semi-worsted Yarns

These are a halfway house, using carded wool but spun along the length of the fibre.

Superwash Wool

This is wool that has been chemically treated with chlorine to remove the overlapping scales on the surface of the fibre before being neutralised and then coated with a layer of a polymer resin called Hercosett (a petroleum-based plastic) to smooth and seal the eroded surface. This removes the ability of wool to full so it can be washed in a washing machine without shrinking or felting.

https://farmfiberknits.com/what-is-the-superwash-process-and-what-does-it-do-to-wool (Accessed 28 April 2025)

ARTISTS' LINKS

Peter Collingwood: www.roseuniacke.com
www.petercollingwoodtextiles.com

Jane Deane: www.janedeane.co.uk
www.instagram.com/jane.deane

Eileen Hallman: https://newworldtextiles.com/about
www.instagram.com/newworldtextiles

Stacey Harvey-Brown: https://theloomroomfrance.com
www.instagram.com/creativeweaver

Sue Hiley Harris: www.suehileyharris.co.uk

Susan Iverson: www.susaniversonart.com
www.instagram.com/susaniversontapestry

Beth Ross Johnson with forresto: www.forresto.com/sashiko
(Sashiko pattern generator)

Heather Macali: https://heathermacali.com
www.instagram.com/heathermacali

Lesley Millar: https://transitionandinfluence.com/textural-space

Wendy Morris: www.instagram.com/wendymorrisweavings

Sara Nordling: www.saranordling.com
www.facebook.com/sara.nordling

Paul O'Connor: https://coeweaves.com/publications-1#

Melanie Olde: www.melanieolde.com
www.instagram.com/melanie_olde

Kadi Pajupuu: https://kadipuu.ee/en
www.instagram.com/kadipuu

Amy Parker: www.instagram.com/amygwen99
www.ravelry.com/projects/amygwen99

Ann Richards: www.instagram.com/annrichardsweave

Kay Sekimachi: https://browngrotta.com/artists/kay-sekimachi

Norma Smayda: www.saunderstownweavingschool.com

Lynn Smetko: www.lynnsmetkodesigns.com
www.instagram.com/lynnsmetko

Lucy Smyth: www.lucysmyth.com

Frances Stevens: https://katealbertaweaving.com
www.instagram.com/katealbertaweaving

Susie Taylor: http://susietaylorart.com
www.instagram.com/weaving.origami

Dianne Totten: https://diannetottenhandwovens.com
www.facebook.com/crimpcloth

Suzanne Townshend: www.instagram.com/suzannetownshend

Pauline van Asperen: www.paulienvanasperen.nl
www.instagram.com/paulienweaves

Hannah White: www.hannahwhitestudio.com
www.instagram.com/hannahwhitestudio

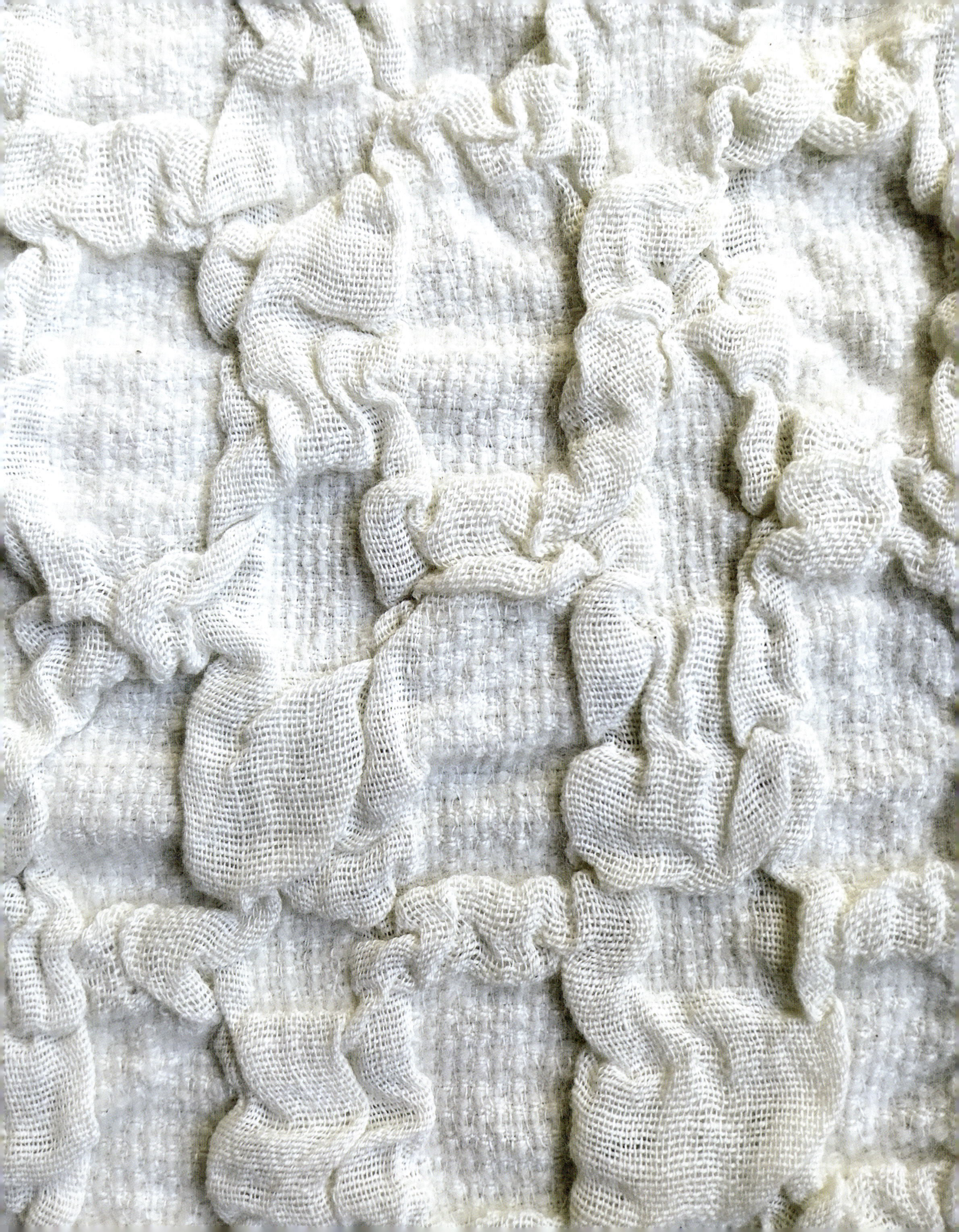

GLOSSARY

DRAFTING CONVENTIONS

- **Advancing draft** – An advancing draft, whether in threading or liftplan, is a pattern which – if repeated and moved on by one or more shafts each time – moves progressively through the shafts. In music, this kind of pattern is called a sequence.
- **Extended draft** – An extended draft is one where a pattern is repeated an increasing number of times. For instance, if a block is threaded on shafts 1 & 2, which lasts for six ends, and another on shafts 3 & 4, which lasts for six ends, and the first block is further repeated but adding an extra four ends on to the new block, then that is extending the block/draft.
- **Extending advancing draft** – An extending advancing draft is one that moves on in sequence, each repetition varying the number of ends in the sequence. This allows for a feeling of movement in the fabric.

A–Z GLOSSARY

Accordion pleats: Even-sided pleats.

Active yarns: Yarns that have the propensity to shrink, such as wool, overtwist and elastane. (*See* Chapter 1.)

Advancing threadings/treadlings: Whether in threading or treadling, a pattern which – if repeated and moved on by one or more shafts each time – moves progressively through the shafts. In music, this kind of pattern is called a sequence.

Bedford cord: A block effect for weaving vertical pleats using alternating wefts to weave selected blocks and floating above or behind other blocks. The two wefts between them weave all the blocks.

Blocks: Two or more shafts in threading or treadling that are repeated a number of times to create a specific area of the same weave. They are then repeated on another sequence of two or more shafts to create block designs.

Clasped weft: A tapestry weft technique where two wefts from opposite sides of the warp come to meet in the same shed, turn around each other and return back to the side from which they started.

Cloqué: A French word to denote a blistered or puckered surface to a fabric.

Crammed-and-spaced: A sleying method of putting multiple warp ends into the same dents for a certain number of dents, followed by several empty dents. This can be a regular or irregular pattern.

Deflected double weave: A member of the colour-and-weave family of effects, which uses two warps and wefts. Each weft weaves its own warp and the two separate layers are connected through the action of the warp and weft floats, which are selected either to be raised above the current weft being used or to remain underneath the weft.

Design line: The overview of a threading or treadling plan. This can be in profile mode or threading mode.

Dimensional texture: The generic name of fabrics utilising methods that raise the surface of the cloth above the flat plane.

Grids in double cloth surrounding single cloth blocks create dimensional outlines.

Discontinuous weft: A tapestry weft effect using a weft thread for a selected distance of the weft. It does not run from one side of the warp to the other.

Divided parallel threading: (See *Parallel threading*)

Double cloth: Two layers of cloth being woven at the same time with two warps and two wefts that can be kept separate, interchanged or joined together in various ways.

Double width: Two layers of weaving joined at one selvedge and woven with one weft in a C-shape, weaving in one direction across the bottom layer, then in the opposite direction across the top layer, returning back across the top layer for the next pick and then returning in the opposite direction across the bottom layer.

Expanded advancing threadings: These are threading and treadling patterns that allow a run of an advancing design to be extended by repeating the four-end twill repeat one or more times.

Extended parallel threading: (See *Parallel threading*)

Face down: Where the design to be viewed is on the reverse (underneath) side of the cloth, usually woven to reduce the amount of shafts lifted in each pick.

Fell: The edge of the fabric where the next pick is woven into place.

Felting: The result of woollen yarns being wet-finished until the individual yarns are totally meshed together.

Floats: Any length of warp or weft that goes over or under two or more consecutive ends or picks. In dimensional weaving, floats are usually longer than three ends or picks.

Four-colour double weave: Creates four different effects through mixing two warp yarns and two weft yarns. In dimensional weaving, one warp and one weft usually use an active yarn to create texture on wet-finishing.

Fulling: The process of shrinking cloth by heat, pressure and water.

Ground weave/warp/weft: The underlying constructed fabric, often in plain weave, underpinning more decorative elements such as supplementary warps and wefts.

Honeycomb: A weave structure comprised of woven cells alternating with warp and weft floats, outlined with two or more picks of plain weave.

Horizontal pleats: Created through weave structure and folding in the warp direction to give a horizontal effect.

Inclusions: Additional soft or hard elements inserted into a piece of fabric sculpture to aid in its sculptural aspects.

Integrating layers: When two or more layers in a fabric are combined.

Interchanging layers: When two or more layers in a fabric change their position, i.e. from being on top to being underneath.

Knife pleats: Pleats with one side longer than the other, which lean over to one side.

Liftplan: The information that tells table and dobby loom weavers which shafts are lifted for each pick in the weaving.

Matelassé*:* A French word to describe a quilted or stitched effect in fabric, using two layers of fabric and often incorporating a wadding.

Meet & separate: A tapestry weft effect where two wefts coming from each side of the warp meet each other but do not twist around each other, before returning to their respective sides in the next shed.

Motif: An independent design shape, often created with the aid of a point draft. Not a background weave.

Multiple wefts for one pick: The use of several different weft threads covering selected autonomous areas of the warp in order to make one complete pick.

Network-drafted threadings: Threadings belonging to an underlying network that allows for 'legal' moves to ensure that tie-ups and treadling plans will create the underlying structure. They can be based on three, four or more ends for the underlying weave.

Overshot: A style of weaving that incorporates supplementary weft threads to give a pattern, interspersed with a tabby ground weft (alternating plain weave).

Parallel threading (inc. divided and extended parallel threading): A system of threading that allows for different methods of repeating threading patterns a number of shafts above or below the original threading, alternating the threading end by end. Divided parallel threading copies the original threading and adds it above or below, effectively doubling the number of shafts required to weave the design. The two sets of threadings do not overlap each other. Extended parallel threading copies the original threading and intersperses it above or below the original line starting half the total number of shafts away from the start. For example, an eight-shaft extended parallel threading starting on shaft 1 will have its copy beginning with end 2 on shaft 5.

Parallel treadling: The same principles apply in treadling as in parallel threading – the original treadling alternates with its 'echo' pick by pick, often using an extended tie-up.

Passive yarns: Yarns that remain stable (i.e. no significant shrinkage) on wet-finishing, such as cotton, linen and silk. (*See* Chapter 1)

Piqué: A French word to describe a stitched dimensional effect in cloth, with two warps, with the second warp woven (fast-backed) or left as floats (loose-backed). Sometimes used with a wadding weft.

Profile draft: An overview of a design showing only the main design blocks.

Pulled warps: Used in tapestry weaving, warp threads are left unwoven during weaving and pulled gently but firmly through the weaving after removing from the loom to create three-dimensional sculptural shapes in the fabric.

Quad cloth: Four layers of cloth being woven on the loom at the same time. Four warps and four wefts, which can be woven separately, interchanged or combined in different ways.

Ratio: The amount of active to passive yarns used in threading and treadling. Higher ratios usually involve more passive yarns and fewer active yarns.

Sashiko: A Japanese design aesthetic found in embroidery and adapted for weave, where it is known as *sashiko ori.*

Satin: A family of weaves created with long floats in warp and weft, where one side is weft-dominant and one side is warp-dominant. Interlacements are set intermittently in a diagonal formation.

Sculpture: The formation of dimensional shapes that hang or are mounted in space so that they can be viewed from all angles.

Seersucker: A fabric with vertical stripes of puckered fabric created by differing tensions applied to warp bands of plain weave and (often) rib. Increased tension on the warp rib bands, whether in an active yarn or not, will generate puckering in the plain weave bands.

Sett: The number of ends or picks per inch/cm. Open setts allow for more shrinkage potential while closer setts give a firmer fabric.

Shibori: Used in dimensional texture to gather up cloth in a selected pattern, with gathering threads that are removed after the cloth is wet-finished through washing or steaming.

Skeleton tie-up: A shorthand way on a treadle loom of using two treadles to create a larger number of shaft combinations. Suitable for a jack loom or some countermarch looms.

Stitched double cloth: Joining one layer of double cloth to another through selected individual or multiple shafts for a limited time. Used in dimensional texture to create puckered patterns.

Supplementary warp/weft: Separate warps and/or wefts in addition to the main warp and weft, which are often used for patterning.

Tabby: Plain weave used while alternating with pattern wefts.

Telescoped threading: This takes a design line that is taller than the number of shafts available and truncates it, dividing up the design into the requisite number of squares tall, and taking anything above that line and transposing them directly on to the available shafts.

Tie-up (including parallel, quadrant fashion and extended parallel and multi-treadle and skeleton): The area of a weaving draft that shows how the shafts work together. Combined with the treadling, the tie-up enables a defined pattern to be woven. Tie-ups can be extended to any number of 'treadles' for a table or dobby loom weaver, but floor loom weavers are restricted to a set number of pedals for their individual floor loom. Parallel tie-ups are two tie-ups designed to work together, often for different sides of a fabric, and treadled alternately. Quadrant tie-ups, even or uneven, have designated areas (quadrants), which denote a ground weave and/or a series of shafts that are required to work alongside pattern shafts to create the design. Multi-treadle tie-ups use two treadles at the same time for one pick. Skeleton tie-ups (where possible) give a basic tie-up of a minimum number of shafts that can be used in combination to weave a given design without the need for re-tying shafts on a treadle loom.

Treadling: Used in conjunction with the tie-up to create the order of picks required for the selected design.

Triple cloth: Three layers of weaving (three warps and wefts) being woven at the same time on the loom. They can interchange, combine with each other, or be kept separate.

Tubular weaving: Weaving two layers of plain or other weaves in a circular form with one weft, weaving the top layer in one direction and the bottom layer in the opposite direction, forming an O shape.

Twill: A diagonal progression of lifts creating diagonal lines and diamonds in a cloth, depending on the threading.

Unwoven warps: Usually found in tapestry, this is where wefts are woven in selected areas only, leaving other areas free of weaving with just the warp threads.

Upright pleats: Pleats that are comprised of two warps, where one warp weaves both sides of the pleat, which is then pulled up tightly to the fell of the other layer and woven in.

Vertical pleats: Created by threading blocks and interaction of the weft, and running in the vertical direction.

Wadding: A thicker, often spongy weft or warp yarn used to bulk out a dimensional effect, often seen in matelassé, piqué and stitched double cloth.

Waffle: A weave consisting largely of floats and minimal plain weave, usually designed with a point threading to create a highly dimensional fabric.

Wet-finishing: The process of finishing fabric by immersing it in water by hand or machine or steaming it. In dimensional texture, this is where certain effects are created through the amount of manipulation of the fabric and the interaction of pressure, moisture and soap. This can also include using extremes of temperature in order to 'shock' wool, for example, and tumble-drying.

Woollen-spun yarns: (*See* Chapter 1.)

Worsted/semi-worsted-spun yarns: (*See* Chapter 1.)

Woven as drawn in (a.k.a tromp as writ): The treadling plan is the same design as the threading line. It gives a balanced design around the diagonals.

BIBLIOGRAPHY

Albers, A., *On Weaving* (Wesleyan University Press, 1965)

Alderman, S., *Mastering Weave Structures: Transforming ideas into great cloth* (Interweave Press, 2004)

Aldersley-Williams, H., *Zoomorphic: New animal architecture* (Laurence King Publishing, 2003)

Arn-Grischott, U., *Doubleweave: On four to eight shafts* (English version) (Interweave Press, 1999)

Becker, J. with Wagner, D.B, (2014) *Pattern and Loom: A practical study of the development of weaving techniques in China, Western Asia and Europe* (NIAS Press, 1986)

Braddock, S.E. and O'Mahony, M., *Techno Textiles: Revolutionary fabrics for fashion and design* (Thames & Hudson, 1998)

Braddock Clarke, S.E. and Harris, J., *Digital Visions for Fashion + Textiles: Made in code* (Thames & Hudson, 2012)

Briscoe, S., *The Ultimate Sashiko Sourcebook: Patterns, projects and inspirations* (David & Charles, 2004)

Byrd, S.J., *A Song of Praise for Shifu: Shifu Sanka* (The Legacy Press, 2013)

Callender, J., *Stitched Shibori: Technique, innovation, pattern, design* (Search Press, 2017)

Colchester, C., *The New Textiles: Trends & traditions* (Thames & Hudson, 1991)

Constantine, M and Larson, J.L., *Beyond Craft: The art fabric* (Van Nostrand Reinhold Company, 1973)

Constantine, M and Larson, J.L., *The Art Fabric: Mainstream* (Van Nostrand Reinhold Company, 1981)

Coxon, A., Fer, B. and Muller-Schareck, M. (eds) *Anni Albers* (Tate Modern, 2018)

Coxon, A., Jacob, M.J. (eds) *Magdalena Abakanowicz* (Tate Modern, 2022)

Craft and Folk Art Museum LA, *Kay Sekimachi: Simple Complexity* – Exhibition Catalogue (2016)

Dalgaard, L., and Adam, P., *Thread Magic: Weaving for shape and texture* (Forlaget Mellemvaerk, 2020)

Dalgaard, L. (trans Richards, A., 2009), *Magical Materials to Weave: Blending Traditional and Innovative Yarns* (FiberFeber, 2007)

Davison, M.P., *A Handweaver's Pattern Book* (Churchill & Dunn Ltd., 2014)

Davison, M.P. (ed.), *A Handweaver's Pattern Book* (Marguerite P. Davison, 1953)

Demand, T., *Model Studies* (Ivory Press, 2011)

Domingo, E. (ed.), *92 motivos de Sashiko: Modelos tradicionales con diseños actuales* (Editoria El Drac, 2018)

Ellis, C., *Woven Shibori* (Interweave Press, 2005)

Emery, I., *The Primary Structure of Fabrics: An illustrated clarification* (Thames & Hudson, 1966, 1980, 1994)

Eyring, S., *3-D Hand Loom Weaving: Sculptural tools and techniques* (Schiffer Publishing, 2020)

Field, A., *Collapse Weave: Creating three-dimensional cloth* (A & C Black, 2008)

Fisch, A.M., *Textile Techniques in Metal: For jewelers, textile artists, & sculptors* (Echo Point Books & Media, 1996, 2016)

Garibi, I., *Origami Tessellations for Everyone* (Self-published, 2018)

Gjerde, E., *Origami Tessellations: Awe-inspiring geometric designs* (CRC Press, 2009)

Gordon, J.E., *Structures: Or why things don't fall down* (Da Capo Press, 1978)

Inouye, B., *Exploring Multishaft Design* (Weavingdance Press, 2000)

Iverson, S., *Tapestry with Pulled Warp: Inspiration, technique, and the creative process* (Shiffer Craft, 2024)

Jackson, P., *Folding Techniques for Designers: From sheet to form* (Laurence King Publishing, 2011)

Jackson, P., *Complete Pleats: Pleating techniques for fashion, architecture and design* (Laurence King Publishing, 2021)

Karuno, H., *Kigami and Kami-ito: Japanese handmade paper and paper thread* (2013)

Keasbey, D., *Pattern Techniques for Handweavers* (Doramay Keasbey, 2005)

Keasbey, D., *Designing with Blocks for Handweaving*, 2nd ed. (Keasbey Publications, 2011), p. 18

Kovnat, D., *Weaving Outside the Box: 12 projects for creating dimensional cloth* (Purple Cow Creations, 2022)

Larsen, J.L. and Freudenheim, B. *Interlacing: The elemental fabric* (Kodansha International/Harper & Row, 1986)

Leitner, C., *Paper Textiles* (A&C Black Publishers, 2005)

Lukasheva, E., *Curved Origami: Unlocking the Secrets of Curved Folding in Easy Steps* (Self-published, 2021)

Manchester Art Gallery, *The First Cut* (Exhibition catalogue, 2012/2013)

McArthur, M. and Lang, R.J. *Folding Paper: The infinite possibilities of origami* (Tuttle Publishing, 2013)

Miller, C.K., *Weaving with Wire: Creating Woven Metal Fabric* (Schiffer Craft, 2023)

Moore, J., *Doubleweave* (Interweave Press, 2010)

Nathan, H., Sekimachi Stocksdale, K. and Mayfield, S., *The Weaver's Weaver: Explorations in multiple layers and three-dimensional fiber art* (Fiber Arts Oral History Series, University of California, Berkeley, 1995)

Oelsner, G.H., *A Handbook of Weaves: 1875 Illustrations* (Dover Publications Ltd, 1915)

Osterkamp, P., *Warping Your Loom & Tying On New Warps* (Lease Sticks Press, 2015)

Pearson, D., *New Organic Architecture: The breaking wave* (Gaia Books Ltd, 2001)

Pollock, N. (ed.), *Reiko Sudo NUNO Visionary Japanese Textiles* (Thames & Hudson, 2021)

Richards, A., *Weaving Textiles That Shape Themselves* (The Crowood Press, 2012)

Richards, A., *Weaving: Structure and Substance* (The Crowood Press, 2021)

Ridgway, E and Salthe, V. (eds), *Ruth Asawa: Citizen of the universe* (Thames & Hudson, 2022)

Ruthin Craft Centre, *Nuno Nuno Books: Zokuzoku* (Ruthin Craft Centre, 2012)

Sandu Publishing, *Paper Play* (Gingko Press, 2014)

Schoeser, M., *International Textile Design* (Laurence King Publishing, 1995)

Scott, J., *Textile Perspectives in Mixed-Media Sculpture* (The Crowood Press, 2003)

Shenton, J., *Woven Textile Design* (Laurence King Publishing, 2014)

Schlein, A., *Network Drafting: An Introduction* (Bridgewater Press, 1994)

Schlein, A., *The Liftplan Connection: Designing for dobby looms with Photoshop and Photoshop Elements* (Bridgewater Press, 2010)

Simpson, J., *Experiments in Deflected Double Weave* (Long Thread Media LLC, 2023)

Slowman, P. (ed), *Paper: Tear, fold, rip, crease, cut* (Black Dog Publishing, 2009)

Smayda, N. (with G. White), *Ondulé Textiles: Weaving Contours with a Fan Reed* (Schiffer Publishing, 2017)

Spuybroek, L. (ed.), *The Architecture of Variation* (Thames & Hudson, 2009)

Spuybroek, L. (ed.), *Textile Tectonics* (NAi Publishers, 2011)

Strickler, C., *A Weaver's Book of 8-Shaft Patterns* (Interweave, 1991), p. 120

Stuart Thorpe, A. and Larsen, J.L., *Elements of Weaving* (Doubleday & Co., 1967)

Stubenitsky, M., *Weaving with Echo and Iris* (Uitgeverij Stubenitsky, 2014)

Stubenitsky, M., *Double with a Twist* (Uitgeverij Stubenitsky, 2019)

Sullivan, D.L. *Pique: Plain and Patterned* (Sullivan Publications, 1998)

Sutton, A., *British Craft Textiles* (William Collins Sons & Co Ltd., 1985)

Sutton, A. and Sheehan, D., *Ideas in Weaving* (B.T.Batsford Ltd., 1989)

Sutton, A., *The Structure of Weaving* (Hutchinson & Co Publishers Ltd., 1982)

van der Hoogt, M. (ed.), *Fabrics That Go Bump* (XRX Books, 2002)

van der Hoogt, M. (ed.), *Twill Thrills: 35 Projects in the new twills* (XRX Books, 2004)

Wada, Y.I., Kellog Rice, M., Barton, J., *Shibori: The inventive art of Japanese shaped resist dyeing* (Kodansha Jane, 1983, 1999)

Wada, Y.I., *Memory on Cloth: Shibori now* (Kodansha, 2002)

Waller, I., *Thread: An art form* (Studio Vista, 1973)

Waller, I. *Textile sculptures* (Taplinger Publishing Co, 1977)

Watson, W., *Textile Design and Colour, Sixth Edition* (Ariel Books, 1954)

Watson, W., *Advanced Textile Design (Third Edition)* (Ariel Books, 1946)

Wertenberger, K., *8, 12... 20: An introduction to multishift weaving* (Interweave Press, 1988)

COMPLEX WEAVERS' JOURNAL

#64 Sept 2000
#65 Jan 2001
#66 May 2001
#70 Sept 2002
#82 Oct 2006
#83 Feb 2007
#84 June 2007
#86 Feb 2008
#87 June 2008
#89 Feb 2009
#93 June 2010
#97 Oct 2011
#100 Oct 2012
#101 Feb 2013
#102 June 2013
#103 Oct 2013
#106 Oct 2014
#108 June 2015
#110 Feb 2016
#117 June 2018
#118 Oct 2018
#119 Feb 2019
#121 Oct 2019
#124 Oct 2020
#126 June 2021

WEAVER'S

#17 Summer 1992
#22 Fall 1993
#24 Summer 1994
#31 Spring 1996
#36 Summer 1997
#37 Fall 1997
#44 Summer 1999

HEDDLECRAFT

2020 Harvey-Brown, S March/April

INDEX

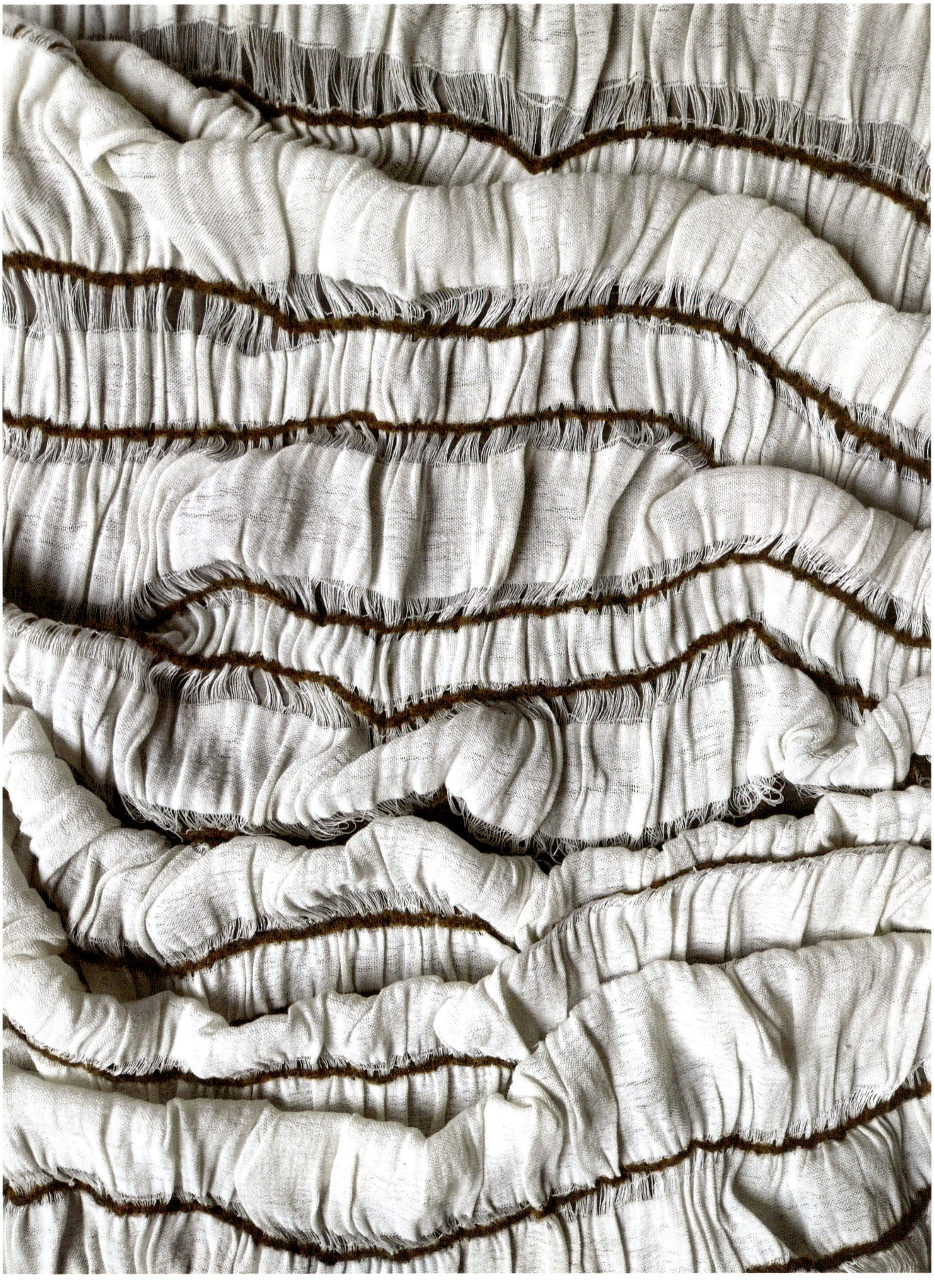

Strata Wall II detail: Wet-finishing in a washing machine gives organic movement to a seersucker effect.

First published in 2026 by
The Crowood Press Ltd
Ramsbury, Marlborough
Wiltshire SN8 2HR
enquiries@crowood.com
www.crowood.com

British Library Cataloguing-in-Publication Data
A catalogue record for this book is available from the British Library.

For product safety-related questions, contact:
productsafety@crowood.com

ISBN 978 0 7198 4595 6

Typeset by Envisage IT
Cover design by Sergey Tsvetkov
Printed and bound in India by Parksons Graphics

Acknowledgements
Usually, our knowledge as weavers is built on those who come before us and also those who share the journey with us. Ruby Leslie got me going on this particular path and Bonnie Inouye challenged and inspired me to dig ever deeper with her incredible knowledge, high expectations and innovation in weaving. Wendy Morris is generous with her knowledge, her considerable expertise, her warmth and her wonderful weaving, including contributing to Chapter 3. She has also provided me with a critical eye in the editing of this book. Any errors are totally mine.

Many weavers have contributed to this book and to all, my grateful thanks. Their work is inspirational. Special mention to Susan Iverson who allowed me to share her technique for pulling warps to create sculptural shaping.

Thanks to Colin Usher who is both friend and photographer, and to the team at Crowood for bringing this book to life.

Finally, the culinary support of my husband and his patience with my weaving obsession is legendary! Thank you, Graham!

The author's website:
www.theloomroomfrance.com

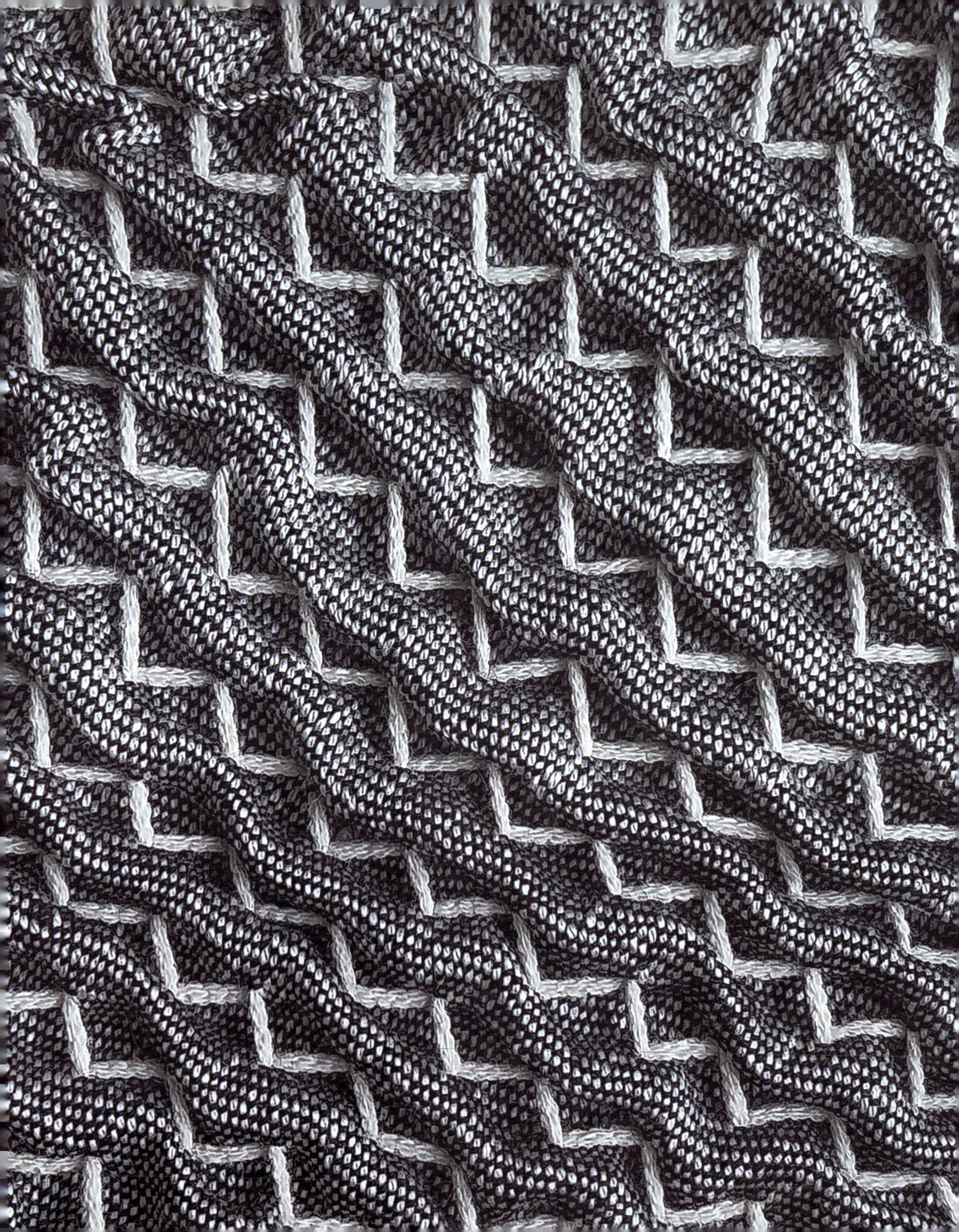